# WISE CHOICES

*Decisions, Games, and Negotiations*

EDITED BY

Richard J. Zeckhauser
Ralph L. Keeney
James K. Sebenius

HARVARD BUSINESS SCHOOL PRESS
BOSTON, MASSACHUSETTS

Library of Congress Cataloging-in-Publication Data

Wise choices : decisions, games, and negotiations / edited by
   Richard J. Zeckhauser, Ralph L. Keeney, James K. Sebenius.
       p.   cm.
   Includes bibliographical references and index.
   ISBN 0-87584-677-7
       1. Decision-making—Mathematical models.   2. Management games.
   3. Negotiation in business.   I. Zeckhauser, Richard.   II. Keeney,
   Ralph L., 1944–      .   III. Sebenius, James K., 1953–      .
   HD30.23.W563      1996
   658.4′0353—dc20                                                    95-39962
                                                                        CIP

*HD*
*30.23*
*.W563*
*1996*

Chapter 9 of the present work is reprinted with permission from *Energy Policy*, vol. 23, Thomas C. Schelling, "Intergeneral Discounting," 1995, Elsevier Science Ltd, Butterworth Heinemann imprint, Oxford, England.

*To Howard Raiffa*
*our mentor, teacher, and friend*

# CONTENTS

# FOREWORD

This book grows out of the remarkable career of a distinguished scholar, teacher, and human being: Howard Raiffa.

As Howard neared his retirement from the Harvard Business School faculty in December 1994, members of the academic community—not only here at the Harvard Business School, but at institutions around the world—began looking for a way to celebrate his career of astonishing achievement. This was far from easy. Several times, Howard has either invented an entirely new field, or has changed an existing field so fundamentally that he earned recognition as its reinventor. To cite just one example (from Irving H. LaValle's essay at the end of this volume), before 1968 few people called themselves "decision analysts." But after the publication in that year of Howard's seminal *Decision Analysis*, many in both business and the academy applied new labels to themselves. He has had equally dramatic impacts in game theory and negotiation analysis.

Howard's colleagues decided to celebrate his accomplishments with a colloquium that would bring together participants from around the world to build upon the intellectual foundations that he had laid. The colloquium, sponsored by this School, was held in October 1994 and included scholars from a broad range of disciplines and affiliations. The papers presented at that colloquium, subsequently refined through vigorous debate and individual scholarship, make up the chapters of this volume.

The editors of *Wise Choices*—Richard J. Zeckhauser, Ralph L. Keeney, and James K. Sebenius—provide a substantive overview of its contents in their concise and integrative Introduction. Here I simply would like to express a few thoughts about what Howard Raiffa has meant to the intellectual community at the Harvard Business School. I'm sure my thoughts will resonate with Howard's friends, followers, and admirers at many other institutions.

Howard came to the Harvard Business School in 1957. He was one of a small cadre of discipline-based scholars who were brought to the School through the generosity of the Ford Foundation, as part of a larger movement to broaden the intellectual base of business schools nationwide. I don't speak from personal knowledge—I was in grade school at the time—but I'm told that there was a collective holding of the breath as brilliant young minds like Howard Raiffa's began to descend on this institution with their strange new tools. Did a Ph.D.-holding mathematician and statistician have a chance of assimilating here, or would he become part of a self-contained intellectual enclave? Could we learn from him, and vice versa?

Of course, as it turned out, the association created the structure for a "win-win" game. Howard was intensely interested in decision making under conditions of uncertainty and competition—and this was exactly what the Harvard Business School had long professed to study and teach. Moreover, he was a wonderful teacher. As he once said, he took to the case method like a duck to water. But unlike most ducks, Howard reshaped, deepened, and expanded the pond, and linked it to other ponds near and far. Partly this was due to the power of his ideas; just as important was his ability to attract talented young scholars to the Harvard Business School and engage them in the kind of cross-disciplinary, problem-focused teaching and research that is his hallmark.

The result was that in what was then called the managerial economics (ME) area, Howard and his colleagues created not an isolated enclave, but a welcoming gateway to this School. Over the years, many of the best young faculty they attracted moved from ME to become leaders in technology and operations, in finance, in marketing, in strategy. As I look around me today, almost forty years after Howard's arrival here, it is clear that much of the leadership of this School is testimony to the success of that "seeding" process. And the seeds he has planted will continue to bear fruit well into the future. His young colleagues will continue to meet the challenge that Howard set for himself so long ago: bringing sophisticated analytical tools to bear on important problems of practice. My peers on faculties here and elsewhere, and also our counterparts in business, know just how hard this is to achieve.

Like the man himself, the Raiffa vision of scholarship is broad and deep. What is most remarkable about Howard (of course, excepting his formidable intellect) is his willingness to go far more than halfway to engage his colleagues here and elsewhere, irrespective of discipline. He is astoundingly open to good ideas wherever he finds them. His is a disciplined mind that cuts across disciplines. Indeed, he is walking testimony to the power of the collaborative intellectual venture. The Negotiation Roundtable that he founded here has been a monthly attraction for scholars from many schools at Harvard and other universities. Under its auspices, Howard and his colleagues have analyzed dozens of cases, produced important books, and guided many doctoral students.

Howard's impact on cross-disciplinary teaching and course development has been no less powerful. Not only are courses in negotiation and decision making part of the required curriculum in our MBA program, but the group responsible for those courses is now engaged in building—with Howard's help and guidance—an interdisciplinary community that integrates the relevant behavioral and mathematical sciences. This, I think, is a process that resonates throughout *Wise Choices.*

As Harvard and other leading universities increasingly emphasize just this sort of venture, we become only more aware of Howard's four highly productive decades in the cross-disciplinary vineyards. The real risk in cataloging his proud record of collaborations—here, at the Kennedy School, the Law School, the School of Public Health, and at the International Institute for Applied Systems Analysis, where he was the founding director—is that I'll overlook something of vital importance. Suffice it to say that wherever he has gone, Howard has won deep and abiding friends for the concept of intellectual teamwork.

I have already lauded Howard's teaching skills. I should also state unequivocally that he is one of the world's great listeners. (We can all conjure up a mental image of Howard with his coat off, sleeves rolled up, and brow furrowed, listening *hard* to one or more of us.) He is a wonderful writer. He is a gentle and demanding mentor. And, as this book so amply demonstrates, he has proven that theory can be brought to bear on action—wisely and gainfully—and that thoughtful action and practice inspire good theory. The fact that he is a charming, thoroughly decent, enthusiastic, and cheerful human being is just a bonus. We are lucky to be his associates—and his students.

Kim B. Clark
Dean, Harvard Business School

# ACKNOWLEDGMENTS

This volume grew out of a conference sponsored by the Research Division of the Harvard Business School to celebrate Howard Raiffa's extraordinary contributions to scholarship and teaching. The participants, in addition to Howard Raiffa himself, were his colleagues, collaborators, and students, including some from as far as Europe, the Middle East, and Asia.

Our overwhelming debt is to Howard Raiffa, a friend, teacher, and inspiration to the individuals who contributed to this volume. We hope that some portion of his wisdom is distilled on these pages.

We also thank Miriam Avins, who skillfully edited this volume; Wendy Wyatt, who expertly administered its preparation; and Barbara Roth of the Harvard Business School Press, who deftly guided it to publication. The work of Keeney and Zeckhauser on this volume was supported by National Science Foundation Grants SBR-9308660 and SES-9111056, respectively.

# INTRODUCTION

To live life is to make decisions. This is true for organizations and individuals, for self-interested choices and for actions that affect the decisions and welfare of others. This volume asks how such decisions can be made effectively. It is inspired by the lifetime intellectual odyssey of Howard Raiffa, pioneer decision analyst, game theorist, and scholar of negotiation. As his own work has progressed from statistical decision theory to game theory to decision analysis to negotiation analysis, his central question has always been: How can we make wise choices?

The papers presented here reflect the methodological unity of three fields—decision analysis, game theory, and negotiation analysis—and play on the common themes they embrace. Analysis is always front and center. Possible decisions are disaggregated into their component elements to be analyzed; there is virtually no role for holistic assessments. Two profound sets of methodological contributions—game theory and utility theory from John Von Neumann and Oskar Morgenstern, and Bayesian decision theory from Leonard J. Savage—provide the underpinnings for this volume.[1] In a few short intellectual generations, these methodologies have come to influence our understanding of a vast array of decisions that are made by individuals, groups, and interdependent parties.

The titles of three of Howard Raiffa's books form our major section titles. In "Decision Analysis" we explore individual decision making under uncertainty. The uncertainties are generated by natural phenomena, such as weather or seismic conditions, or by the confluence of actions of many individuals, as with market prices.[2] In "Games and Decisions" we turn to games of strategy, situations where one player's actions influence another player's welfare directly, creating an interplay among their actions. In "The Art and Science of Negotiation" we examine negotiation analysis, which draws together decision analysis and game theory in assessing how agreements can and do get struck. Negotiation analysis proceeds in the sequential manner of decision analysis; the principal uncertainties relate to the values, information, and behavior of negotiation partners. In our final section, we turn to the Art and Science of Howard Raiffa, whose contributions span and help unite these three fields. All of our authors are students of Raiffa, be they his senior or junior, dissertation advisee, colleague, or collaborator.

These papers reflect the power of the distinctions, sharply etched by David Bell, Raiffa, and Amos Tversky, among normative, prescriptive, and descriptive points of view in decision research.[3] Normative analyses tell us what should be done, usually from the perspective of more than one individual, possibly from the perspective of society as a whole. Thus, normative analysis tells us that all favorable bargains should be struck, and possibly describes the appropriate division of gains from trade.

Prescriptive analysis details how decisions should be made by rational individuals choosing on their own behalf. Societal norms and tradeoffs, the well-being of others, are not considered except to the extent that the individual values them or that they affect the payoffs to his choices. Descriptive analysis, by contrast with normative and prescriptive analysis, looks not at what should be, but what is. It examines and diagnoses the ways individuals actually make decisions. Recent years have witnessed a growth of behavioral decision analysis, which is well represented in some of these analyses. It demonstrates that what decision makers should do and do do are frequently quite different.

Several of our chapters are predominantly methodological. The authors offer improvements in probabilistic assessment, the valuation of monetary consequences, the varieties and measures of risk, the creation and valuation of decision options, and discounting over long periods of time. Others revisit the axioms of choice, questioning their behavioral fidelity and investigating alternatives. The consideration of strategic uncertainty—uncertainty about the choices of others—is a recurring element in this work. A number of chapters investigate gaming methods, taking how individuals actually behave in choice situations as a guideline to predicting and understanding the outcomes that will pertain in markets and other interactive contexts.

The payoff to all the decisions examined in *Wise Choices* is to improve welfare, whether of individuals or of society. Most chapters illustrate with at least some applications, and a number focus on practicable methods for coping with real-world problems. Applications of decision analysis discuss medical decision making, both in general and in relation to Down's Syndrome, risks to life and limb, and the environment.

Taken together, this body of papers points to a modern decision research that is not imprisoned in separate methodological cells, but that rigorously and aptly draws from many related sources in search of truly wise decisions. Thus we have game-theoretic treatments of market entry or coalition formation that utilize behavioral insights and experimental findings as well as abstract equilibrium characterizations. Negotiation analyses explicitly proceed in the sequential manner of decision analysis, attending to how uncertainties unfold. Empirically informed assessments of how negotiation partners or market competitors behave complement traditional insights from game theory. Ethical reasoning is infused with strategic logic and, pleasingly, the converse is true as well.

Despite the tremendous range of decision situations addressed here, the choices have much in common: Their consequences are important. They confront uncertainty. The alternatives are not clearly delineated. Indeed, a first step in many real decisions is to recognize that a decision must be made.

The substance of the decisions analyzed in this volume ranges from personal medical problems to national public policies, from business investment to international diplomacy, from decisions based on the monetary bottom line to those founded on fundamental moral principles. The central theme for all is that wise choices flow from systematic analysis.

## NOTES

1. John Von Neumann and Oskar Morgenstern, *Theory of Games and Economic Behavior* (Princeton, NJ: Princeton University Press, 1944); and Leonard J. Savage, *Foundations of Statistics* (New York: Wiley, 1954).
2. Statistical decision theory addresses similar situations, but is more appropriate for decisions where there is an abundance of directly relevant data. Decision analysis, by contrast, is more appropriate for one-of-a-kind decisions that must rely more on judgments about the potential resolution of

uncertainties, on indirectly relevant information, and on the structure of values.

3. David E. Bell, Howard Raiffa, and Amos Tversky, *Decision Making: Descriptive, Normative, and Prescriptive Interactions* (New York: Cambridge University Press, 1988).

# PART 1

## Decision Analysis

# PART 1.1

## Interpretation of Information

# CHAPTER 1

# CONTRASTING RATIONAL AND PSYCHOLOGICAL PRINCIPLES OF CHOICE

## Amos Tversky

Casual observations as well as controlled experiments indicate that people often make decisions that are at variance with the rational theory of choice. Indeed, the tension between rational analysis and psychological intuition has characterized the study of individual choice from its beginning in the eighteenth century, and its implications have been the subject of a lively debate ever since. Many rational theorists have attempted to reconcile lay choices with the standard rational model either by relaxing the requirements of rationality (for example, giving up the independence axiom of expected utility theory) or by rationalizing observed behavior through the introduction of additional considerations (such as utility for gambling, limited memory, or cost of thinking). This approach, which is particularly popular among economists, seeks to eliminate the apparent gap between normative and descriptive theory and use the rational theory to predict observed choices. This chapter argues that a complete reconciliation between normative and descriptive theories is not possible, that the analysis of normative and psychological intuitions call for different accounts, and that the tension between them is essential for understanding, predicting, and improving human decision making.[1]

This thesis, I believe, is closely related to Howard Raiffa's philosophy. Perhaps more than any other decision theorist, Raiffa has acknowledged and explored the contrast between normative and psychological intuitions, which he has regarded as the raison d'être of decision analysis. Moreover, as he taught people how to structure choice problems and make more reasonable decisions, Raiffa discovered some of the major obstacles to rational choice, such as the prevalence of over-confidence in the assessment of subjective probability distributions and the impact of the reference point in decision under uncertainty.[2] He also found ways to frame decision problems so as to enhance the appeal of the normative theory.[3] Although Raiffa's orientation was prescriptive rather than descriptive, he pioneered the study of judgmental biases, reference points, and framing effects.

This paper contrasts the rational theory of choice with a psychological analysis of decision making. It focuses on three basic assumptions that underlie the rational theory: description invariance, procedure invariance, and context independence. Description invariance demands that preferences among options should not depend on the manner in which they are represented or displayed. Two representations that the decision maker, on reflection, would view as equivalent descriptions of the same problem should lead to the same choice—even without the benefit of such reflection.[4] Procedure invariance requires that strategically equivalent methods of elicitation reveal the same preference order. For example, the standard theory assumes that a preference between $x$ and $y$ can be established either by offering an individual a direct choice between $x$ and $y$ or by comparing their reservation prices, and that the two procedures should yield the same order. Although description invariance and procedure invariance are essential to the rational theory of choice, they are usually treated as implicit constraints on the interpretation of the model, not as explicit assumptions. In some cases, invariance is "built into" the primitives of the model. For example, if gambles are represented as random variables, then any two realizations of the same random variable must be mapped into the same object.

Context independence, often called the principle of independence of other alternatives, demands that the preference order between $x$ and $y$ should not depend on whether $z$ is available or not, provided the presence of $z$ does not provide new information about $x$ or $y$. This is an immediate consequence of the standard maximization model, which assumes that the decision maker has a complete preference order and that—given an offered set—the decision maker selects the option that is highest in that order.

Description invariance, procedure invariance, and context independence are routinely assumed in applications of the rational model. Although these assumptions are compelling from a normative standpoint, they are not descriptively valid. The evidence suggests that people often do not have well-articulated preferences and that their choices are actually constructed—not merely revealed—in the evaluation process. Furthermore, people's choices depend on the framing of the problem, the method of elicitation, and the context of choice.[5] Thus, alternative descriptions of the same choice problem lead to systematically different responses; strategically equivalent elicitation procedures give rise to different decisions; and the choice between options often depends on the choice set in which they are embedded. This paper illustrates these phenomena and discusses the psychological principles that generate them. This treatment, which can be viewed as a constructive analysis of choice, cannot compete with the rational model in scope, rigor, or elegance. It is approximate, incomplete, and occasionally vague. Its virtue lies in its potential to explain behavior that is inconsistent with the rational model and to address problems that are not treated by the standard theory. The inevitable tension between normative and descriptive principles is discussed in the final section.

## Description Invariance and Framing Effects

A number of participants in a survey were asked to choose between two economic programs that differ in the expected rates of inflation and unemployment.[6] They were told that if program A is adopted, 10 percent of the work force would be unemployed and the rate of inflation would be 12 percent; whereas if program B is adopted, 5 percent of the work force would be unemployed and the rate of inflation would be 17 percent. Most respondents favored program B, which promises lower unemployment. A second group was told that if program A is adopted, 90 percent of the work force would be employed and the rate of inflation would be 12 percent; whereas, if program B is adopted, 95 percent of the work force would be employed and the rate of inflation would be 17 percent. The majority of respondents in the second version favored program A, which promises lower inflation, contrary to the modal choice in the first version. Thus, equivalent formulations of the same decision problem yield systematically different preferences. The same information has a greater impact when it is framed as the difference between 5 percent and 10 percent unemployment than when it is framed as the difference between 95 percent and 90 percent employment. These observations suggest that, contrary to description invariance, people choose, in effect, between descriptions of options rather than between the options themselves.

Framing effects are quite common in the choices of both naive and sophisticated respondents. For example, experienced physicians made markedly different choices between two treatments for lung cancer— surgery and radiation therapy—depending on whether the outcomes of these treatments were described in terms of mortality rates or in terms of survival rates: the difference between 0 percent and 10 percent mortality had more impact than the difference between 90 percent and 100 percent survival. Surprisingly, the physicians were just as susceptible to the effect of framing as were graduate students or clinic patients.[7]

These observations illustrate what might be called the acceptance principle: people tend to accept the frame presented in a problem and evaluate the outcomes in terms of that frame. As a consequence, people are likely to either avoid or seek risk, depending on whether a problem is described in terms of gains or losses.[8] Similarly, people are likely to prefer indexed or non-indexed contracts depending on whether the outcomes of the relevant transaction are described in nominal or in real terms. In one study, subjects were asked to imagine that they worked for a company that produced computers in Singapore and had to sign a contract to sell some specified number of new computers to be delivered and paid for a year later.[9] The computers were currently selling for $1,000 each; but due to inflation, all prices, including production costs and computer prices, were expected to increase by about 20 percent. Subjects had to choose between Contract A: selling the computers a year later for $1,200 (20 percent higher than the current price), and Contract B: selling the computers a year later for the going price at that time. For one group of subjects the options were described in nominal terms, relative to $1,200. In this frame, Contract A appears riskless since the computers are guaranteed to sell for $1,200 no matter what; whereas Contract B appears risky since the computers' future price would be less than $1,200 if inflation is low, and more than $1,200 if inflation is high. A second group of subjects was presented with the same alternatives described in real terms, relative to the computers' expected future price. Here, Contract B appears riskless because the computers would be sold for their actual price, regardless of the rate of inflation. Contract A, on the other hand, appears risky: the computers are to be sold for $1,200, which may be more than they are worth if inflation is lower than the anticipated 20 percent, and less than they are worth if inflation exceeds 20 percent. The contract that appeared riskless in each frame was relatively more attractive than the one that appeared risky; thus, contract A was chosen more often in the former case, when it was framed as riskless, than in the latter, when it was framed as risky.

A striking framing effect that relies on people's tendency to maintain the status quo has been observed in insurance decisions. New Jersey and Pennsylvania have recently introduced the option of allowing automobile drivers to limit their own right to sue in exchange for lower insurance rates. In New Jersey, motorists must request the full right to sue, whereas in Pennsylvania the full right to sue is the default.

When offered the choice, only about 20 percent of New Jersey drivers chose to acquire the full right to sue, while approximately 75 percent of Pennsylvania drivers chose to retain it. The difference in adoption rates due to the different frames had financial repercussions that are estimated at around $200 million.[10]

In these examples, as in most violations of description invariance reported in the literature, subjects appear to adopt the frame presented in the problem without considering alternative frames. The question of how people reconcile competing frames is discussed in the last section.

## Procedure Invariance and Preference Reversals

In axiomatic theories of choice, the preference order appears as an abstract relation that is given an empirical interpretation in terms of specific methods of elicitation such as choice or pricing. Procedure invariance demands that normatively equivalent elicitation procedures should reveal the same preference order. This requirement plays an essential role in measurement theories. For example, one can establish which of two objects is heavier either by placing each object separately on a scale or by placing both objects on the two sides of a pan balance; the two procedures yield the same results, within the limit of measurement errors. Analogously, the rational theory of choice assumes that each individual has a well-defined preference order that can be elicited either by offering people a choice between options or by observing their reservation price. Just as it would be difficult to attribute weight to objects if different measurement procedures produced different results, it is difficult to attribute utility to options if different methods of elicitation yield different choices.

In fact, people systematically violate procedure invariance. This phenomenon, called *preference reversal*, was first demonstrated more than three decades ago by Sarah Lichtenstein and Paul Slovic.[11] They presented subjects with two prospects having similar expected values. One prospect, the *H* bet, offers a high chance of winning a relatively small prize (for example, 8 chances in 9 to win $4); whereas the other prospect, the *L* bet, offers a lower chance to win a larger prize (a 1 in 9 chance to win $40). When asked to choose between these prospects, most subjects choose the *H* bet. Subjects were also asked to state the lowest price at which they would be willing to sell each bet if they owned it. Surprisingly, most subjects put a higher price on the *L* bet. (In a recent study that used this particular pair of bets, for example, 71 percent of the subjects chose the *H* bet, but only 33 percent priced *H* above *L*.) Numerous experiments replicated this phenomenon, using different bets, monetary incentives, and even a market setting. What is the cause of preference reversal? Why do people charge more for the low probability bet that they choose less often?

Recent work suggests that the major cause of preference reversal is the compatibility between the response mode and the attributes of the prospects: an attribute of an object is given more weight when it is compatible with the response mode than when it is not.[12] Because the cash equivalence of a bet is expressed in dollars, compatibility implies that the payoffs, which are expressed in the same units, will be weighted more heavily in pricing than in choice. Consequently, the $L$ bet is overpriced relative to the $H$ bet, which gives rise to the observed preference reversals. This account has been supported by several additional studies. In one experiment, subjects were presented with $H$ and $L$ bets involving nonmonetary outcomes, such as a one-week pass for all movie theaters in town or a dinner for two at a local restaurant.[13] If preference reversals are due primarily to the compatibility of prices and payoffs, which are both expressed in dollars, they should be substantially less frequent when the outcome is nonmonetary. Indeed, the prevalence of preference reversal was reduced by half.

Note that the compatibility hypothesis does not depend on the presence of risk. It implies a similar discrepancy between choice and pricing for riskless options, such as a prospect that offers a payment of $x$ dollars, $t$ years from now. Consider a long-term prospect $L$ that pays $2,500 five years from now, and a short-term prospect $S$ that pays $1,600 in one and a half years. Subjects were asked to choose between $L$ and $S$ and to price both prospects by stating the smallest immediate cash payment for which they would be willing to exchange each delayed payment.[14] In accord with the compatibility hypothesis, subjects chose the short-term option 74 percent of the time but priced the short-term option above the long-term option only 25 percent of the time. This observation indicates that preference reversal is a general pattern, not a peculiar characteristic of betting behavior.

Another psychological mechanism that leads to violations of procedure invariance involves the notion of relative prominence. In many cases, people agree that one attribute (say, safety) is more important than another (say, cost). Although the interpretation of such a claim is not entirely clear, there is evidence that the attribute that is judged more important looms larger in choice than in pricing.[15] For example, consider two programs designed to reduce the number of fatalities due to traffic accidents, each characterized by the expected reduction in the number of casualties and an estimated cost. Because human lives are regarded as more important than money, the prominence hypothesis predicts that this dimension will be given more weight in choice than in pricing. When given a choice between programs X and Y below, the great majority of respondents favored X, the more expensive program that saves more lives.

| | Expected number of casualties | Cost |
|---|---|---|
| Program X | 500 | $55 Million |
| Program Y | 570 | $12 Million |

However, when the cost of one of the programs was removed and subjects were asked to determine the missing cost so that the two programs were equally attractive, nearly all subjects assigned values that imply a preference for Y, the less expensive program that saves fewer lives. For example, when the cost of Program X is removed, the median estimate of the missing cost that renders the two programs equally attractive was $40 million. This implies that at $55 million, Program X should not be chosen over Program Y, contrary to the afore-mentioned choice. Thus, the prominent attribute (saving lives) dominates the choice but not the pricing. This discrepancy suggests that different public policies would be supported depending on whether people are asked which policy they prefer, or how much they think each policy ought to cost.

Further applications of the prominence hypothesis were reported in a study of people's responses to environmental problems.[16] Several pairs of issues were selected where one issue involves human health or safety and the other concerns protection of the environment. Each issue included a brief statement of a problem along with a suggested form of intervention, as illustrated below.

PROBLEM: Skin cancer from sun exposure is common among farm workers.

INTERVENTION: Support free medical checkups for threatened groups.

PROBLEM: Several Australian mammal species are nearly wiped out by hunters.

INTERVENTION: Contribute to a fund to provide safe breeding areas for these species.

One group of subjects was asked to choose which of the two interventions they would rather support; a second group of subjects was presented with one issue at a time and asked to determine the largest amount they would be willing to pay for the suggested intervention. Because the treatment of cancer in humans is generally viewed as more important than the protection of Australian mammals, the prominence hypothesis predicts that the former will receive greater support in direct choice than when the two problems are evaluated independently. This prediction was confirmed. When asked to evaluate each intervention separately, subjects were willing to pay more, on average, for safe breeding of Australian mammals than for free checkups for skin cancer. However, when faced with a direct choice, most subjects favored free checkups for humans over safe breeding for mammals. Thus, people may evaluate one alternative more positively than another when each is evaluated independently, but then reverse their evaluation when the alternatives are directly compared, which accentuates the prominent attribute.

## Context Independence and Tradeoff Contrast

One of the basic assumptions of the rational theory of choice is that each option has a utility, or subjective value, that depends only on the option. Given a set of options, the decision maker always selects the one with the highest value. If you prefer salmon to steak in a binary choice, for example, you should never select steak from a menu that includes salmon—unless the other entrees provide some information about the relative quality of the steak or the salmon. In particular, a nonpreferred option cannot be made preferred by adding new alternatives to the choice set; this assumption is called context independence. Despite its simplicity and intuitive appeal, there is evidence that people's preferences are influenced by the choice set, and that the popularity of an option can be increased by enlarging the set. We focus here on a particular psychological mechanism, called tradeoff contrast, that generates systematic violations of context independence.

Contrast effects are ubiquitous in perception and judgment. For example, a circle appears larger when surrounded by small circles than when surrounded by large ones (see Figure 1-1). Similarly, a product may appear attractive on a background of less attractive products and unattractive on a background of more attractive products. Contrast effects apply not only to a single attribute, such as size or attractiveness, but also to the tradeoff between attributes. Consider, for example, products that vary on two attributes; suppose $x$ is of higher quality but $y$ has a better price. The decision between $x$ and $y$, then, depends on whether the quality difference outweighs the price difference, that is, the price/quality tradeoff. I propose that decision makers tend to prefer

**Figure 1-1**
*Contrast Effect*
*The middle circle on the right appears larger than the*
*middle circle on the left due to contrast*

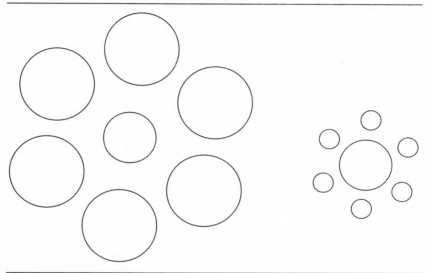

x over y more often if they have encountered other choices in which a comparable improvement in quality is associated with a larger difference in price. This is the *tradeoff contrast hypothesis.*

Perhaps the simplest demonstration of the tradeoff contrast hypothesis involves manipulation of the background context defined by the choices encountered in the past. In one experiment, half the subjects were given a choice between options x' and y', and the second half chose between x" and y" (see Figure 1-2).[17] Following the initial choice, all subjects were given a choice between x and y. The tradeoff contrast hypothesis predicts that the tendency to prefer x over y will be stronger among subjects who first chose between x' and y' than among those who first chose between x" and y". Table 1-1 presents the results for two experiments: choosing among tires that vary in warranty and price, and gifts consisting of a combination of cash and coupons. Each coupon could be redeemed for a book or compact disk at local stores. Subjects were informed that some of them, selected randomly, would actually receive the gifts they selected.

Table 1-1 shows that the background influenced subsequent choice as predicted. The results for tires indicate that subjects exposed to Background B', in which a small difference in price ($91 versus $85)

**Figure 1-2**
*A Test of Background Tradeoff*

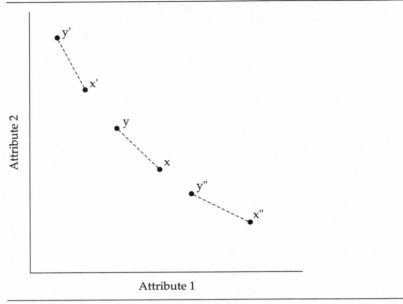

was associated with a large difference in warranty (75,000 versus 55,000 miles), were more likely to select from the target set the less expensive tire than those exposed to Background B″, in which a relatively large difference in price ($49 versus $25) was associated with a small difference in warranty (35,000 versus 30,000 miles). The same pattern was observed for gifts, as seen in the lower part of Table 1-1. Here the rate of exchange was $15 per coupon in Background B′, $5 per coupon in Background B″, and $10 per coupon in the target set. Subjects exposed to the background in which coupons were fairly expensive were significantly more likely to select from the target set the gift with more coupons than subjects exposed to the background in which coupons were relatively inexpensive.

It may be argued that the subjects' choices can be justified by the information provided by the context. I wish to make two points in response. First, regardless of whether the observed pattern of preferences can be rationalized, the data are inconsistent with the standard maximization model. If people commonly rely on the set of alternatives under consideration in order to assess the value of an option, then the standard theory of the consumer should be revised to accommodate decisions based on such inferences. Second, an account based on ra-

## Table 1-1
### Background Contrast

**Category: Tires**

| Warranty | Price | Background Set B' ($n = 111$) | Background Set B" ($n = 109$) |
|---|---|---|---|
| $x'$: 55,000 miles | $85 | 12% | |
| $y'$: 75,000 miles | $91 | 88% | |
| $x''$: 30,000 miles | $25 | | 84% |
| $y''$: 35,000 miles | $49 | | 16% |

| Warranty | Price | Target Set | |
|---|---|---|---|
| $x$: 40,000 miles | $60 | 57% | 33% |
| $y$: 50,000 miles | $75 | 43% | 67% |

**Category: Gifts**

| Cash | Coupons | Background Set B' ($n = 51$) | Background Set B" ($n = 49$) |
|---|---|---|---|
| $x'$: $52 | 3 | 92% | |
| $y'$: $22 | 5 | 8% | |
| $x''$: $77 | 4 | | 40% |
| $y''$: $67 | 6 | | 60% |

| Cash | Coupons | Target Set | |
|---|---|---|---|
| $x$: $47 | 5 | 47% | 77% |
| $y$: $37 | 6 | 53% | 23% |

tional inference can explain some examples, such as the tires, but not others, such as the gifts. A consumer who is uncertain about the price of a warranty may use the information provided by the background to evaluate whether paying $15 for 10,000 miles of warranty is a good deal; here the background contrast effect can be interpreted as rational inference based on the information provided by the context. This account, however, cannot explain the background contrast effect in the choice between gifts. Suppose you are just willing to trade $10 in cash for one coupon. Why should you change your mind after observing gifts in which the corresponding tradeoff is $5 or $15? The effect of the background was no stronger for tires than for books—it appears that people's choices exhibit tradeoff contrast whether or not it is normatively justified.

Another implication of the tradeoff contrast hypothesis is that the "market share" of $x$ can be increased by adding to $\{x, y\}$ a third alternative $z$ that is clearly inferior to $x$ but not to $y$.[18] In one demonstration, a group of subjects was offered a choice between $6 and an elegant Cross pen.[19] The pen was selected by 36 percent of the subjects and the remaining 64 percent chose the cash. A second group was given a choice among three options: $6 in cash, the same Cross pen, and a second, less attractive pen. The second pen appears to be dominated by the first pen but not by the cash. Indeed, only 2 percent of the subjects chose the less attractive pen, but its presence increased the percentage of subjects who chose the Cross pen from 36 percent to 46 percent.

Similar effects have been observed in the marketplace. For example, Williams-Sonoma, a mail order and retail business located in San Francisco, used to offer one bread-baking appliance priced at $275. Later it added a second bread-baking appliance, which was similar to the first but somewhat larger. The price of this item was $429, more than 50 percent higher than the original appliance. Not surprisingly, perhaps, Williams-Sonoma did not sell many units of the new item, but the sales of the less expensive appliance almost doubled. To my knowledge, Williams-Sonoma did not anticipate this effect. In other situations, salespeople intentionally exploit context effects. A common tactic used to convince consumers to purchase a given product is to present an additional less attractive product and argue that the former is a bargain in comparison with the latter.

Context effects induced by contrast are not confined to consumer choice. In an experiment that tested legal judgment, subjects were presented with a trial case involving a broker who concealed from the would-be buyer of a house information regarding substantial dry rot damage to the foundation.[20] The repair cost is estimated at about $100,000. The jury convicted the defendant of knowingly withholding material information, and each subject was asked to act as a judge and select an appropriate sentence.

One group of subjects was asked to choose either the prosecutor's recommendation of a $2,500 fine and one month in jail, or the probation department's recommendation of a $2,500 fine and six months of probation, during which the defendant would perform 50 hours of community service. A second group of subjects was given an additional suggestion by the probation department: a $2,500 fine and six months probation with 50 hours of counseling sessions on "ethical business practices and the connection between dishonesty and impaired self-esteem." Given the prevailing skepticism about the utility of counseling, this option is expected to appear less appropriate than community service. Thus the addition of the counseling option should enhance the attractiveness of community service. The data support this prediction; very few subjects in the second group selected the probation and counseling, but its presence significantly increased the percentage who chose the probation and community service.

These violations of context dependence indicate that people do not maximize a precomputed preference order, but construct their choices in light of the available options. As a consequence, variations in the offered set produce decisions that are inconsistent with simple maximization. The systematic failure of the standard model, I suggest, is not due to its complexity, but rather to the fact that people sometimes do not have clear preferences and, as a result, they use the context to identify what appears to be the "best buy." While some normative models require a great deal of memory and difficult computations, the application of utility maximization in the present context requires only an ordering of options. It is hard to conceive of a simpler model; any descriptive model of such decisions is bound to be considerably more complicated.[21]

The preceding examples illustrate that people sometimes err by complicating rather than by simplifying the task; they often perform unnecessary computations and attend to irrelevant aspects of a situation. For example, in order to judge which of two circles in Figure 1-1 is bigger, it seems simplest to evaluate the critical figures and ignore the "irrelevant" circles in the background. Similarly, to decide which of two options is preferable, it seems easiest to compare them directly and ignore the other options. The fact that people do not behave in this manner indicates that many departures from classical models of rational choice cannot be easily explained merely as an attempt to reduce computational complexity.

## On the Resolution of Inconsistency

The studies reviewed in the preceding sections show that human behavior is often inconsistent with the basic tenets of the standard rational model. It appears that people do not always have a well-defined preference order and that their choices depend on the framing of the problem, the method of elicitation, and the context of the choice. Unlike the early counterexamples to expected utility theory, devised by Maurice Allais and Daniel Ellsberg, whose normative status has been debated extensively, the demonstrations reviewed in this chapter are noncontroversial from a normative perspective. The experiments reviewed here show that people consistently violate normative principles they wish to obey. Because the assumptions of description and procedure invariance are normatively unassailable but descriptively inadequate, normative and descriptive accounts of individual choice cannot be reconciled.

The rational theory of choice seems to provide a better account of people's intuition than of their actual behavior. When faced with their inconsistent choices, people often (but not always) revise their preferences in accord with the rational model. This is especially true with respect to violations of stochastic dominance and transitivity.[22] The situation is less clear with respect to violations of independence, say, in the Allais or Ellsberg problems. Here, many subjects are not moved by Leonard J. Savage's and Raiffa's arguments; to use Samuelson's phrase, they choose to satisfy their preferences and let the axioms satisfy themselves.[23] Thus, stochastic dominance has an undeniable normative appeal; transitivity comes second, whereas independence trails behind. This ordering of axioms with respect to normative appeal is based on decisions in which the application of the axiom in question is made transparent to the respondents. In a nontransparent context, even stochastic dominance can be systematically violated.[24]

Violations of description invariance are also commonly viewed as errors, although people are often at a loss as to which frame to adopt. As one subject put it, "I prefer the sure outcome over the risky prospect when the problem is framed in terms of lives saved; I prefer the risky prospect over the sure outcome when the problem is framed in terms of lives lost; and I also like to give consistent responses to the two versions." In this respect, framing effects resemble visual illusions; the recognition of an error does not eliminate its appeal. In some cases, however, there appears to be a dominant frame. When presented with both the employment and the unemployment versions of our opening problem, people's responses are much closer to the unemployment version than to the employment version. Similarly, the responses of physicians who were presented with both the mortality and the survival data for the lung cancer problem were much closer to those induced by the mortality frame than to those induced by the survival frame.[25] Evidently, the descriptions in terms of mortality and unemployment tend to dominate the descriptions in terms of survival or employment.

The question of which frame dominates sometimes depends on the order in which they are encountered. An earlier study of framing (involving hypothetical choices) revealed that people who lost a ticket for a show that costs $20 are less likely to buy another ticket than people who lost a $20 bill.[26] In the original demonstration the two questions were presented to two different groups of subjects. In a follow-up study the two questions were posed to the same subjects in different orders. This manipulation produced an interesting pattern. The great majority of subjects expressed willingness to buy a ticket after losing a $20 bill regardless of whether this problem appeared first or second. However, the expressed willingness to buy a second ticket after losing the first was considerably greater among those who first encountered the lost cash problem than among those who did not. Once you realize that you would buy a ticket after losing a $20 bill, you are more inclined to do so after losing a ticket. The reverse argument does not have much force, presumably because it is less natural to construe the lost money as a lost ticket than to construe the lost ticket as lost money. In this case, the juxtaposition of the two frames in the proper order favors the "lost money" frame. How people choose among competing frames is an intriguing topic from both descriptive and prescriptive standpoints.

I have argued that both normative and descriptive analyses of choice are essentially empirical. The descriptive analysis of choice is concerned with the principles that govern actual decisions; the normative analysis of choice is concerned with human intuitions about what constitutes rational behavior. Description invariance, transitivity, and stochastic dominance are generally endorsed by people as principles of rational choice, but this endorsement does not ensure that people's choices will generally satisfy these principles.

An analogy with ethics may be instructive. A normative ethical account is concerned with the principles that underlie moral judgments. A descriptive ethical account is concerned with human conduct. Both enterprises are essentially empirical, but the first refers to people's moral intuitions whereas the second refers to people's actual behavior. The two analyses, of course, are interrelated, but they do not coincide. People generally agree that one should pay income tax or contribute to worthy causes, even if they do not always do so. Similarly, people may accept the normative force of description invariance, even though it is often violated in their own choices. Although the separation between normative and descriptive analyses has been widely accepted in ethics, it is somewhat controversial in decision theory—perhaps because the discrepancy between normative and descriptive theories in ethics stems primarily from motivational considerations, whereas the analogous discrepancy in choice stems primarily from cognitive limitations. It is apparently easier to accept violations of norms that stem from self-interest than violations of norms that result from fallible reasoning.

## Notes

1. Amos Tversky and Daniel Kahneman, "Rational Choice and the Framing of Decisions," *Journal of Business* 59 (1986): 251–278.
2. See Marc Alpert and Howard Raiffa, "A Progress Report on the Training of Probability Assessors," in *Judgment under Uncertainty: Heuristics and Biases*, eds. Daniel Kahneman, Paul Slovic, and Amos Tversky (New York: Cambridge University Press, 1982), pp. 294–305; and Howard Raiffa, *Decision Analysis: Introductory Lectures on Choices Under Uncertainty* (Reading, MA: Addison-Wesley, 1968).
3. Howard Raiffa, "Risk, Ambiguity, and the Savage Axioms: Comment," *Quarterly Journal of Economics* 75 (1961): 690–694.
4. See Kenneth J. Arrow, "Risk Perception in Psychology and Economics," *Economic Inquiry* 20 (1982): 1–9; and Tversky and Kahneman, "Rational Choice."
5. See, for example, Colin Camerer, "Individual Decision Making," in *Handbook of Experimental Economics*, eds. John Kagel and Alvin Roth (Princeton, NJ: Princeton University Press, 1995), pp. 587–703; and John W. Payne, James R. Bettman, and Eric J. Johnson, "Behavioral Decision Research: A Constructive Processing Perspective," *Annual Review of Psychology* 43 (1992): 87–131.
6. George A. Quattrone and Amos Tversky, "Causal Versus Diagnostic Contingencies: On Self-Deception and on the Voter's Illusion," *Journal of Personality and Social Psychology* 46 (1984): 237–248.
7. Barbara J. McNeil, Steven G. Pauker, Hal Sox, and Amos Tversky, "On the Elicitation of Preferences for Alternative Therapies," *New England Journal of Medicine* 306 (1982): 1259–1262.
8. Tversky and Kahneman, "Rational Choice."
9. Eldar Shafir, Peter Diamond, and Amos Tversky, "On Money Illusion," *Quarterly Journal of Economics* (forthcoming).
10. Eric J. Johnson et al., "Framing, Probability Distortions, and Insurance Decisions," *Journal of Risk and Uncertainty* 7 (1993): 35–51.
11. Sarah Lichtenstein and Paul Slovic, "Reversals of Preference Between Bids and Choices in Gambling Decisions," *Journal of Experimental Psychology* 89 (1971): 46–55; and Sarah Lichtenstein and Paul Slovic, "Response-Induced Reversals of Preference in Gambling: An Extended Replication in Las Vegas," *Journal of Experimental Psychology* 101 (1973): 16–20.
12. Amos Tversky, Paul Slovic, and Daniel Kahneman, "The Causes of Preference Reversal," *American Economic Review* 80 (1990): 204–217.
13. Paul Slovic, Dale Griffin, and Amos Tversky, "Compatibility Effects in

Judgment and Choice," in *Insights in Decision Making: Theory and Applications*, ed. Robin M. Hogarth (Chicago: University of Chicago Press, 1990).

14. Tversky, Slovic, and Kahneman, "The Causes of Preference Reversal."

15. Amos Tversky, Shmuel Sattath, and Paul Slovic, "Contingent Weighting in Judgment and Choice," *Psychological Review* 95 (1988): 371–384.

16. Daniel Kahneman and Ilana Ritov, "Determinants of Stated Willingness to Pay for Public Goods: A Study in the Headline Method," *Journal of Risk and Uncertainty* 9 (1994): 5–31.

17. Itamar Simonson and Amos Tversky, "Choice in Context: Tradeoff Contrast and Extremeness Aversion," *Journal of Marketing Research,* 14 (1992): 281–295.

18. Joel Huber, John W. Payne, and Christopher Puto, "Adding Asymmetrically Dominated Alternatives: Violations of Regularity and the Similarity Hypothesis," *Journal of Consumer Research* 9 (1982): 90–98.

19. Simonson and Tversky, "Choice in Context."

20. Mark Kelman, Yuval Rottenstreich, and Amos Tversky, "Context-Dependent Legal Decision Making," *The Journal of Legal Studies* (forthcoming).

21. Amos Tversky and Itamar Simonson, "Context-Dependent Preferences," *Management Science* 39 (1993): 1179–1189.

22. For results on stochastic dominance, see Tversky and Kahneman, "Rational Choice"; for results on transitivity, see Amos Tversky, "The Intransitivity of Preferences," *Psychological Review* 76 (1969): 31–48.

23. See Leonard J. Savage, *The Foundation of Statistics* (New York: Wiley, 1954); Raiffa, "Risk, Ambiguity, and the Savage Axioms"; and Paul Slovic and Amos Tversky, "Who Accepts Savage's Axiom?" *Behavioral Science* 19 (1974): 368–373.

24. Tversky and Kahneman, "Rational Choice."

25. Barbara J. McNeil, Steven G. Pauker, and Amos Tversky, "On the Framing of Medical Decisions," in *Decision Making: Descriptive, Normative, and Prescriptive Interactions,* eds. David E. Bell, Howard Raiffa, and Amos Tversky (New York: Cambridge University Press, 1988).

26. Amos Tversky and Daniel Kahneman, "The Framing of Decisions and the Psychology of Choice," *Science* 211 (1981): 453–458.

# CHAPTER 2

# SIGN POSTING: THE SELECTIVE REVELATION OF PRODUCT INFORMATION

## Richard J. Zeckhauser and David V. P. Marks

Sellers post countless signs to convey information about their wares, ranging from "LO MILEAGE" on a used car, to past performance statistics on a mutual fund, to the experience and education listed on a resume. For reasons we will explore, the information revealed in signs is usually truthful, but the whole truth is rarely presented. The LO MILEAGE car is rusting out underneath; the mutual fund had a few lousy years before the period reported; much of the $50 million budget mentioned on the applicant's resume is outside his authority.

We refer to the process of providing information to prospective buyers as "sign posting."[1] This process conveys information that would otherwise be costly or impossible to acquire. Though some information is provided and other information hidden, buyers untangle the message, at least to some degree. They may be suspicious that the mutual fund did not mention volatility, nor the job applicant the number of people who report to him, and may draw appropriate inferences. Below we study how the game of sign posting is played.

Our concern originates in a multi-attribute world: Buyers care about many characteristics of a product, and quality is not easily captured in a single number. Moreover, different individuals have different preferences, making it more difficult to convey information,

Scott Feira, Mary Frangakis, Laurie King, and David Kuo provided able research assistance. Miriam Avins, Gerhard Holt, Ralph Keeney, and James Sebenius provided valuable comments. Richard Zeckhauser's work was supported by the National Science Foundation.

say, about customer satisfaction. In many cases, potential buyers will not even know what other information may be relevant. In other cases, buyers will falter in the complex process of statistical inference, though in theory a grand Bayesian approach could handle matters.

When we examine ads in newspapers or on television, or seek to winnow down a list of colleges using their admissions materials, we are engaged in a subtle game. We must be simultaneously expert at inference, multi-attribute utility theory, decision theory, and game theory. Students of Howard Raiffa—who has written books in all of these areas—should be well prepared.

We also examine sign posting as a critical ingredient in a modern economic system. Sign posting helps deal with situations where information flows poorly, and where multiple attributes matter. But it offers only a partial solution to the problem of poor information flow. Recognizing the dangers of, or at least the welfare losses associated with, selective revelation by sellers, government frequently mandates the provision of information. A final section shows that such requirements can significantly affect the market.

## The Game

We present sign posting as an informal game. Sellers provide signs containing selective, but generally truthful, information about their products. Consumers decode the signs, perhaps imperfectly. Consumers have preferences for products with multiple attributes.[2] Since preferences vary, quality is not a single numeraire. On the basis of what they can infer about particular products, consumers choose what to buy. When posting and decoding are expensive, there will be important effects on product characteristics and market function, no matter how expert the participants.[3]

### The Content of Signs

Sellers provide their prospective customers with selective information about their products; that is, they post signs. This section discusses sellers' choices about what information to post, and how to present it, as well as the limitations on their choices.[4]

As is already evident, advertisements and signs are related but distinct concepts. An advertisement is a notice intended to induce consumers to purchase a good, and is disseminated in printed or electronic media. But signs also include price tags and product tags affixed to goods, job applicants' oral statements about themselves made to prospective employers, resumes, and campus photographs in

**Figure 2-1**
*The Penalty for Exaggerating Claims about Characteristics in Signs*

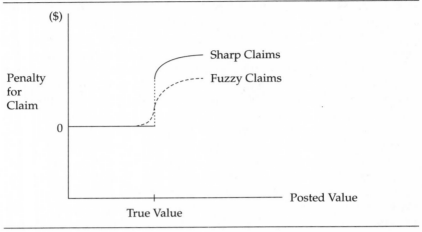

college catalogs. The selection of samples can be a form of sign posting; witness the attractive and diverse students in the catalogs.[5]

*Variable or fixed.* The characteristics posted in signs may either be variable, within the seller's control, or fixed, beyond his control. For example, the price of a condo is normally within the seller's control, but its square footage is not.[6] For fixed characteristics, the seller has one decision: whether or not to post the characteristic. For variable characteristics, the seller must decide which characteristics to post, and at what level to set them. A seller's decision about how much of a variable characteristic to provide may well be affected by his expectations about whether he will post it. Colleges utilizing federal loans have recently been required to inform applicants about the percentage of students graduating within 150 percent of the normal time. Presumably, this gives them an incentive to boost their graduation percentage.

*Sharp or fuzzy.* A good's posted characteristics may also be "sharp" ("magna cum laude graduate of Princeton") or "fuzzy" ("excellent student"). Price is generally sharp, but curiously (to an economist) is frequently not posted.

It is generally more costly to exaggerate about sharp characteristics than about fuzzy characteristics. (See Figure 2-1.) First, false statements may be illegal. For example, while it may be illegal for a breakfast cereal manufacturer to state falsely that "One serving contains 100 percent of the minimum daily requirements," the seller is unlikely to be penalized for claiming that "This cereal is nutritious," no matter how low the nutritional content of the cereal. Recently, however, the Food and Drug Administration began to regulate terms such as "low cholesterol" and "light" in relation to manufactured foodstuffs.

Second, false statements may injure the sign poster's reputation. For example, even if it were legal to do so, General Motors would be unlikely to state that a car has 18 cubic feet of trunk space if it has only 17. If the misrepresentation became known, it would damage the firm's public image. But the company might be less reluctant to describe the trunk as "large." Similarly, someone selling a used car through a classified ad would be ill-advised to overstate the condition of the body; a prospective buyer will see the body for herself. The seller would hardly be credible stating, "I admit that I lied about the body, but the engine is as good as I claimed."

When a seller posts accurate or even understated information about fuzzy characteristics, a prospective buyer may wrongly conclude that the seller exaggerated. Suppose that someone correctly writes in a letter of recommendation that "John is very smart." The reader, upon meeting John, may erroneously judge John to be less than "very smart," and the possibility of such disagreement may impose a cost even if the writer intended to understate John's qualities.[7] Sign-posters' inclination to exaggerate on fuzzy signs may be tempered by the discomfort caused by so doing; the tug of such costs prevents excessive exaggeration. Marks and Zeckhauser provide a model of the outcome when exaggeration costs are understood, and incurred, and messages get unravelled.[8]

*What characteristics are postable?* As a practical matter, sellers cannot post information about all of a product's characteristics, and buyers cannot confirm all information by inspection. That is, not all of a product's characteristics are both postable and observable. A characteristic is "postable" by a seller if a depiction or brief description of the good, or of the specific characteristic, enables a prospective buyer to assess, at low cost, the good's endowment of the characteristic,[9] or if the seller can assess, at low cost, the good's endowment of the characteristic and convey his assessment to the buyer.

A characteristic is observable by buyers if a prospective buyer can, at low cost, inspect the good and assess its endowment of the characteristic. For example, a car's paint job is observable, but the state of its engine is less so. As a practical matter, the energy efficiency of an air conditioner, though postable by the manufacturer, is unobservable by the consumer. At modest cost, the manufacturer can determine the unit's energy efficiency and post it for all buyers, while for any single buyer the cost of determining the unit's energy efficiency would be prohibitive. In contrast, the flavor of a new prepared food may be observable but not postable; the seller may be unable to describe the taste.

If a characteristic, such as the energy efficiency of air conditioners, is important and postable but not observable, then government may be tempted to mandate posting. The seller can realize economies of scale in producing information; individual buyers cannot.

Testimonials are one way to post information about characteristics that are not directly postable. For example, it may be impossible to post the charm of a resort, but if a celebrity attests to the resort's charm, then the seller has, in effect, posted the charm. Similarly, celebrity endorsements allow insurance companies to post their soundness, and charities to post their legitimacy.

*Signals as signs.* A "signal" is an observable characteristic (e.g., a college degree) whose cost of adjustment varies inversely with the level of a desirable unobservable attribute (e.g., aptitude). Sellers can use signals to demonstrate that their products possess unobservable attributes.[10]

Signals are a special case of sign posting. Signaling models are concerned with how sellers communicate information about a single underlying characteristic whose level cannot be revealed directly; sign posting models are often concerned with how sellers decide which of many characteristics to post. Signals convey information about unobservable characteristics; signs often post observable characteristics. In signaling models, the seller can vary the amount of the signaling variable that he produces; sign posting models concern both characteristics that the seller can vary and characteristics that are fixed.

Posting signs is frequently inexpensive; generating signals is expensive. The cost of posting a signal differs across individuals; the cost of posting signs is often the same across individuals. Signaling models assume that the seller can costlessly transmit information about the signaling variable; sign posting models typically assume that it is costly for sellers to post, and buyers to decipher, information about characteristics. The key to signaling models is the cost of producing the signal, which depends upon the amount of the underlying characteristic the product possesses; the key to sign posting models is the cost of posting and decoding information about characteristics.

Sellers post "signals" about an underlying attribute, rather than the attribute itself, for several reasons. First, bald assertions that are not objectively verifiable may not be credible; sellers may have little incentive to be truthful in describing characteristics that are difficult for buyers to verify. Signals provide a way to convey credible information about such characteristics. For example, describing oneself as smart may not be credible; displaying a Harvard Business School diploma may credibly suggest that one is smart. Second, signals may provide an innocuous way to convey information that would be obnoxious if posted. For example, bluntly posting one's wealth would also, as a side effect, suggest that the person is status conscious. But making large donations to the symphony may signal wealth—and generosity and culture—without suggesting status consciousness.[11]

*Posting price.* Though prices play a central role in economic models of competition, signs often omit price, for at least two reasons: First, posting prices only makes sense if the product's other characteristics are posted or understood. With nonstandardized products, it is difficult to quote a price that buyers can compare to others. For example, a physician's services are customized to each patient's needs, making it difficult to state in advance the cost of treatment.[12]

Second, posting a low price may promote unfavorable inferences about a product's quality. One suspects that many prospective patients would be put off by a doctor's claim that he has the lowest prices around. Price is particularly likely to be omitted from a sign when quality is difficult to assess, and is important relative to price, as with medicine, where most consumers pay only a small fraction of the costs they incur. Advertising a good's price as being "X percent off the original price" is presumably intended to negate the unfavorable quality inference.[13]

*Omissions and truth.* Sellers generally post highly incomplete information about their products. First, it is costly to produce and post signs. Posting more information (e.g., by placing a larger ad) costs more. Second, given buyers' finite ability to process information, a less complete sign may actually be more informative. The disclosure requirements of the Securities Act of 1933 are criticized on such grounds; prospectuses that are too complete may be less helpful to investors. California's recent chemical-labeling legislation has been criticized on similar grounds; there may be so many carcinogens that labeling all of them would overwhelm consumers.[14]

Third, as discussed above, certain characteristics are difficult to describe. Fourth, incomplete signs may cause prospective buyers to overestimate a good's undisclosed characteristics. A photograph of a house's beautiful living room may cause buyers to infer that the rest of the house is of comparable quality. The more even the quality of a product, the more information the seller may want to provide, lest prospective buyers wrongly infer that the unposted characteristics are inferior.[15]

While signs tend to be incomplete, they probably tend to be truthful. First, the law may require it. For example, specific statutes prohibit false advertising, and consumer protection legislation prohibits false and misleading statements by retailers. Second, the prospect of bad publicity, of injury to reputation, and of losing repeat business may deter sellers from posting false signs.[16] Third, in many transactions, the buyer can inspect or test the good before the purchase becomes final, or can return it if dissatisfied. In such cases, the seller would probably gain nothing by lying, and might well suffer.

Fourth, when characteristics are fuzzy, it is difficult to demonstrate that someone lied. A good student can safely describe himself as an "excellent" student, but not as being in the "top 10 percent" of his class. Finally, being truthful may not be expensive. Everyone expects signs to be incomplete; this allows the sign poster to choose, and he can usually find a good characteristic to post.

The choice of how complete to make a sign can have interesting consequences. College applications are, in effect, a sign, though the consumer—the admissions office—can impose requirements on what must be included. Lafayette College made submitting Scholastic Aptitude Test (SAT) scores optional for applicants starting in 1995. One might expect there to be a threshold SAT score, with scores exceeding that threshold being reported, and scores below it not. But then a student whose score was just below the threshold would choose to report rather than have the admissions committee assume his score to be at the mean of the other unreported scores. If he reports, then both the threshold and the mean score among nonreporting applicants declines slightly. The threshold might unravel until only the applicant with the lowest score would not report.

In practice, this complete unraveling process probably does not occur for at least two reasons: First, not everyone is a sophisticated decision theorist expecting everyone else to be the same. If some students with scores of 1200 will not report, perhaps mistakenly, then a rational student who scored 1150 may actually be better off not reporting. Second, it is expensive to take the SAT. In time, people who expect to do relatively poorly will simply avoid the expense.

In a world of fully rational expectations and behavior, where the posting and consumption of information is costless, sign posting will reveal all information. The real world, being neither fully rational nor costless, experiences extensive sign posting with information systematically omitted.

### How Consumers Decode Signs

Sellers have considerable leeway in creating the signs they post about their products. They may make truthful but fuzzy statements, and provide only the most favorable facts. So why do prospective buyers look at sellers' signs? First, signs are frequently the only available source of information. Second, some consumers are gullible, and fail to discount for information not given. Third, many consumers are good Bayesians; they are adept at decoding signs, just as producers are good at constructing them.[17]

A sign is often valuable to a prospective buyer as the first step in learning about a product. For example, a house hunter who sees a house advertisement that includes a beautiful living room will learn more about the property before committing herself to making the purchase. In contrast, when ordering from a catalog, one generally cannot inspect the product before buying. This enhances the importance and value of the vendor's reputation for integrity.

Search costs increase the value to consumers of signs. If a homeowner's display ad featuring his beautiful living room induces a buyer to look at the house, then the seller has a substantial advantage. Similarly, stores do not like to facilitate comparison shopping by quoting prices over the telephone; they know that if a buyer must come into the store, she is more likely to buy. And antiques stores display their beautiful wares in the window, without prices, knowing that there is some stickiness once a prospective shopper steps across the threshold, since stopping in a new store will be costly.

Evidence suggests that individuals search less than they should. John Pratt, David Wise, and Zeckhauser find unreasonably high price variability for standardized goods; the implied search costs are unrealistically high.[18] The cognitive strategies that people use to compensate for their limited ability to absorb information may be less than fully rational. For example, "status quo bias" leads people to stick too much with decisions already made, or with whatever alternatives they encounter early on.

Despite consumers' limited ability to rationally assimilate information, many decode signs well. The reader can try a self-test with the following letter, a redacted version of an actual letter of recommendation received at the Kennedy School from a distinguished economist:

> To the Hiring Committee:
> Mr. John Doe has taken three graduate seminars with me, was for two years my teaching assistant in an upper-level course on game theory, was head teaching assistant when I taught our introductory economics course, and is writing his dissertation under my supervision.
> He is the only student to whom I have given a general examination grade of "distinction" in 20 years of teaching here and at [another major university]. His scholarly work reflects not only his training here but his three years of research at. . . .

His dissertation examines . . . [long factual description]. His
work cannot fail to attract attention.

The first paragraph of the letter indicates the professor knows Doe
well. The naive reader might conclude Doe was selected in some
competition for teaching assistant positions; the sophisticated reader
might wonder why more was not said about that. Might the better
students get fellowships? To identify Doe as the only student in 20
years to get a distinction is certainly to post a sign. Impressive, but it
would be more so if we were told that there was no grade above
distinction, and that the professor had examined many dozens of
students, not just a small number. The careful reader of signs will
inquire about information not given. Why does the professor not describe Doe as bright, incisive, or original? Is he merely capable and
extremely conscientious? The final sentence appears to be carefully
crafted. The thesis may be widely noticed, but have little lasting impact. The naive reader will be wowed by this letter; the savvy reader
will be skeptical.[19]

Even if all consumers are skilled at inference and deduction, and
even if all information is ultimately communicated, the practice of sign
posting still imposes deadweight costs. For example, those who post
fuzzy signs must exaggerate their claims if they are to communicate them accurately, since consumers will routinely discount fuzzy
claims. The sign posters then must bear the cost of being considered
exaggerators.

In reality, of course, most consumers are not perfectly rational
decision makers. Rather, they make decisions using a variety of heuristics of the sort explored by Daniel Kahneman, Paul Slovic, and Amos
Tversky.[20] Sellers know this and surely capitalize on it when designing
their signs. To take an extremely simple example, sellers frequently
price goods at a penny below the round dollar figure—$5.99 instead
of $6.00—presumably because they find that buyers perceive the for-
mer figure to be significantly lower than the latter.

## Effects of Sign Posting on Competition

Many markets function where only partial information is provided
about competitors' products. The competitors also have the ability to
improve selected characteristics of their products, although doing so
may be costly. A critical question is how the practice of sign posting
affects competition in a market.

In many contexts, one product will be known for one attribute,
and a second for another. For example, many colleges have fewer than

2,000 students and are known for having faculties who pay careful attention to students. Other colleges, mostly at research universities, have much larger undergraduate bodies, and focus on the extraordinary intellectual resources available. The middle range is almost unpopulated, though many prospective students might welcome a mix of significant faculty attention and strong research. It would be simply too expensive for a Harvard to restructure itself to give, and get credit for giving, careful attention to students, or for Swarthmore to become, and become recognized as, a research institution.

Given less than perfect information flow, and the practice of sign posting, this outcome is possible even if there are no economies of scale or returns to specialization, and even if the consuming public mostly wants a mix of characteristics. Thus, Harvard Business School is loath to give up its reputation for the case method. Stanford, in part to illustrate its rigor, demands that its students learn calculus; advertising that now 60 percent of its teaching is by the case method would accomplish little.

This phenomenon of strength building in one area is also well known in professional firms. Wesleyan College was recently searching for a new president. It could hire the executive search firm Hedrick and Struggles, a good firm with conventional candidates, or Spencer Stuart, which is best known for nonconventional choices. Wesleyan would have liked a mix of these two worlds, but the producers had differentiated themselves.[21]

On the other hand, sometimes sign posting may only increase *perceived* differentiation: sellers can divide the market by attracting buyers' attention to different features of similar or identical products. For example, one car manufacturer's signs may stress acceleration and another's may emphasize seating capacity, while the cars may be very similar in other respects, or perhaps similar even in acceleration and seating capacity. Those who long for glamour will tend to buy from the first manufacturer, and those with large families will tend to buy from the second.[22] In sum, sign posting may promote product differentiation, both real and perceived.[23]

In some circumstances, the cost of processing information leads the purchaser to ask for selected information. Applicants for teaching positions in economics are asked to present a single paper, since it is costly for the hiring committee to read more materials. The feedback loop has led to a situation where most candidates focus on their job-talk papers to the detriment of the rest of their theses, and many theses now consist of three papers, rather than an integrated analysis.

Sign posting can foster incentives to produce high-quality products.[24] A company that owns a brand name has an incentive to maintain or improve the quality of its product to protect the value of the brand name. For example, suppose that two competing firms sell similar versions of a product, but that only one firm's product has a brand name. If the brand is well established, consumers will know the quality of the branded good, but will likely assume that the unbranded good has the average quality of unbranded goods of this type. Since shoppers will never know the quality of the unbranded good, the producer has no incentive to improve quality. In contrast, the seller of the branded good has an incentive to improve its quality, so long as the increased price associated with a higher-quality good exceeds the greater cost of producing it.[25] Buyers displaying brand-name products—e.g., wearing Calvin Klein jeans—post signs about themselves.[26]

The role of brand names as signs of quality is reflected in prices for corporate acquisitions. A firm that produces the highest-quality good in a market will command a disproportionate price relative to its earnings. One obvious explanation for this is that the acquirer will be able to use the acquired firm's brand name as a sign of quality for other products. For example, when Beatrice acquired Sara Lee, the former renamed itself the Sara Lee Corporation.

In at least some situations, posting signs yields surprisingly high rewards. Anecdotal evidence suggests that by distributing flyers posting their availability, free-lance house cleaners in Cambridge, Massachusetts, can earn wages considerably above the going rate for such work. Apparently, the buyers do not investigate the market. Similarly, anecdotal evidence suggests that people who place personal ads obtain better results than people who actively read and respond to such ads.

### Government and Sign Posting

To correct for market failures, to ensure that markets are fair, and to pursue other social goals (such as energy conservation), the government frequently exploits the ability of signs to affect buyers and sellers.[27]

Government—federal, state, and local—has long engaged both in sign posting and in regulating sign posting by others.[28] First, the government often posts its own signs regarding sellers' products. For example, the Food and Drug Administration (FDA) posts signs about the efficacy of drugs, and the U.S. Department of Transportation posts signs about airlines' punctuality.[29]

Second, in some contexts, the government requires that sellers' signs be truthful. For example, the Federal Trade Commission (FTC) generally requires that advertising be truthful.[30] Third, the government sometimes regulates the completeness of the information in signs. For example, as mentioned earlier, the Securities and Exchange Commission (SEC) requires that prospectuses provide complete disclosure.[31]

Fourth, in some cases the government requires that sellers post information about certain characteristics of a product (for example, the energy efficiency of air conditioners) and prescribes a standardized format for posting such information.[32] Such mandated posting has at least two effects: First, it may help consumers to identify products possessing the desirable characteristic. Second, it may induce sellers to produce products that possess the desirable characteristic.[33] Other such characteristics include the tar and nicotine content of cigarettes, automobiles' fuel efficiency, mutual funds' fees and performance, and, under recent legislation in California, carcinogens in the workplace.[34]

Not surprisingly, sellers whose ratings on these standardized scales are particularly high tend to post their ratings prominently. For example, advertisements for low-tar cigarettes tend to highlight their low-tar content, whereas advertisements for high-tar cigarettes tend to focus on other characteristics, such as the product's taste. During the period from 1967 (when the government began requiring tar content to be posted) to 1986, the market share held by low-tar cigarettes in the United States increased from 2 percent to 53 percent.[35]

We suspect that smokers responding to information about tar content, and manufacturers changing their product in response to smoker preferences, played a major role in the growth of market share for low-tar cigarettes. We call this the "C&M" ("consume and manufacture") effect: Consumers increase their demand for products possessing the newly posted characteristic, and sellers increase their production of such products. The C&M effect surely also helps account for the increase in fuel efficiency that followed institution of the Environmental Protection Agency's requirement that automobile manufacturers post fuel efficiency.

Only in recent years have mutual funds been required to post their fees in a standardized format. These fee structures tend to be complex because of the use of "soft dollars" and other arrangements. We expect that the new regulation will lead funds to restructure their fees in ways that reduce reported fees. For example, they might seek to increase their brokerage commissions, which do not count as fees, and reduce other charges that do count as fees.[36]

When the government engages in or requires sign posting, it may not be an ordinary agent for the consumer. It may be engaging in paternalism, say, by requiring that health warnings be posted on cigarette packages. It may be seeking to correct a mispriced resource, such as energy under price controls, or it may just be trying to use increased information to foster competition.

Sometimes the government's posting requirement may be the result, rather than the cause, of increased attention to the importance of particular characteristics. The government may begin to require that sellers post information about particular characteristics after people have decided that the characteristic is important—witness the FDA's recent initiatives with foods listed as "light" or "low in cholesterol."

How effective is government sign posting? Early experience with airline promptness is suggestive. In November 1987, the U.S. Department of Transportation began publishing monthly reports on major airlines' on-time performance to foster the C&M effect, i.e., to enable passengers to make informed choices among flights, and to increase the airlines' incentives to minimize delays.[37]

Some evidence suggests that passengers pay little attention to the reports. For example, a poll of 1,500 travel agents in June 1988 revealed that 72 percent of them had never been asked by a customer for information about on-time performance, even though flight-by-flight ratings had been available for six months on travel agents' computers. There are several possible explanations for this finding: First, many consumers may be unaware of the data's availability. Second, factors other than promptness affect flight choices, including price, customer loyalty to particular airlines, and frequent flier programs.[38]

Nonetheless, airlines with good on-time records often do include this information in their advertisements. And on-time performance among the airlines has improved. For example, in September 1987, 77 percent of flights were on time. In June 1988, 84.3 percent were on time.[39] On the other hand, in at least some cases, airlines have merely increased the stated length of flights to give themselves more leeway, so reported improvements in on-time performance may be overstated.

Government manipulation of sign posting to increase competition or awareness of certain characteristics may decrease the quality of, or competition over, other characteristics. For example, the government's monthly publication of on-time performance data may have succeeded in increasing competition along this dimension. But perhaps focusing competition on promptness has caused airlines to be less attentive to other product features, such as passenger comfort. Similarly, as already mentioned, the SEC's disclosure requirements may cause companies to provide too much information.

## Conclusions

The foregoing discussion suggests several conclusions, drawn on concepts from multi-attribute utility theory, game theory, and decision theory.

First, sellers will tend to overproduce characteristics that can be posted in signs, and underproduce characteristics that cannot be posted. For example, if accounting rules require firms to post current earnings but prohibit them from posting projected earnings, then firms may focus excessively on producing good current earnings, to the detriment of their longer-term interests.[40]

Second, if sellers can choose which characteristics to post, they may post characteristics that their competitors are not posting; that is, sign posting may facilitate actual or perceived product differentiation, reducing competition.

Third, if a firm can vary the level of particular characteristics of its product (in addition to choosing which characteristics to post), then it may choose to differentiate its product by producing more or less of particular postable characteristics than its competitors do. This too could reduce competition.

Fourth, because prices may serve as a signal of quality, sellers may have a disincentive to post low prices.

Fifth, government regulation of signs—for example, requiring truthfulness or completeness, or imposing standardized reporting arrangements—affects not only what information is conveyed but also product design and ultimately market structure.

Throughout our lives—from a toddler's cry to be cuddled, through a college student's careful choice of essay topic, to a corporate executive's skillful explanation of diminished earnings—we are all engaged in the game of sign posting, the selective revelation and partial decoding of information. In our private lives, sign posting plays a pivotal role in activities ranging from casual conversation to courtship. In the business world, the ability to post truthful but likely incomplete signs profoundly affects both product attributes and market structures.

## NOTES

1. The relation between "sign posting" and "signaling," as the term is used in economics, is discussed below.
2. Ralph Keeney and Howard Raiffa, *Decision and Multiple Objectives: Preferences and Value Tradeoffs* (New York: Cambridge University Press, 1993).
3. We assume in this paper that sellers post signs about their products, and that buyers decode the signs; this reflects the division of labor observed in practice. But why don't buyers post signs about what they are looking for? There are several reasons.

   First, in "product space," the seller's product occupies a *point* (e.g., he is offering an apartment with three rooms, one bath, and a fireplace), but the buyer has an *indifference curve* (e.g., he might give up a fireplace to get a second bath). It is probably easier for the seller to describe his point than for the buyer to describe his curve.

Second, it may be easier for the seller to describe the characteristics of a product than it is for the buyer to describe what he seeks in a product. For example, a seller can use photographs to communicate what his apartment looks like. It may be more difficult for buyers to describe what they want an apartment to look like.

Third, sellers will typically be able to exploit greater economies of scale in sign posting than could buyers. A company that makes and sells thousands of cars can spread among all of its sales the cost of posting signs; the car buyer typically buys just one car and therefore cannot similarly spread such cost. (Of course, when buyers can exploit economies of scale—as can, say, Walmart's wholesale buyers—then they may well post signs.)

4. Sellers will typically post only favorable information about their products, but may occasionally post unfavorable information, for at least five reasons. First, if the seller chooses a sufficiently insignificant flaw, the benefit of demonstrating his honesty by posting it may outweigh the detriment of having revealed it. Second, posting unfavorable information about a "bad" characteristic that the buyer does not care strongly about may counteract the otherwise problematic effect—discussed below—that low price is often a signal of low quality.

Third, posting unfavorable information ("We're number two") may indicate complementary favorable characteristics ("We try harder"). Fourth, sellers may post bad characteristics because prospective buyers ask them to.

Fifth, a seller may post an unfavorable characteristic in the belief that buyers will misunderstand it. For example, a seller might truthfully report that his car has a certain compression ratio. The stated ratio may actually be bad, but naive buyers will assume that it must be good or the seller would not mention it. Similarly, a bank might post its CD rates in a large sign, or a gas station its gas prices, even if the posted numbers are not really competitive.

Interestingly, sellers appear to be less likely to post bad characteristics of their competitors' products. (The conspicuous exception is politicians, who commonly engage in negative campaigning.) One reason is probably that mentioning a competitor's name—even in the context of making a negative comment—promotes awareness of that name.

An *excuse* is a sign intended to cause observers to interpret an apparently bad characteristic less harshly than they otherwise would. For example, explaining to a visitor that the seller just returned from out of town could cause the visitor to discount the messiness of the seller's office.

5. Steve Johnson, Co-CEO of Johnson-Grace, the leading image compression

company on the Internet, observes: "We present our potential customers with a range of examples of compressed images. Naturally, the greater our advantage over the competition for an image, the more likely it is to be included." Personal communication, May 1995.

6. While price is generally a variable characteristic, there may be exceptions, as with government-imposed price controls.

7. Thus, buyers sometimes determine the requirements that will be imposed on sellers. Consider the problem facing an employer who wishes to hire a research leader with administrative and research responsibilities. Should the job description require a Ph.D.? On the face of it, an employer might be inclined to omit this requirement, believing that some qualified candidates may not hold a Ph.D. But then potential applicants with Ph.D.s might not apply, either because they do not wish to take a job that does not require a Ph.D., or because they wrongly infer that the job is primarily administrative. On the other hand, an applicant without a Ph.D. who does receive a job offer will be very happy.

8. David Marks and Richard Zeckhauser, "Sign Posting: Selected Product Information and Market Function," working paper, 1994.

9. This suggests that signs are postable if they contain objectively rebuttable information. For example, the number of tennis courts is postable because sellers will be reluctant to say they have four courts if they only have two. On the other hand, there may be a tendency to exaggerate subjective items.

10. See Michael Spence, *Market Signaling: Informational Transfer in Hiring and Related Screening Processes* (Cambridge, MA: Harvard University Press, 1974).

11. There has been much discussion of advertising as a signal. See, for example, Philip Nelson, "Advertising as Information," *Journal of Political Economy* 81 (1974): 729–754; Richard Kihlstrom and Michael Riordan, "Advertising as a Signal," *Journal of Political Economy* 92 (1984): 427–450; and Paul Milgrom and John Roberts, "Prices and Advertising Signals of Product Quality," *Journal of Political Economy* 94 (1986): 796–821.

   This paper employs a different approach to explain the use of signs. Whereas the signaling models generally assume that advertising is uninformative, we assume that signs *are* informative.

12. Rizzo and Zeckhauser show that advertising has no effect on price in physician markets. John Rizzo and Richard Zeckhauser, "Advertising and the Price and Quality of Primary Care Physician Services," *Journal of Human Resources* 27 (1992): 381–421.

13. Thus, New York City consumer protection laws prohibit a seller from advertising a product as being sold at a marked-down price unless the seller actually sold the product at the original price. The posted price of new cars is the point from which expected discounts are computed. The major long distance telephone services offer so many discount programs

that most people do not pay the full listed rates; therefore, discount percentages are uninformative, and some long distance advertising mentions comparative prices, rather than percentage discounts.

14. Marketing experts tend to believe that it is often better to provide less information in signs. A widely accepted principle in marketing is that advertisements should focus on no more than a few of a product's features.

15. Posting just one characteristic, rather than a few, may be less likely to prompt prospective buyers to think about which characteristics are *not* posted. This may help explain why sellers often post only one characteristic, even when their product has a large number of characteristics. Car ads, for example, often focus on just one feature.

16. The cost of being known to have made a false statement can be high. (For example, at a university the penalty for falsely denying a true allegation of plagiarism may be more severe than the penalty for having plagiarized.) This cost increases the likelihood that signs are truthful and therefore increases the effectiveness of sign posting.

17. It is important to be careful about our assumptions about buyers and sellers. Sometimes a naive buyer can rely on the fact that other buyers are informed. This might be true if the salesman could not distinguish between sophisticated and unsophisticated buyers, and was targeting both groups. In this case, the seller might not make a claim unless it would impress a sophisticated buyer. But if the seller only counts on selling cars to naive buyers, this reasoning does not apply. In some models, it will be sufficient for naive buyers to know that some buyers are sophisticated. However, this will not work if the product is targeted at unsophisticated buyers.

18. John Pratt, David Wise, and Richard Zeckhauser, "Price Differences in Almost Competitive Markets," *Quarterly Journal of Economics* 53 (1979): 189–211.

19. In reality, different prospective buyers have different inferential abilities, and sellers presumably try to exploit this, by posting different kinds of signs for different target audiences. Times Square signs saying "GOING OUT OF BUSINESS, 50% OFF" may fool unsophisticated tourists, but are not likely to fool more sophisticated New Yorkers.

20. Daniel Kahneman, Paul Slovic, and Amos Tversky, eds., *Judgement Under Uncertainty: Heuristics and Biases* (New York: Cambridge University Press, 1982).

21. Richard Cavanaugh, search committee member, personal communication, October 3, 1994.

22. Because of the advantage to a seller of posting different characteristics than his competitors post, a seller may choose to post signs that his competitors can't imitate (e.g., "oldest restaurant in Boston").

23. For a related discussion, see Asher Wolinksy, "True Monopolistic Compe-

tition as a Result of Imperfect Information," *Quarterly Journal of Economics* 101 (1986): 493–511.

24. For example, posting referees' names on journal articles would reward their effort, provide incentives for better assessments, and guide prospective readers.

25. The differing quality of Korean and Taiwanese manufactured exports illustrates this. See Dani Rodrik, "Industrial Organization and Product Quality: Evidence from South Korean and Taiwanese Exports," in *Empirical Studies of Strategic Trade Policy*, eds. Paul Krugman and Alasdair Smith (Chicago: University of Chicago Press, 1994). Rodrik found that the quality of Korean manufactured exports is higher, at least as indicated by price received, and attributes this to the superior ability of Korean firms to internalize reputational externalities. Korean industry is dominated by large conglomerates, whereas Taiwanese industry is less concentrated. The large Korean firms, with well-known brand names (such as Hyundai, Samsung, and Lucky Goldstar), have a greater incentive to provide high quality goods.

Rodrik found that Korean goods sell for about 20 percent more than their Taiwanese counterparts, reflecting that Korean goods have systematically higher quality. Country names could also function as signs of quality, as brand names do. For example, Korean products could come to have a reputation for being of higher quality than Taiwanese products.

26. While signs create incentives for sellers to enhance postable characteristics, sellers also have other incentives to enhance unpostable characteristics. First, if a buyer can observe certain characteristics before a purchase becomes final, then the seller has an incentive to improve those characteristics even if they are not postable. Second, if the seller hopes for repeat business or referrals, he will be concerned that his product's nonpostable characteristics satisfy the buyer's expectations. Third, the seller may have legal or moral obligations to produce the characteristics or, as master woodworkers will tell you, may take pleasure in producing excellent hidden work.

Sellers may also try to imply that unpostable characteristics are better than they actually are: A freshly painted home interior suggests a fastidious homeowner and better conditions under the walls. Slovenly homeowners can capitalize on this to paint a false picture.

27. Private organizations, such as Consumers Union or Underwriters Laboratories, can also affect product quality by posting signs of their own, or by allowing their signs to be posted.

28. For example, the Pure Food and Drug Act of 1906 prohibits shipment of misbranded food and drugs. The Federal Trade Commission Act of 1914 established the FTC, which is today the single most important government agency concerned with advertising. The Lanham Trademark Act of 1947

protects firms' interests in trademarks and slogans. The Fair Packaging and Labeling Act of 1966 requires that manufacturers label packages with the content, the manufacturer, and the quantity. The Public Health Cigarette Smoking Act of 1970 banned cigarette advertising on the broadcast media, and required health warnings on cigarette ads in the print media. See C. Bovee and W. Arens, *Contemporary Advertising* (Homewood, IL: Irwin, 1986), pp. 50–51.

29. Independent private entities may also post signs about sellers' products. For example, *Consumer Reports* posts detailed signs evaluating different brands of particular products.

30. There are exceptions to this requirement. For example, "puffing" is generally permitted, on the grounds that most consumers will correctly unravel the seller's hyperbole. Thus, a beer seller might be permitted to assert that his beer has "the smoothest taste."

31. Interestingly, government regulations sometimes *bar* sellers from posting truthful information. For example, drug companies are not allowed to post the beneficial effects for unapproved uses of drugs approved for certain uses. Liquor companies are not allowed to post the nutritional content of alcoholic beverages.

32. The use of standardized methods of accounting is an important example of this, albeit regulated by the Financial Accounting Standards Board, a private, nonprofit organization.

    Some products do not lend themselves to standardized labeling or reporting. When the government began to regulate the labeling of juice beverages several years ago, it required beverages being called a "juice drink" to contain no more than a certain percentage of water. This particularly hurt cranberry juice producers because undiluted cranberry juice is practically unpotable, and producers must add a lot of water. Ocean Spray's "Cranberry Juice" had to be renamed "Cranberry Juice Cocktail."

33. Whether insurance packages should be standardized was a critical issue in the national health insurance debate of 1994. Already Supplementary Insurance for Medicare must be sold in one of a number of standardized packages. Economists usually talk about the benefits of standardization in avoiding adverse selection, and the costs in terms of discouraging innovation or product diversity. Sign posting concerns suggest that standardization facilitates comparison shopping.

34. Such labeling is hardly helpful, however, if individuals have difficulty understanding the risks. Kip Viscusi and Wesley Magat, *Informational Approaches to Regulation* (Cambridge, MA: MIT Press, 1992).

35. *Reducing the Health Consequences of Smoking: 25 Years of Progress,* a Report of the Surgeon General (Rockville, MD: Office on Smoking and Health, Center for Chronic Disease Prevention and Health Promotion, Centers for

Disease Control, Public Health Service, U.S. Department of Health and Human Services, 1989).

36. Mutual funds also must now report their performance in a standardized way. We would not expect this to affect significantly their incentives to perform well because such incentives have always existed. But it may now be easier for investors to learn about funds' past performance. Thus, in this case, the "consumer" effect will probably be large compared to the "manufacturer" effect.

37. I. Molotsky, "Major Airlines Are Ranked on Delays and Other Woes," *New York Times*, November 11, 1987, p. B9. A flight is deemed to have arrived on time if it arrives within 15 minutes of the scheduled time. Thus, being 16 minutes late and being 5 hours late have the same effect on an airline's rating.

38. T. Waite, "Q. and A.: Airline Ratings a Year Later," *New York Times*, August 28, 1988, Travel Section, pp. 12, 26.

39. Ibid.

40. Inhibitions on and difficulties in portraying the future are thought to be an important cause of leveraged buyouts.

# CHAPTER 3

# Normative Validity of Graphical Aids for Designing and Using Estimation Studies

## Rex V. Brown and John W. Pratt

One of Howard Raiffa's signal contributions to decision science has been to focus attention on prescriptive analysis, which acknowledges that the normative must be tempered by the descriptive if it is to be useful.[1] A rich analytic theory addresses normative decision making,[2] but algorithms that embody the theory typically require many difficult judgmental inputs that professionals and decision makers cannot or will not effectively supply, and produce outputs that they find uncongenial. Rigorous decision aids are not helpful if ordinary mortals cannot provide the inputs or interpret the output. An aid is no longer damned by acknowledgment that it has logical flaws if they permit a better fit with the intended use or user.[3] Furthermore, a simpler, disaggregated model is not necessarily weaker normatively than a complex one; it just relies more heavily on intuition, which may or may not be made sounder by being decomposed (that is, modeled).

An aid's effectiveness is thus measured by criteria beyond theoretical rigor.[4] It should draw on all relevant knowledge, elicit sensible inputs, and produce readily interpreted outputs. Its costs must be acceptable—inputs not too burdensome, nor calculation too expensive.

This paper was supported by the National Science Foundation, Division of Social Sciences, under grant number #ISI-8722149. Illustrative material draws heavily on Rex Brown, Gary Lilien, and Jacob Ulvila, "New Methods for Estimating Business Markets," *Journal of Business-to-Business Marketing* 1 (1993): 33–65.

It should fit the institutional culture and meet organizational needs. Aids that satisfy these requirements often sacrifice some logical soundness, yet are successfully adopted. Imperfectly fitting additive multi-attribute utility functions have been used successfully in many executive "decision conferences." Graphic analogs have been found to be particularly appealing for their cognitive accessibility, economy, and communication power. For example, box-and-whisker charts are helpful in communicating univariate probability distributions, and decision trees in communicating contingent choices.[5]

It is nonetheless important to understand what is lost in a normatively imperfect analysis.[6] In this paper, we evaluate the normative soundness of two visual aids for making quantitative estimates based on judgments and data.[7] Both were developed in the context of business-to-business marketing, to help decide, for example, how much to spend on what research activities before launching a new product, and how to combine the complex, disparate, and inconclusive data accumulated in the research. The standardized sample surveys and inference procedures common in consumer marketing do not apply to such problems. Rather, reliance on seasoned professional judgment is unavoidable, yet the knowledge of experts and the information available may be troublesome to incorporate even informally.

## Linked Error Assessment Triangles

A central—but largely neglected—problem in market research, and quantitative research more generally, is the failure to make accurate total error assessments.[8] Total error assessments are needed both to design a quantitative research strategy and to base decisions on the estimates obtained. For example, an estimate of market size is built up from estimates of the number of customers and demand per customer, and each of these may be based on a sample survey or other estimating study. The credibility of the estimate of market size, either before or after the study is performed, will depend in part on assessments of survey errors due to mismeasurement, random fluctuation, nonresponse, and sampling frame mismatch—including any judged dependence between them.

Suppose a manager is deciding whether to use 1,000 mail questionnaires or 80 more expensive personal interviews to estimate what fraction of the population is likely to buy his product. The total sample error can be decomposed into measurement error and representativeness error. The fraction of the population who will actually buy is the target variable $p$. If $s$ is the fraction of the sample that will *actually* buy and if *s'* is the fraction of the sample that *claims* it will buy, then the total error equals the representativeness error plus the measurement error, or

$$p - s' = (p - s) + (s - s').$$

The assessed or estimated sizes (standard deviations, say) of two component errors and their total can be represented by the three sides of a triangle. If the components are uncorrelated, then they are represented by the legs of a right triangle and the hypotenuse represents the total (because the variance of the sum of uncorrelated variables is the sum of their variances). Generalizations to other measures of size and to correlated, multiplicative, and multiple components are discussed below.

Figure 3-1 shows a right triangle for each type of survey. The estimate of the total error is the hypotenuse, and the component errors, which are taken to be uncorrelated, are the legs. For the mail survey, measurement error dominates representativeness error; doubling or

**Figure 3-1**
*Comparing Errors in Two Surveys Using Triangles*

A: MAIL SURVEY (n = 1000):

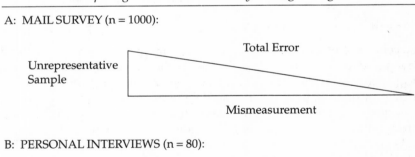

Total Error

Unrepresentative
Sample

Mismeasurement

B: PERSONAL INTERVIEWS (n = 80):

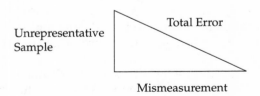

Total Error

Unrepresentative
Sample

Mismeasurement

CONCLUSION: Strategy B is more accurate in spite of the unrepresentative sample because mismeasurement dominates sample error.

**Figure 3-2**
*Assessing Total Error from Its Independent Components*

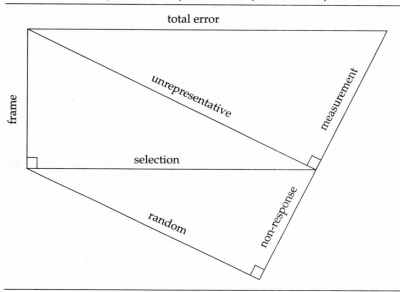

halving this error can be seen to have a relatively small effect on total error in diagram A. In contrast, reducing the measurement error, even at the cost of relatively large increases in representativeness error, substantially decreases the total error.[9]

Component errors can be decomposed further.[10] Any error decomposition can be represented graphically by appropriately linked triangles; Figure 3-2 shows representativeness error decomposed into three components:

- Frame Error: The sample is drawn from a list (or frame) where the value, $f$, of the variable of interest (fraction buying) is not identical to the value, $p$, in the target population.

- Random Sampling Error: The value, $d$, in the sample selected differs from the value, $f$, in the frame it was selected from, due to random fluctuations.

- Non-Response Error: The value, $s$, for the respondents in the sample differs from the value, $d$, in the entire sample selected including "non-respondents."

Thus, the representativeness error equals the sum of the frame error, the random sampling error, and the non-response error, or

$$p - s = (p - f) + (f - d) + (d - s).$$

The chain of triangles in Figure 3-2 decomposes the total error assessment into increasingly fine components. The figure shows the contribution of each error component and makes apparent the potential reduction in total error from reducing any component error.[11] Any hierarchical type of decomposition is possible, not merely a single sequence of triangles; for example, measurement error could be decomposed further.[12] A still more complex variant was developed and successfully used to help choose between random and quota sample designs in market research.[13]

*Case Study*

The marketing research manager of a large manufacturer of personal computers (PCs) wished to estimate the number of PCs in business use in the United States at the end of 1988. He could take either a sample survey of 8,000 PC users or a survey of shipment data from PC vendors. With a consultant's help, he used an adaptation of the linked-triangle approach to make his choice (see Figure 3-3). During a two-hour meeting, the manager discussed the errors in the two approaches with market research specialists. The consultant attempted to represent the argument in triangle format on a blackboard, subject to confirmation and correction by the participants.

For the user survey, the error in estimating the number of PCs in business use at the end of 1988 was decomposed into error in estimating the number of PC-using establishments and error in estimating the number of installed PCs per establishment. The latter was further decomposed into the unrepresentativeness of the establishments sampled and the error in measuring establishments. (Further decomposition of representativeness error into random, frame, and non-response error was performed but is not shown here.)

The length of each line was initially a judgment of proportional error by a market research specialist, based on information available from the survey organizations and on her experience with similar surveys. The lines show the magnitudes of the errors remaining after judgmental allowance, prompted by the consultant, for any likely biases (in this case expected underestimation). For example, the specialist judged that errors in estimating the population of establishments would be small compared to the error in estimating the number of

**Figure 3-3**

*Probable Errors in Estimating 1988 PCs Installed Using Two Approaches*

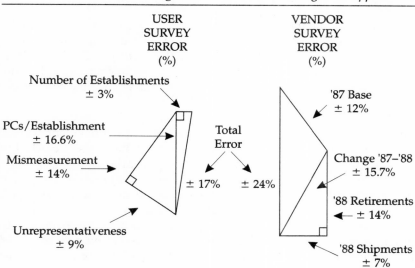

installed PCs per establishment, and would have a negligible impact on total error.

Specifically, she judged that, even after adjustment for bias, the true numbers of PCs per establishment could still be 14% more or less than the reported numbers (with 90% probability). A similar assessment of ±9% for residual error due to sample unrepresentativeness (including random error) brings the total error in PCs per establishment to ±16.6% (because $14^2 + 9^2 = 16.6^2$). Combining this with an assessed error of ±3% in the total number of establishments gives a total error in the number of PCs of about ±17%. The manager accepted this assessment after satisfying himself, with input from others in the room, that the triangles "looked right."

For the vendor survey, the total error in estimating PCs was decomposed into the error in the estimate for the previous year (±12%) and the error in the estimate of the net increase over the intervening year. The latter was derived from errors in shipments (±7%) and retirements (±14%); it equaled ±15.7%. Estimates of the 1987 base and of the increase between 1987 and 1988 were judged likely to suffer from common errors and hence positively correlated. To reflect this, the angle between the corresponding lines is not a right angle, but is obtuse, in fact 120°. This corresponds to a correlation about halfway between none and complete. The resulting total error for the vendor survey is ±24%.

These judgments imply that the user survey is more accurate than the vendor survey. The geometry permits a simple comparison of these accuracies by comparing the lengths of the corresponding lines. This visual inspection will probably provide all the insight needed to determine if any plausible change in inputs would change the conclusion.

### Normative Validity

The client found the triangles on a blackboard a convenient way to evaluate the relative merits of alternative estimation strategies. But does the triangle aid convey *logically* the appropriate messages?

*Interpretation of a single triangle.* The simplest exact interpretation of a single triangle is that the sides are proportional to the standard deviations of additive errors. In this case, all sides must be expressed in identical units, such as number of PCs. If inputs are expressed in different units, they must be converted to common units; for example, the error in the percentage of retirements could be converted to the error in the number of retirements by multiplying it by the number in place. Additive errors can all be percentages as long as they are percentages of the same thing, at least roughly. That is, 1988 shipments and 1988 retirements could both be percentages of the 1987 base, and the falsification introduced by thinking of 1988 retirements as a percentage of the 1988 base will not be great if the 1988 base is close to the 1987 base.

A second interpretation of a single triangle is that the sides are proportional to the uncertainties of multiplicative errors. In this case, all sides must be expressed in percentages. The units of the quantities to which the percentages refer must also multiply appropriately; for example, the number of establishments times PCs per establishment equals the number of PCs. To make this interpretation exact, one could take logarithms; the sides of the triangles would then be proportional to the standard deviations of the logarithms of the multiplicative errors. However, it is hard to imagine that assessments would ever be made directly in this form.

There is no difficulty if the errors lie in the range where (natural) $\log(1 + x) = x$ is an adequate approximation, or, more or less equivalently, $(1 + x)(1 + y) = 1 + x + y$ is an adequate approximation. For errors up to 20%, the error in $\log(1 + x) = x$ is less than 12% (since $\log(1 - 0.2) = -0.2231 = (-0.2) \times 1.12$); this is within tolerance for most error assessments. For larger multiplicative errors, the question of scaling needs attention.

For example, if a component of error is assessed as ±50%, does this mean that specified fractiles of the distribution of the multiplicative error factor are 1.5 and $1/1.5 = 2/3$, or 1.5 and 0.5, or even 0.5 and $1/0.5 = 2$? If we compromise on the geometric mean of $1 + x$ and $1/(1 - x)$, which is $[(1 + x)/(1 - x)]^{1/2}$, then the factor and its reciprocal differ by approximately $2x$. Under this interpretation, a 50% error would mean a factor $[1.5/0.5]^{1/2} = 1.732$, making factors above 1.732 and below $1/1.732 = 0.577$ equally likely. The approximation $2x$ is in error by less than 16% even for $x = 0.5$, as we see by comparing $1.732 - 0.577 = 1.155$ to $2 \times 0.5 = 1.0$. The corresponding range on the logarithmic scale is $\log(1 + x) - \log(1 - x) = \log[(1 + x)/(1 - x)] = 2x$ approximately, with error less than 10% for $x \le 0.5$ (since $\log[1.5/0.5] = 1.099$).

Thus multiplicative errors, unless they are very large, can if necessary be converted to additive errors with adequate accuracy.

*Linking triangles.* Adjacent triangles need not use identical units. Their common side can have one unit in one triangle and another in the other, thus establishing the relation of the two scales. Similarly, a sequence of triangles fixes the relations among all scales used. For example, in the diagram of user survey error in Figure 3-3, one can interpret the sides of the first triangle as errors in numbers of PCs per establishment due to mismeasurement, unrepresentativeness, and both together, but the second triangle must refer to percentage errors, since it is multiplicative. Thus, additive and multiplicative formulations are being combined. If the common edge represents a number in the first triangle and a percentage in the second, this fixes the relation between the number and percentage scales.

*Comparing decompositions.* When comparing two decompositions into linked triangles, or their total errors, their scales must be appropriately related to each other. If an edge somewhere in one decomposition has the same units as an edge in the other, or can be so interpreted, this determines the factor by which one decomposition must be rescaled, either arithmetically or graphically, to achieve comparability. In Figure 3-3, where no such relationship stands out, one can be created, for example, by considering or converting the error in the 1987 base to be the percentage error in the vendor survey. The scales of the two diagrams can then be made comparable by rescaling either the user survey or the vendor survey so that the percentage error scales in the two diagrams agree.

*Choice of uncertainty measure.* Another issue is the interpretation of the length or numerical value used to represent an error in relation to the distribution of that error. One might take it to be the standard deviation, mean absolute error, semi-interquartile range, or any other scale parameter. Those providing the judgmental inputs presumably

**Figure 3-4**
*Relation between Angle and Correlation*

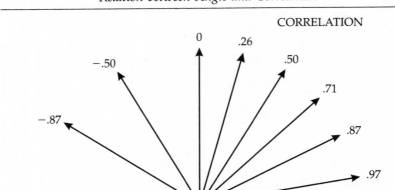

have no such specific feature of the distribution in mind, but their assessments should all be consistent with some common interpretation. Right triangles can represent uncorrelated errors exactly if the lengths of the sides are equal to the standard deviations. But so can they if the sides differ from the standard deviations by a factor $k$ that is the same for all. And the factor $k$ need not be known as long as the purpose is only to compare approaches with one another, rather than, for example, to compare them with their costs. Thus, the method of linked triangles will work as long as the opinion about each error can be adequately represented by *some* distribution with a standard deviation equal to $k$ times the length of the corresponding side, with the same $k$ for all errors. The constancy and value of $k$ are empirical questions worth investigating.

*Correlation.* The correlation between errors in the same triangle is represented by the angle between the corresponding sides. A right angle represents zero correlation. Positive correlations between component errors are represented by obtuse angles and negative correlations by acute angles. The exact relationship between the correlation $\rho$ and the angle $\alpha$ is $\rho = -\cos \alpha$, since this makes the variance and squared length agree. (Specifically, if the components have variances equal to the squared lengths $\sigma_x^2$ and $\sigma_y^2$, then their sum has variance $\sigma_{x+y}^2 = \sigma_x^2 + \sigma_y^2 + 2\rho\sigma_x\sigma_y$ and squared length $\sigma_{x+y}^2 = \sigma_x^2 + \sigma_y^2 - 2(\cos \alpha)$ $\sigma_x\sigma_y$ by the law of cosines.) Figure 3-4 displays examples of angles and corresponding correlations.

Because correlations are not easy to assess directly, other perspectives on them may be useful, especially for the more common case of positive correlation. We mention two. First, suppose that the components are themselves sums of independent terms with equal variances $\sigma^2$. If they have $m$ and $n$ terms respectively, including $k$ terms in common, then $\sigma_x^2 = m\sigma^2$, $\sigma_y^2 = n\sigma^2$, $\sigma_{x+y}^2 = (m + n + 2k)\sigma^2$, and $\rho = k/\sqrt{mn}$. The terms in common are a fraction $k/m$ of the first component and $k/n$ of the second, and $\rho$ is the geometric mean of these fractions. Unfortunately the natural graphical view of this is three-dimensional and therefore perhaps not a useful assessment aid: let a tetrahedron have three right-triangular faces as shown in Figure 3-5a; then the edges of the fourth face represent the two correlated components of error and their sum.

Negative correlation would arise if the $k$ common terms had opposite effects on the two errors (opposite signs in $x$ and $y$). Then $\sigma_{x+y}^2 = (m + n - 2k)\sigma^2$ and $\rho = -k/\sqrt{mn}$. The graphical view is actually simpler for negative correlations; all the right angles are at the same vertex (see Figure 3-5b).

A second perspective uses the degree to which one component of error can predict the other. Specifically, the linear regression of $y$ on $x$, say $\beta x$, is uncorrelated with the residual, $y - \beta x$. Hence we may represent their standard deviations as the legs of a right triangle with hypotenuse $\sigma_y$, and this triangle represents the sum of uncorrelated components of error as before (see Figure 3-5c). If $\rho > 0$ and the $\beta x$ leg is plotted as an extension of the $x$ leg, then the $x$ and $y$ legs will be angled correctly. Of course $x$ could be regressed on $y$ instead or in addition. The regressions of $y$ on $x$ and $x$ on $y$ have standard deviations $\rho\sigma_y$ and $\rho\sigma_x$, which are different unless $\sigma_y = \sigma_x$. In the rare case $\rho < 0$, we have $\beta < 0$ and the direction of the regression leg $\beta x$ reverses. To use this perspective for assessment, one would adjust the angle until the lengths of the altitude $\sigma_{y-\beta x}$ and base $\sigma_{\beta x}$ agreed with one's opinion about the fractions of $y$ that are respectively unpredictable and predictable by $x$ (see Figure 3-5d).

## Representing Information in Several Assessments by Overlapping Areas

Information about a given target quantity is often at hand or obtainable from several sources. Estimates may come from a variety of experts, or be arrived at by different approaches. Resource constraints often force a choice between one source and another, or between combinations of sources; a decision maker would then like to maximize the total information, in some sense, to be expected from the sources chosen. Both the relative amounts of information and the amount of overlap among the actual or potential sources of information must be

**Figure 3-5**
*Component Error Triangles*

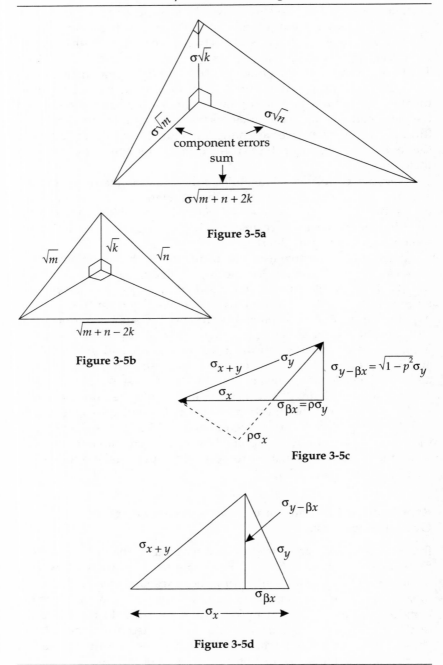

$\sigma\sqrt{k}$

$\sigma\sqrt{m}$   $\sigma\sqrt{n}$

component errors

sum

$\sigma\sqrt{m + n + 2k}$

**Figure 3-5a**

$\sqrt{m}$   $\sqrt{k}$   $\sqrt{n}$

$\sqrt{m + n - 2k}$

**Figure 3-5b**

$\sigma_{x+y}$   $\sigma_y$

$\sigma_x$

$\sigma_{y-\beta x} = \sqrt{1-p^2}\,\sigma_y$

$\sigma_{\beta x} = \rho\sigma_y$

$\rho\sigma_x$

**Figure 3-5c**

$\sigma_{y-\beta x}$

$\sigma_{x+y}$   $\sigma_y$

$\sigma_{\beta x}$

$\sigma_x$

**Figure 3-5d**

assessed somehow. It would be useful to have some practical way of expressing these assessments and seeing their implications, without having to deal explicitly with difficult concepts such as variances and covariances.

One possibility is to represent the amount of information embodied in each source by the area of a circle and the common information by the overlap of the circles, and then to interpret the union of the areas as the total information.[14]

As an example, suppose that three research services, X, Y, and Z, will each forecast a product's sales for the same cost, but only two services can be afforded. An assessor has the most confidence in X and next most in Y. However, X and Y use similar methods, whereas Z's approach is entirely different. If Figures 3-6a and 3-6b represent the assessor's judgment, she would prefer X and Z over X and Y because the union of areas in 3-6a is greater than in 3-6b.

*Normative Validity*

Much research remains to be done on the normative validity of this aid. We present some first steps and ideas.

*Circles.*    If circles are used for more than two sources, geometry unfortunately greatly constrains the possible overlaps and hence what commonalities or correlations can be represented. For example, if Dick and Ralph have different though possibly overlapping information, as in Figure 3-6c, and if Howard knows everything they know, then he must know a lot that neither of them knows. If John has told both Dick and Ralph all that he knows, then there must be much that both know but John does not.

It is easy to see that circles impose far more constraints than other shapes do, especially if a flexible family of other shapes is allowed, even if the family is restricted to convex shapes. For example, if the intersection AB of two circles A and B is not a large fraction of either, then AB will be much longer than wide. If a third circle C is contained in AB, then it can be at most a small fraction of it, a fraction approaching 0 as the width-to-length ratio of AB approaches 0. Thus the information in C cannot be close to—and may be limited to an arbitrarily small fraction of—the common information in A and B. Similarly, a circle C that contains AB must be quite a bit larger than AB. Even if the circles A and B have equal size and overlap by 1 radius (39%), as in Figure 3-6d, a circle contained in AB can be only 25% as large as A and B and hence at most 64% of AB, while a circle containing AB must be almost twice its size.[15] If A and B do not overlap and C contains both, it must be larger than their union by at least twice the area of the smaller. (See Figure 3-6e.) If A and B do overlap, then C cannot overlap

**Figure 3-6**
*Use of Circles to Represent Information Overlap*

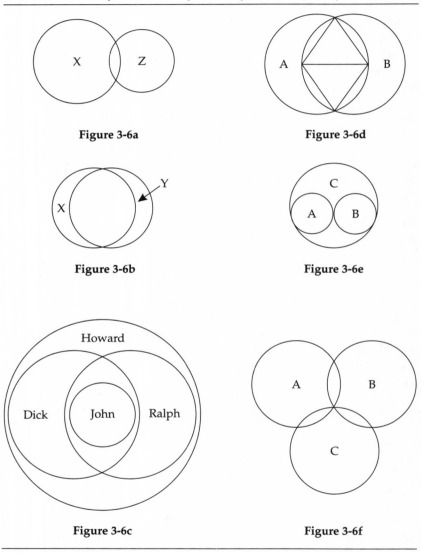

Figure 3-6a

Figure 3-6d

Figure 3-6b

Figure 3-6e

Figure 3-6c

Figure 3-6f

both substantially without also overlapping their intersection. (See Figure 3-6f.) Except for the last, these problems could be handled by omitting redundant sources of information from the diagram, but they make amply clear the inadequacy of circles to represent information overlap from more than two sources.

*Noncircular areas.*   There may be mathematical restrictions on the relative size of the $2^m - 1$ elementary subsets in the field of sets generated by $m$ convex sets. It seems conceivable that connectedness alone could impose restrictions for large $m$. For $m = 4$, however, Figure 3-7 has $2^4 - 1 = 15$ non-empty elementary subsets and it appears that almost any relative sizes could be achieved while keeping A, B, C, and D convex.

Thus, when there are four or fewer sources of information, if shapes are flexible, the only constraint imposed by geometry is that intersections cannot have negative area. This may also be the only constraint when there are more than four sources—we have not investigated this question beyond counting equations and variables (see below). In any event, with more than four sources the graphical aid would be hard to use, except perhaps in specially structured situations.

*Relation between area and information.*   It is not clear how well people can match up area, information, sample size ($n$), and so on. It is obviously hard to understand how area increases with linear dimensions, how variance increases with standard deviation and relates to the size of errors, and how all these relate to $n$ and $\sqrt{n}$; the failings of unaided intuition here are well documented.[16] Sometimes failings may

**Figure 3-7**
*Use of Noncircular Areas*

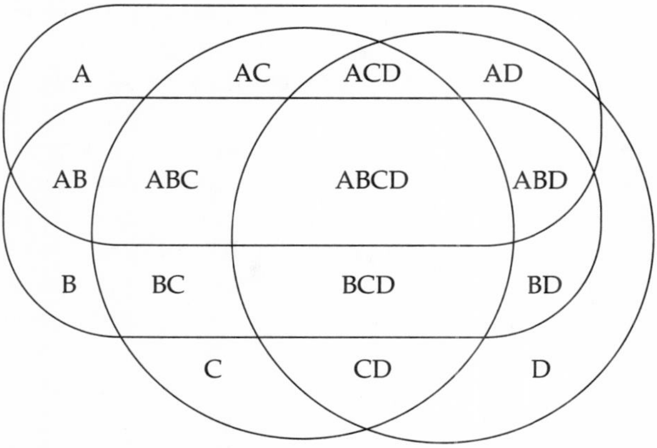

partially offset one another. To us, casual intuition suggests that area may be a good psychological surrogate for amount of information, appropriately defined.

If area represents information about the target variable, and if information equals 1 divided by the variance (which is proportional to $n$ if the only error is random sampling), should it be taken to include or exclude prior information? Technically, it would be expected posterior information in the first case and expected new information or an increase in information in the second. Which sense is chosen may well affect the psychological or geometric ease of drawing regions, and conceivably the logical possibility of making the regions convex.

*Equations versus variables.* Let $A_i$ be the region representing approach $i$, $\mathbb{A}$ = area, $a_i = \mathbb{A}(A_i)$ = the information that $i$ has about $\mu$ (the quantity of interest), $a_{ij} = \mathbb{A}(A_i \cap A_j)$ = common information of $i$ and $j$ about $\mu$, $a_{ijk} = \mathbb{A}(A_i \cap A_j \cap A_k)$, etc. Including the empty set (no information), there are $2^m$ possible information sets if $m$ approaches are considered (each fully specified), hence $2^m$ equations for areas $\mathbb{A}(\cup_{i \in S} A_i)$, where $S$ is a subset of $\{1, 2, ..., m\}$. There are also $2^m$ elementary sets $\cap_i B_i$, where $B_i$ is either $A_i$ or its complement. The areas $\mathbb{A}(\cup_{i \in S} A_i)$ are determined by the areas of the elementary sets and vice versa. So the geometry supplies enough free variables without equality constraints to represent everything needed; however, it imposes restrictions corresponding to the non-negativity of the area of each elementary set. This may make representation infeasible, though the "common information" interpretation suggests infeasibility will seldom occur.[17]

## Concluding Discussion

We have investigated the normative validity of two low-tech graphical analog devices intended to aid research design and estimation. While they are not always exactly valid, in most situations where one would think of using them, over wide ranges, they approximate a rigorous normative procedure adequately for practical purposes. Hence their usefulness may ordinarily be decided on the basis of psychological and cognitive attractiveness and effectiveness and other practical considerations. A nontrivial cognitive issue that remains, however, is how closely the judgment being modeled fits the interpretation that the aid assumes. Do the sides and angles of triangles and the areas and overlaps of circles, as assessed, reasonably correspond to the intended features of the assessor's probability distribution?

We have used these aids primarily in situations where research users and suppliers jointly explore the implications of only somewhat disaggregated judgments that are represented quantitatively. The role of the analyst (when not the same person as either the user or supplier) has been no more than that of a facilitator, especially in group deliberations.

A promising alternative use would be as a communication device between an analyst and a technically untrained client. A complex analysis could be translated into a close graphical approximation, which the client would check for plausibility, and might adjust or override with direct judgment. This practice would be an adaptation of the use of "coarse" models to manage and integrate refined analytic models, at different levels of granularity. Such coarse models have been used by managers to help direct policy research and merge it with their own judgment. Interactive but nongraphic software has been used to make complex probabilistic risk assessment models usable by nuclear regulators when deciding on requirements for reactors.[18] Perhaps graphic analog versions of such software can be developed to further enhance the practical value of such models in applications beyond "simple" estimation.

Although the analog aids discussed here have been implemented satisfactorily on a blackboard, they probably must be computerized to realize their greatest potential. Other analog devices, for example, summing the areas of rectangles to represent additive utility functions,[19] may need to be computerized to be really useful at all. It may also be possible to incorporate software that helps gauge the impact of departures from normative validity.

We cannot, of course, infer much directly from two decision aids. The two here are, however, reasonably representative of a dozen or so such aids we have employed on the decision and assessment problems of consulting clients. Our general feeling is that a graphic analog that plausibly represents an analysis is typically valid enough normatively to be valuable to a professional user. The practical effectiveness of a decision aid usually depends more on the user's understanding, and hence trusting, what the analysis is saying, than on just how logically coherent it is. A graphic analog may make clear any unrealism in the analysis, and therefore how to allow for it. Paradoxically, a moderately "invalid" aid may actually increase the normative validity—in the sense of drawing legitimate inferences from available knowledge and judgment—of what the user concludes from an analysis.

## NOTES

1. David E. Bell, Howard Raiffa, Amos Tversky, eds., *Decision Making: Descriptive, Normative, and Prescriptive Interactions* (New York: Cambridge University Press, 1988).

2. John W. Pratt, Howard Raiffa, and Robert Schlaifer, *Introduction to Statistical Decision Theory* (Cambridge, MA: MIT Press, 1995).

3. Some controversy surrounds this issue. See, for example, Rex V. Brown, "The State of the Art of Decision Analysis: A Personal Perspective," *Interfaces* 22 (November–December 1992): 5–14; and Ronald A. Howard, "Heathens, Cults and Heretics: The Religious Spectrum of Decision Analysis," *Interfaces* 22 (November–December 1992): 15–19.

4. Rex V. Brown, "Toward a Prescriptive Science and Technology of Decision Aiding," *Annals of Operations Research* 19 (1989): 467–483.

5. See John W. Tukey, *Exploratory Data Analysis* (Reading, MA: Addison-Wesley, 1977); and Robert Schlaifer, *Analysis of Decisions under Uncertainty* (New York: McGraw-Hill, 1969). Another graphical aid, in early stages of development, whose unresolved issues are primarily behavioral rather than normative, is feedback-adjusted reconciliation, or "jiggling." See Rex V. Brown, J. W. Ulvila, and D. von Winterfeldt, "Plural Analysis: Developing Multiple Approaches to Quantitative Research" (Falls Church, VA: Decision Science Consortium, Inc., NTIS PB87–116331/A05, 1984). This aid involves reconciling discrepant assessments from alternative models of the same target variable by having an assessor adjust (jiggle) the models' assessed inputs until their outputs coincide. In psychological experiments by von Winterfeldt, Eppel, and Ford, subjects comfortably and successfully used a computerized (but non-graphical) jiggling procedure to reconcile predictions of compact disk recorder sales five years ahead. See D. von Winterfeldt, T. Eppel, and C. Ford, "An Experimental Investigation of Plural Analysis: Estimating the Market Share of Compact Disc Players in 1990," *Behavioral Science* 33 (1988): 187–195.

6. A graphical aid whose unresolved issues are primarily normative is "adding information/cost graphs," discussed in the symposium draft of this paper. The graph of information against cost for one research approach is added to the mirror image of that for another with the origin at the total available budget. The maximum information achievable, and sensitivity to misallocation, are readily seen. The primary normative issues are what measures of information are additive, under what assumptions, taking into account uncertainty, nuisance parameters, and conditioning.

7. Ease of use and other descriptive issues are not addressed here. They are discussed at a general level in R. V. Brown and A. Vari, "Toward a Prescriptive Science and Technology of Decision Research: The Normative Tempered by the Descriptive," *Acta Psychologica* 80 (1992): 33–47.

8. See Rex V. Brown, "The Evaluation of Total Survey Error," *The Statistician* 17 (1968): 335–355; and Rex V. Brown, *Research and the Credibility of Estimates* (Boston: Division of Research, Harvard Business School, 1969).

9. Representativeness error is not inversely proportional to the square root of sample size because it has components other than random sampling

fluctuations that are not reduced by sample size; these contribute to the representativeness errors shown in diagrams A and B.

10. The "decomposed error analysis" of Brown, *Research and the Credibility of Estimates,* explores this possibility, using the statistical theory of the distribution of functions of random variables to infer the accuracy of an estimate.

11. Even if the decision appears to affect only one type of error (e.g., sample size affects random error), there are often indirect effects on other variables. In this case, a larger sample requires economizing on interviews, thereby increasing measurement error.

12. Contortion lovers will note that the representation of a hierarchical decomposition by triangles is a graph-theoretic dual of the rooted bifurcating tree or dendrogram representing the hierarchy, with the sides of the triangles corresponding to the branches of the tree.

13. C. S. Mayer and Rex V. Brown, "A Search for the Rationale of Nonprobability Sample Designs," in *Marketing and Economic Development, Fall Conference Proceedings,* ed. P. D. Bennett (Chicago: American Marketing Association, 1965), pp. 295–308.

14. Anthony Freeling, 1984. Private communication to Rex Brown.

15. The figure is drawn with A and B of equal radius and overlapping by 1 radius. In this case, AB is 1 radius wide and $\sqrt{3}$ times as long, a circle C in AB can be at most 1/4 as big as A, a circle C that contains AB must be at least 3/4 as big as A, while AB is exactly $k = 2/3 - \sqrt{3}/2\pi = 0.391$ times as big as A. We have $1/4k = 0.64$ and $3/4k = 1.92$, almost 2.

16. Daniel Kahneman, Paul Slovic, and Amos Tversky, eds., *Judgment Under Uncertainty: Heuristics and Biases* (New York: Cambridge University Press, 1982).

17. Infeasibility corresponds to something like negatively correlated errors.

18. Rex V. Brown and J. W. Ulvila, "Does a Reactor Need a Safety Backfit? Case Study on Communicating Decision and Risk Analysis Information to Managers," *Risk Analysis* 8 (1988): 271–282.

19. O. I. Larichev, R. V. Brown, E. Andreyeva, and N. E. Flanders, "Categorical Decision Analysis for Environmental Management: A Siberian Gas Distribution Case," in *Contributions to Decision Making,* eds. J. P. Caverni, Maya Bar Hillel, and H. Jungermann (Amsterdam: North-Holland Elsevier, 1995), pp. 255–286.

# PART 1.2

## Valuation

# CHAPTER 4

# VALUING BILLIONS OF DOLLARS

Ralph L. Keeney

The government often makes decisions that impose large economic costs, as well as significant non-economic impacts, on taxpayers and businesses. Should it appropriate $10 billion for some social program? Make a regulation that would reduce air pollution but cost individuals and businesses $15 to $20 billion? Spend over $100 billion to clean up hazardous waste at Department of Energy facilities in the United States? This paper explores how people do and should think about the value of enormous economic costs and balance them against the expected benefits of public programs and regulations.

To make responsible decisions about the use of limited funds requires three steps: specifying the program costs, specifying the expected benefits, and comparing the costs and benefits. When carried out explicitly, this third step usually involves making value tradeoffs to assign equivalent dollar values to the benefits.[1] Many feel that the main challenges to making responsible decisions about expensive programs are the difficulties in specifying benefits and making the value tradeoffs between the costs and benefits.[2] It seems to be assumed that the economic costs can be relatively clearly specified and that the value of a billion dollars is well understood. I do not believe this is so: the difficulty in specifying and valuing economic costs also seriously impedes good decision making.

This paper was written with the support of the Electric Power Research Institute, Project Numbers RP-3231-12 and RP-2560-3, and the National Science Foundation, Grant SBR-9308660. I thank Robin Gregory, Gordon Hester, Jeff Keisler, Elke Weber, and Richard Zeckhauser for comments on an earlier draft of this paper.

We, meaning the politicians, regulators, interveners, and general public, often advocate decisions that suggest that dollars do not much matter. We focus on environmental, social, health, and safety impacts, not economic costs. For example, legal interpretations of the Clean Air Act state that economic costs should not be considered in setting appropriate national ambient air quality standards. Some regulations require expenditures of over $100 million to prevent one case of cancer due to some carcinogens, while regulations for other carcinogens imply that avoiding a case of cancer is worth less than $1 million.[3]

This paper addresses two issues: how to value large economic costs, and how to compare them with non-economic impacts. I make a few observations about how we evaluate large economic costs. Then, I suggest some guidelines for how we should evaluate large economic costs. There are two reasons for examining both descriptive and pre-scriptive aspects of valuing large costs—to broaden our thinking about large economic costs and contribute to understanding the complexity of such valuations, and to promote more reasoned valuation of the costs and non-economic impacts of potential programs and regulations, and, through this process, contribute to improved decision making.[4]

## Costs Are Complex

Why is it so difficult to understand the value of large economic sums? Several different kinds of costs are paid for by different people or organizations for different reasons, and it is often uncertain how large they will be. If costs do not occur all at once, costs over time become an issue. There are necessarily value tradeoffs among all these different costs, as well as value tradeoffs between each of these costs and non-economic impacts. That is, a dollar is not always a dollar.

### Types of Costs

*Costs* will mean economic costs, typically measured in dollars. We are particularly interested here in costs of millions or billions of dollars.[5] I define costs with respect to three characteristics: their relationship to an activity, the degree to which payers can recognize this relationship, and why the costs are paid. All costs have all three characteristics.

*Direct costs* are economic costs that are attributable to a specific activity. *Indirect costs* are associated with, but not directly attributable to, an activity. For example, when a firm purchases air pollution equip-ment, the direct costs are those of purchasing the equipment only; the costs of installing and operating the equipment are indirect costs. However, if the activity is to "install specific air pollution devices," the direct costs are those of purchasing and installing the equipment; indirect costs may be associated with operating the equipment. *Unforeseen costs* are costs that, prior to an activity, were not attributed to or associated with that activity. They may have been overlooked or considered insignificant. For example, unforeseen costs of moving a transmission line underground could result from a lawsuit because of alleged inconvenience.

Direct, indirect, and unforeseen costs will all occur in the future. In contrast, *sunk costs* are direct, indirect, and originally unforeseen costs that have already been expended and cannot be changed or recovered, no matter what decisions are made later.

*Identifiable costs* can be identified by payers as attributable to a specific decision. For example, the purchaser of a motorcycle helmet recognizes that the need to purchase and pay for the helmet is a result of a motorcycle helmet regulation. *Statistical costs* cannot be traced by payers to a specific decision. For example, a regulation might increase the costs of building transmission lines for electricity. This cost would be passed to individuals through the cost of electricity and the costs of products from firms that use electricity. Statistical costs are usually calculated as the expected (or average) costs for all payers with similar characteristics.

*Voluntary costs* are costs for which payers can decide whether or not to pay. For example, the additional costs of radial tires, above those for standard tires, are voluntary costs. Such costs are also called discretionary costs. *Involuntary costs* are costs that the payer is required to pay for but would prefer not to. For example, regulations require expenditures that would not be voluntary purchases for most people, such as smog control devices on vehicles, tamper-proof packaging, and providing health care and schooling for illegal immigrants. I define *necessary costs* as those that fall between voluntary and involuntary costs; no one requires that you buy food and shelter, but you do not have much choice.

### Certainty of Costs

*Certain costs* can be attributed to or associated with a specific activity, and their amounts are known with certainty before the activity is begun. *Uncertain costs* are costs whose amounts are uncertain when the activity is started. The costs of needed materials to move a portion of an overhead electricity transmission line underground may be certain, whereas the construction costs may be uncertain if no one knows how long it will take to dig the trenches. These uncertain costs may be described by probability distributions. One could argue that all costs are uncertain—that it is merely the degree of uncertainty that differentiates various costs. However, the distinction between certain and uncertain costs clarifies discussions.

### Costs over Time

The economic costs of many major activities do not all accrue at the same time. Hence, it is necessary to distinguish when the costs occur because the value of costs in one period is not the same as the value of equal costs in another period. *Costs accruing over time* are described by indicating how much cost occurred in each period.[6] The *discounted cost* of a cost accruing in the future is its value as a cost today (that is, the present value cost). This requires a value tradeoff between future and present costs. For example, if one dollar today is worth two dollars in eight years, the value tradeoff between cost today and cost in eight years is 1 to 2. The *net present value cost* is the cost today that is equivalent in value to a series of costs accruing over time. It is typically calculated by discounting the costs in each of the future periods, and then summing these amounts.

### Who Pays the Costs

A *payer* is an individual or organization paying the costs. Among organizations, it is useful to distinguish between government and business payers. It might be appropriate to consider that the government is really the public. However, I choose to use the government as the payer because the individuals who make up the public ultimately pay for all expenditures, whether passed on by government expenditures or paid initially by individuals. *Initial payers* first pay the costs associated with an activity. A regulation requiring the installation of pollution control equipment on industrial facilities is initially paid for by the companies owning those industrial facilities; however, these costs are necessarily passed to other payers who are customers, shareholders, or employees. The *ultimate payers* are those whose purchasing power is reduced because of the costs associated with any activity; it is they who must forego other purchases because of the costs.

With large costs, it is often important to know whether the costs are fairly borne by the payers. The *distribution of costs* is a complete description of how costs are borne by the ultimate payers. A summary description would indicate who paid, and how much. With uncertain costs, it would indicate the probabilities of different costs being borne by each payer. In evaluating such distributions, it seems to matter if a payer is a *deep-pocket payer,* one with access to large amounts of money for expenditures; they are most commonly government, big business, or wealthy individuals.

## Value Tradeoffs

*Value tradeoffs* are prescriptive in nature; they indicate specific amounts of two goods that have an equivalent value. Because there are different types of costs, there is a need for value tradeoffs among them. For example, one dollar of identifiable costs may be worth the same as three dollars of statistical costs—a value tradeoff of 1 to 3.

*Non-economic impacts* include anything not typically measured in dollars, such as environmental, social, and health and safety consequences. To integrate costs and non-economic impacts into a common framework for decision making, one must make value tradeoffs between various costs and non-economic impacts. For example, if avoiding a $10,000 cost is equivalent in value to saving an acre of mature northern pine forest from fire, then the value tradeoff is $10,000 to 1 acre of forest. On the other hand, if a mandated government program saves acres of mature northern pine forest at a cost of $25,000 per acre, this cost provides no direct indication of the relative values of $25,000 and 1 acre of forest.

## How We Tend to Value Billions of Dollars

This section presents several observations about how people seem to value large amounts of money. Together, these observations illustrate the complexity inherent in valuing large sums, and suggest why we often do not do a good job at such valuation.

I am interested in evaluating dollars both just before they are spent and just afterward, when they become costs for whatever was purchased. With all other things equal, having $2 billion is obviously preferred to having $1 billion, but spending $1 billion is preferred to spending $2 billion. Thus, to avoid ambiguity, I will use "valued more" to mean "more important" rather than "preferred to."

### Observation 1. We Value Dollars by the Value of What We Actually Get for Them, Not What We Could Have Gotten.

The vast majority of experience that most people have in dealing with money concerns their own money. It is therefore natural that people draw an analogy between their own costs and large economic costs of programs and activities.

When we think about the value of a dollar, it is one we can spend today on a cost that is identifiable, voluntary, direct, and certain. Consider an individual who can spend $1,000 a month as she chooses. To her, it is very clear which and whose dollars are being used for what. She knows the value of what she buys. The tradeoffs are also readily apparent; if she buys one product or service, she will not have the money to buy something else. With large economic costs, these consequences—whose dollars are spent, what one gets for these dollars, and what one forgoes—are not as clear. These costs are typically statistical, involuntary, indirect or unforeseen, uncertain, and spread over the future—and the initial payer is often somebody else. With government or government-mandated expenditures we do not have any direct choice about purchases, so we value all dollars according to what they actually purchase. If we could choose what was to be purchased, dollars would be valued in terms of where they could best be spent.

### Observation 2. We Value Today's Dollars Spent for Direct, Identifiable, Voluntary, Certain Costs More Than Other Dollars.

More specifically, a direct cost is valued more than an equal indirect cost, which is valued more than an equal unforeseen cost. Sunk costs are not disregarded. It is easier to identify the direct costs of a program than its indirect costs; naturally, recognized direct costs are valued more than unrecognized indirect costs. By their nature, unforeseen costs are unrecognized when a program, regulation, or purchase is approved, so they are not valued at all. Once costs have been sunk into a project, the desire to get one's money's worth makes most people willing to spend additional funds to justify the sunk costs.

Identifiable costs are valued more than equal statistical costs. Identified costs are scrutinized more than statistical costs to determine whether one is getting one's money's worth, and many feel that they have more control over identifiable costs than statistical costs. Perhaps for both these reasons, identifiable costs tend to be valued more than statistical costs.[7]

Voluntary costs are valued more than equal involuntary costs. When people choose to spend money, presumably they are getting their money's worth. When costs are imposed involuntarily, they may often feel that they do not get their money's worth. This is reasonable; the costs would often not have been imposed if people voluntarily bought the product or service. Since voluntary purchases generally bring more value to the payer, voluntary costs are valued more than involuntary costs.

With equal expected costs, certain costs are valued more than uncertain costs. Certain costs are likely identifiable and their amounts known for sure, while the amounts of uncertain costs are not known for sure. Estimates of costs for large projects usually assume "business as usual" and tend to neglect possible material or expertise shortages, strikes, or changing circumstances that can greatly increase costs. As a result, some uncertain costs are unrecognized, so uncertain costs tend to be undervalued relative to certain costs.[8]

Costs that will accrue in the future are frequently undervalued. It is easier to estimate short-term costs than long-term costs, partly because longer-term costs are more likely to be indirect or unforeseen, and there is more uncertainty that can affect costs. Since uncertain indirect and unforeseen costs are less valued than certain direct costs, future costs are undervalued as well.

Government decision makers know that some costs will occur after they leave office, or at least after the next election. Costs attributed to others matter less than costs attributed to us, so future costs are undervalued. In contrast, short-term pork barrel costs are valued highly by the officials who benefit from promoting them.

### Observation 3. We Value Costs in Terms of Who the Initial Payers Are and the Distribution of Costs among Them.

Most individuals value their own dollars more than the dollars of other individuals, government, or business. Costs to initial payers are more easily recognized than costs to ultimate payers. The cost of a program can be easily traced to the expenditures of initial payers for those costs, which are often identifiable, direct, and relatively certain. In contrast, costs to the ultimate payer are often statistical, indirect, and relatively uncertain. For example, a company that is required to install specific safety equipment can easily recognize and tabulate those identifiable costs, but by the time the individuals who must ultimately pay for the regulation accrue these costs, they will be blurred through numerous transactions that link the cost of the safety equipment to the costs of products of the company to the costs of purchasers of those products. If those purchasers are other businesses, then there is an additional link to the ultimate payers, who might be individual customers of that second business. The ultimate payers would have a hard time recognizing how the safety regulations affect the cost of the products they buy.

It is not generally recognized that individuals ultimately pay all costs initially paid by businesses or government. When a business incurs costs, they must be passed on to customers, employees, or shareholders—in other words, individuals. Government costs are paid by taxpayers, both individual and business, and business taxes are passed on to individuals. Because the paths of these costs are murky, some people do not recognize that individuals pay these costs. Others may recognize it, but think the costs fall mainly on other individuals; after all, few people are employees, stockholders, and significant purchasers of a product from one company. And even then, most costs to businesses affect other companies. With government costs, most may be paid by others, including those who have not been born yet.

Costs to government and business are valued less than equal costs to individuals. Costs to government and business are at least partially viewed as costs to others, so they are less valued than costs to us. Also, most individuals feel that government and businesses can more easily afford costs than other payers, which also reduces the value of their costs.

With costs to government and business, we feel we get less for a given cost than if we spent the same amount. With big business, often we feel it is not a voluntary choice to purchase their products. Sometimes government regulations require it and at other times they are necessary for our way of life (e.g., cars, electricity, health care). We also believe that government is not particularly efficient in many endeavors, and so we get less for our money here too.

### Observation 4. We *Undervalue Costs Relative to Non-economic Impacts.*

The costs of large government programs are typically indirect, statistical, uncertain, far in the future, and paid by others. Thus, the dollar costs are undervalued relative to what you could purchase for such amounts. Non-economic impacts are typically overvalued because for some constituency, the non-economic benefits are direct, identifiable, certain, and will occur soon; to these constituents it is worth spending the additional money to get those benefits. No similar constituency is concerned about saving that specific money. Depending on how the money would otherwise be spent, some constituency might worry about losing the potential benefits they could gain from the money. It is much more likely that the beneficiaries of a particular program would work to ensure that their benefits are valued highly than that another constituency would try to ensure that the money remains available to possibly fund its program. Perhaps this is one reason why so many government programs are funded, putting our country in ever greater debt. Our national debt may also indicate that the non-economic impacts of programs are valued more highly than their costs.

Government does not spend its money; it spends our money or requires us to spend it in certain ways. Since our money is "others' money" from the government's viewpoint, it is undervalued. Congress is supposed to make the value tradeoffs, providing each department with a budget that corresponds to the value citizens should get from the department's services. Partially due to the magnitude of this task, some efficiency is lost and much of the money ends up where it cannot do the most good. Within departments, money is sometimes sought after as a means to power, prestige, and job security. This inefficient dividing process deprives the public of the full value of its dollars.

Large cost differences are undervalued. To many individuals, the differences between $5.6 million and $6.7 million and between $5.6 billion and $6.7 billion seem similar. The two sets of costs have the same percentage difference, and anything less than a 20 percent difference does not seem significant.[9] Most people do recognize that a difference in billions is more significant than a difference in millions, but not that one is a thousand times bigger than the other. In some sense, $1.1 billion does not seem very big; $1,100 million seems bigger.

Value tradeoffs between different types of costs are rarely made explicit. To appraise expensive programs, the costs are often combined into a single cost figure although attempts are sometimes made to differentiate direct and indirect costs. However, rarely are other types of costs mentioned explicitly; there is usually little attention to statistical and identifiable costs, uncertainties, costs over time, and who must pay. As a result, one cannot meaningfully consider the value tradeoffs between all the different types of costs.[10]

Value tradeoffs between costs and non-economic impacts are rarely made explicit. Making value tradeoffs between costs and non-economic impacts is difficult; it requires soul-searching judgments about values. The implications of these judgments are that some programs should be pursued, and others should not.[11] While explicit value tradeoffs invite criticism, they are important. For example, a recent analysis of more than 500 life-saving programs in the United States found that costs paid for a year of life saved ranged up to $10 billion, with a median of $42,000. The median cost for 144 toxin control programs was $2,782,000 per life-year saved. Value tradeoffs place the value per year of life saved in the range of $10,000 to $100,000. The study implies that thousands of additional deaths could be averted and billions of dollars of expenditures avoided if economic resources were transferred from the more expensive intervention procedures to the more effective ones.[12]

## Prescriptive Guidelines for Valuing Large Amounts of Money

How should we evaluate large amounts of money? If we want responsible and defensible decisions about activities and programs of interest, then funds spent should contribute as much to the quality of life in our country as they can. It is appropriate, if not easy, to find ways to decrease the amount of funds spent and maintain the contribution to quality of life or find better ways to spend the same amount of funds.

The following four guidelines suggest how to achieve a considerable improvement in decision making, through better evaluating the economic costs of large programs, and reasonably comparing them to non-economic impacts.

### Guideline 1. Value Dollars by What We Can Get for Them.

If the world only had money and there was nothing it could buy, then money would have no value. Money has value because it can be traded for goods and services. Before being spent, the value of a large amount of money must depend on what can be bought for it. The costs of various goods and services provide a useful indication of the value of large amounts of money. However, these costs provide little insight about the value of those goods and services.

In appraising large investments, one need not only search for similar programs to help determine an appropriate value for the dollar: If $10 billion were not spent on highway safety, it might be spent on educational programs, creating jobs, or improving the environment. It is important to know what the costs of specific contributions in all of these areas would be. Table 4-1 shows the costs of various activities that many people feel are worthwhile. It includes the cost per unit of benefit, as well as the number of units that can be purchased for costs typical of major programs.

### Guideline 2. Value Different Kinds of Dollars Equally and Use Net Present Value Costs for Costs Accruing over Time.

Give the same value to a dollar of direct, indirect, and unforeseen costs, to a dollar of statistical and identifiable costs, to a dollar of voluntary, involuntary, and necessary costs, and to a dollar of certain costs and an expected dollar of uncertain costs. All of these costs are eventually borne by individuals. Although these individuals recognize some costs more easily than other types of costs, every expenditure has the same effect on them—it eliminates options.

The costs of expensive programs are distributed very broadly; hundreds of thousands and usually millions of people are typically the ultimate payers for any particular program. As a result, the economic costs, which may be uncertain to each individual, will be relatively small. Hence it does not make sense to be risk averse; using the expected cost in valuing such circumstances is appropriate.

Many programs are pursued at any time, and most of these programs have costs that accrue over time, so it makes sense to use the net present value in valuing the costs of these programs. There is an important issue about what discount rate should be used to calculate the net present value, but it is reasonable to use a consistent rate for

**Table 4-1**

*Costs of Various Activities (To Help Formulate
Appropriate Value Tradeoffs)*

| Activity | Cost | Number of Units of the Activity That Can Be Purchased for | |
| --- | --- | --- | --- |
| | | $10 Million | $1 Billion |
| Rookie police officer for one year | $42,000 | 238 | 23,800 |
| Retrofit 10,000 sq. ft. pre-1934 building to current California seismic standards | $75,000 | 133 | 13,300 |
| Purchase a smoke detector | $25 | 400,000 | 40 million |
| Incarcerate a prisoner for one year | $16,000 | 625 | 62,500 |
| Retrofit a car with driver's side air bag | $900 | 11,100 | 1.11 million |
| Have a mammogram | $100 | 100,000 | 10 million |
| Summer job for a teenager | $1,400 | 7,143 | 714,300 |
| Unemployment benefits for one year | $8,840 | 1,131 | 113,100 |
| School lunch program for one year | $152 | 65,790 | 6.58 million |
| Sponsor a child through Feed the Children for one year | $240 | 41,670 | 4.17 million |
| Complete set of immunization shots for one child | $200 | 50,000 | 5 million |
| Include a child in Head Start for one year | $2,800 | 3,571 | 357,100 |

Sources: *LA Weekly*, "LAPD Wages Compared to Other California Departments," June 24–30, 1994, p. 15; *Los Angeles Times*, "U.S. to Offer Quake Building Guidelines," May 27, 1986, p. 17; *Consumer Reports*, May 1994, p. 338; Bureau of Justice Statistics, "Prisons and Prisoners in the United States," Washington, DC: U.S. Department of Justice, 1992; *New York Times*, "Retrofitting Old Cars with Driver's-Side Air Bags," February 2, 1994, p. D5; *New York Times*, "Mammogram Debate Moving from Test's Merits to Its Costs," December 27, 1993, p. A1; *Los Angeles Times*, "The Job for America Is More Jobs for Youths," June 14, 1993, p. B6; Department of Commerce, *Statistical Abstract of the United States* (Washington, DC: U.S. Government Printing Office, 1993), Table 597; ibid., Table 608; Feed the Children, "Investing in Their Future," brochure (Oklahoma City, Child Sponsorship); *Los Angeles Times*, "Health: Clinton Said to Soften Vaccine Plan," May 5, 1993, p. A21; and *New York Times*, "Census Report Shows a Rise in Child Care and Its Cost," August 16, 1990, p. A20.

all programs. For programs with costs accruing over very long periods, particularly over multiple generations, a different discounting procedure should perhaps be used to account for any intergenerational transfer of costs of a program.[13] But again, it is reasonable to do this in a consistent manner so that we could calculate the net present value, and use this result in appraising alternative actions.

*Guideline 3. Value Costs in Terms of Who the Ultimate Payers Are and the Distribution of Costs among Them.*

It is important to know who ultimately pays for any expensive program or activity. Since the ultimate payers are always individuals, it is also important to know how much each individual will pay. Thus, each proposed program should be carefully examined to make all of the costs explicit, and to show their distribution. This allows a more reasoned evaluation of whether anticipated benefits are worth the costs and whether the costs are appropriately distributed.

*Guideline 4. Establish Explicit Value Tradeoffs Between Economic Costs and Non-economic Impacts; Alternative Uses of Money Should Guide These Value Tradeoffs.*

The value tradeoffs relate a program under consideration to all the other possible programs that are out of the limelight for the moment. Suppose one is trying to decide whether to spend $10 billion on a specific program that would make travel in automobiles safer through improved highway maintenance. Suppose it was estimated that 200 people might be saved. Dividing 200 into $10 billion yields a cost of $50 million for each saved life. If other highway safety programs could avoid potential fatalities at costs in the range of $1 million to $5 million per life saved, is it appropriate to spend $50 million to save a life through the maintenance program? Of course, one should also consider the reductions in injuries and property damage that might result from the proposed program and with the alternative programs, but if after such considerations the insights remained the same, we should not spend $50 million to avoid 1 fatality in an automobile accident when we could spend the same amount of money to avoid 10 to 50 fatalities. The more cost-effective programs reduce the chance of death for everybody who uses the highways.

Consider another example. Suppose there is a proposal that the United States fund a massive food support package to an area with a long-raging civil war. The cost is estimated to be $200 million annually for the next two years. With this $400 million investment, advocates estimate that 100,000 people could be fed until the famine due to war ends. Such a contribution is obviously important, but it should be considered in light of similar opportunities to invest $400 million. For example, through Feed the Children, $400 million would support 834,000 children with food, clothing, educational opportunities, and medical attention for two years. Would it make sense to invest the $400 million in the war zone rather than around the world in places where equal investments might have a greater impact?

One alternative to the implementation of any program is to implement another program. Another alternative is to not implement any program. If that highway safety program or food support program were not implemented, citizens could keep their money. In effect, this allows the individuals to decide how to use the additional funds to improve their own quality of life. The statistics indicate that individuals tend to use money in ways that improve their health and safety. Specifically, it has been calculated that if individuals are collectively $5 million to $12 million better off, there would be one less fatality because of the manner in which that money would be used.[14] Does it make sense for government programs to save one life at a cost of $50 million, when individuals can spend their own money in ways that save a life for between $5 million and $12 million, and also yields them a higher quality of life? Such considerations must be recognized in setting appropriate value tradeoffs between large economic expenditures and non-economic impacts.

## Relationships Between Prescriptive and Descriptive Value Tradeoffs

Some interesting insights about the importance of making value tradeoffs explicit can be illustrated with a simple example. Consider the value tradeoffs between costs and statistical lives indicated in Figure 4-1. Suppose that the value tradeoff (VT) for this is set at $3 million, meaning that we are indifferent between a cost of $3 million and avoiding risks resulting in one statistical fatality. Suppose also that there are many government programs that already reduce statistical fatalities. Their costs range up to a high (HI$) of $200 million per statistical life saved. Many other possible programs could also save statistical lives; each of these programs has a dollar cost necessary to avoid a statistical fatality. The lowest such cost (LO$) is the most cost-effective way to save statistical lives of the programs not funded.

Obviously, if we canceled the program corresponding to the HI$ and used the newly available funds to support the program with the LO$ and the next most cost-effective programs, additional statistical lives can be saved for the same cost. If this process continues until the new HI$ equals the new LO$, then the maximum number of statistical

**Figure 4-1**

*Value Tradeoffs between Costs and Statistical Lives*
*(The x's indicate costs per statistical life saved of existing government programs and the o's indicate costs per statistical life saved of other possible programs.)*

| $/statistical life saved (millions) | 0 | | 3 | | 200 | |
| --- | --- | --- | --- | --- | --- | --- |
| | LO$ | | VT | | HI$ | |

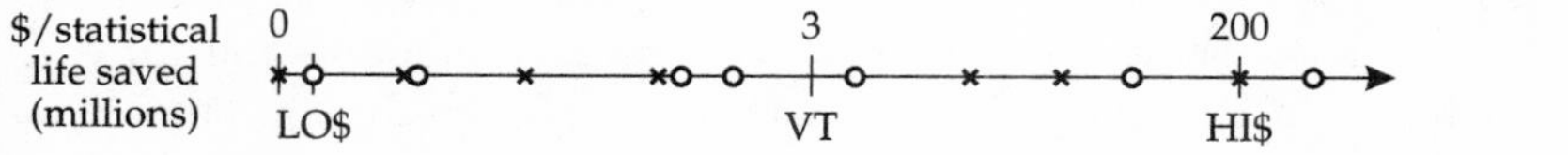

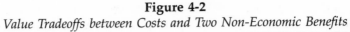

**Figure 4-2**
*Value Tradeoffs between Costs and Two Non-Economic Benefits*

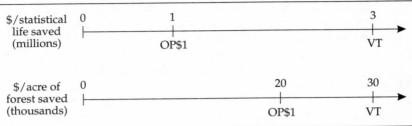

lives would be saved for the cost invested. At this point, the number of statistical lives saved and the cost of saving them defines what I call the operational value tradeoff (OP$1), which indicates the amount of money that should be exchanged for a unit of a non-economic benefit in order to maximize the total benefits given the total dollars invested by government for that non-economic benefit. By definition, when HI$ equals LO$, then OP$1 is equal to each of them.

If OP$1 is greater than VT, then clearly there is too much investment in purchasing this benefit. But if OP$1 is less than VT, there may be too much, too little, or an appropriate level of investment, as we shall see. Furthermore, if the cost of a unit of benefit for a proposed program is greater than OP$1 but less than VT, it provides a benefit greater than the cost of investing in the program; however, that investment is not warranted as there are better investments for the money.

Suppose the VT for saving acres of forest is $30,000 per acre saved. Thus, one statistical life saved is equal to the benefit of 100 acres of forest saved, since $3 million is indifferent to each. Now, consider the interesting situation where the OP$1 is less than the VT for both statistical fatalities and acres of forest (see Figure 4-2). We can define the surplus value (SV) of the investments in both benefits by

$$SV = (VT - OP\$1)_{lives} \text{ (statistical lives saved)}$$
$$+ (VT - OP\$1)_{forest} \text{ (acres of forest saved)}.$$

To maximize this surplus value, the total dollars invested in either saving statistical lives or acres of forest should be rearranged so the VT:OP$1 ratio is the same for both non-economic benefits. When any appropriate changes in investments are made to reach this condition, the HI$ and LO$ for both benefits change but remain equal for each benefit. I now define the operational value tradeoff (OP$2) as the dollar cost that should be exchanged for a unit of a non-economic benefit in order to maximize the surplus value of both benefits if the total dollars invested by government for both non-economic benefits is fixed. The reinvestments will lead to a new OP$1 for each benefit, equal to OP$2. In the example in Figure 4-2, the OP$1 for acres of forest will drop and that for statistical lives will increase in order to maximize SV. Hence, considering investments to preserve forest acreage in isolation would result in too much investment in such benefits; a shift of some funds to save statistical lives would be appropriate. This illustrates that all investments in programs below the original OP$1 are not necessarily good ones.

As before, if OP$2 is greater than VT for either good, there is too much investment in these benefits. If OP$2 is less than VT, there still may be too much, too little, or an appropriate amount of investment, depending on the appropriate amount of government investment. To establish this requires maximizing the surplus value for the different allocations of funds to individuals and to government. However, this would be difficult to do for some benefits pursued by government, such as peace and freedom, and some benefits pursued by individuals, such as fun, excitement, and learning. But for benefits that are pursued by both the government and individuals—such as life saving and preserving the environment—prescriptive guidance for government investment may be helpful. If individuals, without necessarily making optimal or rational decisions, end up saving one statistical life for every $5 million to $12 million they spend, then this should place an upper bound on the operational value tradeoff used by government to pursue statistical life saving. Otherwise, government life saving programs lose more lives than they save.

Suppose the process above led to determining the operational value tradeoffs (OP$3) for some non-economic benefits, which indicated the dollar costs that should be exchanged for a unit of those benefits given that the surplus value of investing these dollars by government or privately was the same. The amount of money transferred by individuals to government in this situation would be the appropriate amount transferred for those benefits. The OP$3s would be the appropriate value tradeoffs to use in evaluating programs involving both costs and non-economic benefits. These operational value tradeoffs would not likely be equal to the value tradeoffs, but they would depend on the value tradeoffs; the surplus value of any investment depends on the differences between the operational value tradeoffs and the value tradeoffs. If a value tradeoff increases, the corresponding OP$3 would increase proportionally.

## Conclusion

Significant government decisions have both large economic and non-economic consequences. To appraise the alternatives, a balancing of these consequences is necessary. There is a wide gap between how this is done and how it should be done (see Table 4-2 for a summary).

Many studies have sought to better understand investments intended to provide benefits that are direct or indirect, identifiable or statistical, voluntary or involuntary, and certain or uncertain. These studies assumed that money is money. This paper turns things around and examines investments where the dollar costs are direct or indirect, identifiable or statistical, voluntary or involuntary, and certain or uncertain. The intention is to promote research about how billions of dollars of government costs are valued and why and to investigate the role of standards for value tradeoffs in this process. The potential benefits are tremendous.[15] We do not need to reach an optimal allocation of resources to receive substantial benefits. Rather, we just need to avoid being demonstrably stupid. Reasonable common-sense decisions would make a tremendous positive difference.

**Table 4-2**
*Summary of How We Do and Should*
*Evaluate Billions of Dollars*

| Descriptively<br>How We Evaluate Dollars | Prescriptively<br>How We Should Evaluate Dollars |
| --- | --- |
| We value dollars by what we get for them. | We should value dollars by what we *could* get for them. |
| We value different kinds of dollars differently and undervalue future costs. | We should value different kinds of dollars the same and use net present value costs for future costs. |
| We value costs in terms of who the *initial* payers are and the distribution of costs among them. | We should value costs in terms of who the *ultimate* payers are and the distribution of costs among them. |
| We undervalue costs relative to non-economic impacts. | We should establish explicit value tradeoffs for the relative value of costs and non-economic impacts. |

## NOTES

1. See, for example, Alan J. Krupnick and Paul R. Portney, "Controlling Urban Air Pollution: A Benefit-Cost Assessment," *Science* 252 (1991): 522–527.
2. Committee on Risk and Decision Making, Howard Raiffa, Chair, *Risk and*

*Decision Making: Perspectives and Research* (Washington, DC: National Academy Press, 1982).

3. See Randall Lutter and John F. Morrall, "Health-Health Analysis: A New Way to Evaluate Health and Safety Regulation," *Journal of Risk and Uncertainty* 8 (1994): 43–66. Several additional cases in which large sums of money are spent for relatively insignificant non-economic benefits are discussed in Stephen Breyer, *Breaking the Vicious Circle: Toward Effective Risk Regulation* (Cambridge, MA: Harvard University Press, 1993).

4. For background on the prescriptive and descriptive orientations, see David E. Bell, Howard Raiffa, and Amos Tversky, eds., *Decision Making: Descriptive, Normative, and Prescriptive Interactions* (New York: Cambridge University Press, 1988).

5. These large costs might more accurately be referred to as "perceived costs," and the concepts for addressing them correspond to concepts for addressing perceived risks. See Paul Slovic, "Perception of Risk," *Science* 236 (1987): 280–285.

6. Costs over time have been extensively studied in the literature. See, for example, Tjalling C. Koopmans, "Representation of Preference Orderings over Time," in *Decision and Organization,* eds. C. Bart McGuire and Roy Radner (Amsterdam: North-Holland Publishing Company, 1972), and Richard F. Meyer, "Preferences over Time," in *Decisions with Multiple Objectives,* Ralph L. Keeney and Howard Raiffa (New York: Cambridge University Press, 1993).

7. This is analogous to the situation where identifiable lives tend to be considered more valuable than statistical lives in evaluating programs to reduce the loss of life. See Howard Raiffa, William B. Schwartz, and Milton C. Weinstein, "Evaluating Health Effects of Societal Decisions and Programs," in *EPA Decision Making* (Washington, DC: National Academy of Sciences, 1978).

8. If an explicit analysis of uncertainties were conducted and if the decision maker were risk averse, uncertain costs should be valued more than certain costs. However, empirical studies suggest that even when the costs are all recognized, avoiding certain costs is valued more than avoiding uncertain costs. See Daniel Kahneman and Amos Tversky, "Prospect Theory: An Analysis of Decision under Risk," *Econometrica* 47 (1979): 263–291.

9. Some evidence suggests that individuals evaluate differences in costs by their percentage difference. See Amos Tversky and Daniel Kahneman, "The Framing of Decisions and the Psychology of Choice," *Science* 221 (1981): 453–458.

10. In Ralph L. Keeney, "Structuring Objectives for Problems of Public Interest," *Operations Research* 36 (1988): 396–405, the costs of transporting nuclear wastes to a repository were categorized into costs initially borne by the federal government, state governments, and utility companies based

on the elicitation of objectives from about 50 concerned individuals. A subsequent assessment of a utility function over these and other objectives indicated that at least one individual valued a billion dollars of cost to the federal government as less significant than an equivalent cost to the state governments or utility companies. Details are found in Westinghouse Electric Corporation, "Phase 1 Study of Metallic Cask Systems for Spent Fuel Management from Reactor to Repository" (Waste Technology Services Division, Report WTSD-TME-085, Madison, PA, 1986).

11.  A sound methodology, multi-attribute utility theory, exists to quantify and use value tradeoffs in evaluation. See Ralph L. Keeney and Howard Raiffa, *Decisions with Multiple Objectives.* Analyses using explicit value tradeoffs indicated that the Department of Energy chose an inferior set of sites for final consideration as a nuclear waste repository, and that a strategy to investigate sites sequentially was better than the required strategy of checking three sites simultaneously. See Miley W. Merkhofer and Ralph L. Keeney, "A Multiattribute Utility Analysis of Alternative Sites for the Disposal of Nuclear Waste," *Risk Analysis* 7 (1987): 173–194, and Ralph L. Keeney, "An Analysis of the Portfolio of Sites to Characterize for Selecting a Nuclear Repository," *Risk Analysis* 7 (1987): 195–218. Partially as a result of these insights, the Nuclear Waste Policy Act was amended.

12.  Tammy O. Tengs et al., "Five-Hundred Life-Saving Interventions and Their Cost-Effectiveness," *Risk Analysis* 15 (1995): 369–390.

13.  Thomas C. Schelling, "Global Decisions for the Very Long Term: Intergenerational and International Discounting," in *Wise Choices: Decisions, Games, and Negotiations,* eds. Richard J. Zeckhauser, Ralph L. Keeney, and James K. Sebenius (Boston: Harvard Business School Press, 1996).

14.  Ralph L. Keeney, "Mortality Risks Due to Economic Expenditures," *Risk Analysis* 10 (1990): 147–159.

15.  For just the 587 life-saving interventions examined in Tengs et al., "Five-Hundred Life-Saving Interventions," approximately 60,000 additional deaths could be avoided annually by reallocating the same amount of funds spent on more cost-effective programs. Viewed another way, our country could save the same number of people and save $31 billion each year. See David Stipp, "Prevention May Be Costlier than a Cure," *Wall Street Journal,* July 6, 1994, p. B1.

CHAPTER 5

# OPTIONS

## Ronald A. Howard

My purpose is to increase the use of options in decision making. By an option, I mean not simply any alternative, but rather *an alternative that permits or may permit a future decision following revelation of information.* This meaning encompasses common options in financial affairs, but also extends, as we shall see, to many other areas of personal and professional life. The expanded concept of an option is both one of the most fundamental notions of decision analysis and an important aid to decision synthesis.

Crucial to the idea of an option is the exercise of human will in the future decision. Engaging in research and development in the hope of finding profitable products is an option because human will is exercised throughout the development and commercialization process as information is revealed. Purchasing a lottery ticket is an option; a prize can still be declined. Contracting lung cancer after a life of heavy cigarette smoking is not an option, but choosing to smoke is an option that may provide a later unwelcome decision about cancer treatment. Common options are carrying a pocket knife, installing extra wiring for possible future use, and making freeway bridges wider than freeways.

Options can be contractual or non-contractual. Contractual options are agreements with other parties to provide future decision alterna-

This paper has benefited greatly from the contributions of several people on issues that range from references through concepts to structure. I thank Miriam Avins, Ron Beaver, Rick Giarrusso, Ralph Keeney, David Luenberger, Jim Matheson, Gerry Sauer, and Richard Zeckhauser for their help.

tives that would not otherwise be available. For example, one type of contractual option is the exclusive right, usually obtained for a fee, to buy or sell property within a specified time and for a specified price. Escrow is a contractual option that allows one party to withdraw from an agreement easily if other parties do not fulfill their commitments.

Non-contractual options exist when we recognize or create the possibility of deciding after the revelation of information with the same or a modified set of alternatives. Non-contractual options may involve the acquisition of contractual options. Furthermore, the new information may be gathered as a result of creating the option. To illustrate both these points, consider the idea of buying an option to purchase oil rights to a property, commissioning and paying for a test drilling program, and deciding whether to buy the oil rights based on the test drilling results. This idea is a non-contractual option that contains a contractual option and the creation of information that would otherwise not be available.

I have observed that the opportunity to recognize and create options is too frequently overlooked in the framing and structuring of decision problems. This stems from a failure to recognize the sequential nature of most decision situations. For example, an analysis of an actual business decision problem that might result in litigation was performed by an executive who had limited decision analysis training. He carefully laid out in a decision tree a series of steps on the road to litigation and the possible results of a suit with their probabilities. He based his decision on the analysis. At no point in the sequence of decisions did he introduce alternatives of offering to settle for various amounts. Such alternatives represent free, non-contractual options that may well have increased the value of the decision.

An important concept in decision analysis is clairvoyance on one or more of the uncertainties faced by the decision maker. Clairvoyance is an option that permits one to make all decisions after revelation of specified uncertainties. Clairvoyance with limited flexibility is an option that permits one to make a limited set of decisions or of alternatives for decisions after revelation of specified uncertainties. Since any experiment or information gathering activity can be viewed as providing clairvoyance on the results of that experiment or activity, any experiment or other information gathering activity can be viewed as an option.

This paper begins with a discussion of fundamental concepts that will be used in the development. Then we present examples of options to illustrate the breadth of application. The evaluation of a simple option is followed by a more extensive discussion of a decision about where to throw a party, which allows us to explore issues of time and information gathering. We illustrate financial options using the case of an option to call a security. We show how options create value (and how the lack of them can curtail value) in the "venture capitalist's" problem. We then illustrate the power of inventing and designing options to create value.

## Fundamentals

Our discussion of options will apply to decision makers who follow the five rules of actional thought.[1] In brief, they are:

> THE PROBABILITY RULE. The decision maker can describe the alternatives as deals composed of possibilities and associated probabilities.

> THE ORDER RULE. The decision maker can order from best to worst the possibilities for all alternatives considered as prospects; two or more may be at the same level.

> THE EQUIVALENCE RULE. Given three prospects at different levels, the decision maker can assign a probability (a preference probability) to receiving the best versus the worst that would make the decision maker indifferent to receiving this deal or the middle prospect.

> THE SUBSTITUTION RULE. The decision maker maintains the indifference established in the equivalence rule if faced with a real choice and a probability the decision maker believes is equal to the preference probability.

> THE CHOICE RULE. Given a choice between two deals involving the same two prospects at different levels, the decision maker must choose the deal with the higher probability of the better prospect.

The rules permit choosing among any alternatives; those who adopt the rules are "rulepeople." As long as they prefer more money to less, rulepeople have a risk attitude described by a $u$-curve for dollars that allows them to calculate a certain equivalent in dollars for any deal consisting of dollar prospects and associated probabilities. The certain equivalent is the inverse of the $u$-curve evaluated at the sum of the probability of each prospect, multiplied by the value of the $u$-curve for each dollar amount.

If the certain equivalent is always equal to the sum of the probabilities times the dollar amounts, then the decision maker is risk neutral; otherwise, the decision maker is risk sensitive. If the certain equivalent is less than that for a risk neutral person, the decision maker is risk averse. When we use any of these terms without restricting the range in which they apply, we mean that they apply for any deal.

## Deltapeople

The value of an option depends on the buyer's or seller's risk attitude. Our discussion generally applies to any risk attitude, but we illustrate it only for rulepeople who satisfy the delta property: their certain equivalent for a deal will increase or decrease by delta if all dollar prospects in the deal are increased or decreased by delta. We call such a person a "deltaperson." Considering only deltapeople simplifies the computation of option values because we need not be concerned with wealth effects. Deltapeople are risk neutral or have an exponential risk attitude,

$$u(x) = a - be^{-x/\rho}, b > 0,$$

with constant risk tolerance $r$. Risk-averse deltapeople have positive risk tolerances.

## Price and Value

Acquiring or creating an option may require paying a price in terms of a value measure; this is the option price. Choosing an alternative provided by the option may require an additional payment of value measure, the exercise price for that alternative. When the same exercise price is associated with some of the alternatives, and no exercise price is associated with the others, we shall speak simply of the exercise price of the option.

Given the exercise price or prices, the value of an option to be acquired is the option price at which the decision maker is indifferent about buying it. Generally the option value will increase with uncertainty and the number of the alternatives.

The usual value of clairvoyance is the value of the clairvoyance option with a zero exercise price. Below we examine both this case and the case of non-zero exercise price. The usual value of an experiment is the value of the clairvoyance option on the results of the experiment with a zero exercise price. The notion of option allows us to expand the concept of value of clairvoyance. Each exercise price will have an associated option value.

## Option Examples from Everyday Life

There are many examples of this expanded notion of option. In every case there is a tradeoff between the option price and the exercise price.

Car owners have many options. They can carry a spare tire, or a mini–spare tire. The mini has a lower option price, both in initial cost and saving of storage space, but a lower exercise value because it can be used at a limited speed for a limited distance. They can also carry tools, subscribe to a tow service, or buy a fire extinguisher. Buying a car equipped with an air bag or an automatic braking system are alternatives that are not options because using them is not an exercise of human will. In contrast, buying a car with a seat belt or with cruise control are options; they allow future decision making.

The purchase of insurance is a very common option. The option price is usually called the premium. The exercise prices may be fixed (e.g., payments per doctor visit for medical insurance or deductible amounts for automobile collision and comprehensive insurance) or a function of loss (e.g., piece-wise linear copayments for medical insurance above a deductible). Note that the option will not be exercised—no claim will be filed—when the loss is less than the deductible amount, unless deductible payments accumulate to satisfy a maximum annual deductible amount.

Not only is buying insurance an option, there are also options to buy insurance. Purchasing an extended warranty on a new car or appliance is buying insurance. Often the seller will extend the opportunity to buy the insurance for some period after the original purchase, usually at no charge. The buyer thus has the alternative of buying insurance after observing the initial performance of the product: an option on an option. In the same vein, life or health insurance policies may confer options to increase coverage without additional proof of insurability.

## Simple Option Analysis

An option affords us at least the possibility of adjusting our decisions in the light of experience. The value of the option derives from the likelihood and benefit of such adjustment. Consider the simplified option decision shown in Figure 5-1.

You can buy an option for an option price $p_o$. If you do, then with probability $q$ the exercise condition $E$ will arise (e.g., a fire, or stock price doubling). If you exercise the option you will incur the exercise price $p_e$ and the payoff $c$. If you do not exercise the option, then the payoff will be $b$; if the exercise condition does not arise, then the payoff will be $a$. In all cases where you buy the option, payoffs are reduced by the option price $p_o$. If you do not buy the option, then the payoff will be $b$ under the exercise condition, and otherwise $a$. A risk neutral person would exercise the option if the gain from exercising it, $c - b$, would be greater than the exercise price

$$c - b > p_e.$$

The net value would be $c - b - p_e$, which will occur with probability $q$. Therefore, the value of the option is $q(c - b - p_e)$, and it should be bought if the value exceeds its price $p_o$,

$$q(c - b - p_e) > p_o.$$

For a risk sensitive ruleperson, the option will be exercised under the same conditions, but will be attractive only if the certain equivalent of the option deal,[2]

$$[q, (c - p_e - p_o); (1 - q), (a - p_o)],$$

is greater than the certain equivalent of the no option deal,

$$[q, b; (1 - q), a].$$

**Figure 5-1**
*Option Decision Tree*

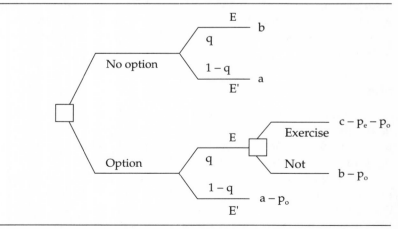

**Figure 5-2**
*Effect of Exercise Price on Option Value*

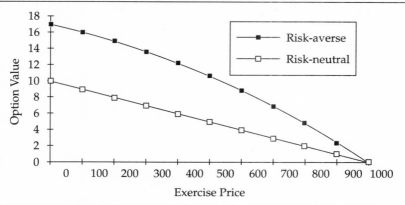

To illustrate, consider someone facing a 1 percent chance of a $1,000 loss. He is offered an option that will reimburse the loss at different exercise prices (deductibles). Figure 5-2 shows how the option value will vary with the exercise price if the person is risk neutral and if the person is a risk averse deltaperson with a risk tolerance of $1,000. As we would expect, the option is considerably more valuable to the risk averse person when the exercise price is low, because without the option this person has a larger negative certain equivalent of the deal. The value of the option falls about the same amount to both people with initial increases in the exercise price.

## The Party Problem

To illustrate the use of options, consider the party problem. Jane is planning a party. She has three alternatives: have the party outdoors (*O*), on the porch (*P*), exposed to the weather on the sides, or indoors (*I*). She is concerned about the weather, which will be sunny (*S*) or rainy (*R*); she assigns probability .4 to *S*. She is risk neutral and assigns dollar values to various combinations of location and weather, as shown in Figure 5-3.

Jane's certain equivalents of the three alternatives are 40, 48, and 46; she chooses a porch party. If she knew it would be sunny, she would have an outdoor party and make 100; if she knew it would be rainy, she would have an indoor party and make 50. Since the probabilities

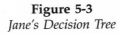

**Figure 5-3**
*Jane's Decision Tree*

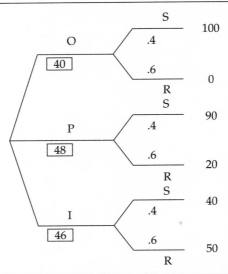

of sunny and rainy are .4 and .6, free clairvoyance would provide her with a valuation of 70, an increase of 22. This means that the value of the option represented by clairvoyance on the weather is 22.

The party problem is a useful paradigm for several reasons. First, it is clearly contrived, so little energy is spent on deciding whether it mirrors some real-life decision. Second, although it is almost the simplest nontrivial decision problem, it presents many challenging questions. Third, in form it is close to many common decisions.

For example, in the case of seismic risk to nuclear power plants, think of *R* as a serious seismic event in the operating life of the plant. Then *O* could be the alternative of no structural modification for this risk; *I* the alternative of extensive, expensive, and effective modification; and *P* a limited and less effective modification alternative. With suitable changes in probabilities and values, the process of analysis is unchanged. Similar illustrations for business and medical decisions are readily constructed.

Returning to the party problem, note that Jane can create the clairvoyance option by setting up the party both outdoors and indoors. If she can do this for an option price of less than 22, she will come out ahead. She can also decrease the option price by increasing the exercise price—she could partially set up the party both indoors and outdoors, with the rest of the party facilities arranged so they can be moved to the party location once the weather is known. Since rain is more likely, she would set up these movable features for an indoor party and move them outdoors if necessary. If she could have the partial set-up for an option price of 10 and an exercise price of 5 given sunshine, then the valuation of the option would be $22 - 10 - .4(5) = 10$. For Jane, creating this option would raise the value of the party from 48 to 58.

### Party Problem with Many Days: Sequential Decisions

Suppose Jane has an option to have the party on any of the next $n$ days after observing the weather each morning. She assigns the same .4 probability to the weather's being sunny on any day, regardless of the weather on preceding days. Under these conditions, she will hold her party outdoors on the first sunny day, with a value of 100. If she waits until $n = 1$, the last day, she will have the party on that day in the location best suited to the day's weather—that is, with clairvoyance. The value of the option when $n = 1$ is therefore 22, as we calculated above.

With this option for $n$ days, Jane will be able to enjoy an outdoor party in the sunshine if at least one of the $n$ days is sunny. This will happen with the probability that not every day is rainy, $1 - .6^n$. For example, if the option covers two days, there is a .64 chance that at least one will be sunny. She will have a .64 chance of a party worth 100 outdoors, and a .36 chance of a party worth 50 indoors, for a valuation of 82. Without the ability to plan the party after observing the weather she would have a porch party worth 48, so the two-day option is worth 34.

As $n$ increases, the option becomes more valuable, up to a point. As Figure 5-4 shows, for $n$ greater than 9, the option is worth about 52, the difference between the value of the best party, 100, and the value of the porch party, 48.

### Information Options

As we have said, the opportunity to gain information before acting is an option. To explore such options further and to allow for risk aversion, suppose the party decision is faced by Jane's friend Kim, a deltaperson with a constant risk tolerance of $72.13 (exactly, 50/ln 2). Aside from this difference, Kim and Jane face identical problems.

As shown in Figure 5-5, Kim's certain equivalents for the alternatives differ from Jane's. Kim would have the party indoors, with a certain equivalent of 45.83. The option of clairvoyance on the weather

**Figure 5-4**
*Change in Option Value*

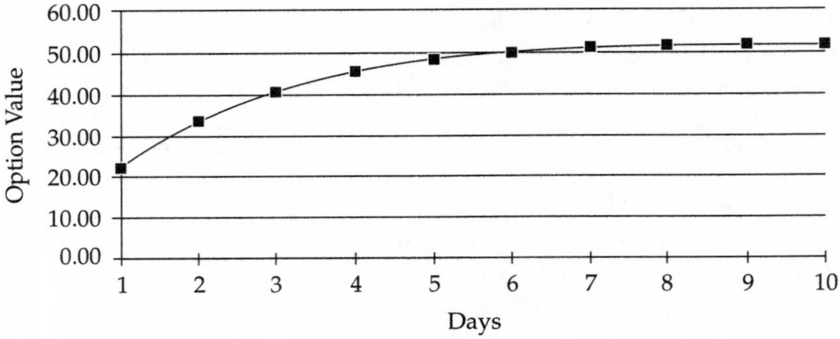

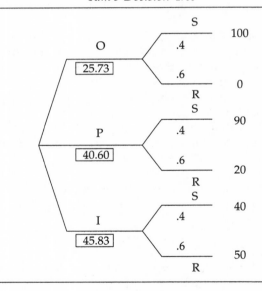

**Figure 5-5**
*Kim's Decision Tree*

would give her a deal in which with probability .4 she will have an outdoor party with value 100, and otherwise an indoor party with value 50; this deal has a certain equivalent of 66.10. Since Kim is a deltaperson, her value for the clairvoyance option is 66.10 − 45.83, or 20.27.

Now suppose Kim is offered the services, not of a clairvoyant, but of the Acme Rain Detector. She assigns .8 probability to the detector's saying Sunny (*S*) when the weather will, in fact, be sunshine, and the same probability to Rainy (*R*) when the weather will be rain, as shown in Figure 5-6.

Reversing the tree, as in Figure 5-7, shows the chance she will receive each report and the implications for the probability of sunshine.

Figure 5-8 shows the decision tree for using the Rain Detector if it is free; arrows indicate the best alternative.

**Figure 5-6**
*Rain Detector's Probability Assessments*

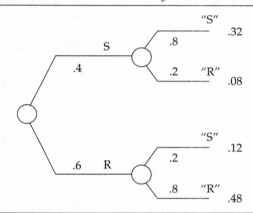

**Figure 5-7**
*Detector's Probability Tree in Inferential Form*

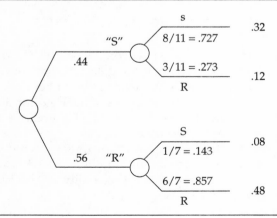

**Figure 5-8**
*Kim's Decision Tree for Use of Rain Detector*

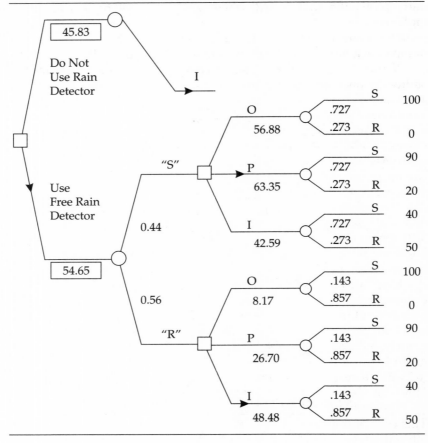

Note that Kim will have the party on the porch if the detector says Sunny, but she will stay indoors if the detector says Rainy. As Kim is a deltaperson, the value of the detector option to her is 54.65 − 45.83, or 8.82. If Kim is given free use of the Rain Detector, her value of clairvoyance falls to 66.10 − 54.65, or 11.45. She would not accept the services of a clairvoyant who charges $12.

But suppose the clairvoyant asks, "How much would you pay me for an option on my services at any time for $12?" Kim reasons, "If Acme says Sunny, which it will with probability .44, I would have the party on the porch with a certain equivalent of 63.35 and a .727 chance of sunshine. If I then obtained clairvoyance, I would have a .727 chance of an outdoor party with a value of 100 and a .273 chance of an indoor party with value 50. Such a deal would be worth 82.59 to me, an increase of 19.24 over the 63.35 value I would otherwise face. I would certainly pay $12 for clairvoyance under these circumstances, leaving me with a net 7.24 improvement.

"On the other hand, if Acme says Rainy, which it will with probability .56, I would have the party indoors with a certain equivalent of 48.48 and a .143 chance of sunshine. If I then obtained clairvoyance, I would have a .143 chance of an outdoor party with a value of 100 and a .857 chance of an indoor party with value 50. Such a deal would be worth 55.35 to me, an increase of 6.87 over the 48.48 value I would otherwise face. I would not pay $12 for clairvoyance under these circumstances; I would not exercise the option and would receive no value from it.

"Therefore the value of the option to me is the certain equivalent of a deal with a .44 chance of 7.24 and a .56 chance of nothing; namely, 3.10. Given that I have free use of the Acme Rain Detector, but do not know yet what it will indicate, I would pay no more than $3.10 for an option on clairvoyance with an exercise price of $12."

Kim can now investigate how the option value depends on the exercise price. If the exercise price were zero, then she would always exercise and the value of the option to her would be the value of a deal that with probability .44 pays 19.24 and with probability .56 pays 6.87; namely, $12.05. Yet earlier, we computed the value of clairvoyance, given free use of the Rain Detector, as $11.45, the clairvoyant wanted $12, and Kim refused. Now it looks like she should have accepted. How can we reconcile these results?

The problem lies in using incremental deals to evaluate the option. This type of thinking will work in the risk neutral case, but not generally otherwise. Let us change the reasoning this way. If the detector says Sunny, which it will with probability .44, then after paying the $12 for clairvoyance, Kim will have a deal worth 70.59 (82.59 − 12), and this is greater than the 63.35 value deal she otherwise faced. If the detector says Rainy, which it will with probability .56, then free clairvoyance would give her a 55.35 value, and after paying the $12 she would be left with less than the 48.48 value she faces without clairvoyance, so she would not exercise the option.

Therefore, the option with an exercise price of 12 would create a deal with a .44 chance of 70.59 and a .56 chance of 48.48. The certain equivalent of this deal is 57.39. Without the option, her certain equivalent of the free detector deal is 54.65. Therefore, given that Kim has

**Figure 5-9**
*Clairvoyance Option Value*

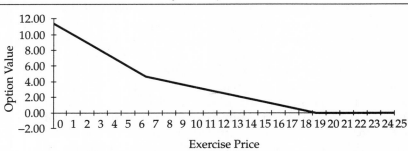

free use of the Acme Rain Detector, but does not know yet what it will indicate, she would pay no more than $2.74 for an option on clairvoyance with an exercise price of $12.

Now we can return to our investigation of how the option value depends on the exercise price. If the exercise price were zero, Kim would always use the clairvoyant's service and the value of the option to her would be the value of a deal that with probability .44 pays 82.59 and with probability .56 pays 55.35; namely, 66.10, less the value without the option (54.65), or 11.45, just the value of clairvoyance. If the exercise price were $19.24 (i.e., 82.59 − 63.35) or greater, then she would never exercise and the option would be worthless.

As Figure 5-9 shows, below an exercise price of 6.87, the option is exercised regardless of the detector indication; above this price it is exercised only if the detector indicates Sunny. The option has no value when the exercise price exceeds 19.24.

Calculating option value is more involved when the decision maker is risk sensitive but not a deltaperson. We can no longer find the value of the option by subtracting the certain equivalent of the deal without the option from the certain equivalent of the deal with a free option.

### Financial Options

Financial instruments are a common type of contractual option. We illustrate how an individual investor might value call options, which give the holder the right to buy something, often a share of stock, at a specified price—the exercise price—within a certain period.[3]

To illustrate, suppose a share of stock can sell in the market for

**Table 5-1**
*Price Transition Probabilities*

| | | To | | | | |
|---|---|---|---|---|---|---|
| | | 200 | 150 | 100 | 50 | 0 |
| From | 200 | .717 | .133 | .05 | .05 | .05 |
| | 150 | .133 | .633 | .133 | .05 | .05 |
| | 100 | .05 | .133 | .633 | .133 | .05 |
| | 50 | .05 | .05 | .133 | .633 | .133 |
| | 0 | .05 | .05 | .05 | .133 | .717 |

five different prices: 200, 150, 100, 50, and 0. The prices change from day to day, with transition probabilities given by Table 5-1.

Consider a call option that will allow a share of the stock to be bought at any time within the next $n$ days for 100. For a risk neutral person, how does the value of this option change with the current price of the stock and the number of days remaining in the option? The value is established by recursion. If tomorrow is the last day to exercise the option, then it will be exercised if tomorrow's price is greater than 100; the profit will be 100 if the price is 200 and 50 if the price is 150. If today's price is 200, the value of the option tomorrow will be .717(100) + .133(50) = 78.35. Since it is worth 100 today, it should be exercised for a profit of 100. If today's price is 150, the value of the option tomorrow will be .133(100) + .633(50) = 44.95; however, it is worth 50 today and should be exercised for that profit. If today's price is 100, there is no point in exercising the option today—it should be held, since its value tomorrow is .05(100) + .133(50) = 11.65. Similar calculations for the current prices of 50 and 0 both produce a value of 7.50, so the option should be held.

Now we know that the value of the option with one day remaining is 100, 50, 11.65, 7.50, or 7.50, according to whether the price of the share with one day remaining is 200, 150, ..., 0. If two days remain, we repeat the calculation using these values and the transition probabilities. For example, if the price is 150 and two days remain, then the value of holding the option is .133(100) + .633(50) + .133(11.65) + .05(7.50) + .05(7.50) = 47.25, and the option should be exercised for a profit of 50.

The results are summarized in Table 5-2. Once we know the value of holding the option, we know whether to exercise it today. As in the party problem, the more days remaining, the greater the value of the option; not surprisingly, the option should always be exercised if the

**Table 5-2**
*Option Strategy and Value*

| | | | | | Days Remaining | | | | | |
|---|---|---|---|---|---|---|---|---|---|---|
| PRICE | 10 | 9 | 8 | 7 | 6 | 5 | 4 | 3 | 2 | 1 |

| | | | | | Option Values | | | | | |
|---|---|---|---|---|---|---|---|---|---|---|
| 200 | 87.57 | 86.7 | 85.77 | 84.8 | 83.8 | 82.79 | 81.82 | 80.82 | 79.67 | 78.33 |
| 150 | 64.84 | 62.44 | 59.95 | 57.4 | 54.89 | 52.58 | 50.76 | 49.19 | 47.31 | 45 |
| 100 | 55.75 | 52.61 | 49.26 | 45.67 | 41.81 | 37.6 | 32.87 | 27.3 | 20.43 | 11.67 |
| 50 | 53.25 | 49.84 | 46.15 | 42.14 | 37.76 | 32.93 | 27.56 | 21.53 | 14.81 | 7.5 |
| 0 | 52.59 | 49.11 | 45.34 | 41.26 | 36.82 | 31.98 | 26.68 | 20.86 | 14.46 | 7.5 |

| | | | | | Better Action: Call (C) or Hold (H) | | | | | |
|---|---|---|---|---|---|---|---|---|---|---|
| 200 | C | C | C | C | C | C | C | C | C | C |
| 150 | H | H | H | H | H | H | C | C | C | C |
| 100 | H | H | H | H | H | H | H | H | H | H |
| 50 | H | H | H | H | H | H | H | H | H | H |
| 0 | H | H | H | H | H | H | H | H | H | H |

| | | | | | Profit from Better Action | | | | | |
|---|---|---|---|---|---|---|---|---|---|---|
| 200 | 100 | 100 | 100 | 100 | 100 | 100 | 100 | 100 | 100 | 100 |
| 150 | 62.44 | 59.95 | 57.4 | 54.89 | 52.58 | 50.76 | 50 | 50 | 50 | 50 |
| 100 | 52.61 | 49.26 | 45.67 | 41.81 | 37.6 | 32.87 | 27.3 | 20.43 | 11.67 | 0 |
| 50 | 49.84 | 46.15 | 42.14 | 37.76 | 32.93 | 27.56 | 21.53 | 14.81 | 7.5 | 0 |
| 0 | 49.11 | 45.34 | 41.26 | 36.82 | 31.98 | 26.68 | 20.86 | 14.46 | 7.5 | 0 |

share price reaches 200; and the option should be exercised if the share price reaches 150 and four or fewer days remain. The value of a ten-day call option at 100 when the current price is 100 is 55.75.

## The Venture Capitalist's Problem

When a sequential decision is represented as a simple decision, serious decision errors can result. We demonstrate this with a simple example that is similar in form to a venture capital investment. Suppose that a risk neutral person is offered the opportunity to participate in an investment determined by three Success (S) − Failure (F) trials. The probability of Success on each trial is the same, but unknown, and has initially been assigned a uniform distribution between 0 and 1. As successive trials are performed, the probability of Success will change according to the rules of probability, as shown in Figure 5-10.[4] Success makes a later Success more likely; Failure makes a later Failure more likely.

The investment pays $100 for a Success and costs $80 for a Failure. Since, a priori, there is a .5 chance of Success on each of the three trials, each trial contributes .5(100) + .5(−80), or $10, to the value of the deal for a total value of $30.

Suppose now that the investor is offered an option to stop participating at any point. What is the value of this option? Figure 5-11 shows the analysis.

We begin by anticipating the third trial. For the four possible histories at that point—SS, SF, FS, and FF—the valuations of the third trial are 55, 10, 10, and −35. An investor would choose to exercise his option and stop if he had observed two failures; otherwise, he would continue. If he had observed only one trial and it was a Success, then he would have a 2/3 chance of receiving 100 + 55 and a 1/3 chance of receiving −80 + 10 for a valuation of 80. However, if the first trial was a Failure, he would have a 1/3 chance of receiving 100 + 10 and a 2/3 chance of −80 (since he would then stop). This valuation is −50/3, and he would again exercise his option to stop. At the beginning of the process the overall value is .5(100 + 80) + .5(−80) = 50. The value of the option is thus 50 − 30, or $20. Thus, the option to stop participating increases the value of the investment from $30 to $50.

**Figure 5-10**
*Success-Failure Probability Tree*

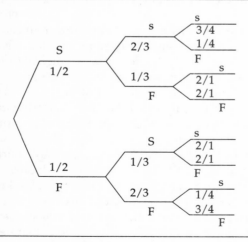

**Figure 5-11**
*Strategy and Certain Equivalents for Venture Capitalist's Problem*

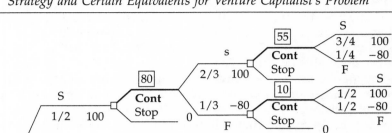

If the option allows the investor to not participate in any trial, rather than to stop participating in the process, then it would be slightly more valuable. The investor would choose not to participate in the second trial if the first trial was a failure, but to participate in the third trial if the second trial was a success. This would increase the valuation of the process and the value of the option by .5(1/3)(10), or $1.67.

If the payoffs for Success and Failure are reduced by $10 to $90 and −$90, the investment would have no value to a risk neutral person, unless there was an option to stop at any time. With this option, the analysis proceeds as before with the results in Figure 5-12.

The option to stop will be exercised if there is a failure on the first trial. The value of the option and therefore the value of the process is $30. In this case, there is no additional value of an option to pass on any trial rather than to stop.

Thus, options that permit a decision maker to cut losses in the face of unfavorable information can be extremely valuable, and a failure to represent such options in a decision problem can lead to serious error. The case of the executive facing litigation discussed in the introduction is one example; product warranties, return privileges, and money back guarantees are more common. Similarly, options that permit a decision maker to reap profits following the revelation of favorable information can be extremely valuable; these are often bought with "sweat equity" in startup companies.

## Creating Options

Every discussion on generating alternatives for a decision asks, "What options could and should we create?" Options result from recognizing or creating new decision opportunities in anticipation of the total or partial resolution of uncertainty.

Suppose a man is on a motoring vacation and is concerned about whether he will be able to find a motel room at his desired destination, though he assigns only a 50 percent chance of reaching it given the highway's bad traffic conditions. He calls ahead and finds that he can have a room if he pays for it now by credit card. His alternatives are to guarantee the reservation or not.

Suppose that he offers to guarantee the innkeeper half the cost of the room (the option price) and to pay an additional three-quarters of the cost of the room if he arrives (the exercise price). If he is risk neutral, his evaluation of the cost of the option is .5 + .5(3/4), or 7/8 the cost of the room, which is less than the cost of the guarantee. If the innkeeper is also risk neutral and assigns the same .5 chance of the traveler's appearing, then the value to the innkeeper is also 7/8. The

**Figure 5-12**

*Venture Capitalist's Problem with Value Created by Options*

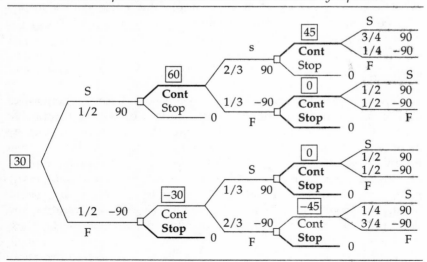

option will be a good deal to an innkeeper who assigns less than a 7/8 probability to renting the room to someone else.

One can adjust the option to fit other situations. For example, if the exercise price is one half the room cost, the option cost is 3/4; selling this option will be desirable to the innkeeper if there is otherwise less than a .75 chance of renting the room.

Options such as these should have an important place in selecting business strategies. Customarily, to define possible strategies, a decision maker first identifies every decision required to define the strategy and then specify the alternatives for that decision.[5] Strategies to be investigated are the few most promising coherent selections of one alternative for each decision. For example, a cosmetic company developing possible strategies for a new perfume would have to decide what type of product the scent is; alternatives might include medium-priced mass market, very high priced and exclusive. Alternatives for the distribution channel might include top-level department stores and discount chains. A strategy that incorporated the exclusive, very high priced product and discount chain distribution would not be coherent.

As useful as this notion of strategy construction is, the framing of the choices for each decision as alternatives may lead to insufficient consideration of strategies that contain options and hence sequential decisions. One can evoke options by asking first whether one would be in a better position to make some decision after the revelation of one or more uncertainties. If so, one can ask what options one could create to provide the improved decision opportunity. Then, using the type of analysis illustrated here, we would evaluate whether the options make sense. In the perfume example, one might choose to pay for an option on manufacturing facilities rather than commit before the results of a market survey are available.

## Summary

We have now explored some of the ways to extend our thinking about decisions by expanding the notion of options beyond the contractual sphere. We have seen how many everyday alternatives may be viewed as options. We have examined how options add value, how to treat information-gathering opportunities as options, and how to evaluate options that extend over time. We have seen the importance of recognizing and modeling options in avoiding loss and creating value. Finally, we have illustrated how a proactive view toward creating and designing options can have major benefits in personal and business decisions.

One final comment. Performing a decision analysis permits one to make a future decision following the revelation of information, namely, the insights from the analysis. Therefore performing a decision analysis is itself an option, and can be valued as such. The answer to the question "When should I do a formal decision analysis?" should be "When its option value exceeds its cost."

## NOTES

1. These rules are based on a Laplace-Jaynes view of probability and von Neumann–Morgenstern axioms for decision under uncertainty. See Ronald A. Howard, "In Praise of the Old Time Religion," in *Utility Theories: Measurements and Applications*, ed. W. Edwards (Boston: Kluwer Academic Publishers, 1992), pp. 27–55.
2. The brackets specify a deal. The probability and value of each prospect are separated by commas; the prospect descriptions are separated by semicolons.
3. Options have a substantial literature. See, for example, John C. Cox, and Mark Rubenstein, *Options Markets* (Englewood Cliffs, NJ: Prentice-Hall, 1985); and John Hull, *Options, Futures, and Other Derivative Securities*, 2nd ed. (Englewood Cliffs, NJ: Prentice-Hall, 1993). Most analysts are concerned with market and investor models based on the avoidance of arbitrage possibilities. In contrast, we take the point of view of an individual investor with beliefs about security movements and personal preferences.
4. Probabilities follow Laplace's Law of Succession.
5. Ronald A. Howard, "Decision Analysis: Practice and Promise," *Management Science* 34 (1988): 679–695.

# CHAPTER 6

# MEASURING RISK AND RETURN FOR PORTFOLIOS

## David E. Bell

Though the concept of utility as a way to model degrees of satisfaction can be traced back at least two hundred years, it was von Neumann and Morgenstern's clever axiomatization of the concept that sparked a heightened level of activity with it.[1] Amplified, explained, and popularized by Howard Raiffa's landmark book *Decision Analysis*,[2] the new discipline took hold in universities and consulting firms across the world. Great excitement and anticipation permeated the field. Many of us believed that this methodology was the universal solution to difficult decision problems in general, and financial decisions under uncertainty in particular.

Decision analysis has been a big success. It has enlightened economic analyses in diverse areas of application and had notable success in matters of health, safety, and the environment. One area where it has enjoyed less success than might have been expected has been in the financial community.

While there is nothing inherently inappropriate about the application of decision analysis in finance, the two areas have developed separately, and with their own conventions, making technology transfer problematic. For example, decision analysts think in terms of holistic alternatives (as if this was to be the last financial decision you'll ever make), whereas in finance decisions are viewed as dynamic and inherently reversible. Decision analysts have historically viewed payoffs as being incremental to existing wealth (plus $10) rather than as returns (plus 10 percent). Finally, decision analysts have viewed with satisfaction that the concept of utility subsumes the labile concept of risk, whereas in finance measures of risk are in the forefront of theories.

In recent papers I have tried to close the gap between these two fields by exploring the degree to which utility may be reinterpreted in terms of risk and return. In an early paper, I showed that there is a surprisingly rich set of utility functions that are compatible with a measure of risk.[3] More recently, I have identified all utility functions that may be represented in terms of risk and return,[4] and provided a behavioral axiom that, when added to the original set prescribed by von Neumann and Morgenstern, leads to a theory of decision making that is entirely compatible with risk and return.[5]

All of these papers were written from the traditional decision analysis perspective that assumes payoffs are additive with respect to current wealth. In this paper, I present the same theory but assume that payoffs are multiplicative. One unexpected by-product of this research concerns the role of the mean as the benchmark measure of a distribution's value "were it not for the risk." In the world of multiplicative returns, its preeminent role seems suspect.

In the next section I review the necessary background in a little more detail. In the succeeding sections I describe the main results. Proofs are sketched in the Appendix.

## Background

Investors are constantly seeking attractive prospects for their capital, many evaluating the attractiveness of prospects in terms of two measures, risk and return.[6] However, since von Neumann and Morgenstern first axiomatized expected utility, it has been accepted that the rational way to make decisions of this kind involves constructing a utility function defined over the domain of potential outcomes, in this case levels of net worth. The best choice is the one with the highest expected utility. This approach ignores the intuitive concepts of risk and return.

For example, suppose an investor with current wealth $w$ is considering two possible investments. One investment, $\tilde{x}$ is equally likely to give a rate of return on invested capital of either 10% or $-5\%$. The second investment, $\tilde{y}$, has a probability .10 of doubling an initial investment, and a probability .90 of losing 20%. If the investor has a utility function $u$, then the first investment is to be preferred over the second if

$$Eu(w\tilde{x}) = 0.5u(1.1w) + 0.5u(0.95w)$$
$$> 0.1u(2w) + 0.9u(0.80w) = Eu(w\tilde{y}),$$

where $E$ symbolizes the taking of a probabilistic average.

This evaluation process is theoretically sound, but it is very difficult to specify an appropriate utility function for a particular investor. It is generally agreed that an appropriate utility function for wealth will usually be "smooth" (there is no critical or target level of wealth), increasing (more money is better than less), and risk averse (a "fair" gamble, say a coin toss to win or lose $10, is unattractive). Most people also agree with John Pratt, Raiffa, and Robert Schlaifer, who all argue that a utility function should be decreasingly risk averse.[7] But these conditions provide only limited guidance for an investor, and no satisfactory process for selecting a specific function has been found. In part, this stems from inevitable inconsistencies in investors' answers to both hypothetical and real choices.

Even if the selection process were to be performed satisfactorily, the very nature of an expected utility analysis seems unsatisfactory to many people: the output of such an analysis is a ranking of the alternatives, yet the value of an analysis often stems from the insight it yields into *why* one alternative is better than another. Might it be possible to explain these decisions in terms of risk and return? "Return" is a measure of the attractiveness of an alternative, were it possible to average across the possible outcomes. "Risk" concerns the level of disparity among possible outcomes. Utility analysis should be more intuitively helpful if its results could be explained in terms of risk and return. This paper determines the extent to which utility analysis may be interpreted in terms of risk and return, thus combining the theoretical power of utility with the intuitive appeal of risk and return.

Ideally there would exist, for alternatives $\tilde{x}$, a function $r(\tilde{x})$ measuring return, a function $R(\tilde{x})$ measuring risk, and a risk-return tradeoff function $f(r, R, w)$ that evaluates the overall attractiveness of an alternative $\tilde{x}$ assuming the investor currently has wealth $w$. The functions $r$, $R$, and $f$ might vary across decision makers.

In earlier papers, I reported results along these lines for investments that provide outcomes that are incremental to current wealth ($w + \tilde{x}$ rather than $w\tilde{x}$).[8] The multiplicative case is worthy of separate development because investments are an important potential area of application for utility analysis, and also because of some interesting implications for the measurement of risk and return.

## Utility Functions Compatible with Risk and Return

The most common use of a risk-return framework for investments is one in which return is measured by the mean $\tilde{x}$, and risk is measured by the variance $E(\tilde{x} - \bar{x})^2$. As Harry Markowitz showed, these measures lead to a mathematically elegant, and pragmatic, evaluation of portfolio alternatives.[9] A mean-variance evaluation system can be compatible with the axioms of utility, since a quadratic utility function, $u(w) = aw + bw^2$, leads to a portfolio measure of $Eu(w\tilde{x}) = aw\bar{x} + bw^2E(\tilde{x})^2 = aw\bar{x} + bw^2E(\tilde{x} - \bar{x})^2 + bw^2\bar{x}^2$, which is of the form $f(\bar{x}, E(\tilde{x} - \bar{x})^2, w)$. However, the quadratic utility function has some disturbing properties; in particular, it is *increasingly* risk averse for all $w$; that is, a risky portfolio becomes relatively *less* desirable as a person gets richer. In this paper, we investigate whether there are sensible risk-return frameworks that are compatible with sensible utility functions.

We assert that a sensible utility function satisfies these properties:

$U_0$: (Smooth) $u(w)$ is continuous and infinitely differentiable.

$U_1$: (More Money is Better) $u(w)$ is increasing in $w$.

$U_2$: (Risk Aversion) $\bar{\tilde{x}} < \bar{x}$ for all $\tilde{x}$ other than $\tilde{x} = \bar{x}$.

$U_3$: (Decreasing Risk Aversion) If $\tilde{x}$ is indifferent to a fixed payoff $y$ at wealth $w$, then $\tilde{x}$ is preferred to $y$ at higher levels of wealth.

We also suggest the following properties of a risk-return function $f(r, R, w)$:

$R_0$: (Smooth) $f$ is continuous and infinitely differentiable.

$R_1$: (More Money is Better) $f$ is increasing in $r$, and in $w$.

$R_2$: (Risk Aversion) $f$ is decreasing in $R$.

$R_3$: (Decreasing Risk Aversion) If $\tilde{x}$ is indifferent to $\tilde{y}$ at wealth $w$, then $\tilde{x}$ is preferred to $\tilde{y}$ at higher levels of wealth if and only if $R(\tilde{x}) > R(\tilde{y})$.

We can show the following:

THEOREM 1.   The ordering of portfolios $\tilde{x}$ by an expected utility measure $Eu(w\tilde{x})$, satisfying $U_0$, $U_1$, $U_2$, and $U_3$ is consistent with a risk-return function $f(r(\tilde{x}), R(\tilde{x}), w)$ satisfying $R_0$, $R_1$, $R_2$, and $R_3$ if and only if $u$ belongs to one of the following two families:

(i)   $u(w) = aw^d + bw^c$   $ad > 0, d \leq 1, bc > 0, c < 1$, or

(ii)   $u(w) = a\log w + bw^c$   $a > 0, bc > 0, c \leq 1$.

A proof of this result is in the Appendix of this paper. It is easy to see that these functions do satisfy the various conditions of the Theorem. As a simple example, consider $u(w) = w - w^{-1}$, which is of type (i) above with $a = d = 1$ and $b = c = -1$. It is continuous and differentiable (for $w > 0$), it is increasing ($u'(w) = 1 + w^{-2} > 0$), and it is risk averse ($u''(w) = -2w^{-3} < 0$). It is also decreasingly risk averse. Pratt defines risk aversion by the quantity $-u''(w)/u'(w)$ or $2w^{-3}/(1 + w^{-2})$.[10] This quantity decreases with $w$.

Now consider the risk-return representation of this utility function. We have $Eu(w\tilde{x}) = w\tilde{x} - w^{-1}E(1/\tilde{x})$. If we say $r(\tilde{x}) = \tilde{x}$ and $R(\tilde{x}) = E(1/\tilde{x})$, then $f(r, R, w) = wr - R/w$. This is continuous and differentiable in $r$, $R$, and $w$ (for $w > 0$). It is increasing in $r$ and decreasing in $R$. Finally, it satisfies the decreasing risk-aversion condition because $r$ becomes increasingly weighted as $w$ increases. Note that a given utility function does not have a *unique* representation in terms of risk and return. For example, an alternative definition of $r(\tilde{x}) = \tilde{x}$ and $R(\tilde{x}) = E(\tilde{x}/\tilde{x})$ yields $f(r, R, w) = wr - R/(rw)$, which also satisfies $R_0$, $R_1$, $R_2$, and $R_3$.

It is easy to generate measures of risk and return that are compatible with each of the utility families of Theorem 1 and with conditions $R_1$, $R_2$, and $R_3$. Each utility function of Theorem 1 may be expressed, in the obvious way, as the sum of two utility functions, $u(w) = u_1(w) + u_2(w)$, and in such a way that $u_1$ is always less risk averse than $u_2$ for any particular level of $w$. For example, if $u(w) = aw^d + bw^c$, and if $d > c$, we may set $u_1(w) = aw^d$ and $u_2(w) = bw^c$. If we define $r(\tilde{x}) = E(\tilde{x}^d)$ and $R(\tilde{x}) = -(1/c)E(\tilde{x}^c)$, then $f(r, R, w) = aw^d r - bcw^c R$, and this satisfies $R_0$, $R_1$, $R_2$, and $R_3$.

If $u(w) = a\log w + bw^c$ then there are two cases; $c$ can be positive or negative. If $c$ is positive then $w^c$ is less risk averse than $\log w$ and so we set $u_1(w) = bw^c$ and $u_2(w) = a\log w$. In this case $r(\tilde{x}) = E(\tilde{x}^c)$, $R(\tilde{x}) = -E\log\tilde{x}$, and $f(r, R, w) = bw^c r + a\log w - aR$. If $c$ is negative, then $\log w$ is less risk averse than $w^c$ and so we set $u_1(w) = a\log w$ and $u_2(w) = bw^c$. In this case $r(\tilde{x}) = E\log\tilde{x}$, $R(\tilde{x}) = -(1/c)E(\tilde{x}^c)$, and $f(r, R, w) = a\log w + ar - bcR$.

## Alternative Measures of Risk and Return

The risk-return functions we derived in the last section were each equivalent to the general form $r(\tilde{x}) - k(w)R(\tilde{x})$, where $k(w)$ represents the tradeoff factor between $r$ and $R$ (which declines as $w$ increases). This form is appealing due to its simple linear structure. However, do the risk and return measures that we have been using come close to representing a decision maker's intuitive thinking about risk and return? While there is considerable debate about how people wish to measure risk,[11] it is reasonable to suppose that most people measure return by the mean, $\tilde{x}$, the statistic used in all elementary analyses with decision trees.

THEOREM 2. If we add the requirement that $r(\tilde{x}) = \tilde{x}$ to the list of conditions in Theorem 1, then the compatible utility functions are:

(i) $u(w) = w - bw^{-c}$ $b > 0, c > 0$, and

(ii) $u(w) = w + a\log w$ $a > 0$.

While a direct proof of this result is fairly easy,[12] it can also be understood in the context of the representation $u(w) = u_1(w) + u_2(w)$ described in the previous section of this paper. The functions in Theorem 2 are those from Theorem 1 for which $u_1(w) = w$.

What are some desirable properties of a risk measure? Although each investor will have a unique risk measure, for our purpose the general form of the measure can be defined by an investor's answers to three questions:

1. Is a guaranteed payoff of 5% less risky, more risky, or equally risky than a guaranteed payoff of 10%?

2. If an investment is equally likely to pay off 5% or 10%, is this risky?

3. If any investment is combined with a second (independent) alternative offering a 50–50 payoff of either +1% or −1%, does the investment necessarily become riskier?

I believe that an investment with a guaranteed fixed payoff has no risk. Therefore, a guaranteed payoff of 5 percent has the same risk as a guaranteed payoff of 10 percent—none. On the other hand, I believe that alternatives that are uncertain, but guaranteed to leave the decision maker better off (as in question 2 above), are risky, since the payoff is uncertain. Finally, I believe that any alternative is made riskier (and less attractive) by the manipulation described in question 3. Indeed, someone who believes that all guaranteed payoffs are riskless, and agrees with the premise in question 3, cannot logically also believe that the alternative described in question 2 is riskless.

Fortunately, a wide range of risk and return measures are compatible with the utility functions of Theorems 1 and 2. The following conditions summarize my own predispositions.

$R_4$: All sure things have zero risk.

$R_5$: Assuming the decision maker begins with a known fixed wealth, the riskiness of an alternative depends only upon the probability distribution of final wealth.

To explain $R_5$, consider a person with initial wealth $w$ investing in $\tilde{x}$, and another person with initial wealth $w/2$ investing in $2\tilde{x}$. How much risk does each face? It seems to me that they face the same risk since their distribution of final wealth is the same. This view emphasizes the concept of risk as an indication of variability in outcome rather than as a measure of "decision correctness" represented by concepts such as probability of loss or regret.[13] Finally, for reasons explained in the next section of the paper, to assume that $r(\tilde{x}) = \tilde{x}$ seems hasty, yet a measure of return should be some form of average across possible outcomes. I suggest the following condition:

$R_6$: A measure of return should be a utility function.

The mean averages the raw percentage payoffs across the possible scenarios. $R_6$ simply allows more flexibility in the definition of return; what we average may be *any* function of the percentage payoff associated with a particular outcome. Of course, $R_6$ also permits the mean.

THEOREM 3. Given the conditions of Theorem 1, and further assuming $R_4$, $R_5$, and $R_6$, three cases are possible:

(i)    $u(w) = aw^d + bw^c$ with $1 \geq d > c$, $bc \geq 0$, $ad \geq 0$,
       $r(\tilde{x}) = (1/d)E\tilde{x}^d$, and
       $R(\tilde{x}) = (1/d)\log E\tilde{x}^d - (1/c)\log E\tilde{x}^c$.

(ii)   $u(w) = a\log w + bw^c$   $a, b, c > 0$   $c \leq 1$,
       $r(\tilde{x}) = (1/c)E\tilde{x}^c$, and
       $R(\tilde{x}) = (1/c)\log E\tilde{x}^c - E\log\tilde{x}$.

(iii)  $u(w) = a\log w + bw^c$   $a > 0$, $b < 0$, $c < 0$,
       $r(\tilde{x}) = E\log\tilde{x}$, and
       $R(\tilde{x}) = E\log\tilde{x} - (1/c)\log E\tilde{x}^c$.

A sample proof is given in the appendix.

## Numerical Examples

This section graphs some numerical examples, using, for illustrative purposes, the case $r(\tilde{x}) = \tilde{x}$, $u(w) = w - bw^{-c}$ ($b > 0$, $c > 0$), $R(\tilde{x}) = \log\tilde{x} + (1/c)\log E(\tilde{x}^{-c})$. The risk measure has only one parameter to be assessed, $c$. As $c$ increases from zero, the measure of risk becomes more and more influenced by the size of the worse outcome; it approaches

**Table 6-1**

| Alternative | Possible Payoffs | Probability | Average Payoff |
|---|---|---|---|
| A | 100% | .20 | 12% |
|   | −10% | .80 |  |
| B | 100% | .50 | 50% |
|   | 0% | .50 |  |
| C | 70% | .75 | 48% |
|   | −20% | .25 |  |
| D | 40% | .95 | 36% |
|   | −40% | .05 |  |

**Table 6-2**

| | Relative Riskiness | | | | | | |
|---|---|---|---|---|---|---|---|
| Alternative | c = .01 | c = 0.3 | c = 1 | c = 3 | c = 5 | c = 6 | c = 10 |
| A | 1 | 2 | 3 | 3 | 4 | 4 | 4 |
| B | 2 | 1 | 1 | 2 | 2 | 3 | 3 |
| C | 3 | 3 | 2 | 1 | 1 | 1 | 2 |
| D | 4 | 4 | 4 | 4 | 3 | 2 | 1 |

a "maximin" mentality. Consider the four alternatives A, B, C, and D in Table 6-1. They are discrete for expositional purposes; the risk-return framework works just as well for continuous distributions.

Table 6-2 shows the relative riskiness of each alternative for each of seven values of $c$, ranging from 0.01 to 10. The four alternatives are ranked, for each value of $c$, from 1 (most risky) to 4 (least risky); for example, the risk of alternative A would be calculated as:

$$R(A) = \log(1.12) + (1/c)\log(.2 \times 2^{-c} + .8 \times .9^{-c}).$$

Table 6-2 highlights the reversal in riskiness of the investments A, B, C, and D as we move from $c = 0.01$ to $c = 10$. The seven values of $c$ were selected to show the sequence in which each pair of alternatives switches rank. (For example, A and B switch between $c = .01$ and $c = 0.3$.) Figure 6-1 shows risk-return graphs of these alternatives for four of the $c$ values.

**Figure 6-1**
*Risk-Return Graphs*

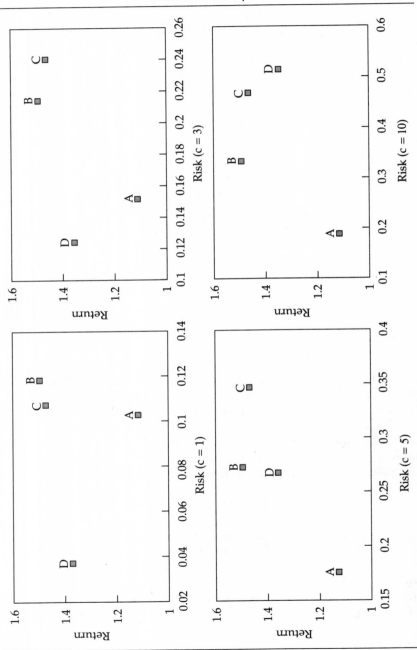

## Is the Mean the Right Measure of Return?

Why is the mean so favored as a measure of the "non-risk" attractiveness of an alternative? Clearly, it is a convenient statistic, it is the first moment approximation, and it represents a "base case" of linear utility. But what guide to action does it represent? In the context of *additive* gambles ($w + \tilde{x}$, rather than $w\tilde{x}$), I think the following is the behavioral implication most people have in mind:

$M_1$: Consider repeating the same investment (independently) an infinite number of times. You are guaranteed to make money if and only if the mean of the investment is positive.

Or, for those who dislike the thought of infinite repetition:

$M_2$: Suppose you repeat the same investment many times and it happens that the outcomes occur in exact proportion to their probability. You will make money if and only if the investment has a positive mean.

To me, those embody exactly the right notions for a measure of return. Return should measure the average performance of an alternative. (Risk, on the other hand, is a recognition that a long-term view is not always realistic.) But in the context of *multiplicative* investment returns, $M_1$ and $M_2$ are no longer true. For example, consider an investment that, with equal probability, increases wealth by 60 percent or decreases it by 50 percent. The mean is positive. Yet in two trials, one good, one bad, the investor's wealth goes from $w$ to $.8w$. If this investment is taken independently, many times, the investor's capital will plunge rapidly.

The appropriate modifications of $M_1$ and $M_2$ for the multiplicative investment scenario are:

$M_1'$: Consider repeating the same investment (independently) an infinite number of times. You are guaranteed to make money if and only if the expected logarithm of the investment is positive.

$M_2'$: Suppose you repeat the same investment many times and it happens that the outcomes occur in exact proportion to their probability. You will make money if and only if the expected logarithm of the investment is positive.

Thus, it may be inappropriate to label as "risk averse" an investor who rejects a 50–50 gamble between +60% return and a −50% return. The following definition of risk aversion seems more natural in the investment context.

PORTFOLIO RISK AVERSION.    An investor is risk averse only if he or she judges some investment with a positive expected logarithm unacceptable.

Using this definition as a basis for measuring portfolio risk aversion, we may deduce that $u(w) = \log w$ is the "risk neutral" utility function and $u(w) = w^{-c}$ ($c > 0$) is the family of utility functions exhibiting constant portfolio risk aversion.

Note that in the additive context, $u(w) = w$ is the natural risk neutral utility function, since $Eu(w + \tilde{x}) = w + \bar{x}$, and $\bar{x}$ is the benchmark measure of return. In the multiplicative context, $u(w) = \log w$ is the risk neutral utility function, since $Eu(w\tilde{x}) = \log w + E\log\tilde{x}$, and $E\log\tilde{x}$ is the benchmark measure of return. This does not mean that the best portfolio is the one that maximizes $E\log\tilde{x}$. Though this criterion has received much attention in the finance literature,[14] such a criterion would only be appropriate for an investor who is not concerned about risk. If $r(\tilde{x}) = E\log\tilde{x}$ is the appropriate definition of return, then Theorem 3 suggests that risk should be measured as $R(\tilde{x}) = E\log\tilde{x} - (1/c)\log E\tilde{x}^c$, for some parameter $c$ that varies with the individual.

## Uncertainty of Initial Wealth

This paper assumes that a risk-return interpretation of expected utility is a desirable objective in itself, and most utility functions are ruled out of consideration simply because they do not permit such an interpretation, not because they stand accused of making aberrant recommendations. However, these ruled-out utility functions *do* make aberrant recommendations when initial wealth $w$ is uncertain. This can occur if, for example, an investor rolls over one asset into another without knowing precisely what the asset to be sold is currently worth.

Suppose that an investor must choose between two investments, but her wealth is uncertain due to two *prior* investments. One of the two prior investments was much more risky (in a way we will define shortly). Now clearly it cannot hurt, and would probably help, if she could know the outcome of either or both of these prior investments before having to make the pending choice. But suppose she is allowed to know the outcome of only one of the two prior investments. Which should she choose? The following condition asserts she should elect to hear the resolution of the more risky prior investment.

CONTEXTUAL UNCERTAINTY CONDITION.   Suppose that an investor must commit all available wealth to one of two investments, $\tilde{x}$ or $\tilde{y}$. Suppose further that this decision must be made before learning of the outcomes of two earlier (independent) investment decisions $\tilde{z}_1$ and $\tilde{z}_2$. The investor is, in effect, selecting either $\tilde{z}_1\tilde{z}_2\tilde{x}$ or $\tilde{z}_1\tilde{z}_2\tilde{y}$. Now suppose that, while $\tilde{z}_1$ and $\tilde{z}_2$ are independent, it is the case that for some constant $k > 1$ we have $\tilde{z}_2 = k\tilde{z}_1$. That is, $\tilde{z}_2$ has the same distribution as $\tilde{z}_1$ but with more extreme outcomes. Suppose we now offer the investor the possibility of knowing the outcome of *either* $\tilde{z}_1$ or $\tilde{z}_2$ *before* the need to select between $\tilde{x}$ and $\tilde{y}$. We assume that the investor will never find it advantageous to select the resolution of $\tilde{z}_1$ over the resolution of $\tilde{z}_2$.

THEOREM 4.   The only utility functions that satisfy the Contextual Uncertainty Condition and $U_1$, $U_2$, and $U_3$ are:

(i)   $u(w) = aw^d - bw^{-c}$     $(a, b, c, d > 0 \quad d \leq 1)$, and

(ii)  $u(w) = a\log w - bw^{-c}$     $(a, b, c > 0)$.

The proof is by consideration of the function $v(w) = Eu(w\tilde{x}) - Eu(w\tilde{y})$ for arbitrary alternatives $\tilde{x}$ and $\tilde{y}$. The Contextual Uncertainty Condition is equivalent to the condition that, for all $\tilde{x}$ and $\tilde{y}$ for which $v(w)$ can be zero, $v$ is monotonic in $w$. The intuition is that $v$ should have no local optima that might lead an investor to prefer localized information of investment outcomes.[15]

While this theorem makes no reference to measures of risk and return, any utility function satisfying the condition is representable in terms of risk and return.

## Conclusions

We have shown that it is possible to interpret expected utility analysis for investments in terms of risk and return tradeoffs. And, while we have argued for consideration of the measure $E\log\tilde{x}$ as a more appropriate measure of return than $\tilde{x}$, both are consistent with well-behaved utility functions. While academic opinions on the appropriate functional form for return are quite firm, there is very little consensus on an appropriate functional form for risk. This paper shows that if consistency with expected utility is to be required, the definition of return severely constrains the selection of $R(\tilde{x})$.

Finally, there is good reason to believe that the popular view of investment decisions as a tradeoff between risk and return has some sound basis. The Contextual Uncertainty Condition is, to my mind, a sensible prescriptive assumption. If the condition deserves a normative status on a par with risk aversion and decreasing risk aversion, then a risk-return view of decisions under uncertainty is correct; if the condition is regarded only as a convenient approximation, it nevertheless demonstrates that any subtleties of evaluation lost by assuming a risk-return framework are exceedingly fine.

## Appendix

### Proof of Theorem 1

Since we require that the equation $Eu(w\tilde{x}) = f(r(\tilde{x}), R(\tilde{x}), w)$ be an identity for all $w$ and $\tilde{x}$, we may take any two values for $w$, say $w_1$ and $w_2$, to obtain: $Eu(w_1\tilde{x}) = f(r(\tilde{x}), R(\tilde{x}), w_1)$, and $Eu(w_2\tilde{x}) = f(r(\tilde{x}), R(\tilde{x}), w_2)$. These equations may be inverted to solve for $r(\tilde{x})$ and $R(\tilde{x})$. The inverse function theorem,[16] requires only that the tradeoff between $r$ and $R$ be different at $w_1$ and $w_2$, and this is so because of $R_3$.

Hence, $r(\tilde{x}) = g_1(Eu(w_1\tilde{x}), Eu(w_2\tilde{x}), w)$, and $R(\tilde{x}) = g_2(Eu(w_1\tilde{x}), Eu(w_2\tilde{x}), w)$ for some functions $g_1$ and $g_2$. Substituting $r$ and $R$ back into $f$, we conclude that $Eu(w\tilde{x}) = g(Eu(w_1\tilde{x}), Eu(w_2\tilde{x}), w)$ for some function $g$. This representation is at the heart of a risk-return relationship: it says that only two "statistics" of $\tilde{x}$ (in this case $Eu(w_1\tilde{x})$, $Eu(w_2\tilde{x})$) are needed to specify $Eu(w\tilde{x})$.

We can show that $g$ must be linear in its first two arguments. Consider a case in which $\tilde{x}$ has only $n$ possible outcomes, $x_i$ with probability $p_i$, $i = 1, ..., n$. Then

$$g(Eu(w_1\tilde{x}), Eu(w_2\tilde{x}), w) = Eu(w\tilde{x}) = \sum_{i=1}^{n} p_i Eu(wx_i)$$

$$= \sum_{i=1}^{n} p_i g(u(w_1x_i), u(w_2x_i), w) = Eg(u(w_1\tilde{x}), u(w_2\tilde{x}), w).$$

We conclude that the expectation operator, $E$, may be exchanged with the function $g$. From this, we may conclude that $g$ is linear in $Eu(w_1\tilde{x})$, and $Eu(w_2\tilde{x})$. So $Eu(w\tilde{x}) = a_0(w) + a_1(w)Eu(w_1\tilde{x}) + a_2(w)Eu(w_2\tilde{x})$ for some functions $a_0$, $a_1$, and $a_2$. More simply, $u(wx) = a_0(w) + a_1(w)b_1(x) + a_2(w)b_2(x)$, where $b_1(x) = u(w_1x)$ and $b_2(x) = u(w_2x)$. This functional relationship has only five solutions in $u$:

    (i)   $u(w) = aw^d + bw^c$,

    (ii)   $u(w) = a\log w + bw^c$,

    (iii)   $u(w) = a(\log w)^2 + b\log w$,

    (iv)   $u(w) = (a\log w + b)w^c$, and

    (v)   $u(w) = w^a\cos(b\log w)$,

for arbitrary coefficients $a$, $b$, $c$, and $d$. Note that the quadratic function is in family (i) where $d = 1$, $c = 2$. While these are the only utility families to have a risk-return representation, only families (i) and (ii) satisfy conditions $U_1$, $U_2$, and $U_3$. Family (v) violates $U_1$ if $b \neq 0$. Families (iii) and (iv) are increasingly risk averse if $a \neq 0$.

It remains to show that these families have risk-return interpretations satisfying $R_1$, $R_2$, and $R_3$. If $u(w) = aw^d + bw^c$, then $Eu(w\tilde{x}) = aw^d E(\tilde{x})^d + bw^c E(\tilde{x}^c)$. If $a$ and $b$ are both positive and if $d > c$, let $r(\tilde{x}) = E(\tilde{x})^d$ and $R(\tilde{x}) = -E(\tilde{x}^c)$, which satisfies $R_1$ and $R_2$. Since $d > c$, as $w$ increases, $r(\tilde{x})$ becomes relatively more weighted, thus satisfying $R_3$. If $d < c$, let $r(\tilde{x}) = E(\tilde{x}^c)$ and $R(\tilde{x}) = -E(\tilde{x}^d)$. Other variations are similar.

Note that these choices of $r$ and $R$ may not match our intuition about *sensible* measures for $r$ and $R$; we are merely establishing that at least one *possible* definition exists for each.

## Proof of Theorem 3

Consider the important case $u(w) = a\log w + bw$, where $Eu(w\tilde{x}) = a\log w + aE\log \tilde{x} + bw\tilde{x}$. For some functions $g$ and $h$ we must have $r(\tilde{x}) = g(E\log \tilde{x}, \tilde{x})$ and $R(\tilde{x}) = h(E\log \tilde{x}, \tilde{x})$. If $r$ is a utility function then $g(E\log \tilde{x}, \tilde{x}) = E_{\tilde{x}}g(\log x, x)$, which is possible only if $g$ is linear in its arguments. That is, for some constants $\alpha$, $\beta$, we have $r(\tilde{x}) = \alpha E\log \tilde{x} + \beta \tilde{x}$. Consider the case where $\tilde{x}$ is a constant, say $k$, so $r(\tilde{x}) = \alpha \log k + \beta k$. Because of assumption $R_1$, we know that $r$ is increasing in $k$, so $\alpha \geq 0$, $\beta \geq 0$, and $\alpha + \beta > 0$.

But now consider some nonconstant alternative $\tilde{y}$ for which $r(\tilde{y}) = r(k)$. We have $\alpha E\log \tilde{y} + \beta \tilde{y} = \alpha \log k + \beta k$. Since $r(\tilde{y}) = r(k)$, the preference ordering of $\tilde{x}$ $(=k)$ and $\tilde{y}$ must be the same for all $w$; it depends only on the ordering of $R(\tilde{x})$ and $R(\tilde{y})$. That is, $(a\log k + bwk) - (aE\log \tilde{y} + bw\tilde{y})$ has the same sign for all $w$. This means that the signs of $\log k - E\log \tilde{y}$ and $k - \tilde{y}$ must be equal. But this is inconsistent with our earlier conclusion (based on the relation $r(\tilde{y}) = r(k)$), that $\alpha E\log \tilde{y} + \beta \tilde{y} = \alpha \log k + \beta k$. We conclude that either $\alpha = 0$ or $\beta = 0$.

Suppose $r(\tilde{x}) = E\log \tilde{x}$. Now consider arbitrary alternatives $\tilde{x}$ and $\tilde{y}$ that happen to be indifferent at $w$. That is, $(aE\log \tilde{x} + bw\tilde{x}) - (aE\log \tilde{y} + bw\tilde{y}) = 0$. As $w$ increases, $\tilde{x}$ will be preferred over $\tilde{y}$ if and only if $\tilde{x} > \tilde{y}$ (since $b > 0$). But by condition $R_3$, $\tilde{x}$ is to be preferred to $\tilde{y}$ as $w$ increases if and only if $r(\tilde{x}) > r(\tilde{y})$ or $E\log \tilde{x} > E\log \tilde{y}$. But for the equation in this paragraph to hold, it must be that $E\log \tilde{x} < E\log \tilde{y}$. This is inconsistent. But if $r(\tilde{x}) = \tilde{x}$, then the above argument is consistent.

Now consider $R(\tilde{x}) = h(E\log \tilde{x}, \tilde{x})$. Since $R_5$ tells us that $R(k\tilde{x}) = R(\tilde{x})$, we may arbitrarily standardize $R(\tilde{x})$ as $R(\tilde{x}/\bar{x})$. Hence $R(\tilde{x}) = h(E\log \tilde{x} - E\log \bar{x}, 1)$, or simply $h(E\log \tilde{x}/\bar{x})$. We know that $Eu(w\tilde{x}) =$

$a\log w + a\log(\tilde{x}/\bar{x}) + a\log\bar{x} + bw\bar{x}$, and by $R_2$ that this expression is decreasing in $R(\tilde{x})$. Hence $h$ is decreasing in $E\log(\tilde{x}/\bar{x})$. Since the definition of $R(\tilde{x})$ is arbitrary up to monotonic transformations, we may assume that $R(\tilde{x}) = E\log(\tilde{x}/\bar{x})$.

Arguments for the other cases are similar.

## Portfolio Risk Aversion

Following Pratt, we may determine a suitable measure of portfolio risk aversion for an investor with utility function for wealth $u(w)$.[17] We may write $Eu(w\tilde{x}) = Eu\exp(\log w + \log\tilde{x})$, where $u\exp$ is the convolution of $u$ with the exponential function. Changing notation, let $v = u\exp$. Assume $E\log\tilde{x} = 0$ and that $\tilde{x}$ is "small." Then

$$E\, v(\log w + \log\tilde{x}) \simeq v(\log w) + \frac{[E(\log\tilde{x})]^2}{2}\, v''(\log w).$$

Let $c(w, \tilde{x})$ be the certainty equivalent of $\tilde{x}$ at wealth $w$ so that $Eu(wc) = Eu(w\tilde{x})$ and, approximately,

$$E\, v\,(\log w + \log c) = v(\log w) + \log c\; v'(\log w).$$

Hence

$$\log c \simeq \frac{E(\log\tilde{x})^2}{2}\, \frac{v''(\log w)}{v'(\log w)}.$$

Translating back into the $u$ notation, since $u(w) = v(\log w)$, we have $u'(w) = \dfrac{1}{w}\, v'(\log w)$ and

$$u''(w) = -\frac{1}{w^2}\, v'(\log w) + \frac{1}{w^2}\, v''(\log w),$$

so that $v'(\log w) = wu'(w)$ and $v''(\log w) = w^2 u''(w) + wu'(w)$. Hence

$$\log c \simeq \frac{E(\log\tilde{x})^2}{2}\left(w\, \frac{u''(w)}{u'(w)} + 1\right).$$

Now $\tilde{x}$ is undesirable only if $\log c < 0$, so a suitable measure of *portfolio risk aversion* is

$$-\left(w\, \frac{u''(w)}{u'(w)} + 1\right).$$

This is equivalent to Pratt's *relative risk aversion* $\left(-\dfrac{wu''(w)}{u'(w)}\right)$ less one.

NOTES

1. John von Neumann and Oskar Morgenstern, *Theory of Games and Economic Behavior,* 2nd ed. (Princeton, NJ: Princeton University Press, 1947).
2. Howard Raiffa, *Decision Analysis: Introductory Lectures on Choices Under Uncertainty* (Reading, MA: Addison-Wesley, 1968).
3. David E. Bell, "One-Switch Utility Functions and a Measure of Risk," *Management Science* 34 (1988): 1416–1424.
4. David E. Bell, "Risk, Return and Utility," *Management Science* 41 (1995): 23–30.
5. David E. Bell, "A Contextual Uncertainty Condition for Behavior Under Risk," *Management Science* 41 (1995): 1145–1150.
6. Investors will typically divide their capital among many prospects. Measuring the risk of an individual prospect is made complicated by the potential correlation of its rate of return with other constitutents of the investor's portfolio; see Robert C. Merton, *Continuous-Time Finance* (Oxford: Blackwell, 1990), ch. 2. We will be concerned here with finding risk and return measures for portfolios viewed in their entirety.
7. John W. Pratt, "Risk Aversion in the Small and in the Large," *Econometrica* 32 (1964): 91; Raiffa, *Decision Analysis;* and Robert O. Schlaifer, *Analysis of Decision under Uncertainty* (New York: McGraw-Hill, 1969), p. 146.
8. Bell, "One-Switch Utility Functions"; Bell, "Risk, Return and Utility"; and Bell, "A Contextual Uncertainty Condition."
9. Harry M. Markowitz, "Portfolio Selection," *Journal of Finance* 7 (1952): 77–91.
10. Pratt, "Risk Aversion."
11. R. Duncan Luce and Elke U. Weber, "An Axiomatic Theory of Conjoint, Expected Risk," *Journal of Mathematical Psychology* 30 (1986): 188–205.
12. Bell, "Risk, Return and Utility."
13. On the concept of the probability of loss, see Peter C. Fishburn, "Foundations of Risk Measurement, Part II: Effects of Gains on Risk," *Journal of Mathematical Psychology* 25 (1982): 226–242; and Peter C. Fishburn, "Foundations of Risk Measurement, Part I: Risk as Probable Loss," *Management Science* 30 (1984): 396–406. On the concept of regret, see David E. Bell, "Regret in Decision Making under Uncertainty," *Operations Research* 30 (1982): 961–981.
14. Edwin J. Elton and Martin J. Gruber, *Modern Portfolio Theory and Investment Analysis* (New York: Wiley, 1981), section 3.
15. A detailed proof may be derived from that in Bell, "A Contextual Uncertainty Condition."
16. Thomas M. Apostol, *Mathematical Analysis* (Reading, MA: Addison-Wesley, 1957), p. 144.
17. Pratt, "Risk Aversion."

# CHAPTER 7

# Upside Opportunity and Downside Risk

## Richard F. Meyer

From his earliest to his most recent writings, Howard Raiffa has been unwavering both in his skepticism of equilibrium concepts in game theory and his enthusiasm for SEU (subjective expected utility) decision theory. Commenting on the epistemic assumptions of game theory, he wrote in *Games and Decisions*: "It hardly seems necessary to point out that this is a serious idealization which only rarely is met in actual situations. If one systematically examines the several features of a game in extensive form, it is clear that human beings do not generally have the knowledge assumed." After exploring equilibrium solutions for a number of non-cooperative games, he continues, "Do these examples sound the death knell for the equilibrium concept as the principal ingredient of a theory of non-cooperative non-zero-sum games? In our opinion, the answer must be yes if one demands a realistic theory for all possible non-cooperative non-zero-sum-games. . . ." A few lines later, "It is unfortunate (or fortunate, depending upon your viewpoint) that a unified theory for all non-cooperative games does not seem possible."[1]

A very different tone pervades his 1985 defense of SEU theory. "Back in the 1950s when someone like Allais or Ellsberg concocted an ingenious example that showed that people violated the fundamental axioms of the SEU theory, I exploited such observations. I argued that if people, in making intuitive choices, always satisfied the norms of the SEU theory, then there would be no raison d'être for teaching people how to choose wisely." And a few pages later, "Kahneman and Tversky . . . brilliantly portray what's wrong with SEU theory as a *descriptive* or predictive theory. They systematically codify behavioral departures from the normative SEU model. . . . I now would like to discuss some informal attempts I have made to get subjects to change their minds or to think more deeply about choices they have made that are inconsistent with SEU theory. In some cases, my therapeutic interventions have convinced some of these subjects that they have made choices that are not appropriate for their deeply held basic feelings and they actually reverse some choices. . . . In other cases, I conclude that the subjects are right in registering so-called inconsistencies, and the theory is wrong or that the theory is being applied in too gross and insensitive a manner."[2]

In essence, Raiffa is saying that the discipline of SEU theory is a good starting point for prescriptive analysis, and that inconsistencies that are discovered should first be treated under the presumption that SEU theory is "right," and only accepted if that presumption proves insupportable. It is an approach that I shall call PEU theory—Presumed Expected Utility theory.

Both equilibrium game theory and SEU theory have a thorough axiomatic foundation, and neither corresponds to ordinary human behavior. Furthermore, Raiffa was a pioneer in early experimental work demonstrating cognitive biases in probability assessment,[3] and a faithful reporter of such discoveries by others in all his writings. So why this strong affection for prescriptive SEU analysis and this unease with equilibrium-based game theory as a guide to action? This paper will not give an altogether satisfactory answer, but broadly speaking, I believe that we become rightly suspicious of a theory if:

1. a highly stylized structure is used to characterize real-world situations that are far richer than the imposed structure; and

2. strong results follow from the imposed structure; but

3. these results would no longer follow even approximately if the structure were modified in ways that still leave it a reasonable proxy for the real-world situations.

Such a lack of robustness is unsettling; it destroys our confidence in the implications of the theory. In this sense, game theory is far less robust than SEU theory.

Another example of this lack of robustness is found in Arrow-Debreu theory.[4] If the number of "states of the world" is sufficiently small for complete contingent markets to exist, prices in an uncertain world become determinate. But if the markets are not complete, additional arguments are required. Such a result, in a world with an indeterminate number of states (if indeed there are "states" at all) is clearly suspect. We shall see an example of "incomplete markets" in this paper. But such suspect idiosyncratic theories can be redeemed if we can show that essential features of some of their conclusions remain valid under less restrictive (or differently restrictive) assumptions.

Why do we construct these theories? It has, of course, been argued broadly that we are reasoning creatures, seeking understanding, full of curiosity. This portrayal of "scientific man" has been overdone. At least as important, and apparently unique to humans, is our desire to *justify* our actions, not in the sense of excuses, but in the sense of a convincing rationale. This is the more believable meaning of "rational economic man": we seek a rationale, a "theory of the case," to strengthen our confidence and the confidence of others in the righteousness of our actions. PEU theory must be seen in this light; and in this light, a healthy dose of skepticism—"is this voodoo?"—is always appropriate.

This paper is devoted to a class of problems where PEU theory does not fit without alteration, but the alterations are very much in the spirit of PEU theory, and so are the conclusions. We observe that for many economic decisions, there is a tendency to view outcomes as gains or losses relative to a perceived status quo.[5] When this attitude is appropriate, it conflicts with the "substitution axiom" of SEU theory, so the theory needs revision. The changes we propose are formally reminiscent of prospect theory, although their motivation is different. The revised theory permits the local risk aversion to be different for losses and for gains, and this has potentially major implications for the valuation of financial derivatives.

## Anchoring on a Status Quo

This paper follows the usual SEU formalism of representing an uncertain event by a discrete probability distribution of outcomes, each resulting in different aggregate levels of wealth. We have, however, some reservations about the use of a substitution or independence axiom.

### Some Elementary Observations

Typically, the real-world events we face can be likened to a cityscape in a fog: the details and sometimes even the general outline of the possible outcomes are far from clear. Instead of capitulating to the pervasive vagueness, and assessing a CE (certainty equivalent) directly, we bravely push the analysis one stage further in hope of achieving a little more insight, and assess CEs one stage further out.

Suppose that, proceeding this way, we structure the tree shown in Figure 7-1. If our CE for the (B, C, D) lottery happens to be 300 (which we will assume for expository purposes), then at the initial position we ostensibly face the same lottery as (B, C, D), so the CE is 300 by simple substitution. But do we? Not if knowledge that A and E did not occur at the first stage is informative, i.e., affects our preference ordering for lotteries at the second stage. In that case, we need an additional state variable to show that at endpositions B, C, and D, we are in a different state from A or E. However, the observation that, with a sufficient number of state descriptors, we can always force the substitution axiom to hold is a tautology: there will never be true substitution if the preference orderings on wealth alone are different in every part of the tree. The crux of the problem is that we are trying, with an *excessively* summarized descriptor of consequences, to make headway in the fog. Some apparent contradictions may well be the result. We should explore these, but we should not mechanically postulate the substitution axiom to hold.

We will assume that dominance (that is, if any one endposition is improved, the lottery will be preferred) and transitivity hold, so that there is a complete ordering over lotteries, and therefore CEs exist for all lotteries. We shall also assume risk aversion throughout the interval of consequences, i.e., the CE is always less than the lottery's expected value.[6] But we shall not always assume the substitution axiom.

It is customary in the profession to speak of risk both for downside and for upside uncertainty. To the layman, "upside risk" sounds silly; we shall therefore refer to downside risk and upside opportunity. Of

### Figure 7-1

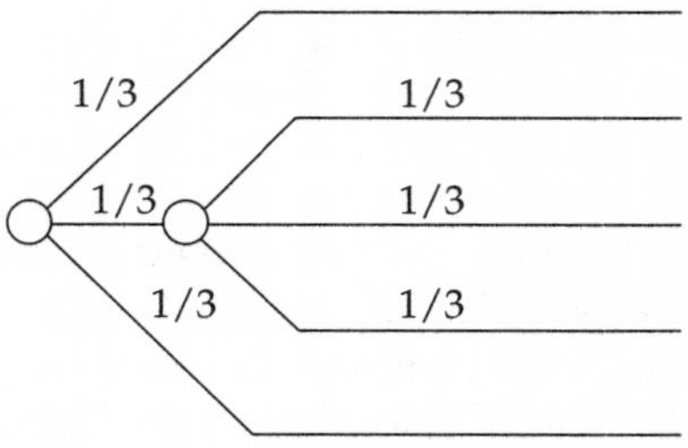

| | END POSITION VALUE | |
|---|---|---|
| | CE (WEALTH) | LABEL |
| | 1000 | A |
| | 1000 | B |
| | 300 | C |
| | 100 | D |
| | 100 | E |

## Figure 7-2

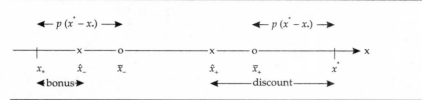

course, to speak of upside and downside at all requires some notion of a status quo, an anchor relative to which changes are measured. People do this in any case, possibly to excess:[7] it is uncomfortable to keep one's eyes unfocussed and contemplate the entire fog of possible outcomes as one holistic Gestalt. Here we shall not predetermine a status quo, but express all consequences in terms of aggregate wealth and let a status quo be defined implicitly.

### The Upside and the Downside

Let $x_*$ and $x^*$ denote the worst and best outcomes we consider. We shall confine ourselves to discrete lotteries, and assume risk aversion throughout $(x_*, x^*)$.

Consider first two lotteries, $L_-$ and $L_+$ defined as:

$$L_-: \{x_*, 1 - p; x^*, p\} \text{ and } L_+: \{x_*, p; x^*, 1 - p\},$$

where $p$ is a small probability, $<<.5$. In words, $L_-$ is a two-pronged lottery with a chance $1 - p$ at outcome $x_*$ and a chance $p$ at outcome $x^*$. $L_-$ represents a poor person with a long shot at becoming wealthy, and $L_+$ is a rich person with a small chance of losing it. The implicit status quos are near $x_*$ and $x^*$. Figure 7-2 shows the relative configuration of the points of interest, where the respective means are denoted by $\bar{x}_-$ and $\bar{x}_+$, and the CEs by $\hat{x}_-$ and $\hat{x}_+$. The total *bonus* $(\hat{x}_- - x_*)$ accorded $L_-$ for its upside opportunity is clearly less than the *discount* $(x^* - \hat{x}_+)$ given $L_+$ for its downside risk. It is reassuring that this follows strictly from positive risk aversion; it requires neither the substitution axiom, nor decreasing risk aversion. A more subtle question is whether the risk premia for the upside and downside lotteries must always be ordered in a particular way. It can be shown that this is not so, even when SEU theory applies.

The situation is a little more complicated in our second prototype problem. Let $\bar{x} = (x_* + x^*)/2$ denote the mean of a 50-50 lottery, and

**Figure 7-3**

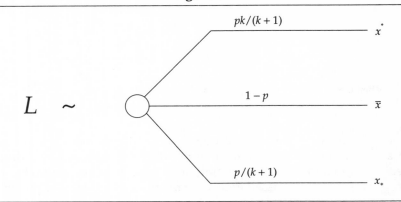

consider upside and downside lotteries relative to $\bar{x}$, which is viewed as the status quo:

$$L_+: \{\bar{x}, 1 - p; x^*, p\} \text{ and } L_-: \{x_*, p; \bar{x}, 1 - p\}.$$

If the *bonus* of the upside opportunity is named $h$, and the *discount* for downside risk $kh$, then:

$$\hat{x}_+ = \bar{x} + h \text{ and } \hat{x}_- = \bar{x} - kh. \qquad \textbf{(7-1)}$$

Can or must $k$ be larger than 1, and if so, how much larger can it be? To answer this, consider the lottery $L: \{\hat{x}_-, 1/(k + 1); \hat{x}_+, k/(k + 1)\}$, which has mean $\bar{x}$ because of (7-1). If the substitution axiom applies, we can substitute $L_+$ and $L_-$, and obtain the equivalent three-pronged representation for $L$ that is shown in Figure 7-3. For sufficiently large $k$, we see that $L$ would have a CE in excess of $\bar{x}$. Hence we would be risk-seeking, which contradicts our initial assumption. The substitution axiom therefore puts an upper limit on $k$. How large can $k$ be?

Since the substitution axiom is supposed to apply, there is a con-cave utility function $u(x)$, which we may choose to be 0 at $x_*$ and 1 at $x^*$. By risk aversion, $u(\bar{x}) > \frac{1}{2}$, so call the excess $r$:

$$u(\bar{x}) = \frac{1}{2} + r. \qquad \textbf{(7-2)}$$

In fact, this $r$ is an overall measure of the degree of risk aversion in the interval $(x_*, x^*)$. If we substitute (7-2) for the middle outcome in Figure 7-3, we find that $L$ has utility equal to $(\frac{1}{2} + r) - p(\frac{1}{2} + r - k/(k + 1))$.

But since $L$ has expectation $\bar{x}$, $L$ will be risk seeking (which is a contradiction) if its expected utility is greater than $\frac{1}{2} + r$. This implies $(\frac{1}{2} + r - k/(k + 1)) < 0$, or equivalently,

$$k > (\tfrac{1}{2} + r)/(\tfrac{1}{2} - r). \qquad \text{(7-3)}$$

For reasonable values of $r$, such as $r \leq .1$, we find $k \leq 1.5$ as an upper limit on $k$. That is, we may not *discount* downside risk by more than 1.5 times the *bonus* we give for upside opportunity. Furthermore, as the interval $(x_*, x^*)$ is reduced, $r$ should approach zero, so $k$ must approach 1. Therefore, for small gambles, the downside discount and the upside bonus must become equal.

If we do not like this, we don't like the substitution axiom. A reasonable appearing behavioral condition is only as good as its implications. It is not difficult to construct formal preference structures that allow any limiting ratio between the "prices" for downside risk and upside opportunity. Consider, for example, the following implicit definition of the CE $\hat{x}$ for any discrete lottery $\{(x_i, p_i), i = 1, ..., n\}$:

$$\sum_{x_i > \hat{x}} p_i(x_i - \hat{x}) = k \sum_{x_i < \hat{x}} p_i(\hat{x} - x_i).$$

For $k > 1$, this preference ordering is risk averse, and downside risk is $k$ times as "expensive" as upside opportunity. For $k = 1$, we see that $\hat{x} = \bar{x}$, so by subtraction the risk premium for any $k$ is

$$\bar{x} - \hat{x} = (k - 1) \sum_{x_i < \hat{x}} p_i (\hat{x} - x_i).$$

We see that the risk premium is proportional to the expected downside, and hence linear in the dispersion of the lottery. This contrasts with the Pratt-Arrow findings (within the confines of SEU theory) of risk premia which, for narrow lotteries, are quadratic in the dispersion. Furthermore, if we now introduce nonlinear functions of the $p$'s and the deviations from the "status quo" $\hat{x}$, we immediately have the prospect theory formalism,[8] but based on aggregate levels of wealth.

## Derivative Valuation

In the latter half of the 1980s, Howard Raiffa taught a course in Risk Management for several years. For the public risk issues (such as toxic chemicals, nuclear reactor failure, etc.) covered in the course, he had been actively involved in research and practice for several decades. But the issues of financial risk management, which had been more in my sphere of interest, were new to him. So one day I met him coming out

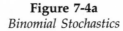

**Figure 7-4a**
*Binomial Stochastics*

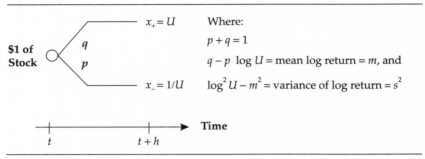

of his office, looking very pleased, and saying, "I now really understand pseudo-probabilities."

Pseudo-probabilities (also called "risk neutral" probabilities) occur
in the valuation of options and other financial derivatives.[9] They permit the valuation to be done by using an "expected value" rule, but
with probabilities that are not the underlying stochastic process probabilities. Figures 7-4a and 7-4b show the simplest example, which is
pricing a derivative of a stock whose price movement follows a binomial process: in a short period of time $h$, \$1 of the stock can either
move up to a value $\$U$ ($U > 1$) or down to a value $\$1/U$, with
probabilities $q$ and $p$ respectively (where $p + q = 1$). To determine $p$,
$q$, and $U$ (given an $h$), we must replicate the mean return $m$ and the
variance of return $s^2$ (per time period $h$) that we estimate the stock to
have in reality. In Figure 4a the appropriate relationships are shown
for the log of the returns. The values of $m$ and $s^2$ could correspond to
historical values, or they could be forward looking. In any case, the
resulting *process* values for $p$ and $q$ are not the probabilities used in
valuing the derivative correctly.

Instead (see Figure 7-4b), we think in terms of the prices of two
"elementary" options *ccall* and *pput*: they pay an amount $e^{rh}$ after time
$h$ if the stock rises (ccall) or falls (pput), where $r$ is the risk-free rate. If
these two elementary options have market prices $\gamma$ and $\pi$ respectively,
then an arbitrary derivative that pays $V_+$ if the stock rises and $V_-$ if
the stock falls can be priced by arbitrage (see relation 3 in Figure 7-4b).
Furthermore, by two other arbitrage relationships that must hold for
the risk-free security and the stock (since a portfolio of one ccall and
one pput replicates the risk-free security, and a portfolio of $Ue^{-rh}$ ccalls
and $e^{-rh}/U$ pputs replicates the stock), we can determine $\gamma$ and $\pi$ in
terms of $U$ and $h$. Note that $p$ and $q$ no longer appear, and $\gamma$ and $\pi$

take on the role of pseudo-probabilities, in that the stock and the derivative are valued by a discounted expected value formula that uses $\gamma$ and $\pi$ as probabilities, and $e^{-rh}$ as the discount factor. It is interesting to observe the similarity with "prospect theory": we adjust the *probabilities* used in the valuation. We do not discount expected values at a risky rate, nor do we discount risk-adjusted CEs at a risk-free rate.

What happens when the more realistic assumption is made that the stock price can stay constant, as well as rise or fall? Figure 7-5a shows the stochastics for the resulting trinomial process. If we only want to match the mean and the variance of the log returns of the real process, we can now choose $h$ and $U$ independently. For a given $h$, there will be a minimum value of $U$ (call this $U_*$) for which $p' + q' = 1$, so that the trinomial process degenerates to the binomial process we studied earlier. It therefore follows from Figure 7-4a that this minimum value of $U$ is given by

$$\log^2 U_* = m^2 + s^2.$$

For any $U > U_*$, it follows from the second relation in Figure 7-5a that $p' + q' < 1$, so that we have a bona fide trinomial process. As $U$ is

## Figure 7-4b
### *The Binomial Valuation Model*

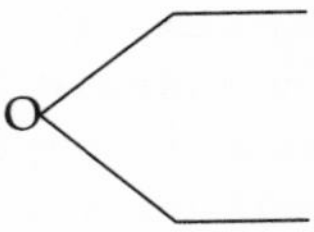

| | Stock | Risk-Free | Ccall | Pput | Derivative |
|---|---|---|---|---|---|
| Payoffs (at $t + h$): | | | | | |
| $U$ | $U$ | $e^{rh}$ | $e^{rh}$ | $0$ | $V_+$ |
| $1/U$ | $1/U$ | $e^{rh}$ | $0$ | $e^{rh}$ | $V_-$ |
| Prices (at $t$): | | | | | |
| | $\$1$ | $\$1$ | $\$\gamma$ | $\$\pi$ | $\$V$ |

Three Arbitrage Relations:

1. ccall + pput = risk-free, so $\gamma + \pi = 1$

2. Stock parity, so $e^{-rh}(\gamma U + \pi/U) = 1$

3. Derivative Replication, so $V = e^{-rh}(\gamma V_+ + \pi V_-)$

### Figure 7-5a
*Trinomial Stochastics*

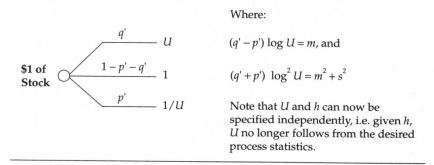

Where:

$(q' - p') \log U = m$, and

$(q' + p') \log^2 U = m^2 + s^2$

Note that $U$ and $h$ can now be specified independently, i.e. given $h$, $U$ no longer follows from the desired process statistics.

increased, $p' + q'$ decreases, so that the process looks increasingly like a jump process: with high probability $(1 - p' - q')$ the stock price will be unchanged, with small probability $(p' + q')$ the price will change (up or down) by a large factor $U$. The process becomes increasingly skewed, and the log returns increasingly leptokurtic. If the preference structures of the market participants are non-SEU, as described at the end of the previous section, the value of $U$ can be expected to affect market prices, so great care must be taken in modeling the stochastic process.

There is another line of reasoning showing the treacherous nature of simple substitution arguments. Suppose we choose $U$ such that $\sqrt{p'} + \sqrt{q'} = 1$; denote this value of $U$ by $U_c$. In that case the resulting trinomial process is equivalent to observing at every other epoch a binomial process with $p = \sqrt{p'}$, $q = \sqrt{q'}$, $U = \sqrt{U_c}$ and epoch $h/2$. In other words, the trinomial process corresponding to $U_c$ is the "square" of a binomial process. A little algebra yields readily that $U_c$ must satisfy $\log^2 U_c = m^2 + 2s^2$.

May we now evaluate derivative securities defined on the trinomial process (with epoch $h$) as if they were defined on the "square root" binomial process (with epoch $h/2$), and use the arbitrage argument given in Figure 7-4b? It would seem so, if a preference-based substitution argument is acceptable. Yet notice that, if a true arbitrage argument is required, we can only carry out the required portfolio rebalancing every $h$ (not every $h/2$), so that half the time we face uncertainty with an imperfectly synthesized portfolio. We therefore fail to mimic perfectly the derivative to be synthesized, and may not equate the value of the synthesized trading strategy to the value of the derivative. A similar argument may be levied against the standard methodology of continuous time finance: processes that generated near-normal log returns over long periods of time may derive from log return distributions for very short time intervals that are very far from normal.

Figure 7-5b shows the arbitrage relationships that must hold in the trinomial case. Thus the stock can be replicated by holding $e^{-rh}$ units of the risk-free security, $(U - 1)e^{-rh}$ ccalls and $-(1 - 1/U)e^{-rh}$ pputs. "Pseudo-expected risk-free discounting" remains the valuation rule, but there are no longer a sufficient number of relations to determine $\gamma$ and $\pi$ unless *multiple derivatives* on the same underlying stock are trading. And if multiple derivatives are trading, there is no longer a requirement that "upside bonuses" and "downside discounts" are priced "alike," as the substitution axiom would have us do. In other words, the substitution axiom may well be violated by observable market prices, without an opportunity for corrective arbitrage.

In summary, the same type of valuation rule remains valid when the stock price can remain unchanged, but the pseudo-probabilities are not subjective Bayesian probabilities, and the so called "implied volatility" has to do with upside versus downside pricing, not with process volatility, or even forward-looking process volatility. Even the term "derivative" becomes a misnomer. If we only observe stock prices over time, we can estimate the process stochastics (that is $p'$ and $q'$) given

**Figure 7-5b**
*The Trinomial Valuation Model*

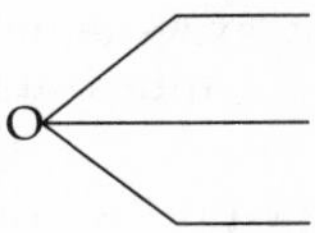

| | Stock | Risk-Free | Ccall | Pput | Derivative |
|---|---|---|---|---|---|
| Payoffs (at $t + h$): | | | | | |
| $U$ | | $e^{rh}$ | $e^{rh}$ | $0$ | $V_+$ |
| $\$1$ $\ \ \ 1$ | | $e^{rh}$ | $0$ | $0$ | $V_o$ |
| $1/U$ | | $e^{rh}$ | $0$ | $e^{rh}$ | $V_-$ |
| Prices (at $t$): | | | | | |
| | $\$1$ | $\$1$ | $\$\gamma$ | $\$\pi$ | $\$V$ |

Arbitrage Relations:

1. Stock parity, $1 = e^{-rh} + \gamma(U - 1)e^{-rh} - \pi(1 - 1/U)e^{-rh}$

2. Derivative Replication, $V = [(1 - \gamma - \pi)V_o + \gamma V_+ + \pi V_-]e^{-rh}$

$h$ and $U$, but we cannot infer both $\gamma$ and $\pi$. The "stock parity" relation gives us only one relation for two parameters. Hence we cannot in general value derivatives, unless we observe at least one derivative that is trading in addition to the stock. This is also the likely explanation for the "equity premium" puzzle: the fact that observed market risk-premia are much larger than would be expected from typically observed levels of risk aversion for consumption.[10] If upside and downside risk are priced differently, so that $k$ is not 1, but we persist in using a PEU theory that ignores this violation of the substitution axiom, then the falsely imputed levels of risk aversion (which assume that $k = 1$) need not be consistent.

## Epilogue on Science

The eminent historian of science, Gerald Holton, has recently commented, in the context of the natural sciences, on the neither linear nor unified mode of progress toward scientific understanding. In a paper entitled "The Controversy over the End of Science," he first identifies the two principal reigning views regarding the progress of science as those of the *linearist*, who is driven by a motivating hope for continued progress toward the target of a unified theory, and the *cyclicist*, who believes in an end to the current progress in physics, when civilization in the sense of a codified social, religious, and political fabric will again take over. But then he goes on to point out that these are not the only "theories about the eventual fate of science":

> To mention just one divergence, a small but growing group of scientists appears now to be quite comfortable with a style of work that is on neither the linearist nor the cyclicist trajectory, but opts frankly for an inherent pluralism. They disclaim any expectation for an ultimate coherence of all parts even within a given science. These might be called splitters rather than lumpers. They have an important role in the advancement of science, for that often depends on the interaction and alternation of these two traits of research—as if science moves on two feet. . . .
>
> A second "minority" type of divergence from the two main models for the fate of science is represented by the belief of the physicist P. W. Anderson. Anderson sees a "hierarchical structure of science" that does not permit in principle a reduction to one set of fundamental laws from which one could then "reconstruct the universe." For example, the problems of scale and of complexity do not allow the properties of large aggregates of elementary particles to be understood merely by extrapolation of the behavior

of individual particles. Rather, by a process analogous to the old conception of "emergence," in each level of complexity there can be imagined to arise entirely new properties; hence each is likely to have a conceptual structure of its own, and presumably also its own rate and direction of progress.[11]

What Holton describes as "divergences" in the natural sciences must certainly be in the mainstream course of progress of the social sciences, where the richness and variety of problem settings require a multitude of parallel as well as hierarchical approaches. Fortunately, Howard Raiffa has never fallen prey to the minimalist ideals of the unifiers. He has spoken frequently of his "divide and conquer" principle: first attack and solve the simplest but still relevant form of a problem, and then add complexity later. Yet he has never insisted that all such stylized abstractions must derive from the same small set of assumptions, attempting a complete unification that, in the social sciences, would have been barren. Instead, he has always had a keen eye for fields where progress was possible, he has been eclectic in developing an appropriate methodology for each without abandoning rigor, and he has had an uncanny ability to involve us all in his passions.

## Notes

1. R. Duncan Luce and Howard Raiffa, *Games and Decisions* (New York: John Wiley and Sons, 1957), pp. 49 and 104.
2. Howard Raiffa, "Back from Prospect Theory to Utility Theory," in *Plural Rationality and Interactive Decision Processes*, eds. M. Grauer, M. Thompson, and A. P. Wierzbicki (New York: Springer Verlag, 1985), pp. 100 and 102.
3. Marc Alpert and Howard Raiffa, "A Progress Report on the Training of Probability Assessors," in *Judgment Under Uncertainty: Heuristics and Biases*, eds. Daniel Kahneman, Paul Slovik, and Amos Tversky (New York: Cambridge University Press, 1982), pp. 294–305.
4. Peter Newman, Murray Milgate, and John Eatwell, eds., *The New Palgrave Dictionary of Money and Finance* (London: Macmillan Press, 1992). See articles on "Arrow-Debreu," vol. 1, p. 59, and "Incomplete Markets," vol. 2, p. 355.
5. William Samuelson and Richard Zeckhauser, "Status Quo Bias in Decision Making," *Journal of Risk and Uncertainty* 1 (1988): 7–59.
6. Other definitions, such as that given in David E. Bell and Howard Raiffa, "Risky Choice Revisited," in *Decision Making: Descriptive, Normative and Prescriptive Interactions*, eds. David E. Bell, Howard Raiffa, and Amos Tversky (New York: Cambridge University Press, 1988), pp. 99–112, may be used where convenient.

7. Samuelson and Zeckhauser, "Status Quo Bias."

8. Daniel Kahneman and Amos Tversky, "Prospect Theory: An Analysis of Decisions under Risk," *Econometrica* 47 (1979): 276–287.

9. John C. Cox and Mark Rubinstein, *Options Markets* (Englewood Cliffs, NJ: Prentice Hall, 1985), p. 174.

10. Mao-Wei Hung, "The Interaction between Nonexpected Utility and Asymmetric Market Fundamentals," *Journal of Finance* 49 (1994): 325–343.

11. In Gerald Holton, *Science and Anti-Science* (Cambridge, MA: Harvard University Press, 1993), pp. 126–144, extract from pp. 140–142.

CHAPTER 8

# DOES SOCIETY MISMANAGE RISK?

## Joanne Linnerooth-Bayer

Is society's system for managing risks to life and limb deeply flawed, as Richard Zeckhauser and Kip Viscusi have claimed?[1] Do our public officials overreact to unlikely but very visible risks, such as those posed by nuclear power or hazardous waste facilities? Do they put too little effort into ameliorating risks with a far greater death toll, such as those involving automobiles, diet, and smoking? In our zeal to prevent the "worst case," do our public authorities, as Albert Nichols and Zeckhauser suggest, sanction conservative assessments of risks?[2]

What priority our public policy makers should place on saving lives is an issue as topical today as it was in the late 1970s, when Howard Raiffa and his colleagues first addressed the economic valuation of life-saving measures.[3] The U.S. Environmental Protection Agency's recent policy of "rational risk management," aimed at optimizing the benefits of risk reduction policies, has rekindled a longstanding debate on the value of reducing risks to life and limb and the meaning of the concept of rational risk management.

No one in this debate advocates strict adherence to an objective of maximizing the number of lives or life-years saved and injuries reduced (which I will refer to in this paper as a lives-saved objective). This would exclude public perceptions and concerns about the context

This paper was partly supported by the Center for Risk Management, Resources for the Future, Washington, DC. I sincerely thank Ralph Keeney and Richard Zeckhauser for their extensive comments and help. I am also indebted to Kip Viscusi, Dominic Golding, Howard Kunreuther, David Ball, and Louis Goossens for their suggestions. Of course, I take full responsibility for all views expressed in this paper.

of the risks, for example the anxiety surrounding the risks of nuclear power as distinct from driving automobiles. Yet many commentators see a lives-saved objective, appropriately adjusted to take account of factors such as public anxiety, as a guiding principle for setting public risk reduction priorities (which I will refer to in this paper as a lives-saved principle). This principle does not generally permit the large deviations from the lives-saved objective that can be observed in government life-saving programs and regulations. Adopting the lives-saved principle would result in far fewer deaths overall.

Opponents to the lives-saved principle are concerned about how public anxiety and other concerns enter this type of reasoning. Focusing narrowly on such factors as lives and injuries, even with adjustments for public anxiety, might exclude other subtle but legitimate concerns about the risks of our technological societies. Who controls the risk-generating process? Who estimates the risks? Who determines what fears are legitimate? And how are the risks distributed? Rejecting an expert-based model of public risk management, many opponents view risk as a social construct that cannot be fully expressed by expert estimates of the probability of death. They advocate wider participation in the public discourse and eventual policies. At its core, this debate is about the role of expertise in democratic societies, the nature of social consent in pluralistic societies, and difficult issues of equity in life-saving policies.

This paper examines the issue of whether and how far public policy makers are justified in straying from a lives-saved objective in the case of extreme or catastrophic risks that occur with very low probability. I begin by asking how the welfare economist would evaluate the choice between risk neutrality and risk aversion, that is, between pursuing a lives-saved objective and deviating from this objective to account for public concerns about catastrophic events. The economist's reasoning depends on how the affected individuals themselves would decide; however, individual choice is often described as irrational. Advocates of the lives-saved principle, therefore, suggest that only justified or "rational" anxiety be admitted to the public decision. I show that the concept of rational choice is very complex even in risk situations void of most real-world context. For this reason, making adjustments for deviations from rational choice to account for public anxiety requires a subjective judgment by the policy maker about what is rational. This leads to an expert-dominated priority setting process.

I argue instead that seemingly irrational personal risk preferences should not disqualify informed public preferences as a legitimate input to policy decisions involving risk, even if this means substantial deviations from the lives-saved objective. I illustrate my arguments with a case involving the transportation of nuclear materials through New York City. Whereas the economist's cost-benefit reasoning can, in theory, accommodate public preferences, research on the sociology and political culture of risk controversies sheds doubt on whether the precepts of economic welfare theory can provide an acceptable normative decision rule for making controversial risk choices. Ultimately, the priority setting process and the legitimacy of the lives-saved principle is a matter of political culture.

## The Economist's Case for a Lives-Saved Objective

A risk averse policy maker would prefer a policy that results in 10 statistical deaths over a gamble with an expected loss of 10 lives but a possibility of a large number of deaths. Public risk aversion is thus usually thought of as a preference for individual "statistical" deaths over more catastrophic events. As a result, collective disasters are given more regulatory attention even if more lives could be saved with the same resources were they allocated to saving "statistical" persons. This seeming mismanagement of social resources can be compared to the distortions in the valuation of "billions of dollars" discussed by Ralph Keeney in this volume.[4]

Opponents of risk aversion in public policy argue for the lives-saved principle in order to save as many lives as possible given the available resources and with appropriate adjustments for public anxiety about catastrophic events. Alternatively, opponents of the lives-saved principle argue that if people display extreme preferences for avoiding collective deaths,[5] for example for reducing their risk of flying as opposed to their risk of driving, the public decision maker is justified in making large differential expenditures in assuring safety in the two areas. The two differ primarily with regard to the issue of the appropriate adjustment for public anxiety.

One way to view this issue is to ask how justifiable or "rational" are individual preferences for personal and social risk reduction strategies. Do deviations from a maximum life-expectancy objective on the personal level reflect genuine anxiety or do they result from misinformed and irrational choices? As Zeckhauser and Viscusi query,[6] does behavior that does not maximize the odds of survival illustrate the limits of human rationality, and, if so, how should we proceed once we admit that individuals do not correctly react to many risks? Whether individuals correctly or rationally react to risks is clouded by many factors characterizing risk situations in addition to the odds of survival, for instance, whether the risk is taken voluntarily, whether it is controllable, and so forth. Yet even abstracting from these contextual factors, the question of rational choice is not clear.

To illustrate, consider two hypothetical risk situations. In Situation A, each of 1,000 persons is exposed to an annual chance of death of 1/1,000, resulting in 1 expected fatality. The probabilities are generated independently—each person flips his or her own coin—so no person's fate depends on the fates of the others. This scenario could apply to a group of people with high cholesterol where each person's annual chance of death from heart failure is 1/1,000, or it could apply to a group of high-risk drivers. The fatalities will likely be anonymous or statistical in the sense that little public attention will be focused on them.

Situation B takes the form of a group lottery; there is a 1/1,000 chance of a disastrous event taking the lives of all 1,000 persons, and a 999/1,000 chance of no fatalities at all. As in Situation A, each person faces the grim prospect of a 1/1,000 chance of death, and the statistical expectation is still one death. Yet here the probabilities are not independently generated—one flip of the coin determines the fate of the entire group. If we learn that 1 person dies, then we can assume that all 1,000 die. In such cases, the deaths usually occur simultaneously at one place and draw considerable public attention.

Situations A and B have equivalent expected outcomes—namely, one fatality. If the costs are the same, the lives-saved objective would require the policy maker to be indifferent between reducing the two risks. Clearly, these risk situations are highly abstracted; yet this level of abstraction underlies much of the analytical discussion of risk aversion. There is no ambivalence or uncertainty with respect to the probabilities, and full agreement is assumed for the probability estimates. The outcome concerns only the number of fatalities, excluding concerns such as the dignity of the death and the control each individual feels in the risk situation. The deaths are assumed to occur to present generations, the age of the victims is irrelevant, and there is no social or political context.

In this hypothetical and abstracted situation, the economist, given the expected utility model of rationality, would endorse the lives-saved objective. A fundamental notion of economic welfare theory is that public programs should be valued as those affected would value them. Economists assume that this valuation exercise should occur ex ante, before the uncertainty is resolved.[7] Since Situations A and B both pose a personal ex ante mortality risk of 1/1,000, economists assume that each of the 1,000 individuals, acting as expected utility maximizers, would be willing to pay the same sum to ameliorate either risk. A risk averse policy of placing priority on reducing the risks in Situation B is inefficient or "Pareto-inferior"; a reallocation with appropriate compensation could improve the position of all involved. Because an equal allocation is preferred by all, a lives-saved objective is consistent with the Pareto-efficient solution and would therefore be recommended by economists.

Risk aversion is therefore inefficient, and as Ralph Keeney has argued, it is also inconsistent with a preference for an equitable distribution of risks.[8] To illustrate, consider Situation C. Two people are exposed to an extremely high chance of dying and the other 998 face no risk at all. Like Situations A and B, the expected loss of life is one person. A policy maker who makes choices in a manner consistent with the expected utility model cannot be both risk averse (or prefer to reduce the risks in Situation B over A) and at the same time display a preference for distributing risks in an equitable manner (or prefer to reduce the risks in Situation C over A).

Keeney's conclusion can be understood as follows: The more inequitably the risks are spread or the more they are concentrated among a few people, the less likely is the chance of a large number of deaths or the chance of exceeding the statistical expectation (in this case, one fatality). While Situation A distributes the risks over many people, there is a very small chance of a large number of deaths—as many as 1,000. In contrast, the worst possible case for Situation C is two fatalities. If one prefers Situation A over C to achieve equity, one must also accept the remote possibility of many deaths; this is consistent only with a risk-prone utility function. A preference for Situation A over C implies risk proneness; a preference for A over B implies risk aversion. One cannot be both risk averse and risk prone.

Thus, not only are risk averse policies inconsistent with rational individual choices and inefficient in actually saving lives, but they are also inconsistent with policies promoting an equitable risk distribution. To the economist, the lives-saved objective thus finds strong justification on both efficiency and equity grounds. This does not mean that advocates of this objective do not recognize that other factors should be taken into consideration. The age and the pain and suffering of the victims are certainly factors, as are concerns about social disruption in the case of catastrophes. Those strongly in favor of a modified lives-saved objective, or the lives-saved principle, will allow some adjustment to reflect citizens' concerns, but large deviations may be considered irrational. For example, Martin Bailey writes:

> Although there is no rational case for spending a huge sum to avoid a death from one cause while refusing to spend a relatively small sum to avoid a death from another cause, it can be shown

that rational, well-informed citizens do not equalize these incremental sums precisely in private choices. Hence a policy based on such choices will allow some, albeit minor, differences in these sums to remain.[9]

## The Economist's Case against a Lives-Saved Objective

Yet even in the abstract case considered above, the lives-saved objective is not as solid as it might seem. First, the Keeney efficiency-equity tradeoff is based on the von Neumann–Morgenstern axioms of individual rationality underlying the expected utility model;[10] as Keeney notes, these may not be entirely appropriate in the case of mortality risk evaluation. Second, the ex ante valuation of the three risk situations may not promote an unambiguously positive change in social welfare, especially for high-risk situations.

### *Reexamining the Rational Case against Risk Aversion*

For those who feel uncomfortable with Keeney's result, or persist in preferring A to B to C, some more explanation is called for. If risk-averse preferences are based only on the notion of a nonlinear disutility function, for example, where the disutility of two fatalities is greater than twice the disutility of one fatality (which is implicit in most economic analysis), then risk aversion might easily be challenged, as Keeney did, on moral grounds. The implication is that one values lives lost collectively more than those same lives lost individually, and this leads to an inequitable distribution of risks.

But there is another plausible concept of risk aversion that allows the preference, A to B to C. This version of risk aversion is a distaste for collective trials, where the coin is not flipped for each person but is flipped to determine the fate of the collective group. A preference for how the odds are generated, however, violates the expected utility model and may for this reason be considered irrational. It seems that those who admit to the preference of A to B to C (they are both risk averse and prefer a more equitable spread of the risks) are either irrational or, by displaying a nonlinear utility function over lives, immoral.

But what constitutes irrationality? According to the expected utility model, which drives Keeney's results, only outcomes have a utility— not procedure, nor how the probabilities are generated. In other words, "who flips the coin and how it is flipped" cannot be a factor in a person's preference function. This seems innocuous and reasonable at first blush, but may be inconsistent with how people actually view even hypothetical risk situations. If a person prefers the independent trials of Situation A (each flips his or her own coin) to the collective trial of Situation B (one coin is flipped to determine the fate of all 1,000 people), then the preference of A to B to C is no longer inconsistent. In fact, it is well documented that individuals prefer risk situations where they feel they have some control over the odds. Of course, the independent flip of the coin is not genuine control, but only perceived control; yet, there is little denying that many individuals prefer a risk context with even an appearance of personal control. Keeney and R. L. Winkler confronted this dilemma of following the von Neumann–Morgenstern axioms and reconciling preferences for equity in the distribution of risks.[11] A reconciliation, in some cases, meant allowing preferences concerning the *process* by which the consequences are distributed.

The fact that individuals often do not maximize expected utility might strengthen the case for more formal decision analysis (and more explicit risk-benefit tradeoffs) to improve decisions. Paul Schoemaker, however, points to experimental results that could undermine even the normative appeal of the model.[12] For example, some of the biases that lead people to behave differently than the model would predict may be so basic as to render the normative theory inoperative. In addition, many individuals persist in violating the model even when their biases are made apparent to them.

### Reexamining Ex Ante Valuation in High-Risk Cases

A second problem with the lives-saved objective is the priority it implies for reducing very high risks in individual cases. Strict neutrality would place the same priority on reducing the risks in Situation A, B, and C, since each has the same expected outcome. Yet, we would expect a greater aggregate willingness-to-pay value for C, where two people face a very high risk. The reason is that people are willing to pay disproportionately more to decrease higher mortality risks, which has been empirically verified for the risk of death and injury.[13] Indeed, as the probabilities approach 1, an individual is likely to be willing to pay all he or she can beg and borrow to decrease the risk by even a very small amount. At the other end of the probability scale, people may be willing to pay a large premium to reduce a very small risk to zero. This is a form of risk taking. In these cases, the welfare economist is clearly obliged to stray from the risk-neutral position.

This brings us to the issue of the budget constraint. According to the willingness-to-pay model, the value of a reduction in risk is bounded by each individual's budget or wealth. This may be troubling for those who are unhappy with the current distribution of wealth.

Moreover, many feel that public expenditures on health and safety should be independent of the wealth of the beneficiaries. Yet, the economist rightly points out that society's resources are finite, and that these scarce resources should be allocated so that the benefits of risk reduction at the margin are just equal to the social costs of this risk reduction.

This logic is convincing in the aggregate, but may not be entirely appropriate for individual cases of risk reduction. Even those who advocate the willingness-to-pay approach for valuing mortality risk may find the budget constraint inappropriate in some cases; in fact, economic welfare criteria impose a second criterion that asks what an individual would have to be compensated if the risk reduction program were not undertaken. This is referred to as a person's willingness to accept. Most people would not accept even infinite compensation for certain immediate death, but can only pay a finite sum to avoid it. The higher the risk, the greater the likely difference between a person's willingness to pay and to accept.

When the two measures lead to different results in the benefit-cost calculations, Ezra Mishan advises that the economist forego his or her mandate to recommend a course of action.[14] Both measures must lead to the same result for unambiguous fulfillment of the Pareto criterion. The economist can thus only justify use of the willingness-to-pay measure for very small changes in mortality risks.[15] This does not undermine the lives-saved position for the low-probability events considered here, but does challenge the logic when applied to higher-risk situations where the potential victims are identifiable people.

In sum, rationality as defined by the expected utility model leads the welfare economist to accept the lives-saved objective for small risks, but to reject it for lotteries involving higher mortality risks. The expected utility model, however, is not fully appropriate as a basis for judging how individuals should rationally value different risk situations, and therefore it cannot lend support to the lives-saved principle by deeming large deviations in public preferences irrational. Of course, economists recognize that in the real world, many of the factors that must be taken into account require adjustments in the lives-saved objective. The point of this discussion is that there may be adjustments to this objective that have heretofore been considered inappropriate because they appear to arise from irrational public preferences. A broader view of rationality will lead the economist further from the lives-saved objective than the deviations usually sanctioned by the concept of public anxiety. In fact, the concepts of irrationality and anxiety are difficult to separate, which ultimately reduces the prescriptive appeal of the lives-saved principle.

## The Lives-Saved Objective and Citizen Choice

Besides appealing to public irrationality, another line of argument against large deviations from the lives-saved objective is that the economist's welfare principles, which endorse public preferences as a guide to public choices, are not appropriate for "life and limb" decisions. Sarah Lichtenstein et al. thus ask if it is not the moral obligation of our social decision makers to save as many lives as possible given the constraints of the public budget.[16]

To illustrate the issue of the appropriate model of political choice, consider a case involving the transportation of radioactive materials. In 1976, New York City banned the road transport of large shipments of radioactive materials through the city. Five years later, the U.S. Department of Transportation (DOT) published a Final Rule, HM-164, that overruled this local prohibition. DOT's decision was based on a quantitative risk assessment that showed the most lethal credible accident to be one involving plutonium shipments that could cause an estimated 5 early fatalities, 1,800 latent cancer fatalities, and 290 early morbidities, but only with the very low probability of around one in a million.[17] The estimate excluded the possibility of sabotage, which another report crudely estimated could result in as many as a million latent cancer fatalities.[18]

New York City challenged HM-164 on the basis that DOT misjudged the significance of the unlikely possibility of a catastrophic accident, and the District Court upheld New York City's challenge. The ruling judge, Judge Sofaer, acknowledged that "significance depends on the estimation of the credible consequences discounted by their improbability," i.e., risk neutrality. Yet, he stated, "In some circumstances, significance will depend heavily on the gravity of the potential consequences, for some consequences are so grave that, however unlikely, their mere 'credibility' makes the impact of an agency action significant."[19]

If "mere credibility" of disastrous consequences is significant, then the expected value rule and risk neutrality are rejected.[20] Judge Sofaer justifies his position on the grounds that adhering to an expected value rule bypasses any consideration of public concern about catastrophic events. Although the legal authority on which to base decisions involving catastrophic risks is at best vague, Judge Sofaer nonetheless claimed that DOT unjustifiably dismissed public concern. Moreover, in the judge's opinion, the public's perceptions are not misperceptions. Rather, "public reaction is a manifestation of collective wisdom based on human experience. It should not be lightly dismissed as unscientific."[21] Judge Sofaer's decision was reversed by an Appeals Court judge, who wrote: "Disquieting as it may be even to contemplate such matters," DOT's decision that a remote possibility of a serious accident does not pose a significant risk for the human environment "cannot be said to be an abuse of discretion."[22]

This case encapsulates the controversy and judicial insecurity regarding the treatment of potentially catastrophic events and, ultimately, the issue whether to adhere to a lives-saved objective. To what extent should public concerns about catastrophic risks be considered in the public policy decision? DOT was clearly against weighing public risk aversion in its considerations. The public, DOT stated, is incapable of rationally appraising the consequences of accidents; it tends to be disproportionately influenced by potentially large consequences.[23] The DOT would not, therefore, regulate with a view to relieving public concern it finds unjustified.[24] Moreover, DOT claimed that irrational public anxiety is responsible for actions such as New York City's transport ban, so that local governments may be unfit to legislate in some areas.

Are local governments unfit to legislate risk-reducing policies if they reject the lives-saved objective by responding to "irrational" public anxiety? While judging the anxiety of the public to be irrational is necessarily subjective, there is no question that the public has different perceptions of the seriousness of many risks than that of the experts.[25] A large literature in cognitive psychology shows that people rely on various rules of thumb, or "heuristics," in estimating probabilities.[26]

Thus, it is hard not to conclude, as did DOT, that the public's judgments are inappropriate for guiding public policies. If policies must be based on individual choice, do we force policy makers to make decisions according to how many people will be frightened, rather than how many will be killed?[27] More fundamentally, do misperceptions of probability and inconsistent choices involving risk, even in areas where the public is adequately informed and knowledgeable, constitute reasonable grounds for rejecting public preferences and citizen choice as a basis for public risk-affecting programs?

At least three arguments suggest the contrary:

- We do not demand perceptional astuteness and consistency in other areas of private and public choice.

- Expert judgments are also affected by biases and heuristics.

- Experts' probability estimates often do not reflect the full essence of the risk issue, and therefore perceptual accuracy may play only a minor role.

In few other areas of individual or public choice has so much attention been focused on whether personal choices are perceptionally correct or rational. Nobody cares if consumers rate the performance of detergents, toothpastes, or automobiles correctly, or if they are affected by packaging. Liberal, individualistic societies tolerate a large amount of seeming misjudgment in private choices because they prize individual autonomy. Misjudgment should be minimized by policies that encourage honest information and truth in advertising, but in the end each person is free to decide, and we generally do not scrutinize these choices for consistency and perceptional bias.

So why should we single out "risk" as an area where individual choice should be disqualified? One response is that risk choices involve life and death, and therefore inconsistency and misperceptions should not be tolerated as a basis for public policy. Proponents of the lives-saved principle sometimes point out that if the government does not pursue schemes that save the "cheapest" lives first, then it is responsible for the sacrifice in lives caused by this inefficiency.[28] Even those who generally feel that public input leads to better social decisions may hope that decision makers will go against public opinion in certain circumstances in order to make a better decision.[29]

While the question of governmental authority and public consent is a matter of political culture, the grounds for singling out risk as a special case has little merit; virtually *all* private and public expenditures, not only those directly reducing mortality risks, have an opportunity cost in terms of lives.[30] The idea of blaming the government for not allocating resources in such a way as to maximize life expectancy is therefore misleading; it obscures the fact that we trade life expectancy for other amenities every day, and even within programs that aim to increase life span there are other dimensions that may be worth the sacrifice in this objective.

While appealing to the lives-saved principle across a myriad of noncontroversial public expenditures can only enlighten the political process, in controversial areas such as nuclear power, hazardous waste incineration, or biotechnology, appeals to the principle may reduce the credibility of our political decision makers and regulatory institutions. In these cases, the importance that advocates of the lives-saved principle place on saving lives may appear more as a cloak for discrediting the public's concerns about certain technologies.

To this point, we have tacitly assumed that the expert estimates of risk are in some sense correct, but expert estimates may exhibit biases similar to those found in nonexperts' judgments. Among others, Brian Wynne argues that both the experts and the lay public base their perceptions on social biases and assumptions that are usually inadvertent and implicit in technical analyses.[31] The assumptions of the experts may be no better than the lay public's, and may be worse. Strictly following expert-driven assessments of risk loses its policy appeal to the extent that subjectivism enters the scientific process and analysis.

A third reservation about rejecting the perceptions of the public is that experts' probability estimates may not take account of a range of legitimate public concerns, such as the voluntariness of the risk, the effects on future generations, and the equity of the risk distribution.[32] As expressed by Slovic, although individuals tend to misjudge probabilities, their conceptualization of risk is often much broader and richer than the experts' reliance on quantitative estimates of lives, injuries, and property damage.[33] Risk perception research originated in the belief that the factors leading to misperceptions could be identified and to some extent corrected. Yet this research shows that perceptions of risk that differ from the probability estimates do not always reflect ignorance of the statistics or a misinformed judgment about reacting to the odds. That is, the perceptions are not for the most part correctable.

As advocates of the lives-saved principle acknowledge, the risk perception research reveals that the lives-saved objective cannot be applied without making exceptions for risks that are perceived to be especially serious and threatening by the public. This means that it is problematic to apply a single value to risk reduction or saving a life across a range of different risk situations. However, a large body of empirical literature has striven to isolate this value by imputing a person's money tradeoff for risk taking. Most of the empirical findings are based on compensating wage differentials, although some empirical evidence also exists on the implicit value of risks derived from consumer behavior and from contingent valuations based on questionnaires. In a comprehensive review, Viscusi documents the wide range of results, as well as the limitations of the methodologies employed.[34] He notes the obvious difficulty in controlling for the complex reasons why people do hazardous work, in addition to the purported money-for-risk tradeoff these studies try to isolate. Aggregate data tend to miss the heterogeneity of the workers and the firms, and extrapolating from one point on the tradeoff curve necessarily invokes assumptions of rational response. Directly asking people what they are willing to pay to reduce mortality risk is also problematical; responses to questionnaires are notoriously unreliable predictors of actual behavior.

A more fundamental problem with these studies is their purpose. If it is to identify a range of individual valuations of risk reduction to assure that government programs do not deviate significantly from this range, then arguably the studies are only of limited value. For example, ascertaining what workers are willing to pay to reduce their risk from exposure to a carcinogen is useful for valuing public programs that regulate this carcinogen and perhaps others that pose similar risks. However, these valuations cannot be transplanted to other types of risks, for example, those posed by genetically altered organisms, nuclear technologies, or the transportation of hazardous substances, at least not without making the adjustments that advocates of the lives-saved principle call for.[35]

These adjustments have been attempted, for instance, in the form of exponential weighting functions on consequences with multiple, simultaneous fatalities.[36] This form of risk aversion has been adopted in the safety targets of the U.S. Nuclear Regulatory Agency, and has been proposed by the International Atomic Energy Agency.[37] In the Netherlands, risk aversion has been formalized in legislation specifying safety targets for industrial facilities. It bears emphasis, however, that these weighting functions are essentially arbitrary. How much more society wishes to spend to avoid catastrophic risks, or how far our social decision makers should stray from the lives-saved objective, will depend on how these weights are determined. As an alternative to expert-decided weights, the economist's welfarist model dictates that the valuation depends on how much the affected individuals wish to spend. Ultimately, this means that the lives-saved principle is replaced by one of citizen preference.

## The Lives-Saved Principle and Political Culture

So far, the most challenging aspect to the lives-saved principle has been making appropriate adjustments to account for the rich contextual concerns brought to light by risk perception studies. However, the framing of the debate in terms of differential perceptions has been recently challenged by a growing literature in sociology and anthropology that postulates that risks and the scientific discourse surrounding environmental risk issues are to an important extent socially constructed; that is, the scientific knowledge on risks cannot be created and validated independently of social influences.[38] This has been documented by numerous case studies showing that organized interest groups interpret the evidence on risk differently than their opponents. While these contradictory interpretations might be characterized as "bad science," where the evidence is biased to reflect personal or group interests, cultural anthropologists argue that interests are themselves grounded in social context.[39] They suggest that individuals choose what to fear in order to support their way of life and give more or less attention to risks according to world views or ideologies that entail deeply held values and beliefs. These values, in turn, reinforce patterns of social relations and ways of life. According to research by Aaron Wildavsky and Karl Dake, these social relations can predict risk-taking preferences better than measures of knowledge of the probabilities and outcomes.[40]

From this cultural perspective, the lives-saved principle appeals more to individualistic and hierarchical groups than to egalitarian groups. Indeed, economists, whose discipline is strongly individualistic, and the bureaucratic forces of the Environmental Protection Agency call for more rational risk management policies. We find the critics of this approach especially in the ranks of egalitarian groups calling for environmental justice, and they often reject the logic of the lives-saved principle on the grounds that it is simply a cover to justify sweeping policies of deregulation.

More profoundly, if individual preferences are determined more by adherence to different world views than by perceptions of the benefits or costs of a policy, the welfarist model of public choice may be neither meaningful nor useful for valuing controversial risk programs. Conflicting groups will likely not accept a welfare concept based on a Pareto improvement (and potential compensation of the losers) when they are strongly committed to a position far beyond their personal risks or disbenefits. The economist's welfare principles, therefore, may make little political sense when debates are so polarized that conflicting groups view each other's preferences as unreasonable. Therefore, citizens' participation in public risk controversies may be a more effective way to accommodate citizens' concerns than aggregating preferences over a culturally diverse public.

## Summary

The validity of a lives-saved principle as a guide to public life-saving programs and regulations depends on the extent to which the principle must be adjusted to reflect public anxiety about dissimilar risks. The principle is valid if the deviations are for the most part minor and occasional, but the principle loses its normative appeal if the deviations become significant and pervasive. Following the economist's reasoning, the issue of how far to stray from the lives-saved objective translates into the question of how far those affected would deviate from this objective in their personal choices, and whether deviant and seemingly irrational preferences disqualify citizen choice as legitimate for guiding public life-saving policies.

People tend to make choices that appear grossly inconsistent with their interest in self-protection. The risk perception studies provide the most acknowledged justification for these inconsistencies by establishing risk as a multidimensional concept that cannot easily be reduced to a probability of death or injury. Insofar as these inconsistencies reflect reasonable public anxiety, advocates of the lives-saved principle suggest that the objective be compromised to reflect public perceptions. Unreasonable inconsistencies are those that appear uninformed or irrational.

However, since there is no fully satisfactory model to establish rational choice, determining which preferences are a legitimate basis for public policy requires a subjective judgment about their reasonableness. Were the citizens of New York City reasonable in their demands to reject the transport of radioactive materials through the city? If public preferences appear unreasonable to policy makers, are there grounds for rejecting the economist's welfare basis of public choice in order to more closely adhere to the lives-saved objective?

While there is always room for improvement in the public understanding of technical risks, informed public preferences should influence "life and limb" policy decisions, even if this means *substantially* deviating from the lives-saved objective. Deviations from this objective imply a loss of life, but this does not justify exceptional treatment of life-saving and life-risking choices; all allocative decisions have an opportunity cost in terms of human lives. Ignoring seemingly unreasonable public preferences for risk-reduction expenditures endorses an expert-based model of public choice, and experts' estimates of risk are subject to the same heuristics and biases as private perceptions. Promoting a goal of saving as many lives as possible, therefore, may inadvertently endorse a risk management process that is contrary to the values of our democratic societies.

This does not mean that expert-based arguments of risk reduction based on the lives-saved principle are not a valuable input to the policy discussions. Public decision makers should have access to comparative estimates of risk, and they should be accountable for large disparities in public risk-reducing expenditures. The important point is that, following economic logic, policy makers can justify substantial deviations from the lives-saved objective if they are based on the public's concerns about the risk situation. If the stakeholders are well informed, even seemingly irrational or unreasonable concerns should not be dismissed as illegitimate, even if this means greater deviations from a lives-saved objective than the lives-saved principle allows.

However, in controversial risk issues, the economist's welfare model may not be appropriate for determining the value of a risk-reduction or risk-imposing policy. If cultural biases permeate the way people perceive risks, and if people are committed to strongly held values that are reinforced by their attitudes to risk, it is unlikely that they will be willing to accept the cost-benefit logic, which aggregates the benefits and costs over disparate groups. The Pareto criterion may make little political sense when risk debates are strongly polarized.

Because of this social plurality, there is no one right procedure for determining the priority our social decision makers should place on risk-reducing or risk-increasing policies. Rather, we can expect continual competition among the groups bidding for political influence. This competition can be a constructive dialogue if all groups can respect and recognize as legitimate the claims of the others. Although adhering to the lives-saved principle is a constructive argument in this dialogue, society's system for managing risks to life and limb is not necessarily flawed by deviations from this principle. The system is flawed if the concerns of informed citizens are ignored or deemed irrational.

## NOTES

1. Richard Zeckhauser and Kip Viscusi, "Risk Within Reason," *Science* 248 (1990): 559–564.
2. Albert Nichols and Richard Zeckhauser, "The Perils of Prudence: How Conservative Risk Assessments Distort Regulation," *Regulation* 10 (1986): 13–24.
3. Howard Raiffa, William Schwartz, and Milton Weinstein, "Evaluating Health Effects of Societal Decisions and Programs," in *EPA Decision Making* (Washington, DC: National Academy of Sciences, 1978).
4. Ralph L. Keeney, "Valuing Billions of Dollars," in *Wise Choices: Decisions, Games, and Negotiations,* eds. Richard J. Zeckhauser, Ralph L. Keeney, and James K. Sebenius (Boston: Harvard Business School Press, 1996).
5. Richard Zeckhauser has noted that some people may actually prefer collective deaths when their family and friends are mutual victims.
6. Zeckhauser and Viscusi, "Risk Within Reason," p. 560.
7. See Ezra Mishan, "Evaluation of Life and Limb: A Theoretical Approach," *Journal of Political Economy* 79 (1979): 687–705; Thomas Schelling, "The Life You Save May Be Your Own," in *Problems in Public Expenditure and Analysis,* ed. W. Chase (Washington, DC: Brookings Institute, 1968), pp. 74–86; and Myron A. Freeman, "Ex Ante and Ex Post Values for Changes in Risks," *Risk Analysis* 9 (1989): 309–317.
8. Ralph Keeney, "Utility Functions for Equity and Public Risk," *Management Science* 26 (1980): 345–353.
9. Martin Bailey, "Reducing Risks to Life: Measurement of the Benefits" (Washington, DC: American Enterprise Institute, 1980).

10. John von Neumann and Oskar Morgenstern, *Theory of Games and Economic Behavior* (Princeton, NJ: Princeton University Press, 1953).

11. Ralph Keeney and R. L. Winkler, "Evaluating Decision Strategies for Equity of Public Risks," *Operations Research* 33 (1985): 955–970.

12. Paul Schoemaker, "The Expected Utility Model: Its Variants, Purposes, Evidence and Limitations," *Journal of Economic Literature* 20 (1982): 529–563.

13. Kip Viscusi and William Evans, "Utility Functions That Depend on Health Status: Estimates and Economic Implications," *American Economic Review* 803 (1990): 353–374.

14. Ezra Mishan, *Cost-Benefit Analysis* (London: Unwin Hyman Press, 1988).

15. Joanne Linnerooth, "Murdering Statistical Lives . . . ?" in *The Value of Life and Safety,* ed. Michael Jones-Lee (Amsterdam: North Holland, 1982), pp. 229–261.

16. Sarah Lichtenstein et al., "When Lives Are in Your Hands: Dilemmas of the Societal Decision Maker," in *Insights in Decision Making: A Tribute to Hillel J. Einhorn,* ed. Robin Hogarth (Chicago: University of Chicago Press, 1990), pp. 91–106.

17. Sandia National Laboratories, "Transportation of Radionuclides in Urban Environs: Draft Environmental Assessment," report prepared for the U.S. Nuclear Regulatory Commission (Washington, DC, July 1980).

18. See "Calculations of Radiological Consequences from Sabotage of Shipping Casks for Spent Fuel and High-Level Waste," referred to in *Final Environmental Statement in the Transportation of Radioactive Material by Air and Other Modes* (NUREG-0170) (Washington, DC: Nuclear Regulatory Commission, 1977).

19. A. D. Sofaer, "Opinion," United States District Court, Southern District of New York, 81 Civ. 1778 (ADS), 1982.

20. It is perhaps of interest that this "expected value rule" was not new to the courts. It was introduced into judicial interpretations of tort law as early as the 1920s by Judge Learned Hand, who gave the standard for negligent conduct a simple mathematical interpretation: risk is expressed as the product of probability times consequences. Provided the product remains constant, an accident with low probability and high consequences is weighted equally in assessing liability with an accident with high probability and low consequences. See J. Yellin, "Judicial Review and Nuclear Power: Assessing the Risks of Environmental Catastrophe," *George Washington Law Review* 45 (1977): 969–992.

21. Sofaer, "Opinion," p. 76.

22. H. Newman, "Appeal from the May 6, 1982, Judgment of the District Court for the Southern District of New York," 539 F. Supp. 1237 (dissenting statement, U.S. Court of Appeals for the Second Circuit, Nos. 415, 451, August Term, 1983).

23. *Federal Register* 45 (1980): 7141.
24. Department of Transportation, Summary of Comments, DOT Motion, EX. E, pt.H.4., p. 4.
25. Paul Slovic, "Perception of Risk," *Science* 236 (1987): 280–285.
26. Amos Tversky and Daniel Kahneman, "Availability: A Heuristic for Judging Frequency and Probability," *Cognitive Psychology* 5 (1973): 207–232; Amos Tversky and Daniel Kahneman, "Exceptional vs. Intuitive Reasoning: The Conjunction Fallacy in Probability Judgment," *Psychological Review* 90 (1983): 293–315; and Paul Slovic, Sarah Lichtenstein, and Baruch Fischhoff, "Facts and Fears: Understanding Perceived Risk," in *Societal Risk Assessment: How Safe Is Safe Enough?* eds. Richard Schwing and William Albers (New York: Plenum, 1980), pp. 181–216.
27. Andreas Treuber, "Justifying Risk," *Daedalus* 119 (1991): 235–254.
28. For example, see Karin Schraeder-Frechette, "Risk-Cost-Benefit Methodology and Equal Protection," in *Risk Evaluation and Management*, ed. Vince Covello, John Menkes, and Jerald Mumpower (New York: Plenum, 1986), pp. 275–296.
29. Lichtenstein et al., "When Lives Are in Your Hands."
30. Ralph Keeney, "Morality Risks Induced by Economic Expenditures," *Risk Analysis* 10 (1990): 74–81.
31. Brian Wynne, "Frameworks of Rationality in Risk Management: Towards the Testing of Naive Sociology," in *Environmental Threats: Social Science Approaches to Public Risk Perceptions*, ed. J. Brown (London: Belhaven, 1989), pp. 70–93.
32. Slovic, Lichtenstein, and Fischhoff, "Facts and Fears"; and Vince Covello, "Social and Behavioral Research on Risk: Uses in Risk Management Decisionmaking," *Environmental International* (December 1984): 87–96.
33. Slovic, "Perception of Risk."
34. Kip Viscusi, "The Value of Risks to Life and Health," *Journal of Economic Literature* 31 (1993): 1912–1946.
35. John Graham and James Vaupel, "The Value of Life: What Difference Does It Make?" *Risk Analysis* 1 (1981): 89–95.
36. F. R. Farmer, "Reactor Safety and Siting: A Proposed Risk Criterion," *Nuclear Safety* 8 (1967): 539–548; Richard Wilson, "The Costs of Safety," *New Scientist* 68 (1975): 274–275; and James Griesmeyer and David Okrent, "Risk Management and Decision Rules for Light Water Reactors," in *An Approach to Quantitative Safety Goals for Nuclear Power Plants*, NUREG-0739 (Washington, DC: U.S. Nuclear Regulatory Commission, 1980), pp. 234–251.
37. Friedrich Niehaus, "Status, Experience, and Future Prospects for the Development of Probabilistic Safety Criteria," draft report (Vienna: International Atomic Energy Agency, 1986).

38. Sheila Jasanoff, *Risk Management and Political Culture* (New York: Russell Sage Foundation, 1986).
39. See Mary Douglas, "Cultural Bias," Occasional Paper No. 35 (London: Royal Anthropological Institute of Great Britain and Ireland, 1976); Mary Douglas, *Essays in the Sociology of Perception* (London: Routledge and Paul Kegan, 1982); Mary Douglas and Aaron Wildavsky, *Risk and Culture* (Berkeley: University of California Press, 1982); Michael Thompson, "Postscript: A Cultural Basis for Comparison," in *Risk Analysis and Decision Processes,* eds. Howard Kunreuther and Joanne Linnerooth (Berlin: Springer Verlag, 1983), pp. 363–387; Jonathan Gross and Steve Rayner, *Measuring Culture* (New York: Columbia University Press, 1985); and Aaron Wildavsky and Karl Dake, "Theories of Risk Perception: Who Fears What and Why?" *Daedulus* 119 (1991): 41–61.
40. Wildavsky and Dake, "Theories of Risk Perception."

# Global Decisions for the Very Long Term: Intergenerational and International Discounting

## Thomas C. Schelling

Economists who deal with very long-term policy issues, like greenhouse gas emissions over the next century or two, are nearly unanimous that future benefits that take the form of additions to future consumption need to be discounted to be commensurable with each other and with the consumption earlier foregone to produce those benefits. And there is a near consensus—I can mention William Cline, Samuel Fankhauser, Alan Manne, and William Nordhaus—that the appropriate discount rate should be conceptualized as consisting of two components.[1]

One is pure time preference and, according to Fankhauser, "deals with the impatience of consumers and reflects their inborn preference of immediate over postponed consumption."[2] The second reflects the changing marginal utility of consumption with the passage of time, and is decomposed into a rate of growth of consumption per capita and an elasticity of marginal utility with respect to consumption. The two components, pure preference for early over later utility, and declining marginal utility with growing per capita consumption, are used to compare not only utility increments in the year, say, 2050 with costs incurred in 2000, but to compare utility increments in the year 2150 with increments in the year 2050.

I discuss "pure time preference" and then the relevance of the elasticity of marginal utility with respect to income or consumption. But first, since I am going to argue that "discounting" is not the appropriate concept for dealing with the benefits of reduced greenhouse gas emissions in the distant future, I should clarify that I find traditional discounting perfectly appropriate for comparing costs and benefits of, say, hazardous waste cleanup, as in the United States "Superfund" program. In that kind of program discounting with appropriate rates of interest is crucial to determining which sites are worth cleaning up, how much they should be cleaned up, and when or in what order of priority they should be cleaned up. In that kind of program "we" who pay the costs are saving and investing—foregoing some current consumption—in order to reap future benefits, along with our children and grandchildren. It makes sense to "optimize" our investment portfolio by reference to appropriate discount rates. Global greenhouse gas abatement, I shall argue, is not like cleaning up our own land for our own benefit. *Costs* we incur for greenhouse gas abatement need to be discounted; *benefits* need an altogether different treatment.

Another preliminary note. This essay is directed only at the valuation of future material consumption by individuals in GNP projections. That is what the typical greenhouse-abatement optimization models assess. This essay does not examine the projections themselves, and it has omitted any reference to values other than those conventionally included in material consumption. It omits damages and benefits relating to nature, biodiversity, wildlife, etc. It omits environmental influences on public health, which are potentially important, for good or ill, in poor countries where the hazards remain more biological than chemical. It omits the possibility that in developed countries the income elasticity of demand for environmental and recreational benefits may be high enough to bring developed-country benefits back into the picture. Any implications for greenhouse policy are limited accordingly, as they are in typical greenhouse-abatement optimization models.

## Pure Time Preference

Roy Harrod characterized time preference as "a polite expression for rapacity and the conquest of reason by passion." Fankhauser mentioned "impatience" and an inborn preference of immediate over postponed consumption. I am dubious about the ubiquity of that inborn impatience of consumers, at least for adults with decent levels of income. But even if it exists, a time preference pertinent to discounting the long-term costs and benefits of greenhouse gas abatement cannot have anything to do with the "pure rate of time preference" defined in this fashion. That is because the alleged inborn preference for earlier rather than later consumption is exclusively concerned with the consumer's impatience with respect to his or her *own* consumption.

Alan Manne begins by asking us to "consider an economy in which there is a single agent acting as producer, consumer, investor and saver."[3] An agent, it should be noticed, that is immortal. I suppose such an agent could have an inborn impatience about consumption. But greenhouse policy is not about saving for later consumption. It is about foregoing consumption in order that *somebody else* at a later time enjoy more consumption than would otherwise be available.

This assumption of the immortal agent, explicit in Manne, makes the issue one of "optimization over time"—one of maximizing the utilities of myriad heterogeneous peoples spread over continents and centuries as if they were all one family, all one "agent." It supposes that whoever pays for the investments that lead to increments in future consumption values increments in other people's utility *as if they were increments in his or her own utility.* It is this willingness to model all humankind as a single agent that makes optimization models attractive, feasible, and inappropriate.

Additionally, the optimization models have no provision for redistributing current income; they redistribute only forward in time. Contemporary Chinese get nothing from us, but future Chinese are part of the family.

I myself feel no impatience about an increment of consumption that will accrue to people whom I shall never know and who do not now exist in the year 2150, compared with an increment that will accrue to the people whom I shall never know and who do not now exist in the year 2100, or even in the year 2050.

I can imagine reasons—some of them may even appeal to me—for preferring a boost to consumption in 2025 to the same boost of consumption in 2075, but it is hard to see that it has anything to do with impatience and the inborn preference of immediate over postponed consumption. In 2025 my oldest son will be the age I am today and his brothers a little younger; with a little luck they will be alive and healthy and my grandchildren will be the ages that my children are today, and my great grandchildren (whom I do not yet know) will have most of their lives ahead of them. Seventy-five years later they will all be strangers to me. My genes may be as plentiful in the population at the later date but they will be spread thinner. I probably would prefer the benefits to accrue to my own grandchildren rather than to their grandchildren, but when I remind myself that my grandchildren's happiness may depend on their perceived prospects for their own grandchildren, my "time preference" becomes attenuated.

The point is that we may have grounds for preferring utility increments to accrue to earlier rather than later descendants of people now alive, but it cannot have anything to do with the kind of time preference that Harrod, Fankhauser, Manne, or Nordhaus was talking about.

Actually, time may serve as a kind of measure of "distance." The people who are going to be living in 2150 I may consider "farther away" than the people who will be living in 2050. They will also be different in racial composition and geographical distribution from the people I most identify with. I observe that in redistributing income via transfer payments, in providing foreign aid, in contributing to charity, etc., people are expected to differentiate, and do differentiate, among recipient peoples according to several kinds of distance or proximity. One is geographical: Americans are expected to be more interested in their own cities than in distant cities, their own country than distant countries. Another is political: east coast Americans are more interested in the people of Los Angeles than in the people of Quebec. Another is cultural: some people are closer in language, religion, and other kinds of heritage. Sheer familiarity seems to matter, and of course kinship does. (Kinship distance has both horizontal and vertical dimensions; just as children are closer than grandchildren, children are closer than nieces and nephews. Time just happens to correlate with vertical distance.)

To be less interested in the welfare of East Africans than former Yugoslavians is less like "discounting" than, perhaps, "depreciating," putting a lesser value on. When we count future welfare less than our own we are depreciating generations that are distant in time, in familiarity, in culture, in kinship, and along other dimensions. (There is no reason to suppose that the depreciation would be exponential. Beyond certain distances there may be no further depreciation for time, culture, geography, race, or kinship. Discounting, at least in the presence of a capital market, is expected to be exponential.)

The crucial point is that decisions to invest in greenhouse emissions abatement for the benefit of future generations are not "saving" decisions, not decisions about postponing our own consumption, but decisions about redistributing income—our income. To invest resources now in reduced greenhouse emissions is to transfer consumption from ourselves—whoever "we" are who are making these sacrifices—for the benefit of people distant in the future. It is very much like making sacrifices now for people who are distant geographically or distant culturally. Deciding whether I care more about the people who will be alive in 2150 than the people who will be alive in 2050 is a little like deciding whether I care more about people in one continent than in another, or about English-speaking people more than people who speak other languages, or about people who share my history and my culture more than people who do not. People do have preferences about whom to help; the preferences show up in charitable giving, in foreign aid, in immigration policy, in military intervention.

What we are talking about is very much like a foreign aid program. Some of the foreigners are our own descendants who live not on another continent but in another century.

Cline half agrees with me. He, too, argues that impatience ("myopia") "may be a legitimate basis for a single individual's preferring consumption earlier rather than later in his lifetime" but is "hardly a justifiable basis for making intergenerational comparisons."[4] He disagrees in believing that we should not prefer—except on marginal utility grounds, which I am about to discuss—our own consumption to the consumption of future people. I expect that, whether or not we should, we all do. If we do not there is a most extraordinary anomaly: we greatly prefer our own consumption to that of distant contemporaries, or even quite close ones, but not to that of people distant in time. It would be strange to forego a percent or two of GNP for 50 years for the benefit of Indians, Chinese, Indonesians, and others who will be living 50 to 100 years from now—and likely much better off than today's Indians, Chinese, and Indonesians—and not a tenth of that amount to increase the consumption of contemporary Indians, Chinese, and Indonesians. At its peak the Marshall Plan took about 1.5 percent of U.S. GNP; it went to the foreigners "closest" to the Americans in most respects; and it was recognized as a short-run emergency. Americans do nothing like that now for anybody alive, except other living Americans. Whether that is good or bad, I do not see why we should expect them to prefer so much to help the unborn.

## Marginal Utility

The second component of the proposed discount rate is the rate of change over time of the marginal utility of consumption. The argument for including that component must be that in transferring income, or redistributing income, an important goal is to maximize the aggregate utility of consumption over time. The expectation is that on average the marginal utility of global consumption will decline over time as a result of rising consumption per capita. Resources invested now out of our own incomes will benefit people in the future who are expected to be better off than we are—an unaccustomed direction for redistributing income!

Both within countries and among countries, we expect civilized governments to redistribute toward the poorer countries and toward the poorer elements of their own populations. Doing it that way probably, as Abba Lerner argued in *The Economics of Control* 50 years ago, increases total utility.[5] But I doubt whether that is the only reason why people prefer to see income redistributed from rich to poor rather than the other way around.

The argument for transferring consumption from the poor to the rich, or from the decently well off to the much better off, would be that the resources transferred grow in the process, and grow so much that though the marginal utility of the recipient is lower than that of the donor, the magnitude that the gift achieves in transit more than compensates. (That the resources so invested "grow" by forestalling decrements does not affect the argument.)

There is not much room for this idea in *contemporary* transfers. If a poor farmer has some poor soil and a richer farmer has rich soil, somebody could argue that taking seed from the poor farmer and giving it to the rich farmer will so enhance the resulting crop that the somewhat utility-satiated rich farmer will gain more utility than the poor farmer loses. But that is just an argument for trade: the poor farmer is better off selling the seed to the rich farmer, and their joint utility is even higher. The ethical interest arises only if trade is not possible, as when we outfit somebody who will emigrate to the new world, become rich, and never be heard from again, or as we contemplate transferring consumption forward in time to people who have no way to reciprocate.

Arthur Okun introduced the "leaky bucket" in his 1974 Godkin lecture, "Equality and Efficiency: The Big Tradeoff."[6] Transferring consumption from those who have plenty to those who do not typically entails inefficiency—some administrative costs, some deadweight losses due to tax avoidance or transfer seeking, some transfers going to unintended and undeserving recipients. His analogy was carrying water from where it was plentiful to where it was scarce in a leaky bucket. The "big tradeoff" was how leaky the bucket can be before we judge the effort not worthwhile. Clearly, if the bucket arrives dry the effort was a mistake; if the bucket arrives three-quarters full or one-quarter, or even a sixteenth, somebody in charge has to consider what discount ratio or augmentation ratio is acceptable.

Somebody might—not many people will—use some elasticity to calculate the marginal utility of consumption (Okun's water) where it is scarce and where it is not and decide whether total utility goes up with the leaky-bucket transfer. Marginal utility is clearly pertinent, for those who understand it, but probably rarely decisive even for them. Enough attention was paid to John Rawls's *Theory of Justice* by quite sophisticated people to somewhat dethrone utility maximization, at least to deny it exclusive status.[7] And Rawls was talking about transferring from rich to poor.

Okun never got around to talking about the other bucket, the "incubation bucket" in which the good things multiply in transit so that more arrives at the destination than was removed from the origin. The tradeoff question here would be, what sacrifice of food where it is scarce is worthwhile if, in being transported to where it is abundant, it grows handsomely. Or, recognizing the advantage of moving resources from where they are less fruitful to where they are more fruitful, how much do we want to "discount" the greater fruitfulness when it accrues to people who already enjoy bountiful supply? Of course Okun, concerned with contemporary transfers, could not be interested: the market would take care of the efficiency problem, and nobody is interested in helping the rich at the expense of the poor.

The conclusion I reach is that "optimization" models are inappropriate for dealing with very long-term public investments, especially when the beneficiaries will be spread over the planet. Optimization models imply that it is our own consumption that we are promoting in the future; it is not. Not only do these models incorporate an irrelevant "time preference," they imply that we want to treat increments in other people's utility from consumption as if they were our own. I can see no acceptance of the principle that consumption should be so distributed (redistributed) as to maximize utility. No such contemporary redistribution has ever been witnessed; and it would be strange to feel a strong obligation to redistribute income from ourselves to others in the future, *valuing their utility from consumption as if it were our own,* and no corresponding obligation to contemporaries who are poorer than we (with higher marginal utilities of consumption) and probably poorer than their own descendants.

Depreciating the consumption of high-income future people makes sense; but the "optimization" approach is based on the principle that if the material benefits we procure for those future high-income people are large enough to offset their reduced marginal utilities, we should procure those future utilities just as if those utilities were our own. Few citizens who understood this principle would ever vote for it.

I conclude that most of us will want to discount or depreciate heavily the extra consumption provided for (or conserved for) descendants of the current population, because they are distant and because they are likely to be better off, and it is *our* hard-earned consumption that somebody is proposing we transfer forward in time. The analogy, or at least a better analogy than "optimization of consumption over time," is transferring resources from North America and Western

Europe to Africa or the Middle East, South or Southeast Asia, China, Russia, or deserving peoples anywhere. It is an aid program, not a savings program. There may be some reason for some people to prefer consumption increments that occur in 2075 over consumption increments that occur in 2125, just as there may be people who prefer consumption increments to occur in West Africa rather than East Africa, Russia rather than in Ukraine, or Boston rather than Los Angeles. And I have no quarrel with people who, when they are prepared to contribute large amounts to charity, indulge their own preferences about who should benefit.

What should matter is your expectation about the course of per capita consumption over the next century or two. If the developed and the developing worlds both continue to grow in per capita consumption as they have done for the past 40 years, the people in most countries are likely to be much better off in material welfare 50, 75, or 100 years from now than they are now. What we ought to feel we owe them is an ethical issue we do not have much practice with, because we are not used to thinking about making our own sacrifices, or imposing sacrifices on our contemporaries, for the benefit of people who are substantially better off.

## The Need to Disaggregate

We must avoid a fallacy here. If average per capita income rises in every country for the next hundred years, and if the poorer populations grow more rapidly than the wealthier populations, and if most of the economic sacrifices in the interest of carbon abatement are borne by the countries that can best afford it, the transfers will tend to be from the well-to-do people of Western Europe, North America, and Japan to the residents of what we now call the "developing" countries, who should be far better off a century from now than they are now, but may not yet be as well off, during most of the intervening century, as we are today in Western Europe, North America, and Japan.

The significance of that point is that in deciding how to value consumption increments over the coming century or two we need to disaggregate consumption according to the levels of per capita consumption at which they accrue. The optimization models err, on their own terms, in aggregating all future consumption and applying a uniform discount rate for declining marginal utility. Correctly, all increments in consumption should be valued at their own marginal utilities. In the optimization models, increments for poor people are discounted equally with increments for the rich; there is no adjustment for the fact that when Chinese per capita income has doubled, and

Chinese marginal utility may have been halved—using the popular but arbitrary logarithmic utility function—Chinese marginal utility will still be many times greater than that of the current populations most likely to pay for greenhouse abatement.

In neglecting to disaggregate, the optimization models make three assumptions in deriving a discount rate that are either dubious or wrong.

> They assume that elasticities of utility with respect to consumption are the same at all levels of consumption. (A logarithmic or power function meets that condition.) I count this one dubious.

> They assume that growth rates are uniform. Actually, the optimization models themselves do not; they recognize that China may develop much more rapidly than the currently advanced countries. But the discount-rate calculations use a single average growth rate.

> They assume that those who pay for abatement and those who benefit—or whose descendants benefit—are the same. Because all populations—all nations or regions—are assumed to enjoy increasing consumption per capita, and because investments in abatement precede benefits, the benefitting populations are assumed to have higher consumption levels and lower marginal utilities than the populations that finance the abatement.

I start from the premise that investments in greenhouse abatement, for the first 50 years, will be paid for by the countries that can afford it, the developed countries of Western Europe, North America, and Japan, and a few others. The beneficiaries of abatement will mainly be the descendants of those now living in the undeveloped countries, for several reasons explained below. Thus the consumption transfers will be from well-to-do countries that will mainly pay for abatement over the coming 50 years to the developing countries that, though probably better off progressively over the next 50 years, will have lower consumption levels 50 years from now than the current consumption levels of the developed countries. (Benefits from abatement during the first 50 years will almost surely be negligible compared with benefits during the second 50 years.) Thus the consumption transfers, despite the hoped-for uniformly (not uniform) positive growth in GDP per capita everywhere, will be generally from rich to poor. That is, from lower marginal utility to higher marginal utility. The implications are startling, but first I should explain why the beneficiaries will be mainly the descendants of the populations now poor.

First, if the benefits of abatement were shared uniformly over the global population, about 90 percent of the benefits would accrue to the countries now considered undeveloped. The well-to-do are now about a fifth of the world's population; in 2075 the populations in countries now undeveloped are expected to be somewhere between seven-eighths and eleven-twelfths of the global population. So those populations will comprise most of the beneficiaries.

Second, material productivity in the developed countries currently appears to be substantially immune to weather and climate; production in less developed countries depends much more on outdoor activities, especially agriculture, and is potentially much more susceptible to adverse effects of climate change. So besides outnumbering the descendants of the currently developed countries, they can suffer greater greenhouse damage per capita. (In absolute terms, the more developed countries could incur more lost GDP per capita, though the damage might not be noticeable.)

Finally, the currently developed countries enjoy GDP per capita 10 times or more that of the undeveloped; during the second half of the coming century they will probably still be ahead by a factor of four or more. So the marginal utility of consumption of the poorer nine-tenths of the population will be several times that of the richer tenth, and the benefits in utility increments from material consumption will therefore be overwhelmingly inherited by the descendants of those who are currently poor.

(If Chinese per capita income increased at 4 percent per year for the next 50 years and 2 percent for the following 50 years, and U.S. per capita income increased at 1 percent over the 100 years, Chinese per capita income would still be less than half the U.S. level at the end of the century. At those rates of improvement, the Chinese will be about up to the present U.S. level toward the end of the century, and before then we shall probably lose interest in further increments.)

I said the implications are startling. One has already been mentioned: virtually all the benefits from enhanced consumption will accrue to countries that will not participate much in financing the abatement. The transfers will be from the currently rich to the descendants of the currently poor, who will, when the benefits begin to be felt, be much less poor than they are now but still poorer than the descendants of the currently rich and probably still significantly poorer than the abatement-financing countries are now.

Second, the implicit "discount rate" based on marginal utility comparisons will be negative. The currently popular optimization models cannot show this negative rate, because GDP per capita is assumed to rise everywhere. But even if it does, disaggregating shows that the beneficiaries will be both poorer and more numerous than those who finance the increments in consumption.

Third, if GDP per capita continues to increase in most of the developing world, as I expect and as the optimization models assume, marginal utilities of the beneficiaries will be much higher during the first 50 years—before abatement benefits become significant—than in the second 50 years. This factor substantially tilts the priority toward whatever investments can raise living standards in the first and second generations. And those are likely to be direct investments in economic development (which also should reduce dependence on climate) rather than investment in climate stabilization.

Even more drastic: if marginal utilities will be higher in the fifth decade than in the sixth, in the third than in the fourth, and in the first than in the second, today's undeveloped populations have stronger claims, on the basis of marginal utility, than the populations two or four generations in the future. Once we disaggregate the world's population by income level, it becomes logically absurd to ignore present needs and concentrate on the later decades of the coming century. An initial interest in climate and its impact on welfare should not insulate us from alternative means to the same end.

And that means that no framework for considering the benefits and costs of greenhouse abatement can isolate itself from the opportunity cost: direct investment in the economic improvement of the undeveloped countries. Abatement expenditures should have to compete with alternative ways of raising consumption utility in the developing world.

## A Policy Approach

Once we abandon the immortal-agent (optimization) approach, there are two pertinent policy questions. First, do we want to help the future populations of China, Bangladesh, and Nigeria at our expense because they are poor and will still be poor for some time? Second, assuming that we who pay for greenhouse abatement do not want to time-discount the consumption utility of poor countries, what mix of programs maximizes the integral of their consumption utility over time? We can choose among greenhouse abatement, direct investment in their economic improvement, or direct subsidies to their consumption.

Nothing in this formulation can directly answer the question of *how much* to help the Chinese and the others. That remains a choice, not an analytical result. Just as there is no accepted formula for how much people want to help the Somalis, the Indians, the Chinese, or anybody else with current consumption, there is no formula that tells us how much people want to help with future consumption, whether with development aid or with greenhouse abatement. (I emphasize helping the poor; but there is likewise no analytical formula that could tell us how much to expect people to want to redistribute toward future Americans and Europeans.)

A different question is how to distribute increments to the consumption of Chinese and others over time when the marginal utility of their consumption is declining. The Chinese themselves may have a strong preference for current and near-term consumption over the distant, more than diminishing marginal utility would prescribe. We then have to decide whether to depreciate the consumption of future Chinese less than today's Chinese would depreciate it. (The Chinese preference for earlier rather than later increments is likely to be enhanced when they are contemplating *income,* not just consumption, because earlier increments can be partly invested to enlarge consumption later. With greenhouse abatement we have no control over Chinese allocation between consumption and investment.)

If we abandon optimization based on the immortal-agent image, what analytical procedure do we replace it with? A first approximation may be:

For *alternative levels* of greenhouse abatement, assess benefits as consumption increments for each country or for regions that are homogeneous with respect to per capita income.

Identify a utility function by which to convert the consumption increments into commensurable "utility" increments. (This function should not be chosen for mathematical simplicity or tractability.)

Treat the results as a menu of what we get for our money when we invest alternative amounts of greenhouse abatement in the enhanced welfare of currently poor countries, not as an optimization that tells us how much to invest.

Estimate the increments in consumption, and corresponding "utilities," that could be procured in a sample of different countries with direct investment in infrastructure, industry, public health, education, research and development, etc., to identify—for any level of aggregate contribution to future welfare—the efficient mix of investments in abatement and economic development. This has to be done by sample, because we cannot allocate resources between greenhouse abatement and economic development country by country. Greenhouse abatement is necessarily uniform worldwide (in $CO_2$ concentration); we cannot give India public health and education, and Indonesia greenhouse abatement, on the basis of comparative advantage.

## The Rate of Interest

Optimization models often look to the market rate of interest—some rate, somewhere—to get a handle on an appropriate discount rate. What role does my analysis ascribe to the market rate of interest? First, the market rate of interest cannot tell us anything about *how much* people would like to contribute now to help others in the future. Second, it does tell us something about *when* people would like to contribute: the earlier, the more it costs. Third, it tells us little, if anything, about what return we would get on public investments in poor countries, investments that may be alternatives to greenhouse abatement. Fourth, our domestic rate of interest does help to identify an interesting opportunity cost: instead of investing in greenhouse abatement or in economic development, we could invest commercially and dedicate the proceeds to somebody's future consumption.

## The Utility-Function Approach

The question of what discount rate to use should disappear. In its place is the question, what utility function should be used in valuing future increments in other people's consumption? This is a real question, not a matter of mathematical convenience. It is not a question economists have much practice with. The policy implications of emphasizing a utility function, rather than a discount rate, are troublesome—unavoidable, but troublesome. The discounting procedure has a disarming familiarity; the analogy with saving for future consumption has appeal. Everybody knows about interest rates, and they are genuinely pertinent to much national public investment. In contrast, marginal utilities from consumption are alien to most policy thinking. People usually understand the argument for redistributing from rich to poor, but no legislator ever wonders whether the utility function is a power function, a logarithmic function, or a polynomial; whether there should be a universal utility function for all cultures and all times; whether material consumption is the only argument of the function; or anything of the sort.

My procedure—properly—gives no answer to the question, how

much? An optimization model answers that question—incorrectly, but it gives an answer. Facing an optimization, a policy maker can say, "I'll do half that, no more," but at least the policy maker thinks that he or she is doing half of something objectively arrived at. My procedure requires a *choice* of how much, with no benchmark.

Furthermore, it is hard to think about the future with my procedure and not be forced to think about the present. If marginal utilities of consumption are the correct target for investing in future welfare, they must be just as pertinent to today's welfare. But today's welfare vanishes from the greenhouse-optimization models because there is no greenhouse-abatement increment in current or near-term consumption. Greenhouse abatement, which is largely identified with energy policy, is insulated in optimization models from economic development. An answer to how much (and when) to abate is given in optimization models independently of what else is going on. When greenhouse abatement is identified as a mechanism for making income transfers to future generations, especially to those whose consumption levels are still comparatively low, it should have to compete with transfers for investment in economic development.

Carbon dioxide abatement is probably "target efficient," helping mainly those we would prefer to help. Poorer countries are usually going to be more vulnerable to climate change than wealthier countries. But direct investments in public health, birth control, training and education, research, physical infrastructure, water resources, etc., can also be directed to target populations, so abatement does not necessarily have the advantage.

I doubt that developing countries would choose to defer consumption increments to later generations, whether what is deferred comes out of their own resources or out of resources made available by wealthier countries. I would expect, if offered a choice of immediate development assistance or equivalent investments in carbon abatement, potential aid recipients would elect the immediate. So if we, the developed, elect carbon abatement for their benefit, it is *we* who choose their descendants over themselves.

Whichever we choose, there is no reliable way we can constrain our own descendants' choices to continue or to discontinue what we began. We can invest in the consumption of future generations through carbon abatement or through direct investments; in 2050 our descendants can discontinue the direct investments, or they can discontinue the carbon abatement. There may be institutional reasons for expecting discontinuance to be more likely with one approach or the other, but the choice is not self-evident.

## Notes

1. William R. Cline, *The Economics of Global Warming* (Washington, DC: Institute for International Economics, 1992); Alan S. Manne, "The Rate of Time Preference: Implications for the Greenhouse Debate," in *Integrative Assessment of Mitigation, Impacts, and Adaptation to Climate Change*, eds. N. Nakicenovic et al. (Laxenburg, Austria: International Institute for Applied Systems Analysis, 1994); William D. Nordhaus, *Managing the Global Commons: The Economics of Climate Change* (Cambridge, MA: MIT Press, 1994), pp. 11–19, 154–56; and Samuel Fankhauser, "The Social Costs of Greenhouse Gas Emissions: An Expected Value Approach" (Centre for Social and Economic Research on the Global Environment, University College and University of East Anglia, 1993).
2. Fankhauser, "The Social Costs," p. 13.
3. Manne, "The Rate of Time Preference," p. 469.
4. Cline, *The Economics of Global Warming*, p. 249.
5. Abba P. Lerner, *The Economics of Control: Principles of Welfare Economics* (New York: Macmillan, 1994).
6. Arthur Okun, *Equality and Efficiency: The Big Tradeoff* (Washington, DC: The Brookings Institution, 1975).
7. John Rawls, *A Theory of Justice* (Cambridge, MA: Harvard University Press, 1971).

# PART 1.3

## Applications

# CHAPTER 10

# DECISION ANALYSIS IN HEALTH AND MEDICINE: TWO DECADES OF PROGRESS AND CHALLENGES

## Milton C. Weinstein

The origins of decision analysis are usually traced to its early applications in business, but Howard Raiffa always had a passion for decision problems in health and medicine. He supervised several doctoral dissertations at Harvard Business School and the Graduate School of Arts and Sciences on applications of decision analysis to medicine. He worked on the difficult problem of how to allocate dialysis machines before Congress decided to provide dialysis to anyone whose kidneys had failed. This paper comments on what medicine has learned from decision analysis during the 25 years since the publication of Howard Raiffa's classic text,[1] and also on how the art and science of decision analysis has been enriched by its exposure to the fascinating decision problems in health care. A physician reading *Decision Analysis* cannot help but be struck by how relevant are the six steps in the "process of decision analysis" to decision making in the clinical setting:

"1. List the viable options available to you for gathering information, for experimentation, and for action." What diagnostic tests can I order? What treatments can I use?

"2. List the events that may possibly occur." What might the diagnostic tests reveal? What disease, if any, does the patient have? Will the patient's symptoms resolve or get worse? Will the patient survive?

"3. Arrange in chronological order the information you may acquire and the choices you may make as time goes on." Physicians are comfortable with decision trees as aids in organizing their reasoning.

"4. Decide how well you like the consequences that result from the various courses of action open to you." Is the reduced risk of death worth the side effects? Is the pain relief worth the risk of dying on the operating table? Physicians are uncomfortable quantifying utilities for life and death, but they know these tradeoffs underlie their decisions.

"5. Judge what the chances are that any particular event will occur." Assigning probabilities to events is at the heart of modern clinical epidemiology, and the melding of scientific data and expert judgment remains a challenge.

6. The final step is to "make a series of calculations and then fix on a certain strategy that . . . seems the best of the many that are available to you." The formal, quantitative process of analyzing a decision tree is not yet part of the repertoire of most practicing physicians, and may never be, but the compelling logic of decision analysis has influenced the minds of a generation of doctors.

## The Influence of Decision Analysis in Clinical Medicine

Twenty-five years after the publication of *Decision Analysis,* medicine has embraced decision analysis as a core discipline. For example, Jerome Kassirer, the current editor in chief of *The New England Journal of Medicine,* is best known for his research on decision analysis in medical decision making.[2] Although he is also a noted kidney specialist and has published extensively in specialty journals, his pathbreaking articles on how decision trees can help doctors think more clearly about their practices have been more influential. The journal now runs a regular feature on clinical decision making, which often incorporates decision trees, Bayesian logic, and utility concepts to convey messages to practicing physicians. As a second example, medical board examinations now include questions on the essentials of decision analysis. Decision analysis also affects clinical practice directly, through medical specialty organizations and government panels that formulate clinical guidelines or policy recommendations.

A widely discussed example of the use of decision analysis in health policy was the effort in Oregon to rank medical practices according to their cost-effectiveness for purposes of allocating the state Medicaid budget.[3] The measure of effectiveness used was the gain in quality-adjusted life years, a special example of expected utility used in health-related decision analysis (to which I return later). Although the expected utility basis for the rankings was abandoned, this may have been more a result of the necessarily crude way in which the method was applied than of the shortcomings of decision analysis itself.

A classic example of decision making in which patients make the ultimate decision but the physician is expected to provide counseling is a couple's decision whether to undergo amniocentesis to detect fetal abnormalities such as Down's Syndrome. Susan Pauker and Stephen Pauker have developed a simple but compelling decision analysis model that has been used in counseling hundreds of patients.[4] The model involves eliciting the couple's utilities for adverse events such as the birth of an affected child, an elective abortion, and a spontaneous abortion that may have been caused by the amniocentesis procedure. The authors report that satisfaction with the model is high among patients and physicians.

Another influential decision analysis was that by David Eddy of the decision of how often to perform pap smears to screen for cervical cancer.[5] This analysis was cited as influential in the recommendation by the American Cancer Society to alter its recommended screening frequency from once a year to once every three years.

The analysis by Lee Goldman et al. of the decision whether to give cholesterol-lowering drugs to patients who have had a heart attack resulted in a change in recommendations between the first and second reports of the National Cholesterol Education Program on lowering cholesterol in adults.[6] The first report had emphasized the treatment of asymptomatic persons who had not had a heart attack, while the second report, following the conclusions of the Goldman study, urged physicians to give priority for cholesterol reduction to patients who have already had a heart attack or who are at particularly high risk of having a heart attack for reasons other than high cholesterol.[7]

Decision analysis was recommended by a panel of the Institute of Medicine of the National Academy of Sciences as the best procedure for setting priorities for new vaccine development in the National Institutes of Health (NIH).[8] The model developed by the panel is being used at the NIH as a basis for priority setting, and a new panel is being established to update the model and to extend it to new vaccine candidates.

## Current Issues in Medical Decision Analysis

The relationship between decision analysis and clinical medicine has been one of mutual education and synergistic development. Concepts from decision analysis, such as Bayesian probability revision and utility assessment, have become assimilated into the language of physicians, at least as represented in the leading research journals. Conversely, the exposure of decision analysis to medical problems has resulted in new analytical methods and insights whose significance goes beyond medical applications. This reciprocal relationship is illustrated in this section, which covers six current issues in medical decision analysis.

### Who Is the Decision Maker?

To whom should decision analysts address their work? A glib answer is that the physician is the agent for the patient's interests. Often, however, physicians override their best honest assessment of the patient's interest; fear of malpractice litigation, or psychological consequences such as guilt and regret, or the promise of financial gain may drive a decision. For example, surgeons may be reluctant to perform appendectomies for patients with acute abdominal pain, because they are more averse to deaths caused by surgery than to deaths caused by the natural course of appendicitis.

The pure principal-agent model of decision making loses force when the health of more than one individual is at stake. The decision to perform a cesarean section is influenced by concerns for the health of both mother and child. The decision to immunize a patient is influenced not only by the benefit to the patient, but also by the community's benefit from a reduction in the risk of transmission of the infectious disease. Physicians who are placed in the role of gatekeeper of resources, as in health maintenance organizations, may also wish to protect the interests of patients who may arrive later. These concerns complicate the task of patient care, bringing it into the domain of social policy.

While physicians might seem to be natural consumers of decision analyses, they do not generally have the time to analyze in detail each medical decision they make. They rely on guidelines, rules of thumb, and even formal algorithms to help them in their daily decisions. For this reason, decision analyses in medicine are rarely performed for an individual case. (A notable exception is the clinical consulting service in the Division of Clinical Decision Making at the New England Medical Center Hospital).[9] Most medical decision analyses are aimed at groups of physicians and seek to clarify issues for a class of problems, rather than assisting in a particular decision. Some analyses are targeted at medical specialty societies, government panels, or others charged with developing decision guidelines on a medical diagnosis or treatment problem.

Other users of medical decision analyses are those who manage medical resources for society as a whole. Decisions about public funding for procedures ranging from immunizations to organ transplants have been informed by decision analyses.[10]

Because medical decision analyses are typically intended to influence medical practice by informing debate about a controversial decision problem, they are usually communicated through media that can reach large numbers of physicians, such as medical journals. Clinical guidelines, such as those developed by medical specialty societies and government panels, are sometimes accompanied by supporting analysis. In recent years, dissemination of decision analysis in an electronic form that allows users to enter patient-specific probability and utility data is becoming more prevalent.

The complex and interrelated network of users and beneficiaries of medical decision analyses presents a challenge to the classic client-analyst relationship. Decision analysts in medicine must always be cognizant of the broader population affected, and the myriad of decision makers who may one day read the analysis and be influenced by it.

### How Complex Should Decision Models Be?

Effective decision models should be just complex enough to satisfy the decision maker that all important alternatives, outcomes, and contingencies have been considered.[11] A decision tree that becomes a "bushy mess" loses its effectiveness because insights are obfuscated by complexity.

Medical decision problems are inherently complex by virtue of the unfolding of clinical events over time, and this has led to the development of a variety of analytical tools particularly suited to the medical context. While these tools offer more realistic models of problem structure, probabilities, and utilities, they could reduce the impact of decision analysis in medicine by making the models less accessible to clients. Here, I consider three modeling techniques that have been developed and considerably refined in response to the needs of medical decision modeling.

Medical decision analysts needed a modeling tool that combines the recursive aspects of Markov state-transition models, which lend themselves to modeling the course of illness through time, and decision trees, which flexibly model discrete events.[12] The result was the "Markov cycle tree," which is essentially a decision tree in which some paths end in a Markov chain.[13] The notion of a "Markov node" was invented to accommodate this feature into decision tree software. Using Markov cycle trees, modelers can make transition probabilities—such as the annual probability of death, relapse, or infection—conditional upon previous events in the tree, such as treatments chosen or nonfatal events.

Unfortunately, Markov models are "memoryless"; they cannot accommodate situations in which the time a patient spends in one health state affects the probabilities that the patient will move from that state to other states. Rather than create separate states for each amount of time in some state, a device called the "tunnel state" was developed to model passage through a series of substates differentiated only by the duration spent in the tunnel. For example, the time since infection with the AIDS virus could be modeled as a Markov tunnel, where the probability of developing AIDS-related complications depends on the length of time since infection.[14] The tunnel is really not a conceptual breakthrough; it is a computational device that facilitates the use of software for Markov modeling of recursive, time-dependent clinical processes.

A second area of spectacular development in medical decision analysis is the use of biostatistical models of survival to generate sequences of mortality probabilities for recursive modeling as patients age. Most models begin with life tables of annual mortality probabilities by age, sex, and sometimes race. The question is how to model the effects of disease and treatment on the baseline probabilities. Typically, the first step is to transform annual probabilities ($p$) into instantaneous rates ($\mu$), where $p = \exp(-\mu)$. Next, one can model the effects of disease and treatment as either additive or multiplicative. Additive models superimpose effects of treatment and disease additively upon the baseline mortality rate.[15] Multiplicative models, such as Cox proportional hazard regression models, posit that the baseline hazard function $\mu_0(t)$, is multiplied by an exponential function of covariates, that is, $\mu(t) = \mu_0(t)*\exp(\beta Z)$, where $Z$ is a vector of covariates including disease status and treatment status. The choice of model is crucial; Karen Kuntz and I have shown that dramatic differences in conclusions can result from the choice of extrapolating survival functions according to additive or multiplicative models.[16]

An interesting offshoot of work on modeling survival probabilities is a "bedside" approximation of life expectancy, known as the declining exponential approximation to life expectancy, or DEALE.[17] The DEALE models the baseline annual mortality rate as a constant equal to the reciprocal of life expectancy, $\mu_0 = 1/L$. ($L$ comes from life tables.) Effects of disease and treatment are modeled additively. More sophisticated variants of DEALE account for increasing mortality with age and other features.[18]

The third aspect of model complexity concerns the modeling of utilities. In early applications of decision analysis to medicine, the outcome at the end of each branch of a decision tree was assessed, one by one. The classic method used was the basic reference gamble, where the respondent was asked to place each outcome on a scale between the best of all possible outcomes (usually "cure" or "return to full health") and the worst (usually death).[19] The practicality of direct utility assignment depends on a small number of possible outcomes. As models became more complex, and the range of outcomes grew to a virtual continuum of survival and health status possibilities, modelers tackled the problem of assigning a utility function to a multi-attribute space whose dimensions include length of survival and many attributes of quality of life.[20] A method previously used by health status researchers, wherein weights were assigned to time spent in various health states to produce a measure called Healthy Life Years was related to utility theory and renamed Quality-Adjusted Years of Life (QALYs).[21] The problem with QALYs is that strong assumptions about the patient's preferences (such as mutual utility independence between longevity and quality of life) are required for a decision maker to want to make decisions based on maximizing expected QALYs.[22] They can be adjusted for attitudes toward risk and time preference,[23] but they cannot easily incorporate preferences that assign different weights to health states depending on the duration of time spent or the sequence in which they are experienced. Some argue that QALYs should be abandoned as a proxy for utility, despite their relative ease of assessment, in favor of an essentially holistic assessment of sequences of health states.[24]

With all the new medical decision-analytic tools, decision trees have become too complicated for analysis by hand. Software packages, including SML-TREE and Decision Maker, feature Markov nodes; automatic calculation of quality-adjusted and discounted life expectancy; choices of models for Bayesian probability revision; and a wide range of sensitivity analysis options.[25] A model of decisions about prevention and treatment of coronary heart disease, which contains thousands of states, once ran in 30 minutes on a mainframe computer,[26] but can now run in 30 seconds on a personal computer.

As the inner workings of models become less accessible, even to the modelers, the challenge to the analyst is to ensure that the results can be explained well enough that the client trusts them. Physicians and opinion leaders in health policy will not and should not trust models blindly; they must be convinced that the model behaves realistically. If it produces counterintuitive results, these must be explicable in intuitive terms. So Howard Raiffa warned us three decades ago, when computers could barely outperform humans in computation.

## Utilities

No element of the decision-analytic paradigm has received as much attention in medical applications as utilities. Three issues surface in almost every medical decision problem: Who should assign utilities to health outcomes? Are outcome scales that are not firmly based in subjective expected utility theory acceptable for decision analysis in lieu of formal utilities? What is the prescriptive role of psychologically valued outcomes such as anxiety and regret?

People who live with long-term health problems assign higher utilities to such outcomes than people who are relatively healthy. For example, people who are blind or require renal dialysis assign higher utilities to those health states (on a scale from perfect health to death) than do people who have not experienced those states. Perhaps this is because healthy people underestimate their ability to adapt to these conditions, or perhaps people adjust to such conditions by creating a new "self." Which "self" should represent the patient: the healthy individual who may develop the condition, the person with the condition, or the person who has been relieved of the condition?

There is no solution to this problem of "multiple selves," and it presents challenges to clinical investigators, who are becoming convinced that data on patient preferences should be routinely collected as part of clinical trials and other forms of clinical research. Two approaches are currently being debated. One approach is to obtain utility assessments from patients who are being followed in clinical studies, thereby directly assessing the utility for the health state of each patient. For example, patients in a study of heart disease might be asked to weigh their current health against a gamble between good cardiac health and death. This approach assumes that the patients experiencing a health state should assign utility to that state. The other approach is to obtain utilities for health states from a community survey. Unfortunately, respondents may not have sufficient knowledge to assess various health states. Research has addressed ways to formulate questions so that respondents have the knowledge to give thoughtful answers. For example, people may not understand what it means to have congestive heart failure, but they may be able to understand a state of health defined according to the activities they can and cannot perform, their emotional outlook, and their ability to work or attend school. However, symptoms such as pain remain elusive. The best solution to the problem of measuring utility may be to rely on patient utilities for decisions involving treatment of existing conditions, and community-based utilities for decisions involving prevention or for resource allocation.

The second question surrounding utility analysis in medical decision problems concerns the validity of various outcome scales. The QALY numeraire represents utility only under the stringent assumption of a constant proportional time-tradeoff of quality of life for longevity;[27] this assumption is needed to make a multidimensional outcome space tractable. An unresolved question is whether the weights assigned to time spent in health states should be based on utility or value equivalence (such as standard gambles or time-tradeoffs), or whether it is sufficient to use ordinal rating scales. Ordinal rating scales are easier to understand, and they are administered routinely as part of quality-of-life questionnaires now commercially available to health researchers and clinicians; but they often produce results with little validity when interpreted as utilities. For example, respondents may assign a 70, on a 100-point scale, to a bad sore throat. Does that mean they would accept a 30 percent chance of death to avoid living the rest of life with this sore throat? If not, this number has no meaning as a utility and should not be used in expected value calculations. Despite their drawbacks, the use of rating scales is proliferating because they are much easier to administer than time-tradeoff or standard gamble questions. Several computer-assisted utility assessment tools have been developed to help physicians help patients assess utilities the "right way."[28]

The third and most challenging of the utility-related problems in medical decision making concerns the psychological consequences of decisions. Preference structures for medical problems incorporate anxiety and reassurance, and regret and blame,[29] as legitimate arguments in utility functions for health decisions.

The inclusion of anxiety and reassurance undercuts a familiar teaching of decision analysis—that a decision to acquire information cannot be optimal unless a subsequent decision is nontrivially conditional upon the information. Reassurance is the primary motivation for performing ultrasound tests in apparently normal pregnancies.[30] Likewise, the decision whether to perform the safer amniocentesis or the riskier chorionic villus sampling is influenced by the desire for information about fetal health sooner rather than later.[31] Sometimes the value of information can be negative, as in the decision to screen for early prostate cancer, because most such cancers would otherwise go undetected and without ill effects throughout life.

The possibility that a decision will later result in regret also plays a role in many health decisions. Resource allocations guided by expected utility considerations tend to give less priority to last-ditch life-saving interventions than some critics think appropriate,[32] possibly because the analysis leaves out the psychological and perhaps moral imperative to attempt to save a life in jeopardy. This is sometimes labeled ex ante identifiability, and it is also a variant of regret.[33] Prevention, which saves statistical lives, is less urgently advocated than life-saving treatments.

Ex post identifiability also plays a role in medical decision making that is not captured by conventional decision analyses. The Hippocratic dictum, "do no harm," is cited by a physician who argues that lives lost as a result of a medical decision should weigh more heavily than lives lost as a result of a failure to act.[34] In the decision to perform an appendectomy for a patient with equivocal signs of appendicitis, should the physician assign a lower utility to death on the operating table than to death from a ruptured appendix? The patient who wants to survive would say "no," but the physician who must live with the wrong decision might regret errors of omission and commission differently. While some patients die of ruptured appendices even with surgery, death from anesthesia is possible only with surgery.

The patient may also be motivated by regret. A postmenopausal woman may be reluctant to follow the advice of a decision analysis that says her expected utility would increase if she undergoes hormone replacement therapy. While the benefits of avoiding hip fractures and preventing heart disease may outweigh the risks of cancer, the latter may weigh more heavily; should cancer occur, there is a greater chance that it would have been caused by the therapy, than that a heart attack or hip fracture could have been prevented.

The question of whether such psychological attributes as anxiety and regret should be incorporated into prescriptive and normative analyses is nowhere more pertinent than in medical decision making. Should people be trained to resist their influence, or are they as legitimate as, say, risk aversion? We do not know whether training or psychotherapy makes a difference; nor can we say whether we want them to.

### Probabilities

The growing number of physicians trained in clinical epidemiology are taught to be skeptical of subjectivity and to demand scientific proof of effectiveness. They are taught a research methodology based on hypothesis testing, not Bayesian updating. This training is an effective counterbalance to the proliferation of medical practices whose effectiveness is highly uncertain, but it is at odds with the subjectivist underpinnings of decision analysis, and often leads to mistrust of probability assessments based on "statistically insignificant" empirical data, let alone expert judgment. Randomized clinical trials in which statistically significant results are achieved are viewed in some circles as the only legitimate data for decision making. Meta-analyses that combine data from multiple trials are held in suspicion by some, as are observational data of the type collected in "outcomes research."

Data collection can be defended by decision analysts as worthwhile investments in sampling about uncertain probabilities, although the decision-analytic conclusion that sometimes it is better to act without further information often falls on deaf ears. In decision-theoretic terms, the highly charged political debate over the use of experimental AIDS drugs hinges on the relative disutilities attached to errors of commission (Type I) and errors of omission (Type II), and judgments about prior probabilities of effectiveness.

Deeper differences in outlook relate to the purpose of clinical research: should it reveal truth or guide decisions? Decision analysis views clinical research as gathering information to guide decisions, rather than to establish truth. But physicians presented with their first elementary example of a worked decision tree invariably ask for a significance level to accompany the conclusion, or a confidence interval around the expected utility difference. One could construct some sort of confidence interval based on sampling error in the probability estimates, but this would not really be meaningful to a clinician; a scientist may fail to reject a null hypothesis, but to the clinician, not to act is to act.

Nonetheless, the physician-researcher's mistrust of subjectivity has led to a healthy respect for data among medical decision analysts. Because most medical decision analyses are targeted at physicians at large, the more objective the basis for probability assessments, the more credible and widely applicable is the analysis. A decision analysis built on subjective probabilities is less likely to be published in medical journals than an analysis based on empirical data.

## Roles for Sensitivity Analysis

Medical decision analyses must be useful to physicians with different beliefs and different opinions of the validity of data in the medical literature; patients with varying clinical characteristics and, therefore, different probabilities; and patients with differing utilities. Sensitivity analysis helps physicians adapt a generic decision analysis to themselves and to their patients. In fact, the decision analysis software programs designed for medical applications have some of the most sophisticated graphics for sensitivity analysis available.

Another role of sensitivity analysis in medical decision making is to focus debate about controversial decisions. Sensitivity analysis can identify the probabilities and values to which a decision is most sensitive, thereby defusing disputes over probabilities that do not matter.

The technique of Monte Carlo sensitivity analysis, also used in risk analysis, has become routine in medical decision analysis.[35] The inputs to such analyses include probability distributions of all uncertain probabilities, taking into account interdependencies. The output is a probability distribution on the expected utility of each alternative action, as well as a probability that each action is optimal. In medicine, there is great demand for confidence.

### Teaching Physicians and Health Professionals

No tribute to Howard Raiffa would be complete without mention of teaching. His love of teaching is legendary, and his skill is unsurpassed. Those of us who teach decision analysis to physicians and dentists draw inspiration from him every day.

The role of decision analyst as teacher is perhaps more critical in medicine than in other arenas. A generation of physicians has been exposed to the essentials of decision analysis in medical school and in residency programs. Two textbooks have sold several thousand copies each, and are used internationally.[36] Physicians elect postdoctoral fellowships in medical decision science to complement their clinical training in cardiology, oncology, and infectious diseases. A generation of academic medical leaders consider decision analysis their major contribution to research and education. The editor of the *New England Journal of Medicine,* the chiefs of medicine at Dartmouth and Georgetown Medical Schools, and the dean of the Harvard School of Public Health are all important contributors to the literature and practice of medical decision analysis. Following them are many more future department heads, journal editors, and deans who know the difference between chance nodes and decision nodes, and many of whom know the formulas for the beta density function and a constant risk aversion utility function.

The Society for Medical Decision Making was established in 1979 to promote the discipline of decision analysis as equal to medicine's biological and clinical disciplines. *Medical Decision Making,* published since 1981, has included papers of importance not only to medicine but to decision science more generally. A cottage industry of short

courses and software programs in decision analysis, with clients ranging from government agencies to pharmaceutical firms to medical
specialty societies, is thriving.

While it would be naive to claim that decision analysis has joined
the mainstream of medicine on an equal footing with other disciplines
such as anatomy and physiology, it has made enormous strides in that
direction. The penetration in medicine is arguably deeper and broader
than in business. No small part of the credit for these developments
belongs to Howard Raiffa.

## NOTES

1. Howard Raiffa, *Decision Analysis: Introductory Lectures on Choices Under
   Uncertainty* (Reading, MA: Addison-Wesley, 1968).
2. For example, see Stephen G. Pauker and Jerome P. Kassirer, "Therapeutic
   Decision Making: A Cost-Benefit Analysis," *New England Journal of Medicine*
   293 (1975): 229–234; Jerome P. Kassirer, "The Principles of Clinical Decision
   Making: An Introduction to Decision Analysis," *Yale Journal of Biology and
   Medicine* 49 (1976): 149–164; Jerome P. Kassirer and Stephen G. Pauker,
   "The Toss-Up," *New England Journal of Medicine* 305 (1981): 1467–1469;
   Stephen G. Pauker and Jerome P. Kassirer, "Decision Analysis," *New Eng-
   land Journal of Medicine* 316 (1987): 250–258; and Jerome P. Kassirer et al.,
   "Decision Analysis: A Progress Report," *Annals of Internal Medicine* 106
   (1987): 275–291.
3. Harvey D. Klevit et al., "Prioritization of Health Care Services: A Progress
   Report by the Oregon Health Services Commission," *Archives of Internal
   Medicine* 151 (1991): 912–916.
4. Susan P. Pauker and Stephen G. Pauker, "The Amniocentesis Decision: Ten
   Years of Decision Analytic Experience," *Birth Defects* 23 (1987): 151–169.
5. David M. Eddy, *Screening for Cancer: Theory, Analysis, and Design* (Englewood Cliffs, NJ: Prentice-Hall, 1980).
6. Lee Goldman et al., "Cost-Effectiveness of HMG-CoA Reductase Inhibition
   for Primary and Secondary Prevention of Coronary Heart Disease," *Journal
   of the American Medical Association* 265 (1991): 1145–1151.
7. National Cholesterol Education Program, "Report of the NCEP Expert
   Panel on Detection, Evaluation, and Treatment of High Blood Cholesterol
   in Adults," *Archives of Internal Medicine* 148 (1988): 36–39; and Expert Panel
   on Detection, Evaluation, and Treatment of High Blood Cholesterol in
   Adults, "Summary of the Second Report of the National Cholesterol Education Program Expert Panel on Detection, Evaluation, and Treatment of
   High Blood Cholesterol in Adults," *Journal of the American Medical Association* 269 (1993): 3015–3023.

8. Institute of Medicine, National Academy of Sciences, Diseases of Importance in the United States, vol. 1 of *New Vaccine Development: Establishing Priorities* (Washington, DC: National Academy Press, 1985).

9. Dennis A. Plante et al., "Clinical Decision Consultation Service," *American Journal of Medicine* 80 (1986): 1169–1174.

10. See, for example, Alan R. Hinman and Jeffrey P. Koplan, "Pertussis and Pertussis Vaccine: Reanalysis of Benefits, Risks, and Costs," *Journal of the American Medical Association* 251 (1984): 3109–3113; and David G. Simon, "A Cost-Effectiveness Analysis of Cyclosporin in Cadaveric Kidney Transplantation," *Medical Decision Making* 6 (1986): 199–207.

11. Raiffa, *Decision Analysis*, pp. 240–243.

12. On Markov state-transition models, see J. Robert Beck and Stephen G. Pauker, "The Markov Process in Medical Prognosis," *Medical Decision Making* 3 (1983): 419–458; and Frank A. Sonnenberg and J. Robert Beck, "Markov Models in Medical Decision Making: A Practical Guide," *Medical Decision Making* 13 (1993): 322–338.

13. See James P. Hollenberg, "Markov Cycle Trees: A New Representation for Complex Markov Processes," *Medical Decision Making* 4 (1984): 529 (abstract).

14. Joanna E. Siegel, Milton C. Weinstein, and Harvey V. Fineberg, "Bleach Programs for Preventing AIDS among IV Drug Users: Modeling the Impact of HIV Prevalence," *American Journal of Public Health* 81 (1991): 1273–1279.

15. J. Robert Beck, Jerome P. Kassirer, and Stephen G. Pauker, "A Convenient Approximation of Life Expectancy (The 'DEALE')," *American Journal of Medicine* 73 (1982): 883–897.

16. Karen M. Kuntz and Milton C. Weinstein, "Life Expectancy Biases in Clinical Decision Modeling," *Medical Decision Making* 15 (1995): in press.

17. Beck, Kassirer, and Pauker, "A Convenient Approximation."

18. Emmett Keeler and Robert Bell, "New DEALEs: Other Approximations to Life Expectancy," *Medical Decision Making* 12 (1992): 307–311.

19. See, for example, Allen S. Ginsberg and Fred L. Offensend, "An Application of Decision Theory to a Medical Diagnosis-Treatment Problem," *IEEE Transactions on Systems Science and Cybernetics* SSC-4 (1968): 355–362.

20. Joseph S. Pliskin, Donald S. Shepard, and Milton C. Weinstein, "Utility Functions for Life Years and Health Status," *Operations Research* 28 (1980): 206–224.

21. On Healthy Life Years, see George W. Torrance, Warren H. Thomas, and David L. Sackett, "A Utility Maximization Model for Evaluation of Health Care Programs," *Health Services Research* 7 (1972): 118–133; and James W. Bush, Milton M. Chen, and Donald L. Patrick, "Health Status Index in Cost Effectiveness: Analysis of a PKU Program," in *Health Status Indexes*, ed. Robert L. Berg (Chicago: Hospital Research and Educational Trust, 1973).

On QALYs, see Milton C. Weinstein and William B. Stason, *Hypertension: A Policy Perspective.* (Cambridge, MA: Harvard University Press, 1976); and Richard Zeckhauser and Donald Shepard, "Where Now for Saving Lives?" *Law and Contemporary Problems* 40 (1976): 5–45.

22. Pliskin, Shepard, and Weinstein, "Utility Functions."

23. Magnus Johannesson, Joseph S. Pliskin, and Milton C. Weinstein, "A Note on QALYs, Time Tradeoff, and Discounting," *Medical Decision Making* 14 (1994): 188–193.

24. Abraham Mehrez and Amiram Gafni, "Quality-Adjusted Life Years, Utility Theory, and Healthy-Years Equivalents," *Medical Decision Making* 9 (1989): 142–149; and Magnus Johannesson, Joseph S. Pliskin, and Milton C. Weinstein, "Are Healthy-Years Equivalents an Improvement over Quality-Adjusted Life Years?" *Medical Decision Making* 13 (1993): 281–286.

25. See James P. Hollenberg, "SMLTREE: The All-Purpose Decision Tree Builder," Boston: Pratt Medical Group, 1985; and Frank A. Sonnenberg and Stephen G. Pauker, "Decision Maker 6.0," in *MEDINFO86: Proceedings of the Fifth Conference on Medical Informatics,* eds. R. Salamon, B. Blum, and M. Jørgensen (Washington, DC: North-Holland, 1986).

26. Milton C. Weinstein et al., "Forecasting Coronary Heart Disease Incidence, Mortality, and Cost: The Coronary Heart Disease Policy Model," *American Journal of Public Health* 77 (1987): 1417–1426.

27. Pliskin, Shepard, and Weinstein, "Utility Functions."

28. Walton Sumner II, Robert F. Nease, and Benjamin Littenberg, "Status Report on Automated Utility Assessment with U-Titer," *Medical Decision Making* 13 (1993): 399 (abstract).

29. Donald M. Berwick and Milton C. Weinstein, "What Do Patients Value? Willingness to Pay for Ultrasound in Normal Pregnancy," *Medical Care* 23 (1985): 881–893; David A. Asch, James P. Patton, and John C. Hershey, "Knowing for the Sake of Knowing: The Value of Prognostic Information," *Medical Decision Making* 10 (1990): 47–57; Scott B. Cantor, "A Decision Analytic Approach to Prenatal Diagnosis" (doctoral dissertation, Harvard University, 1991); David E. Bell, "Regret in Decision Making under Uncertainty," *Operations Research* 30 (1982): 961–981; and Milton C. Weinstein and Robert J. Quinn, "Psychological Considerations in Valuing Health Risk Reductions," *Natural Resources Journal* 23 (1983): 659–673.

30. Berwick and Weinstein, "What Do Patients Value?"

31. Cantor, "A Decision Analytic Approach."

32. David C. Hadorn, "Setting Health Care Priorities in Oregon: Cost-Effectiveness Meets the Rule of Rescue," *Journal of the American Medical Association* 265 (1991): 2218–2225.

33. Weinstein and Quinn, "Psychological Considerations."

34. Allen S. Brett, "Hidden Ethical Issues in Clinical Decision Analysis," *New England Journal of Medicine* 305 (1981): 1150–1152.

35. Peter Doubilet et al., "Probabilistic Sensitivity Analysis Using Monte Carlo Simulation: A Practical Approach," *Medical Decision Making* 5 (1985): 157–177; and Gregory C. Critchfield and Keith E. Willard, "Probabilistic Analysis of Decision Trees Using Monte Carlo Simulation," *Medical Decision Making* 6 (1986): 85–92.
36. Milton C. Weinstein et al., *Clinical Decision Analysis* (Philadelphia: W.B. Saunders, 1980); and Harold C. Sox et al., *Medical Decision Making* (Boston: Butterworths, 1988).

# CHAPTER 11

# Optimizing the Prenatal Detection of Down's Syndrome: A Decision-Analytic Economic Policy Analysis

## Joseph S. Pliskin, Orit Refaely, Yitzhak Romem, and Rivka Carmi

Many birth defects, especially ones resulting from chromosomal abnormalities, are now detected prenatally. A chromosomal abnormality is a disorder that affects 1 of the 23 pairs of human chromosomes; such an abnormality increases the likelihood of a miscarriage but may go undetected until birth. The more frequent abnormalities involve having too few or too many chromosomes. Down's syndrome, also known as Trisomy 21, is a condition where there exists an extra (third) twenty-first chromosome. It is the most common serious chromosomal abnormality; it appears in 12 out of every 10,000 newborns and is responsible for approximately 25 percent of severely mentally handicapped children. It is characterized by several physical and mental factors, and most cases involve moderate retardation. The prevention of Down's syndrome has received much attention during the past decades.

Amniocentesis, which is usually performed between the fifteenth and seventeenth week of pregnancy, is considered to offer a definitive diagnosis of the presence or absence of Down's syndrome and other chromosomal abnormalities. The procedure involves inserting a long needle through the woman's abdomen to extract amniotic fluid for chromosomal analysis. It is believed to increase the risk of a spontane-

We want to thank Dr. Lea Friedman for her valuable assistance in the statistical analysis.

ous abortion by .5 percent, or 1 miscarriage in 200 procedures.[1] Amniocentesis usually costs $400 to $1,000.

The occurrence of Down's syndrome, and other chromosomal abnormalities, is highly correlated with advanced maternal age (see Figure 11-1),[2] so screening programs to prevent Down's syndrome have focused on older women who are pregnant. In the United States, women above 35 years of age are offered free amniocentesis;[3] in Great Britain the age is 40; and in Israel the age has just been reduced to 35 from 37. The rationale for offering free amniocentesis is usually both economic and humanitarian: the costs of screening all women above some threshold should be outweighed by the savings incurred through the reduction in the number of people with Down's syndrome, who require increased medical care, special education, special home or institutional care, and sheltered work.

Other explanations for the age threshold are not uncommon. Some would look at Figure 11-1 and find a "steep" change in the curve around ages 35 to 40. Others argue that age 37 is the point at which the risk of Down's syndrome just equals the added risk of an amniocentesis-induced abortion. Of course, such an argument is very faulty: it puts all the decision weight on probabilities, with complete disregard for the utility of the various outcomes. As a matter of fact, it implies that all the negative outcomes are equally valued by society and all positive outcomes are also equally, but differently, valued.

Deciding whether to perform amniocentesis is a decision with large financial and social stakes. In the past, the mother's age has been the sole factor used to determine whether amniocentesis is offered, but several new and cheap blood tests indicate the likelihood that a fetus has Down's syndrome without endangering the mother or fetus. Thus, deciding who should be offered amniocentesis has become a more complicated question; this is the focus of the present analysis.

## The Amniocentesis Decision

A screening policy that offers amniocentesis to women above some age threshold reflects a societal perspective; it reflects the economic considerations of society at large. There remains a very important individual decision problem for every pregnant woman (or expectant couple). The decision whether or not to undergo amniocentesis can be very emotional, and reflects individual preferences for the various outcomes: normal fetus, spontaneous abortion, amniocentesis-induced abortion, and Down's syndrome fetus. The decision problem involves attitudes toward risk, regret, disappointment, and loss

**Figure 11-1**

*Risk of Down's Syndrome Births by Maternal Age*
*(per 1,000 live births)*

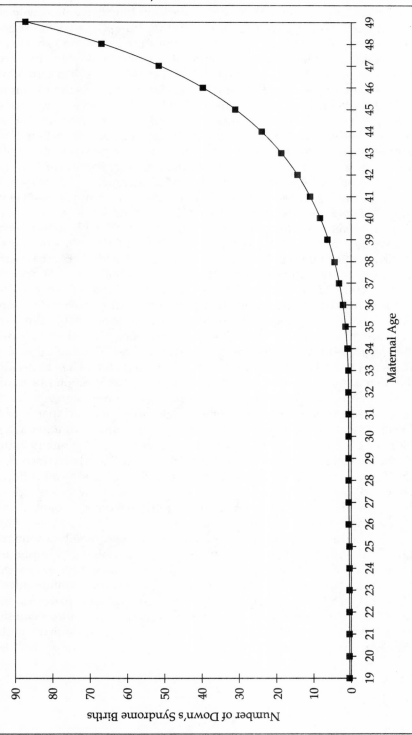

of opportunity. Individuals face this decision whether amniocentesis is available free of charge or for some payment.[4] (Cost simply becomes one of the many attributes in the problem.) One can easily envision that a couple with several healthy children would avoid any risk of having a Down's syndrome child, even if the risks of terminating a pregnancy would be huge. Conversely, a couple facing the same risk of a Down's syndrome fetus, but who had achieved pregnancy after many years of painful, expensive, and frustrating fertility treatments, may not want any added risk of a spontaneous abortion. The former couple would easily opt for an amniocentesis while the latter would refuse it (and risk a Down's syndrome child), regardless of whether society offers amniocentesis free of charge.

This paper focuses on the societal decision. In recent years, several biochemical factors have been found to correlate with Down's syndrome. Lower than normal levels of maternal serum alpha-fetoprotein (AFP) are correlated with a higher incidence of Down's syndrome, regardless of maternal age.[5] In Israel, the current Ministry of Health policy is to offer amniocentesis to any woman above age 35 and to women from 32 to 35 with a low AFP level.

Recently other tracers, including maternal serum levels of chorionic gonadotropin (HCG) and unconjugated oestriol (UE3), have also been found to correlate with Down's syndrome.[6] One blood sample suffices to test for all three tracers. Using the three biochemical measurements (AFP, HCG, UE3) in conjunction with maternal age to decide whether amniocentesis is appropriate increases the detection rate to 65 percent and reduces the number of unnecessary amniocenteses.[7]

The screening of older women can detect only about 40 percent of Down's syndrome cases, since most pregnancies are at younger ages. Figure 11-2 presents the distribution of deliveries in Israel in 1990 by maternal age. Israel's current policy, by which AFP levels are incorporated for women aged 32–35 and amniocentesis is offered to all women above 35, can only detect 54.6 percent of expected Down's syndrome cases, assuming that all women entering the screening program undergo amniocentesis if so recommended.

This study evaluates what combination of the three biochemical tests and maternal age should be used in determining whether to recommend amniocentesis. First, a decision-analytic approach is used to find an optimal risk threshold for providing free amniocentesis. Once this threshold is established, a cost-benefit analysis can determine the optimal combination of biochemical tests, and hence an optimal overall screening strategy. We assume that all fetuses with Down's syndrome are aborted.

**Figure 11-2**

*Distribution of Live Births in Israel by Maternal Age (1990)*

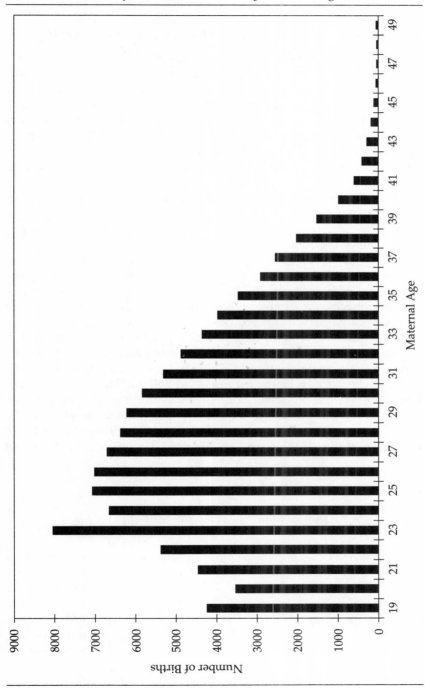

## Determining the Optimal Risk Threshold for Amniocentesis

We assume that a woman's age and levels of maternal serum markers will be used to determine whether her fetus is at "high risk" or "low risk" for Down's syndrome, and thus also determine if she will be offered free amniocentesis no matter what her age. The possible outcomes of this process are depicted in Table 11-1. We assume that there are no incremental costs for making a "right" decision; that is, that the consequences of not performing an amniocentesis in a normal pregnancy and those of performing one in an affected pregnancy imply no economic costs.

Our objective now is to minimize a loss function for the total costs of misclassification:

$$\min\{\text{expected loss}\} = \min\{\text{CFP} \times P(\text{FP}) + \text{CFN} \times P(\text{FN})\},$$

where $P(\text{FP})$ is the probability of a false positive; $P(\text{FN})$ is the probability of a false negative; CFP is the economic costs of a false positive screen (unnecessary amniocentesis); and CFN is the economic costs of a false negative screen (missed case of Down's syndrome).

An equivalent way to look at this problem is to find an optimal probability threshold. Women whose risk of carrying a Down's syndrome fetus exceeds this threshold will be offered amniocentesis, while women whose risk is below the threshold will not. Up to four parameters can affect the probability of Down's syndrome—the levels of the three biochemical markers and maternal age. These parameters can be considered as a vector $X = (\text{age, AFP, HCG, UE3})$, or perhaps of lesser dimension if not all three markers are used. Given a vector $X$ we can

**Table 11-1**

*Risk Classification versus Fetus State*

|  |  | Actual Fetus | |
| --- | --- | --- | --- |
|  |  | Down | Non-Down |
| Screening Result | High Risk (positive) | True Positive | False Positive |
|  | Low Risk (negative) | False Negative | True Negative |

**Figure 11-3**

*Decision-Analytic Approach to Determine Optimal Threshold*

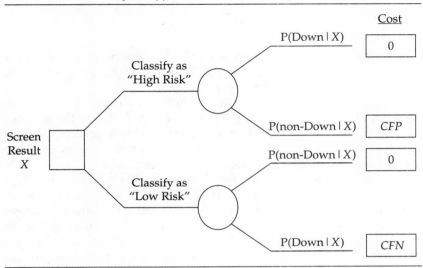

calculate a posterior probability of Down's syndrome, so in a sense we are looking for an optimal X. Figure 11-3 presents the decision problem facing the policy makers.

The optimal threshold, the probability of Down's syndrome that minimizes the above loss function, equalizes the expected costs of the two decision branches. This implies that

$$P(\text{non-Down}|X) \times \text{CFP} = P(\text{Down}|X) \times \text{CFN}.$$

Using Bayes's formula we obtain

$$\frac{P(\text{Down})}{P(\text{non-Down})} \times \frac{P(X|\text{Down})}{P(X|\text{non-Down})} = \frac{\text{CFP}}{\text{CFN}}.$$

The left side of the equation consists of the product of the ratio of prior probabilities (the odds for Down's syndrome) multiplied by the likelihood ratio. The right side is the cost ratio of misclassification. Hence, the optimal threshold is determined by the ratio of the cost of a false positive screen, which results in an unnecessary amniocentesis, to the cost of a false negative, which results in an undetected case of Down's syndrome.

For any vector X of test results, a woman will be referred for free amniocentesis only if her risk of Down's syndrome exceeds the cost ratio. To determine this ratio we must now calculate the various economic costs.

## Cost Calculation

Two economic cost elements are needed to determine the threshold for offering free amniocentesis: CFP, the costs of a false positive screen, and CFN, the cost of a false negative screen.

The cost of a false positive screen includes the cost of amniocentesis, an ultrasound to verify gestational age (to validate the findings of the biochemical tests), and an abortion (if a Down's syndrome fetus is detected) or a spontaneous abortion following amniocentesis. Since we are interested only in incremental costs beyond those that would be incurred if amniocentesis is not performed, we omit all costs except the amniocentesis procedure itself. Ultrasounds to determine gestational age are routinely performed for all pregnant women; the costs of terminating a pregnancy or of a spontaneous abortion are similar to the costs of a regular delivery. In Israel, the cost for an amniocentesis was calculated to be $477. This includes genetic counseling, administration, personnel and materials for the actual procedure, genetic analysis of the amniotic fluid, and a pathological consultation.[8]

The second component of the threshold ratio is the economic cost of an undetected case of Down's syndrome. It is the net discounted present value of the cost of caring for and raising a person with Down's syndrome for his or her lifetime, estimated at 35–47 years. It includes some direct medical costs and the costs of special education, rehabilitation, institutional as well as home care, and a sheltered work place. Studies assessing the costs of caring for the handicapped usually equate home care costs with those of institutional care to account for the opportunity costs of parents and siblings who engage in providing care.

In Israel, this cost averaged U.S. $154,266 (discount rate of 5 percent), with a range of $113,150 to $204,900. One study estimates this cost at $397,200.[9] Another study estimates lifetime costs of caring for people with various handicaps from $1,000,000 to $4,000,000 in the state of New York.[10]

Taking the calculated costs into account, for Israel the optimal amniocentesis threshold is CFP/CFN = $477/$154,266 = 1/323. If age alone is used to determine risk, we should offer amniocentesis to all women 36 and older.

If we perform a similar analysis for U.S. data, the threshold would be lower than 1/1,000; the costs of amniocentesis are only slightly higher than in Israel while the costs of a Down's syndrome child could

**Figure 11-4**
*Optimal Threshold versus Cost of Down's Syndrome Case*

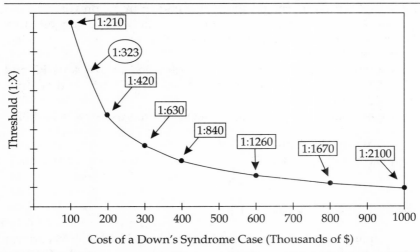

Cost of a Down's Syndrome Case (Thousands of $)

be much higher. This implies that amniocentesis should be offered much more often. Figure 11-4 shows the change in the optimal threshold as a function of the cost of a Down's syndrome case, holding the cost of amniocentesis constant at $477. A similar analysis can be performed for the costs of amniocentesis, which have an inverse effect on the cutoff ratio. (Doubling the costs of amniocentesis will halve the cutoff ratio.)

## Screening Strategies

Which biochemical tests should be performed? We consider all plausible combinations to determine which one, in combination with maternal age, will yield the largest net economic benefit.

With the advancement of pregnancy, the concentration of the biochemical variables in the maternal blood changes; therefore, the unit of measurement used for each parameter is multiples of the median (MOM) of normal levels for that gestational week. This enables a comparison of levels for different weeks of pregnancy and reduces variation among laboratories. When expressed in MOMs, the logarithmic levels of AFP and HCG are roughly normally distributed. There is no need for such a transformation for the UE3 levels expressed in MOMs. In addition, low levels of AFP, high levels of HCG, and low values of UE3 correlate with an increased risk of Down's syndrome. The three parameters are nearly independent. The joint distribution of any subset is multi-normal both for Down's syndrome pregnancies and normal pregnancies, and our calculations follow those suggested by Anderson.[11] The means and covariance matrix for the three parameters are independent of maternal age.

The cost of an AFP analysis was estimated at $16; an AFP and HCG, $24; an HCG and UE3, $23; an AFP and UE3, $27; and all three tests, $33.

We evaluate four screening strategies for the risk threshold 1:323.

1.  Age + AFP + HCG

2.  Age + HCG + UE3

3.  Age + AFP + UE3

4.  Age + AFP + HCG + UE3

We compare these to the current Ministry of Health policy: to perform the AFP test for women between the ages of 32 and 35, and refer them for amniocentesis if the AFP level is below 0.5 MOM, and also to refer all women 35 and older.

## Cost-Benefit Analysis

Costs of screening include the costs of obtaining the blood specimens, costs of analysis, costs of amniocentesis, and other related costs. The number of amniocenteses performed reflects the age distribution of the pregnant women and the joint distribution of the various biochemical parameters within each age group. The benefits (or savings) reflect the averted costs of caring for people with Down's syndrome. Table 11-2 shows each strategy's potential detection rate and rate of unnecessary amniocentesis (false positive rate). As can be clearly seen, Strategy 4, which uses all three biochemical parameters in conjunction with maternal age, outperforms every other strategy on both dimensions. It is clearly superior to the current practice in Israel. In fact, all four strategies considered dominate Israel's current policy. The reason for this dominance is the increased focusing of amniocentesis as a result of the screening. The various calculations take into account that the number of pregnancies that will enter screening exceeds the number of births by nearly 30 percent because of third trimester spontaneous abortions, many of which involve fetuses with various problems. We did not assume that screening will be offered to all pregnant women; rather, we incrementally analyzed each age group starting with older women.

**Table 11-2**

*Strategy Performance*

| Strategy | Detection Rate | False Positive Rate |
|---|---|---|
| 1. Age + AFP + HCG | 69.9% (121) | 10.1% (10,558) |
| 2. Age + HCG + UE3 | 70.9% (123) | 9.9% (10,391) |
| 3. Age + AFP + UE3 | 62.3% (108) | 10.8% (11,382) |
| 4. Age + AFP + HCG + UE3 | 73.7% (128) | 9.3% ( 9,824) |
| 5. Ministry of Health | 54.6% ( 95) | 15.3% (16,084) |

The numbers in parentheses represent the expected number of Down's syndrome cases detected in 1990 (for column 2), totaling 173; and the number of amniocenteses that would find an unaffected fetus (column 3), totaling 104,671 in 1990. For example, Strategy 4 can detect 128 out of 173 Down syndrome cases, and will result in 9,824 amniocenteses in a normal pregnancy.

We found that screening with even one biochemical marker is so valuable and cost-beneficial that it is justified for pregnant women of any age.

When turning to the economic aspects of each strategy, the dominance of the triple-test strategy is further enhanced. Table 11-3 presents the total costs, total savings, and net savings of each strategy assuming that all pregnant women are screened. Strategy 4 could save Israel about $11.5 million, more than double the potential savings of the current policy. It is interesting that the total screening costs of the Ministry of Health policy are larger than for any of the other strategies, even though less screening is performed. This is because amniocentesis is offered to all women above 35.

The triple test is clearly superior to all other screening strategies. It detects more cases of Down's syndrome, generates fewer false positives, and saves money. Rarely does one find such multi-attribute dominance.

Following the strong conclusions of this analysis, Israel's Ministry of Health is currently adopting the policy recommended here. The optimal strategy calls for offering the triple test *free of charge* to all pregnant women, regardless of age. The major health maintenance organizations are adopting a similar approach already, even though from their perspective, only direct medical costs that are averted as a result of screening are relevant.

## Discussion

Averting a case of Down's syndrome has more than economic benefits. The usually negative impact of a Down's syndrome child on the rest

**Table 11-3**
*Cost-Benefit Analysis (millions of 1992 U.S. dollars)*

| Strategy | Cost of Blood Tests | Cost of Amnio-centesis | Total Screening Costs | Total Cost Savings | Net Savings |
|----------|------|------|------|------|------|
| Age + AFP + HCG | 2.51 | 5.02 | 7.53 | 18.67 | 11.14 |
| Age + HCG + UE3 | 2.47 | 4.94 | 7.41 | 18.93 | 11.52 |
| Age + AFP + UE3 | 2.81 | 5.40 | 8.21 | 16.63 | 8.42 |
| Age + AFP + HCG + UE3 | 3.48 | 4.68 | 8.16 | 19.69 | 11.53 |
| Ministry of Health | 1.44 | 7.59 | 9.03 | 14.59 | 5.56 |

of the family, the psychological burdens, and the limitations on normal routines are all important and not quantifiable economically. The anxiety during pregnancy and testing, the burdens and possible guilt feelings following an abortion or terminations of pregnancy are also relevant, for each parent as well as society. It is generally accepted that the prevention of a Down's syndrome case involves many additional noneconomic benefits and hence any screening program can only warrant expansion.

Our analysis assumed that screening for the three blood markers only detects Down's syndrome. However, AFP testing reveals cases of neural tube defects, and amniocentesis can discover a variety of other chromosomal abnormalities. Thus, at the same cost of screening, individuals and society can reap additional benefits.

We did not assume that a couple will have a normal baby following the abortion of a Down's syndrome fetus. If the couple has another normal child, this can be viewed as a positive economic contribution to society, thus further enhancing the potential benefits of screening.

The cost-benefit calculations assumed that all pregnant women are screened, but in Israel only 60 to 70 percent actually come for screening. Noncompliance seems to be correlated with some ethnic backgrounds and with a high degree of Jewish observance, not with age. The incidence of Down's syndrome does not seem to vary significantly across ethnicities and degree of religious observance, so the net benefits should be proportional. The value of screening as expressed in detection rates and false positive rates in the screened populations will remain the same. Hence the analysis is valid for subsets of the population.

Another important issue not addressed by our analysis, which bears both on the individual choice and on social benefits, relates to actions following amniocentesis. In many societies, it is implicitly understood that a woman who agrees to undergo amniocentesis will end the pregnancy if a Down's syndrome fetus is detected. If this is not the case, then the screening costs remain the same, but the benefits of Down's syndrome prevention are diminished.

Our analysis suggests that if the biochemical tests reveal that there is less than a 1/323 chance that a fetus has Down's syndrome, the woman should not be offered free amniocentesis. Thus, women above 35 may find themselves denied free amniocentesis. Such a policy has been justified in the recent literature, but may face considerable political opposition; it is difficult to take away a public good that society has learned to take for granted. Thus, a new policy may continue to offer amniocentesis to women above 35, resulting in lower cost savings and more unnecessary amniocenteses.

The large-scale introduction of the biochemical blood screening of every pregnant woman has raised various ethical issues that are only partially addressed in the literature. Screening programs promote an exaggerated public awareness of the syndrome, beyond its proportional societal importance and burden. On the one hand, the public is being educated on the achievement potential of Down's syndrome children; on the other hand, prenatal screening programs to prevent the birth of these children are constantly being nationally promoted. (This double message is very confusing, and probably contributes to the underutilization of screening programs that many centers report.)

The ethical concerns raised by prenatal diagnosis include balancing the parental desire to produce the perfect offspring and the financial burden of the handicapped, with the view that increasing social tolerance for less perfect individuals is important, as is the moral commitment of the community to provide for the less fortunate. Thus, the question as to what should influence public health policy regarding prenatal screening programs cannot solely address economic issues and should not be detached from changing societal attitudes.

Another concern raised by screening for Down's syndrome is the general anxiety it causes. It is suggested that the test highlights the possibility, however small, that anyone may have an affected baby. This might be a cause for anxiety throughout the entire pregnancy. Even the best counseling cannot effectively meet this issue since it is difficult and often impossible for many people to understand how the concepts of risk and definitive diagnosis differ.

The fact that amniocentesis is associated with a risk of losing the pregnancy is another concern. A cutoff risk figure at the same level as the risk of the procedure is used for the medical recommendation of amniocentesis. However, anxiety often prompts women to choose amniocentesis when the risk of Down's syndrome is lower than the threshold but higher than expected for their age. No doubt, this significantly increases the loss of normal pregnancies and also, although to a lesser extent, increases the risk of maternal complications.

Therefore, a cost-benefit evaluation of the prenatal biochemical screening for Down's syndrome should not be the only basis for policy. Although it is very difficult to quantify the ethical and psychological issues, they should be considered in any analysis of a screening program.

## NOTES

1. B. F. Crandall et al., "Follow-up of 2000 Second Trimester Amniocenteses," *Obstetrics and Gynecology* 56 (1980): 625.
2. G. E. Palomaki and J. E. Haddow, "Maternal Serum Alpha-fetoprotein, Age, and Down Syndrome Risk," *American Journal of Obstetrics and Gynecology* 156 (1987): 460–463.
3. J. E. Haddow et al., "Reducing the Need for Amniocentesis in Women 35 Years of Age or Older with Serum Markers for Screening," *New England Journal of Medicine* 330 (1994): 1114–1118.
4. Susan P. Pauker and Stephen G. Pauker, "The Amniocentesis Decision: Ten Years of Decision Analytic Experience," in *Genetic Risk, Risk Perception, and Decision Making*, eds. G. Evers-Kiebooms et al. (New York: Alan R. Liss, 1987), pp. 151–169.
5. See H. S. Cuckle, N. J. Wald, and R. H. Lindenbaum, "Maternal Serum Alpha-Fetoprotein Measurement: A Screening Test for Down Syndrome," *Lancet* 1(1984): 926–929; and I. R. Merkatz et al., "An Association between Low Maternal Serum Alpha-Fetoprotein and Fetal Chromosomal Abnormalities," *American Journal of Obstetrics and Gynecology* 148 (1984): 886–894.
6. See M. H. Bogart, "Prospective Evaluation of Maternal Serum HCG Levels in 3428 Pregnancies," *American Journal of Obstetrics and Gynecology* 165 (1991): 663–667; J. A. Canick and G. J. Knight, "Low Second Trimester Maternal Serum Unconjugated Oestriol in Pregnancies with Down's Syndrome," *British Journal of Obstetrics and Gynaecology* 95 (1988): 330–333; and N. J. Wald et al., "Maternal Serum Screening for Down's Syndrome in Early Pregnancy," *British Medical Journal* 297 (1988): 883–887.
7. J. E. Haddow et al., "Prenatal Screening for Down's Syndrome with Use of Maternal Serum Markers," *New England Journal of Medicine* 327 (1992): 588–593.
8. All costs are in 1992 U.S. dollars.
9. S. H. Taplin and R. S. Tompson, "Cost-Justification Analysis of Prenatal Maternal Serum AFP Screening," *Medical Care* 26 (1988): 1185–1201.
10. S. L. Nolin and D. A. Snider, "Fragile X Screening Program in New York State," *American Journal of Medical Genetics* 38 (1991): 251–255.
11. T. W. Anderson, *An Introduction to Multivariate Statistical Analysis* (New York: Wiley, 1958), ch. 6.

CHAPTER 12

# EXPECTED VALUES OF INFORMATION AND COOPERATION FOR ABATING GLOBAL CLIMATE CHANGE

## James K. Hammitt

Activities as central to present human society as burning fossil fuels and clearing forests for rice paddies and livestock pastures may change the composition of the atmosphere, and with it the climate and sea level of the planet; this possibility is one of the most serious of environmental issues.[1] The sensitivity of the climate to human activities and the consequences of climatic change for society and the environment are highly uncertain, but a failure to limit climate change could be costly or even catastrophic. While some changes might be viewed as improvements, these would likely be offset by the cost of adapting to the new conditions; for example, some regions would need to replace water supply systems and others would need to develop new agricultural practices. Animals and unmanaged ecosystems might find adaptation more difficult. The costs to humans of adapting to a new climate and a rising sea could impose severe hardship. Particularly in developing nations, millions of people might lose their homes, raising the specter of environmental refugees and international disputes over fresh water and other environmental resources.[2]

I thank John Adams for assistance in model formulation and analysis; James Sebenius, Albert Nichols, and other colloquium participants for valuable comments; and NOAA and the Harvard Center for Risk Analysis for support. Above all, I thank Howard Raiffa for stimulating my interest in decision analysis and game theory, and for his intellectual guidance and warm support.

Yet actions to prevent or minimize global climate change could themselves be costly, disruptive, and potentially catastrophic. About 95 percent of the world's commercially produced energy comes from fossil fuels, the primary contributor to potential climate change.[3] The annual cost of limiting carbon dioxide ($CO_2$) emissions from fossil fuel combustion to its 1990 level through the next century has been estimated as 2 to 4 percent of the gross world economic product,[4] but stabilizing the climate is expected to require reducing emissions, not stabilizing them. Committing a large share of economic output to abating climate change could impede efforts to address numerous other important environmental and social problems.

Tremendous uncertainties surround the problem. First, we cannot predict the consequences of actions we might take. We do not know the effects of government regulation on economic activities and emissions of $CO_2$ and other greenhouse gases; how changing emissions would affect atmospheric composition; how a changing atmosphere would affect the speed of regional climate change; how climate change affects human activities, unmanaged ecosystems, and environmental conditions; or how we can adapt to climate change and what effects adaptation would have on anthropogenic emissions. These are "outcome" uncertainties. But even if by some miracle we could resolve these uncertainties, fundamental "value" uncertainties would remain: which of the many alternative outcomes should be chosen? How do we choose a level of environmental quality and economic consumption, their distribution across people and time, and the probability that they will occur? Uncertainties about social values or preferences limit our ability to evaluate tradeoffs among outcomes, and to decide how much we as a society are willing to alter our behavior to reduce the chance of various harms.

The problem would be hard enough if global cooperation could be assumed. In fact, climate change is a global "commons" problem:[5] greenhouse gases are well mixed in the global atmosphere and remain there for decades or centuries after they are released, so the effects of anthropogenic emissions do not depend on where an emission (or reduction in one) occurs, and within the time scale of human interest, scarcely depend on when. Any actions to abate climate change will be taken by autonomous agents: individuals, communities, firms, and national governments. Because most of the costs of abatement fall on those taking action, but others cannot be excluded from sharing the benefits, climate-change abatement is a public good and is likely to be underprovided, or provided inefficiently.[6]

Given the potential magnitude of the costs of climate change and of policies to avert it, the staggering uncertainties about virtually every important factor in the problem, and the public-good nature of abatement, it is hard to determine what levels of abatement, promotion of international cooperation, and climate research are desirable. Consequently, climate change appears to be fertile ground for the application of two fields to which Howard Raiffa has made seminal contributions: decision analysis and game theory. In this paper, tools from these fields are used to generate insight into the merits of alternative actions. For simplicity, the climate problem is framed as a two-period game of incomplete information between the industrialized and developing nations. Each region chooses a first-period abatement policy, expecting to revise it for the second period when new information about outcomes and values is obtained. The environmental and economic consequences of alternative choices are simulated using a numerical integrated-assessment model.

Some perspective on the relative importance of uncertainty and the lack of a unified decision maker may be obtained by comparing the expected values of information and of cooperation. The expected value of information is defined as the difference in expected costs between cases where the values of important parameters are more or less certain. The expected value of cooperation is defined as the expected cost difference between game solutions in which the regions do not and do cooperate. Each value depends upon the other. Illustrative calculations of these values and their mutual dependence are reported herein. Such information may help policy makers determine the emphasis to place on international negotiation and scientific research.

## A Two-Region Abatement Game

This section explains the model used to simulate international actions on greenhouse gas abatement. The first subsection lays out the analytical framework; the second specifies the values used in the model, and how they were determined.

### Analytic Structure

The analysis is structured as a two-period, two-party game of incomplete information. In the first period (1990–2010), the North (industrialized nations) and the South (developing nations) each select an abatement policy. At the beginning of the second period (2010), it is assumed that all uncertainties about climate change are resolved and the two regions will have negotiated an agreement that limits climate change to an acceptable level and allocates abatement costs between them in accordance with an agreed "burden-sharing rule." Each region attempts to minimize its own costs of limiting climate change to the acceptable level.

The assumptions of perfect information and an international agreement by 2010, and the existence of only two agents, are clearly oversimplifications. The perfect-information assumption provides terminal conditions for a problem that has an indefinite planning horizon. The calculated costs from the beginning of the second period, conditional on first-period actions, may be viewed as approximations to the optimal-value function, the expected cost assuming optimal action (under uncertainty) thereafter. In contrast to a more realistic assumption of continuing uncertainty, second-period perfect information will reduce the expected value of information. The assumption that international agreement is reached by 2010 allows a comparison of abatement costs if cooperative abatement begins sooner rather than later; in fact, regions might never cooperate. This optimistic assumption biases the expected value of cooperation downward, since the losses from a failure to cooperate can accumulate for only 20 years. Limiting the game to two agents also biases the value of cooperation downward; at least one must receive a large share of the global benefits of first-period abatement, and so the noncooperative solution will be closer to the cooperative solution than it might be with a larger number of parties.

In the first period, both the level of climate change that will be judged acceptable and the burden-sharing rule are uncertain. These are determined in part by the negotiation leading to second-period agreement, but for this analysis they are assumed to be exogenous; information about them is represented by a prior probability distribution.[7] The prior distribution is assumed to be common knowledge; it is known to each region, known to be known to each region, and so on. In fact, much of the information about climate change, its consequences for various regions, abatement opportunities, and even historical factors that may affect the allocation of future costs is scientific information that is routinely made available. Significant efforts are made to ensure that all parties have access to the best available information through programs such as the periodic Intergovernmental Panel on Climate Change (IPCC) reports.[8]

The expected present value of each region's abatement costs as a function of its first-period actions is summarized by a payoff matrix. The cooperative solution is the first-period strategy pair that minimizes global abatement costs. A noncooperative solution is a pure-strategy Nash equilibrium, that is, a pair of regional strategies such that neither region can unilaterally improve its expected payoff if the other does not change its action. The game may have zero, one, or more such equilibria. If a unique Nash equilibrium exists, it defines each region's

**Figure 12-1**
*Costs to North and South for a Hypothetical Game*

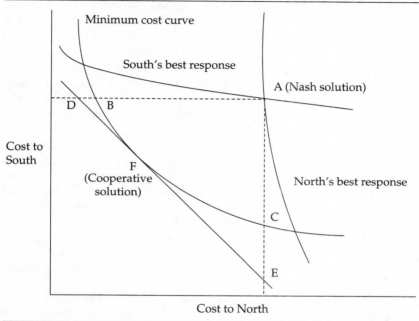

Minimum cost curve

South's best response

A (Nash solution)

D    B

Cost to
South

F
(Cooperative
solution)

North's best response

C

E

Cost to North

reservation price for a negotiated solution, since either region can withdraw from negotiations and bear the expected costs associated with the Nash outcome (unless the other region is willing to worsen its own outcome to inflict punishment). Mixed-strategy equilibria are not considered here; it does not seem plausible that a region or nation could effectively randomize its strategy.

Regional abatement costs are illustrated in Figure 12-1. The best-response functions describe each region's best action conditional on the other region's choice; their intersection (if any) is a pure-strategy Nash solution. Reflecting the public-good nature of abatement, the Nash solution A may not be Pareto-efficient; both regions' welfare would be improved if they could move from A to any point further left and down. The minimum-cost curve represents the abatement-possibility frontier, and the sector B–C the efficient bargaining range (that is, the set of efficient outcomes that are Pareto-superior to the Nash solution). The regions can reach any point in the bargaining range by coordinated first-period actions; the North could gain between zero and A–B from cooperation, and the South could gain between zero and A–C.

If the regions can make side payments through direct aid, allocation of tradable emission permits, or other mechanisms, the feasible set of cooperative outcomes can be improved. The sum of the regions' costs is minimized at F, where the slope of the minimum-cost curve is $-1$. If costs can be compensated without loss, all points on the tangent at F can be achieved by coordinating abatement actions to achieve F and making side payments between regions as appropriate. To obtain an allocation between F and E, the North would transfer resources to the South; to achieve an outcome between F and D, the transfer would be reversed.[9] If side payments are feasible, the efficient solutions are described by D–E and the possible gains from cooperation extend from zero to A–D for the North and zero to A–E for the South.

How regions expect emissions and abatement costs to be allocated in the second period significantly guide their first-period strategies; the share of second-period emissions a region expects to be permitted determines the extent to which it captures the benefit of any abatement it undertakes in the first period. A region that expects the other to absorb all the second-period abatement costs has no incentive to reduce its emissions in the first period; a region that expects to bear all the second-period costs will efficiently balance its abatement activities between periods.

Two equally probable rules for allocating second-period emissions are considered: the least-cost rule, under which the second-period actions that minimize global abatement costs are adopted, and an equal-rate rule, under which the regions reduce their emissions by equal percentages at all subsequent dates, an outcome that may serve as a focal point in negotiations.[10] Alternative burden-sharing rules that relate emission reductions to regional emissions per capita, emissions per unit output, or other factors could also be considered.[11]

*Integrated-Assessment Model*

Abatement costs are simulated using a regionally disaggregated version of a model that simulates globally aggregated emissions of $CO_2$ and other important greenhouse gases, atmospheric composition, an index of climate change, and abatement costs. Annual global emissions are modeled as the sum of regional emissions. A region can reduce its emissions by either of two types of activities, "energy conservation" and "fuel switching."[12]

"Energy conservation" is relatively inexpensive, quickly implemented, and limited in scope. It requires 20 years for full implementation and reduces emissions by 20 percent. Costs are incurred in the year of operation and are proportional to the emission reduction.

**Table 12-1**

*Cost Parameters ($/ton of avoided carbon emissions)*

| Abatement Technology | North | South |
|---|---|---|
| Conservation | 0 | 52 |
| Low-cost fuel switching (first 50%) | 320 | 130 |
| High-cost fuel switching (last 50%) | 999 | 570 |

Further reductions require "fuel switching," which is more expensive and more slowly implemented. Cost and effectiveness are simulated assuming that all emissions are produced by durable equipment (such as electric generating plants and automobiles) using either emitting (fossil fuel) or non-emitting (nuclear, solar, biomass) technologies; for both technologies, construction and operating periods are 10 and 30 years, respectively. Each region chooses the rate at which it substitutes non-emitting for fossil-fueled capital, eventually achieving complete substitution. To reflect different degrees of substitutability among applications, the marginal cost of substituting for the first 50 percent of fossil-fueled capital is smaller than the cost for the second 50 percent.

Emission and cost parameters are obtained by calibrating model outputs for each region to results of an energy-economy model.[13] Because of the assumed more rapid economic growth in the developing countries, unabated emissions grow much faster in the South than in the North. Between 1990 and 2100, $CO_2$ emissions from the North double from 4.2 to 8.4 billion metric tons (carbon weight) per year, but grow almost 10-fold from 1.6 to 15.1 billion metric tons per year in the South.[14]

Cost parameters are reported in Table 12-1. The costs of conservation are lower in the North than the South, but the costs of fuel switching are lower in the South. This suggests that the North is the least-cost emission avoider in the near term, when conservation is the only mechanism with significant effect, and the South is the least-cost avoider over the longer term, when conservation opportunities are saturated and incremental reductions are achieved by fuel switching. Although uncertain, regional differences in abatement costs are important determinants of abatement-game payoffs and solutions.

The effects of anthropogenic emissions on the atmosphere and climate are simulated using simple physical-science models that are calibrated to results of more complex models. Atmospheric greenhouse gas concentrations are represented using an equation that describes the removal of atmospheric $CO_2$ to the ocean as calculated by a model of ocean circulation.[15]

Climate change is measured by the difference between the global annual mean surface temperature in year $t$ and its pre-industrial value, $\Delta T(t)$. Although the effects of climate change will depend on regional and seasonal changes in temperature, precipitation, wind, and other factors, their magnitudes are likely to correlate with $\Delta T$.[16] $\Delta T(t)$ is simulated using a model that simulates the energy-absorbing properties of atmospheric greenhouse gases and heat transfer to the deep ocean.[17] Uncertainties about climate change are represented by alternative values of the climate sensitivity parameter $\Delta T_{2x}$, defined as the equilibrium $\Delta T$ accompanying a doubling of atmospheric $CO_2$ (from pre-industrial levels). The IPCC suggests that $\Delta T_{2x}$ is between 1.5 and 4.5° C, with a "best estimate" of 2.5° C.[18]

The "acceptable level" of climate change is represented by the climate target $\Delta T^*$, where it is assumed that all time paths of $\Delta T(t)$ with the same maximum value produce equivalent damages. Although clearly an oversimplification, because lags due to capital replacement, atmospheric residence times, and thermal inertia damp the effects of rapid changes in policy on the evolution of $\Delta T(t)$, differences in the timing of climate impacts among scenarios with the same peak are small.[19] The climate target may be motivated by an "acceptable risk" concept: because so little is known about the consequences of climatic change, a limit is set beyond which the risk of serious damages is judged to become too great or to increase sharply. Such a limit is consistent with the 1992 Framework Convention on Climate Change, which commits signatories to the "stabilization of greenhouse gas concentrations at a level which would prevent dangerous anthropogenic interference with the climate system."[20] Several groups have attempted to define climate targets specifying maximum acceptable magnitudes or rates of global average change based on the adaptability of natural ecosystems, the land area that might be lost to a rise in the sea level, and similar factors.[21]

The climate target $\Delta T^*$ and climate sensitivity $\Delta T_{2x}$, together with the requirement that $\Delta T(t)$ does not exceed $\Delta T^*$, constrain allowable emissions. Because the emission constraint is monotonically related to $\Delta T^*/\Delta T_{2x}$, the effect on policy choice of uncertainties in both parameters can be represented by fixing $\Delta T_{2x}$ at 2.5° C and representing the uncertainty about climate change and its consequences by a judgmental distribution on $\Delta T^*$. For this analysis, each of three possible values of $\Delta T^*$, 1.5, 2.0, and 2.5° C, are assigned equal probability (independent of the burden-sharing rule). The lowest value is near the upper end of the 1.0–1.6° C range suggested at the Bellagio and Villach meetings of the World Meteorological Organization/United Nations Environment Programme Climate Impacts Panel;[22] values much smaller than this cannot be achieved with this model because capital replacement constrains the rate at which emissions can be reduced. The upper value was proposed by Florentin Krause et al., and the middle value is simply the midpoint of the range.[23]

## Simulated Game Results

Each region is allowed to choose from the six first-period strategies specified in Table 12-2. The strategies are numbered from least to most stringent; Strategy 1 entails minimal abatement. In the second period, the climate target and burden-sharing rule become known and regional emissions are determined to satisfy the burden-sharing rule and the requirement that $\Delta T(t)$ never exceeds the climate target.

The payoff matrix is presented in Figure 12-2. The cooperative solution, which minimizes expected global abatement costs, requires North to adopt Strategy 3 and South to adopt Strategy 2; this solution is described by the ordered pair [3, 2]. Expected abatement costs, reported as annualized values over the period 1990–2100 at a 5 percent discount rate, are $120 billion per year for the North and $130 billion per year for the South, totaling $250 billion per year globally.

The Nash solution occurs at the intersection of the best-response functions. North's best action is Strategy 1 or 3, depending on South's choice. Both strategies include the slowest fuel-switching rate (50 percent substitution after 140 years), but differ in whether or not North

### Table 12-2
*Available First-Period Strategies*

| Strategy | Initiate Conservation? | Fuel-Switching Rate* |
|---|---|---|
| 1 | No | 140 |
| 2 | No | 100 |
| 3 | Yes | 140 |
| 4 | Yes | 100 |
| 5 | Yes | 40 |
| 6 | Yes | 20 |

*Years from initiation to 50% completion

**Figure 12-2**
*Payoff Matrix for Uncertain Climate Target and Burden-Sharing Rule*

| South's strategy | | | | | | | | |
|---|---|---|---|---|---|---|---|---|
| 6 | N | 67 | 73 | 70 | 75 | 137 | 583 |
|   | S | 330 | 328 | 328 | 327 | 315 | 308 |
| 5 | N | 98 | 109 | 99 | 106 | 162 | 598 |
|   | S | 172 | 164 | 163 | 159 | 145 | 102 |
| 4 | N | 113 | 123 | 115 | 118 | 191 | 627 |
|   | S | 157 | 153 | 150 | 148 | 125 | 82 |
| 3 | N | 121 | 132 | 119 | 129 | 196 | 635 |
|   | S | 151 | 146 | 145 | 142 | 125 | 80 |
| 2 | N | 122 | 130 | *120* | 129 | 190 | 628 |
|   | S | 136 | 132 | *130* | 126 | 110 | 62 |
| 1 | N | 132 | 141 | 126 | 136 | 199 | 636 |
|   | S | 129 | 126 | 125 | 121 | 106 | 61 |
|   |   | 1 | 2 | 3 | 4 | 5 | 6 |

North's strategy

Notes: Regional abatement costs in $billion/yr.
    Best-response functions and Nash solution in **bold**.
    Cooperative solution *centered in italics*.

begins conservation. It is in North's interest to begin conservation in the first period (Strategy 3) only if South selects one of its three least stringent actions. South's Strategy 1 is dominant—it is the South's best response to any of North's choices. The Nash solution is [3, 1], at which the expected global abatement costs are $252 billion per year. The expected benefit of cooperating in the first period is $2.2 billion per year, or 1 percent of the expected cost of the cooperative solution.

The expected values of perfect information and of cooperation can be defined globally or regionally. The global values define the possible gains, while the regional values provide information about the regions' incentives to support research or cooperation. Since information about climate change is freely shared, it may be most useful to evaluate its value globally; even if the regions cannot cooperate on abatement, they may cooperate on climate-change research. Global and regional expected values of information and of cooperation are evaluated in the following subsections.

## Global Values of Information and Cooperation

The global expected value of perfect information is the expected sum of regional abatement-cost savings that could be obtained if the burden-sharing rule and climate target were known before players selected their first-period actions (so they could select the optimal actions); the expectation is taken with respect to the prior distribution for these parameters. The expected value of information depends on whether or not the regions cooperate in the first period; it is $14.8 billion per year at the cooperative solution and $4.7 billion per year at the Nash solution, 6 percent and 2 percent of the expected costs without additional information, respectively.

The value of information can also be evaluated for each of the parameters. First, consider the expected value of information about $\Delta T^*$ if the regions were to agree in advance on the principle governing the allocation of second-period abatement efforts.[24] How would such an agreement affect the expected value of information about $\Delta T^*$?

The value of information about $\Delta T^*$ depends on which burden-sharing rule is selected. If the regions agree in advance to the least-cost rule, thereby minimizing global abatement costs in the second period (and using side payments to achieve any desired cost allocation), the payoff matrix would be as presented in Figure 12-3. In this case, the cooperative and Nash solutions coincide at the strategy pair [3, 1], so there is no value to first-period cooperation. Expected global costs are $238 billion per year, 5 percent or $12 billion per year less than in the original game. This reflects the exclusion of outcomes using the less efficient equal-rate rule. The expected value of perfect information about $\Delta T^*$ is $7 billion per year if the regions cooperate in the first period and $6.3 billion per year if they do not. (The expected value of information differs because the cooperative and Nash solutions to some of the games that would result if the value of $\Delta T^*$ were known are different.)

If the regions agree in advance to the equal-rate rule, expected costs are given by the matrix in Figure 12-4. The cooperative solution is [3, 2] as in the original game, but the expected global costs are $259 billion per year, 4 percent or $9 billion per year higher than in the original game, because the least-cost second-period allocations have been precluded. At the Nash solution [1, 1], neither region undertakes more than minimal abatement and the expected global costs are $269 billion per year, 4 percent or $10 billion per year higher than at the cooperative solution. The expected value of perfect information about $\Delta T^*$ is $20.7 billion per year if the regions cooperate and $6.7 billion per year if they do not.

**Figure 12-3**
*Payoff Matrix for Uncertain Climate Target
and Least-Cost Burden-Sharing Rule*

| South's strategy | | | 1 | 2 | 3 | 4 | 5 | 6 |
|---|---|---|---|---|---|---|---|---|
| | 6 | N | **79** | 84 | 81 | 83 | 142 | 583 |
| | | S | 308 | 309 | 309 | 311 | 308 | 308 |
| | 5 | N | **95** | 108 | 98 | 103 | 140 | 583 |
| | | S | 172 | 163 | 162 | 161 | 159 | 104 |
| | 4 | N | 87 | 91 | 87 | **84** | 143 | 583 |
| | | S | 175 | 172 | 168 | 170 | 148 | 87 |
| | 3 | N | 91 | 99 | **89** | 92 | 139 | 583 |
| | | S | 168 | 165 | 165 | 162 | 150 | 86 |
| | 2 | N | 95 | 99 | **92** | 96 | 136 | 583 |
| | | S | 152 | 151 | 147 | 144 | 137 | 68 |
| | 1 | N | 107 | 109 | *95* | 102 | 139 | 583 |
| | | S | **145** | **142** | *143* | **140** | **132** | **67** |
| | | | 1 | 2 | 3 | 4 | 5 | 6 |
| | | | | | North's strategy | | | |

Notes: Regional abatement costs in $billion/yr.
Best-response functions and Nash solution in **bold**.
Cooperative solution *centered in italics*.

The expected values of cooperation and of information for these games are summarized in Table 12-3. Results are also shown for the games where uncertainty about only the climate target is resolved ex ante, and the games where all uncertainties are resolved in advance.

The expected value of information at the cooperative solution is greater than or equal to its value at the Nash outcome, except when $\Delta T^* = 1.5°$ C and the allocation rule is uncertain. For both cooperative and Nash cases, if regions agree on an allocation rule in advance, the expected value of information about $\Delta T^*$ is greater if they adopt the equal-rate rule. If uncertainty about the climate target is eliminated, the expected value of information about the allocation rule is zero except for $\Delta T^* = 1.5°$ C. For $\Delta T^* = 2.5°$ C, the value of information about the allocation rule and the value of cooperation are both zero, because the cooperative and Nash solutions coincide and do not depend on the allocation rule.

These results suggest that the value of information is likely to

**Figure 12-4**

*Payoff Matrix for Uncertain Climate Target*
*and Equal-Rate Burden-Sharing Rule*

| South's strategy | | | 1 | 2 | 3 | 4 | 5 | 6 |
|---|---|---|---|---|---|---|---|---|
| 6 | N | | **55** | 61 | 59 | 67 | 132 | 583 |
| | S | | 352 | 346 | 347 | 342 | 321 | 308 |
| 5 | N | | 101 | 109 | **99** | 109 | 185 | 612 |
| | S | | 171 | 164 | 164 | 157 | 130 | 100 |
| 4 | N | | **140** | 155 | 142 | 152 | 239 | 672 |
| | S | | 139 | 134 | 132 | 126 | 102 | 77 |
| 3 | N | | 151 | 164 | **149** | 165 | 253 | 686 |
| | S | | 133 | 128 | 126 | 122 | 99 | 74 |
| 2 | N | | 148 | 160 | *147* | 161 | 245 | 674 |
| | S | | 121 | 114 | *113* | 108 | 83 | 55 |
| 1 | N | | **156** | 172 | 158 | 170 | 258 | 689 |
| | S | | **113** | **109** | **108** | **102** | 79 | 54 |

North's strategy

Notes: Regional abatement costs in $billion/yr.
Best-response functions and Nash solution in **bold**.
Cooperative solution *centered in italics*.

exceed the value of cooperation. Moreover, the regions usually benefit more from reducing uncertainty when they coordinate their actions than when they do not. Information is more valuable for the equal-rate than for the least-cost allocation rule, because the least-cost rule provides greater flexibility in adapting second-period emissions to limit abatement costs when the climate target is more stringent than expected. The expected value of information about the allocation rule is largest for the most stringent climate target, because this target is relatively costly to achieve and abatement costs are more sensitive to first-period actions than they are with laxer targets.

Similarly, the expected value of cooperation depends on information about the climate target and rule. With uncertainty about the burden-sharing rule, the expected value of cooperation is much larger for $\Delta T^* = 1.5°$ C ($37 billion per year) than for either of the two less restrictive targets. With uncertainty about the burden-sharing rule resolved as well, the value of cooperation is $69 billion per year (15

**Table 12-3**

Global Expected Values of Cooperation and Information

| Prior Information | | Cooperative Solution | | Nash Solution | | | Expected Value of Information | |
| Burden-sharing rule | ΔT* (°C) | Solution [N, S] | Expected global costs ($b/yr) | Solution [N, S] | Expected global costs ($b/yr) | Expected value of cooperation ($b/yr) | Cooperative solution ($b/yr) | Non-cooperative solution ($b/yr) |
|---|---|---|---|---|---|---|---|---|
| Uncertain | Uncertain | [3, 2] | 250 | [3, 1] | 252 . | 2.2 | 14.8 | 4.7 |
| Least-cost | Uncertain | [3, 1] | 238 | [3, 1] | 238 . | 0 | 7 | 6.3 |
| Equal-rate | Uncertain | [3, 2] | 259 | [1, 1] | 269 . | 10 | 20.7 | 6.7 |
| Uncertain | 1.5 | [3, 5] | 445 | [3, 1] | 482 . | 37 | 2.5 | 4 |
| Uncertain | 2.0 | [1, 2] | 174 | [1, 1] | 175 . | 1.5 | 0. | 0 |
| Uncertain | 2.5 | [1, 1] | 88.5 | [1, 1] | 88.5 . | 0 | 0. | 0 |
| Least-cost | 1.5 | [5, 1] | 438 | [5, 5] | 440 . | 2 | na | na |
| Least-cost | 2.0 | [1, 1] | 169 | [1, 2] | 169 . | 0 | na | na |
| Least-cost | 2.5 | [1, 1] | 85 | [1, 1] | 85. | 0 | na | na |
| Equal-rate | 1.5 | [3, 5] | 446 | [3, 1] | 515 . | 69 | na | na |
| Equal-rate | 2.0 | [1, 2] | 178 | [1, 1] | 181 . | 3 | na | na |
| Equal-rate | 2.5 | [1, 1] | 92 | [1, 1] | 92. | 0 | na | na |

Note: Uncertain prior information denotes uniform prior on alternative burden-sharing rules and values of ΔT*. na = not applicable.

percent of cooperative costs) under the equal-rate rule, but only $2 billion per year under the least-cost rule. The large discrepancy results because the least-cost rule provides flexibility to reduce second-period costs. Under the equal-rate rule, the South undertakes much less first-period abatement at the Nash solution [3, 1] than at the cooperative solution [3, 5], which requires more rapid and costly abatement by both regions in the second period. In contrast, although the Nash and cooperative solutions to the game with the least-cost rule also differ substantially ([5, 5] and [5, 1], respectively), the cost consequences are much smaller since the second-period abatement is allocated quite differently between the two solutions.

### Regional Values of Information and Cooperation

The regional expected values of cooperation and of information are reported in Table 12-4. Although the world always benefits from more information and cooperation, a region may suffer. For the game with uncertainty about both the allocation rule and the climate target, the expected values of cooperation and of information to the North are positive, but the expected values to the South of cooperation and (if the regions cooperate) of information are both negative. This suggests that South would be unwilling to participate in cooperative abatement and research without compensation. This pattern of expected benefits to North and costs to South is common to most of the games where either the burden-sharing rule or the climate target is known. The pattern seems to reflect a greater sensitivity of strategy and costs to first-period information for South than for North.

For example, consider the regional expected value of cooperation, $6.8 billion per year to North and −$4.7 billion per year to South. Shifting from the Nash to the cooperative solution requires South to substitute Strategy 2 for Strategy 1, increasing its first-period costs; North adopts Strategy 3 in both cases. The increase in global first-period abatement allows modest joint cost savings in the second period, but the net effect is an increase in South's expected costs and a decrease in North's. For cooperation to constitute a Pareto improvement, North would need to compensate South between $4.7 billion per year and $6.8 billion per year (about 5 percent of each region's costs).

The expected values of information depend on whether or not the regions cooperate. If they do cooperate in the first period, the expected value of perfect information about the allocation rule and climate target is $21 billion per year for North and −$6.2 billion per year for South; if not, the expected value of information is positive for both regions ($3.2 and $1.5 billion per year for North and South, respectively). If either the allocation rule or climate target is known, the expected value

**Table 12-4**

Regional Expected Values of Cooperation and Information

| Prior Information | | Expected Value of Cooperation ($b/yr) | | Expected Value of Information ($b/yr) | | | |
| --- | --- | --- | --- | --- | --- | --- | --- |
| | | | | With cooperation | | Without cooperation | |
| Burden-sharing rule | ΔT* (°C) | North | South | North | South | North | South |
| Uncertain | Uncertain | 6.8 | -4.7 | 21 | -6.2 | 3.2 | 1.5 |
| Least-cost | Uncertain | 0 | 0 | 8.7 | -1.7 | 2 | 4.3 |
| Equal-rate | Uncertain | 9.3 | 0.7 | 35.7 | -15 | 2.3 | 4.3 |
| Uncertain | 1.5 | 55 | -18 | 9.5 | -7 | -3 | 7 |
| Uncertain | 2.0 | 2.5 | -1 | 2 | -2 | -2 | 2 |
| Uncertain | 2.5 | 0 | 0 | 0 | -0 | 0 | 0 |

Note: Uncertain prior information denotes uniform prior on alternative burden-sharing rules and values of ΔT*.

of information about the other parameter remains positive for North and negative for South if the regions cooperate; if they do not, the value of information is positive for South and may be positive or negative for North.

The pattern of regional expected-information values is due in part to the solutions and abatement costs for the games $\Delta T^* = 1.5°$ C. Consider the case where the regions agree to the equal-rate rule in advance, for which the expected value of information with cooperation is greatest for North and smallest for South. If they learn in advance that $\Delta T^* = 1.5°$ C, the regions shift to [3, 5] from the cooperative solution with uncertainty about $\Delta T^*$, [3, 2]. This shift has a large effect on regional costs, reducing North's costs (conditional on $\Delta T^* = 1.5°$ C) by $95 billion per year (because its second-period abatement actions and costs are more limited) and increasing South's costs by $45 billion per year (because its first-period costs are substantially increased). This case contributes a large part of the expected value of information; the effects on regional costs of learning in advance that $\Delta T^* = 2.0$ or $2.5°$ C are much smaller. In contrast, if the regions do not cooperate, they shift from [1, 1] to [3, 1] on learning that $\Delta T^* = 1.5°$ C. In this case, North's costs decrease $7 billion per year and South's costs decrease $13 billion per year. As a result, the expected value of information is more equal for the two regions under the Nash solution.

The regional expected values of information and cooperation suggest that cooperation on research or abatement might require North to compensate South. In principle, such compensation could be readily incorporated into any agreement on emission limitations through the allocation of tradable emission permits, financial aid, technical assistance, or other means. The positive expected values of information and cooperation for North are consistent with the larger investment in climate research and the greater expressed willingness to undertake abatement in the industrialized than developing countries, although differences in wealth and scientific resources may be more important.

## Conclusions

Decision analysis and game theory provide a framework for formulating and evaluating policy on global climate change. In addition to evaluating the merits of abatement policies, information about the expected value of information and the expected value of cooperation can help policy makers determine the appropriate allocation of resources to research and diplomacy.

In this illustration, the expected value of information about climatic change and its consequences is larger than the expected cost savings that may be achieved by near-term coordination of abatement policies. The expected value of information is usually greater when the regions cooperate on abatement than when they do not. However, the expected value of information about climate is greater when the regions use the inefficient equal-rate allocation rule.

These results may depend on the limited scope of uncertainties, the small number of abatement strategies, and the specification of the integrated-assessment model. An especially important limitation may be the assumption that the regions cooperate in the second period and achieve the climate target. As discussed above, several of the major simplifying assumptions are likely to bias the expected values of information and of cooperation downward; their effect on the relative magnitudes of these quantities is unclear. Despite these limitations, the analysis suggests some insights that may hold for a broader set of cases. For example, the higher value of information when regions cooperate may be fairly general, although one can imagine that exceptions may arise.

An important issue that is not addressed here is whether improved information about exogenous factors stimulates or deters cooperation. It is often argued that agreement, at least on a distributive principle, may be more readily achieved when the parties do not know the precise effects on their own situations. For example, Rawls's theory of justice is motivated by a consideration of the agreements individuals would make behind a "veil of ignorance," before knowing their positions in society.[25] Alternatively, information suggesting that the consequences of climate change will be extremely harmful could stimulate nations to cooperate on abatement, as when a common military or other threat promotes alliance among those threatened. Information suggesting that climate change is not a serious threat could allow nations to reallocate resources to more urgent matters.

Although the present application uses an extremely simplified representation of the climate-policy problem, the tools illustrated can be applied to a much richer integrated-assessment model. In that setting, they may prove useful for evaluating the relative merits of investigating the processes linking human behavior and climatic change and promoting international cooperation.

## NOTES

1. U.S. Environmental Protection Agency, Science Advisory Board, *Reducing Risk: Setting Priorities and Strategies for Environmental Protection* (Washington, DC: U.S. Environmental Protection Agency, 1990).
2. See Stephen H. Schneider, *Global Warming: Are We Entering the Greenhouse*

*Century?* (San Francisco: Sierra Club Books, 1989); and Michael Oppenheimer and Robert H. Boyle, *Dead Heat: The Race Against the Greenhouse Effect* (New York: Basic Books, 1990).

3. World Resources Institute, *World Resources 1990–1991* (Oxford: Oxford University Press, 1990).

4. Alan S. Manne and Richard G. Richels, *Buying Greenhouse Insurance: The Economic Costs of Carbon Dioxide Emission Limits* (Cambridge, MA: MIT Press, 1992).

5. See Garrett Hardin, "The Tragedy of the Commons," *Science* 162 (1968): 1243–1248.

6. See Mancur Olson, Jr., and Richard J. Zeckhauser, "The Efficient Production of External Economies," *American Economic Review* 60 (1970): 512–517.

7. The outcome of the negotiation is uncertain for each player ex ante, and the representation of this uncertainty by a prior distribution accords with the asymmetrically descriptive/prescriptive approach to negotiation analysis described in Howard Raiffa, *The Art and Science of Negotiation* (Cambridge, MA: Harvard University Press, 1982).

8. For example, see John T. Houghton, Geoffrey J. Jenkins, and James J. Ephraums, eds., *Climate Change: The IPCC Scientific Assessment* (Cambridge: Cambridge University Press, 1990); and John T. Houghton, Bruce A. Callander, and Shelagh K. Varney, eds., *Climate Change 1992: The Supplementary Report to the IPCC Scientific Assessment* (Cambridge: Cambridge University Press, 1992).

9. Note that the cooperative solution F may lie outside the range B–C; if so, all the points on the tangent that dominate the Nash solution require side payments in one direction.

10. The Montreal Protocol, which restricts the consumption of compounds that may destroy stratospheric ozone, uses an equal-rate rule to allocate reductions within groups of countries. In the present analysis, percentage reductions are approximately but not exactly equal when only one region begins "conservation," described below, in the first period.

11. See Michael Grubb et al., "Burden Sharing," in *Confronting Climate Change: Risks, Implications and Responses,* ed. Irving Mintzer (Cambridge: Cambridge University Press, 1992); and Michael Hoel, "Efficient International Agreements for Reducing Emissions of $CO_2$," *Energy Journal* 12 (1991): 93–107.

12. Additional detail is provided in James K. Hammitt and John L. Adams, "The Value of International Coordination in Abating Climate Change," in *Reducing Carbon Dioxide Emissions: Costs and Policy Options,* eds. Darius Gaskins and John Weyant (Stanford: Stanford Energy Modeling Forum, 1994). The globally aggregated version of the model is described in James K. Hammitt, Robert J. Lempert, and Michael E. Schlesinger, "A Sequential-Decision Strategy for Abating Climate Change," *Nature* 357 (1992): 315–

318; and Robert J. Lempert, Michael E. Schlesinger, and James K. Hammitt, "The Impact of Potential Abrupt Climate Changes on Near-Term Policy Choices," *Climatic Change* 26 (1994): 351–376.

13. The Edmonds-Reilly model, described in James Edmonds and John Reilly, *Global Energy: Assessing the Future* (Oxford: Oxford University Press, 1985) and in Gaskins and Weyant, *Reducing Carbon Emissions.*

14. The North includes the U.S., other OECD and former Soviet Union regions; the South includes China and the rest of the world.

15. Ernst Maier-Reimer and Klaus Hasselmann, "Transport and Storage of $CO_2$ in the Ocean: An Inorganic Ocean-Circulation Carbon Cycle Model," *Climate Dynamics* 2 (1987): 63–90.

16. See Michael E. Schlesinger and Xingjian Jiang, "A Phased-in Approach to Greenhouse-Gas-Induced Climatic Change," *Eos* 72 (1991): 593–596; and Michael E. Schlesinger and Xingjian Jiang, "Climatic Responses to Increasing Greenhouse Gases," *Eos* 72 (1991): 597.

17. Stephen H. Schneider and Starley L. Thompson, "Atmospheric $CO_2$ and Climate: Importance of the Transient Response," *Journal of Geophysical Research* 86(C4) (1981): 3135–3147.

18. Houghton et al., *Climate Change;* and Houghton et al., *Climate Change 1992.*

19. Hammitt, Lempert, and Schlesinger, "A Sequential-Decision Strategy."

20. Michael Grubb, "The Climate Change Convention: An Assessment," *BNA International Environmental Reporter,* August 12, 1992, pp. 540–543.

21. Florentin Krause, Wilfred Bach, and Jon Koomey, *Energy Policy in the Greenhouse* (New York: Wiley, 1992); Frank R. Rijsberman and Rob J. Swart, *Targets and Indicators of Climate Change* (Stockholm: Stockholm Environment Institute, 1990); Rob J. Swart and Monique J.M. Hootsmans, "A Sound Footing for Controlling Climate Change," *International Environmental Affairs* 3 (1991): 124–136; and David A. Wirth and Daniel A. Lashof, "Beyond Vienna and Montreal: Multilateral Agreements on Greenhouse Gases," *Ambio* 19 (1990): 305–310.

22. Krause, Bach, and Koomey, *Energy Policy in the Greenhouse.*

23. Ibid.

24. The Framework Convention on Climate Change includes language suggesting that signatories may have agreed to a rule under which the industrialized countries compensate the developing countries for the costs of developing national abatement programs and some abatement costs. See Grubb, "The Climate Change Convention."

25. John Rawls, *A Theory of Justice* (Cambridge, MA: Harvard University Press, 1971).

# PART 2

## Games and Decisions

# CHAPTER 13

# STRATEGIC AND STRUCTURAL UNCERTAINTY IN GAMES

## Adam M. Brandenburger

For Howard Raiffa, games have always been about decisions. This chapter describes an emerging theory of games as decisions—call it "interactive decision theory"—that accords very well with Raiffa's sensibilities. After a brief introduction, the chapter places interactive decision theory in historical context. It goes on to review recent work that is giving formal shape to interactive decision theory, and concludes with some current research questions.

### Interactive Decision Theory

All games, whether cooperative or noncooperative, involve several players whose fortunes are interdependent. In noncooperative games, each player is faced with a specified set (or series of sets) of choices; that is, each player faces a decision problem. The players are interdependent in that the consequences of one player's actions typically depend on the other players' actions. Decision theory says that players should handle the interdependence by forming probability assessments of other players' choices. Using these assessments, players should make their choices so as to maximize their expected payoffs. One-person decision theory stops here. But this misses something important.

I thank Bob Aumann and Harborne Stuart for conversations on the subject of this paper, and Miriam Avins, Jim Sebenius, and Richard Zeckhauser for editorial suggestions. Financial support from the Harvard Business School Division of Research is gratefully acknowledged.

A crucial difference between the uncertainty that a player faces in decision problems in the one-person and game contexts is that the game context involves "strategic uncertainty," or uncertainty surrounding the purposeful behavior of players.[1] The distinction is important because strategic uncertainty is amenable to probability assessments in which the player steps into the shoes of other players and recognizes that they, too, face decision problems. In doing so, a player may be able to narrow down the strategic uncertainty he faces by ruling out certain choices of other players as inconsistent with what he knows or believes about their payoff functions, assessments, rationality, and so on.

In assessing the strategic uncertainty in a game, then, players are led also to assess the "structural uncertainty," or uncertainty surrounding the parameters of the game, such as the payoff functions.[2]

Putting oneself in other players' shoes is only the first step. More is possible. A player may be able to narrow down another player's assessment by recognizing that she too is engaged in the exercise of stepping into other players' shoes. Of course, one should then recognize that other players will also recognize this, and so on ad infinitum.

This form of analysis, which can be termed "interactive decision theory," springs very naturally from one-person decision theory. It involves confronting both the strategic and the structural uncertainty inherent in a game. It also involves grappling with potentially infinite chains of reasoning—reasoning about other players, reasoning about other players' reasoning, and so on.

## Historical Context

In their *Theory of Games and Economic Behavior,* von Neumann and Morgenstern discuss rational behavior in a game in terms quite similar to those of interactive decision theory:

> Every participant can determine the variables which describe his own actions but not those of the others. Nevertheless those "alien" variables cannot, from his point of view, be described by statistical assumptions. . . . His actions will be influenced by his expectation of these [variables], and they in turn reflect the other participants' expectation of his actions.[3]

But noncooperative game theory did not develop as interactive decision theory. Instead, the subject started with the minimax theory for zero-sum games, and extended its reach to include non-zero-sum games with the notion of strategic equilibrium.[4] Since then, the idea of a Nash equilibrium, together with its refinements, has become the principal analytical tool of noncooperative game theory.

Equilibrium theory does not accord an important role to strategic uncertainty. More precisely, an equilibrium profile of strategies can always be taken to be common knowledge among the players. If mixed strategies are involved, these too can be assumed to be common knowledge. Strategic uncertainty enters the picture only in the limited sense that there is uncertainty about the pure realizations of the mixed strategies. This is very different from interactive decision theory, which places strategic uncertainty at center stage.

Structural uncertainty, on the other hand, has been emphasized within equilibrium theory in recent years. The now vast field of information economics studies the implications of structural uncertainty in games. The basic idea is not new; von Neumann and Morgenstern distinguished between games with "complete information" and games with "incomplete information."[5] In the present terminology, the former are games that do not exhibit structural uncertainty, and the latter are games that do. Similarly, R. Duncan Luce and Raiffa stated their assumption that the parameters of a game were transparent to the players.[6]

Early game theorists did not attempt to analyze games with structural uncertainty. Then came John Harsanyi's bold formulation.[7] Harsanyi asserted that each player could be thought of as being one of several different possible "types." A type encodes all of a player's beliefs—beliefs about the parameters of the game, beliefs about the other players' beliefs, and so on. It is supposed that each player knows only his own type, not the types of the other players. Each type, however, is associated with a "given" probability distribution over the possible profiles of types of the other players. Harsanyi went on to define an equilibrium concept, "Bayesian equilibrium," for games with incomplete information. His work prepared the ground for the subsequent blossoming of information economics.

Two aspects of Harsanyi's formulation should be noted. First, his arguments were informal; it was left to others to provide rigorous support for his assertions (see below). Second, Harsanyi chose to analyze only structural uncertainty. He did not view strategic uncertainty as suitable for probability assessment by players:

> Every player $i$ . . . will assign a *subjective* joint probability distribution $P_i$ to all variables unknown to him—or at least to all unknown *independent* variables, i.e., to all variables not depending on the players' own strategy choices.[8]

The Bayesian equilibrium concept stood in place of explicit consideration of strategic uncertainty.

## The Mathematics of Types

Formal arguments in support of Harsanyi's construction have emerged
in a number of papers;[9] here we sketch the mathematics of types,
following the approach of Brandenburger and Eddie Dekel.

Start with an abstract space $S$. The exact interpretation of $S$ will
depend on the context; for example, a particular element in $S$ might
specify the players' payoff functions. Each player is imagined to form
a first-order belief over $S$.[10] A player's second-order belief is then a
probability measure over the product of $S$ and the space of possible
first-order beliefs of the other players.[11] A third-order belief is a probability measure over the product of $S$, the space of first-order beliefs
of other players, and the space of second-order beliefs of other players.
Fourth-order beliefs, fifth-order beliefs, and so on are defined similarly.
A "type" of a player is simply an infinite hierarchy of beliefs—a
particular first-order belief, a particular second-order belief, a particular third-order belief, etc.

Does this construction specify all the beliefs of a player? Not
necessarily. We do not yet know what probabilities a player assigns to
the different possible types of another player. So it seems we must
construct a "second-level" hierarchy of beliefs, comprising beliefs over
types, beliefs over beliefs over types, and so on. But then we would
need a "third-level" hierarchy. And so on. The construction becomes
mathematically daunting, to say the least.

However, if a player's first-level hierarchy satisfies a natural "coherency" condition—that the different orders of belief of the player do
not contradict one another—then the player's belief about what types
the other players might be are, in fact, already determined. This belief
need not and cannot be independently specified. To understand the
coherency condition, recall that a player's first-order belief is an assessment over $S$ while his second-order belief is a joint assessment over $S$
and the space of first-order beliefs of the other players. Coherency says
that the marginal distribution on $S$ of the second-order belief must be
equal to the first-order belief. Analogous conditions are imposed on
pairs of higher-order beliefs.

The point is that a coherent type of a player naturally induces a
probability measure on the product of $S$ and the space of profiles of
types of the other players. Indeed, there is a homeomorphism between
the space of coherent types of a player, and the space of probability
measures on the product of $S$ and the space of profiles of types of the

other players. Mathematically, this is an immediate consequence of Kolmogorov's Existence Theorem from the theory of stochastic processes.[12]

The construction is not yet quite complete; while a coherent type induces a belief over the possible types of the other players, this belief is not necessarily concentrated on the space of coherent types of the other players. This means that a coherent type does not necessarily induce a belief over the other players' beliefs over types; nor are beliefs over beliefs over beliefs over types necessarily determined; and so on. The answer is to require that each type assign probability 1 to the event that the other players' types are coherent, probability 1 to the event that the other players' types assign probability 1 to the previous event, and so on ad infinitum. That is, common knowledge of coherency is assumed.

Let $T$ denote the subset of the space of all possible types of a player that satisfies the above restrictions. A straightforward argument shows that the space $T$ is homeomorphic to the space of probability measures on the product space $S \times T^{n-1}$, where $n$ is the number of players. This finishes the construction.

This construction shows that there is complete generality in a model that specifies a set of possible types for each player, where each player knows only his own type and not the types of the other players, and where a probability measure over the space of possible profiles of types of the other players is associated with each type. Harsanyi's bold vision is vindicated.

## Unified Treatment of Strategic and Structural Uncertainty

Several ideas in decision and game theory have come together recently, resulting in the development of a mathematical model that allows for a unified treatment of strategic and structural uncertainty in games. Key ingredients in this synthesis are Harsanyi's theory of games with incomplete information and the subsequent work on the mathematics of types (discussed above), and Robert Aumann's formalization of the notion of common knowledge.[13]

Aumann and Brandenburger present a formal model, termed an "interactive belief system," that treats strategic and structural uncertainty equally. In an interactive belief system, all uncertainty facing a player in a game is subject to probability assessment, whether the uncertainty is about other players' strategic choices, their payoff functions, or their assessments.

To see how this approach works, start with a "strategic game form," that is, a set of players $\{1, ..., n\}$ and for each player $i$ a (finite) set of possible strategies $A_i$. An interactive belief system for this strategic game form consists of:

    1.  for each player $i$, a set of types $T_i$,[14]

and for each type $t_i$ of $i$,

    2.  a probability distribution on the set $T_1 \times \cdots \times T_{i-1} \times T_{i+1} \times \cdots \times T_n$,

    3.  a strategy $a_i$ from $A_i$, and

    4.  a payoff function $g_i\colon A_1 \times \cdots \times A_n \to \mathbb{R}$.

Each player, then, may be one of several different possible types, where a particular type is associated with a certain belief over the profiles of types of the other players (item 2), a certain choice of strategy (item 3), and a certain payoff function (item 4).

    Call a particular profile of types $(t_1, \ldots, t_n)$ a "state of the world." The specification of an interactive belief system and of a state of the world in that system fully describes each player's strategic choice and payoff function, each player's beliefs about the other players' choices, payoff functions, and beliefs about these matters, and so on. Interactive belief systems are thus a formal tool for doing interactive decision theory.

    How general is this approach? Can it handle all the uncertainty that might be present in a game? Yes. The formal construction of types outlined above guarantees it.[15] Thus it is tempting to point to Kolmogorov's Existence Theorem as playing a crucial foundational role in interactive decision theory, analogous to that played by Brouwer's Fixed Point Theorem in equilibrium theory.

## Current Research Directions

Aumann and Brandenburger use the interactive belief system technology to identify decision-theoretic conditions that yield Nash equilibrium. The approach can also be applied much more widely. This section sketches four current directions for research, all of which extend the scope of interactive decision theory.

### Elimination of the Game Form

In the formalism of the interactive belief system, the notion of a given game has, rather like the Cheshire cat, all but vanished; only the game form remains. The final step would be to eliminate the game form as well, instead including the players' beliefs about who is actually playing the game and what strategies the players can adopt (as well as beliefs about beliefs about these matters, and so on, as usual) in the interactive belief system.

Would this extra step result in any greater generality? Harsanyi asserted that it would not.[16] Suppose, for example, that there is uncertainty as to whether a particular strategy is at the disposal of some player. Harsanyi argued that this could be adequately analyzed by including the strategy in the player's given strategy space, with uncertainty about which of two payoff functions the player possesses. The payoff functions would be designed so that the player's use of the strategy in question would yield a very large and negative payoff regardless of other players' choices when the strategy is "absent," but not when the strategy is "present."

At first glance, Harsanyi's argument appears to involve an assumption that the player in question is rational.[17] Or is the assumption that the player is rational and also that the other players believe this? Or must we go all the way and assume common knowledge of rationality? Whatever the requirement, any such assumption would be troublesome. The interactive belief system should stand independent of the extent of uncertainty about the players' rationality.

To scrutinize Harsanyi's argument, Hong Hu defines a generalized interactive belief system that admits uncertainty as to the players' strategy spaces.[18] She shows that any such generalized system can be transformed into an interactive belief system without changing the extent of uncertainty about the players' rationality. In other words, explicitly allowing for uncertainty about the strategy spaces adds nothing, just as Harsanyi asserted. The apparent difficulty with Harsanyi's argument turns out—at least as far as strategy spaces are concerned—to be illusory.

### Extension to Game Trees

To date, interactive belief systems have been defined for strategic-form games, in which each player chooses a complete contingent plan of action (that is, a strategy). An active area of research concerns the extension of the formalism to game trees, to take explicit account of the sequential nature of much interactive decision making.[19]

Games with perfect information are a good starting point. For such games, the backward induction algorithm has long been accepted as uncontroversial, but the algorithm has recently become subject to critical examination.[20] A formalism for doing interactive decision theory in game trees should help determine the exact status of backward induction logic. Aumann has developed an interactive formalism for perfect information games in which, if rationality is common knowledge, the backward induction outcome results.[21]

One approach to developing an interactive formalism that applies to games with imperfect or perfect information is to replace each type's standard probability distribution (item 2 in the definition of an interactive belief system) with a "conditional probability system."[22] With this apparatus, one can talk formally about the players' beliefs at different points in the tree, their rationality at various points, and so on. It remains to be seen where this approach will lead.

Replacing the standard probability measures in an interactive belief system with conditional probability systems also raises a foundational question: What becomes of the construction of types of players outlined here? Can it still be carried through?

### Extensions of the Strategic-Form Approach

A question within the strategic-form approach is how to extend the interactive belief system technology to incorporate admissibility (that is, avoidance of weakly dominated choices). Admissibility plays an important role in basic one-person decision theory,[23] and also in strategic-form refinements of Nash equilibrium. Larry Blume, Brandenburger, and Dekel have developed a one-person decision theory, involving "lexicographic probability systems," that combines a form of subjective expected utility maximization with admissibility.[24] Grafting this theory onto the interactive belief system may prove fruitful. There is also a foundational question, similar to that for conditional probability systems, as to how the construction of types works when lexicographic probability systems take the place of standard probability distributions.

### Applications

Relatively little has been done so far in applying interactive decision theory to games of economic interest.

Aumann has considered Robert Rosenthal's "centipede" game.[25] Applying the backward induction algorithm to this game leads to the conclusion that the first player will choose to "go out," thereby ending the game immediately. The same answer obtains if, in an interactive decision-theoretic treatment, one assumes that the rationality of the players is commonly known and that there is a common prior. Aumann shows, however, that even a very small departure from common knowledge of rationality can produce a very different outcome in which the players choose to "stay in" until quite late in the game.

Harborne Stuart has studied the finitely repeated Prisoner's Dilemma.[26] He demonstrates that if rationality is commonly known, and a mutual absolute continuity assumption holds, then the players choose to "defect" throughout the game (the backward induction outcome). Given this benchmark, Stuart goes on to explore what cooperative behavior involves in terms of levels of knowledge of rationality and amounts of irrationality.

David Roth has examined predation.[27] He shows that in the presence of strategic uncertainty, an entrant might well enter an industry, experience a hostile ("predatory") response from an incumbent, and then exit. This cannot happen within the confines of equilibrium theory, absent structural uncertainty.[28] The objective of this work is not to deny the relevance of structural uncertainty, but to emphasize the importance of strategic uncertainty. As Roth points out, strategic uncertainty is likely to loom large in entrant-incumbent games: by definition, the players have no experience competing with each other.

Roth and Amanda Bayer have studied bargaining from a similar perspective.[29] They demonstrate that delayed agreement is possible, even in the absence of structural uncertainty, as long as there is strategic uncertainty.

Brandenburger and Pankaj Ghemawat have looked at wars of attrition.[30] They show that under common knowledge of rationality, a fight of any duration is possible; and both players can have strictly positive expected payoffs, even though both may incur overall losses. These two conditions can hold not only at the start of the game, but also throughout the game. Equilibrium analysis of the war of attrition yields two pure equilibria in which one or the other player concedes immediately. Fighting can occur only in mixed equilibria. In a mixed equilibrium, the players are indifferent between fighting and conceding at each point in the game; in fact, they have zero expected payoffs. By contrast, interactive decision analysis of the war of attrition brings out the irreducible "fog of war": both players may well expect to come out ahead, and both may well end up with large losses.[31]

## NOTES

1. The term "strategic uncertainty" appears in J. Van Huyck, R. Battalio, and R. Beil, "Tacit Coordination Games, Strategic Uncertainty, and Coordination Failure," *American Economic Review* 80 (1990): 234–248; Vincent Crawford, "Adaptive Dynamics in Coordination Games" (Department of Economics, University of California, San Diego, 1992); David Roth, "Rationalizable Predatory Pricing" (Department of Economics, University of Michigan, January 1993); and elsewhere.
2. Roth, "Rationalizable Predatory Pricing."

3. John von Neumann and Oskar Morgenstern, *Theory of Games and Economic Behavior* (Princeton, NJ: Princeton University Press, 1944), pp. 11–12.

4. John Nash, "Non-Cooperative Games," *Annals of Mathematics* 54 (1951): 286–295.

5. von Neumann and Morgenstern, *Theory of Games*, p. 30.

6. R. Duncan Luce and Howard Raiffa, *Games and Decisions* (New York: Wiley, 1957), p. 49.

7. John Harsanyi, "Games with Incomplete Information Played by 'Bayesian' Players," Parts I–III, *Management Science* 14 (1967–1968): 159–182, 320–334, 486–502.

8. Ibid., p. 167.

9. See W. Armbruster and W. Böge, "Bayesian Game Theory," in *Game Theory and Related Topics*, ed. O. Moeschlin and D. Pallaschke (Amsterdam: North-Holland, 1979), pp. 17–28; W. Böge and Th. Eisele, "On Solutions of Bayesian Games," *International Journal of Game Theory* 8 (1979): 193–215; Jean-Francois Mertens and Shmuel Zamir, "Formulation of Bayesian Analysis for Games with Incomplete Information," *International Journal of Game Theory* 14 (1985): 1–29; Aviad Heifetz, "The Bayesian Formulation of Incomplete Information—The Non-Compact Case" (School of Mathematical Sciences, Tel Aviv University, November 1991); and Adam Brandenburger and Eddie Dekel, "Hierarchies of Beliefs and Common Knowledge," *Journal of Economic Theory* 59 (1993): 189–198.

10. A natural requirement to impose on the construction is that players are not uncertain about their own payoff functions. This can be done without difficulty.

11. One's first instinct might be to define a second-order belief as a probability measure over the space of possible first-order beliefs of the other players alone, rather than over the product of $S$ and this space. This would not be a satisfactory approach, however, since it would not specify a player's joint assessment over the two spaces. A complete construction of beliefs, beliefs about beliefs, etc., must encode the answers to all conceivable questions that could be posed to a player concerning his probability assessments.

12. See, for example, Kai Lai Chung, *A Course in Probability Theory*, 2nd ed. (New York: Academic Press, 1974), p. 60. In the theory of stochastic processes, the term "consistency" is often used to refer to agreement between probability measures of different orders. Harsanyi used "consistency" to mean something else, which is why Brandenburger and Dekel employ the term "coherency" in this context.

13. Robert Aumann, "Agreeing to Disagree," *Annals of Statistics* 4 (1976): 1236–1239. Other relevant papers include John Harsanyi, "Games with Randomly Disturbed Payoffs: A New Rationale for Mixed Strategy Equilibrium Points," *International Journal of Game Theory* 2 (1973): 1–23;

Armbruster and Böge, "Bayesian Game Theory"; B. Douglas Bernheim, "Rationalizable Strategic Behavior," *Econometrica* 52 (1984): 1007–1028; David Pearce, "Rationalizable Strategic Behavior and the Problem of Perfection," *Econometrica* 52 (1984): 1029–1050; Robert Aumann, "Correlated Equilibrium as an Expression of Bayesian Rationality," *Econometrica* 55 (1987): 1–18; Tommy Tan and Sergio Werlang, "The Bayesian Foundations of Solution Concepts of Games," *Journal of Economic Theory* 45 (1988): 370–391; Adam Brandenburger and Eddie Dekel, "The Role of Common Knowledge Assumptions in Game Theory," in *The Economics of Missing Markets, Information, and Games*, ed. Frank Hahn (Oxford: Oxford University Press, 1989), pp. 46–61; and Robert Aumann and Adam Brandenburger, "Epistemic Conditions for Nash Equilibrium," Working Paper No. 91-042, Harvard Business School, forthcoming in *Econometrica*.

14. For concreteness, think of the type spaces $T_i$ as finite. Conceptually, it is important to allow for infinite types spaces; see Aumann and Brandenburger, "Epistemic Conditions," Section 6, for further discussion.

15. See also the discussion on the elimination of the game form, below.

16. Harsanyi, "Games with Incomplete Information," pp. 167–168.

17. This was pointed out to me by Hong Hu and Thomas Sjostrom.

18. Hong Hu, "Can't Do or Won't Do? On Harsanyi's Economization of Structural Uncertainty in Games" (Harvard Business School, July 1994).

19. Arguably, no such extension should be necessary. The very definition of a strategy, it may be asserted, ensures the adequacy of the strategic form. Whatever the merits of this position, a direct formulation of interactive decision theory for game trees seems likely to yield insight.

20. See, for example, Kaushik Basu, "On the Non-Existence of a Rationality Definition for Extensive Games," *International Journal of Game Theory* 19 (1990): 33–44; Elchanan Ben Porath, "Rationality, Nash Equilibrium and Backward Induction in Perfect Information Games," Working Paper No. 14-92, Department of Economics, Tel-Aviv University, 1992; Cristina Bicchieri, "Self-Refuting Theories of Strategic Interaction: A Paradox of Common Knowledge," *Erkenntniss* 30 (1989): 69–85; Cristina Bicchieri, "Knowledge-Dependent Games: Backward Induction," in *Knowledge, Belief and Strategic Interaction*, ed. Cristina Bicchieri and M. Della Chiara (Cambridge: Cambridge University Press, 1992); Ken Binmore, "Modeling Rational Players: Part I," *Economics and Philosophy* 3 (1987): 179–214; Giacomo Bonnano, "The Logic of Rational Play in Games with Perfect Information," *Economics and Philosophy* 7 (1991): 37–65; Philip Reny, "Rationality in Extensive Form Games," *Journal of Economic Perspectives* 6 (1992): 103–118; and Philip Reny, "Common Belief and the Theory of Games with Perfect Information," *Journal of Economic Theory* 59 (1993): 257–274.

21. Robert Aumann, "Backward Induction and Common Knowledge of Rationality," *Games and Economic Behavior* 8 (1995): 6–19.

22. For a definition, see Roger Myerson, "Multistage Games with Communication," *Econometrica* 54 (1986): 323–358. As Hammond has pointed out, the concept of a conditional probability system goes back to the probabilists Rényi, Császár, and de Finetti, among others. See John Hammond, "Elementary Non-Archimedean Representations of Probability for Decision Theory and Games" (Department of Economics, Stanford University, 1992), to appear in *Patrick Suppes: Scientific Philosopher,* ed. P. Humphreys (Boston: Kluwer Academic Publishers, forthcoming).

23. Luce and Raiffa, *Games and Decisions,* ch. 13.

24. Larry Blume, Adam Brandenburger, and Eddie Dekel, "Lexicographic Probabilities and Choice under Uncertainty," *Econometrica* 59 (1991): 61–79. Hammond has established connections between conditional probability systems, lexicographic probability systems, and other extended probability concepts. See Hammond, "Elementary Non-Archimedean Representations"; and John Hammond, "Consequentialism, Non-Archimedean Probabilities, and Lexicographic Expected Utility," Department of Economics, Stanford University, 1992, to appear in *Proceedings of the Second Workshop on Knowledge, Belief and Strategic Interaction,* ed. Cristina Bicchieri (Cambridge: Cambridge University Press, forthcoming).

25. Robert Aumann, "Irrationality in Game Theory," in *Economic Analysis of Markets and Games: Essays in Honor of Frank Hahn,* ed. Partha Dasgupta et al. (Cambridge, MA: MIT Press, 1992), pp. 214–227. See also Robert Rosenthal, "Games of Perfect Information, Predatory Pricing, and the Chain Store Paradox," *Journal of Economic Theory* 25 (1982): 92–100.

26. Harborne Stuart, "Common Belief of Rationality in the Finitely Repeated Prisoner's Dilemma" (Working Paper No. 93-066, Harvard Business School, 1992).

27. Roth, "Rationalizable Predatory Pricing."

28. More precisely, such behavior cannot arise in a pure-strategy equilibrium. It can happen in a mixed-strategy equilibrium, but this then requires the players to be indifferent between various pure choices. This is hard to swallow—at least in the context under discussion.

29. David Roth and Amanda Bayer, "Delay in Bargaining as a Coordination Failure" (Department of Economics, University of Michigan, 1992).

30. Adam Brandenburger and Pankaj Ghemawat, "The War of Attrition between British Satellite Broadcasting and Sky Television" (Harvard Business School, 1993).

31. Here too, the equilibrium analysis can be embellished by introducing structural uncertainty. The goal of the interactive decision analysis is to highlight the effect of strategic uncertainty.

CHAPTER 14

# What Can You Learn from a Game?

## Edward A. Parson

This paper considers ways that simulation games can be used to inform difficult and complex problems of policy and decision. The use of games for serious purposes, as opposed to recreation, originated more than a century ago in the field of military planning; manual or map games served as devices to test battle plans, coordinate actions, train commanders, and predict the outcome of battles.[1] In the postwar period, interest in gaming has increased, driven partly by advances in game theory and computing power, and has broadened from military planning to the study of foreign policy crises and, occasionally, other areas of policy and decision.[2]

Despite several substantial contributions to the field, questions concerning the appropriate uses and goals of simulation gaming remain confused, and discussions of purposes seem to have had little influence on the practice of gaming or game development.[3] Several factors may have contributed to this confusion. Writers on game purposes have sought to construct extremely broad taxonomies including essentially all games and design methods, including those for recreational and commercial use, while the viability and implications of particular objectives likely depend strongly on the particular method and application. Categories of use have not been sharply drawn, so some applications of games fall into more than one, or none. Because most gaming experience is still in the military and security fields, discussions of uses have tended to emphasize those likely to arise in this field, while others less likely to do so have received less careful consideration. Finally, the relationship between purposes of games and criteria for their design and implementation has not been elaborated.

This paper seeks to elaborate and clarify a particular set of uses of simulation gaming applied to a particular class of problems: informing complex, difficult, and high-stakes policy and decision problems, particularly problems outside the field of military and security affairs. Problems that might merit investigation through simulation gaming are those with high enough stakes to merit substantial investment in knowledge or insight to guide decision making, but whose complexity, novelty, or perverse characteristics impose sharp limits on the usefulness of standard decision-making procedures, historical analogy, or conventional forms of analysis. In "informing" such problems we include all heuristic purposes of simulation gaming: uses of gaming intended to help actors with significant responsibilities to understand decisions they may face and their implications, or to understand the context in which continuing decisions take place.

The characteristics of these problems that make them so difficult, and that limit the usefulness of other forms of analysis, can be of several kinds. Key outcomes may depend upon the interacting decisions of multiple agents, which may be particularly complex when agents' interests are partly aligned and partly in opposition. Decisions may be drawn from choice sets that are ambiguous, poorly known, or changing. Large numbers of complex organizational routines may be required to work together.[4] Consequences may be poorly known, fall on unidentified or remote people, or occur far in the future. Or finally, knowledge about agents' interests and choices, and relevant properties of the world, may be seriously incomplete or contested.

Two classes of such problems are particularly salient: the management of rapidly developing crises, and problems involving major changes in laws, regulations, or institutions. Crisis management is the area of gaming application that most closely resembles its traditional use in military planning, but can also include, for example, disaster preparedness, energy supply interruption, and international macroeconomic or debt crises.[5] Problems of decision making under major changes of rules or institutions could include corporate strategy in industries in transition; domestic policy reform in health care or welfare; long-horizon policy issues such as public pension reform under demographic shifts; the fundamental redesign of institutions, policies, and laws, as has been under way for several years in Eastern Europe and the former Soviet Union; and international policy making on imperfectly understood but potentially grave global environmental threats such as climate change.[6]

Focusing attention on this limited set of applications of simulation gaming—applications to inform complex policy or decision problems—this paper discusses four models of how simulation gaming can contribute, seeking to assess the relative strength and weakness of each, and to sketch out the implications of each for the design and implementation of simulation games. The next section outlines the basic characteristics of simulation-gaming methods, and their central methodological challenges. Subsequent sections lay out and assess the four models, summarize the implications of each for simulation design, and offer concluding observations on the benefits and limits of informing complex policy and decision problems through simulation gaming.

## Simulation Gaming: Basic Characteristics and Challenges

Simulation games, like other forms of simulation, are representations; they seek to represent a complex system by constructing a simpler one with relevant behavioral similarity.[7] The behavioral similarity to the real system of concern makes a simulation useful, for if it is realized, one can learn about the real system by observing, and manipulating, the simpler simulated one.

Simulation gaming differs from other kinds of simulation in how it represents human decision making and problem solving. While other kinds of simulation may exclude human agency from the system studied, or represent it entirely through formal or computer models, simulation gaming represents it through the behavior of human participants. It seeks to represent the information processing, cognition, negotiation, and decision making of senior decision makers, organizations, or governments, by engaging people to participate in a simulation, giving them roles, information, tasks, and responsibilities, and placing them in a vivid, demanding, realistic situation in which they must act.

While some simulations may employ a single human participant interacting with a complex mechanical system—e.g., flight simulators used for pilot training, practice, and testing control systems—simulation gaming involves multiple participants and focuses on their collective decisions and the interactions among them. While the interactions of decisions can be structured in many ways, two characteristics are generally deemed essential to making a simulation a game: rules structuring the interactions among participants' decisions; and separate centers of thought or decision (teams or individuals) that do not observe each others' planning and deliberation, and so must interpret and respond to statements and actions that they did not compose.[8]

The use of multiple human participants in a structured interaction without full information defines a simulation game; other design elements, which support and constrain participants' decisions, can vary widely. Simulation games may include rich narrative "scenarios" that provide context for, and identify the essential elements in, participants' decision problems;[9] some combination of an expert control team, formal models, or fixed rules that determine the consequences of participants' joint decisions;[10] or general information resources or formal planning and analysis tools to support participants' deliberations.[11]

Lines of simulation gaming work include political-military exercises, crisis gaming, policy exercises, adaptive environmental assessment and management, and the experimental negotiation studies pioneered by Howard Raiffa.[12] Since the broadening of interest in gaming in the 1950s, the history of simulation gaming has been marked by great promise, cyclic periods of enthusiasm and reaction, and instances of both excessive claims by advocates and impossible standards imposed by detractors.[13]

Achieving the necessary degree of "relevant behavioral similarity" to the real problem to be investigated is the essential problem of designing and using a simulation-gaming exercise. How much of what kind of similarity is required, and how persuasively it must be demonstrated, depend on the particular application and objectives for the exercise.

Possible requirements for achieving it may include participants who sufficiently resemble the decision makers they represent; reasonably realistic data to define the scope and context for decision in the simulation; and roles that are both sufficiently accurately portrayed, and sufficiently intense and vivid, that participants act on them, exert themselves, and worry about the consequences of their actions. It is essential, for example, that participants' interests in the social context of the simulation itself—their desire to win, to make mischief, or to be a good citizen—do not overwhelm or trivialize the interests of their roles or teams.[14] Finally, certain unavoidable artifacts of simulation— arbitrary time, the heightened salience of the issue studied, and participants' limited information-processing ability compared to the organizations or governments they represent—must not so dominate the simulation that all significant insights are attributable to them.[15]

## Proposed Models for the Use of Simulation Gaming

This section lays out four possible models of how simulation games can help inform complex decision and policy problems. These differ in the kind of things to be learned, by whom, and through what mechanism, and they imply different design criteria for the development and implementation of simulations. Two of these models are problematic, while two show substantial promise.

## Simulations as Experiments

It is sometimes suggested that simulations can serve as experiments, or quasi-experiments, to test hypotheses about the behavior of people, negotiations, organizations, decision makers in crisis, governments, or the international system. This capability, if realized, would represent a great increase in our power to understand the world. Simulations could serve as artificial worlds to test conjectures for which history failed to offer sharp empirical cases, and for which real-world experimentation would be impossible, too costly, too risky, or morally prohibited. The potential benefits for both enhanced understanding and better decisions and policies would be vast.[16]

The claim of experimental validity imposes stringent standards on the correspondence of a simulation to reality. The simulation must embody enough behavioral similarity to the situation investigated that hypotheses about the real situation imply expected behavior in the simulation, and hence that running the simulation exposes the hypothesis to the risk of falsification that can suggest the limits of its credibility, and increase our provisional willingness to accept it and act on its implications.[17]

In meeting this standard, the simulation itself, like a theory, must be validated; its "relevant behavioral similarity" to the real system must be demonstrated with sufficient confidence. This test can in part be met by validation of the simulations' components: participants enough like the real decision makers, and roles, structures, and rules that embody well verified relationships. But simulations are so complex by standards of experiments that full correspondence cannot even be approximately achieved, and how much similarity is enough is judgmental, not obvious, and sometimes contested. Simulations can fail to achieve the required similarity in many ways: observed behaviors may be artifacts of the particular individuals participating, of arbitrary details of simulation design, or of the unavoidable artificiality inherent in any simulation.

For example, how much and in what ways must simulation participants resemble real decision makers? It is frequently argued that simulation validity requires participants who are real experts, equivalent in knowledge, skills, authority, resolve, and temperament to those who would make decisions in the real system, lest ludicrous behavior occur.[18] Others, also reporting simulation experience, contend that if psychological profiles are well matched then high-school students can in some respects reliably replicate behavior representative of generals and cabinet ministers; that there are only insignificant differences between the performance of middle and top-level officials, and between military and civilian officials; and that if tasks are appropriately defined and intensely demanding, then any participants sufficiently smart, skilled, and motivated will generate instructive and relevant behavior, even if they know little about the particular decision makers they represent or their institutional setting.[19]

Since the validity of a simulation cannot be determined absolutely from the representational accuracy of its components, validation of a simulation must depend on controlled replication. Simulations, to persuade, must generate behavior that resembles the situation of interest, in a manner that persuades knowledgeable and skeptical people that the similarity is solid, reliable, and not obtained through cheating. Replication must be conducted with different participants, to verify that behavior is not an artifact of a particular group; and with variation in design details, to verify that behavior is not an artifact of some particular arbitrary design feature. Except for intentional variation of the factors being investigated, this replication must be closely controlled.

The need for controlled replication strongly shapes simulation design. Sparser decision environments are preferable, to reduce the number of potentially confounding factors. Moreover, while the decision setting might appear quite open-ended, participants' license to redefine the problem or change the rules must in fact be quite limited, lest their simulation become noncomparable with others. Authority over the simulation remains strongly with the experimenters, while participants serve largely as experimental subjects.

This replication requirement is a daunting task, but one characteristic of simulation slightly offsets it. Because of simulations' richness and complexity, their outputs contain huge amounts of information. The main narrative observed in a simulation, and participants' observations, admit detailed examination at both large and small scales, and so include many opportunities to demonstrate either realism or unrealism. Thus, simulations provide many more opportunities to establish validity than if each simulation run were treated as a single datapoint.[20]

Despite this partially offsetting factor, there are two basic difficulties with the model of simulations as experiments, one conceptual, and one practical and often decisive.

The conceptual difficulty is a basic conflict between the presumed novelty and uniqueness of the policy problem to be investigated, and the pursuit of generalizable hypotheses bearing on it. Simulations treated as experiments seek to identify and test regularities that generalize across instances. To this end, their focus even in novel situations is on aspects of the situation that are potentially generalizable and subject to abstraction. This inevitably leads them to concentrate on regularities in the normal course of policy and decision (e.g., general principles of foreign policy and international relations),[21] or on small components of the situation that can be abstracted, and that might occur in many situations. Relevant examples include studies of simple abstract negotiations, prisoner's dilemmas or commons problems, and simple coalition exercises, plus a variety of psychological research in individual decision making and communication. Such studies are more easily replicable because they are less elaborate, costly, and time consuming, and because they depend less on domain-specific expertise and so admit a much wider pool of potential participants.

While simulations as experiments tend to address those aspects of a situation that are most normal and replicable, the essential difficulties associated with complex policy problems concern their uniqueness and novelty. Those aspects that are liable to treatment by simulations as experiments are thus likely to be peripheral to the main difficulties for which insights are required. Of course, no issue, decision, or policy problem can be unique in all its dimensions, and it may be extremely valuable to decompose novel, unique problems into familiar or routine components, to the extent possible. But important elements of the real problem are likely to remain unaddressed, and even if well validated insights into component pieces are attained, the experimental approach cannot recombine the component insights to yield aggregate judgments about the issue. Even if simulation experiments lead us to understand the separate 10 elements that comprise a problem, we have no information about how to combine these insights, and make judgments about the relative influence of the different factors, in the aggregate problem.

The practical difficulty with simulations as experiments concerns the low likelihood of sufficiently replicating an experimental simulation with the right participants, or to control it tightly enough, to achieve a persuasive level of validity. To the extent that participants must be expert in the issue studied, the required participants are likely to be few in number, busy, not substitutable, and likely unwilling to participate in an exercise that casts them as passive experimental subjects. The people who must participate for the exercise to have validity as research are unlikely to participate in an exercise tightly designed for research. The more unique and novel the problem to be studied, the sharper this difficulty is likely to be.

In summary, the model of simulation games as experiments is deeply problematic as a description of how such exercises can help to inform complex policy and decision problems. Simulations can act as experiments, but principally for simple abstract repeatable situations that may occur as components of complex policy problems but are unlikely to represent their most important elements. It may happen that a particular insight arises cogently enough, in enough varied simulations, and with enough external basis for confidence in it that it can come to be accepted as generalizable; but this cannot describe the normal use of simulation games to inform policy.[22]

### Simulations to Instruct Decision Makers

Every discussion of simulation games highlights their value as vehicles for instruction. When simulations are applied to complex policy problems, several forms of instruction may be relevant. Of these, several are persuasive and potentially important, but normally tangential to the core of what makes the problem investigated difficult. Instruction in the essential character of the problem itself may occasionally be valid, but is usually deeply problematic.

Simulations can offer instruction on many levels. Because of their vividness, they can be rapid vehicles for learning large volumes of prosaic facts about an issue, an organization, or a location. Because they involve intense collective work by teams of diversely skilled and knowledgeable experts, they can be powerful devices for the transfer of skills and knowledge among participants. They can instruct in such generic skills as processing large volumes of information, clear communication, negotiation, group problem solving, and decision making under uncertainty. These are all important, potentially valuable forms of instruction. All exploit the vividness and concreteness of simulation to provide a learning experience more salient, durable, or workable than may be available from other means. But none of these bears on the core of the complex problem being investigated. Indeed, these forms of instruction depend very little on the representational accuracy of the simulation. It need only be persuasive enough to get participants engaged in their tasks, and be supported by accurate background information. The simulation structure may be little more than a pretext to bring the right set of participants together.

Seeking to use simulation gaming to instruct decision makers in the essential character of a complex policy problem is a much more problematic enterprise. This mode of instruction presumes that the simulation structure embodies insights into the essence of the problem that are true, important, relatively enduring, and not dominated in practical settings by other factors that the participants understand better than the analysts, and consequently that decision makers should understand them and would act differently if they did.

These conditions are likely to be very seldom attained. Specific pieces of policy-relevant scientific knowledge will seldom warrant this form of instruction, partly because they are liable to major revisions. (For example, recent advances in understanding the radiative effects of chlorofluorocarbons and sulfate aerosols have sharply altered the policy debate around global climate change.) The insights that may merit such instruction will typically be deep insights into the basic structure of a problem. Examples might include the basic logic of nuclear deterrence, or the implications of the long time-horizon of global climate change.

### Simulations to Promote Creativity and Insights

Simulations can be powerful devices to provoke participants to think creatively about the problem, and hence to promote the generation of new ideas and insights. Simulations can achieve this through their pressure, relevance, and distance. A well-designed simulation game is an intense, demanding experience for the participants, and should resemble their real responsibilities closely enough to engage their professional skills and knowledge, but not so closely that they rely on their standard habits, heuristics, and bargaining positions. The experience of uncertainty that comes from teams' not knowing what other teams plan or intend may also serve to push people away from habitual ways of thinking.

The insights that may arise can be of many kinds. They might include changed views of the relative importance of different aspects of a problem, including seeing that something previously overlooked is important; new ideas for negotiating stances, policy design, institutions, or responses to specific contingencies; and ideas about plausible consequences of specific proposals, including unanticipated potential pitfalls. They may include practical ideas for officials, and hypotheses for researchers. Thomas Schelling reports that a participant realized that the supply of jet fuel in Teheran was 10 times larger than had been thought, because kerosene (an acceptably close substitute) was used for domestic cooking.[23] Parson reported that when participants sought to revise an international environmental regime, the new regime only attained stable levels of compliance when it had been adopted unanimously.[24]

Of course, it is not certain that novel, valuable, or useful ideas will emerge in any particular simulation, but the likelihood can be increased by the appropriate selection of participants and careful management of their decision context to maintain required pressure, relevance, and distance.

Even if novel insights appear in a simulation, it is not certain how relevant or applicable they will be to the real problem being investigated. Nor is this necessarily easy to determine. The simulation itself does not offer such a test, for the same reasons that simulations are not viable for hypothesis testing, but the more closely the simulation design has succeeded in capturing essential behavioral features of the real system, the more likely the simulation insights are to be relevant.

The participants' collective judgment provides the first test for the relevance, generalizability, and practicality of the supposed insights generated in the heat of the simulation. Consequently, this testing is much more reliable, and the practical value of simulations greatly enhanced, when participants are real experts. Granting participants the standing to critique the relevance of simulation insights, and consequently the simulation design that conditioned them, implies an equality of standing between simulation participants and designers that is not present in the experimental or the instructional model. Participants are not just experimental subjects or recipients of instruction; nor is the simulation reduced to a mere pretext for bringing them together.

Taking effective advantage of participants' expertise in this way imposes two requirements on simulation design. First, the rules and structure of the simulation should not be rigidly fixed, but should be open to challenge by participants and renegotiation among participants and designers. Second, a sober, critical postsimulation debriefing is an essential component of the learning effect of the simulation. It is here that the significance and legitimacy of the problem posed is explored, potential implications and consequences of decisions taken and plausible alternatives not taken are explored, and the practical applicability and generalizability of strategies and insights from the simulation is tested against participants' knowledge and experience. If these conditions are adequately met, the model of simulation games as generators of new ideas and insights is persuasive and promising.

### Simulations for the Integration of Knowledge

To advance understanding and policy on global environmental change issues, the most important knowledge need is increasingly asserted to be "integrated assessment," the synthesis and organization of knowledge across domains to serve the needs of practical understanding, policy making, and decisions of a variety of actors.[25] The required integration or synthesis can be across a variety of dimensions: across research fields or disciplines, and also across degrees of formalism and confidence, and across people holding knowledge. Three purposes are normally identified for integrated assessment: to bound the importance of particular problems to determine which issues merit attention; to assess the potential consequences of specific policy or decision opportunities; and to identify and prioritize knowledge needs to help inform decisions. Meeting these needs for global environmental change issues and other complex policy problems can require integration or synthesis because disciplinary knowledge is not normally motivated or prioritized by its utility for decision needs, does not normally attend to the linkages between disciplinary domains that can be essential for drawing practical conclusions about the consequences of decisions, and does not normally provide any basis for accommodating informal or intuitive expert judgment.

To inform complex policy problems such as global environmental change, the breadth of integration potentially required is vast. Even if the issues are conceived narrowly, as assessing the environmental consequences of specified, fixed human activities, the breadth of knowledge about the physical and biological world that must be synthesized can be vast. For example, understanding the consequences of specified patterns of acid emissions requires integrating knowledge of atmospheric transport, chemistry, and deposition with knowledge about responses of lakes, forests, and soils under multiple forms of environmental change and other stresses. But since no single decision maker has the authority to determine the level of human emissions, assessing the consequences of particular feasible decisions or policies also requires knowledge of the behavioral, social, economic, political, and organizational factors that determine whether policies are feasible, how much they cost, and what effects they have on the human behavior that is ultimately of concern, plus understanding of ways of valuing the complex, multi-attribute environmental changes that will result.

Two standard methods attempt such integration of knowledge: formal integrated models, and multidisciplinary advisory panels. While these can each be informative and helpful, both suffer from basic limitations, concerned with limits on the breadth of the relevant knowledge that they are able to synthesize, and limits on their ability to clarify preferences or values at stake in the issue considered, or to accommodate diverse preferences.[26] Alternative methods have been proposed to seek aggregation of expert knowledge and opinion without requiring full consensus, such as the Delphi method and expert elicitation techniques.[27] Some of these methods show substantial promise for assessing collective expert views of well-posed uncertain quantities, but they are of little help in the problems of making integrated knowledge serve decision needs, or of accommodating diverse preferences and values that bear on policy choices.

Simulation-gaming methods can help fill some of the important gaps that are left by present assessment methodologies. In pursuing this goal, simulation methods have three salient advantages. First, their open structure permits them to focus and bring together into a transparent, structured, and common forum knowledge from an extremely wide variety of sources—the participants' knowledge, skills, and intuition; technical knowledge embedded in formal models; and research results and disciplinary knowledge from a variety of fields made available within a simulation in text or data. Because of the breadth of knowledge sources that can be represented, simulations can permit a comprehensive treatment of sources of uncertainty in an issue that arise from all sources: limitations of knowledge about the world, as well as strategic uncertainty about the preferences, choices sets, and resources of other actors.

Second, simulations require simulated decisions, and if well designed are sufficiently intense that participants take their decisions very seriously. The pressure on participants, and the requirement for practical action, can force participants to use the available sources of knowledge more aggressively, integrate them more broadly, and organize them more coherently to support their required decisions than they would do in a lower-pressure setting such as a panel meeting or a workshop. Among other benefits, this orientation toward practical decisions can force a sharper consideration than other assessment methods of what current knowledge is most valuable for informing present decisions, and what new knowledge would most help inform required future decisions.

Third, simulations can help to focus and elaborate the criteria by which the consequences are assessed, and the implications of different preferences and values bearing on the issue. Simulations can promote this clarification both by requiring participants to live through the simulated consequences of their choices, and by promoting the airing and elaboration of disparate views through team discussions and interteam negotiations.

The broad implications for simulation design of taking integrated assessment as a major objective are relatively clear. To realize the benefits of the ability to integrate from a wide set of knowledge domains, such knowledge must be made available within the simulation. Two design tradeoffs are likely to arise. First, where the amount of potentially relevant information is vast, there may be a choice between prescreening what is made available, hence the risk of introducing bias in what participants choose to use, and providing a vast ocean of information that could overwhelm the participants or make the simulation even longer and more unwieldy than such exercises already inevitably are (and hence, make it less likely to attract the required senior and expert participants). Second, where there are important gaps in present policy-relevant knowledge, there is a design tradeoff between responsibly characterizing the present state of knowledge, and keeping the decision environment of the simulation sufficiently simple, consistent, and vivid, which may argue for some fictitious extensions or filing of gaps in current knowledge. This second tension is more salient for simulations set in the future, when more knowledge may plausibly be available. This tension may be at the heart of the often denounced data problems and inaccuracies that plague simulation games.[28]

To realize the benefits of the practical decision-orientation of simulation, the exercise must require specific decisions and provide some plausible method of generating consequences, rather than, say, merely consisting of participant teams developing and elaborating scenarios. Such exercises may also have substantial value, but they do not help elaborate the information needs of policy choices; the two forms might complement each other, perhaps by alternating between the two.[29]

Simulation gaming may promise to be a more effective device for the broad integration of knowledge in support of decision and policy needs, in particular the integration of technical and strategic knowledge, than other currently available methods of "integrated assessment" such as formal integrated models. They are not the only effective integrated assessment methods, but they may have key advantages in certain aspects of integration, in particular in integrating scientific with strategic, behavioral, and judgmental knowledge, and in clarifying and exploring the implications of diverse preferences and values. The price is likely to be a lower-resolution treatment of scientific knowledge; while simulation methods can integrate such knowledge, with limited time and attention these are likely to be treated in less detail. Which forms, dimensions, and degrees of integration are likely to be the highest priorities will depend on the issue. Multiple forms of integrated assessment are likely to bring complementary benefits.

Though several commentators on simulation gaming have identified knowledge integration as potentially one of its strongest contributions, few exercises have yet taken this as a primary purpose.[30] Consequently, this application of simulation-gaming methods, while promising, remains relatively undeveloped.

## The Value of Simulation Games

This paper has presented four models of how simulation gaming can inform decision making on difficult, complex policy problems, and has argued that two of these models—simulations as experiments, and simulations to instruct decision makers—are either flawed or irrelevant in application to problems of this kind, while two—simulations to promote creativity and insights, or to integrate knowledge—are persuasive and promising. In sum, the potential contributions to better understanding and decision making that could result from the wider use of simulation methods according to the two persuasive models are great enough to justify their more widespread use.

Certain risks and conditions limit this endorsement; they do not negate the potential contribution of simulation, but do require vigilance. These risks are principally associated with the ambiguous status of predictive claims ascribed to simulations. Predictions, whether derived from simulations or other methods, are difficult, usually wrong, rarely done well, and not much improved by analytic complexity or size of modeling effort.[31] Still, analysts continue to make predictions— some through recognition that intellectually honest development of social theory requires taking the risk of making specific, falsifiable predictions,[32] and some for profit, in a flourishing industry of predictors ranging from the responsible and qualified through the enthusiastic, naive, and disreputable.[33]

The risks of inappropriate or excessive claims of predictive power take two forms: bias, and generalization from small samples. Bias can arise in the simulation's design or structure, in suggestions participants may unintentionally be given about how to act, or in the basic specification of what is relevant and important that is essential to simulation design.[34] It may be accidental, or introduced intentionally.[35] The risk of too-confident generalization arises because the rich narrative experience of a simulation lies somewhere between history and experiment—less rich and more replicable than the former, but much richer and less replicable than the latter. With few simulation runs, each yielding a complex narrative outcome, much of what happens is inevitably nongeneralizable variance.

As are other methods of analysis and assessment, simulation gaming is liable to tempt its users and audiences to ascribe stronger predictive power to the exercise than is appropriate, neglecting the risks of bias and generalizing excessively from tiny samples. Simulation methods may be more liable to fall into this trap than other methods, because the prediction of battle outcomes was their earliest objective and because they generate narrative outcomes of a vividness and specificity that can mislead the enthusiastic or naive, but formal analytic methods are also at risk. Formal models are more opaque, while simulations are more vivid and engaging; which approach is more likely to mislead no doubt will vary from case to case. Indeed, decision makers' unique experiences of real-life events also create a significant risk of excessive generalization from samples of one.[36]

Despite these risks, the potential contributions of simulation games, as of other methods for thinking about important decisions with enduring consequences, does depend on attaining a limited kind of predictive power. This consists of identifying contingencies and consequences that are sufficiently likely that they are relevant to consider in decision making, and of drawing broad comparative judgments regarding relative salience, likelihood, and consequences of particular choices.[37]

Consequently, the merit of simulation depends on sustaining a claim for a limited, qualified predictive power that, with qualifications and subject to corroboration through other means, provides a sufficient basis to justify some action under some conditions. The characteristics of this limited predictive power have resisted precise definition. Consequently, advocates of simulation and of other methods have sought to claim this ambiguous middle ground, asserting that their work makes valuable contributions to decision making and planning that do not depend upon specific (or even probabilistic) predictions. Both modelers and gamers tend to urge their audiences to disregard their exercise's specific results while taking very seriously its deeper and more general insights.[38]

Since these limited claims to quasipredictive power are not amenable to strong verification or refutation, they turn on other means of judging their plausibility and relevance that are necessarily informal and consensual. These other means can include correspondence with real system behavior, and the sober, retrospective reflection of participants and other experienced and knowledgeable people on the relevance, generalizability, and practicability of insights and ideas derived from the simulation.

In fact, inappropriate generalization may be more avoidable in simulation than in other methods or in inference from real events, for two reasons. First, simulations have a capability for replication, albeit a highly limited one. There might be particular value in running heterogeneous sets of simulations, with the same participants having different experiences, playing different roles, and engaging different specific problems, all within the same problem area. Second, simulation's risks are mitigated in the debriefing, when participants can question the simulation's relevance and generalizability, present other possibilities, and reflect critically on their experience, at some distance from the experience they have just lived through.

One must approach complex policy problems with some humility, whatever means is used to study them. While the potential contributions of simulation gaming are large, and complementary to those of other methods, it is undeniable that despite 40 years of experience, simulation-gaming methods have not yet lived up to their perceived promise. The reasons are not clear. Garry Brewer and Martin Shubik, reviewing the experience with both simulation games and formal models in military planning, cite a variety of reasons including limited publication and limited forums to develop and support professional standards.[39] Outside security, the sparser experience with simulations makes these problems more severe. Current technological advances in communications, computing power, interfaces, and modeling tools are substantially advancing what can be achieved in simulation, and making feasible alternative forms of simulation that would no longer require assembling a large number of expert participants for a week. How these new tools could advance the standards of simulation gaming as presently practiced, and the merits and limits posed by such new fora as distributed simulation, are not yet explored.

## Notes

1. Alfred H. Hausrath, *Venture Simulation in War, Business, and Politics* (New York: McGraw-Hill, 1971), pp. 1–5.
2. Garry D. Brewer and Martin Shubik, *The War Game: A Critique of Military Problem-Solving* (Cambridge, MA: Harvard University Press, 1979).
3. See, for example, Martin Shubik, *The Uses and Methods of Gaming* (New York: Elsevier, 1975), Table 2.1, p. 28; K. C. Bowen, *Research Games* (London: Taylor and Francis, 1978), pp. 11–17; and William M. Jones, *On the Adapting of Political-Military Games for Various Purposes* (Santa Monica, CA: RAND Corporation, N-2413-AF/A, March 1986).
4. Paul Bracken, "Gaming in Hierarchical Defense Organizations," in *Avoiding the Brink: Theory and Practice in Crisis Management*, eds. Andrew C. Goldberg, Debra Van Opstal, and James H. Barkley (London: Brassey's, 1990), pp. 81–98.
5. See, for example, Margaret A. Thomas, *An Energy Crisis Management Simulation for the State of California* (Santa Monica, CA: RAND Corporation, R-2899-CEC, August 1982).
6. See, for example, Edward A. Parson, *Negotiating Climate Cooperation: Learning from Theory, Simulations, and History*, doctoral dissertation, Harvard University, 1992; Robert J. Lempert and William Schwabe, "Transition to Sustainable Waste Management: A Simulation Gaming Approach" (Santa Monica, CA: RAND Corporation, European-American Center for Policy Analysis, 1993); Jill Jager et al., "The Challenge of Sustainable Development in a Greenhouse World: Some Visions of the Future" (Stockholm: Stockholm Environment Institute, 1991); and Laura Cornwell and Robert Costanza, "An Experimental Analysis of the Effectiveness of an Environmental Bonding System on Player Behavior in a Simulated Firm," *Ecological Economics* 11 (1994): 213–226.
7. Shubik, *The Uses and Methods*, p. 7. Other forms of simulation include

physical models such as wind tunnels, formal mathematical representations such as predator-prey models, and computer models.

8. Thomas C. Schelling, "An Uninhibited Sales Pitch for Crisis Games," Internal Research Memorandum, RAND Corporation, circulated Summer 1964 and published in "Crisis Games 27 Years Later: plus c'est deja vu" (Santa Monica, CA: RAND Corporation, P-7719, 1964).

9. Harvey DeWeerd, "A Contextual Approach to Scenario Construction," *Simulation and Games* 5 (1975): 403–414; and Peter de Leon, "Scenario Designs: An Overview," *Simulation and Games* 6 (1975): 39–60.

10. Lincoln Bloomfield, "Reflections on Gaming," *Orbis* 27 (1984): 783–790; William M. Jones, *On Free-Form Gaming* (Santa Monica, CA: RAND Corporation, N-2322-RC, 1985).

11. Nihajlo D. Mesarovic, *Globesight: A System for Integrated Assessment of Climate Change* (Cleveland, OH: Systems Applications, 1994).

12. Howard Raiffa, *The Art and Science of Negotiation* (Cambridge, MA: Harvard University Press, 1982); Garry D. Brewer, "Methods for Synthesis: Policy Exercises," in *Sustainable Development of the Biosphere*, eds. William C. Clark and R. E. Munn (Cambridge: Cambridge University Press, 1986), pp. 455–473; Ferenc L. Toth, "Models and Games for Long-Term Policy Problems," paper presented to the 1994 Meeting of the International Simulation and Gaming Association (ISAGA), Ann Arbor, MI, 1994; Ferenc L. Toth, "Policy Exercises: Objectives and Design Elements," reprinted as International Institute for Applied Systems Analysis (IIASA) RR-89-2, *Simulation and Games* 19 (September 1988): 256–276; Ferenc L. Toth, "Policy Exercises: Procedures and Implementation," reprinted as IIASA, RR-89-2, *Simulation and Games* 19 (September 1988): 256–276; Ferenc L. Toth, "Policy Exercises: The First Ten Years," paper presented to the 1994 Meeting of ISAGA, Ann Arbor, MI, 1994; and C. S. Holling, ed., *Adaptive Environmental Assessment and Management* (Chichester: Wiley, 1978); Nicholas C. Sonntag, "Commentary," in *Sustainable Development of the Biosphere*, eds. Clark and Munn, pp. 472–475.

13. See, for example, Robert A. Levine, *Crisis Games for Adults*, Internal Research Memorandum, RAND Corporation, circulated Summer 1964 and published in "Crisis Games 27 Years Later: plus c'est deja vu"; Randall L. Schultz and Edward M. Sullivan, "Developments in Simulation in Social and Administrative Science," in *Simulation in the Social and Administrative Sciences*, eds. Harold Guetzkow, Philip Kotler, and Randall L. Schultz (Englewood Cliffs, NJ: Prentice-Hall, 1972); and Brewer and Shubik, *The War Game*.

14. Experimental economists, studying decisions whose most important outcomes are monetary, achieve this confidence by paying participants according to their outcomes. See, for example, Alvin E. Roth, "Laboratory

Experimentation in Economics," *The Economic Journal* 98 (1988): 974–1031. For decision problems whose important outcomes are not purely monetary, it is not clear that payments would achieve the intended effect.

15. Guetzkow has pointed out that in simulating foreign policy, the most central problems of realism are time and memory, in particular the absence in the accelerated simulated world of slow processes of learning, adaptation, reconciliation, cooling of tempers, and forgetting that occur over the time-scales of real government decision making. In crisis management, though, the relationship of real and simulated time-scales can be reversed; a major purpose of simulation can be to permit more leisurely or repeated "dress rehearsal" of organizational responses to crises that demand response too fast for reflection. Harold G. Guetzkow, "Six Continuing Queries for Global Modelers: A Self-Critique," in *Simulated International Processes: Theories and Research in Global Modeling* (Beverly Hills, CA: Sage Publications, 1981), pp. 331–358.

16. This aspiration for simulations has been stated most cogently by Harold Guetzkow and his colleagues. See, in particular, Harold Guetzkow, "Simulations in the Consolidation and Utilization of Knowledge about International Relations," in *Theory and Research on the Causes of War*, eds. Dean G. Pruitt and Richard C. Snyder (Englewood Cliffs, NJ: Prentice-Hall, 1969); Richard C. Snyder, "Some Perspectives on the Use of Experimental Techniques in the Study of International Relations," in *Simulation in International Relations: Developments for Research and Teaching,* eds. Harold Guetzkow et al. (Englewood Cliffs, NJ: Prentice-Hall, 1963); and the essays collected in Michael Don Ward, ed., *Theories, Models, and Simulations in International Relations: Essays in Honor of Harold Guetzkow* (Boulder, CO: Westview Press, 1985). In addition, Robert Mandel summarizes the use of political games to test hypotheses about systematic perceptual biases of decision-makers in crises, in "Political Gaming and Foreign Policy Making during Crises," *World Politics* 29 (1977): 610–625.

17. Karl Popper, *The Logic of Scientific Discovery* (New York: Harper and Row, 1968).

18. Levine, *Crisis Games for Adults;* and K. C. Bowen, *Research Games.*

19. Harold Guetzkow and Joseph J. Valadez, "Simulation and 'Reality': Validation Research," in *Simulated International Processes*, eds. Guetzkow and Valadez, pp. 253–330; Mandel, "Political Gaming"; and Schelling, "An Uninhibited Sales Pitch."

20. James G. March, Lee S. Sproull, and Michal Tamuz, "Learning from Samples of One and Fewer," *Organization Science* 2 (1991): 1–13.

21. Guetzkow and Valadez, "Simulation and 'Reality'"; and Mandel, "Political Gaming."

22. For example, Schelling reports a consistent difficulty in keeping a crisis boiling across many simulations with disparate settings, contexts, and

participants, and advances a cogent explanation based on how teams manage internal differences over how forcefully they should act. Thomas C. Schelling, "The Role of War Games and Exercises," in *Managing Nuclear Operations*, eds. Ashton B. Carter, John D. Steinbruner, and Charles A. Zraket, pp. 426–444 (Washington, DC: Brookings Institution, 1987).

23. Schelling, "An Uninhibited Sales Pitch."

24. Parson, *Negotiating Climate Cooperation.*

25. Edward A. Parson, "Searching for Integrated Assessment," paper presented to the 3rd meeting of the CIESIN Commission on Global Environmental Change Information Policy, Washington, DC, February 17, 1994; Hadi Dowlatabadi and M. Granger Morgan, "Integrated Assessment of Climate Change," *Science* 259 (1993): 1813; Edward S. Rubin et al., "Integrated Assessment of Acid-Deposition Effects on Lake Acidification," *Journal of Environmental Engineering* 118 (1992): 120–134; and Brewer, "Methods for Synthesis."

26. See, for example, William C. Clark, "Themes for a Research Program," in *Sustainable Development of the Biosphere*, eds. Clark and Munn; and William C. Clark and Giandomenico Majone, "The Critical Use of Scientific Inquiries with Policy Implications," *Science, Technology, and Human Values* 10 (1985): 6–19.

27. Norman C. Dalkey, *Studies in the Quality of Life: Delphi and Decision-Making* (Lexington, MA: Lexington Books, 1972); M. Granger Morgan and Max Henrion, *Uncertainty: A Guide to Dealing with Uncertainty in Quantitative Risk and Policy Analysis* (New York: Cambridge University Press, 1990); David Keith and M. Granger Morgan, "Elicitation of Expert Opinion Regarding Climate Uncertainty," *Environmental Science and Technology*, forthcoming.

28. See, for example, Brewer and Shubik, *The War Game*; Martin Shubik, *Games for Society, Business, and War* (New York: Elsevier, 1972), esp. pp. 299–308; and Garry D. Brewer and Bruce Blair, "War Games and National Security with a Grain of SALT," *The Bulletin of the Atomic Scientists* (June 1979): 18–26.

29. William M. Jones, *On Free-Form Gaming* (Santa Monica, CA: RAND Corporation, N-2322-RC, 1985), p. 42; Robert Mandel, "Professional-Level War Gaming: A Critical Assessment," in *Theories, Models, and Simulations*, ed. Ward, pp. 483–500.

30. See Brewer, "Methods for Synthesis"; Uno Svedin and Britt Aniansson, eds., *Surprising Futures*, Report 87:1 (Stockholm: Swedish Council for Planning and Coordination of Research, 1987); Jager et al., *The Challenge of Sustainable Development*; and Toth, "Policy Exercises: The First Ten Years."

31. William Ascher, *Forecasting: An Appraisal for Policy-Makers and Planners* (Baltimore, MD: Johns Hopkins University Press, 1978).

32. Ithiel de Sola Pool, "The Art of the Social Science Soothsayer," in *Forecasting*

*in International Relations: Theory, Methods, Problems, Prospects,* eds. Nazli Choucri and Thomas W. Robinson (San Francisco: W. H. Freeman and Company, 1978).

33. Herbert L. Smith, "The Social Forecasting Industry," in *Forecasting in the Social and Natural Sciences,* eds. Kenneth C. Land and Stephen H. Schneider (Dordrecht: Reidel, 1987).

34. Harey DeWeerd, "A Contextual Approach to Scenario Construction," *Simulation and Games* 5 (1975): 403.

35. Paul Bracken, "Unintended Consequences of Strategic Gaming," *Simulation and Games* 8 (1977): 283–318.

36. Lloyd S. Etheredge, *Can Governments Learn?* (New York: Pergamon, 1985).

37. Garry D. Brewer, "Discovery Is Not Prediction," in *Avoiding the Brink: Theory and Practice in Crisis Management,* eds. Andrew C. Goldberg, Debra Van Opstal, and James H. Barkley (London: Brassey's, 1990), pp. 99–107.

38. Schwarz et al. observe, ironically, that researchers working in predictive methodologies never say "prediction," and only call other peoples' work "forecasts"; their own products are called "projections" or "scenarios." Brita Schwarz, Uno Svedin, and B. Wittrock, *Methods in Futures Studies: Problems and Applications* (Boulder, CO: Westview Press, 1982), p. 109.

39. Brewer and Shubik, *The War Game,* pp. 272–274.

# CHAPTER 15

# COALITION FORMATION, COMMUNICATION, AND COORDINATION: AN EXPLORATORY EXPERIMENT

## Gary E Bolton and Kalyan Chatterjee

Most negotiations are multilateral. International treaty negotiations, such as those on the law of the sea,[1] the conference on global warming, and recent peace treaties have all been explicitly multilateral. Even many seemingly bilateral negotiations actually involve several players. When a seller negotiates with a buyer, usually both players could approach alternative partners if the negotiation falters. A negotiator is sometimes an agent for a coalition; this is often true for purchases of consumer durables like a house or a car, where a husband and wife need to form a coalition, and is even more prevalent in the sale of industrial products, where engineering and sales, for example, need to agree.

The two-person bargaining game has received the most attention in the academic literature, for the very good reason that one should probably not try to run before one can walk. Recent work, however, has investigatied how coalitions form, a phenomenon that highlights many of the issues that are important to multilateral negotiations. The conceptual distinctions are clearly enunciated by Howard Raiffa.[2] He points out that in a multiparty game, even if there is an impasse with one potential partner, "you can still cooperate with a coalition of some of the others. If there is only one other party, this complexity can't be

---

We thank Jim Sebenius and Kathleen Valley for their comments on the manuscript.

formulated. But even if there are two other negotiating parties—say, B and C—you might consider what you could do with B alone, or with C alone, or with both." Raiffa then discusses the new strategic issues involved. "Should you first approach B and compromise . . . before jointly approaching C? What would be your reaction if B and C collude before you can get into the act? . . . The complexities can become surprisingly rich with just three players, even if we concentrate on the polar extreme where each party faces a world of certainty and where there is only one issue involved."

This paper seeks to enrich our understanding of the questions identified by Raiffa through the study of one particular game: Suppose Player 1 must purchase a design for a one-way diffusive membrane that will be used in the manufacture of Player 1's own product. There are two potential sellers, Players 2 and 3, who can both develop the membrane but cannot produce the final product. Player 1 can develop the membrane with either player or he can sign an agreement with both. While the second seller will not contribute as much as the first, he will still contribute some positive amount, because the two sellers working together can reduce development time. We model this as a game in which the worth or value of the coalition $\{1, 2, 3\}$ denoted by $v(1, 2, 3)$ is 144, while $v(1, 2)$ and $v(1, 3) = 100$. The coalition $\{2, 3\}$ as well as the individual players by themselves can get nothing.

In this game, Player 1 (the buyer) is prima facie in a strong position; the other two are unable to obtain a positive payoff without his participation. As explained in the next section, game theory provides varying estimates of Player 1's strength. Other arguments imply that the buyer's strength may be decreased by equity concerns and the tendency for an equal split to become a focal split.

We study two basic issues. The first is the role of communication. One type of communication consists of making formal offers. If negotiators are bargaining in good faith, this is relatively costly; it implies some commitment to the offer made. There is also informal communication, in which issues are discussed without any implied commitment to a specific offer. This type of communication can explore alternatives in a manner that is less costly in the commitment sense, though it does take up time.[3]

The second issue we explore is the extent to which existing theory describes actual negotiating patterns. In the real world, negotiations proceed in many ways. Telephone calls or private meetings between two parties often supplement or even displace meetings among all three parties, and may lead to the development of informal coalitions. Sometimes, a procedure is followed, such as repeated simultaneous offers. Other negotiations appear to have far less structure.

Our experiment was intended to explore how communication and the structure of negotiations influence multilateral bargaining outcomes. There were two treatments, both face to face, one with a well-defined extensive form, and the other with no structure but with a seven-minute deadline.[4] We chose face-to-face interaction to account for the possible confounding effects discussed below. By examining the differences in behavior across the two treatments, and the differences between theoretical predictions and actual results, we are able to draw conclusions about the directions in which the theory should be modified and extended. We find that different communication structures have significant effects in determining what coalitions will form and how the payoff will be divided. We also find that a restricted communication structure allows the buyer to exploit his power better than an unrestricted one. One can, of course, read too much into the results of a single experiment. However, our results are striking enough, as we hope the sequel will show, that we believe that replications will find similar behavior.

In the next section we discuss the game-theoretic literature associated with this problem. The third section discusses previous experimental work on two-party and coalitional bargaining. The fourth section sets out the experimental design and methodology, and the following section presents the results. The final section suggests directions for future research.[5]

## The Game-Theoretic Literature on Coalitional Bargaining

There are two basic approaches to modeling games in characteristic function form (the form in which we presented coalitional values in the last section). The first, associated with "cooperative" game theory, lays down principles or axioms about the game and then derives implications about how the gains from coalition formation will be allocated. Most work in this genre assumes that when the grand coalition of all players is efficient, as in the game described above, it will form. The "core" of a characteristic function game is, in essence, the set of payoffs such that no other coalition can do better for all of its members. For example, in the game discussed above, two core allocations for Players 1, 2, and 3 are (56, 44, 44) and (142, 1, 1). Coalition {1, 2} or {1, 3} can get 100 by itself. Consequently, in any core allocation, the sum of the payoffs to 1 and 2, and to 1 and 3 must be at least 100. Players 2 and 3 cannot get a positive amount on their own and all players together can get 144, so that the two allocations shown (and many others besides) are in the core. Note, however, that (48, 48, 48) is not; nor is (50, 50, 0). The Shapley value, another popular solution concept, is an average of marginal contributions. One can picture the grand coalition being formed by players arriving in a sequence, with each player allotted the entire amount he adds to the value of the coalition in place when the player arrives. The Shapley value is the average allocation computed over all possible sequences of arrival. For our game it would predict a grand coalition formation with an allocation of (81.33, 31.33, 31.33).

Raiffa introduces these classic solution concepts by asking "What's fair?"[6] The axioms are, therefore, interpreted as arbitration principles. Some game theorists argue that the axioms define descriptively valid principles; rather than explicitly modeling the offer and counter-offer sequence, they capture general characteristics of the process of bargaining.[7] The problem with this interpretation is that it is not clear whether the axioms reflect all bargaining processes or just a particular class. We use it, however, since we are concerned here with descriptive rather than normative issues.

The second game-theoretic approach is "noncooperative"; that is, the process of decision making is explicitly modeled by an extensive form.[8] Recently, there has been a revival of interest in such models.[9] A model by Reinhard Selten admits a multiplicity of equilibria, while one by Faruk Gul focuses on a specific procedure that generates the Shapley value. Similarly, Motty Perry and Philip Reny investigate the noncooperative justification for the core. Chatterjee et al. consider an extensive form where one player begins by proposing a coalition and an allocation. The other players named in the proposal respond sequentially, either accepting or rejecting, and the first rejecter makes a new proposal. As time elapses, payoffs are discounted. There is no exogenous limit on the duration of the game. (Selten's model has the same sequential offers structure, but no discounting, and permits only a single coalition to form.) The stationary equilibrium allocation predicted by Chatterjee et al. for the game above (as the discount factor goes to 1) is (50, 50, 0) or (50, 0, 50). That is, a two-player coalition, {1, 2} or {1, 3}, is predicted to form and to share the coalitional payoff 50–50.

The extensive form treatment of our experiment consists of a finite number of stages. In each stage, a player is randomly chosen to propose a coalition and allocation of the coalition's value. If all members of the proposed coalition accept the proposal, then the game ends and each player receives the stipulated payoff. If one of them rejects the proposal, the game proceeds to the next stage. If there is a rejection in the last stage, the game ends and every player receives a payoff of zero. When there are two stages, the equilibrium predicts agreement in the first stage, with Player 1 getting an expected payoff of 49.34 percent and Players 2 and 3 getting 25.34 percent each. If there are four or more stages, and we assume that if Player 1 receives the same payoff from coalitions {1, 2} and {1, 3} he will choose either with equal probability, the equilibrium prediction is (64, 40, 40) no matter who makes the proposal.[10] This prediction is in the core, but is a far lower estimate of Player 1's power than is given by the Shapley value. In contrast, Chatterjee et al. would predict a two-player coalition with Player 1 getting only 50, considerably less than either of the two above. Thus, different extensive forms predict very different coalitions and allocations of surplus. The usefulness of the extensive form approach is that it gives negotiators some indication of which procedure might be most advantageous; it also enables analysts to compare different predictions to the outcomes of free-form negotiation to see how theory must be extended—one of the purposes of this paper.

To summarize, we have two kinds of prediction for our game. The first kind of prediction is independent of the bargaining procedure; such predictions are supposed to hold especially in free form and also for all extensive forms. In this category are the Shapley value, which predicts 81.33 for Player 1 and 31.33 for each of the other players, and the core, a set of payoffs that range from 56 to 144 for Player 1. The second kind of prediction is specific to the procedure; however, to the extent that the procedure matches what happens in the free-form negotiation, this is relevant also for the analysis of the free form. The prediction for the extensive form we use in our experiment is a payoff of 64 for Player 1 and 40 for each of the others. Chatterjee et al. would predict a two-player coalition between Player 1 and one of the other players, with each getting approximately 50, and the excluded player getting 0. Equal split focal points would be 48 for each player with all three getting together, or 50–50 with Player 1 and one other getting together. Note that the two-player coalition is inefficient, since the third player can add a value of 44.

## The Experimental Literature on Bargaining

Recent experimental work in two-person bargaining has led to debate on some of the more fundamental tenets of human behavior—concern for equity or fairness in distributing gains versus various forms of self-interest. Some work has addressed bargainers' ability to reason, and has challenged the empirical validity of backwards induction (that is, looking ahead to the last stage of the game and reasoning backwards to the beginning). This section reviews some of the findings from that literature.[11]

The recent burst of research on two-person bargaining began with

Werner Güth, Rolf Schmittberger, and Bernd Schwarze, who studied a simple bargaining game in which one bargainer proposes a split of a fixed amount of cash.[12] The other bargainer can accept the proposal, in which case the cash is divided according to the proposal, or reject it, in which case both bargainers receive nothing. The standard game-theoretic analysis of this game begins with the assumption that each bargainer's sole objective is to obtain the most money possible. If so, the responding bargainer should accept any proposal that gives him a positive amount of cash. Consequently, the first player should propose to give the second no more than the smallest positive payoff allowed. In perfect equilibrium, the game ends with the proposer getting virtually all the money. But in the experiment, proposers tended to offer responders amounts significantly higher than the minimum allowed (although rarely more than half), responders frequently rejected proposals that offered them a positive value, and smaller offers were generally rejected more often than larger ones. Later work by two groups studied a multistage generalization of this game in which the perfect equilibrium is found using the same reasoning as in the single-stage case. Other researchers have reported that Güth et al.'s original findings are robust with regard to the cultural background of the subjects, framing and experimenter observation, the amount of cash negotiated over (up to $100), as well as other minor variations.[13]

One explanation for these results is that a bargainer cares about the amount of money he receives, and also about how favorable the relative division of the money is for him—each bargainer cares about whether he receives his *own* fair share.[14] The implications of this hypothesis are basically consistent with the experimental observations (at least for the one- and two-stage games). A second hypothesis is that bargainers learn by adaptation.[15] The rate at which a strategy is played depends on its past performance, with higher past payoffs leading to faster adaptation. This implies that responders learn to accept small offers more slowly than large offers. Proposers will therefore have an incentive to move away from very small offers to obtain the higher expected value of larger offers. Simulations show a pattern of play similar to that observed in experiments. It is not clear whether or to what extent explanations based on fairness and those based on learning are complementary or mutually exclusive. Nor is it clear whether (or in what sense) learning explanations by themselves are sufficient to explain why responders must "learn" to accept a proposal that gives them money.

Bargaining among several parties to form coalitions highlights several issues, notably the lack of a single standard of equity (what should be equally divided, the grand coalition payoff or the two-player payoff?), and the introduction of competition among potential partners. Much experimental work has been done in coalitional bargaining.[16] Selten analyzes several experiments on coalition formation, focusing mainly on experiments that allow unrestricted face-to-face communication and forbid secret negotiations or precommitment to coalitions. Selten also reports an experiment by Maschler that used a game similar to the one we consider, but sets the grand coalition value at 125 (we use 144). The grand coalition actually forms on average and splits the payoff (55, 35, 35).[17]

The results most relevant for our work are reported by Raiffa.[18] In one experiment, where subjects negotiate face-to-face and private meetings are permitted, over 90 percent of the teams formed three-way coalitions, and split the entire grand coalition payoff of 121. (The game has a strong player, Player A, whose coalition with B has a worth of 118 and with C a worth of 84. B and C get 50 together and all three get 121.) On average, A got 69 in these experiments. In a second experiment, subjects communicated by computer. Three out of 67 triads did not settle at all and only 3 triads formed the grand coalition. Raiffa's explanation for this striking difference is that "people probably find it easier to act tough if they are not looking at the other negotiators—if the others are anonymous. It's hard to squeeze out someone else from a coalition when that person is looking at you." Raiffa warns that more experimentation needs to be done.

With regard to communication, our experiment complements those reported by Raiffa (and run by him and Elon Kohlberg). In one treatment, communication is restricted to what is allowed by the extensive form, while in the other subjects may communicate with no restriction. Both treatments of our experiment, however, were face to face.

Finally, in this section, we discuss an experiment by Chatterjee and Bettina Kuon that sheds some light on how equity can motivate behavior.[19] The experiment used a game with one strong player and two weak ones, as in the Raiffa-Kohlberg games and this paper. Bargaining was done over a computer, and communication was restricted to actual offers. Players followed the Chatterjee et al. extensive form with the modification that the game would stop after nearly 800 rounds, perhaps as close to an infinite number of stages as one can do in the lab.

The following game was played: $v(1, 2, 3) = 100 + \mu$; $v(1, 2) = v(1, 3) = 100$; $v(2, 3) = \in < 100$, $v(\cdot) = 0$ for all other coalitions. For $50 > \mu > 0$, the stationary equilibrium predicts payoffs of (50, 0, 50) or (50, 50, 0), but for $\mu > 50$, the grand coalition would form and divide equally. Four values for $\mu$ of 0, 30, 40, and 60 and two for $\in$ of 5 and 40 were chosen. (The current paper studies a game similar to Chatterjee and Kuon with $\mu = 44$ and $\in = 0$.) Several results are relevant. First, for most ($\mu$, $\in$) combinations, there is a difference in outcome between the first 20 games and the next 40 games. (Each group of six players were rotated through 60 games.) In the first 20 games, the grand coalition formed less often; Player 1 received payoffs of around 50; and there was more immediate resolution (for values of $\mu < 50$). The first 20 games therefore exhibit more two-player coalitions forming and splitting equally. As players become more experienced, Player 1's pay-off increases to about 70 and the grand coalition forms more often. While the initial pattern of coalition formation was more consistent with the Chatterjee et al. game-theoretic predictions and a two-player equal split theory, Player 1, the strong player, increased his payoff substantially as the number of repetitions increased. Thus, equity did not seem to be the driving force behind the payoff allocations in all stages of the experiment.

## Experimental Design and Methodology

Our experiment involved two treatments of a three-person coalition game. Two Sellers, A and C, competed to make a contract with one Buyer. (Written directions provided to subjects are included in the Appendix.) Feasible coalitions and their payoffs were identical for the two treatments:

| Contracting Parties | Total Profit of Contract |
|---|---|
| Buyer and Seller A | 100 |
| Buyer and Seller C | 100 |
| Buyer, Seller A, and Seller C | 144 |
| No contract | 0 |

In both treatments, all three players sat at a table, so that each player could see the other two. Each player's role and payoff were known to all.

In the free form treatment, players had seven minutes to negotiate a contract; no structure was imposed, but raised voices and threatening gestures were banned for the purpose of maintaining order. The game ended when a "contracting form," specifying how profits would be distributed among coalition members, had been signed by all parties within an agreeing coalition. A two-person coalition did not need the consent of the excluded party. If, at the end of seven minutes, no contract had been signed, then the game ended and each player received a profit of zero.

In the extensive form treatment, players negotiated within the confines of a strict extensive form game. The game was played in a maximum of four stages. At the beginning of each stage, one player was randomly selected to propose both a coalition and how profits should be distributed among its members. The proposer wrote this information on a form and passed it clockwise to each of the other proposed coalition members. Proposed members examined the proposal and then checked either "accept" or "reject" on the form. If all proposed partners accepted, then the game ended and each coalition member received the proposed share of the profits. If any one of the proposed partners rejected, then the game proceeded to a new stage. All players not in a contract at the end of the game received a profit of zero. No communication beyond the proposal forms was permitted; in particular, players were not allowed to talk during or between the games.

In all other ways, the methodology for both treatments was the same. At the beginning of each session, written rules were read aloud to the whole group. Subjects were divided into randomly selected, equal-sized groups of Buyers, Sellers A, and Sellers C. They then played several games (five in the extensive form treatment and six in the free-form treatment) in round robin fashion. Each subject had the same role in every game. No three subjects played together more than once. All players kept records of their payoffs in each game for reference.

At the end of the session, one game was selected by lottery as the payoff game. Each subject's payment depended on the profit he earned in the payoff game relative to the profit each of the other players with the same role earned in that game. For example, the Seller A who earned the highest profit among all Sellers A received the highest payment; the Seller A with the second-highest profit among all Sellers A received the second-highest payoff, etc. The payoff schedule was identical for all three roles. (See the Appendix for the schedules.) In case of a tie, the players received the average of the relevant awards. The payoff schedule was announced before play started, and each subject received a written copy. After each game, profits received were sorted and a list of what cash payment each profit level would receive if that game were the payoff game was displayed to subjects on an overhead projector. Profit levels were displayed by player role without identifying individual players.

This tournament payoff schedule provides an incentive for each player to gain profits during each game. While we could have accomplished this more directly, we hoped that the tournament schedule would diminish the equity considerations that play an important part in many experiments, and which face-to-face negotiation could magnify. Players' concern about equity usually leads to symmetric splits even when strategic strength is unequally distributed, as in this game. (We are primarily concerned here with strategic strength, so reducing the salience of the equal split makes our results more striking.) Since each player's cash payoff depends on his performance relative to others with the same role, a unit of game profit probably would not have the same cash value to, say, a Buyer as it would to, say, a Seller A. Consequently, appeals to value comparisons during bargaining are more difficult, and to the extent that they persist, they may very well be compatible with nonsymmetrical profit proposals. In fact, any outcome, no matter how asymmetrical in terms of game profits, may lead to equal cash payoffs depending on the performance of the group as a whole. Bolton provides some evidence that tournament schedules for two-person bargaining games tend to encourage asymmetrical splits. In addition, since real-world negotiators and salespeople are often compensated in a tournament style, our payoff scheme seemed likely to enhance the implications of our results.

All subjects were students at Pennsylvania State University, and were recruited through signs posted around campus. Participants were required to appear at a specified time and place. Cash was the only incentive offered. Each subject participated in a single treatment. Fifteen subjects participated in the extensive form treatment, and 18 participated in the free-form treatment. The average earning for both treatments was $15.

## Results

This section compares the coalitions formed and the allocations of profit within those coalitions for the two treatments. In addition, we summarize stage-by-stage play of the extensive form.

The difference in coalition formation is stark. In the free-form treatment, the grand coalition formed all but four times (32 out of 36 games, or 89 percent). Four two-player coalitions formed; two in round 2, and one each in rounds 3 and 6. All four involved Seller A and the Buyer. No games ended without a contract. In the extensive form treatment, the grand coalition formed only once (in round 2) and one game ended without a contract (in round 3). In all of the other games, two-person coalitions formed (23 of 25 games, or 92 percent). Of these, Seller A entered a coalition with the Buyer in 61 percent of the games and Seller C entered with the Buyer in the remaining 39 percent.

Table 15-1 exhibits the average profit earned by each type of player in each treatment. One Buyer in the extensive form treatment consistently earned a much higher profit than other Buyers. With or without the outlier, average payoffs tend to be somewhat higher for the ex-

**Table 15-1**

*Average Player Profit over all Coalitions by Treatment*
*(standard deviation)*

|                   | Buyer   | Seller A | Seller C |
|-------------------|---------|----------|----------|
| Free Form         | 49.6    | 47.4     | 47.3     |
|                   | (1.61)  | (2.23)   | (0.66)   |
| Extensive Form    | 54.7    | 43.3     | 48.2     |
|                   | (11.41) | (9.47)   | (3.05)   |
| Extensive Form*   | 51.4    | 48.7     | 48.0     |
|                   | (3.00)  | (2.87)   | (3.16)   |

*Excludes games played by an outlier Buyer

tensive form. The scattergram displayed in Figure 15-1 tends to confirm this.

For the extensive form treatment, the average number of stages played per round ranged from 2 to 3 (overall average of 2.4 and median of 2), and did not consistently increase or decrease across rounds. About an equal number of games ended in 1, 2, 3, and 4 stages (mode of 2). Only one game ended without a contract. Interestingly, the grand coalition was proposed in 12 of 25 (48 percent) of the games, even though only 1 game ended with a three-player coalition.

## Discussion and Conclusions

The most striking feature of the data is the difference in coalition formation patterns between the extensive form and the free-form versions. In the extensive form version, the grand coalition formed only once in 25 games, while two-person coalitions formed in 23 out of 25 games. In the free-form exercise, behavior was almost completely reversed; 32 of 36 games resulted in the grand coalition. This difference cannot be ascribed to face-to-face versus computerized interactions; both experiments were done face to face. A possible explanation is that the free-form treatment allowed for nearly unrestricted communication, and therefore allowed the two weak players to make informal arrangements among themselves that they later found difficult to break. In the extensive form, there was no "cheap talk"; the only way to exchange information was through the offers. Experimentation was therefore more costly in the extensive form, since with probability 2/3 the proposer cannot make a new proposal in the next period. In the extensive form, this could have led to a tendency to play it safe by trying to structure an offer that only one player, not two, would have

**Figure 15-1**
*Buyer's Profit from Coalition Agreement (by round)*

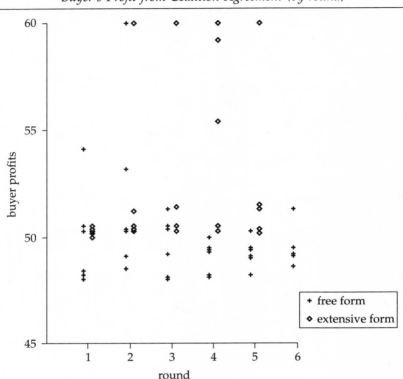

to find acceptable. Indeed, only one grand coalition proposal was accepted; experience with these offers was mostly negative. This suggests that a theory of negotiation must explicitly incorporate the increased cost of experimentation when larger coalitions must be formed.

The free-form payoffs were split three ways almost equally. The Buyer (the strong player) usually obtained a little more than one-third of the total payoff, but only slightly more. None of the grand coalition allocations was in the core, and the Shapley value also did extremely poorly in predicting this allocation. It seems that the powerful draw of the egalitarian solution overwhelmed any power that the strong player might possess. Possibly the tournament structure of payoffs led individuals to reason that a payoff slightly higher than one-third the total would be enough, since other triads would also focus on the equal split; however, in this case the strong player could be expected to ask for and obtain higher payoffs in succeeding rounds. Yet the allocation was remarkably stable over the six rounds of the game, although six rounds may not be long enough for any dynamics to emerge.

In the extensive form, the strong player's payoffs tended to increase somewhat over time. Based on this experiment, the strong player is better off in the structured environment of the extensive form than in the free form, with average payoffs that were a little higher than 50, as opposed to 48 for the free form. The extensive form results are not compatible with the theoretical predictions, and even less so with popular cooperative game theory concepts. Our data might be viewed as corroboration of Janet Neelin et al., who found that subjects played as if they used backwards induction but looked ahead only one stage in the future.[20] Such a policy in this game would yield the two-player coalition with the strong player getting a little less than 50. The Chatterjee et al. extensive form would also produce a two-player coalition with the proposer getting a little more than 50.

What conclusions do these results suggest about bargaining theory? The cooperative solution concepts of the Shapley value and the core proved to be far off the mark even in the unstructured environment where they should be applicable. The extensive form theories were not accurate predictors of the free form, though a two-stage extensive form (rather than the four-stage one used here) would have generated predictions close to what happened in the restricted communication experiment. The focal point/equal split theories fared somewhat better, except that in the free form the equity standard was a three-player one and in the extensive form a two-player split appeared to have been the focal point. Comparing these conclusions with the indications from the Chatterjee-Kuon experiment, it does not appear that equal splits are a sufficient explanation for what occurs in coalitional bargaining, unless one can predict when the standard will shift from the two-player to the three-player one and when players would be able to defeat equity standards over time, as they appear to have done in those experiments. A satisfactory explanation of our results requires a better understanding of how communication affects bargaining to form coalitions.

A final comment from the asymmetric prescriptive/descriptive viewpoint advocated by Raiffa may be appropriate. The "outlier" in our extensive form experiment, who as a buyer obtained an average payoff somewhat higher than the others (56.8 versus 51.4), was a Ph.D. student with training in game theory. He experimented with highly asymmetric splits, proposing 80–20 in one game. While his average payoff was higher, so was his risk: he was involved in the only game in either treatment that ended without a contract.

## Appendix: Written Instructions and Payoff Schedules for the Experiment

### General

Please read the instructions carefully. If at any time you have questions or problems, raise your hand and the monitor will be happy to assist you. From now until the end of the session, unauthorized communication of any nature with other participants is prohibited.

During the session, you will play a series of games with other participants. Each game gives you an opportunity to earn cash.

### Description of the Game

The game concerns three players: a Buyer, Seller A, and Seller C. During the game, Seller A and Seller C compete to enter into a contract to supply the Buyer. Only one contract can be made per game. Each contract has a fixed total profit that can be distributed among the contracting parties. The following schedule shows the profit value of all possible contracts:

| Contracting Parties | Total Profit of Contract |
|---|---|
| Buyer and Seller A | 100 |
| Buyer and Seller C | 100 |
| Buyer, Seller A, and Seller C | 144 |

Before entering into a contract, the contracting parties must agree on how to divide the profits. The goal of each individual buyer and each individual seller is to get as big of a profit as possible for himself or herself.

[*This paragraph appeared in the free-form treatment only.*] For each game, players will be given exactly seven minutes to agree on a contract. During this seven minutes, players may discuss and bargain as they please. However, raised voices and threatening gestures are not allowed. Once a contract is reached, the contracting parties must complete a "contracting form." There are blank forms on each table. In order for the contract to be valid, a contracting form must be *completed* by the time the monitor announces the end of the seven-minute period. A contract is not complete until all parties to the contract have signed the form. Any contract that has total profits exceeding the limits set by the above schedule will be considered invalid.

All players not in a contract at the end of the game receive zero (0) profit.

[*This paragraph appeared in the extensive form treatment only.*] The game is played over four rounds. At the beginning of each round, one player is selected as the "proposer." Selection is by random draw, with each player having an equal chance of being selected. The chosen proposer then completes a "Game Form" (blanks are on the table). On the form, the proposer specifies which players should be in the contract and how much profit each should receive. The proposer then passes the form to the other players starting with the player on the left. If a player is a proposed contract partner, he or she checks either "accept" or "reject" on the form. If the player is not included in the contract proposal, then he or she just passes the form to the left. If all proposed partners accept, then a contract is formed, each partner receives the profit indicated on the form, and the game ends. If any proposed partner rejects, then the contract is rejected and a new round is started. The game is played for a maximum of four rounds. All players not in a contract at the end of the game receive zero (0) profit.

## Role Assignments

You will have the same role, Buyer or Seller A or Seller C, for all games. Your role is determined by the "B" (for Buyer) or "A" or "C" (the sellers) that precedes the folder number you drew when you entered the room.

## Grouping Procedure

Each game you will be grouped with two people having different roles than yourself. The people you are grouped with will change for each game. You will never play the game with any particular individual more than once.

You will play the game at one of the tables in the room. Note that each table is labeled with a number. At the conclusion of each game, new groups are formed for the next game by having players rotate according to the following schedule: Sellers A move to the table with the next highest number; Sellers C move to the table with the next lowest number; Buyers stay at the same table for every game.

## Game Record

Several blank "History" forms are provided in your folder. At the conclusion of each game, fill out one of these forms. Completed forms provide you with a history of your past games, and you may refer to them at any time during the session.

## Profits

How much money you make for a game depends on how much profit you earn compared with how much profit each of the other players *having the same role as you* earns. For example, the Seller A who earns the highest profit among all Sellers A will receive the highest payoff. The Seller A with the second-highest profit among all Sellers A will receive the second-highest payoff, etc. Payoffs for Sellers C as well as Buyers are determined in the same way, using the same schedule. In case of a tie, the players involved will receive the average of the relevant awards. A copy of the payoff schedule has been provided for you in your folder. Please examine this schedule.

## Session Earnings

You will actually be paid for one game. We will play more than one game. The one that you are paid for will be selected by a lottery after all games have been completed. There will be a separate lottery for each of the three types of players, so it is possible that different participants will be paid for different games. Each game has an equal chance of being selected, so it is in your interest to make as much profit as you can in each and every game. Immediately upon conclusion of the session, you will be paid your earnings in cash.

## Consent Forms

If you wish to participate in this study, please read and sign the accompanying consent form. Please note: In order to collect your earnings from the game, you must stay until the end of the session, which will last about 90 minutes.

*Payoff Schedule for 15 Participants*
*(Same Schedule for As, Buyers, and Cs)*

| Total Points | Award |
| --- | --- |
| Highest | $20 |
| Second | $17 |
| Third | $15 |
| Fourth | $13 |
| Fifth | $10 |

*Payoff Schedule for 18 Participants*
*(Same Schedule for As, Buyers, and Cs)*

| Total Points | Award |
|---|---|
| Highest | $20 |
| Second | $18 |
| Third | $16 |
| Fourth | $14 |
| Fifth | $12 |
| Lowest | $10 |

## NOTES

1. James K. Sebenius, *Negotiating the Law of the Sea* (Cambridge, MA: Harvard University Press, 1984).
2. Howard Raiffa, *The Art and Science of Negotiation* (Cambridge, MA: Harvard University Press, 1982), pp. 252–254.
3. This has been dubbed "cheap talk" in the literature. See Joseph Farrell and Robert Gibbons, "Cheap Talk Can Matter in Bargaining," *Journal of Economic Theory* 48 (1989): 221–237.
4. Telephone bargaining is therefore excluded. We plan to pursue this in future work.
5. Purely for convenience, we use the pronoun "he" throughout the paper.
6. Raiffa, *The Art and Science of Negotiation*, pp. 267–269.
7. See, for example, Alvin E. Roth, *Axiomatic Models of Bargaining* (New York: Springer-Verlag, 1979).
8. Historically, the term "noncooperative" arose to denote that the analysis was not "cooperative."
9. An early model of this kind appears in John C. Harsanyi, "A Simplified Model of the $n$-Person Cooperative Game," *International Economic Review* 4 (1963): 194–220. See also Reinhard Selten, "A Non-Cooperative Model of Characteristic Function Bargaining," in Volker Böhm and Hans Nachtkamp, eds., *Essays in Game Theory and Mathematical Economics, in Honor of Oskar Morgenstern* (Bibliographisches Institut, Mannheim, 1981), pp. 131–151; Faruk Gul, "Bargaining Foundations of the Shapley Value," *Econometrica* 57 (1989): 81–95; Motty Perry and Philip J. Reny, "A Noncooperative View of Coalition Formation and the Core," *Econometrica* 62 (1994): 795–817; and Kalyan Chatterjee et al., "A Non-Cooperative Theory of Coalitional Bargaining," *Review of Economic Studies* 60 (1993): 463–477.
10. Akira Okada, "A Non-Cooperative Coalitional Bargaining Model with Random Proposers," Kyoto Institute of Economic Research, mimeo, 1993, considers an extensive form with randomly chosen proposers but a poten-

tially infinite number of rounds. This is similar to the extensive form we use here.

11. Few papers deal explicitly with communication in bargaining games. One we are aware of is Kathleen M. Valley et al., "Is Talk Really Cheap? Using Communication to Outperform Equilibrium Predictions in Bargaining Games" (Harvard Business School, 1994), which considers communication in two-person bargaining with incomplete information.

12. Werner Güth, Rolf Schmittberger, and Bernd Schwarze, "An Experimental Analysis of Ultimatum Bargaining," *Journal of Economic Behavior and Organization* 3 (1982): 367–388.

13. Kenneth Binmore, Avner Shaked, and John Sutton, "Testing Noncooperative Bargaining Theory: A Preliminary Study," *American Economic Review* 75 (1985): 1178–1180; and Janet Neelin, Hugo Sonnenschein, and Matthew Spiegel, "A Further Test of Noncooperative Game Theory," *American Economic Review* 78 (1988): 824–836. Jack Ochs and Alvin E. Roth, "An Experimental Study of Sequential Bargaining," *American Economic Review* 79 (1989): 355–384, describe additional experiments and compare their results with earlier studies. Experiments by Alvin E. Roth et al., "Bargaining and Market Behavior in Jerusalem, Ljubljana, Pittsburgh, and Tokyo: An Experimental Study," *American Economic Review* 81 (1991): 1068–1095; and John R. Carter and Michael D. Irons, "Are Economists Different, and if So, Why?" *Journal of Economic Perspectives* 5 (1991): 171–177 examine the influence of social and cultural background. Framing and experimenter observation are studied in Elizabeth Hoffman et al., "Preferences, Property Rights and Anonymity in Bargaining Games," *Games and Economic Behavior* 7 (1994): 346–380. Gary E Bolton and Rami Zwick, "Anonymity versus Punishment in Ultimatum Bargaining," *Games and Economic Behavior* (in press); Rachel T. A. Croson, "Ultimatum Bargaining with Incomplete Information," mimeo, 1994; and Elizabeth Hoffman, Kevin McCabe, and Vernon Smith, "Degrees of Anonymity and Outcomes in Dictator Games," mimeo, 1993, vary the amount of cash in the negotiation. Other variations are considered by Robert Forsythe et al., "Fairness in Simple Bargaining Experiments," *Games and Economic Behavior* 6 (1994): 347–369; and Eythan Weg and Vernon Smith, "On the Failure to Induce Meager Offers in Ultimatum Games," *Journal of Economic Psychology* 14 (1993): 17–32. Alvin E. Roth, "Bargaining Experiments," in *Handbook of Experimental Economics*, eds. John Kagel and Alvin E. Roth (Princeton, NJ: Princeton University Press, in press) provides a comprehensive survey.

14. Gary E Bolton, "A Comparative Model of Bargaining: Theory and Evidence," *American Economic Review* 81 (1991): 1096–1136.

15. Alvin E. Roth and Ido Erev, "Learning in Extensive-Form Games: Experimental Data and Simple Dynamic Models in the Intermediate Term," *Games and Economic Behavior* (in press). Kenneth Binmore, John Gale, and

Larry Samuelson, "Learning to Be Imperfect: The Ultimatum Game," *Games and Economic Behavior* (in press), propose a model with a somewhat different learning dynamic but a similar flavor.

16. Joseph Kahan and Amnon Rapaport, *Theories of Coalition Formation* (Hillsdale, NJ.: Erlbaum Associates, 1984), survey some early efforts.

17. Reinhard Selten, "Equal Share Analysis of Characteristic Function Experiments," in *Beiträge experimentellen wirtschaftsforschung* [*Contributions to Experimental Economics*], vol. 3, ed. Heinz Savermann (Tübingen: J.C.B. Mohr, 1977), pp. 130–165.

18. Raiffa, *The Art and Science of Negotiation*, p. 266.

19. Kalyan Chatterjee and Bettina Kuon, manuscript in preparation.

20. Neelin, Sonnenschein, and Spiegel, "A Further Test."

# CHAPTER 16

# MARKET ENTRY UNDER INCOMPLETE INFORMATION

## William F. Samuelson

Firms must frequently decide whether to enter a new market while uncertain about whether potential rivals intend to enter. A firm's decision depends not only on demand in the market but also on a forecast of the number of other firms that might enter; typically, there are many more potential entrants than the number of firms the market can ultimately support. Two examples are the markets for personal computers and computer software. Scores of firms have entered these markets, but only the most efficient firms can survive; less efficient firms exit in predictable industry shakeouts.

The present study constructs a simple entry game under imperfect information to investigate the strategic issues surrounding firms' entry decisions. In the main version of the model, firms make simultaneous and independent entry decisions. A two-stage variant in which firms can enter or exit in either period is also briefly described. We examine equilibrium outcomes in which firms make optimal entry (and exit) decisions while anticipating optimal behavior by their rivals. Our analysis goes on to test this simple game-theoretic model through a series of controlled experiments involving student subjects.

The model also casts light on the welfare implications of decentralized market entry. A main finding is that decentralized entry is inefficient ex ante; it is suboptimal even given the constraints posed by incomplete information. To the extent that an entrant's expected profit falls short of the full social benefit, the frequency of entry is deficient. A second result is that increasing the number of potential entrants may or may not bring competitive benefits. The conventional wisdom, which favors greater numbers, is confirmed only when cost differences among would-be entrants are sufficiently large. However, when firms have similar costs, increasing the number of potential entrants can so reduce the individual firm's entry incentive that fewer firms enter on average and social welfare declines.[1]

Beginning with the work of A. Michael Spence, Christian von Weiszacker, and Joseph Stiglitz, understanding the private and social benefits associated with market entry has been very important to researchers.[2] The majority of market-entry work considers the strategic behavior of incumbents and entrants. Mankiw and Whinston review much of this work and provide a unifying model. A second strand of research has focused on sequential entry under perfect information. Sequential models have been examined by Prescott and Visscher, Waldman, and Eaton and Ware.[3] The focus on incomplete information and simultaneous decisions distinguishes the present study from these predecessors.

The next section develops and analyzes the basic model and discusses dynamic extensions. The third section considers an experimental test of the model. Equilibrium behavior, the main normative benchmark provided by game theory, finds moderate experimental support. Over a variety of conditions that vary demand, the number of potential entrants, and the distribution of costs, the equilibrium prediction marks the central tendency of the subjects' actions. Nonetheless, there is considerable dispersion around the equilibrium predictions, and, across several conditions, the average frequency of entry falls short of the equilibrium benchmark. In a dynamic entry experiment, many subjects fail to assess correctly rivals' costs, and deviations from equilibrium behavior are more numerous.

## Equilibrium Entry

The market entry model considered here is probably the simplest one that captures the strategic behavior of firms and its ensuing welfare consequences. There are a known number ($n$) of potential entrants. These firms make their entry decisions simultaneously and independently.[4] If $x$ number of firms enter the market, the gross profit of each is $\pi(x)$, where $\pi(x)$ is a decreasing function of $x$. Though we do not explicitly model the firms' ex post competition, almost all game-theoretic models imply that equilibrium profits decline with the number of entrants. Thus, entrant $i$'s net profit is: $\pi(x) - c_i$, where $c_i$ is the firm's cost of entering and serving the market. The fixed cost $c_i$ is "sunk" upon entry. Each firm's cost is known only to itself and independently drawn from the common probability distribution $F(c)$ with supports $\underline{c}$ and $\bar{c}$. With costs exogenous, we choose to abstract from the firms' strategic cost decisions (as might be relevant in a research and development race).

To set the stage, let us compare the incomplete information framework with the "ideal" model of free entry under perfect information. In the latter case, each firm's entry cost $c_i$ is known to all the firms. For convenience, index these known costs in ascending order: $c_1 \leq c_2 \leq \ldots,$ $c_n$. The standard model would predict entry by $x^*$ number of firms, namely the least-cost firms, $c_1, c_2, \ldots, c_{x^*}$, where $x^*$ is the largest integer satisfying $\pi(x^*) \geq c_{x^*}$. In addition, if firms behave competitively (as price takers) after entry, the resulting Walrasian equilibrium achieves a first-best welfare optimum. An optimal quantity of output is supplied by the least-cost producers.

However, this least-cost entry equilibrium is problematic at best. There is no explicit explanation why only the lowest-cost firms enter. Indeed, one can fashion sequential entry games with different equilibria—where one or more "not quite lowest-cost" firms enter the market (displacing a lower-cost firm). Alternatively, suppose that the $n$ potential entrants have identical costs, but the market can support only $x^*$ firms profitably, where $x^* < n$. Now there are numerous asymmetric entry equilibria (with identities of the entering firms interchanged) in which exactly $x^*$ firms enter. Which specific firms will enter and how the firms, acting independently, might coordinate their entry behavior are questions left hanging.[5]

Entry under incomplete information provides a much more realistic description of behavior in new markets. The model rests on two basic tenets. First, each firm is unaware of competitors' entry intentions at the time of its decision. Second, an entry decision cannot be costlessly reversed; that is, certain nonrecoverable entry costs are incurred by firms. Industry economics prohibit a firm from either waiting to observe competitors' entry choices before entering (because of latecomer disadvantages) or from entering, observing market conditions, and then costlessly exiting. Thus, while entry may be profitable if few other firms enter, it may lead to unavoidable losses if the firm finds itself one of too many entrants.

### Entry Incentives

The entry strategy of a typical firm takes the form: enter if and only if $c_i \leq c^*$, where $c^*$ is the break-even level of cost such that the firm earns a zero expected profit from entry. Consider a symmetric entry equilibrium in which all firms use the common cost threshold $c^*$.[6] Holding cost $c_i$, the firm's expected profit from entry is:

$$E[\pi|c_i] = \sum_{x=1}^{n} q(x)\pi(x) - c_i, \qquad (16\text{-}1)$$

where $q(x)$ is the probability that a total of $x$ firms enter the market. In a symmetric Bayesian equilibrium, $c^*$ is determined according to

$$E[\pi|c^*] = 0. \qquad (16\text{-}2)$$

Furthermore, $q(x)$ equals the binomial probability $B(n-1, x-1, p)$—that is, the chance that $x-1$ of the other $n-1$ firms enter, each with probability $p = F(c^*)$. We presume that: $\pi(n) - \underline{c} < 0 < \pi(1) - \bar{c}$. In short, entry by a single firm is always profitable and entry by all firms is never profitable. With these assumptions, and invoking the intermediate-value theorem, there is a unique solution for $c^*$ in equation (16-2) because $\pi(x)$ is monotonically declining in $x$. To summarize, we have:

> PROPOSITION ONE. Under the conditions above, there is a unique symmetric entry equilibrium, summarized by $c^*$, satisfying (16-2). Other things equal, an increase in the number of potential entrants ($n$), and/or a decrease in the elements $\pi(x)$ will reduce the individual frequency of entry, $F(c^*)$.

To check the second part of the proposition, suppose $c^*$ satisfies equation (16-2) in the base case. For fixed $c^*$, an increase in $n$ causes a probability shift (in the sense of first-order stochastic dominance) toward greater numbers of entrants, implying $E[\pi|c^*] < 0$. Thus, a decline in $c^*$ is needed to restore the equality in equation (16-2). An analogous argument applies to a downward shift in $\pi(x)$. In either case, the frequency of individual entry, $F(c^*)$, declines.

### Entry and Welfare

Depending on the firms' actual costs, the independent decisions of the $n$ firms can lead to too much or too little entry. Obviously, the first-best full-information outcome cannot be achieved. The interesting comparison is between equilibrium entry and the second-best optimum. Let $B(x)$ denote the gross consumer benefit generated when $x$ firms enter and supply the market. Attainment of the second-best outcome requires maximizing

$$W = E[B(x)] - E[\sum_{i=1}^{n} c_i] \qquad (16\text{-}3)$$

with respect to each firm's entry threshold. Consider firm $i$ with cost $c_i$. If it enters, the change in $W$ is:

$$\Delta W_i = \sum_{i=1}^{n} q(x)\Delta B(x) - c_i, \qquad \textbf{(16-4)}$$

where $\Delta B(x) = B(x) - B(x-1)$ denotes the additional consumer benefit when the entrance of firm $i$ increases the number of entrants from $x-1$ to $x$. Necessary conditions for an optimum are $\Delta W_i = 0$ for all firms $i$. Let $\hat{c}_1, ..., \hat{c}_n$ denote the welfare-maximizing entry values.

By comparison, the firm's expected profit from entry is given by expression (16-1), and equilibrium behavior satisfies equation (16-2). Notice the roles played by $\pi(x)$ and $\Delta B(x)$ in expressions (16-1) and (16-4). If the functions $\pi(x)$ and $\Delta B(x)$ were identical, then equilibrium entry would implement the second-best optimum, $c_i^* = \hat{c}_i$. However, there is no a priori reason for such an equality to hold. The behavior of $\pi(x)$ and $\Delta B(x)$ depend on the shape of the consumer welfare function and on the type of ex post competition played out by entrants. Thus, only by pure coincidence can equilibrium entry achieve the second-best outcome. Even by the second-best standard, there may be too much or too little entry in equilibrium.

*Price taking.* As a special case, suppose that each entering firm produces a standardized level of output (normalized to one unit) regardless of how many other firms enter. If $x$ firms enter, then total output $(x)$ determines the market price according to the inverse demand curve $P = P(x)$, which is known to all firms. In this case, the typical firm faces the profit function $\pi(x) = P(x)$. More numerous entrants drive down the market price (and firms' profits), but firms do not vary their outputs to influence price. Provided the inverse demand curve slopes downward, it immediately follows that $\Delta B(x) > P(x)$ for all $x$. That is, the increase in consumer benefit for the discrete output change $x-1$ to $x$ is larger than the market clearing price at $x$. (The difference represents the consumer surplus triangle.) The immediate implication is that $\Delta W_i$ is positive at $c_i^*$. Thus, the equilibrium frequency of entry falls short of the second-best optimum, $c_i^* < \hat{c}_i$.

Obviously, if the typical firm's standard level of output is very small relative to the total market (the market can support a great many firms), the difference between $\Delta B(x)$ and $P(x)$ will also be small; equilibrium entry will be nearly at the second-best frequency. Indeed, in the limit, $dB(x) = P(x)$. However, if the market can support only a small number of firms—four firms (at $c^*$) when $n = 8$, let's say—then the entry shortfall can have a significant welfare impact. Entry falls short of the second-best optimum because the individual firm's expected profit incentive is lower than the full marginal social benefit. (For costs in the interval $[c_i^*, \hat{c}_i]$, firm $i$ will choose not to enter; adding its output would lower the market price sufficiently so as to imply a loss on average—even though expected social welfare would be improved.) However, in one special circumstance, equilibrium entry does achieve the second-best outcome—when industry demand is perfectly elastic or the demand curve is a declining horizontal step function. In either case, $\Delta B(x) = P(x)$ for all $x$, so that $c_i^* = \hat{c}_i$ for all $i$. Obviously, if demand is perfectly elastic (price is constant), there is no need to coordinate the entry of firms. Independent entry with $c^* = P$ generates the first-best optimum.[7]

> PROPOSITION TWO. In general, equilibrium entry fails to achieve the second-best optimum: entry can be deficient or excessive. For downward-sloping demand and price-taking behavior, the frequency of equilibrium entry falls short of the second-best optimum.

### The Number of Entrants

Now consider the welfare implications of varying the number of entrants. The welfare effect of increasing $n$ is ambiguous; depending on the circumstances, expected welfare may increase or decline. To achieve tractable comparative static results, consider the special case of price-taking behavior and a linear profit function: $\pi(x) = P(x) = a - bx$. Now the typical firm's equilibrium entry condition in (16-2) becomes:

$$\begin{aligned} E[\pi|c^*] &= a - bE[x] - c^* \\ &= a - b[1 + (n-1)F(c^*)] - c^* = 0. \end{aligned} \quad \text{(16-5)}$$

The restriction, $\pi(n) - \underline{c} < 0 < \pi(1) - \bar{c}$, ensures a unique solution $c^*$ in the interval $[\underline{c}, \bar{c}]$.

Under linear demand, expected social welfare can be expressed as

$$W = E[ax - .5bx^2] - nF(c^*)E[c|c \le c^*]. \quad \text{(16-6)}$$

Here, the first term measures the expected consumption benefit associated with output $x$ and the second term the entrants' expected costs. We can rewrite $W$ as

$$\begin{aligned} W &= aE[x] - .5b[\sigma^2(x) + (E[x])^2] - nF(c*)E[c \mid c \le c*] \\ &= anF(c*) - .5b[n(n-1)F(c*)^2 + nF(c*)] - n\int_{\underline{c}}^{c*} c\, dF(c). \end{aligned} \quad \text{(16-7)}$$

In turn, the derivative of $W$ with respect to the threshold value $c^*$ is

$$dW/dc^* = nf(c^*)[a - b(n - 1)F(c^*) - .5b - c^*]. \quad \textbf{(16-8)}$$

Since the equilibrium entry threshold satisfies equation (16-5), then $dW/dc^* = .5bnf(c^*) > 0$ in equilibrium. In short, expected welfare would increase if entry occurred more frequently than the equilibrium rate. As noted above, when demand slopes downward and entrants are price takers, equilibrium entry is deficient.

*Identical costs.* To emphasize the pure coordination issues under equilibrium entry, we first provide a complete analysis for the case when all firms are known to hold identical costs (i.e., $c = \underline{c} = \bar{c}$). Here, each entrant earns profit: $a - bx - c$, implying that the maximum number of firms supportable by the market is $x^* = (a - c)/b$. The value $x^*$ is also the optimal number of entrants—that is, social welfare, $W = (a - c)x - .5bx^2$, achieves a global maximum at $x = x^*$.[8] Obviously, if $n < x^*$, all firms will enter since each is assured of a positive profit.

The more interesting case is when there is a surplus of potential entrants: $n > x^*$. In the mixed-strategy equilibrium,

$$E[\pi|c] = a - c - b(1 + (n - 1)p). \quad \textbf{(16-9)}$$

This is simply a special case of (16-5). Setting this equal to zero implies $p = [a - b - c]/[b(n - 1)]$, or equivalently

$$p = (x^* - 1)/(n - 1), \quad \textbf{(16-10)}$$

after making the substitution $x^* = (a - c)/b$. As long as the number of potential entrants exceeds the number supportable by the market ($n \geq x^*$), the frequency of individual entry varies inversely with the size of the supply-demand imbalance. In this sense, the number of firms entering the market is self-regulating. The expected number of entrants is: $E[x] = n \cdot p = [n/(n - 1)][x^* - 1]$. For $n \geq x^*$, $E[x]$ is smaller than $x^*$; once again entry is insufficient on average.

Now consider the welfare implications of equilibrium entry. Two issues are examined: the effect of varying $n$ for fixed $x^*$, and the separate effect of varying $x^*$. In this latter case, assume that market demand is constant and that an increase in $x^*$ is caused by a proportional reduction in the efficient scale of output of the typical firm. In particular, we choose parameter values (for $a$, $b$, and $c$) such that the maximum level of welfare $W^*$ (achieved at $x^*$) is normalized to be 1. After some manipulation, expected welfare can be reduced to:

$$W = \left[\frac{n}{n-1}\right]\left[\frac{x^*-1}{x^*}\right],$$  (16-11)

valid for $n \geq x^*$. Clearly, expected welfare is maximized when $n = x^*$, in which case exactly $x^*$ firms actually enter. As the surplus of potential entrants $(n-x^*)$ grows, expected welfare strictly declines.[9] As $n$ grows without bound,

$$\Psi = \lim_{n \to \infty} W = (x^*-1)/x^*.$$  (16-12)

Though welfare is strictly declining in $n$, the limiting value of $\Psi$ shows that the welfare shortfall due to a surplus of potential entrants is relatively small. In the limit, the shortfall is $1/x^*$ (10 percent if $x^* = 10$ for instance).[10] Finally, letting the number of supportable firms become infinitely large, $\lim_{x^* \to \infty} \Psi = 1$. As the scale of the typical firm becomes vanishingly small (and $x^*$ becomes increasingly large), the law of large numbers implies that the number of entrants converges to $x^*$ (in probability) and attainable welfare approaches the first-best optimum.

*Differing costs.* Cost differences constitute a potential basis for welfare-improving competition. Increasing the number of potential entrants raises the likelihood that a "low-cost" firm will be part of the population and subsequently enter the market. This is the *efficiency* benefit of increasing the number of potential entrants. But as shown above, increasing the number of entrants makes *coordination* more difficult, reducing expected welfare. Whether welfare increases or decreases in $n$ depends on the relative strength of these countervailing effects.

Again, let the profit function take the linear form: $\pi(x) = a - bx$, and suppose that $\pi(n) - \bar{c} < 0$. (If the reverse inequality holds, all firms will enter with certainty and raising $n$ necessarily increases welfare. We abstract from this uninteresting case.) By the chain rule, the welfare effect of varying the number of entrants is given by:

$$\frac{dW}{dn} = \frac{\partial W}{\partial n} + \frac{\partial W}{\partial c}\frac{\partial c}{\partial n}.$$

From equation (16-7), this derivative (at the equilibrium entry value $c^*$) is

$$\frac{dW}{dn} = -.5bF^2 + .5bF^2[1-bf][F + (a - b - c^*)f] + \int_{\underline{c}}^{c^*} F(c)dc,$$  (16-13)

where $F$ denotes the value of the distribution function $F(c^*)$ and $f$ denotes the corresponding density function $f(c^*)$.

To illustrate this welfare effect, suppose firm costs are uniformly distributed with supports $\underline{c}$ and $\underline{c}+d$. Expression (16-13) reduces to

$$\frac{dW}{dn} = .5[d - b][(c* - \underline{c})^2 / d^2][(a - \underline{c}) / (a - \underline{c} - b)]. \quad \textbf{(16-14)}$$

Clearly, the sign of $dW/dn$ depends on the sign of $[d - b]$. First, consider the extreme case $d = 0$: all firms' costs are identical. Here, adding potential entrants has no effect on efficiency; raising $n$ simply increases coordination costs and lowers expected welfare. Conversely, if $d$ is positive and $b = 0$, demand is perfectly elastic, so coordination costs vanish; the behavior of other firms has no effect on the firm's cost threshold (or the consumer benefit its entry generates). Raising the number of potential entrants increases the number of low-cost firms, thereby generating a pure efficiency benefit. Finally, if $b$ and $d$ are both positive, their relative magnitudes determine whether welfare increases or declines with $n$. For instance, if demand is steeply sloped ($b$ is large), or cost differences are minor ($d$ is small), the welfare shortfall due to uncoordinated entry (entry by too few or too many firms) is large relative to the potential efficiency benefits of enlisting lower-cost firms.[11] Consequently, welfare declines with increasing numbers.

> PROPOSITION THREE. Given cost differences among firms, increasing the number of potential entrants involves a basic tradeoff between efficiency benefits and the costs of uncoordinated entry. If cost differences are sufficiently large (small), expected welfare is increasing (decreasing) in $n$.

### Entry Dynamics

The framework above describes the entry decisions of potential competitors when each has only one chance to enter. Though the model is instructive, it can be fairly criticized for omitting the dynamics of firm entry. In fact, a firm can decide to enter at any time. If it has not entered already, it can choose to do so at time $t_2$, $t_3$, and so on. If it and numerous rivals have entered, the firm can exit the market now or later. Allowing for asymmetric timing issues, the firm may have the opportunity to enter before others, or may find itself preempted by others. The firm predicates its decisions on knowledge of the number of entrants to date and on its assessment of the probable number of future entrants.

To illustrate the nature of dynamic equilibrium behavior, consider the simplest possible setting—one involving two potential entrants and two periods. Entry and exit are costless and the rate of discount is zero.[12] The firms' private costs are independently drawn from the distribution $F(c)$. In the symmetric equilibrium:

1. A firm enters in period one if and only if its cost is no greater than $c^*$.

2. If only one firm enters in period one, that firm remains in the market in period two and the other firm stays out.

3. If neither firm enters in period one, then each enters in period two if and only if its cost is no greater than $c^E$.

4. If both firms enter in period one, then each remains in the market in period two if and only if its cost is no greater than $c^X$.

As an example, suppose that $\pi(1) = 2.0$, $\pi(2) = 1.2$, and each firm's cost is uniformly distributed on the interval $[1, 2]$. Then, the equilibrium cutoff values can be computed as $c^* = 1.61$, $c^E = 1.74$, and $c^X = 1.43$ respectively.[13] By contrast, if there were no opportunity to enter or exit in the second period (as in the one-period game already discussed), the equilibrium cutoff value would be $c^* = 1.555$. Initial entry is more frequent in the two-period model than in the single-period model for two reasons. With a single period, entry is all or nothing. In the two-period setting, a firm's entry is reversible; if its rival also enters, the firm can exit gracefully. Moreover, early entry offers the chance to preempt the market either by precluding the rival's later entry or by inducing the rival to exit. Both reasons provide added incentives for early entry—incentives not found in the one-period model where such strategic interactions are absent.

In addition, firms draw the obvious inferences from initial entry behavior. If neither firm enters initially, both reveal that their costs are greater than $c^* = 1.61$. Thus, each is willing to enter at higher costs ($c^E = 1.74$) in the second period. If both firms enter in period one, both must have costs below $c^* = 1.61$. Thus, each will remain in the market only for relatively low costs, $c^X = 1.43$. It is straightforward to show that both properties hold generally for the two-period, two-player model—that is, for arbitrary cost distributions.

Does the added opportunity for entry and exit in the two-period model increase social welfare? In the present example, yes. A direct computation shows that expected welfare is about 5 percent greater in the two-period model than in the one-shot model, where firms must commit to entry for both periods. (Obviously, the firms themselves are better off because the threshold cost has increased from 1.555 to 1.61.) More generally, one would expect that enhancing entry and exit flexibility—shortening the time between entry/exit periods and increasing the number of periods—would raise expected welfare. Nonetheless, like the one-shot entry model, the dynamic model still faces a tradeoff between coordination and efficiency.[14]

## Experimental Tests and Results

The predictions and welfare results of the model presented in the previous section depend on firms' undertaking equilibrium entry behavior. Anecdotal evidence from the business press and case studies of entry in new markets are two sources of empirical evidence bearing on actual managerial behavior.[15] An additional source is the evidence gleaned from controlled experiments. This section reports the results of experiments involving graduate management students.

### Description of the Experiments

The experiments were conducted in four graduate courses at Boston University School of Management. All were conducted in class: in two sections of "Managerial Economics" (including an executive MBA offering) and in two sections of "Competitive Decision Making." Two features of the experiments are noteworthy. First, each student's performance was evaluated and contributed to his or her grade in the course. Thus, students did not view their responses as purely hypothetical.[16] Each student's overall score was calculated by pitting his or her entry strategy against the entry strategies of all other students in the class. This "tournament design" meant that the average performance of each student's strategy was evaluated in comparison to the cross section of class strategies.[17] This design was intended to encourage risk neutrality on the part of subjects. (Students were freed from the risk of being matched with idiosyncratic partners.) From previous experience in other in-class exercises, students understood that their objective was to adopt a strategy that performed well against the cross-section of actions taken by the class.[18]

The second key feature of the experiments was the opportunity for subjects to learn about making entry decisions. In the end, subjects reported their chosen entry strategies (their personal entry thresholds) in different economic settings, but first they engaged in practice sessions to gain experience in making entry choices. In a typical session, 2, 4, or 11 students would play the roles of potential entrants. After being assigned a private cost estimate, each student would determine his or her entry decision, and these entry decisions would be reported to all members of the group. The number of practice sessions varied by group size: four sessions for 2-person groups, two sessions for

4-person groups, and one or two sessions for 11-person groups. Each subject's cost estimates varied over the sessions. The intent of the practice sessions was to ensure that subjects fully understood the ground rules of the entry game, and to provide subjects with feedback on how their strategies performed in comparison to the entry behavior of other students. The subjects' conduct during the experiments suggested that both of these objectives were achieved. The practice sessions allowed students to gain experience making entry decisions (and to observe others' decisions) without being "trained" in their entry behavior.[19]

### Results

The experiments were conducted in seven different conditions. These included one-shot entry competition between 2 firms (two conditions), one-shot entry involving 4 firms (two conditions), one-shot entry involving 11 firms (two conditions), and a two-period, 2-firm entry competition (one condition). We begin with a description of the 2-firm and 4-firm results.

In conditions I and II, the firm's gross profit function was: $\pi(x) = 2.8 - .8x$, and each firm's private cost was drawn independently from a uniform distribution on the interval [1.0, 2.0]. In Condition I, each subject faced one other potential entrant ($n = 2$); in Condition II, the subject faced three other entrants ($n = 4$). The equilibrium cost thresholds for these conditions are $c^* = 1.555$ and $c^* = 1.294$, respectively.

To what extent did subjects' reported entry strategies approximate these benchmarks? Table 16-1 reports the cross section of subject responses. In Condition I, most responses are tightly bunched in the 1.5 and 1.6 intervals. The mean response, 1.49, is near the equilibrium benchmark, 1.55. During post-experiment debriefings, students revealed something of the thinking behind these responses. Many students reported reasoning along the following lines:

> What if my rival were to enter for costs below 1.5? [The midpoint of the cost range seemed to be an appealing focal point.] Then, he or she will enter half the time. This means my gross entry profit will be either 2.0 or 1.2, with each equally likely. Thus, my break-even cost is $c^* = 1.6$.

A student who stopped here would be apt to report $c^* = 1.6$ (44 percent of all responses) or possibly $c^* = 1.5$ to allow a margin of safety. Reports in the 1.5 interval accounted for 30 percent of all responses.[20]

What might account for the scatter of lower reports? The down-

**Table 16-1**

*Experimental Results*

---

Condition I (two firms)

$n = 2$, $\pi(x) = 2.8 - .8x$
$c \in [1, 2]$, $c^* = 1.555$

|           | Distribution of Student $c^*$'s | | | | | | | | |
|-----------|------|------|------|------|------|------|------|------|-------|
|           | 1.0  | 1.1  | 1.2  | 1.3  | 1.4  | 1.5  | 1.6  | 1.7  | Total |
| Number of |      |      |      |      |      |      |      |      |       |
| Responses | 1    | 0    | 4    | 1    | 7    | 15   | 22   | 0    | 50    |

Mean: 1.49         Standard Deviation: .135         $t$-value: $-3.59$

Condition II (four firms)

$n = 4$, $\pi(x) = 2.8 - .8x$
$c \in [1, 2]$, $c^* = 1.294$

|           | Distribution of Student $c^*$'s | | | | | | | | |
|-----------|------|------|------|------|------|------|------|------|-------|
|           | 1.0  | 1.1  | 1.2  | 1.3  | 1.4  | 1.5  | 1.6  | 1.7  | Total |
| Number of |      |      |      |      |      |      |      |      |       |
| Responses | 11   | 2    | 18   | 12   | 3    | 4    | 0    | 0    | 50    |

Mean: 1.21         Standard Deviation: .143         $t$-value: $-4.04$

---

*Note:* Each cost category includes responses in the surrounding neighborhood. For
example, 1.5 includes all responses from 1.45 to 1.54, and so on.

ward bias is mainly attributable to the four 1.2 responses. A firm breaks
even at a cost of 1.2 even if a rival enters *all the time* (in which case
$\pi(2) = 1.2$). It appears that some subjects readily adopted this "ultra-
conservative" strategy. A $t$-test rejects the hypothesis that the sample
mean equals the equilibrium benchmark (1.55) at the 99 percent confidence level ($t$-value $= -3.59$). In short, subject responses are biased
downward.

In Condition II, the increase in the number of potential rivals
dramatically alters the distribution of responses: 60 percent of responses are in the 1.2 and 1.3 intervals. The rationale for this behavior
was along the following lines:

Suppose a firm only enters for relatively low costs, say one-
third of the time. Then, on average, I can expect to face one
entrant, and can profitably enter up to $c^* = 1.2$. If entry is slightly
less frequent, I can profitably enter up to some higher cost, say,
$c^* = 1.3$.

However, the response distribution is bimodal, displaying a second congregation of responses at $c^* = 1.0$. A significant proportion of subjects would *never* enter the market; these students apparently reckoned that entry would be unprofitable on average because one or more competitors would enter. As in the two-entrant condition, the sample mean of subject responses was below the equilibrium benchmark, $c^* = 1.294$. This bias is significant at the 99 percent confidence level ($t$-value $= -4.04$).

In Conditions III and IV, a different set of student subjects confronted a variation of the basic entry game. As before, there were two or four potential entrants, and costs ranged over a unit interval—in this case, the interval [2, 3]. The new profit function was $\pi(x) = 7.0 - 2.5x$. Here, the equilibrium cost thresholds are $c^* = 2.71$ and $c^* = 2.294$ for two and four entrants respectively. Table 16-2 lists the experimental results. For $n = 2$, more than two-thirds of responses fall in the 2.6, 2.7, and 2.8 intervals—that is, near the equilibrium entry value, $c^* = 2.71$. The remaining responses are roughly split between the 2.5 and 3.0

### Table 16-2
*Experimental Results*

Condition III (two firms)

$n = 2, \pi(x) = 7.0 - 2.5x$
$c \in [2, 3], c^* = 2.71$

| | | | | Distribution of Student $c^*$'s | | | | |
|---|---|---|---|---|---|---|---|---|
| | 2.3 | 2.4 | 2.5 | 2.6 | 2.7 | 2.8 | 2.9 | 3.0 | Total |
| Number of Responses | 0 | 0 | 4 | 4 | 11 | 8 | 1 | 5 | 33 |

Mean: 2.74     Standard Deviation: .148     $t$-value: .987

Condition IV (four firms)

$n = 4, \pi(x) = 7.0 - 2.5x$
$c \in [2, 3], c^* = 2.294$

| | | | | Distribution of Student $c^*$'s | | | | |
|---|---|---|---|---|---|---|---|---|
| | 2.0 | 2.1 | 2.2 | 2.3 | 2.4 | 2.5 | 2.6 | 2.7 | Total |
| Number of Responses | 8 | 3 | 8 | 7 | 4 | 3 | 0 | 0 | 33 |

Mean: 2.22     Standard Deviation: .159     $t$-value: $-2.73$

*Note:* Each cost category includes responses in the surrounding neighborhood. For example, 2.5 includes all responses from 2.45 to 2.54, and so on.

extremes. A subject would rationally choose $c^* = 3.0$ (always entering) if he or she expected the typical rival to use $c^* = 2.5$ (that is, to enter half the time). Conversely, $c^* = 2.5$ is optimal against a rival who is expected to enter 80 percent of the time. In short, these responses are consistent with differing but plausible expectations about rivals' behavior. The mean response, 2.74, is very close to the equilibrium benchmark, $c^* = 2.71$, and the associated $t$-value is only .974.

The responses in Condition IV ($n = 4$) show a similar pattern to those of Condition II, except for the shift in scale. Almost half of the responses are in the 2.2 and 2.3 intervals, near the equilibrium value, $c^* = 2.294$. However, one-quarter of students reported 2.0, that is, a strategy of never entering. As in Condition II, the sample mean 2.22 is significantly lower than the equilibrium benchmark ($t$-value $= -2.73$).

In Conditions V and VI, subjects faced 10 potential rivals ($n = 11$) under two different profit conditions: $\pi(x) = 2.1 - .2x$ and $\pi(x) = 3.3 - .2x$, respectively. Costs were drawn from the interval $[1, 2]$. For these profit functions, the equilibrium cutoff values are $c^* = 1.3$ and $c^* = 1.7$. Surprisingly, the increased number of rivals seemed to make the entry task slightly easier. Table 16-3 lists the complete results. In each condition, the majority of responses were near the equilibrium benchmark. In each, the mean response, 1.25 or 1.68, was not significantly different from the equilibrium benchmark. In the debriefing, many students reported formulating their entry strategy strictly on the basis of the expected number of rival entrants. For instance, in Condition VI a subject might guess that a typical rival will enter 70 percent of the time ($c^* = 1.7$) in which case one would expect seven rivals on average. If the subject enters, the resulting gross profit is $3.3 - (.2)(8) = 1.7$, and this would be his or her cutoff value. Provided subjects guess the average entry propensity with reasonable accuracy, entry behavior will tend toward the equilibrium benchmark. The overall pattern of responses in Conditions V and VI bears out this result.

*Entry dynamics.* Subjects who participated in Condition I later reported entry strategies for a two-period, two-entrant game (Condition VII). As in the earlier conditions, the profit function was $\pi(x) = 2.8 - .8x$, and costs were drawn on the interval $[1, 2]$. As noted earlier, equilibrium behavior is described by the first-period cutoff value, $c^* = 1.61$, and the second-period entry and exit values, $c^E = 1.74$ and $c^X = 1.43$, respectively.

Table 16-4 lists subjects' responses and underscores four main results. First, the subjects' first-period entry behavior is nearly identical to their entry behavior in the single-period game. In the two-period condition, the mean cutoff value is 1.50, nearly identical to the single-period mean, 1.49. Because the same subjects participated in both

**Table 16-3**

*Experimental Results*

Condition V (11 firms)

$n = 11$, $\pi(x) = 2.1 - .2x$
$c \in [1, 2]$, $c^* = 1.3$

Distribution of Student $c^*$'s

|                        | 1.0 | 1.1 | 1.2 | 1.3 | 1.4 | 1.5 | 1.6 | 1.7 | 1.8 | Total |
|------------------------|-----|-----|-----|-----|-----|-----|-----|-----|-----|-------|
| Number of Responses    | 6   | 4   | 8   | 13  | 3   | 1   | 2   | 0   | 1   | 38    |

Mean: 1.25     Standard Deviation: .178     $t$-value: $-1.61$

Condition VI (11 firms)

$n = 11$, $\pi(x) = 3.3 - .2x$
$c \in [1, 2]$, $c^* = 1.7$

Distribution of Student $c^*$'s

|                        | 1.1 | 1.2 | 1.3 | 1.4 | 1.5 | 1.6 | 1.7 | 1.8 | 1.9 | 2.0 | Total |
|------------------------|-----|-----|-----|-----|-----|-----|-----|-----|-----|-----|-------|
| Number of Responses    | 0   | 1   | 1   | 2   | 5   | 8   | 8   | 6   | 1   | 6   | 38    |

Mean: 1.68     Standard Deviation: .200     $t$-value: $-.625$

*Note:* Each cost category includes responses in the surrounding neighborhood. For example, 1.5 includes all responses from 1.45 to 1.54, and so on.

conditions, we can directly measure changes in behavior. Of the 50 subjects, 30 reported the same cutoff values. Fifteen subjects raised their cutoff values (entered more frequently); five lowered them. According to equilibrium behavior, subjects should enter more frequently in the two-period game; they should raise their cutoff value from $c^* = 1.55$ to $c^* = 1.61$. Subject entry behavior in the two-period game clearly deviates from equilibrium ($t$-value $= -5.74$.) Moreover, a $t$-test conducted on the differences between subjects' paired responses in Conditions I and VII cannot reject the hypothesis of identical behavior. In short, subjects saw no reason to alter their entry behavior in the two-period condition from that in the one-period condition; consequently, they entered much less frequently in the first period than the equilibrium benchmark would prescribe.

Second, if both firms enter in period one, subjects are much more likely to exit the market in period two than the equilibrium benchmark predicts. The middle distribution in Table 16-4 shows that responses

**Table 16-4**

*Experimental Results*

Condition VII (two firms, two periods)

$n = 2$, $\pi(x) = 2.8 - .8x$

$c \in [1, 2]$, $c^* = 1.61$, $c^E = 1.74$, $c^X = 1.43$

Distribution of Student $c^*$'s

|               | 1.0 | 1.1 | 1.2 | 1.3 | 1.4 | 1.5 | 1.6 | 1.7 | 1.8 | 1.9 | Total |
|---------------|-----|-----|-----|-----|-----|-----|-----|-----|-----|-----|-------|
| Number of Responses | 1   | 0   | 3   | 3   | 4   | 17  | 20  | 2   | 0   | 0   | 50    |

Mean: 1.50          Standard Deviation: .139          $t$-value: $-5.74$

Distribution of Student $c^X$'s

|               | 1.0 | 1.1 | .12 | 1.3 | 1.4 | 1.5 | 1.6 | 1.7 | 1.8 | 1.9 | Total |
|---------------|-----|-----|-----|-----|-----|-----|-----|-----|-----|-----|-------|
| Number of Responses | 2   | 1   | 24  | 11  | 3   | 5   | 3   | 0   | 0   | 0   | 49    |

Mean: 1.28          Standard Deviation: .136          $t$-value: $-7.76$

Distribution of Student $c^E$'s

|               | 1.0 | 1.1 | 1.2 | 1.3 | 1.4 | 1.5 | 1.6 | 1.7 | 1.8 | 1.9 | Total |
|---------------|-----|-----|-----|-----|-----|-----|-----|-----|-----|-----|-------|
| Number of Responses | 1   | 0   | 2   | 3   | 4   | 12  | 16  | 7   | 1   | 1   | 47    |

Mean: 1.53          Standard Deviation: .161          $t$-value: $-8.77$

*Note:* Each cost category includes responses in the surrounding neighborhood. For example, 1.5 includes all responses from 1.45 to 1.54, and so on.

congregated in the 1.2 and 1.3 intervals. The mean exit cutoff value reported by subjects is 1.28—significantly below the equilibrium benchmark of 1.43 ($t$-value $= -7.76$). Equilibrium behavior calls for a .18 reduction in the cutoff from first period to second (from $c^* = 1.61$ to $c^X = 1.43$). For 23 of 49 subjects, the reduction exceeded .18. For 13 subjects the reduction approximated .18. The remaining 13 students showed little or no change.

Third, if neither firm enters in period one, subjects are much less likely to enter the market in period two than the equilibrium benchmark predicts. The bottom distribution in Table 16-4 shows that responses congregated in the 1.5 and 1.6 intervals. The mean entry cutoff value reported by subjects is 1.53—well below the equilibrium benchmark of 1.74 ($t$-value $= -8.77$). Equilibrium behavior calls for a .13 increase in the cutoff from first period to second (from $c^* = 1.61$ to $c^E = 1.74$). For 30 of 47 subjects, there was little or no change in their cutoff values. For 11 subjects the increase approximated .13, while for 6 subjects, the change exceeded .13. Overall, subjects entered more frequently than in the first period ($t$-value $= 3.84$) but much less frequently than the equilibrium prediction.

Fourth, if only one firm entered in the first period, those who had entered reported that they would remain in the market, and those who had not would remain out of the market. (The sole exceptions were two subjects who reported they would enter in the second period as outsiders.) These actions accord with equilibrium behavior and beliefs.

What might account for the pronounced and systematic deviations from equilibrium behavior? First, consider second-period behavior. Subjects tend to overreact to the presence of a first-period entrant (exiting too frequently) and underreact to its absence (entering too infrequently). Clearly, subjects are concerned about risking a second-period loss if both firms remain in the market. Based on their post-experiment remarks, most students recognized that a rival's first-period entry marks it as a "low-cost" firm. Indeed, as evidenced by their exit behavior, subjects tended to overreact to the rival's entrance.[21] By contrast, the absence of entry made little difference in second-period behavior. A rival's failure to enter *should* be significant—by marking it as a "high cost" firm unlikely to enter in period two. However, as with Sherlock Holmes's dog that didn't bark in the night, this significance was lost on most subjects. The incidence of second-period entry increased only slightly and was well below the equilibrium benchmark.

What about first-period behavior? Most subjects perceived no strategic difference between the one-period and two-period settings and reported the same cutoff values. Some students saw a "first mover" preemptive advantage and entered more frequently in the two-period setting. A few students saw a "second mover" advantage; they chose to enter less frequently in period one, preferring to wait and see if an untapped market would present itself in period two. Overall entry behavior was virtually identical in Conditions I and VII. However, in the post-experiment discussion, two simple questions were enough to spur many students to reassess their entry behavior: If only one firm enters initially, what is your prediction about second-period behavior? (Answer: The incumbent will remain in the market and the outsider will remain on the sideline.) What does such second-period behavior imply about a firm's first-period entry strategy? (Answer: The firm should raise its cost threshold to increase its chance of preempting the market.) In failing to incorporate the impact of second-period behavior, subjects tended to underestimate the advantage of immediate market entry.

*Summary.* Over a variety of conditions, subjects' behavior tended to follow the equilibrium benchmark. Behavior conformed to the qualitative predictions in Proposition One. An increase in the number of potential entrants and/or a downward shift in the gross profit function induced lower cutoff values and less frequent entry by subjects. Nonetheless, responses were considerably dispersed around the equilibrium prediction, and across several conditions, the average frequency of entry fell short of the equilibrium benchmark.

Because the profit function is linear, a subject's expected payoff in the one-shot setting depends only on the average entry behavior (the average cutoff value) of the subject population. For instance, in Condition II, the average cutoff was $c^* = 1.21$, implying $E[\pi|c_i] = 2.8 - (.8)[1 + (3)(.21)] - c_i = 1.496 - c_i$. Thus, when playing against average subject behavior, an "empirically" optimal entry strategy is $c' = 1.496$. Against subjects who enter less frequently than equilibrium, the optimal response is to enter more frequently, and vice versa. Over the seven conditions, average cutoff values were generally near—though somewhat below—equilibrium values. Consequently, a successful route to finding an empirically optimal strategy would have been to start with the symmetric equilibrium strategy and then increase one's cutoff value slightly. Finally, recall that in equilibrium, the frequency of entry is suboptimal—less than the frequency called for in a second-best optimum. The fact that actual entry behavior falls short of the equilibrium benchmark further increases this welfare shortfall.

## Conclusion

Howard Raiffa's *The Art and Science of Negotiation* is widely praised for the power of its models and the range of its practical applications: bargaining, dispute resolution, risk sharing, competitive bidding, and voting.[22] Many of these models and applications arose in the course of his teaching, where it was natural to test the actual behavior of students and executives against various game-theoretic prescriptions. This study has attempted to follow a similar program. The model of entry under incomplete information is intended to capture the strategic issues facing would-be entrants in a new market. The model provides a number of testable predictions concerning firm entry behavior: for instance, that the frequency of individual entry will decline as the number of other potential entrants increases. It is also useful in identifying circumstances in which entry incentives are suboptimal.

The model's welfare findings provide the basis for a number of policy conclusions. The predominant economic wisdom emphasizes freedom of entry as a fundamental basis for market competition. Thus, most antitrust initiatives involve assessing the extent of entry barriers (as well as other pertinent industry conditions). However, for irreversible entry under uncertainty, the absence of entry barriers may not be a guarantee of optimal entry. Under normal conditions, when there are significant cost differences among entrants and demand is elastic, government measures to expand the number of potential entrants are appropriate; but in some circumstances, the number of potential entrants may well be excessive, and a reduction in their number may improve welfare. Frequently, this reduction will be accomplished by natural economic forces. For instance, the scramble to form joint ventures among cable television companies, the "Baby Bells," long distance carriers, and cellular telephone companies is already reducing the number of potential entrants into the emerging markets for multimedia telecommunication services. This development is likely to be pro-competitive rather than anticompetitive.

The possibility of excessive competition is also relevant in non-market settings. In a competitive procurement, a public or private buyer often issues a broad "request for proposals" to maximize the set of potential suppliers. However, when a firm's entrance into the competition involves significant non-recoverable costs and when cost differences among firms are expected to be small, measures to limit the number of bidders may be welfare improving. In the extreme, it may pay to eliminate bidding altogether and to negotiate with a single supplier instead. These same factors may favor the use of joint-bidding by suppliers; the reduction in bid-preparation costs may more than compensate for the reduced level of bidding competition.

## APPENDIX: SAMPLE INSTRUCTIONS

In the following in-class exercise, your role is as the manager of a firm facing the decision of whether or not to enter a new market. As in earlier exercises, your overall payoff will be determined by pitting your chosen strategy against the strategy choices of the other students in the class. You should choose the strategy that in your judgment performs best on average against the expected behavior of the class. Your performance on the exercise will count toward your "exercise" grade in the course.

As manager, you must decide whether your firm should enter a new market without knowing whether a second firm might also enter. If you choose not to enter, your profit is zero. If you enter the market, your predicted profit is:

$$\pi = 2.0 - .8x - c.$$

Here $x$ denotes the number of *other* entrants (either $x = 0$ or $x = 1$) and $c$ denotes your cost of production. For instance, if $c = \$1.5$ million and the other firm stays out, your entry profit is: $2 - (.8)(0) - 1.5 = \$.5$ million. But if the other firm enters, your profit is: $2.0 - .8 - 1.5 = -\$.3$ million. At the time you make your entry decision, you will know your own cost but not the cost of your potential entrant. You judge that the other firm's cost is *independent* of your own and falls in the range \$1 million to \$2 million, with all values in between equally likely.

1. Your production manager is about to provide an estimate of your own firm's cost (somewhere in the \$1 million to \$2 million range). Consider the initial cost listed below. First, indicate in the space provided whether you would enter the market or not. Then, turn to your student partner and tell each other your entry choices. Note your resulting profit. (Report your action to your partner but not your true cost or actual profit or loss.) Repeat this process using the second, third, and fourth costs estimates and changing partners. These are "practice" rounds allowing you to gain experience making entry decisions and to observe others' decisions. After completing these practice rounds, answer the final question below.

Your firm's cost is 1.38. I would _____ (Enter or Not enter)

Your firm's cost is 1.81. I would _____ (E or N)

Your firm's cost is 1.19. I would _____ (E or N)

Your firm's cost is 1.56. I would _____ (E or N)

In general, I would enter only if my cost is _____ or below.

(If it happens you would always enter for any cost estimate, report the cost value 2.0 or simply write "Always Enter." If you would never enter, write in 1.0 or write "Never Enter.")

2. Now suppose there are *three* other potential entrants besides yourself. The typical firm's entry profit remains:

$$\pi = 2.0 - .8x - c,$$

but now $x$ can be 0, 1, 2, or 3 other entrants. As before, the firms' respective costs lie between \$1 million and \$2 million and are independent of one another. Clearly, the market cannot profitably support all four firms. Like you, each firm will enter only if it judges its cost low enough to warrant a profit on average. Starting with the initial cost estimate, indicate whether you would enter the market or not. Then, communicate your entry choice to the three other students in your group. Follow the same process with the second estimate. Answer the last question by reporting your ultimate entry strategy.

Your firm's cost is 1.63. I would _____ (Enter or Not enter)

Your firm's cost is 1.39. I would _____ (E or N)

In general, I would enter only if my cost is _____ or below.

3. Finally, return to the setting in item 1, where your firm faces *one* potential competitor. The profit formula in item 1 pertains, but now there are *two* decision periods. In period one, each firm decides whether to enter or not. In period two (after observing each other's action), each firm makes a second decision whether to serve the market or not (i.e., to enter, stay out, remain in, or exit). Your firm's actual cost is listed below. For this cost, write down whether you would enter the market or not. When your firm number is called, you will be asked to report your entry decision. Your student partner will do likewise. After learning the Period One outcome, write down your entry/exit choice for Period Two. Then you and your partner will be asked to report your second-period decisions. Finally, after this practice session is completed, write down your complete entry and exit strategy (what you would do in each of the listed circumstances).

Your firm's actual cost is 1.42.

With this cost, I would _____ (enter or not) in Period One.

With this cost and given what happened in Period One, I
would _____ (stay out, exit, enter, or stay in) in Period Two.

After completing the practice session, report your general strategy.

Generally, I would enter in Period One only if my cost is
_____ or below.

Suppose you did *not* enter in Period One but your rival did.

I would choose to _____ (enter or not) in Period Two.

Suppose you entered in Period One but your rival did *not*.

I would choose to _____ (remain or exit) in Period Two.

Suppose *both* firms entered in Period One.

I would remain in Period Two only if my cost is _____ or
below.

Suppose *neither* firm entered in Period One.

I would enter in Period Two only if my cost is _____ or
below.

## NOTES

1. This kind of entry deterrence was first raised in Roger Sherman and
   Thomas Willett, "Potential Entrants Discourage Entry," *Journal of Political
   Economy* 75 (1967): 400–403.
2. See A. Michael Spence, "Entry, Capacity, Investment and Oligopolistic
   Pricing," *Bell Journal of Economics* 8 (1977): 534–544; Christian C. von
   Weizsacker, "A Welfare Analysis of Barriers to Entry," *Bell Journal of Eco-
   nomics* 11 (1980): 399–420; and Joseph E. Stiglitz, "Potential Competition
   May Lower Welfare," *American Economic Review* 71 (1981): 184–189.
3. See N. Gregory Mankiw and Michael D. Whinston, "Free Entry and Social
   Inefficiency," *Rand Journal of Economics* 17 (1986): 48–58; Edward C. Prescott
   and Michael Visscher, "Sequential Location among Firms with Foresight,"
   *Bell Journal of Economics* 8 (1977): 378–393; Michael Waldman, "Noncooperative Entry Deterrence, Uncertainty, and the Free Rider Problem," *Review
   of Economic Studies* 54 (1987): 301–310; B. Curtis Eaton and Roger Ware,
   "A Theory of Market Structure with Sequential Entry," *Rand Journal of
   Economics* 18 (1987): 1–16.

4. The crucial assumption is that the firm's entry decision is made in ignorance of the entry intentions of (at least some of) its competitors. Entry decisions need not literally be simultaneous.

5. Clearly, some sort of asymmetry among firms (in reputation or in the timing of entry opportunities) would be necessary as an entry-coordinating device.

6. Dixit and Shapiro argue that the symmetric equilibrium embodies a logical focal point for the players. Avinash Dixit and Carl Shapiro, "Entry Dynamics and Mixed Strategies," in *The Economics of Strategic Planning*, ed. Lacy Glenn Thomas (Lexington, MA: Lexington Books, 1986), pp. 63–79. By contrast, asymmetric equilibria (when they exist) are unconvincing as coordination mechanisms.

7. The assumption that demand follows a step-function is plausible in certain nonmarket settings. For instance, in a procurement, competitive bids determine the winning bidder and the supply price. In this setting, equilibrium entry achieves a second-best optimum. See William Samuelson, "Competitive Bidding with Entry Costs," *Economic Letters* 17 (1985): 53–57.

8. The optimality of free entry depends upon price taking by firms; different assumptions about post-entry behavior can render free entry suboptimal. See von Weizsacker, "A Welfare Analysis of Barriers to Entry."

9. See also Kofi O. Nti, "More Potential Entrants May Lead to Less Competition," *Journal of Economics* 49 (1989): 47–70. In this model, an incumbent monopolist faces a number of potential entrants, all with identical costs. After entry, firm behavior is described by the Cournot quantity equilibrium. The analysis show that increasing the number of potential entrants raises overall welfare while reducing consumer surplus.

10. In a second-best optimum, one sets the entry probability $p$ to maximize (16-7). Setting $\partial W/\partial p = 0$, we arrive at $p = (x^* - .5)/(n-1)$. This optimal entry probability is greater than the equilibrium probability. In addition, maximum welfare is computed to be $W^* = [n/(n-1)][(x^*-1)/x^* + 1/(2x^*)^2]$.

11. Three variations on a simple numerical example illustrate this point. Suppose $\pi(x) = 1.5 - .5x$. If firms have identical costs, $c = .5$, then as $n$ increases, expected welfare declines from 1.0 ($n = 2$) to .5 ($n = \infty$). If instead, costs are uniform on the interval $[0, 1]$, expected welfare increases from 1.0 ($n = 2$) to 1.5 ($n = \infty$). Finally, if the cost interval is $[.25, .75]$, expected welfare is constant (.94) for all $n$. (This is the knife-edge case: $d = b = .5$.) In short, instituting a mean-preserving spread in the cost distribution reverses the welfare impact of increasing the number of potential entrants.

12. Here we assume that a firm's entry profit is the same whether it enters early or late. A more realistic model might confer increased profits to early

entrants. The model can be easily extended to allow for a positive discount rate and entry and exit costs without changing the essential results.

13. For a complete analysis, see William Samuelson, "Market Entry under Incomplete Information" (Boston University Discussion Paper, 1994).

14. Definitive results for such full-fledged dynamic models are limited by their analytic complexity. Bolton and Farrell consider a pair of firms (holding private costs) that can enter at any of a number of points in time but cannot subsequently exit. In equilibrium, a low-cost firm tends to enter early, a higher-cost firm later (if at all). Dixit and Shapiro consider a multiperiod dynamic entry (and exit) game with identical costs and complete information. Over time, entry and exit moves the number of firms toward the stable long-run equilibrium. See Patrick Bolton and Joseph Farrell, "Decentralization, Duplication, and Delay" (Harvard University, 1988), and Dixit and Shapiro, "Entry Dynamics and Mixed Strategies."

15. Interesting examples include the scientific competition to uncover the "cancer gene" and the race to synthesize human insulin. See Natalie Angier, "Fierce Competition Marked Fervid Race for Cancer Gene," *New York Times,* September 20, 1994, p. C1; and Paul Barese, Adam Brandenburger, and Vijay Krishna, "The Race to Develop Human Insulin," Harvard Business School Case 9-191-121, 1992.

16. Overall, student performance on in-class and out-of-class exercises comprised between 25 and 30 percent of the final grade. Though the contribution of this particular exercise was very small, MBA students took this decision exercise (indeed, anything graded) very seriously. For a discussion of the incentives provided by monetary and non-monetary payoffs, see Richard Thaler, "The Psychology of Choice and the Assumptions of Economics," in *Laboratory Experimentation in Economics,* ed. Alvin Roth (Cambridge: Cambridge University Press, 1987), pp. 99–130.

17. Classic examples of this design are the prisoner's dilemma tournaments analyzed in Robert Axelrod, *The Evolution of Cooperation* (New York: Basic Books, 1984).

18. An additional consequence of the tournament design was to confine attention to the symmetric equilibrium benchmark. That is to say, asymmetric behavior (indeed, the expectation of such behavior) was virtually excluded. Asymmetric behavior is viable in a *particular* encounter between entrants. For instance, an asymmetric equilibrium in a two-firm entry game would have one firm always entering and the other always staying out, but the prospect of such behavior is highly unlikely in the tournament setting. Using the "always enter" strategy would be optimal if and only if the vast majority of other subjects always (or almost always) chose to "stay out"—a highly unlikely prospect.

19. In previous class sessions, students had been exposed to two-by-two payoff tables, the Prisoners' Dilemma, and the idea of reflexive thinking.

No games of incomplete information (nor any settings resembling the entry game) had yet been discussed.

20. A few students professed to carry the reasoning one step further: "If I am willing to adopt $c^* = 1.6$, then many of my classmates may do likewise. If my rival enters 60 percent of the time, my break-even cost will be below 1.6, probably around 1.5. (It is 1.52 to be exact.)" Carrying this reasoning to its logical conclusion, one establishes (by trial and error) that the symmetric equilibrium value is $c^* = 1.555$.

21. After one class of students participated in Conditions I, II, and VII, we included an additional decision question for the second class. In Condition IIa, subjects were told that they were one of four firms currently serving the market. They were then asked to report a cutoff value below which they would remain in the market and above which they would exit. Except for the framing of the status quo point, Condition IIa was identical to Condition II. Thus, a subject's reported cutoff value should be the same in the two conditions. The mean cutoff value in the exit frame was .03 lower than the mean value reported in the entry frame. Though this difference was not statistically significant ($t$-value $= -1.70$), framing alone could account for part of the increased incidence of exit in period two.

22. See Howard Raiffa, *The Art and Science of Negotiation* (Cambridge, MA: Harvard University Press, 1982).

# PART 3

## The Art and Science of Negotiation

# CHAPTER 17

# Rules of the Game, Permissible Harms, and the Principle of Fair Play

## Arthur Isak Applbaum

> However, I saw recently in my neighborhood at Mussidan that those who were forcibly driven out from there by our army, and others of their party, screamed as at treachery because during the discussion of terms, and while the treaty was still in effect, they had been surprised and cut to pieces: a complaint which might have had some plausibility in another century. But as I have just said, our ways are utterly remote from these rules; and parties should not trust one another until the last binding seal has been set. Even then there is plenty of room for wariness. . . .
>
> "To conquer always was a glorious thing, Whether achieved by fortune or by skill" (Ariosto), so they say. But the philosopher Chrysippus would not have been of that opinion, and I just as little. For he used to say that those who run a race should indeed employ their whole strength for speed but that, nevertheless, it was not in the least permissible for them to lay a hand on their adversary to stop him, or to stick out a leg to make him fall.
>
> Michel de Montaigne, "Parley time is dangerous."

This paper is a downpayment to Howard Raiffa on an outstanding promise to write about the ethics of negotiation. Thanks for helpful comments are due to Miriam Avins, David Estlund, Mark Kleiman, Stephen Latham, Frederick Schauer, James Sebenius, Dennis Thompson, Alan Wertheimer, and Richard Zeckhauser. Portions of the section entitled "The Argument from Consent" draw on work written in collaboration with Harold Pollack. The epigraph is from *The Complete Essays of Montaigne*, trans. Donald M. Frame (Stanford, CA: Stanford University Press, 1958).

The notion of a game has two complementary senses: a game as strategic interaction, and a game as rule-governed social practice. As a strategic interaction, a game invites players to engage in harmful tactics that are presumptively wrong, such as deception, coercion, or violence. In defense of at least some use of such tactics, players commonly claim that they are engaged in a game as a rule-governed social practice as well, and that the rules of the game permit the use of tactics that would otherwise be impermissible. I wish to explore various arguments that might be offered in support of the claim that presumptively wrong actions, if permitted by the rules of a game—henceforth called *game-permissible* actions—for that reason are no longer wrong, and so become *morally permissible* actions.

The games I mainly have in mind are middle-level social institutions that order the activities of actors who have at least partly conflicting interests, or who represent others who have such interests. Negotiations are such games, as are lawsuits, political campaigns, and competition in the marketplace. On a smaller scale, so are parlor games and sports, and I will often analogize from deceptive parlor games and violent sports to larger and more complex social institutions. As shorthand, I call these institutions *adversary games*, and the actors whose activities are ordered within them *adversaries*. The adversary legal system, in which lawyers are permitted, within its rules, to make claims they know to be false and advance interests they know to be unjust, is one such game, though not all the players in all the games considered here are adversaries precisely in the way that opposing lawyers are. I use the term "adversary" more loosely.

The biggest game that will be considered is the game of law—not the practice of legal representation by lawyers, but the ordering of society by the rule of law. When asked about the game of law our question of whether game-permissible actions are, for that reason, morally permissible has a familiar ring and a familiar answer. The fact that an action is permitted by the laws of the state does not by itself render the action morally permissible. American law permits all sorts of horrible ways of treating others, and so the exercise of one's legal rights can be morally wrong. There are many perfectly legal ways to be vicious, cruel, hurtful, and deceitful—to wrong others through speech, or by causing psychological distress, or by hurting one's relations. It is often legal to dupe a retiree into investing his life's savings stupidly, to incite racial hatred for political gain, or to sell arms to murderous regimes abroad.

If these practices are wrong, the fact of their legality does not necessarily make them any less wrong. This is so, not only for an imperfect set of existing laws, but for any ideal set of laws. As often noted, the regulation and coercive prevention of all morally wrong action would in itself cause great economic inefficiencies and grave restrictions of liberty, so that there are some morally wrong actions that would be unwise to outlaw, and others that would be morally wrong to outlaw. The optimal amount of legally permissible moral wrongdoing is not zero.

That legality does not, in itself, make presumptively wrong actions morally permissible is no surprise, and this conclusion is widely though not uniformly held. In the case of smaller social games, however, one is more likely to think that game-permission *does* create moral permission. For example, deception and violence are presumptive moral wrongs, but the rules of the game of poker permit deception, and the rules of boxing, football, and hockey permit violence. It is widely believed that lying in poker and tackling in football are morally permissible, and widely believed that this is so because the rules of the games of poker and football permit such actions. Similarly, it is widely believed that the permissive rules of professional games such as lawyering, business management, and elective politics generate moral permissions to engage in deceptive and coercive tactics that, if not for their game-permissibility, would be morally wrong.

Several arguments have been offered to back up the claim that the rules of games provide moral permission to use tactics that would otherwise be wrong, but they are weaker or more limited in scope than is often supposed. The next two sections briefly explore the arguments from consent and tacit consent, and show that they either fail to justify sharp practices or require stringent conditions that are unlikely to be met in practice. The second half of the paper examines the argument from fair play—oddly enough, the most promising way to support at least some deceptive, coercive, and violent practices.

The fair play principle was originally developed by H. L. A. Hart and John Rawls to establish a general obligation for citizens to obey the law even when they have not consented. Roughly, fair play obligates us to do our fair share in schemes of social cooperation from which we willingly benefit, and not to freeride on the burdens shouldered by others. The fair play argument ingeniously retains two important intuitions: that receiving benefits may lead to obligations, but that obligations must be connected to voluntary acts. Fair play thereby offers a grounding for political obligation that depends on voluntary action, but not on voluntary consent to be obligated. The fair play argument is here employed in a novel way, to establish a moral *permission* that otherwise would not exist, rather than to establish a moral obligation that otherwise would not exist. I develop necessary and sufficient conditions for the fair play argument to work in establishing a permission, and, along the way, explore whether the games of business, legal practice, and elective politics meet these conditions.

## The Argument from Consent

One way that game permissions might generate moral permissions is by way of consent. For two well-known and complementary reasons, genuine consent is a very potent permitter of actions that, absent consent, would be wrong. First, some actions are presumptively wrong because they harm the welfare of others, but since we ordinarily presume that people know what is in their own welfare, their consent to a presumptively wrong action against them reverses the presumption that the action in fact harms them. Second, some actions are presumptively wrong because they override or undermine the will of others, and so fail to treat others as autonomous—that is, self-ruling—agents. But performed with consent, these actions properly respect the will of the target, and so become exercises in autonomy, rather than violations of it. Thus, players in a game consent to the rules of the game, and so consent to be subjected to the deception, coercion, or violence the rules of the game permit. So, for one or the other of the two reasons just offered, consent removes the presumptive wrong of actions taken in accordance with the rules of a game, rendering game-permissible deception, coercion, and violence morally permissible. (Alternatively, consent changes the appropriate description of these actions, so that they are no longer instances of deception, coercion, or violence.)

When players have actually consented to the rules of a game, the argument from consent is compelling. But the criteria of genuine consent are stringent, and may not hold for most players in social games with any complexity. Citizens, for example, rarely give genuine consent to obey the laws of the state. We must be careful in particular not to conflate the strong argument from consent with the much weaker claim about expectation, and assume that those who expect to be the targets of adversary tactics have consented to be such targets.

Deception in poker ordinarily is morally permitted because the conditions necessary for genuine consent are ordinarily satisfied: a player who sits down at the felt enters into an actual (not hypothetical), informed (not manipulated), and voluntary (not coerced) agreement to play by the rules. And since he may leave the table at virtually no cost, his acceptance of each deal of the cards signals continued acceptance of the terms of play. The argument from consent straightforwardly gives moral permission to actions permitted by the rules of poker because we presume that the player has chosen to participate and that the choice is both in his own interests and his to make. There are no doubt limits to the authority of self-rule, even when the stringent conditions of free and informed consent are met. Freedoms that destroy the worth of freedom—the classic and most extreme example being the conundrum of voluntary slavery—are deeply problematic. But choosing to play poker does not test the limits of the permission-generating property of consent.

Unlike poker, consent to the rules of larger social games played by business managers, lawyers, and politicians may be absent or defective. First, most public and professional games profoundly affect those who are not players. Campaign mudslingers take aim at opposing candidates, but also cloud public discourse and deceive citizens; defense attorneys aim to defeat the prosecution, but also malign the reputations of reluctant witnesses; a cigarette manufacturer's manipulative advertising aims to take market share away from a competitor, but also harms teenagers. Second, not all players are knowledgeable about the rules of the game. Marketers distract consumers from *caveat emptor*; real estate brokers, who have a fiduciary responsibility to sellers, cultivate trust and dependency in buyers, and in the end work for themselves, depend on ambiguity about their loyalties. Third, even when players are knowledgeable, they may face exit barriers or their alternatives may be so poor that their continued participation in an adversary game cannot be assumed fully voluntary.

When alternatives to participation are poor, expectation of an adversary game does not imply consent to its rules. In buying a used car, you may fully expect to be deceived about its defects. You may also "play the game" by reading *Consumer Reports* and by taking the car to a mechanic. Yet the inference to consent may be too quick. Here, precision about the moral significance of expectation is needed. Suppose you agree to buy a car "as is," with the expectation that the seller might have deceived you about its worth—say such deceptive practices are conventional in the used car market—and it turns out that, indeed, you have been deceived. On a perfectly plausible understanding of consent and its twin defects of coercion and ignorance, there was no defect in your consent to the exchange of money for car. Your agreement was uncoerced: the seller did not threaten to harm your interests if you did not buy his car, he did not cause you to want a car (say, by smashing your old one), and he is under no prior duty or obligation to compensate for your carlessness.[1] Your agreement was informed: you knowledgeably took into account the possibility of deception, and you reasonably believed that the deal was worth the risk. (We might suppose that, because of the widespread expectation, the market price of used cars is already discounted for deception, so that the expected value to a buyer, even with the chance of deception, is positive.)

Since your expectation of deception removed ignorance as a defect in your consent, you indeed have consented to the exchange, but you need not have consented to be deceived, let alone have consented to a regime permitting deception. Consent to one does not necessarily imply consent to the others. Therefore, if the rules of the game require consent for their legitimation, then consent to a transaction does not necessarily legitimate the rules under which the transaction has occurred. The deceptive seller can invoke your agreement, and your knowledge of and expectation of standard practices in the market, only to show that you voluntarily exchanged money for car, not that you volunteered to be deceived. So, though you may be morally obligated to perform your part in the exchange, even if tricked, the seller is not necessarily morally permitted to trick you. If the practice of deception here relies on your consent for its legitimation, the exchange by itself does not legitimate the deceptive practice. The argument from expectation therefore fails to justify adversary action against a target. At most, it denies the target certain remedies, such as canceling the transaction. Of course, consent need not be necessary or sufficient legitimating grounds: some adversary games do not need the consent of the target for their legitimation (for example, the prosecution of just claims in the legal system), while other games are not justified by consent of the target (such as Russian roulette).

### The Argument from Tacit Consent

Consent is a potent way to establish a moral permission to engage in presumptively wrong actions permitted by the rules of a game, but its conditions—free and informed agreement—are stringent. So, not surprisingly, expansive claims are made to impute *tacit* consent to situations where explicit consent is absent. Locke famously makes this argument to establish an obligation to obey the law, claiming that anyone who possesses or enjoys the use of land in the territories of a government—even if only to travel freely on the highway—thereby gives tacit consent to obey the government's laws.[2] The argument from tacit consent is that a class of actions such as participation, compliance, or acceptance of benefit signals or constitutes tacit consent to the rules of an adversary institution, and that tacit consent is a species of genuine consent. Does participation or acceptance of benefit indeed imply tacit consent? If so, how? And does tacit consent have the moral force of explicit consent?

Consider two ways in which tacit consent can be understood to be a species of genuine consent. On the evidentiary view, a set of evidentiary conditions such as participation, compliance, or acceptance of benefit are good evidence that the actor in fact has met the primary conditions of consent—free and informed agreement. Since the power of the evidentiary conditions depends on their contingent connection to the primary conditions, the ascription of consent when the evidentiary conditions are met is merely a presumption, rebuttable by stronger evidence that one has not entered into a free and informed agreement. So, on the evidentiary standard, a citizen who pronounces, every time he walks on the sidewalk, that he refuses to be obligated by the laws of the state, and that his use of public streets should not be construed as tacit consent to the authority of the law, cannot be understood to have offered tacit consent by his use of the sidewalk. There may be *other* reasons that obligate him, and, as we will see, other reasons for which his use and benefit of sidewalks matter, but he is not obligated by way of tacit consent. Similarly for permissions: someone who buys a used car and signs a proclamation that explicitly denies that his participation in the used car market implies his tacit consent to be treated as a target of deception has not, on the evidentiary view, consented to the rules of that market. (Again, there may be other reasons that permit actions against him on account of his participation.) If the evidentiary view of tacit consent is correct, then those activities that are presumed consensual must be grounded empirically in some statistical generalization about actual intentions. If, upon investigation, we find that most sidewalk users are philosophical anarchists, and that most used car buyers expect to be deceived but do not intend to consent to be deceived, then an explicit denial of tacit consent is no longer needed to rebut the presumption of consent. Rather, the presumption runs the other way, absent further evidence that, for this particular actor, some action *does* signal tacit consent.

Against the evidentiary view of tacit consent, consider the constitutive view. Some actions constitute consent: to participate in or to benefit from a game *means* to consent to its rules. On this view, built into the meaning of "playing poker" or "bargaining with a used car salesman" is the notion of consent to certain practices, which cannot be undone by contrary proclamations. What are we to make of the football halfback who, before the game, pins to his jersey a note that reads, in large letters, "I do not consent to be tackled," and then proceeds to take his place on the field, accepts a handoff, and runs with the football towards the goal line? One is tempted to say that he no longer plays football. If so, then he indeed has withdrawn his consent, he may not be tackled—and the referee should eject him from the game. But an equally plausible understanding is that he has not withdrawn his consent, that he cannot coherently deny consent so long as he takes the football in hand. Carrying a football under those circumstances means that one has consented to be tackled, no matter what he may signal or even intend to the contrary.

Consider an analogy. When Magritte adds to his drawing of a pipe the legend "Ceci n'est pas une pipe" (This is not a pipe), he does not undo the pipeness of the image. We don't say, "Oh. Before I read the disclaimer, I thought it was a pipe, but now I understand that it must be something else." Magritte's drawing tweaks at the notion that artists are authoritative interpreters of their art; tacit consent, understood constitutively, denies force to the explicit disclaimer "this is not consent" when one's behavior constitutes consent. The intention of the actor no more determines the meaning of an action than the intention of an artist determines the meaning of a work of art.[3]

Are we then to say that playing a game constitutes tacit consent to the game's rules, so that, if the rules allow deception, coercion, or violence, it is permissible to deceive, coerce, or do violence to the player? Not always. First, even if the possibility of constitutive tacit consent is granted, we must establish which actions do in fact constitute consent. Here the analogy to Magritte's pipe breaks down. Magritte's drawing is unproblematically pipish—hence the air of paradox; but participation in or benefit from adversary games does not unproblematically constitute consent, even if some acts—signing a check or running with a football, say—do so constitute. Even Locke understands that there are limits to what actions can be taken to mean. He holds that tacit consent does not create a permanent obligation to submit to government, and does not denote membership in a society. Without explicit consent, political obligation ceases when one's possession of land or enjoyment of residence in a country ceases.[4]

Alternatively, even if we agree that participation in adversary institutions *does* constitute consent despite the intentions of the actor, then the moral force of this sort of consent to obligate or permit may be questioned. We need then to distinguish between two types of consent, the consent that comes from intentional, free, and informed agreement, and the consent that does not. Consent of the second sort, which fails to satisfy the primary conditions of intention, freedom, and knowledge, quite plausibly does not do the moral work of consent of the first sort, and so is not a powerful presumptive source of permission or obligation.

## The Argument from Fair Play

The most promising argument in support of the claim that game permissions generate moral permissions to deceive, threaten, or hurt another player is the argument from fair play. In the face of the failure of arguments from consent to establish a general obligation for citizens to obey the law, Hart and Rawls ingeniously offered the fair play principle as a grounding for political obligation that depends on voluntary action, but not on voluntary consent to be obligated.[5] This section asks if the logic of fair play can be put to a new use: to permit actions that otherwise would not be permitted, rather than to require actions that otherwise would not be obligatory.

Roughly, the fair play principle obligates us to do our fair share in schemes of social cooperation from which we willingly benefit, and not to freeride on others. Rawls writes:

> This principle holds that a person is required to do his part as defined by the rules of an institution when two conditions are met: first, the institution is just (or fair), that is, it satisfies the two principles of justice; and second, one has voluntarily accepted the benefits of the arrangement or taken advantage of the opportunities it offers to further one's interests. The main idea is that when a number of persons engage in a mutually advantageous cooperative venture according to rules, and thus restrict their liberty in ways necessary to yield advantages for all, those who have submitted to these restrictions have a right to a similar acquiescence on the part of those who have benefitted from their submission. We are not to gain from the cooperative labors of others without doing our fair share.[6]

If political society is such a cooperative venture, and citizens freely accept the benefits of social cooperation, then fairness obligates them to obey the laws of the state. The fair play argument was thought to avoid the obvious difficulty with consent arguments, that citizens have not in fact consented to be obligated, while retaining two important intuitions: that receiving benefits may lead to obligations, but that some kinds of obligation must be connected to voluntary acts. Rather than relying on tortured accounts of consent to obligate anarchic pedestrians or demurring football players to play by the rules, we may simply say that fairness obligates these freeriders, with or without their agreement.

Rawls no longer believes that the argument from fair play obligates all citizens to obey the law, because all citizens may not be advantaged by the scheme of social cooperation, or may not have freely accepted its benefits.[7] But his recantation should not deter our attempt to apply the fair play argument to rules of strategic games. The argument for adversary permission from fair play may be stronger than the case for political obligation from fair play in two ways. First, many of the social institutions constituted by rule-governed games of strategy are more likely to be mutually advantageous cooperative ventures than is the whole of a modern society.[8] Second, establishing a permission to play by the rules of a game may be easier than establishing an obligation to play by them.

Does some version of the fair play argument permit players in adversary games to lie, threaten, and inflict violence in accordance with the rules of the game, even if targets have not consented to play by the rules? To answer, I first lay out a very strong and restrictive formulation of the argument. These strong conditions appeal to our clearest intuitions about consent, benefit, fairness, and freeriding, and anticipate some criticisms that have been leveled against the fair play principle.[9] If any form of the fair play argument establishes an adversary permission, it is this one. I then explore the force of the fair play argument in generating adversary permissions by relaxing each of the conditions in turn.

### Strong Conditions of Fair Play

A player in a game of strategy is morally permitted to take action against a target, so as to restrict the target's liberties or set back the target's interests, even if the target has not consented to be targeted, when five conditions are satisfied:

RULE-PERMISSIBILITY. The rules of the game permit such adversary action.

NECESSITY. The rules permitting such action are necessary for the continued success or stability of the game as a mutually advantageous cooperative venture.

MUTUAL ADVANTAGE. The game is a mutually advantageous cooperative venture in that, considering all benefits and burdens, including the burden of becoming a target, and compared with the baseline alternative of there being no game, the game provides all its players positive expected net benefits. Players are those who voluntarily seek the venture's benefits.

JUSTICE. The venture is just in three ways: (a) on some reasonable conception of justice, this particular target is to receive a just share of the venture's benefits and burdens; (b) the venture generally distributes benefits and burdens justly to its players; and (c) the venture imposes no unjust externalities on those who are not players.

VOLUNTARY BENEFIT. Facing benefits and burdens that are of positive expected net benefit and justly distributed, and preferring the existence of the game with its benefits and burdens to there being no game, the target has voluntarily sought the game's benefits. The voluntary seeking of benefits is understood as an uncoerced and informed choice of action in circumstances where not to benefit is both possible and costless.

If fair play works at all to permit adversary action, it will work under these strong—probably excessively strong—conditions, where a player who claims immunity from targeting *does* seem to be asking for an unfair free ride that other players have no apparent moral reason to grant.

The case of the demurring football player satisfies these conditions. Other players have joined together in a mutually advantageous cooperative venture, football, whose rules permit violence against one another. Let us suppose that there is no injustice in the distribution of benefits and burdens (it is an amateur game, without salaries or shaving cream endorsements to distribute; positions have been assigned fairly in accordance with skills and preferences; the neighbor's rosebushes are not in danger). The demurring player seeks the advantages of running with the football—scoring—without the disadvantages of being tackled. This is unfair to the other players, who are all contributing to the venture and risking injury by playing by the rules. So long as he runs with the ball, fairness permits other players to tackle him. Similarly, fairness permits poker players to bluff those who seek the pleasures and rewards of the game. Others have joined together in a mutually advantageous venture, the game of poker, whose rules permit deception. One cannot voluntarily take the game's rewards and reasonably expect to be free from its burdens.

But are the conditions satisfied in the used car negotiation case? Can we consider the used car market to be a mutually advantageous cooperative venture, governed by the rule *caveat emptor,* so that the concealment of defects is permitted under the principle of fair play? Only if, among other things, benefits and burdens are justly distributed between buyers and sellers. Has a political candidate no reasonable complaint about a rival's appeal to racial bias and fear in campaign advertising? Complain he may, for the success and stability of the game of electoral politics does not depend on a campaign etiquette that admits deceptive and hateful advertising. Is a bar association that prevents its lawyers from advertising to be considered a mutually advantageous cooperative venture for the purpose of establishing and maintaining the monopoly pricing of legal services? If so, clients can hardly be understood to be cooperators, let alone advantaged cooperators, in such a venture. Professional institutions and adversary games are not self-contained systems. Some are designed to affect nonplayers, others inevitably do. What is seen as a mutually advantageous cooperative venture from the inside may be nothing of the sort. Adversary games more complex than poker and football that satisfy all of the strong conditions of fair play are rare indeed. If adversary action in the games of business, law, and politics are to be permitted under fair play, a formulation that is more relaxed but that still generates moral permission is needed. Can some of the specifications be loosened?

## Necessity

Consider first the necessity condition, that the rules of the game allowing adversary action such as lies and threats are necessary for the continued success and stability of the mutually advantageous venture. At the core of the fair play argument is the notion that to not play fair is to be unfair to *someone.* M. B. E. Smith argues that there can be no unfairness if there has not been either harm or loss of benefit, so the fair play principle cannot obligate one to cooperate in a social venture if one's freeriding does not cause some loss to at least one cooperator.[10] Smith's condition puts a serious limit on the likelihood of generating *obligations* to obey rules through fair play, because the marginal harms or losses of benefit of one incident of rulebreaking attributable to the fact of rulebreaking itself (apart from harms that would befall even if the act were not against the rules) is usually zero. If, at a sold-out Yo-Yo Ma concert, a couple sitting in the rear of Symphony Hall unobtrusively takes the seats of no-shows at seventh row center, and nobody notices, no one is worse off than if all complied with the rules and the best seats in the house went unfilled. If other concertgoers found out, they might cry unfair: "Why should they get better seats than they paid for, and not us?" or "Why should we have to pay for the best seats when they take them for less?" But on Smith's view, the cry is unwarranted: no harm, no unfairness, and since no one is worse off than had all complied, no harm has been done here (unless causing feelings of resentment and unfairness is a harm). However, if known freeriding encourages others to do the same, so that concert hall civility descends to the level of Filene's Basement, then the free ride does harm the cooperators in a cooperative venture, and is unfair to others. But whether or not one's rulebreaking encourages others to do the same is a factual matter. Observing noncooperative behavior may instead reinforce the importance of cooperation (our typical reaction to litterbugs). On Smith's view, the morally decisive question is not the hypothetical generalization, "What if others did it?" but the empirical prediction, "Will others do it?" Indeed, many rules are robust against a fair amount of noncompliance. If Smith is right, the necessity condition is not strong *enough:* even when a general rule is necessary for the success and stability of a cooperative venture, if a particular act of noncompliance has no untoward effects on cooperators, either directly or by damaging the scheme of cooperation, then no unfairness has occurred.

Recall, however, that we seek to use the fair play principle to permit players to act in accordance with the rules of a game, not to obligate playing by the rules. Smith's condition—that unfairness requires harm or loss of benefit—is more likely to be met when fair play is invoked to permit, rather than to obligate. A player who cannot take aim at a particular target usually *is* denied a benefit—winning the hand, making the tackle, closing the sale, convincing the jury, gaining the votes. If the would-be target has sought the benefits of the rules of a cooperative scheme, even on Smith's account the fair play principle permits targeting in accordance with those rules.

In any case, Smith's condition does not *need* to be met, for moral permission to follow a rule does not depend on the rule's underlying reasons being satisfied in each particular case, even if a moral obligation to follow a rule does so depend. If a rule allowing sharp adversary tactics is necessary for the success of a cooperative scheme, and the general practice of regulation-by-rule is necessary, each adversary act under the rule need not be necessary for the act to be permitted. If permission to target many but not all is necessary, and there is no relevant distinction to be made among the all, or if requiring players to make such distinctions undermines the usefulness of regulating behavior by general rule, then the targeting of all is fair. Of course, rules can be overly broad, and for that reason be unfair. But rules can be overly narrow as well, as would be a rule that exempted a few named freeriders for no other reason than that the inclusion of each and every player is not necessary. Though the game of poker would survive if players were permitted to bluff anyone but Ernest, Ernest is not treated unfairly if he is not granted immunity from bluffing. The game requires that most players be permissible targets, and Ernest can give no good reason why he should be treated specially. Generalization can make adversary rules fair, so that one has moral permission to follow them in specific cases. This is so, even if specific noncompliance with those same general rules is not unfair, so that one has no moral obligation to obey. Suppose that concertgoers have a general practice of throwing rotten tomatoes at those who move up to unoccupied seats, and the existence of the general practice, and common knowledge of its existence, is necessary to deter widespread freeriding. Even if particular freeriders have no obligation to stay in their assigned seats, because their particular acts of freeriding cause no loss of benefit, they have no justified complaint if they are the targets of tomatoes. If some but no particular tomato-tossing is necessary for the success and stability of concerts, then any particular tomato-tossing is permitted.

But why must an adversary rule contribute to the "success and stability" of a game? An adversary rule may generate benefits and add value to an already mutually advantageous cooperative venture without the rule being necessary for the continued existence of the venture as a mutually advantageous scheme. The adversary legal system would successfully survive the repeal of most any single adversary permission, as it survived the introduction of discovery in civil proceedings, but many of its adversary permissions plausibly make the cooperative venture more advantageous to its players. Rawls appears to require a less stringent test—that rules be necessary to yield advantages for all. This follows from the underlying logic of fair play itself: if the prospect of justly distributed mutual advantage justifies the formation of a rule-governed cooperative venture, additional mutual advantage should justify additional rules.

### Mutual Advantage

Consider now the mutual advantage condition. What constitutes, in games of strategy, a "mutually advantageous cooperative venture?" The strong formulation requires that all players be advantaged, and that the advantage of a player be assessed relative to the baseline of no venture (rather than to the baseline of nonparticipation). Leaving for later the question of who counts as a player, is this criterion of mutual advantage needed for the fair play argument to permit players to harm targets in accordance with the rules of a game?

The requirement of universal advantage seems too strong as long as other conditions, such as justice and voluntary acceptance of benefit, are met. Certainly it is too strong if advantage is assessed ex post: to guarantee good outcomes to all would rule out any venture that involves irremediable risks such as physical harm, even if the ex ante expected advantage to all is great. No barns would be raised, no wells dug. Nor do we want to rule out games that add value over the no-game alternative but are zero sum within the game—for example, purely distributive bargains.

But even ex ante universal advantage is too tough. Why should the permissibility of an entire cooperative venture be called into question simply because one player is mistaken about his interests, preferences, or skills at playing the game? Perhaps the one who is not advantaged is under no obligation to comply with a game's rules, if fair play is invoked to obligate; and perhaps the one who is not advantaged is not a permissible target under an adversary rule. But it is not clear why the disadvantage of a few (if they are not unjustly or involuntarily disadvantaged) should block the fair play principle from obligating others who are advantaged. Rawls's requirement of "yielding advantages for all" seems too strong. Surely, the disadvantage of a few should not block a permission to target the advantaged. A small, one-time litigant may be disadvantaged by rules of the court that permit an adversary to engage in costly delay tactics. But why should that render the tactic unfair if used against players who use the same tactics advantageously? The universal advantage requirement can be saved by considering only the advantaged to be participants or players in the cooperative venture, but such a move simply shifts the question to the voluntary benefit condition: why are those who voluntarily seek the benefits of a just cooperative scheme not to be considered participants in that scheme, merely because they would be better off had they not sought such benefits? It appears that universal mutual advantage is too strong.

Next, consider the baseline condition. Is advantage to be reckoned from the alternative of not receiving the benefits or burdens of the existing cooperative venture, or the alternative of there being no such venture at all? The standard description of circumstances in which the fair play principle is in play does not need to make this distinction. Consider four states: FREERIDING, where the player receives the benefits but shirks the burdens of an existing cooperative venture; COOPERATION, where the player receives the benefits and shoulders the burdens; NONPARTICIPATION, where the player neither receives benefits nor shoulders burdens; and NO VENTURE, where the cooperative venture does not exist. The preferences or interests of players are assumed in the standard case to be ordered so that FREERIDING is superior to COOPERATION, and COOPERATION is superior to both NONPARTICIPATION and NO VENTURE.

But suppose my neighbors have mowed a shortcut through a common meadow. I was more advantaged by the open meadow—I do not like the foot traffic, I did not want to disturb the flowers or rabbits. Now that there is a shortcut, I use it, rather than walk around the long way, because what I valued about the undisturbed meadow has already been ruined. The shortcut *is* convenient, and if I had to pay a small fee to continue using it, I would, though I would rather let the path grow over and have no one use it. The neighbors slip a note under my door asking for a modest annual contribution for the upkeep of the path.

Under this scheme, I prefer NO VENTURE to FREERIDING, FREERIDING to COOPERATION, and COOPERATION to NONPARTICIPATION. Am I advantaged by participation in the cooperative venture? Yes, relative to nonparticipation, but not compared with there being no venture at all.

Do I violate the fair play principle in refusing to pay my share? I think not. The venture was not organized for *my* advantage, and my preferences and interests are frustrated by its existence. Must I refrain from participation, and not use the path? Reasonable intuitions go both ways, but if we consider "freeriding" as an attempt to compensate for the involuntary loss imposed by the cooperative venture, then the free ride (or walk) is not unfair to cooperators on the fair play principle. My situation, after all, is different from theirs: they are made better off by the cooperative venture, and I am made worse off.

Many adversary games share this structure. The introduction of competitive markets for goods that previously were allocated through nonmarket mechanisms has not advantaged all players in the new markets. This is obvious when market forces challenge those who had access to resources through traditional means. Not all wives are advantaged by the opening of labor markets to women, though they may now seek employment; trade liberalization creates many losers who nonetheless compete to cut their losses. When Alexander Hamilton freely accepted Aaron Burr's challenge to duel, perhaps he wished that there were no such institution for settling affairs of honor—and perhaps Burr wished the same. If fairness obligates players in these games to abide by the rules, it must be a notion of fairness different from the one underlying the fair play principle, because these players have been disadvantaged by the existence of the cooperative venture.

Is this strong condition of advantage relative to the no venture alternative necessary to *permit* adversary action? If Hamilton is better off without the institution of dueling, is Burr forbidden to fire? The answer appears to depend on a richer description of the burdens imposed on participants in the cooperative scheme, the disadvantages that befall nonparticipants, and the connections of both to the benefits sought by the disadvantaged player. If the player participates to defend against the disadvantages that are imposed by the existence of the venture, and if the burdens that befall players restrict their liberties or set back their interests in ways that would be wrong in the absence of the venture, then there does not seem to be any moral justification to impose burdens on the disadvantaged participant.

If the correct specification of the mutual advantage criterion is advantage in comparison with there being no venture, the scope of the adversary actions permitted by fair play is severely restricted. But it would be a mistake, I think, to interpret the criterion even more stringently, and require that players be advantaged in comparison with any possible cooperative venture. For any set of rules governing a game, there will almost certainly be a different set of rules or a different game more favorably tailored to a particular player. But one is not treated unfairly just because one does not get the most favorable treatment possible, and a freerider can be understood to take unfair advantage of cooperators, even when the rules upon which one freerides are not one's first choice.

### Voluntary Benefit

We turn now to the voluntary benefit condition. The strong formulation defines players as those, and only those, who have voluntarily sought the benefits of the cooperative venture, where voluntarily seeking benefits is understood as an uncoerced and informed choice of action in circumstances where not to benefit is both possible and costless. But why are not all who benefit from the cooperative venture considered participants or players, whether or not such benefit is voluntary? If voluntary benefit is necessary, why must benefit be actively sought, rather than willingly but passively accepted? If benefit is voluntary, why must the possibility of not benefiting be necessary? Why must the possibility of not benefiting be costless?

In rejecting the fair play principle as a source of obligation, Robert Nozick offers a series of engaging examples: neighbors who take turns playing musical entertainment over a local public address system that you enjoyably overhear; neighbors who mow their lawns more frequently than is your habit; people who throw valuable books into your house for exercise; neighbors who cooperate to sweep the streets. "Must you imagine dirt as you traverse the street, so as not to benefit as a free rider?" he asks rhetorically.[11] Must you take your turn at the neighborhood microphone or mow your lawn more frequently? No, because you have not volunteered for the benefits involved, though, in all, the benefits you receive outweigh the burdens requested of you. Nozick's examples point out the importance of some sort of voluntary action in our intuitions about fairness, and not merely the receipt of benefit, but do not tell against the fair play principle as Rawls understands it.

No voluntary participation in receiving benefits, no obligation to assume burdens under fair play. But does this formulation extend to adversary permissions? Or is it sufficient, in order to permit burdening a target, that he has received greater benefit, willingly or not? Suppose you live downwind from a polluting steel mill. You benefit from the economic activity the mill has brought to your town, and the benefit outweighs the health risks of pollution, but this hardly robs you of reasonable complaint. Just as you are not obligated to pay for uninvited valuable books thrown in your house, the book thrower is not permitted to smash your windows, even if the books are more valuable to you than the glass.

The remaining stipulations in the strong formulation of the voluntary participation condition share an underlying logic: without each, voluntary participation in the cooperative venture is difficult to demonstrate. Passive acceptance of benefit may signal willingness, but may result from indifference, ignorance, or the difficulty of avoiding benefit. If refusing benefit is impossible, as with unavoidable public goods like national defense, voluntariness is hard to demonstrate. Again, if avoiding benefit is possible but in itself burdensome (imagining dirty streets and unkempt lawns, or not walking out of doors), not refusing benefit does not necessarily signal willing acceptance of benefit, even if one is better off with the benefits and its associated burdens than without.

As was seen in the earlier discussion of tacit consent, there is a constitutive and an evidentiary interpretation of the connection of these requirements to voluntary acceptance of benefit—and the evidentiary interpretation is the correct one. When a player passively receives a benefit, cannot refuse it, or can refuse it only at a cost, we may not presume, without further evidence, that acceptance of benefit is voluntary. Here, there is good reason to be *more* stringent in finding adversary permissions to impose burdens than in finding obligations to assume burdens. Since one ordinarily knows the state of one's own will better than others can know it, one may in fact be obligated because of voluntary acceptance of benefit in ways that others cannot detect, though others are not permitted to presume such voluntary acceptance. Given the presumptive wrong in restricting liberties and setting back interests, when it comes to adversary permissions there should be a (rebuttable) presumption against assuming the voluntary participation of others.

Once voluntary acceptance of benefit has been established, however, to require the further condition that exit from the game be costless as well is too stringent. Earlier, easy exit was offered as an evidentiary test of a player's continued consent to play by the rules. But recall that the point of the fair play principle is to establish obligations and permissions when prior or ongoing consent to rules is lacking. Costly exit may block the inference that the acceptance of future benefits will be voluntary, but does not undo the voluntary acceptance of past benefits. As long as the conditions of ex ante mutual advantage and justice are satisfied, exit barriers do not preclude application of the fair play principle to past benefits voluntarily accepted. So, if we are in the middle of a high-stakes round of poker, even though you cannot fold your hand and decline further pleasures of the game without a big loss, I may still bluff you. Hamilton and Burr cannot both freely leave the dueling ground, but this exit barrier is not why the duel is impermissible.[12]

## *Justice*

Finally, consider the justice conditions. How do the justice conditions limit the reach of the fair play principle? Straight away, we should back off from Rawls's particular conception of justice and its two principles. The fair play argument requires *a* theory of justice, but not *A Theory of Justice*. Our strong formulation requires, on some conception of justice, that the cooperative venture be just in three ways: *local justice*, in that this particular target of adversary action receives a just share of the venture's benefits and burdens; *internal justice*, in that the venture generally distributes benefits and burdens justly to its players; and *external justice*, in that the venture does not impose unjust externalities on those who are not players. How do these stipulations work, and why are they needed?

The requirement of local justice for permitting adversary action is straightforward enough: we may not treat others unfairly, and so we may not target others if such targeting is unfair to them. Why one has no *obligation* to obey rules that treat oneself unfairly is a bit more complicated. The reasons given here have a bearing on whether or not one has an obligation to obey rules that treat others unfairly, and whether or not one is permitted to target another fairly under rules that also permit unfair targeting.

Rawls reasons that one cannot acquire an obligation to an unjust institution. He argues that extorted promises are void ab initio, and unjust social arrangements are a kind of extortion, so even direct consent to obey an unjust institution is coerced consent.[13] Similarly, we may draw the implication that no obligation of fair play arises when a cooperative venture is unjust, because what appears to be voluntary acceptance of benefit is coerced acceptance.

Rawls's conclusion that one cannot acquire an obligation to an unjust institution claims too much, however, as Simmons has pointed out.[14] Even if injustice is a form of coercion, unjust institutions do not coerce everyone with respect to everything. Suppose a bank is involved in coercive dealings with others. If the bank has not coerced you, and you borrow money with the promise to repay, you have met all the conditions of free and informed consent, and so you are obligated not to default on the loan. One could perhaps argue that one should not freely consort with and acquire obligations to unjust institutions, and argue further that there sometimes are overriding reasons to break one's obligations to unjust institutions (if, say, keeping one's obligation will cause great further injustice). But those arguments are to be distinguished from the present claim, that one logically cannot freely consort with unjust institutions, and so cannot acquire an obligation to them, even if one tries.

Simmons is right that one can enter into obligations to unjust institutions, but Rawls's claim can be saved in a way that preserves its force for our purposes. Though one can acquire obligations to an unjust institution, one cannot become *generally* obligated to obey its rules. An unjust institution, or an institution that is unjust in certain extortionary ways, does not have the legitimacy to make morally authoritative rules, so the fact that such an institution has issued a rule is not by itself a good reason to obey the rule. (There may be other good moral reasons to act in ways that the rules of an unjust institution demand—the action may lead to good consequences, for instance.) And though I can enter into specific obligations to unjust institutions by way of a voluntary promise, I cannot, by my voluntary promise, grant or contribute to the granting of legitimate rulemaking authority to an unjust institution.

The questions about the local and internal justice conditions can now be answered. By seeking the benefits of a cooperative scheme that treats one unjustly, one has not acquired a specific obligation to shoulder burdens, because actions taken in response to injustice are not fully voluntary.[15] By seeking the benefits of a cooperative scheme that treats others unjustly, one has not acquired a general obligation to submit to the scheme's rules, because the rules of unjust institutions lack moral authority. However, one may have acquired specific obligations to specific players (most likely, to those who are treated unjustly).

Similarly, with regard to adversary permissions, an unfair institution does not have the legitimating power to permit what would otherwise be forbidden, such as deception or threats in a business negotiation. If some business activity as a cooperative venture is unfair (say, workers are wrongfully exploited on some view of exploitation), then the fact that business rules permit adversary practices that further the success of the scheme of cooperation adds no further justification to engage in those practices. If such practices would be wrong without a cooperative scheme, the existence of an unfair cooperative scheme does not legitimate the practice. This is so even if the target of some specific adversary action is not being treated unfairly.

Consider now the external justice condition, that the venture imposes no unjust externalities on those who are not players. Under the rather stringent definition of a player that seems to be required, adversary institutions of any social importance that do not have substantial effects on nonplayers will be extremely rare. All legal and political institutions, by their very purposes, affect nonplayers. (However, some minor schemes of internal governance may have no external effects—rules of etiquette in the Senate's private dining room, or the allocation of corner offices in a law firm.) Despite the game-playing images we have encountered, the effects of business enterprise are neither restricted to an inner arena of competitors nor to a larger market of voluntary customers, suppliers, workers, and investors. Let me be clear: I have not provided a reason to suppose that these externalities will be systematically unjust. But when they *are* unjust, permission to inflict external injustice finds no support in the argument from fair play. That piracy is a mutually advantageous and internally just scheme of social cooperation for pirates does not begin to justify a practice devoted to robbery and kidnapping, Gilbert and Sullivan notwithstanding. Much may turn on whether and when various clients, patients, customers, workers, and voters are to be considered players or outsiders, because what counts as unjust treatment of someone who cannot be understood to have voluntarily sought the benefits of a game may be far more demanding than what counts as an injustice to a player.

## Conclusion

The widely held notion that one is morally permitted to harm another if the rules of a social game permit such harm is harder to justify than one might have thought. The notion is intuitively plausible because consent can generate moral permissions, but mere participation in a game does not imply that one has consented to be harmed in accordance with the game's rules. Just as consent-based arguments to obligate citizens to obey the laws of the state founder on stringent evidentiary requirements, consent-based arguments are likely to fail to permit presumptively wrong actions in adversary games. A more promising route is to appeal to the notion that freeriding in a game is unfair to the players who are willing to risk harm in accordance with the game's rules. Though this argument from fair play may fail to obligate freeriders to play by the rules, we do not need to establish as much. We need only to show that players are permitted to harm freeriders in accordance with the rules, just as they are permitted to harm willing players.

Though the best case for an adversary permission that we have seen rests on the fair play argument, even fair play has limited applicability. It takes its biggest normative bite when the harms of games are internalized among those who seek its benefits, but harms generated by most middle-level social institutions—notably, the practices of the competitive professions—are not so internalized. Even on a loose construction of the conditions for fair play, the targeting of nonplayers is not permissible if, game aside, such targeting would be an impermissible restriction of liberty or a setback of interest. This is so even for nonplayers who on balance benefit, and the specification of a player must remain fairly tight. To call all consumers players in the game of market competition, all voters players in the game of electoral politics, and all litigants players in the game of the adversary legal system is too quick, for many consumers, voters, and litigants neither are advantaged by the game nor voluntarily seek the game's benefits. But business managers, public officials, and lawyers may satisfy the conditions of fair play in their deceptive or coercive dealings with one another, and there may be market segments, political elites, and corporate legal clients who meet the criteria of player. If the burdens and benefits of these games are fairly distributed, a player who is deceived or forced may have no reasonable grounds for complaint.

## NOTES

1. So, even on the view that finds coercion when moral expectations, rather than statistical expectations, are violated, this transaction is not coercive. For the moralized view, which I share, see Robert Nozick, "Coercion," in *Philosophy, Science, and Method,* ed. Sidney Morgenbesser et al. (New York: St. Martins, 1969), and Alan Wertheimer, *Coercion* (Princeton, NJ: Princeton University Press, 1987).

2. See John Locke, *Two Treatises of Government* (1690), *Second Treatise,* Section 119, ed. Peter Laslett (Cambridge: Cambridge University Press, 1963). But Locke holds that tacit consent does not create a permanent obligation to submit to government, and does not confer membership in a society. Without explicit consent, obligation begins and ends with possession or enjoyment. See Sections 121f.

3. Some readers have objected that Magritte intended to make a point about representation, not artistic authority: the drawing is not a pipe, but an *image* of a pipe. But if the constitutive view of artistic meaning is correct, Magritte's intentions about the meaning of his drawing do not determine its meaning, and so do not undermine the use to which I put his pipe.

4. Locke, *Second Treatise,* Sections 121f.

5. H. L. A. Hart, "Are There Any Natural Rights?" *Philosophical Review* 64 (1955): 175–191; John Rawls, "Legal Obligation and the Duty of Fair Play," in *Law and Philosophy,* ed. Sidney Hook (New York: New York University Press, 1964); and John Rawls, *A Theory of Justice* (Cambridge, MA: Harvard University Press, 1971). In *A Theory of Justice,* Rawls refers to fair play as the fairness principle. Since the earlier rubric evokes the sorts of games under discussion here, I revert to it.

6. Rawls, *A Theory of Justice,* pp. 111–112; note citing Hart omitted. The two principles refer to the content of Rawls's theory of justice for the basic

institutions of society. In a recent restatement, they are as follows: "(a) Each person has an equal claim to a fully adequate scheme of equal basic rights and liberties, which scheme is compatible with the same scheme for all; and in this scheme, the equal political liberties, and only those liberties, are to be guaranteed their fair value; (b) Social and economic inequalities are to satisfy two conditions: first, they are to be attached to positions and offices open to all under conditions of fair equality of opportunity; and second, they are to be to the greatest benefit of the least advantaged members of society." See John Rawls, *Political Liberalism* (New York: Columbia University Press, 1993), pp. 5f. But though the logic of fair play requires some conception of justice, it does not appear to require Rawls's conception.

7. Rawls, *Theory of Justice,* pp. 113–114, 335–337, 344, 355. But see George Klosko, *The Political Principle of Fairness and Political Obligation* (Lanham, MD: Rowman & Littlefield, 1992), for a recent attempt at reviving Rawls's earlier view.

8. One might think "mutually advantageous *competitive* venture" is more apt. But there is no contradiction: here competitors cooperate, by their rule-abiding behavior, to create a mutually advantageous institution. Compare the distinction in game theory between cooperative and noncooperative games, where cooperation refers to the ability of competitive players to communicate and make binding agreements. See R. Duncan Luce and Howard Raiffa, *Games and Decisions* (New York: Wiley, 1957), p. 89.

9. See M. B. E. Smith, "Is There a Prima Facie Obligation to Obey the Law?" *Yale Law Journal* 82 (1973); Robert Nozick, *Anarchy, State, and Utopia* (New York: Basic Books, 1974), pp. 90–95; and A. John Simmons, *Moral Principles and Political Obligations* (Princeton, NJ: Princeton University Press, 1979), pp. 101–142.

10. Smith, "Is There a Prima Facie Obligation?" pp. 954–958.

11. Nozick, *Anarchy, State, and Utopia,* pp. 90–95. Quote from p. 94.

12. An observation I owe to Jim Sebenius.

13. Rawls, *A Theory of Justice,* pp. 112, 343.

14. Simmons, *Moral Principles,* pp. 77–79, 109–114.

15. This requires several qualifications. It is not meant that one is not responsible for actions taken in response to injustice, nor that the slightest injustice calls into question the freedom of all action. The claim is limited to the application of the fair play principle: freeriding on a scheme that is substantially unjust to you is not unfair, because, under a moralized understanding of coercion, injustice introduces a defect in the voluntariness of your acceptance of benefit, and the fair play principle requires voluntary acceptance. See Nozick, "Coercion," and Wertheimer, *Coercion,* for moralized conceptions of coercion.

CHAPTER 18

# SEQUENCING TO BUILD COALITIONS: WITH WHOM SHOULD I TALK FIRST?

## James K. Sebenius

Surprisingly little systematic consideration has been given to the processes by which negotiators build coalitions, the logic behind their tactical choices, and how these actions matter to outcomes. This essay explores one part of the issue: what David Lax and I have called "strategic sequencing," or the choice of which parties are approached, in what order, openly or secretly, separately or together.[1] Sequencing choices can be a prominent feature of coalition building, an implicit logic governs the tactics employed, and these tactics may significantly affect the results.

For example, the 1985 Plaza accords represent a virtuoso example of sequencing. When James Baker became U.S. Treasury Secretary in 1985, the strong dollar was taking a severe toll on American industry and generating powerful protectionist reactions. The United States, under former Treasury Secretary Donald Regan, then Chief of Staff at

This essay is an outgrowth of work done jointly with David A. Lax. In particular, it draws from our chapter entitled "Thinking Coalitionally: Party Arithmetic, Process Opportunism, and Strategic Sequencing," in H. Peyton Young, ed., *Negotiation Analysis* (Ann Arbor: University of Michigan Press, 1991), pp. 153–193. Beyond this considerable debt, I am pleased to acknowledge useful suggestions on this topic from Arthur Applbaum, Max Bazerman, Nancy Buck, John Hammond, Ralph Keeney, Robert Keohane, Robert Mnookin, Howard Raiffa, Jeff Rubin, William Ury, Michael Wheeler, Gilbert Winham, H. Peyton Young, I. William Zartman, and Richard Zeckhauser, as well as from participants in the negotiation research seminar at Harvard Law School and the Wise Decisions symposium at Harvard Business School. Financial support from the Division of Research of the Harvard Business School is gratefully acknowledged.

the Reagan White House, had for some time spurned international economic cooperation to bring the dollar down. Baker's efforts to build a domestic and international coalition committed to a coordinated effort to accomplish this goal initially relied on secrecy. According to one insider's account,

"Reagan knew of the [Plaza Hotel ministerial] meeting in advance, of course, but was apprised of the full scope of Baker's plan only two days beforehand. Devaluation was sold to the President as necessary to stem the protectionist tide in Congress," says a Baker intimate. "It was sold to Don Regan as being consistent with an earlier call he had made for an international conference to discuss exchange rates. To this day, I don't think Don understood what we were about to do. We managed [Federal Reserve Chairman Paul] Volcker . . . because we had carefully split his board. Paul had no alternative but to go along."[2]

Armed with this domestic "mandate," Baker used the Plaza Hotel meeting to build the necessary international coalition both to act and to make it very difficult for his domestic rivals to later reverse the resulting policy course. As one finance minister said, "At first he split us just like he split the Fed. He began by using the U.S. and Japan against West Germany. Then he combined those three to bring along the whole Group of Five [including Britain and France]."[3]

Baker carefully sequenced his actions to build the coalition of finance ministers committed to implementing his preferred agreement. The de facto coalition was larger, encompassing both domestic and international players. Secrecy and ambiguity, divide-and-conquer tactics, and a tight deadline were used domestically to gain Baker the right to move into the actual Plaza process. There, with the initial concurrence of the Japanese—whose economic interests and bargaining position on the dollar were firmly allied with that of the United States—it was possible to get German agreement. Then this powerful three-way coalition could press the others into the final agreement. To see the potential importance of sequencing here, imagine other possible orders of approach; for example, suppose that the Germans had in advance forged an ironclad coalition with the British, French, and others against the likely American proposal.

Baker's coalitional machinations are fairly typical of one broad class of sequencing actions intended to create an irreversible commitment to a preferred agreement. They suggest a number of analytic and prescriptive issues. For example, under what conditions does sequencing matter? Why are some potential sequences preferred to others?

When are natural allies likely to be approached first and when is the process most likely to commence among potentially blocking interests? How and why does the openness or secrecy of the process matter? Are there characteristic negotiation sequences when both internal and external actors are involved?

The most powerful advances in negotiation theory have been mainly inspired by the bilateral or two-party case—where issues of sequence inherently cannot arise.[4] While multilateral bargaining has been the subject of considerable investigation, the additional complexities posed by coalitional possibilities render the analytic task much more formidable. As Howard Raiffa observed, "There is a vast difference between conflicts involving two disputants and those involving more than two disputants. Once three or more conflicting parties are involved, coalitions of disputants may form and may act in concert against the other disputants."[5]

Yet while a rich array of sequential tactics pervades studies of multiparty bargaining,[6] these actions are rarely the object of analysis, almost as if their range and variety preclude useful generalization, or as if they were intriguing details, merely epiphenomena. Indeed, the predominant emphasis of coalition theories developed thus far has been on the *outcomes* of coalitional actions rather than on the *processes* and *tactics* involved in reaching those outcomes. The founders of classical game theory, von Neumann and Morgenstern, characterized their work as "thoroughly static."[7] Anatol Rapoport's later assessment of the contributions of $N$-person game theory noted that "If the behavioral scientist thinks about decision-making in conflict systems in the mode suggested by $N$-Person Game Theory, he will focus on two fundamental questions: (1) Which coalitions are likely to form? (2) How will the members of a coalition apportion their joint payoff?"[8] Note that both of these canonical questions are outcome-focused. As Rapoport went on to note, game theory still "lacks almost entirely the dynamic component, i.e., a model of the conflict *process.*"

While there are important exceptions to these generalizations, most notably Steven Brams' 1994 book on the "theory of moves,"[9] the more fundamental question arises of whether process and tactics matter at all or whether it is more fruitful to seek a mapping from game "structure" directly to negotiated equilibrium outcome. Indeed, as Ariel Rubinstein observed in an influential *Econometrica* article, "for forty years, game theory has searched for the grand solution," that would achieve "a prediction regarding the outcome of interaction among human beings, using only data on the order of events, combined with a description of the players' preferences over the feasible outcomes of the situation."[10]

This standard "game structure implies equilibrium outcome" presumption has recently been the subject of considerable assessment and critique, especially by those working in the realm of negotiation analysis. The exploration of the present essay is intended to push beyond these static bounds with respect to the complexities and consequences of the sequencing choice in negotiation. Its underlying premise is that these choices can matter in understandable ways, even if outcome predictions—reasoning solely from structure—remain elusive. Its negotiation-analytic methodology offers prescriptive advice given a descriptive assessment of the behavior of the other side(s), does not necessarily presume full strategic rationality or common knowledge of the structure, and is less focused on deriving equilibrium results than on changing perceptions of the zone of possible agreement among the players as a function of tactical choice.[11]

While game theory has neglected sequencing issues, folk wisdom has not. For example, one standard admonition is to "get your allies on board first." Obviously, this sensible approach is the product of much experience and makes eminent sense in many situations; for example, Baker did just this with the Japanese in the international phase of the Plaza accord process. However, there are striking counterexamples to "allies on board first." For example, as the United States sought to build a global anti-Iraq coalition following the Kuwait invasion, many observers would have argued that Israel was its strongest regional ally. Yet the Israelis were pointedly excluded from the growing coalition: Israel's formal membership would have greatly complicated, if not precluded, numerous Arab states' joining.

A related bit of folk wisdom—and standard diplomatic practice—when preparing "your side" to negotiate with an "external" party is to "get your own house in order first," or "hammer out a common internal position." Ambassadors and bargaining agents often see a required first step for eventual external dealings as thrashing out a consensus internally on negotiating instructions. Evidently, this represents time-honored and often good advice. Yet in preparing for the Gulf War, President George Bush did anything but get the U.S. house in order first and then negotiate externally. Instead, he committed U.S. troops to the region, and then exhaustively built up—in part by virtuoso sequential diplomacy[12]—an external international U.N. coalition behind a Security Council Resolution authorizing "all necessary means" to eject Iraq from Kuwait. Only then did the Bush administration begin negotiating seriously for Congressional authorization to use force in the Gulf. Of course, the prior commitment of U.S. troops along with hard-won international backing for the use of force made it vastly harder for Congress to withhold approval. Had Bush started by seeking the approval of a deeply skeptical U.S. Congress, agreement would have been unlikely at best and, given Congressional refusal, any subsequent American-led international coalition-building enterprise would have been hobbled.

Exceptions to maxims—such as "allies first" or "internal consensus before external negotiation"—only raise more basic questions: when are they right and when are they wrong and why? This essay explores such questions, proposes a more general model for sequencing choices, and concludes with a few observations. In contrast with the "structure implies outcome" tradition, the "path effects" of different sequences will play a central role in the analysis.

## Path Effects I: Sequencing to Exploit "Patterns of Deference"

A common problem for the would-be coalition builder is that approaching the most difficult—and perhaps most critical—party offers slim chances for a deal. One approach is to discern what we will define as the "patterns of deference" involving the target player.[13] An illustration comes from observing the successful sequencing tactic of Bill Daley, President Clinton's key strategist for securing Congressional approval of the controversial North American Free Trade Agreement (NAFTA).

> News might arrive that a representative who had been leaning toward yes had come out as a no. "Weenie," [Daley would] say. When he heard the bad news, he did not take it personally. He'd take more calls. "Can we find the guy who can deliver the guy? We have to call the guy who calls the guy who calls the guy."[14]

More formally, suppose that the subjective probability of Party A saying yes if asked independently is less than the conditional probability of Party A saying yes given that A is informed that Party B has already said yes. In symbols, $P(\text{A says Yes} \mid \text{B says Yes}) > P(\text{A says Yes})$. A's deference to B might be due to several factors: B's perceived greater expertise, status, or reputation for having the same values as A; B may have done A a favor and A might feel the tug of reciprocity; or B's yes may "cover" A's choice and lessen the risk for A of agreement. In all these cases, we could say that "A tends to defer to B," or that a pattern of deference exists. Deference may be weak, strong, or absolute, depending on the situation and the magnitudes of the probabilities.

With such a pattern of deference, sequence matters; there is an optimal sequence that maximizes the probability of the desired winning coalition, and the coalitional outcome can be said to be path-dependent. If B is the "easier" party in the sense that $P$(B says yes) > $P$(A says yes), then we might call the B-then-A sequence a "bootstrapping" approach to coalition building. The process of working out the sequence from this structure could be called "backward mapping" or reasoning from the hardest ultimate target to the easiest: "Can we find the guy who can deliver the [most difficult] guy? Call the guy who calls the guy who calls the guy who can deliver the [most difficult] guy."

For concreteness, suppose that A is the "harder" party in that $P$(A says Yes) = .3 while $P$(B says Yes) = .8. Further, suppose that A defers to B, meaning $P$(A says Yes | B says Yes) = .9, but that B does not defer to A, or $P$(B says Yes) = $P$(B says Yes | A says Yes) = .8. The probability of a successful coalition by approaching the easy party (B) first, then A, is $(.8)(.9) = .72$. In contrast, approaching A first, then B, offers only a $(.3)(.8) = .24$ chance of success. The increase in the subjective probability of a successful coalition from approaching B first is $(.72 - .24) = .48$. This probability increment is the path effect of choosing sequence B-A over A-B.

Does this mean that the most-likely-to-agree party should always be approached first? Not at all. Suppose A is the "harder" party in that $P$(A says Yes) = .4, while $P$(B says Yes) = .5, but that B defers to A, or $P$(B says Yes | A says Yes) = .9, while A shows no deference to B. Approaching the easy party (B) first yields a success probability of $(.5)(.4) = .2$, while the reverse order yields a higher value $(.4)(.9) = .36$. This "harder first" result is driven by the extent of B's deference to A. The path effect of sequence A-B over B-A equals the probability increment, .16, of successful coalition building.

Consider an example in which deference patterns suggested starting with the "harder" players. During the author's years on Wall Street with a new firm trying to raise a billion dollars of equity capital for a limited partnership, months of arduous effort were spent working out terms with the Prudential Insurance Company of America ("Pru") for its investment of $100 million as the "lead" limited partner. Pru had a reputation among institutional investors for exceedingly tough bargaining and its agreement sent a powerful signal to other domestic investors that this was a worthwhile venture. Further, having a "name" commitment such as Prudential greatly facilitated raising money in Asia. A number of other sources of capital would probably have been less difficult than Prudential to secure early on; yet when it became necessary or desirable to bring "heavy hitters" like Pru on board, terms with others would have merely constituted a starting point for the negotiations (and would likely have been renegotiated after Pru finally

**Figure 18-1**

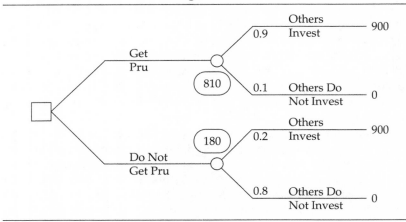

came to an investment agreement). Thus, starting with the hardest player seemed to make the most sense.

Consider a dramatic oversimplification of this case to illustrate the varied effects of deference patterns. Say that the probability that others invest is .9 if Pru is on board, but only .2 if Pru is not on board. Should one endeavor to have Pru on board before approaching the others and, if so, what would having Pru be worth (in millions of dollars)? As Figure 18-1 shows, a path with Pru on board has an expected value of $810 million, while a path without Pru has an expected value of $180 million. The path effect here is an increase of $630 million—if Pru is on board with certainty.

A fuller analysis would also compare the expected value of a path in which one first approaches Pru and then the others to the expected value of an "others-then-Pru" path. Suppose Pru was by far the hardest, with only a .1 chance of investing (whether or not others did) and that the unconditional probability of the others investing was twice as high, or .2. Assume further that the firm seeking investors would trumpet an investment by Pru but would take great pains to ensure that other investors never learned of a Pru turndown. The values of the possible outcomes are shown in Figure 18-2. The expected path effect of "Pru-first" over "others-first" would be $63 million ($253–$190 million) as a result of the expected value of the deference others would show to a favorable Pru decision. Even though the unconditional chance of the others investing (.2) is twice that of Pru investing (.1), it makes sense here to start with the "harder" party.

Of course, the path effects could become much more complex to

**Figure 18-2**

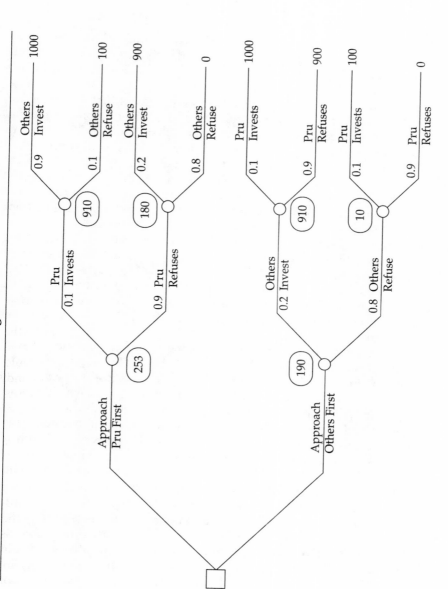

assess, and the implied optimal order could shift under different assumptions. For example, suppose that an early Pru refusal would leak and worsen the odds of others investing from .2 to .1. Then the expected value of a "Pru first" strategy drops to $172 million—below the expected value of approaching the "easy" others first (the expected value of that path is $190 million). Or suppose an additional sequential strategy were considered, such as "others first" but with the option of revisiting them after a turndown if Pru later said yes. In addition, the time and money costs of negotiating could very well depend on the path chosen. For example, the costs of negotiating with others first might rival those of negotiating with Pru first; however, a Pru decision to invest might greatly reduce the costs of subsequent negotiations with others—as well as improve the chances of success.

Thus far, we have seen how deference patterns can influence the costs and success probabilities in subsequent negotiations. By contrast, recall the example of Israel as a potential early U.S. partner in the Gulf War coalition; here a similar assessment would suggest that negotiating for Israeli membership would sharply decrease chances of later recruiting critical potential Arab coalition members. This might be called a "pattern of antagonism."

This style of reasoning is hardly the exclusive province of high politics, war, and finance. Trying to get the "right" participants to a party, a seminar, a panel, or a charity event leads to instinctive but often exquisitely crafted and elaborate sequencing choices. Such choices result from path effects that change what we might call the "expected value of subsequent negotiation," which depends both on the history and the prospective path. Thus far, the path effects have involved changes in conditional agreement probabilities and negotiation costs—both driven by patterns of deference. Yet, as is to be shown below, other elements of subsequent negotiations can change as well.

Prescriptive advice for would-be coalition builders in such cases suggests first, enumerating actual and potential parties relevant to the target coalition; second, assessing their interests, their likely position on joining the target coalition, and their likely alternatives to agreement; third, evaluating potential patterns of deference among the players; and fourth, constructing an optimal sequence by mapping backward from the target coalition to exploit deference patterns.

Thus far we have been investigating the effects of path dependence on sequencing choices that are driven by one important but particular mechanism: patterns of deference. Yet deference patterns comprise only one of several classes of factors that can influence the expected value of subsequent bargaining for a proposed path and given a bargaining history. For example, if the no-agreement alternatives (disagreement values) for subsequent parties worsen or improve as a function of the path so far taken, the chances of their agreement as well as the likely terms of such agreement may change. Further, suppose that an earlier phase of the bargaining changes the expectations of the outcome on the part of later players. Or, suppose that prior negotiations serve to conceal or reveal information that changes the expected value of subsequent bargaining. The next sections of this paper move beyond the path effects of exploiting deference patterns on sequencing choice to explore and illustrate several other such classes of factors that can change the expected value of subsequent bargaining. Then it becomes possible to propose a more general model.

## Path Effects II: Sequencing to Change No-Agreement Alternatives

Considerable evidence suggests that a party is more likely to agree to a proposal, and on less attractive terms, the worse his or her no-agreement alternatives (disagreement utility) appears.[15] An extreme version of this observation would be the Godfather's "offer you can't refuse" with its implied "or else." Popular negotiation accounts have enshrined the acronym BATNA (Best Alternative to Negotiated Agreement) as a standard part of prescriptive advice.[16] In a multiparty negotiation aimed at securing the ultimate agreement of several parties, earlier agreement among some of the players may worsen the no-agreement alternatives of later players. Rather than face the status quo ante, later players may face the prospect of a growing coalition. Often the risk of being left out of such a coalition is quite undesirable, thus increasing the chances of the later players' joining the growing coalition. Sequencing actions, therefore, may lead to higher agreement probabilities and more attractive terms from the point of view of the coalition builder.

### *Worsening No-Deal Alternatives to Improve Agreement Odds: The 1988 Capital Adequacy Accords*

It took a series of crises in the late 1970s and early 1980s to persuade domestic banking regulators in various countries that coordinated regulation was essential in a world of multinational banks and increasingly linked capital markets. In particular, with the onset of the 1982 Mexican debt crisis and the worldwide decline in levels of capital held by banks to cushion losses, regulatory concern grew about the adequacy of bank capital to ensure system safety. The "Basle Committee" at the Bank for International Settlements had been working for some time on this problem. A tortuous path, sketched by Ethan Kapstein and mapped in detail by Glen Tobin, led to agreement on these matters in 1988.[17] While the Basle Committee negotiations ground on without tangible results, the European Community (EC) began to coalesce behind an approach to capital adequacy regulation virtually independently.

Federal Reserve Chairman Paul Volcker, who disliked the emerging EC approach, approached Robin Leigh-Pemberton, his counterpart at the Bank of England, to negotiate a bilateral accord. The Fed's choice to approach the Bank of England to derail the EC process was partly tactical and partly spontaneous. Volcker was aware of British dissatisfaction with details of the emerging EC banking accord; further, U.S. and U.K. regulators had generally compatible views. Moreover, a bilateral agreement between London and New York based on a different regulatory concept would pose a powerful challenge to both the EC and Basle Committee processes.

The bilateral discussions proceeded in great secrecy and were not even mentioned in other multilateral fora that included U.S. and U.K. participation. When an accord was announced in June 1987, it sent shock waves through the community of other banking regulators. While participating in the continuing Basle Committee process, the Federal Reserve also began to follow a "second track" to bring the Japanese into the U.S.-U.K. accord. An agreement among London, New York, and Tokyo would have the potential to virtually determine the multilateral outcome. At the time of these negotiations, Japanese banks were in the midst of making a major strategic thrust into the U.S. market—a move that was causing consternation among U.S. bankers, who saw the lower domestic capital requirements of these new competitors as an "unfair" advantage. The implied threat by the Federal Reserve to stop this profitable Japanese expansion—in the name of domestic banking safety and a "level playing field"—was thus a potent bargaining lever that worsened Japanese alternatives to agreement with the U.S.-U.K. accord. After significant modifications, the Japanese acceded to the proposal. The three-way accord soon overwhelmed the heretofore intractable Bundesbank opposition and formed the basis for the overall 1988 agreement on capital adequacy.

An emerging shared view among banking regulators had clearly raised the desirability of some form of cooperative action on the capital adequacy problem. Yet to craft a winning coalition on its preferred terms, the Federal Reserve used potent sequencing tactics. By the surprise coalition with the British (a deal with the "easiest" party that undercut the separate EC effort) and the later addition of the Japanese, the no-agreement alternatives of the other major countries, especially Germany, to the terms preferred by the Americans were significantly worsened. An increasingly credible commitment to a particular outcome was crafted by the American-led coalition. Deliberate bootstrapping (from easiest to most difficult) progressively worsened the no-agreement alternatives of the later players, and thus drove the regulatory and coalitional outcome desired by the Fed.

## Worsening No-Agreement Alternatives of Internal Blocking Coalitions in Two-Level Games

Despite the conventional wisdom of negotiating "internally" first in order to present a united front in later "external" negotiations, the reverse sequence is often employed when internal would-be blockers are too strong. For example, of the Bush Administration decision to negotiate internationally first for the right to use force against Iraq, National Security Advisor General Brent Scowcroft observed:

> There has been some criticism of us for, in effect, pressuring Congress by building an international coalition and then making the argument, "You mean, Congressman, you're not going to support the President, but the president of Ethiopia is supporting him?" But I don't think we should be apologetic about it. You build consensus in whatever way you can, and when this thing first started, we didn't have support from Congress, and we didn't have support from the American people. . . . We couldn't have gotten the Congress earlier, I don't think, and if there had been no coalition and no UN vote, we would never have gotten Congress.[18]

A similar sequential approach was used by Percy Barnevik to bring about the merger of Asea and Brown Boveri, the Swedish and Swiss predecessors of ABB, the global engineering firm that Barnevik now heads. He noted that:

> When we decided on the merger between Asea and Brown Boveri, we had no choice but to do it secretly and to do it quickly, with our eyes open about discovering skeletons in the closet. There were no lawyers, no auditors, no environmental investigations, and no due diligence. Sure, we tried to value assets as best we could. But then we had to make the move, with an extremely thin legal document, because we were absolutely convinced of the strategic merits. In fact, the documents from the premerger negotiations are locked away in a Swiss bank and won't be released for 20 years.
>
> Why the secrecy? Think of Sweden. Its industrial jewel, Asea—a 100-year-old company that had built much of the country's infrastructure—was moving its headquarters out of Sweden.

The unions were angry: "Decisions will be made in Zurich, we have no influence in Zurich, there is no codetermination in Switzerland." I remember when we called the press conference in Stockholm on August 10. . . . Then came the shock, the fait accompli. . . . The more powerful the strategic logic behind the merger . . . the more powerful the human and organizational obstacles.[19]

Finally, consider a slightly more elaborate sequence in a two-level arms control game with the same objective of overcoming would-be internal blockers. Within the U.S. government, Secretary of State George Shultz and National Security Advisor Robert McFarlane conceived an approach to achieve a "grand compromise" whereby restrictions on the Strategic Defense Initiative ("Star Wars") would be traded for significant reductions in heavy offensive Soviet missiles. In Strobe Talbott's 1988 account:

Shultz and McFarlane developed the idea of getting [President] Reagan to approve, in its vaguest terms, a secret negotiation: The Administration would open a back channel to the Soviets in a way that at least initially excluded the Pentagon civilians; McFarlane would quietly enlist the support of the uniformed military. With luck and skill, the negotiation might produce an agreement that could be presented to the President as virtually a done deal. Nitze would be both the chief designer and the chief negotiator [with the Soviets] of the American position.

Nitze knew that as soon as [Defense Secretary] Weinberger learned what had happened, he would "fight like hell," but by then, he and McFarlane hoped, it would be too late. The alliance between the State Department and the Joint Chiefs of Staff on behalf of a deal that the Soviets had already accepted would be unbeatable. With the grand compromise a fait accompli, and with his own soldiers and diplomats as well as the Soviets lined up to support it, Reagan would impose it on Weinberger.[20]

Talbott reports that the idea was never implemented, largely due to Russian reluctance. Even so, the complex series of intra-U.S. government maneuvers as well as external dealings with the Soviets illustrates coalitional tactics intended by Shultz and McFarlane to commit to an advantageous position within the relevant bargaining range. The intended sequence of dealings envisioned by Shultz—Reagan, the U.S. military, the Russians, and only then the Pentagon civilians—was intended to quietly get domestic allies on board first, generate momentum with an external deal, and then, with public disclosure of the deal, overwhelm potential arms control opponents. In contrast, an initial approach to Weinberger and the Pentagon civilians would presumably have had a far smaller chance of success.

In each of these two-level examples—the Gulf War coalition, ABB, and arms control—an internal faction may well have functioned as a successful blocking coalition to the initiative favored by the protagonist.[21] By choosing to negotiate with outsiders first, the protagonists in these cases hoped to generate an irreversible commitment to a preferred deal. The path effects could overcome the internal blockers and improve the terms of the deal. By examining a number of such instances, the likelihood and effects of an "outside-in" (or, more accurately, a "small inside, then outside, then larger inside") approach may be better assessed in situations with this structure.

## Path Effects III: Shaping Outcome Expectations

Beyond patterns of deference and worsening no-agreement alternatives, a bootstrapper may seek to progressively shape the expectations of later players through the actions taken with earlier ones. Social psychological research points up the potent effects that parties' expectations of the outcome can have on bargaining results.[22] An extraordinary story illustrating this class of path effects on the expected value of subsequent bargaining is how labor organizer Ray Rogers broke the anti-union board coalition at J. P. Stevens, a textile firm.[23]

Although organized labor had sought to gain recognition from Stevens for almost 20 years, frontal bargaining assaults, consumer boycotts, demonizing publicity, and legal action had failed to achieve the union's goals.

The first step of Rogers's bootstrapping approach was a highly publicized demonstration at Stevens's annual meeting, which raised the salience of the new campaign. Rogers's second step was to use labor's clout and sizable business in New York with Manufacturer's Hanover bank to oust Stevens's chairman and another Stevens board member from the Manufacturer's Hanover Board. The surprise success of this effort greatly enhanced the credibility of Rogers's approach both internally at the union, where there was considerable hesitancy about the approach, and with subsequent targets.

The next target was the New York Life Insurance Company, a Stevens creditor that also wrote many union life and health insurance contracts and managed sizable union pension funds. A New York state insurance law permits a sufficient number of policy holders to contest board elections. Rogers threatened New York Life with such an election and that inherently risk averse institution agreed to eject Stevens's chairman from its board.

Next, Rogers targeted Metropolitan Life, a much larger insurance company that, like New York Life, was a major Stevens creditor, wrote many union life and health policies, and managed substantial union pension funds. Rogers's threat to contest the board election at MetLife, combined with the credibility that his campaign had amassed with victories over both Manufacturer's Hanover and New York Life, predisposed MetLife to exert great pressure on J. P. Stevens to make a deal with the union. The anti-union coalition including the Stevens board and management was broken, the union recognized, and a new contract negotiated.

As with deference patterns and worsened no-agreement alternatives, this sequencing strategy depended on early moves to boost Rogers's credibility and share expectations of the outcome for later targets. By starting with the easiest target, Manufacturer's Hanover, raising credibility both internally and externally, and favorably shaping subsequent outcome expectations, Rogers's bootstrapping approach succeeded.

An oft-noted coalitional dynamic, the "bandwagon," normally operates by a combination of worsened no-agreement alternatives and reshaped expectations of the outcome. In getting classic bandwagons rolling, one seeks to get the easy parties on board first and to create the impression of inevitability of the desired final coalition—ideally facing later parties with the choice of (profitably) saying yes to joining or of saying no and being isolated in an undesirable no-agreement alternative.[24]

### Path Effects IV: Sequencing to Conceal or Reveal Information

One use of sequencing is to reveal or withhold information by separating the parties and carefully choosing the order and nature of the negotiating approach. This can prevent irreversible consequences; if near-universal skepticism becomes common knowledge, a successful blocking coalition is almost sure to arise. Negotiations to assemble land for a major project are a good example.

A developer's intentions are highly important; landowners may use this knowledge as a lever to extract maximum price concessions. Thus, the issue of which parcel to try to buy first, second, and so on, may depend on differences in how likely one action or another will be to signal the developer's intentions. Since the intentions will ultimately be made public, however, the developer must also consider the physical relationship of the parcels acquired to those remaining. Knowing whether the parcels already obtained would permit some version of the project to go ahead, or whether they are useless without a later acquisition, can greatly shape subsequent negotiations.[25]

Sometimes, the information consequences of sequencing choices in interlocking negotiations can have unusual process implications. For example, in July 1992, France was dealing both with the European economic and monetary union negotiations as well as with the United States on a major agricultural dispute in GATT's ongoing Uruguay Round. Substantive differences between the United States and France had apparently been dramatically narrowed, and U.S. Secretary of State James Baker was attending dinner with French Foreign Minister Roland Dumas. A senior official overheard their extraordinary exchange:

> "Are you prepared to make a deal?" Mr. Baker asked, referring to the trade talks. Mr. Dumas replied that he was not. "But," said Mr. Baker, "suppose all the conditions you are seeking were fulfilled, would you then be prepared to make a deal?" "No," said Mr. Dumas.[26]

This was not congenital obstructionism; instead, explicitly revealing that government would accede to a trade deal *whose substance was acceptable* prior to the conclusion of the EC negotiation would alienate French farmers, who in turn, would block the EC accord. Negotiating the economic and monetary union agreement first, however, would not mobilize the farmers to block the GATT deal. Thus Dumas wanted to negotiate with Baker on trade last to prevent revealing the government's actual willingness to make the trade deal too early.

A final example of the informational role sequential choice may play in related negotiations comes from trade negotiations. While the United States was in separate talks with Japan, Hong Kong, and Korea over textiles (the "multifiber agreements"), a Korean negotiator said, "We'll ask Hong Kong to go first, then see what they get." Hong Kong officials were regarded as highly skilled and "they have no language problems with the Americans." John Odell reports that, "After waiting for Hong Kong and Japan to go first, Seoul asked for the features they had secured and then also held out for a bit more."[27] In essence, the path effects of the order chosen by the Americans (or encouraged by the Koreans) involved revelations about U.S. reservation prices that were of great value to the Koreans. One wonders whether the Americans should have rethought the sequence and *started* with Seoul.

## More Complex Path Effects

In the most general sense, path effects result from changes in the expected value of subsequent agreement. Thus far, distinct classes of such effects—exploiting patterns of deference, changing no-agreement alternatives, shaping outcome expectations, and revealing or concealing information—have been described and illustrated. However, far more subtle and complex assessments of path effects can lead to more involved sequencing strategies, as the following example illustrates.

Gil Winham (whom I believe coined the phrase "pyramidal" negotiation) described a common sequencing choice in which the major players, who could each block an agreement, separately strike a deal and only then carefully add other parties to the agreement. In the context of the subsidy and countervailing duties issues in the GATT's Tokyo Round, the United States and the EC had powerful disagreements. As a result, these key players first worked on solutions "mainly on the basis of a direct Washington-Brussels exchange."[28] Winham described the rationale behind this process of pyramidal coalition building atop the Washington-Brussels base:

> If the goal is a negotiated agreement, and if each of the two majors has the capacity to prevent that agreement, then the early flow of decision-making probably should occur between the majors at the expense of other nations at the negotiation. Furthermore the incipient agreement would probably be presented to the other nations not in one step, but gradually, in a manner that slowly sought adherents to an evolving accord. This process in fact occurred, and what seems from hindsight a matter of logic was indeed pursued with deliberate care by the U.S. and EC negotiators.[29]

As actually realized, the sequencing actions went as follows:

> Nations were invited to joint the informal US/EC discussions on subsidy/countervail on the basis of their preferential contribution to the potential agreement. In most cases, a nation's trading position was the determining factor, but in some cases personal negotiating skills were also important. In the first dimension, Japan was included, while the second brought in Canada, whose ambassador, Rodney Grey, had long experience in trade negotia-

tion. . . . The Nordic countries were added for reasons of trading interests with the Europeans, and for balance in the informal subsidy/countervail group. Later, when the developing countries were added, the invitation went first to the major nations such as Brazil, Mexico, and India. In this manner, the negotiation developed in a pyramidal pattern . . . adding new delegations to the process, and accommodating, insofar as possible, the new concerns brought by the additional players.[30]

Deference patterns were much less important than the fact that, as the coalition grew, it tended to worsen the no-agreement alternatives of the as-yet left-out parties (in the manner of a bandwagon). The logic that dictated the sequence began with a separate accord among potential blocking parties, and then brought in new adherents according to a tradeoff between the extent of changes they required to join the evolving accord (the smaller the better) and their importance among the so-far left-out parties (the greater the better).

Rather than start the process with this most difficult US-EC base on which to build a higher and higher pyramid of adherents, one might imagine an alternative approach with the principal antagonists recruiting their natural allies into two opposing, polarized, and mutually exclusive blocs. Bringing on board lesser (and easier) players earlier, while adding to the supportive coalition of each adversary, might require concessions to the new members that would also make the eventual reconciliation of the two blocs much more difficult. The path effects of bootstrapping to get allies on board first would likely bequeath a final negotiation that would be both far more costly and risky than a pyramidal approach. From the point of view of path effects, the pyramid appears to trump the bootstrap.

## A More General Account of Sequencing Choice

Return to the general questions posed near the beginning of this essay. In particular, does sequencing matter and, if so, how; further, how should a sequence be chosen? If one were concerned only with patterns of deference, an optimal order exists to maximize success probabilities. Yet the preceding examples and discussion suggests that, at any stage of the coalition process, several other factors potentially influence the choice of who to approach next. Suppose that there are $r$ parties, and thus at least that many potential stages in the sequencing process. Specifically, at stage $m$ of the process, suppose that one is considering expending costs ($c$) in a negotiation to try to win the agreement of party $i$, given negotiating history $h$ (denoting the prior sequence of negotiations and their results). There are four elements of our sequencing decision.

$V_i(m|h)$ is the expected value of gaining the assent of party $i$ at stage $m$ given history $h$. $V_i$ can be conceptually disentangled into two components, the *outcome* value (contribution of $i$ to the ultimate coalition) and the prospective *path effects* (changed probabilities and values of getting other parties on board later) resulting from getting party $i$ on board now. The outcome value is traditional and analogous to outcome values associated with the characteristic function form of a game. The path effects include changed probabilities or values of later success given considerations such as deference patterns, the implications of worsened no-agreement alternatives, reshaped expectations, and bandwagon effects. For example, if parties to be approached later were highly deferential to party $i$, then the process value component would be high. Similarly, if getting one party on board now precluded the formation of a very worrisome potential blocking coalition later, the path effects would reflect this added value.

$C_i(m|h)$ is the expected cost of recruitment of party $i$ at stage $m$ of the process given history $h$. $C_i$ can be conceptually disentangled into the expected costs of dealing with party $i$ and the altered probabilities and costs of getting subsequent parties on board. For example, if getting party $i$ on board now critically antagonized important later parties or prevented their joining, then the value associated with recruiting party $i$ now would be low or negative. Think, for example, of the effect of making Israel the first member of the U.S.-led anti-Iraq coalition. Similarly, if getting $i$ on board stimulated the formation of a countercoalition, the costs would be high. $C_i$ would normally be expected to be negative.

$P_i(m|h)$ is the probability of successful recruitment of party $i$ at stage $m$ given $h$. In more complex calculations, one could make $P_i$ a function of the costs directly associated with recruitment; a greater effort would presumably increase $P_i$.

$F_i(m|h)$ is the cost of a failed effort to recruit $i$ at stage $m$, including resources foregone in the recruitment effort and any process costs, including a loss of reputation, reduction in desired bandwagon effects, and the like. George Bush's decision to build an international anti-Iraq coalition first and then negotiate with the U.S. Congress can be explained by the low probability of success with a "Congress first" strategy and the associated very high cost of failure ($F_i$), which consisted of a radically diminished prospect of a subsequent international coalition if Congress said "no" first. $F_i$ will generally be negative.

Putting these factors together, at stage $m$ in the process, given history $h$, the would-be coalition-builder assesses the following "expected value of subsequent negotiations" (EVSN$_i$) of negotiating with party $i$ as

$$\text{EVSN}_i(m|h) = P_i(m|h)[V_i(m|h) + C_i(m|h)] + [1 - P_i(m|h)]F_i(m|h).$$

Note that a potential recruit will tend to be approached earlier as $V$, $P$, and $F$ are larger and $C$ is smaller; the approach will be later as the reverse is true. An optimal sequence, from among at least $r!$ possibilities, for approaching the $r$ parties will maximize the sum of EVSN$_i(m|h)$ for all $i$. If groups of players (rather than just individual players) could be approached sequentially, or if revisiting those who refused earlier were possible, the number of path possibilities would increase correspondingly. If this process could be expected to take valuable time, the discounted sum could be maximized. Whatever the variant, this expression sets up a backwards induction problem; once values and subjective beliefs are specified, it can be computationally approximated by a method analogous to the algorithm developed by John Wilson in his "subjectivist approach to consecutive conflict."[31] Unfortunately, the required assessments and sheer complexity of the general problem render a computational approach impracticable in most cases of any size. But this formalization suggests at least two useful observations.

First, the very terms that are used in the folk maxims and diplomatic parlance of coalition building are helpful but incomplete when trying to deduce an optimal sequence. Think of "getting *allies* on board first," or "isolating *opponents*," or "starting with the *easy* parties and moving to the *harder* ones," or "thrashing out an *internal* consensus before negotiating *externally*." Indeed, both bootstrapping and pyramiding depend on these categories. An "ally" or "easy" party is presumably characterized by a high probability of recruitment at low cost (high $P$ and low $C$); an opponent or "harder" party would normally have the reverse profile.

The deeper reasons for following or violating received wisdom, however, are driven by the other terms in the expression for EVSN$_i$, in particular the path effects. The sequencing examples in this paper are easily explained by a characterization of the players and process that includes path effects such as the influence of deference patterns, changes in no-agreement alternatives, reshaped outcome expectations, and information revelation. It is not enough to ask "how hard or how easy to get on board is a given player?" but also "how valuable or how costly is that player to recruit?"—being careful to include path effects as well as the path-independent outcome considerations.

Second, to approach EVSN$_i$ calculations, formally or informally, requires a kind of assessment that is not routinely part of multiparty negotiation analyses. Beyond characterizing individual players' interests, beliefs, etc., and coalitional possibilities (e.g., joint payoffs for different coalitions), it is necessary to map the relationships among the players in terms of deference, influence, antagonism, and the like. Given this map, one can assess the relationship between given tactical actions—such as worsening no-deal alternatives or shaping outcome expectations—and the prospects for and terms of subsequent agreements from the current stage of the process to the final target coalition. Ideally, these assessments should be informed by good models and empirical evidence—indeed, stimulating such work is one goal of this essay—but they will inevitably involve subjective judgments. For example, one can imagine using the tools of network theory to map relationships among the parties to discover dense network nodes on which to focus special negotiating attention and isolated segments that may be approached more independently. At present, such assessments in multiparty negotiation are typically made implicitly and informally. A fuller set of tools and concepts is needed to map the different kinds of relationships among parties and to draw out their implications for coalitional negotiations.

## Conclusions

Although sequential tactics have been the focus of the essay, a prior question has been lurking in the background: when should one avoid sequencing and attempt a fully open, collective route to consensus? After all, many sequential moves appear to be—and often are—sneaky, manipulative, deceptive, coercive, and even plainly unethical. It is thus important to think them through both for their ethical *and* their prudential implications. In principle, the choice of a simultaneous or sequential process can be unraveled by specifying and weighing the relevant path effects. Such effects associated with a simultaneous process might include a greater sense of legitimacy and "ownership" of agreement, the possibility of new options generated by brainstorming, as well as altered roles of deference patterns and different possibilities for blocking coalitions to form or to be thwarted.

While sequencing has played a starring role in this essay, supporting roles have been played by other tactical choices—whether to act openly or secretly, whether to meet in subgroups or the full group, how commitments and other actions can be made credibly, how to set the negotiating agenda, which issues to link or separate, whether to bring in a third party or not, etc. A fuller account of coalitional process would obviously devote attention to these actions and their interactions with sequencing. Yet the key notion in this essay is coalitional "process" understood as the link between the structure of a situation and its outcome.

A more basic question is: Under what conditions do sequencing tactics affect outcomes? If a sequential action were costlessly reversible—with no net path or outcome effects—sequencing would not matter and should be relegated to the "frictional."[32] Thus, sequencing can matter only when its effects are costly or impossible to reverse. For example, such cost or irreversibility may occur where some commitments of resources or reputation are made in the process, where information is irretrievably conveyed, where an approach, once made, becomes less feasible or more expensive, where an ironclad blocking coalition is forged, or where a real deadline intervenes.

This essay has focused on such sequential processes ranging from exploiting patterns of deference, to progressively worsening no-agreement alternatives, to preventing private knowledge from becoming common knowledge, to shaping outcome expectations, and the like. It has analyzed common classes of tactical choice such as bootstrapping, pyramiding, and setting bandwagons in motion. It has ultimately urged a new step in coalitional negotiation analyses: Beyond characterizations of individual players (in terms of interests, beliefs, etc.) and coalitional possibilities (e.g., joint payoffs for different coalitions), the would-be coalition builder or negotiation analyst should map the relationships among the different players in terms of deference, influence, antagonism, and the like. Given this map, one can assess the relationship between given tactical actions—such as worsening no-deal alternatives, shaping outcome expectations, or revealing information—and the prospects for and terms of subsequent agreements.

Much of conventional game theory maps the structure of a game—its players, preferences, and order of events—directly into equilibrium predictions of the outcome; ideally, this game structure gives insight into the coalitions that are likely to form and how they will split the payoffs. Yet this analytic presumption effectively rules out the kind of intermediate path effects this essay has explored. Similarly, the ideal organizational types of sociologists have little room for mere "friction" in their accounts. Both traditions have obviously contributed concepts and frameworks critical to understanding the role of sequencing in negotiation. However, if such wheeling and dealing can significantly affect outcomes, then it merits much more attention by negotiation analysts as well as those from game theoretic, psychological, and other methodological traditions.

## NOTES

1. See David A. Lax and James K. Sebenius, *The Manager as Negotiator* (New York: Free Press, 1986), pp. 153–193.

2. Michael Kramer, "Playing the Edge," *Time*, February 13, 1989, p. 32. For considerably more detail, see Yoichi Funabashi, *Managing the Dollar: From the Plaza to the Louvre* (Washington, DC: Institute for International Economics, 1988).

3. Kramer, "Playing the Edge."

4. See, e.g., Thomas Schelling, *Strategy of Conflict* (Cambridge, MA: Harvard University Press, 1960); Thomas Schelling, *Arms and Influence* (New Haven, CT: Yale University Press, 1966); Fred C. Ikle, *How Nations Negotiate* (New York: Harper & Row, 1964); Richard E. Walton and Robert B. McKersie, *A Behavioral Theory of Labor Negotiations* (New York: McGraw-Hill, 1965); Jeffrey Rubin and Bert Brown, *The Social Psychology of Bargaining and Negotiation* (New York: Academic Press, 1975); I. W. Zartman and Maureen Berman, *The Practical Negotiator* (New Haven, CT: Yale University Press, 1982); and Howard Raiffa, *The Art and Science of Negotiation* (Cambridge, MA: Harvard University Press, 1982).

5. Raiffa, *The Art and Science of Negotiation*, p. 11.

6. For examples and numerous references, see Lax and Sebenius, *The Manager as Negotiator.*

7. John von Neumann and Oskar Morgenstern, *Theory of Games and Economic Behavior* (Princeton, NJ: Princeton University Press, 1944; 3rd ed., 1953), p. 44.

8. Anatol Rapoport, *N-Person Game Theory: Concepts and Applications* (Ann Arbor: University of Michigan Press, 1970), p. 286.

9. S. J. Brams, *Theory of Moves* (Cambridge: Cambridge University Press, 1994).

10. A. Rubinstein, "Comments on the Interpretation of Game Theory," *Econometrica* 59 (1991): 923.

11. See, generally, Raiffa, *The Art and Science of Negotiation;* and H. Peyton Young, ed., *Negotiation Analysis* (Ann Arbor: University of Michigan Press, 1991). For a somewhat more methodologically self-conscious characterization and assessment, see James K. Sebenius, "Negotiation Analysis: A Characterization and Review," *Management Science* (1992): 18–38.

12. For a description that focuses on this dimension of the process, see Martin Staniland, "Getting to No—The Diplomacy of the Gulf Conflict, August 2, 1990–January 15, 1991," Case #449, Part 3, Pew Case Studies in International Affairs (Washington, DC: Institute for the Study of Diplomacy, 1993).

13. I first heard this felicitous phrase from Mark Moore.

14. S. Blumenthal, "The Making of a Machine," *New Yorker*, November 29, 1993, p. 93.

15. For evidence, see, for example, Lax and Sebenius, *The Manager as Negotiator,* ch. 3, and the references cited therein.

16. Roger Fisher and William Ury, *Getting to Yes* (Boston: Houghton Mifflin, 1981).

17. Ethan B. Kapstein, "Great Definers," and "Resolving the Regulator's Dilemma: International Coordination of Banking Regulations," *International Organization* 43 (1989): 323–347; and Glenn Tobin, "National Rules and Global Money" (Ph.D. dissertation, Harvard University, 1991).

18. Michael Watkins "The Gulf Crisis: Building a Coalition for War" (Cambridge, MA: Kennedy School of Government Case Program, 1994), p. 53.

19. William Taylor, "The Logic of Global Business: An Interview with ABB's Percy Barnevik," *Harvard Business Review* (March–April 1991): 100–101.

20. Strobe Talbott, *The Master of the Game* (New York: Knopf, 1988), p. 264.

21. See Robert D. Putnam, "Diplomacy and Domestic Politics: The Logic of Two-Level Games," *International Organization* 42 (1988): 427–460 for the first use of the "two-level games" metaphor as well as for the further example of the Bonn Summit in which internal blockers were thwarted by an external coalition.

22. References can be found in V. L. Huber and M. A. Neale, "Effects of Cognitive Heuristics and Goals on Negotiator Performance and Subsequent Goal-Setting," *Organizational Behavior and Human Decision Process* 36 (1986): 342–365.

23. Dedra Hauser, "An Interview with Ray Rogers," *Working Papers* (January–February 1982): 49–57.

24. Steven Brams and others have written several papers that explicitly address the problem of two "proto-coalitions" vying for the membership of an uncommitted party. They derive conditions for the optimal timing for the uncommitted party to join either rival group. These conditions are expressed in terms of a relationship between the probabilities that each proto-coalition will become a winning coalition. S. J. Brams, "A Cost/Benefit Analysis of Coalition Formation in Voting Bodies," in *Probability Models of Collective Decision Making,* eds. R. G. Niemi and H. F. Weisberg (Columbus, OH: Merrill, 1972); S. J. Brams and J. C. Heilman, "When to Join a Coalition and with How Many Others Depends on What You Expect," *The Public Choice* 17 (1974): 11–25; Steven Brams, *Game Theory and Politics* (New York: Free Press, 1975); and S. J. Brams and J. E. Garriga-Pico, "Deadlocks and Bandwagons in Coalition Formation: The 1/2 and 2/3 Rules," *American Behavioral Scientist* 18 (1975): 34–58. This formalized version of the bandwagon effect has been generalized to the case of many parties in Philip Straffin, "The Bandwagon Curve," *American Journal of Political Science* 21 (1977): 695–709.

25. A rich example of sequencing to assemble the block for New York's Citicorp Center can be found in Robert C. Ellickson and A. Dan Tarlock,

*Land-Use Controls* (Boston: Little, Brown, 1981), pp. 1014–1023. Analogous phenomena can be found when investors seek to purchase blocks of stock for a possible takeover or take positions in various debt securities to improve their position in a bankruptcy negotiation—or damage that of rivals.

26. Roger Cohen, "Trade: Limp List of Hopes," *International Herald Tribune,* July 9, 1992, p. 9.

27. John S. Odell, "The Outcomes of International Trade Conflicts: The U.S. and South Korea, 1960–1981," *International Studies Quarterly* 29 (1985): 281–282.

28. Gilbert R. Winham, *International Trade and the Tokyo Round Negotiation* (Princeton, NJ: Princeton University Press, 1986).

29. Ibid., p. 174.

30. Ibid., p. 175.

31. John G. Wilson, "A Subjectivist Approach to Consecutive Conflict," *Journal of Risk and Uncertainty* 5 (1992): 95–97.

32. An example of such an inessential process would be the jockeying around in a three-party noncooperative game in characteristic function form wherein no commitments, whether of resources or reputation, are possible.

# CHAPTER 19

INTERNATIONAL TRADE CONFLICT
AND NEGOTIATION: UNILATERAL
PUNISHMENT, BILATERAL BARGAINING,
AND MULTILATERAL COMMITMENTS

## Heather A. Hazard

This paper evaluates whether the dispute resolution mechanism of the new World Trade Organization (WTO) is compatible with the bilateral bargaining and unilateral punishment frequently undertaken by major trading nations in recent years.[1] Their compatibility is assessed in practice and in theory. Normative conclusions regarding improvement are drawn where these activities and mechanisms do not support trade liberalization.[2]

The primary postwar instrument for promoting international trade liberalization, the General Agreement on Tariffs and Trade (GATT), was a multilateral agreement whose terms were negotiated in periodic multiyear rounds.[3] It was driven by the exchange of concessions, and has reduced tariffs and nontariff barriers to trade. Despite its overall effectiveness, however, the signatories to the GATT routinely became entangled in heated disputes over trade, industrial, and technology policies. According to the terms of the GATT, the disputants could refer

The author would like to thank Jim Sebenius and other members of the symposium, particularly Fritz Mayer and Kalypso Nicolaidis, for their insightful comments. No words would be adequate to thank Howard Raiffa for his intellectual generosity, time, and encouragement over the years. To the extent that we are able to emulate him, let our actions speak louder than our words.

their conflicts to an adjudicatory panel if they could not reach an agreement through bilateral bargaining.[4] The GATT's dispute settlement mechanism allowed punishment only when a panel found that a previously granted concession had been either nullified or impaired, and the signatories agreed to permit punishment.[5] The system was so convoluted, however, that the process inevitably aborted.

The threat posed by the GATT's standing dispute settlement mechanism was intended to deter members from changing from good behavior to bad by increasing the costs of defection. The unsatisfactory performance of the GATT's dispute settlement mechanism led some signatories that were important importers, and therefore had significant trade power, to set up unilateral punishment mechanisms. These nations could retaliate against nations whose trade, industrial, and technology policies they independently deemed damaging and unfair. Their threats of unilateral punishment were intended to compel other nations to end disputed practices and to force them to change from bad behavior to good.

Applying game theory to postwar international trade conflicts allows us to answer a number of contemporary trade policy questions. Does it make sense to pursue unilateral punishment actions, bilateral bargains, and multilateral commitments simultaneously? If it can be shown in theory that unilateral mechanisms support the emergence of cooperation among nations, should not the proliferation of unilateral mechanisms be welcomed? If it makes sense in theory and is consistent legally but causes trouble in practice, how can the practice be improved?

## How Do Nations Bargain?

Once a nation has set its objectives, how does it bargain with other nations to achieve them? When a nation's interests conflict with those of other nations, bargaining outcomes are uncertain; no nation has complete control over them, both because no nation can dictate the behavior of other nations and because of exogenous uncertainty.[6] However, a nation that can influence the behavior of another nation can make strategic decisions and moves. Strategic decisions are interactive decisions in which the decision maker allows for conflict but utilizes the potential for cooperation.[7] Strategic moves are undertaken to influence the other's choice in a manner favorable to one's self by affecting their expectations of one's behavior. Their object "is to set up for one's self and communicate persuasively to the other player a mode of behavior (including conditional responses to the other's behavior) that leaves the other a simple maximization problem whose solution is the optimum for one's self. . . ."[8]

Nations routinely attempt to influence the behavior and choices of other nations, and they must decide which bargaining instrument will be most effective in each situation. Threats and promises are prominent instruments; both are contingent on the partner's behavior.[9] If the other nation is engaging in behavior that one does not approve of, the problem is to convince the "defector" to change its behavior from bad to good—to cooperate. One may use compellent threats or promises, depending upon one's own behavior in the current period.[10] If the defector is already being punished, then one threatens to continue administering the punishment until it cooperates. If the defector is not being punished then one promises to reward it for becoming coopera-tive. (This is equivalent to an implicit threat that the status quo will be continued if it does not alter its behavior.) Both compellent threats and compellent promises assure the defector a higher level of utility if it changes its behavior.[11]

If the other nation is currently cooperative, one must dissuade it from changing its behavior. This can be done through deterrent threats or deterrent promises, depending upon one's own behavior. If the defector is not already being punished, one threatens to punish it if it defects. If the country is receiving compensation, one can promise to continue the compensation so long as it changes its behavior. (This is equivalent to an implicit threat that the standing arrangement will be

**Figure 19-1**

*A Typology of Bargaining Instruments*

|  |  | Statement type | |
| --- | --- | --- | --- |
|  |  | Assurance | Warning |
| Objectives | Dissuade others from changing behavior from good to bad | Deterrent promise | Deterrent threat |
|  | Persuade others to change behavior from bad to good | Compellent promise | Compellent threat |

terminated if it does not alter its behavior.) Deterrent threats and deterrent promises derive their influence from the partner's belief that its utility will fall if it defects.

To be effective, threats and promises must be credible and clearly communicated. Warnings are the instruments for delivering threats; assurances are the instrument for delivering promises. (See Figure 19-1.) If warnings and assurances are not consistent with the issuer's self-interest, the other nation will not find the threats or promises credible.[12] Thus, it is extremely important that the other nation be convinced of the self-interest, particularly when the consequences are not immediately obvious. Communication is not trivial; as Raiffa notes, the main problem in most conflicts is getting the parties to talk and listen to each other.[13]

## Why Use Multilateral Mechanisms?

The notion of threats and promises allows us to develop a new understanding of the variety of mechanisms nations have resorted to in their attempts to resolve trade conflicts. Before World War II, nations relied primarily on bilateral agreements to avoid trade conflicts. The spectacular and destructive period of trade protectionism between the wars, however, combined with the decimation of European industry during World War II, led the United States to champion a number of multilateral financial and economic arrangements, including the creation of multilateral financial institutions. But the U.S. executive branch failed to win ratification from its Congress for an International Trade Organization,[14] and since 1948 the world has hobbled along with the stop-gap, skeletal arrangement of the GATT. The language of the GATT emphasized the noble-sounding objectives of stability and transparency, but its functioning depended on common self-interest.[15] It was in the interest of each of the signatories to have a functioning free trade system, and the principles and rules of the GATT were broadly consistent with this objective.

The GATT incorporated a system of "promise-based reciprocity" for negotiating reductions in tariff and non-tariff barriers to trade. Promise-based reciprocity is based on the principle that cooperation should be met with cooperation, and the practice that concession is swapped for concession. Offers were contingent on counteroffers, so concessions by all countries came simultaneously or not at all. This system of mutual compellent promises functioned well up until the Tokyo Round of the GATT.[16] This system, combined with the non-contingent Most Favored Nation principle, which allowed minor players to share in the progress made by the major players, allowed for rapid trade liberalization.

A signatory that believed the value of a previously granted concession had been diminished by the grantor's subsequent actions was considered to have a reasonable grievance. The structure of the GATT dispute resolution process encouraged the nations that were party to the conflict to seek resolutions bilaterally. If this failed, the complainant could request adjudication. If the request was approved, the nation was found to have been injured, and it was authorized to punish the other nation, then it had the right to retract a concession. This process was designed to reassure the smaller trading nations that disputes would not be resolved on the basis of power alone and that they would be protected by a rule-based system. Unfortunately, this system of deterrent promises worked poorly for a number of reasons.[17] The willingness of nations to even submit disputes eroded markedly after 1967 as the rate of unsuccessful resolutions rose.[18] The heterogeneity of the players and the complexity of the issues increased just as the United States became less and less willing to absorb some of the costs of running the system. The reform of the dispute resolution system was the top negotiating priority of the signatories by the beginning of the Uruguay Round in 1986.

Unfortunately, the hope of substantial reform fell victim to domestic politics. In 1988, a number of countries (particularly the United States) felt a need to demonstrate progress in the negotiations, but no progress had been possible in areas where producers felt their interests were seriously threatened. A decision was made to reach agreements in areas where producers did not perceive their interests to be seriously threatened—such as dispute resolution. As a result, principally minor legalistic reforms were agreed upon (as in previous negotiating rounds) to ease panel formation and speed panel deliberations. Other legalistic reforms, such as not allowing disputants to vote on their dispute and the establishment of an appeals procedure, may prove more significant.

Despite the reforms agreed upon during the Uruguay Round to take effect in the new World Trade Organization (WTO), sanctions will probably continue to be rare. First, the sanctions are generally self-punishing; they reerect barriers, thus raising costs to domestic consumers in the short term. Second, there is strong normative pressure to come to a settlement rather than resort to sanctions. Third, disputants are not required to report the terms of their side agreements; it is possible for them to make agreements that hurt parties not at the negotiating table (by diverting trade instead of creating trade) and that are inconsistent with trade liberalization. Thus, the universe of potential agreements is increased and the incentive for understanding self-punishing sanctions reduced.

The outstanding reasons powerful nations commit to a multilateral dispute resolution system are the credibility it gives to the system in the eyes of smaller nations and the limits it places on damages to any party. The credibility stems from the assurance that intractable disputes will be decided according to rules created and adopted by consensus. Since the worst possible outcome of a dispute is a return to an earlier status quo, and since there are strict prohibitions on responding to retaliation with counterretaliation, the risks of pursuing disputes are safely limited. In the threat-based reciprocity system that prevailed prior to the creation of the GATT, bad was returned for bad, chaos prevailed, and the international trading system simply collapsed. Thus, commitment to a multilateral mechanism is consistent with reinforcing the agreement as a whole, but the resistance to reform (manifested, for example, by the procedural inability to treat complaints as an early warning that rules that have become anachronistic) will continue to make it unsatisfactory.

## Why Threaten Unilateral Punishment?

Threats of unilateral punishment are frequently communicated in international trade disputes despite the existence of multilateral mechanisms. Is this a contradiction? No, unilateral punishments are used for several reasons. First, the performance of the multilateral mechanism is deteriorating (as demonstrated by the rising fraction of disputes with unsuccessful resolution noted earlier). Second, internal bargaining may affect external stances and behavior; for example, a declining industry may successfully lobby for protection for reasons of internal equity rather than economic efficiency. Third, there is enough irrationality in the structure of the international trading regime so that independently dominant strategies yield jointly suboptimal outcomes. This section looks at the second and third reasons more closely.

### Internal versus External Negotiating

While it is readily acknowledged that nations and supranational entities (such as the European Union, EU) consist of many groups with different objectives, the uneasy coexistence of internal and external bargaining is seldom given careful thought.[19] The EU members show markedly different levels of enthusiasm for government intervention in business, with Denmark and Britain anchoring the noninterventionist coalition and France leading the pro-interventionist forces. (See Figure 19-2.) France's record of intransigence allows it to credibly

**Figure 19-2**

*Two-Level Gaming over Trade Policy Rule Formulation*

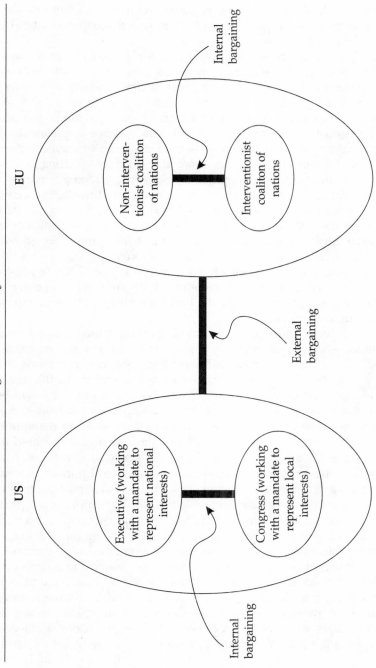

threaten to scuttle external negotiations if it does not get the internal concessions it desires, and gives it a disproportionate ability to influence trade policy at both levels.

The United States' tripartite division of powers leaves many observers from parliamentary countries perplexed. Congress holds the constitutional power to make trade policy. Congress has two sometimes conflicting mandates: to represent local interests and to serve national interests. To its credit, Congress has recognized that the sum of actions taken to protect local interests (particularly considering the short time between elections) is unlikely to be in the best interest of the nation, and corrects this constitutional flaw by delegating negotiating authority to the executive branch for specified periods. It retains the right to ratify the executive branch's commitments.[20] Moreover, the executive branch is generally expected to exchange legislative favors for pro-ratification votes. Thus, the executive branch typically secures international agreements only to bring them home to lengthy debate, criticism, and horse-trading sessions before approval.

Japan's internal gridlock from special interests has led to increasingly urgent calls for electoral reform both internally and externally. In the absence of reform, the United States has pressured Japan on a case-by-case basis.[21]

All these countries' external bargaining stances cannot be understood without analyzing their internal situations. Moreover, as comparative advantage shifts and new geographic concentrations of industry arise, workers face the threat of displacement. To the extent that the costs of displacement are distributed unevenly, there will be calls for protection, retaliation for unfair competition, subsidies to make local products competitive, etc. In short, there will be a demand to take unilateral actions. Some such actions have been incorporated into international trade agreements (such as "safeguard" actions to protect against sudden surges in imports), but unilateral punishment has not. Thus, there is a natural tension between internal demands for unilateral actions and external commitments to abide by multilateral agreements.

Internal political forces tend to encourage protectionist actions, and interest groups lobbying for unilateral government interventions found unexpected support from academic economists during the mid-1980s. Previously, these economists had been unequivocal in their support for unconditional free trade. The revolution of the "new trade theory" was induced by the declining ability of traditional trade theory to explain observed patterns of trade. By the end of the 1980s, it was widely recognized that while neoclassical theory still does a good job of explaining trade in industries where markets clear relatively efficiently and cost reductions for marginal production are limited, an increasing number of industries are driven by externalities and economies of scale.[22] The identification of this latter group of imperfectly competitive industries prepared the intellectual ground for a discussion of government interventions to assist domestic firms by protecting their domestic market positions while claiming shares of foreign markets open to free trade. Early theories neglected the ability of the trading partner to respond to protectionism with more protectionism, which rapidly dissipates any gains.[23] Once the potential for such trade policy retaliation is acknowledged, a social trap structure emerges; the payoff structure is that of prisoner's dilemma.[24] The standard new trade theory hypothesis that in imperfectly competitive industries the highest returns come to the producers in the country that protects when its partner does not is likely true in practice. (See Figure 19-3 for an empirical

**Figure 19-3**

*A Trade Policy Trap? The United States–European Union Beef Dispute*

|  | EU: Free trade | EU: Protectionism |
|---|---|---|
| **US: Free trade** | EU: 456 <br> US: 236 | EU: 456 + .1*236 = 480 <br> US: − .1*3200 = − 320 |
| **US: Protectionism** | EU: − .1*4500 = − 450 <br> US: 236 + .1*456 = 282 | EU: .1*236 = 24 <br> US: .1*456 = 46 |

Assumes: Payoffs equal to producer sales; 10% capture of domestic markets from other player with protection; 10% loss of other foreign markets of exporters if original trade restriction not disputed. Sales given for 1987 in millions of dollars. For further discussion of this example, see Heather A. Hazard, "Risking Reciprocity: Lessons from a U.S.-EC Trade Dispute" in *Global Change and Transformation: Economic Essays in Honor of Karsten Laursen*, ed. Lauge Stetting, Knud Erik Svendsen, and Ebbe Yndgaard (Copenhagen: Handelshøjskolens Forlag, 1993), pp. 90–114.

example.) The problem is that, in practice, most victims retaliate by punishing the defector, leading to losses for both parties.

## Good Strategies, Bad Outcomes

Trade negotiations, conflict, and conflict resolution occur again and again. Moreover, trade is a non-zero-sum game; the amount of trade is constantly growing, and innovations and productivity increases have positive spillover effects that allow all participants' standard of living to rise simultaneously. Thus, a solution concept that is appropriate for single shot, zero-sum games is hardly appropriate for this repeated, non-zero-sum game. The political and economic risk that a defection will trigger a reciprocating defection and make both parties worse off has finally been accepted by leading economists.[25] It will take some time, however, to kill the arguments for defection in populist arguments against trade liberalization, where they still inflame protectionist and nationalist sentiments.

As Duncan R. Luce and Howard Raiffa point out, a "quasi-equilibrium" of cooperate-cooperate emerges in a positive sum, repeated game since "it is not to the advantage of either player to initiate the chaos that results from not conforming, even though the non-conforming strategy is profitable in the short run."[26] As they note, however, the stability of such systems cannot be taken for granted. A robust strategy for surviving and prospering in social traps was not articulated until Anatol Rapoport submitted his now-famous "forgiving tit-for-tat strategy" in Robert Axelrod's computer tournaments.[27] The rules of behavior of Rapoport's strategy are:

1. Avoid unnecessary conflict by cooperating as long as your partner does.

2. Be provocable in the face of an uncalled-for defection by your partner.

3. Forgive your partner after responding to the provocation.

4. Be clear in the signals you send through your behavior so that the other player can adapt to your pattern of action.

There is both anecdotal and theoretical support for adding a "tolerance" rule: do not punish a defection immediately; instead, attempt to verify that a defection has truly occurred.[28] This expanded rule set we can label "virtuous tit-for-tat." While economists have discovered that defection is not a strategy to be recommended, they have paid little attention to such alternative strategies. Once the rules of virtuous tit-for-tat are understood, practices that would otherwise seem incompatible make sense; for example, the threat of unilateral punishment is the embodiment of the second rule of provocability. Thus, the European Union's condemnation of the United States for keeping "a unilateral gun in the holster" cannot be logically supported.[29]

## What About Punishment in Practice?

Immediately after President Bill Clinton's election, the United States' trade partners were nervous that the perceived interventionist tendencies of his administration would undermine free trade. The administration was expected to advance a "strategic trade policy" agenda; that is, a policy consciously undertaken to influence another nation's choice of policies (most frequently their trade, industrial, and technology policies) or a foreign firm's choice of business strategy, in a manner favorable to one's own nation or domestic firms, by affecting their expectations of one's trade policy behavior.[30] Such policies can be classified in many ways, including whether they are one-time or repeated, coercive or cooperative, collusive or competitive, etc.[31] Strategic trade policy instruments are wielded not just to shift rents to domestically headquartered firms by snatching rents from foreign-headquartered firms; they may also be motivated by purposes that aim to increase global economic efficiency. These include increasing the rates of positive technological spillover to promote innovation and productivity increases; correcting market failures and helping to overcome appropriability problems associated with intellectual property; controlling the market power of domestic oligopolists and protecting consumers; and creating additional exports and imports.

The last aim is the raison d'être of the international trade system. To the extent that the multilateral system malfunctions and unilateral systems only compensate for deficiencies, they can be considered trade-creating strategic trade policies. Thus, in theory, U.S. trade partners are right to be nervous about rent-snatching strategic trade policies, but in practice there is no evidence that the Clinton administration has attempted to implement such policies.

We have shown that unilateral punishment makes sense in theory—that it is rational for a nation to do something that damages its interests in the short run but benefits them in the long run.[32] In addition, because these actions reinforce global efficiency gains, it is in the interest of the multilateral system to allow unilateral punishment that adheres to consensus-derived standards of fairness (such as impairment of a previously granted concession and injury) and conduct (such as notification to the other nation of the complaint against the disputed practice). But does unilateral punishment make sense in practice? This question is best treated by examining the character of the implementing instruments, and particularly U.S. trade law, since the United States pioneered their use and still maintains the strongest mechanisms.

Unilateral punishment became a part of the external bargaining stance of the United States as the result of the internal bargaining between the Congress and executive branch described earlier. In 1962, the executive branch required a delegation of authority to pursue multilateral trade liberalization in the Kennedy Round of the GATT. Congress granted this authority, along with the authority to retaliate against certain foreign government actions with trade measures. Congress wanted the executive branch to respond to citizens' complaints more vigilantly than it had,[33] but was not prepared to yield its right to act unilaterally:

> As long as decisions are made on the basis of political consensus of the contracting parties, the United States will have no assurance that questions of consistency with the GATT will be resolved impartially . . . [thus] it is essential that the United States be able to act unilaterally in any situation where *it is unable to obtain* redress through the GATT against practices which discriminate against or unreasonably impair U.S. export opportunities.[34]

Congress reinforced and expanded the United States' unilateral powers with the Trade Act of 1974, particularly Section 301, which established procedures for individuals and firms to bring complaints and petition the U.S. government to take action against harmful foreign activities. The executive branch routinely declined to take action, however, and Congress bolstered the unilateral punishment mechanism in 1979, 1984, and 1986.[35] The 1988 Omnibus Trade and Competitiveness Act introduced a "special 301" procedure for targeting intellectual property rights violations outside the United States and a "Super 301" procedure that allowed for cross-retaliation between sectors and introduced a time frame for identifying specific cases of trade distortions and initiating complaints against the offending nations. After Super 301 lapsed in 1990, measures were introduced into the Senate in 1993 and 1994 to reinstate it, but they were not approved. On March 3, 1994, Super 301 was reinstated by executive order with the intention of giving U.S. trade negotiators a bigger threat to employ in their increasingly frustrated efforts to force the Japanese to compromise on market openings.[36]

## Can Unilateral Punishment and Multilateral Dispute Settlement Coexist?

The European Commission sees the resuscitation of Super 301 as an indication of a U.S. move toward the increased use of unilateral or bilateral measures that damage the world trading system "without reference to, and often in open defiance of, agreed multilateral rules."[37] Is it true that unilateral punishment and multilateral commitments cannot coexist in law and in practice?

The first charge of the European Commission is that the United States will use 301 to circumvent the WTO. This is an empty charge; the 301 legislation requires that all disputes covered by multilateral rules be submitted to multilateral mechanisms. If the United States does attempt to use 301 to circumvent the WTO it will become a candidate for punishment: regardless of the merits underlying the dispute, the WTO cannot condone vigilante action. Super 301 can be seen as a fallback to guarantee citizens and firms that their concerns will not be overlooked simply because no rules governing their area of commerce could be agreed upon or because their areas are not yet subject to the WTO. This coverage is not an unreasonable safety net, but implementation problems remain.

First, the United States is in an awkward position: If it applies sanctions in reaction to a disputed practice not covered by the WTO and its sanctions diminish the value of concessions previously granted by the United States, then the trading partner has grounds for a grievance under the WTO.[38] Second, the usefulness of 301 in sectors that are partially covered (such as cultural products and the audiovisual sector) may be limited.[39] Third, some trade actions that were not covered by the GATT may be covered by the WTO. Again, this should not be a major concern; the United States can withdraw any 301 actions in cases where sanctions are covered by new WTO trade rules, and it can avoid conflict by retaliating only against imports in uncovered areas. Thus, while it is discordant and undiplomatic to strengthen unilateral mechanisms while pursuing multilateral commitments, there is no legal inconsistency.[40] This is significant, since "international [obligations act] as a cost imposed upon any country violating an explicit international agreement"[41] and hence, avoiding violations also avoids such costs. When actions must be taken, nations also seek shelter in ambiguity, designing "the activity to comply with the letter of the obligation, leaving others to argue about the spirit."[42]

Legally, unilateral punishment and multilateral commitments can be compatible, but the question remains: does unilateral punishment restore cooperative behavior in trade policy in practice? If not, why not? The record of 301 in the United States is poor; only a third of the actions led to the withdrawal of the offending measure.[43] Unfortunately, evolutionary forgiving tit-for-tat strategies perform poorly when a nation's signals are misinterpreted—and many nations violate the "clear communication" rule. The United States does not follow the rules of virtuous tit-for-tat in practice. While it seldom defects first and Super 301 allows it to be provocable in the face of conflict, it does not send clear signals, it does not forgive, and it is not tolerant. Finding a violation under Super 301 starts the United States on a punishment path, but there are no provisions that allow it to stop punishment prior to the other nation's stopping the disputed practice. Yet for internal bargaining reasons, ceasing the disputed practice in response to external pressure may be the most difficult path for the trading partner to take. The two-level bargaining game involving the executive branch and Congress generates signals that muddy external communications and make it difficult to be tolerant. Thus, while unilateral punishment mechanisms such as those of the United States can legally and theoretically coexist with multilateral commitments, they have not worked in practice.

One reason to pay attention to unilateral mechanisms now is that they are proliferating. In 1984, the European Community strengthened its "common commercial policy with regard in particular to protection against illicit practices," adding a 301-type avenue for individuals and firms to bring complaints to the government's attention. In the debate surrounding adoption it was argued that countries such as France that routinely seek to influence the Commission will have yet greater opportunity to promote trade-restricting measures.[44] In addition, legal scholars have identified a "tendency for the European Community to follow the United States in many of its import control regimes . . . sometimes the Community says it is emulating U.S. practice in retaliation."[45] The threat to retaliate with "mirror actions" has been noted for its effectiveness by the European Union. Again, the social trap structure appears where a cooperative equilibrium of limited import controls might be hoped for, but in the worst case, mirror actions could create a "vicious circle of trade barriers" if the nations do not follow the virtuous tit-for-tat strategy.[46] During the closing hours of the Uruguay Round, for example, France is believed to have forced changes in the voting rules that will make it much easier for it to invoke actions that protect against import surges. The French claimed that they needed trade weapons as strong as those of the United States.[47] France won this concession in internal bargaining and internal side payments on agriculture in exchange for voting to accept the agreement.

In addition to spreading to other countries, unilateral punishment mechanisms are proliferating within U.S. trade law itself. The Telecommunications Act of 1988 is designed to open foreign markets and includes provisions analogous to Super 301.[48] The U.S. trade representative (of the executive office of the president) has also announced his intention to investigate whether key issues that are not to be covered initially by the WTO should be subjected to new 301 provisions, including a "blue 301" for labor and a "green 301" for environmental protection.

While unilateral punishment mechanisms can complement multilateral commitments and serve the same overall goal of trade liberalization, their proliferation cannot be welcomed for three reasons. First, accidents are more likely as the number of mechanisms and the number of countries using them increases, particularly as nations unfamiliar with them attempt to apply them. Accidents take two forms: muddy signals being misinterpreted by the receiving nation and sparking retaliation, and poorly designed processes having too high a level of automaticity. Second, irrational actors (referred to as "demons" in game theory) are more likely than rational actors to defect and thus trigger conflicts. Third, the joint probability that two nations with defective strategies will become locked into a downward spiral of retaliation and counterretaliation will rise.

Nations can take a number of actions to prevent the proliferation of unilateral mechanisms. In the short run, U.S. and EU trade law should be modified to incorporate forgiveness.[49] Forgiveness is doubly important in the international trade context because the government that is the target of the retaliation must maintain its prestige at home; by forgiving the offending government, the retaliating government provides it with a face-saving opportunity to cease the protectionist practices. National policy makers also need to think of the interests and alternatives of their negotiating partners more carefully and before they make demands; impossible demands lead to heightened trade hostilities. Finally, national political leaderships must stand up to protectionist interests, discourage nationalism, and find mechanisms for spreading the costs and benefits of adjustment more evenly. By arriving at consistent strategies for dealing with turbulent economic times, the major trading nations will be able to send clearer signals abroad. They will then be in a better position to achieve their real objective—not some ill-defined "competitiveness," but a rising standard of living for their citizens.

In the longer run, the United States and the European Union have little choice but to attempt to "disarm," or other nations will mimic them and the mechanisms will multiply and become more and more embedded in domestic law. Disarmament will be best done through sequential, mutual concessions to ensure cooperation and reassure internal constituencies. Such disarming will not take place, however, until the WTO mechanism is first ratified and operative and then expanded. The WTO should be expanded to require reporting of negotiated bilateral agreements terms, provide for stricter enforcement of trade rules, and provide the director general with the authority to intervene and prosecute. In addition, the disputes themselves should become a source of rule renewal; they frequently serve as early warnings that rules are aging, and creative solutions provide new precedents. In this way, a trade problem could be transformed into an opportunity.

Thus, while unilateral punishment and bilateral bargaining can legally and logically coexist with multilateral commitments, the optimum continues to be a multilateral arrangement that is strong enough and comprehensive enough to make them unnecessary.

## NOTES

1. This mechanism was created during the Uruguay Round of the General Agreement on Tariffs and Trade (GATT).
2. This paper is strongly influenced in intent, style, and content by Howard Raiffa, *The Art and Science of Negotiation* (Cambridge, MA: Harvard University Press, 1982). Raiffa advocates the search for solutions to pressing policy problems using the simplest analysis tools appropriate.
3. The GATT was the primary mechanism for trade liberalization from 1947 to 1994. On January 1, 1995, its primacy was overtaken by the WTO; parts of the GATT will remain in force until 1997 to allow for the resolution of outstanding disputes.
4. Panels were ad hoc adjudicatory bodies set up to review disputes in light of the text of the Agreement with the intent of returning a written opinion regarding the existence of fault and the extent of damage.
5. Nullification is a technical legal term for the virtually complete cancellation of the value of a concession as the result of actions by the party that originally granted the concession (as opposed to exogenous conditions such as shifts in consumer demand). Impairment is the partial cancellation of such a concession. The consensus requirement meant that a signatory that was the subject of the complaint (i.e., the respondent) had to approve its own punishment.
6. See R. Duncan Luce and Howard Raiffa, *Games and Decisions* (New York: Wiley, 1957), p. 1.
7. In keeping with Thomas Schelling, *Strategy of Conflict*, 2nd ed. (Cambridge, MA: Harvard University Press, 1980), fn p. 3, "strategic" and

"strategy" are used in the game-theoretic rather than military sense. The focus is on the interdependence of the agents' decisions and on their expectations about each other's behavior. The concept is usefully developed in Avinash Dixit and Barry Nalebuff, *Thinking Strategically: The Competitive Edge in Business, Politics, and Everyday Life* (New York: Norton, 1991), p. 2.

8. Schelling, *Strategy of Conflict*, p. 160, goes on to add ". . . and to destroy the other's ability to do the same"; that is overly restrictive for the non-zero-sum case, where joint gains from cooperation are possible.

9. For clarity, we construct the arguments as though there were only one other nation, but it should be remembered that we are generally referring to multiple other nations. Why is this distinction significant? Because this immediately transforms the game from two-party to multiparty, and multiparty games are inherently more complex than two-party games due to the ability of agents to form coalitions and the importance of reputation (with its linkage effects on games with other agents). See Raiffa, *The Art and Science of Negotiation*, p. 11.

10. See Thomas Schelling, "The Art of Commitment," in *Arms and Influence* (New Haven, CT: Yale University Press, 1966) for the original work on competence and deterrence. This was later insightfully elaborated by Dixit and Nalebuff, *Thinking Strategically*. Roger Fisher, "Deter, Compel, or Negotiate," *Negotiation Journal* (January 1994): 17–32 has made a provocative attempt to fit these concepts into the joint gains negotiating framework and to draw conclusions about their relative efficacy in military security conflicts.

11. Here we use utility as Luce and Raiffa do: an agent faced with risky outcomes (that is, lotteries) is able to rank the lotteries according to their underlying preferences and to select its actions in accordance.

12. See Dixit and Nalebuff, *Thinking Strategically*, p. 126.

13. Raiffa, *The Art and Science of Negotiation*, p. 356.

14. The U.S. trade policy making process and division of powers that made this defeat possible are discussed below.

15. See Robert E. Keohane, "Reciprocity in International Relations," *International Organization* 40 (1986): 1–28; and Robert E. Keohane, "U.S. Compliance with Commitments: Reciprocity and Institutional Enmeshment" (Harvard University, Department of Government, October 1991).

16. In trade, the reduction of one nation's barriers to trade are used to persuade another nation to change its practices and to cooperate by reducing its barriers. Thus, assurances of contingent trade liberalization are compellent promises.

17. In fact, retaliation has only been authorized once in GATT's history. In 1951, the United States accepted retaliation by Denmark and the Netherlands over dairy product restrictions.

18. A case was considered to be successfully resolved if there was a finding or a settlement; the finding or settlement was implemented; and if there was a settlement it was consistent with the GATT. Cases meeting these criteria fell steadily from 100 percent in 1963–1967 to 27 percent in 1983–1987. See Heather A. Hazard, "Resolving Disputes in International Trade" (Ph.D. dissertation, Kennedy School of Government, Harvard University, 1988), pp. 125–128.

19. Notable exceptions include Frederick W. Mayer, "The Dynamics of Internal-External Negotiations: Effects of Domestic Conflict on International Negotiations" (Ph.D. dissertation, Harvard University, 1987); Robert D. Putnam, "Diplomacy and Domestic Politics: The Logic of Two-Level Games," *International Organization* 42 (1988): 427–460; and Frederick W. Mayer, "Domestic Politics and the Strategy of International Trade" (Duke University, Institute of Policy Sciences and Public Affairs, 1990).

20. Trade agreements are usually negotiated under the so-called "fast track" procedure. This allows Congress to vote for or against ratification but denies it the right to modify the agreement.

21. See Peter F. Cowhey, "Domestic Institutions and the Credibility of International Commitments: Japan and the United States," *International Organization* 47 (1993): 324–326.

22. See James A. Brander and Barbara J. Spencer, "Export Subsidies and International Market Share Rivalry," *Journal of International Economics* (February 18, 1985): 83–100; and Paul R. Krugman, *Strategic Trade Policy and the New International Economics* (Cambridge, MA: MIT Press, 1986) for seminal works in this area. See Paul R. Krugman and Alasdair Smith, *Empirical Studies of Strategic Trade Policy* (Chicago: University of Chicago Press, 1994) for a survey of the literature.

23. These models also tended to only look at one industry at a time. Their partial equilibrium nature thus misled economists into neglecting (or at least discounting) the general equilibrium consequences of distorting resource allocation within the economy as a whole.

24. Defecting can be defined as anything one disapproves of. Given the consensus that trade that is not distorted by barriers raises everyone's standard of living in the long run, defecting is equated with trade-restricting or distorting behavior, and cooperating is equated with trade-creating behavior. In a social trap, the reward structure is such that defecting while the other cooperates has the highest payoff (the "temptation" payoff). The next best is both cooperating and receiving the "reward" payoff. This is followed by "punishment," where both defect; the "sucker" payoff comes from cooperating while the other defects. In addition, participants may not eliminate each other, change the reward structure, make enforceable threats, or be certain of the future.

25. Paul R. Krugman, "Free Trade: A Loss of (Theoretical) Nerve? The Narrow

and Broad Arguments for Free Trade," *American Economic Review* 83 (1993): 362–366 also points out that in addition to this broad political economy argument in support of free trade, a narrow economic argument can also be made. That is, "while markets are without question imperfect, the appropriate fix for their imperfections rarely involves trade policy per se. What is wrong with markets is usually a domestic distortion, best fixed by a surgical policy aimed at the source of the market failure."

26. Luce and Raiffa, *Games and Decisions,* p. 98.
27. See Robert Axelrod, "The Emergence of Cooperation among Egoists," *American Political Science Review* 75 (1981): 306–318.
28. See David Lax and James Sebenius, *The Manager as Negotiator: Bargaining for Cooperation and Competitive Gain* (New York: Free Press, 1986), fn, p. 159; and Dixit and Nalebuff, *Thinking Strategically,* pp. 112–115.
29. See Tom Buerkle, "U.S. Criticized for Super 301: EU Calls Trade Law a 'Gun in the Holster,'" *International Herald Tribune,* May 6, 1994, p. 15.
30. This subsumes the more common definition of a strategic trade policy as a government intervention that consciously enables firms to compete with other firms in international markets on altered terms. See David J. Richardson, "Empirical Research on Trade Liberalization with Imperfect Competition: A Survey" (Cambridge, MA: National Bureau of Economic Research, 1989) for a coherent and insightful analysis of trade-diverting strategic trade policies.
31. See Avinash Dixit, "Strategic Aspects of Trade Policy," in *Advances in Economic Theory: Fifth World Congress,* ed. T. Bewley (New York: Cambridge University Press, 1987).
32. It is assumed that we combine short-term and long-term effects through discounting. Short-run damage should not be ignored.
33. See John H. Jackson, *Legal Problems of International Economic Relations,* 2nd ed. (St. Paul: West Publishing Co., 1986), p. 803.
34. U.S. Congressional hearings, 1973, cited in Robert E. Hudec, *The GATT Legal System and World Trade Diplomacy,* 2nd ed. (New York: Butterworth Legal Publishers, 1990), p. 262.
35. See Biswajit Dhar, "The Decline of Free Trade and U.S. Trade Policy Today," *Journal of World Trade* 26 (1992): 133–154 for a useful summary and discussion of U.S. trade legislation with illustrative examples of conflicts where the United States invoked its unilateral mechanisms.
36. 301 mechanisms are generally desired by Congress and thus used as a chip in the bargaining between the executive branch and Congress. The revival of Super 301 by the executive branch without a Congressional request, therefore, came as a surprise. See Reginald Dale, "Free Trade: Idea in Search of a Friend," *International Herald Tribune,* February 15, 1994, p. 9; and "A Dangerous Way to Settle Disputes," *International Herald Tribune,* March 8, 1994, p. 6.

37. Services of the European Commission, *Report on United States Barriers to Trade and Investment,* European Commission, 1994, I194/94, p. 11.

38. See Reginald Dale, "U.S. Threats Shake World Trade Spirit," *International Herald Tribune,* March 8, 1994, p. 9 for a thoughtful commentary on the revival of Super 301.

39. See Richard H. Steinberg, "The Uruguay Round: Preliminary Analysis of the Final Act," in *Laws of International Trade* (Chesterland, OH: Business Laws, 1994) for a more extensive, scholarly analysis of these problems. The U.S. trade representative's office apparently insists, however, that the United States is not in the WTO for any sectors whose provisions it has not committed itself to. See Harry L. Freeman, "A Slam Dunk(el): How Section 301 Could Survive Under the New World Trade Organization," *The International Economy* (March–April 1994): 46.

40. That the U.S. implementing legislation may prove to be in violation of a number of obligations is another issue that must be understood in the internal/external bargaining framework. Congress will have demanded numerous concessions that the executive branch will have no choice but to make to win ratification. After implementation, the United States will come into conflict with the multilateral mechanism, if it is functioning.

41. Dan Kovenock and Marie Thursby, "GATT, Dispute Settlement and Cooperation," *Economics and Politics* 4 (1992): 151–169, p. 153.

42. Abram Chayes and Antonia Handler Chayes, "On Compliance," *International Organization* 47 (1993): 175–205, p. 191.

43. An analysis of all 301 investigations between 1975 and 1990 found that the victories were usually Pyrrhic since they also undermined existing U.S. trade. See "Gunboat Diplomacy," *The Economist,* March 12, 1994, pp. 73–75.

44. See John Jackson, *The World Trading System: Law and Policy of International Economic Relations* (Cambridge, MA: MIT Press, 1989), p. 108.

45. See Robert C. Cassidy, "National Trade Policy Instruments and the GATT: A U.S. Lawyer's Perspective," in *Conflict and Resolution in U.S.-EC Trade Relations at the Opening of the Uruguay Round,* eds. Seymour J. Rubin and Mark L. Jones (New York: Oceana Publications, 1989), p. 161.

46. Marco C. E. J. Bronkers, "National Trade Policy Instruments and the GATT: An EC Lawyer's Perspective," in *Conflict and Resolution in U.S.-EC Trade Relations,* p. 151.

47. This could be an extremely important conclusion of the Round and might lead to heightened trade conflicts. The majority of reporting and analysis, however, has focused on the external goods and services agreements; internal bargains have received relatively little attention, particularly on such procedural matters.

48. See Services of the Commission of the European Community, *Report on United States Trade and Investment Barriers: Problems of Doing Business with the U.S.,* Brussels, April 1994, p. 13.

49. It would be interesting to see whether further insights into practice can be gained from the new models of the emergence of cooperation among egoists, which borrow techniques from statistical thermodynamics. See in particular Natalie S. Glance and Bernardo A. Huberman, "The Outbreak of Cooperation," *Journal of Mathematical Sociology* 17 (1993): 281–302; and Natalie S. Glance and Bernardo A. Huberman, "The Dynamics of Social Dilemmas," *Scientific American* (March 1994): 58–63.

# CHAPTER 20

# DIVIDING THE INDIVISIBLE

## H. Peyton Young

Almost everything can be divided in one way or another. When we say that something is indivisible, we usually mean that it is difficult or costly to divide, not that it cannot be divided. Indivisibles in this sense are commonplace. Children are indivisible. So are houses, paintings, spouses, and jobs. Indivisibles are often the focus of disputes in the family, especially in inheritance and divorce cases. They are frequently bones of contention within the community: Where should the hazardous waste dump or the new hospital be sited? Who must serve in the Army? Who should receive the one available kidney for transplantation? They are also sources of conflict in the international sphere. Prominent examples are territories that are considered indivisible for historical and cultural reasons, such as Berlin, Vienna, or Jerusalem. But things may be indivisible for a variety of other reasons: technological (broadcasting bandwidths), symbolic (the name Macedonia), or aesthetic (the Mona Lisa).

Indivisibles pose a serious stumbling block to negotiations, because they often mislead the claimants into thinking in zero-sum terms: If one gets the object, the other does not. What the parties usually fail to

This chapter is adapted from an article with the same title in *The American Behavioral Scientist* 38 (May 1995): 904–920. I am indebted to Cecilia Albin, Alan Kirman, Robert Mnookin, Kalypso Nicolaidis, Thomas Schelling, James Sebenius, David Victor, and Amanda Wolf for suggesting examples and providing thoughtful comments on earlier drafts. My greatest debt, however, is to Howard Raiffa, whose pioneering work in fair division and negotiation inspired many of the ideas discussed in this paper.

recognize is that there are many methods of dividing a seemingly indivisible object that allow everyone a reasonable portion of the pie.

## Equity, Efficiency, and Indivisibility

Before considering these methods in detail, let us first observe that there is no inherent conflict between indivisibility and efficiency. If the contested object is given to exactly one claimant, it loses none of its intrinsic value. Moreover, if the claimants have different utilities for the object, and if they are allowed to trade after the initial allocation, we can presume that it will end up in the hands of the person who values it most. The crucial problem posed by indivisibles is not efficiency but equity. People have difficulty bargaining over an indivisible item because it does not give them scope to treat everyone even-handedly, to devise a solution that they perceive to be fair. This makes bargaining much more difficult. The key to successful negotiation lies in fashioning an agreement that the parties believe to be both efficient and equitable, as Howard Raiffa was one of the first to point out.[1]

By an equitable distribution I mean, roughly speaking, one that is *appropriate* and *fitting* given the various claims of the parties. Equity in this sense is hard to pin down, especially when the parties have different kinds of claims. Its definition depends on the nature of the distributive problem at hand, as well as the cultural norms and precedents that govern the expectations of the claimants. Yet we usually recognize equity (or the lack of it) when we see it. Indivisibles pose a problem precisely because they make it difficult to satisfy the parties' demands for equity. Thus the key to advancing negotiations over an indivisible object is to find some way to convert it into divisible forms of rights and entitlements.

In this paper I suggest a general framework for thinking systematically about this issue, and then apply the framework to negotiations over child custody, inheritance, medical care, the environment, and international disputes over territory. One of the conclusions is that there is no general recipe for equitable distributions that fits all situations. Philosophical theories of justice notwithstanding, our intuitions about equity are too subtle and varied to be captured in a single formula. Equity is a pluralistic concept that assumes different guises in different contexts.[2] This does not mean, however, that it exists only in the eye of the beholder. As we shall see from the cases, conceptions of equity follow predictable patterns, though they do not conform to simple, all-encompassing rules like Rawls's difference principle. The cases also reveal a set of general techniques for converting indivisibles to divisibles through the definition of property rights. Of course, the identification of techniques does not remove the need to negotiate; people must still make choices. But it does provide a systematic framework for thinking more creatively about solutions.

Let's begin with two current international negotiations that involve indivisible goods. Consider Jerusalem, which is surely one of the greatest stumbling blocks to a peace accord in the Middle East. Here, clustered within a few hundred yards of each other, are some of the holiest sites of three major religions. Here is the accretion of millennia of civilization, almost unbelievable in its complexity and diversity, yet also forming an organic whole. Nevertheless Jerusalem is divisible. We could, for example, build a wall down the middle and top it with barbed wire, somewhat on the model of Berlin. Yet this would be close to sacrilege; it would be like sacrificing a living thing.

Or consider the atmosphere. The air is both a global commons and a global dumping ground. Each year billions of tons of carbon dioxide, particulates, and noxious gases spew forth from factories, cars, and campfires around the globe. Atmospheric scientists believe that their accumulation will, sooner or later, have a major negative impact on the global climate. How should responsibility for maintaining the health of this indivisible resource be shared? Strictly speaking, of course, the atmosphere *is* divisible. One way to divide it, for example, would be to adopt a "greenhouse" solution to the "greenhouse" problem. Countries could encase themselves in huge plastic bubbles, within which they could enjoy their own private climates controlled by their own private thermostats. Yet this would hardly be practical. Quite aside from the expense, it would change the climate in drastic ways— altering currents, rainfall patterns, and temperature. In other words, it would destroy the essential properties of the thing being divided.

When we say that a thing is indivisible, like Jerusalem or the atmosphere, we do not mean that it cannot be divided physically. We mean that the object loses much of its value when divided. The solution is to divide the object notionally rather than physically by creating various kinds of rights to its use. In the case of Jerusalem, for instance, we could conceive of a quasi-autonomous city-state governed by a council of representatives from various religious and ethnic groups. Control of municipal services could be delegated to local neighborhood authorities, and freedom of access would be guaranteed to all the holy sites. This arrangement solves the problem of fair division by assigning powers, rights, and responsibilities in a creative way, not by dividing the object itself.[3]

Similarly, countries can share the atmosphere by creating entitlements to its use. For example, one could issue emissions permits and divide them among the claimants. Such an approach was recently adopted in the United States for dealing with sulfur dioxide emissions from electric power plants. Under the revised Clean Air Act, the federal government allocates emissions permits to each power plant in proportion to its base-period emissions (subject to a specified ceiling), and the plants may then trade their permits within defined geographical areas. A similar approach has been suggested for restricting carbon dioxide emissions globally. Countries would be allocated emissions permits according to some criterion, such as current emissions rates or population (or some combination thereof) and then be allowed to trade them.[4]

## Methods for Creating Divisible Property Rights in Indivisible Goods

These examples illustrate how indivisibles can be made divisible by creating new kinds of property rights. To appreciate the full range of options, however, it is helpful to step back and ask how we allocate indivisibles in the community and in the family. Who gets the children when the marriage breaks up? Who inherits the summer house and who gets the diamond? Who is first in line to receive a kidney for transplantation? Who is admitted to nursery school (or a nursing home)? In whose backyard is the hazardous waste dump located? Society has devised ingenious ways to deal with these local distributive problems, and their solutions offer important clues about how to approach global ones.

Suppose that two heirs have been left equal shares of an estate that contains exactly one object, say a valuable painting. If they cannot agree on how to divide it, the matter will be referred to the courts and the lawyers will take their share, so the heirs have a strong incentive to negotiate a solution. What options are available to them? I suggest eight fairly universal techniques for defining ex ante property rights in an indivisible good. I then suggest that the alternative—giving it all to one claimant—is also perceived to be equitable in a surprising number of situations.

1.  *Physical division.* Cut the painting in two. While this approach is almost always possible, it is typically very wasteful. Indeed this inefficiency is why we say that the good is indivisible, even though it is divisible in fact.

2.  *Lottery.* Use a chance device (for example, flip a fair coin) to determine who gets it. Decision theorists often recommend

this approach, but it is usually shunned in practice for a variety of reasons. One reason is envy: you would rather not take a 50 percent chance that your brother gets sole possession of the painting. Another is regret: if you lose, you will wish that you had chosen another form of property rights; anticipating this reaction, you will not choose to randomize in the first place. A third reason is that randomizing may seem frivolous and even morally wrong when the good is especially valuable (such as a life-saving medical operation), because it abdicates responsibility for making hard choices.[5] For these reasons lotteries tend not to be used except when the good is relatively unimportant in the context of the whole negotiation.

3. *Rotation.* Hang the painting in the heirs' apartments in alternate years.

4. *Common ownership.* Hang the painting on the common stairway leading to the heirs' apartments.

5. *Subtraction.* Destroy the painting or give it away, say to a museum.

6. *Sale.* Sell the painting and divide the money. Or exchange it for two paintings and give one to each heir.

7. *Compensation.* One heir pays the other for exclusive possession of the painting. The compensation need not be in money; for example, one heir could offer a house or a car to the other in return for the painting. The essential idea is that the parties place more goods on the table, which offers them greater scope for making tradeoffs.

8. *Unbundle attributes.* One heir gets exclusive enjoyment of the painting for her lifetime, after which the painting goes to the local museum, which pays the second heir *now* for the right to acquire it later. In other words, the first heir gets to enjoy the painting while the second realizes its money value. This approach is quite general, and amounts to establishing entitlements to different attributes of the indivisible good. In effect this creates more kinds of goods to be traded.[6] The definition of entitlements can be complex and subtle. Under the 1978 Camp David accords, for example, Egypt obtained nominal sovereignty over the Sinai peninsula, with the proviso that it remain forever a demilitarized zone. Thus Israel obtained a valuable covenant—a restriction on the use of the good—while Egypt obtained title. A current example is the negotiation

between Israel and the Palestinians about who has access to particular holy sites, at what times, and who has responsibility for maintaining and protecting them.

These eight methods do not exhaust the possibilities for dividing an indivisible, but I do not know of others that are frequently used.[7] There is another approach, however, which is to frankly acknowledge the indivisibility: someone gets the good, the others do not. This all or nothing approach is actually one of the most common ways of allocating indivisible goods, though it is often overlooked in the literature on fair division. The decision about who gets the good can be based on some notion of need or desert. Alternatively, it can be determined by a social norm or convention. Not long ago, primogeniture was the accepted criterion for awarding inheritances; first discovery still establishes a powerful claim on territory. However, the salience of a norm of priority depends on the situation. In medical care, for example, urgency rather than place in line often determines who is treated first.

## Dividing a Child

The suitability of different methods for creating property rights depends very much on the indivisible item in question. In dividing a work of art, for example, the usual method of division would be sale or compensation, but parents getting divorced would not be likely to divide their child in the same way.[8] Let's consider the eight methods applied to this case.

1. The child could be physically divided. This is what King Solomon threatened in the Biblical story of the two women who claimed they were the mother of the same baby. (We shall return to this case later.)

2. The parents could flip a coin to see who gets custody. This has been proposed as an alternative to lengthy court battles, which are not only expensive but may be emotionally harmful to the child.[9]

3. Rotation or joint custody. This is one of the most common solutions to the problem. Note that the parties need not share equally under this method: one parent might have the child on weekends, for example, and the other have custody during the week.

4. Hold the child in common. In effect this is what they were doing before they divorced.

5. Give the child away, say to a grandparent. This method places both parties on a more equal footing, thus avoiding disputes. It may also be in the best interests of the child in some cases.

6. Sell the child (for example to an adoption agency) and divide the money. Among the various moral dilemmas posed by this solution is that the opportunity to sell children might cause some people to have children for this very purpose.

7. Compensate the person who does not get the child with something else of value, say a summer house.

8. Award different kinds of custody rights to the parents. The mother might have responsibility for rearing the child, for example, and the father for his religious education.

If the court adjudicates the outcome, however, probably the most common solution is to give sole custody to the parent who is judged to be fittest to raise the child. This is an instance of the all or nothing method.

These examples show clearly that the various methods of defining property rights are not equally attractive in all cases. Nevertheless it is important for the parties to recognize how many different approaches there are. Furthermore, it could happen that *all* parties to a negotiation prefer one form of property rights to another, that is, one form is Pareto-superior to the other.[10] For example, if the good in question is a child, one could imagine that both parents prefer a rotation scheme to a lottery. But if the good is a kidney and two patients are waiting for a transplantation, they would no doubt prefer an equal chances lottery to an equal time-sharing scheme. And if the good is a painting, then in most cases the claimants would probably prefer to sell it and divide the proceeds than to time-share it or take their chances in a lottery. In short, there may be a surprising degree of consensus on the appropriate form that the property rights should take. Merely recognizing this may substantially improve the chances of agreement.

## International Negotiations over Indivisibles

The nine preceding methods are also useful in thinking about how to divide indivisibles in the international arena. The first, physical division, is the obvious way to settle territorial claims, but it is not always the most appealing: Witness the Berlin Wall. The second method, lotteries, is seldom used in practice, but is not without precedent. In the Bible, God commanded the Israelites to divide their lands by lot (Numbers 26:55). In the 1947 partition of India and Pakistan, some common property was allocated by the toss of a coin, as I describe below.

The third method, rotation, is a common device for sharing decision making powers. For example, temporary membership on the United Nations Security Council rotates among the nonpermanent members. A similar device was applied to the division of Vienna at the end of World War II. No walls were erected as in Berlin; instead, each of the four occupying powers—Britain, France, the United States, and the Soviet Union—had exclusive jurisdiction over one sector of the city. The area lying inside the Ringstrasse, the city's central core, was administered by a four-power council whose chairmanship rotated among the members.

Common ownership is another method for dealing with territorial disputes. Consider Antarctica, which is claimed by Argentina, Australia, Belgium, Chile, France, Japan, New Zealand, Norway, Poland, South Africa, Russia, the United Kingdom, and the United States. Instead of pressing their claims, they agreed in a 1959 treaty to use the continent only for scientific purposes and not to colonize it or develop its economic resources.

On some occasions nations have given up their claims to disputed territory rather than go to the mat defending them (the subtraction method). Once again Austria provides an example: instead of partitioning the country or going to war over it, the four powers withdrew in 1956 on the condition that Austria be permanently nonaligned. One could conceive of a similar solution in the current negotiations between Israel and Syria over the Golan Heights. Both parties might prefer to give up sovereignty claims and let the territory be administered by a third party than to confront each other across a barbed wire fence.

Method six—sale of the territory with the proceeds divided among the claimants—is quite rare. However, something along these lines is incorporated in the Law of the Sea Treaty, which was negotiated under United Nations auspices in the 1970s.[11] One of the most troublesome issues was how to divide rights to mine the deep ocean floor, which is strewn with nodules rich in nickel, cobalt, manganese, and other valuable minerals. Both then and now only a few industrialized countries have access to the capital and technical know-how to mine these nodules profitably. The developing countries feared that a laissez-faire approach would result in a scramble for the best sites that would leave them out in the cold. Moreover, it would undercut the principle, which had been adopted by the UN General Assembly, that the seabed is part of the common heritage of mankind—a global commons in which all countries have a stake. Yet to give each of them a stake would be meaningless, because the economics of the situation imply that only large-scale enterprises are viable. (This shows how indivisibility can result from increasing returns to scale.) The solution adopted in the Treaty is that the developing countries transferred their rights to an international mining company known as the Enterprise, which collects royalties from development and divides them among its members. In effect, the mining rights are pooled and transferred to a third party in return for a share of the money income.

In some cases, one party has relinquished a territorial claim in return for other goods (the compensation method). A recent example involving nonmonetary compensation is the Camp David Accord, in which Egypt gained sovereignty over the Sinai in return for giving Israel diplomatic recognition, rights to purchase oil, and various other concessions. This agreement also illustrates the unbundling principle: Egypt gained only a circumscribed form of sovereignty that forbade military uses of the Sinai, an arrangement that met Israel's security demands.

### Three Principles of Equitable Distribution

These examples illustrate how the creative definition of property rights can overcome the potential loss of value from dividing an apparently indivisible object. However, defining the form of property rights is merely the first step in a more complex process. At least two other issues must be addressed. One is the basis of the parties' claims on the object: what makes one claim stronger or more credible than another? In territorial disputes, for example, the salient factors establishing a claim include the date of discovery, date of settlement, level of investment, and current political control. Deciding the basis of the parties' claims is an integral and necessary part of the negotiation, distinct from defining the form that the property rights will take. Once this matter is settled, it remains to carry out the distribution. Consider, for example, the division of atmospheric pollution rights among countries. Suppose the parties have decided that the relevant form of property is emissions permits, and that a country's claim to permits is based on its population and economic product. This does not say how many permits each country will actually receive, because the negotiators must still determine the relevant principle of distribution.

Three distributive principles are appropriate in different settings. *Parity* states that claimants should be treated equally and that differences among them should be ignored. *Proportionality* recognizes that salient differences among the claimants exist, and insists that the allotments be in the same ratio as these differences. *Priority* states that the party with the greatest claim should get the object. Each of these principles can be used in conjunction with some or all of the forms of property rights defined earlier.

Parity is consistent with virtually all methods for dividing property rights in an indivisible object. For example, we can give the claimants an equal number of chances at getting the good, or let them have equal time in a rotation scheme. Common ownership is a tacit form of parity, as is giving away. If the good is sold or exchanged for a divisible good, the proceeds can be divided equally. This is also true in a compensation scheme if the additional goods are all divisible.

Parity is not so obviously implementable if there are several indivisible goods on the table, or if the good is divisible but not uniform in quality of attributes (such as a parcel of land). Yet even in these cases a rough form of parity can often be achieved. Consider the problem of how to cut a cake.[12] Cake is divisible but not homogeneous: inevitably one part will not look the same as the other. (Perhaps one piece has more icing and the other has a cherry.) Yet even my children know how to solve this: one of them divides the cake into two pieces and the other gets first choice. This method has the merit that, although the portions may be unequal, the divider can arrange things so that neither prefers the other's piece to his own. Nor does this solution depend on their altruistic impulses. Knowing that his little sister loves cherries, for example, the older brother will no doubt cut the cake so that the smaller piece contains the cherry. In spite of such manipulations, the outcome is a division in which each party prefers what he has to what the other has. This rough form of parity is known in the economics literature as "no envy."[13]

Divide and choose is not merely child's play; it has also been applied in the international arena. For example, the Law of the Sea Treaty contains an ingenious variant of the cake-cutting procedure to allocate rights between the developed countries and the developing ones (represented by the Enterprise). Every time a mining company applies for permission to mine at a given location, it must develop two nearby sites from which the Enterprise chooses one. Thus the Enterprise can expect to receive at least half the royalties from all developed sites.

The second principle, proportionality, is enshrined in law and custom as a standard method for dividing contested objects fairly. Indeed, Aristotle held that it is virtually synonymous with distributive justice: "What is just . . . is what is proportional, and what is unjust is what violates the proportion."[14] In spite of its wide appeal, however, proportionality is more restricted in its application than the parity principle. For example, giving the item away is not consistent with proportionality but it is with parity. Proportionality is also less general than the priority principle, because under proportionality the property rights must be divisible and the claims must be cardinally comparable, whereas under priority the good may be either divisible or indivisible, and the claims need only be ordinally comparable.

Proportionality can be applied to many forms of property rights, including lotteries, rotation, sale, and compensation with divisible goods. A version of it can even be implemented for a collection of heterogeneous indivisible goods: if there are two parties and the ratio of their shares is supposed to be $m:n$, the first allocates the goods into $m + n$ piles, and the second chooses $n$.[15] However, just because the claims are defined on a numerical scale does not mean that proportionality is always the "right" choice. For example, the four powers that occupied Vienna after World War II might well have claimed territory in proportion to the size of their armies. But this does not seem to be the right solution, in part because it is cumbersome, and in part because it makes fine distinctions that do not seem to be worthwhile.

The third principle, priority, works whether the good is divisible or indivisible, though it is not applicable when property is given away or held in common. Moreover, unlike proportionality, it only requires ordinal comparisons among the claimants. The basis for making these comparisons depends on the context. One of the most common is order of arrival; we take it for granted that priority of settlement establishes a bona fide claim to territory, just as we believe that arriving early at a ticket window establishes our priority to get tickets. What makes this work is that priority of arrival is a widely held norm; those who violate it are subjected to social disapproval.

Priority can also be established by utilitarian or ethical arguments. For example, it might be determined by the claimant's suitability for the good in question, as in the award of child custody or the allocation of scarce slots in a public university. Suitability is sometimes determined by a contest—say, who wins a jousting competition for the hand of a lady, or who gets highest marks on an entrance examination. Or it may be determined by a ruse. This was what King Solomon was up to in deciding how to allocate the child between the two claimants. He threatened physical division, but as he lifted his sword, one of the women cried out that she would rather give up her claim than see her baby slain. Thus, in relinquishing her claim, the true claimant revealed herself.

One can also lose one's claim by asserting it. Such a case is recounted by Elizabeth Baxter Hubbard, the daughter of a Harvard professor of botany, in her memoirs about growing up in Cambridge,

Massachusetts, in the early part of this century.[16] The boy next door was the future poet e.e. cummings. One summer day when the children were about ten, they decided to hold a parade. After much negotiation about the details of their attire and the order of events, it came down to the question of who would carry the American flag. Elizabeth asserted boldly that as she was a lady she should carry it. He retorted that if she were a lady she would not have brought the matter up.

Priority can also be established through need. In 1982, the International Whaling Commission, concerned about steep declines in whale populations, imposed a ban on almost all whaling pending a comprehensive assessment of whaling stocks. However, the Alaskan Inuits, for whom whales are a principal source of food, were allowed to continue their traditional hunt.[17] In theory the same number of whales could have been allotted pro rata among all the whaling countries, but this would have made little sense; a handful of whales for Japan or Russia would be as good as none at all. Instead, the whales were awarded to the claimants with the greatest need.

Sometimes priority is determined by a combination of factors. Consider the problem of allocating a kidney among transplant patients. Should it go the person who has been waiting longest (order of arrival)? Or to the one whose case is most urgent (need)? Or to the person who is most likely to survive for a long time (suitability)? The method currently in use in the United States establishes priority by weighting all three factors.[18]

A particularly interesting example of the priority principle is seen in the negotiations over the archipelago of Spitsbergen.[19] Until the turn of the last century, it was a kind of "no man's land" that was not under the jurisdiction of any country, though several claimed an interest in it, including Norway, Sweden, Russia, Germany, Britain, and the United States. The basis of their claims varied: Britain pointed to its discovery by William Barents in the year 1596, though in fact Icelanders had discovered it as early as 1194. (This illustrates the general principle, of which Columbus's discovery of America is a good example, that being the last to discover something is better than being the first.) The United States felt obliged to protect the interests of a U.S. firm that was operating a coal mine there. Norway had a natural interest in the territory because of its proximity, and because some Norwegian firms had mining operations there. All of the claimants routinely used its coasts for fishing and whaling. Their primary objective was to keep their access to mineral and ocean resources, and in the future perhaps to establish settlements. However, the lack of any governmental authority to register claims, enforce property rights, and maintain order was increasingly viewed by everyone as unsatisfactory.

Various efforts were made between 1905 and 1920 to negotiate an administrative framework that would be acceptable to all parties. Initially the focus was on some form of power sharing, but working out the details proved to be so complicated that nothing came of it. The issue was finally settled after World War I by a commission consisting of Britain, France, Italy, and the United States. The moment was ripe, since the defeat of Germany and the chaotic situation in Russia essentially removed two significant claimants from the scene, and the others recognized it was in their interest to resolve the issue swiftly and decisively. They also acknowledged that previous attempts to resolve the issue by a division of powers had failed. Their proposed solution was to award sole sovereignty to one country, Norway, with two provisos: first, that all signatories have equal rights of access to exploit mineral resources and to fish in its waters; and second, that it never be used for military purposes. The logic of this solution was that Norway had a strong natural claim—it is the closest to Spitsbergen—and it was willing to administer the territory under the stated restrictions. Moreover, the others preferred a clean resolution to a complex power-sharing formula that might lead to disputes later. Thus, an all or nothing solution was preferred by all claimants to an outright division.

## Mixing the Methods: The Partition of India and Pakistan

A remarkable division that illustrates different bases for recognizing claims, different forms of property, and different principles of distribution is the partition of India and Pakistan. On the stroke of midnight, August 15, 1947, British rule came to an end and two new countries were born. The magnitude of the enterprise was unprecedented—some 400 million people and a territory the size of Europe was split in two. All government property was divided between India and Pakistan according to principles that they had jointly negotiated. This included bullion in the bank, railroad engines and cars, desks, chairs, books, brooms, typewriters, hat pegs, paper clips, and chamber pots. In charge were two lawyers—Chaudhuri Mohammed Ali for Pakistan and H. M. Patel for India—plus a staff of a hundred bureaucrats who kept handwritten stacks of files, each knotted with a twist of red ribbon.[20]

As in most divorce cases, some of the bitterest disputes were over money. Patel and Mohammed Ali had to be locked in a room until they came to terms. The outcome was that all cash in the bank and government debt was apportioned in the ratio 17.5 percent for Pakistan, 82.5 percent for India, this being roughly the proportion of population in the two countries. All other divisible assets—tables, chairs, typewriters, telephones, army uniforms, brass bands—were divided in the proportions 20 percent for Pakistan and 80 percent for India. (This represented a simple rounding of the monetary criterion.) But some property was not strictly divisible. A notable case was the national libraries. Some books were simply ripped in two; Pakistan got A–K and India L–Z of a dictionary. Sets of encyclopedias were divided with alternate volumes going to each dominion. When only one copy of a book was available, a team of librarians was charged with deciding which country had the greatest natural interest in it, that is, which had priority. People actually came to blows over such questions as whether India or Pakistan had a greater natural interest in *Alice in Wonderland.*

One fascinating episode took place in the stable yards of the Viceroy, Lord Mountbatten. At issue were 12 viceregal carriages, 6 trimmed in gold, 6 in silver. They represented all the pomp, majesty, and mystery that had fascinated and infuriated the raj's subjects. Every visiting dignitary and head of state had paraded through the streets in one of them. Mountbatten's aide-de-camp, Lieutenant Commander Peter Howes, decided that it would be a shame to split up the sets. Instead, they would settle the matter by lottery. He tossed a coin into the air. Major Singh, the Indian representative, shouted "heads." Heads it was, and India took the gold coaches. Lieutenant Howes then proceeded to divide up all the boots, wigs, uniforms, and other paraphernalia that went with each set of carriages. One item remained: the coachman's ceremonial posthorn. The obvious solution was to toss a second coin. Howes hesitated: if India won the toss again, the Pakistani representative, who was already fuming, might boil over. Instead, he invoked the subtraction method by announcing that he would give it to neither, and sauntered out of the courtyard with the horn tucked under his arm.

Thus, different types of property were allocated according to different methods, different principles, and different criteria. Homogeneous property was physically divided according to the proportionality principle, with population shares as the criterion. Some of the books were divided equally, others on the basis of suitability (all or nothing method, priority principle). The viceregal coaches were allocated by the toss of a coin (lottery method, parity principle). The posthorn was taken away (subtraction method, parity principle). Perhaps the most important indivisible—the name India—was retained by the larger half on the grounds that the smaller half (Pakistan) was seceding. This is also an application of the priority principle.

## Gains from Trade

Could the division of India and Pakistan have been improved upon? Certainly one can do better than tearing dictionaries in two. There was a similar case in the 1970s, when the University of Louvain in Belgium separated into two universities along linguistic lines. The old campus of the university became exclusively Flemish and was styled the Katholieke Universiteit van Leuven. A new campus was built for the French-speaking contingent, and called the Université Catholique de Louvain. As in the India-Pakistan partition, a major bone of contention was how to divide the library. Should they, like the Indians and Pakistanis, rip the books in half? A more sensible solution would be to give the Flemish books to the Flemish campus, and the French books to the French campus, with a separate principle used to allocate books in other languages. Yet they did not follow this method, perhaps because the two collections differed in size. Instead, they went down each shelf and gave alternative volumes to each campus—one to Leuven, one to Louvain, one to Leuven, one to Louvain, and so forth. Needless to say, this was extremely wasteful, as it meant splitting up sets of encyclopedias and bound journals. However, in the second stage of the process the parties were allowed to trade. Half of one set of journals was swapped for another to make two complete sets. Flemish books were traded for French ones, and so forth. Although this process was time-consuming, one could argue that it was worth the effort because its outcome was both equitable and efficient: equitable because the parties began from a position in which they had more or less equal shares; efficient because, after trade, both parties could not do better.

## The Role of Equity in Negotiations

What lessons can we draw from these cases? First, indivisibles are not what we say they are. We can divide them, but they lose much of their value when we do so. The challenge is to devise ways of dividing property rights in the indivisible good that preserves as much of its value as possible while treating all claimants equitably.

But how do we know in a concrete case that the outcomes were in fact equitable? One answer is that the parties willingly agreed to their terms; no one was coerced. This explanation is not entirely satisfactory, however, because it is not falsifiable. Under this definition of equity, the outcome of *every* voluntary agreement is fair. It is similar to saying that individuals always make choices that maximize their utility functions. Without saying what properties utility functions have, it is not a useful statement.

In fact, the justice of the agreements we have analyzed is evident from their terms. These are not arbitrary, but follow definite patterns and employ well-established principles that we see in many distributive situations. In each case the three principles—parity, proportionality, and priority—were interpreted differently in the details, but they were clearly recognizable.

Finally, it is worth recalling that these agreements worked. They have proved to be durable even without the benefit of strong institutions to enforce them. This is significant; I doubt that they would have had the same self-policing property if their terms had been arbitrary— the outcome of a contest of wills with no rationale to back them up. Agreements based purely on bargaining power tend to be fragile. First, they are almost impossible to justify to one's constituents. The representatives for Louvain and Leuven will have little trouble justifying a 50:50 division of the books, but a lot of trouble justifying 19:23. It is not good enough to say that the outcome resulted because Leuven did not bargain as hard. Similarly, the representative from Pakistan can say that he agreed to a 20:80 split because this is the approximate ratio of the countries' populations, but he cannot say he agreed to it because Pakistan was in a weaker bargaining position. It may be true but it is not an acceptable reason. Moreover, the Indian representative knows this. Hence they both have an interest in crafting an outcome that is based on widely accepted norms and can be justified to their constituents. This severely constrains what they can agree to.

Second, even when negotiators are not answerable to their constituents, there is an advantage to basing an agreement on distributive norms rather than on balance of power arguments. Power cannot be known precisely and perceptions of it are constantly in flux. It follows that an agreement reached on the basis of balance of power today may have to be renegotiated tomorrow, which is not an appealing prospect. It is better to come to terms on the basis of principles that do not change from one day to the next, for then the agreement is self-policing: if the parties have to renegotiate, they can expect to come to the same terms they did before. This is why negotiations based on equity principles are so attractive—they strike a balance that the parties find satisfying when the agreement is made, and that they continue to find satisfying over time.

## Notes

1. See Howard Raiffa, "Arbitration Schemes for Generalized Two-Person Games," in *The Annals of Mathematics Studies* (Princeton, NJ: Princeton University Press, 1953); R. Duncan Luce and Howard Raiffa, *Games and*

*Decisions* (New York: Wiley, 1957); and Howard Raiffa, *The Art and Science of Negotiation* (Cambridge, MA: Harvard University Press, 1982). Other noteworthy discussions of equity in negotiation include Roger Fisher and William Ury, *Getting to Yes* (Boston: Houghton Mifflin, 1981); William Zartman and Maureen Berman, *The Practical Negotiator* (New Haven: Yale University Press, 1982); James Sebenius, *Negotiating the Law of the Sea* (Cambridge, MA: Harvard University Press, 1984); H. Peyton Young, *Negotiation Analysis* (Ann Arbor: University of Michigan Press, 1991), ch. 1; and H. Peyton Young, *Equity in Theory and Practice* (Princeton, NJ: Princeton University Press, 1994).

2. See Young, *Equity in Theory and Practice,* ch. 1.

3. Detailed proposals for dividing Jerusalem along these lines are discussed by Cecilia Albin, "Negotiating Indivisible Goods: The Case of Jerusalem," *The Jerusalem Journal of International Relations* 13 (1991): 45–76.

4. Joshua Epstein and Raj Gupta, *Controlling the Greenhouse Effect* (Washington, DC: The Brookings Institution, 1990); Michael Grubb, "The Greenhouse Effect: Negotiating Targets," *International Affairs* 66 (1990): 67–89; H. Peyton Young and Amanda Wolf, "Global Warming Negotiations: Does Fairness Matter?" *The Brookings Review* (Spring 1992): 46–51.

5. Guido Calabresi and P. Bobbit, *Tragic Choices* (New York: Norton, 1978).

6. I am indebted to James Sebenius for suggesting unbundling as a general method of division.

7. Arbitration might be considered another method of division. However, since the arbitrator will likely adopt one of the methods suggested here, we may consider these to be the primary methods of division.

8. For a thorough discussion of how courts deal with children in divorce cases, see Robert H. Mnookin, "Child Custody Adjudication: Judicial Functions in the Face of Indeterminacy," *Law and Contemporary Problems* 39 (1975): 226–293; and E. Maccoby and Robert H. Mnookin, *Dividing the Child: Social and Legal Dilemmas of Custody* (Cambridge, MA: Harvard University Press, 1992).

9. Jon Elster, *Solomonic Judgements: Studies in the Limitations of Rationality* (Cambridge: Cambridge University Press, 1989).

10. This idea was hinted at by Luce and Raiffa in *Games and Decisions*, p. 365. For a more complete discussion, see Young, *Equity in Theory and Practice,* pp. 134–135.

11. Sebenius, *Negotiating the Law of the Sea.*

12. Hugo Steinhaus, "The Problem of Fair Division," *Econometrica* 16 (1948): 101–104.

13. Duncan Foley, "Resource Allocation and the Public Sector," *Yale Economic Essays* 7 (1967): 45–98. For various applications of this concept, see William Baumol, *Superfairness* (Cambridge, MA: MIT Press, 1988).

14. Aristotle, *Ethics*, trans. by J. A. K. Thompson (Harmondsworth, UK: Penguin, 1985), pp. 177–179.
15. This idea has been proposed independently by several people, including Thomas Schelling and Dean Foster (personal communication).
16. Elizabeth B. Hubbard, "Life Was Lovely," *Harvard Magazine* 91 (1988): 61–64.
17. J. G. Van Beek, "Historical Review of the Management Measures Taken by the International Whaling Commission," *Lutra* 30 (1987): 166–192.
18. See Jon Elster, *Local Justice* (New York: Russell Sage Foundation, 1993); and Young, *Equity in Theory and Practice*.
19. This account of the Spitsbergen negotiations is based on Elen C. Singh and Artemy A. Saguirian, "The Svalbard Archipelago: The Role of Surrogate Negotiators," in *Polar Politics: Creating International Environmental Regimes*, eds. Oran R. Young and Gail Osherenko (Ithaca, NY: Cornell University Press, 1993), pp. 56–95.
20. This account is based on Larry Collins and Dominique Lapierre, *Freedom at Midnight* (New York: Avon, 1975).

# CHAPTER 21

# MEASURING COOPERATION IN NEGOTIATIONS: THE IMPOSSIBLE DREAM

## Dana R. Clyman

Cooperative bargaining problems are characterized by the dual activities of value creation and value claiming. Indeed, in all but the simplest single-issue negotiations, a fundamental and inescapable tension exists between the actions necessary to create value and those necessary to claim it: "This tension affects virtually all tactical and strategic choice. Analysts must come to grips with it; negotiators must manage it. Neither denial nor discomfort will make it disappear."[1] As a result, to understand negotiations one must distinguish among the cooperative value-creating and distributive value-claiming components so that they may be evaluated separately. Doing so is as necessary for theoreticians and empiricists who want to understand the factors that drive effective performance as it is for teachers and consultants who wish to offer prescriptive advice.

In negotiating experiments, for example, distributive outcomes can be ordered easily. When comparing the settlements achieved by different pairs of negotiators, it is easy to tell when a party in one of the roles achieved a better settlement than another party in the same role simply by comparing the utilities achieved. When measuring coopera-

The author would like to thank the many participants of the Harvard Business School seminar "Wise Choices: Games, Decisions and Negotiations," honoring Howard Raiffa, for their enthusiastic discussion and comments. In addition, the author would like to express his very special thanks to David Bell, John Dell, Sherwood Frey, Howard Raiffa, James Sebenius, and Richard Zeckhauser for their encouragement, support, and detailed suggestions. Naturally, all remaining errors are the author's own.

tion, however, it is not so clear how to tell whether one pair of negotiators achieved a more cooperative agreement than another and, if so,
by how much. Yet, such a measure is needed if we are to assess the
effect of various restrictions, structures, or conditions on the potential
for cooperative outcomes.

Indeed, numerous negotiating experiments have been conducted
to determine the impact on cooperative settlements of restricted communication, principals and agents, relationships, "social trap" situations, instructions concerning the extent of permitted disclosure, and
more or less aggressive goals. And many of these experiments have
led to the conclusion that negotiators are not fully cooperative because
they do not achieve Pareto-efficient solutions; they leave money on the
table. However, without a formal measure, it is impossible to say just
how inefficient the negotiated settlements are or how much value has
been left unrealized.

Moreover, when a scatterplot of the expected utilities achieved by
each of the parties is constructed, the data are typically widely scat-
tered. While those agreements represented by points on the Pareto-
efficient frontier may be defined as maximally cooperative, for those
represented by points inside the frontier it is natural to question which
agreements represent more cooperative outcomes, and how "close"
they are to efficient settlements. How else can one compare the cooperative nature of the outcomes?

To enable these comparisons, several cardinal measures of cooperation have been proposed, most notably joint profit[2]—the most frequently used measure—and the measures proposed by David Lax and
James Sebenius and by Thomas Tripp and Harris Sondak.[3] Each of
these measures allows us to judge which of any two deals is more
cooperative, and by how much. Nevertheless, none of these measures
is valid in all negotiating settings. Indeed, as this paper demonstrates,
a general measure of cooperation that applies to all negotiation settings
cannot exist. This means that successful measures of cooperation must
be specific to the negotiating setting under investigation. Therefore, in
addition to structuring experiments, empirical researchers must also
identify and select an appropriate measure for each particular setting.

None of these measures is valid in all negotiating settings because,
for each of them, there exist settings in which the measure is not
distribution free. In other words, adoption of the measure results in
preferred allocations of resources. Tripp and Sondak, for example, like
many others before them, object to joint profit as a measure of cooperation because its adoption requires that "negotiators should sometimes act against their own interests for the sake of joint profit."[4] To
see this, suppose there is a negotiation over a collection of resources,

all of which are more highly valued by one of the parties to the negotiation than by the other. To maximize joint profit in this negotiation, the parties must agree to give all of the resources to the one who values them more highly. Clearly this bargaining solution is not in the best self-interest of both parties.[5]

It is for this reason that theoreticians have long rejected joint profit as a measure of cooperative performance. This paper demonstrates that, for every other measure of cooperation, negotiating settings can also be constructed in which adoption of the measure also results in preferred distributions of resources. Thus, all measures must be rejected for the same reason that theoreticians rejected joint profit.

The next section examines the best of the proposed measures, the integrativeness quotient of Lax and Sebenius. To build intuition for the final result, this measure is examined in some detail through a stylized negotiating setting wherein adoption of the measure establishes preferred distributions of resources. The third section presents the impossibility theorem—a generic counterexample. The proof consists of the construction of two negotiating settings, and an argument that demonstrates that no measure of cooperation can work in both settings by showing that every conceivable measure will fail to be distribution free in at least one of them. The final section offers reflections on the implications of the result.

## A Proposed Measure of Cooperation

As already indicated in the discussion of joint profit, for a measure of cooperation to be distribution free, all settlements represented by points on the Pareto frontier must be considered equally cooperative; otherwise, some distributions of resources are preferred to others. The measure of cooperation discussed here—the integrativeness quotient proposed by Lax and Sebenius—like all measures based on the idea of integrativeness, has this property. Formally, we say that settlement A is more integrative than settlement B whenever the expected utility of settlement A is greater than that of settlement B for at least one of the two parties, and not worse for the other. In other words, settlement A is more integrative than settlement B whenever it (weakly) Pareto-dominates settlement B in expected-utility space. (This idea of integrativeness is also known as the Pareto condition.)

The idea is intuitively appealing; by definition, all Pareto-efficient settlements are maximally and therefore equally integrative. Because any measure of cooperation based on integrativeness shares this property—that all settlements represented by points on the Pareto frontier are equally cooperative—it seems that such a measure would be distribution free.

However, integrativeness alone is not sufficient to compare settlements off the Pareto frontier; too many pairs are not comparable. The issue becomes how to determine which of a pair of noncomparable settlements is closer to the frontier, and therefore more cooperative. This question has led to various proposals for measuring cooperation, each based on its own cardinal measure of closeness.

The best of these measures, the integrativeness quotient proposed by Lax and Sebenius, is defined as 1 minus a ratio of areas. The numerator of the ratio is the area represented by agreements that are Pareto-superior to the negotiated agreement (denoted by $S$ in Figure 21-1); the denominator of the ratio is the total area under the Pareto frontier (denoted by $P$). Thus, the Lax and Sebenius integrativeness quotient is given by $IQ = 1 - \dfrac{S}{P}$.

The measure has several appealing features. First, all deals represented by points on the Pareto frontier are equally and maximally cooperative, with an IQ of 1. Second, as a sequence of deals approaches a Pareto-optimal deal, the sequence of areas, $S$, approaches 0, so the

**Figure 21-1**
*Lax and Sebenius's Integrativeness Quotient*

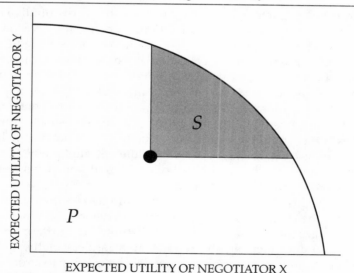

EXPECTED UTILITY OF NEGOTIATOR Y

$S$

$P$

EXPECTED UTILITY OF NEGOTIATOR X

sequence of IQs approaches 1. This provides a concept akin to continuity. Third, the measure is simple to calculate (although the calculus is needed when the frontier is curved), easy to understand, and intuitively appealing. Fourth (and this is the feature that makes this measure better than any of the alternative proposals), the measure is independent of changes in scale in the utility functions of the two parties; that is, positive affine transformations of the utility functions leave the measure unchanged. This is important because utility functions are unique only up to such transformations. Finally and most important, because all deals on the Pareto frontier are equally and maximally cooperative, no particular distribution of resources is established as the single optimal preferred distribution.

To examine this measure more deeply, however, we need to consider a structure that enables us to compare settlements off the frontier. To do that, we construct a simple stylized negotiating setting in which the distributive and cooperative issues are easily and completely separable.[6] In this negotiation, the two parties are trying to agree on the division of some collection of resources represented by a pile of chips. For simplicity, assume that side payments are not possible. In addition, assume that the parties have different capabilities, priorities, and values, so that they value the chips differently. In particular, assume that negotiator $X$'s utility for chips is linear and equal to $1 a chip, but that negotiator $Y$'s utility for $c$ chips is given by $\sqrt{c}$, a common risk-averse utility function.

How the negotiators divide the chips is a strictly distributive issue; furthermore, since we will allow fractions of chips, the division may be as refined as the negotiators like. To make this a mixed-motive negotiation, suppose there is a collection of rooms, each with a different number of chips, and that the negotiators must also pick the room in which to negotiate—and thus the pile of chips to divide. Suppose, further, that the room with the largest number of chips contains 100 chips, and that every other room contains a different, smaller number of chips. When thinking about this structure, it sometimes helps to think in terms of 10 rooms, each with a different multiple of 10 chips, and other times it helps to think about an infinity of rooms to make the negotiating structure continuous.

Thus, in this stylized negotiation there are two issues: the number of chips to be divided and the percentage division. The first issue is strictly congruent; the second, strictly distributive. Furthermore, the issues are independent in the sense that regardless of the division agreed upon, joint gains are always possible by moving to a room with more chips, even if the percentage distribution of chips is held fixed.

**Figure 21-2**
*Lax and Sebenius's Integrativeness Quotient: S Is Not Constant*

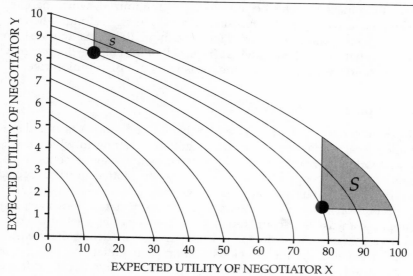

Because the only issue in any given room is strictly distributive, all deals struck in any particular room must be equally cooperative.

The Pareto frontier for this negotiation can be expressed as the function $y = \sqrt{100 - x}$, where $x$ and $y$ represent the respective negotiators' utilities. The utility-space representation of this negotiation is presented in Figure 21-2. In addition to the Pareto frontier, Figure 21-2 presents the "interior" frontiers for deals struck in several other rooms, and the areas $S$ for two deals struck in the room with 80 chips.

From the structure of the stylized negotiation, we know that any two deals struck in the same room are equally cooperative because the only issue in that room is distributive—who gets what percentage. Thus, just as all deals struck in the room with all 100 chips must be equally cooperative, so too must all deals struck in the room with 80 chips. But while the Lax and Sebenius measure does rate all deals for 100 chips as equally cooperative, it does not assign the same value to each deal for 80 chips. To see this, note that the two areas $S$ presented in Figure 21-2 do not have the same size. Thus, the measure differentiates among the set of deals for 80 chips, even though these deals differ only in their distributive component.

Furthermore, because the measure discriminates among these equally cooperative deals, it is possible to find the division that maximizes the measure. This occurs when $S$ is minimized, which happens when Y receives all of the resources. In fact, in this setting, whenever a deal is struck in a room with fewer than all 100 chips, the measure dictates that the settlement where Y gets all of the chips is the preferred allocation of resources. Thus, the measure is not distribution free.

### An Impossibility Theorem

To demonstrate that the Lax and Sebenius measure was not distribution free, we first constructed a negotiating setting in which it was easy to identify natural sets of equally cooperative agreements. These sets of equally cooperative agreements, when plotted in the expected utility-space representation of the negotiation, were represented by a collection of isocooperative curves. By its very nature, however, any proposed measure of cooperation must also result in a set of isocooperative curves. Indeed, in some sense, the curves define the measure and vice versa. In the previous section, a negotiation setting was constructed where the natural sets of isocooperative curves differed from the set of isocooperative curves defined by the measure.

As is easily seen from Figure 21-3, whenever these two sets of isocooperative curves are not identical they must intersect, and from the manner in which they intersect we can identify preferred distributions of resources.[7]

To prove that there cannot exist any measure of cooperation that works in every negotiating setting, we follow the same approach. We first construct two negotiation settings, with identical Pareto frontiers but distinct sets of isocooperative curves. Loosely, the argument then proceeds by noting that because the frontiers are identical, any measure of cooperation must treat the two settings identically, but because the natural sets of isocooperative curves differ, none can.

More formally, assume the existence of a measure of cooperation. Because the utility-space representations of the two negotiation settings are identical, the measure must apply to the two negotiations in exactly the same way. But the measure also establishes a set of isocooperative curves, and this set of curves can only agree with one of the distinct sets of isocooperative curves from the two negotiation settings. Therefore, it cannot be identical with both. As a result, in at least one of the two settings, the curves will intersect. Thus, the measure differentiates from among sets of equally cooperative settlements, thereby establishing preferred allocations of resources, proving that the measure cannot be distribution free. Thus, the supposition of the existence of

**Figure 21-3**

*Lax and Sebenius's Integrativeness Quotient: Intersecting
Sets of Isocooperative Curves*

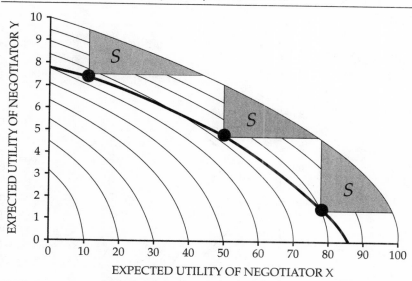

such a measure leads to a contradiction: no measure of cooperation can work in all negotiating settings.

To create the two negotiating structures, we add a second issue to the negotiation. Instead of dividing one pile of chips, suppose the negotiators must divide two piles of chips: a blue pile and a red pile. In both settings, the room with the most chips has 50 of each color. In setting one, the rooms have either only blue chips, or 50 blue chips and some red chips. In setting two, the opposite is true—each room has either only red chips, or 50 red chips and some blue chips.

Both negotiators' utilities for blue chips will be $1 apiece. To add asymmetry to the structure, suppose negotiator X's utility for red chips is $1 apiece, while negotiator Y's utility for red chips is $2 apiece.[8]

The Pareto frontiers, and hence the utility-space representations, of both negotiations are identical. Although these negotiations are not strictly distributive in each room (value is created whenever Y trades blue chips for red ones), it is still in the common interest of both negotiators to choose a room with more chips. More important, there are still natural, easily identified, well-defined sets of isocooperative curves. Moreover, the distributive and congruent issues are still inde-

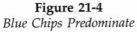

**Figure 21-4**
*Blue Chips Predominate*

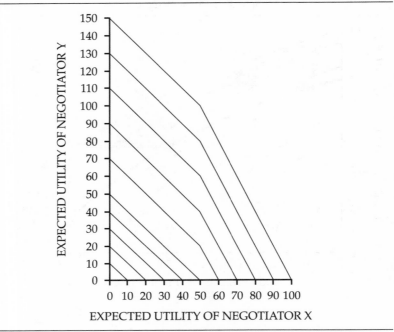

pendent in the sense that regardless of the agreed-upon division, joint gains are always possible by moving to a room with more chips, even if the percentage distributions of both types of chips are held fixed.

The utility representations of these negotiations, along with a series of isocooperative curves from a collection of alternate rooms, are presented in Figures 21-4 and 21-5. As the figures show, the Pareto frontiers are identical—the utility-space representations are the same. Nevertheless, by construction, the isocooperative curves are different. Therefore, no measure of cooperation can exist that is distribution free in both of these negotiating settings, as it is impossible for the isocooperative curves from any measure to agree with both sets of isocooperative curves.

### Implications for Future Research

The impossibility theorem does not show that it is impossible to construct a distribution-free measure of cooperation for particular negoti-

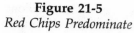

**Figure 21-5**
*Red Chips Predominate*

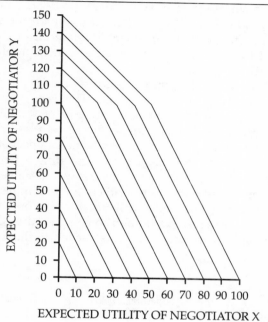

ating settings, only that it is impossible to construct one distribution-free measure for all negotiating settings. Indeed, for the stylized negotiations discussed in this paper, it is easy to identify distribution-free measures.

But, what does this mean for researchers who want to conduct experiments that measure the impact of changes in conditions on the ability of negotiators to be cooperative? There are two possibilities. First, one could drop the requirement that measures of cooperation be distribution free. This would mean that even joint profit would again become a feasible alternative, and once joint profit is allowed, one would have to accept conclusions about noncooperativeness based on nothing more than one party refusing to allow the other to have all of the resources. This would be unacceptable.

Second, one could insist on retaining the distribution-free requirement. This means that measures of cooperation must be specific to particular negotiation settings, or perhaps classes of settings. Finding a way to identify specific measures for particular settings will not be simple. Whatever mechanism or methodology is adopted will have to cope with the richness, structure, and complexity of the multi-dimensional spaces in which terms and conditions are defined and deals are struck. Clearly, no measure that is defined solely on the utility-space representation of negotiated agreements (as are all of the measures currently used by experimental researchers) can be applicable to all negotiation settings.

The good news is that all measures satisfying the Pareto condition must give rise to highly correlated results. This is so because all such measures must agree on how to rank any pair of settlements where one Pareto dominates the other. This, in fact, is why switching among measures of cooperation based on integrativeness appears to have little effect on the results and conclusions of negotiating experiments. The bad news, however, is that different measures will disagree, specifically when comparing settlements where neither Pareto dominates the other. That is, the experimental results will differ when our experimental methodologies become refined enough to compare those pairs of settlements for which a better measure was needed in the first place.

## NOTES

1. David A. Lax and James K. Sebenius, *The Manager as Negotiator* (New York: Free Press, 1986), p. 30.
2. In its simplest form, joint profit is the sum of the values received by the two parties. When we refer to joint profit, we mean its more general form: the sum of the expected utilities achieved by the two parties.
3. David A. Lax and James K. Sebenius, "Measuring the Degree of Joint Gains Achieved by Negotiators" (Harvard University, 1987); and Thomas M. Tripp and Harris Sondak, "An Evaluation of Dependent Variables in Experimental Negotiation Studies: Impasse Rates and Pareto Efficiency," *Organizational Behavior and Human Decision Processes* 51 (1992): 273–295. For a more complete discussion of these two measures, see Dana R. Clyman, "Measures of Joint Performance in Dyadic Mixed-Motive Negotiations," *Organizational Behavior and Human Decision Processes* 64 (October 1995): 38–48.
4. Tripp and Sondak, "An Evaluation of Dependent Variables in Experimental Negotiation Studies."
5. Many believe that when side payments are allowed, joint profit regains its lost status as the preferred measure of cooperation. This is not true. It is easy to demonstrate that even when side payments are allowed, joint profit is unlikely to provide a distribution-free measure of cooperation. Indeed, the only time joint profit is distribution free, except for pathological cases where the two parties have particular pairs of risk-averse and risk-seeking

utility functions (or particular pairs of utility functions that are mixtures of both), is when both parties share exactly the same linear utility function (up to translation by a constant). Even changes of scale, which do not affect preference orderings, cause joint-profit maximization to result in bargaining solutions with preferred resource distributions.

To see this, consider a simple negotiation over $N$ dollars (so whether side payments are allowed is irrelevant) and suppose both parties have non-risk-seeking utility functions $U$ and $V$ respectively—that is, the first derivatives are strictly positive and the second derivatives are never positive. Then, because a joint-profit maximizing agreement is a solution to the problem

$$Max \quad U(z) + V(N - z),$$
$$0 \leq z \leq N$$

we know from the first-order condition that the solution occurs where $U'(z) = V'(N - z)$. But we also know that if the measure is distribution free, then all choices of $z$ must be equally joint-profit maximizing. However, given the conditions on the first and second derivatives of the utility functions, this can only be true for all $z$ in $[0,N]$ if both first derivatives are equal to the same constant. Thus, not only must both utility functions be linear, they must be identical up to translation. Even changes in scale (positive affine transformations) result in particular optimal solutions (e.g., preferred distributions of resources).

6. David Bell's suggestion for this framing of the stylized negotiation is gratefully acknowledged.

7. The isocooperative line presented in Figure 21-3 for the Lax and Sebenius measure is representative only; it is not drawn to scale.

8. It is important to note that this construction was possible using only simple additive linear utility functions.

# CHAPTER 22

# SIGNALING IN NEGOTIATIONS

## Robert Wilson

Effective preparation for negotiation requires a combination of prescriptive and descriptive analyses—this is a central theme of Howard Raiffa's influential book *The Art and Science of Negotiation*.[1] Raiffa's prescriptive/descriptive approach is a main ingredient of negotiation analysis wherever it is taught or practiced. Its thesis is that effective analysis of one party's negotiation strategies from a normative perspective must be accompanied by good description of the other party's motives and likely strategies. In part, the intention is to avoid unrealistic predictions about the other's behavior.

Referring to the prescriptive aspects, Raiffa emphasizes that "there is no question as to the value of applying decision-theoretic concepts: analysis can help." The descriptive mode aims to improve predictions about the other party's behavior, such as responses to settlement proposals. Raiffa asks, "How could analysis be used to help one party in a competitive conflict situation without assuming excessive rationality on the part of the 'others?'" and concludes that, "The concepts of decision analysis seemed to me much more applicable than those of game theory" due to "the limitations of iterative, back-and-forth, gamelike thinking." This aversion to game-theoretic reasoning has, however, limited prescriptive/descriptive analyses of the role of signaling, which is important whenever the parties bring different information to a negotiation.

The important role of each party's private information is a latent

The preparation of this paper was supported by grants from the Hewlett Foundation and the National Science Foundation.

theme in Raiffa's book. For example, his exposition of analytical models focuses initially on the development of a probability assessment by one party of the other's reservation price—the prototypical example of private information. Informational effects deserve a more prominent role in the further development of the prescriptive/descriptive approach to negotiation analysis. In various kinds of disputes, such as litigation and wage negotiations, informational disparities provide the best explanation of the general patterns observed in the data. To substantiate this conclusion, I offer casual evidence from several contexts of bilateral bargaining over a wage or price. These examples suggest that implicit communication via credible signaling is a key part of many negotiations. It accounts in part for the familiar phenomenon that disputes are not resolved until sufficient revelation ripens the issues for settlement.

Of course, descriptive analysis addresses some aspects of private information. For example, it is often used to assess a probability distribution over the possible reservation prices of the other party. It can be used to interpret the signals provided by the other party's offers or delays, and to refine a probability assessment of that party's reservation prices. There remains, however, a central problem of negotiation analysis that has not been addressed by the prescriptive/descriptive approach: how to predict the effect of the signals that one's own offers and delays provide to the other party. The heart of this problem is predicting the interpretation and credibility of an intended signal. If a potential buyer wants to convey credibly that his reservation price is low, what offers, delays, or other behaviors provide probative demonstrations to the seller? Negotiation analysis requires a criterion to identify behaviors that signal credibly—in this case, behavior that provides evidence to the seller that dispels her conjecture that his reservation price might be high.

Game-theoretic models provide this criterion via incentive compatibility constraints. By confining attention to an equilibrium in which each party's strategy is a best response to the other's strategy, these models exclude inferences inconsistent with self-interested behavior. For instance, an equilibrium precludes the seller's inferring that the buyer's reservation price must be low if his observed behavior would also be profitable were his reservation price high. Thus, a credible signal that his reservation price is low must be a behavior that could not be profitably imitated if his reservation price were high.

As usually practiced, asymmetric prescriptive/descriptive analysis excludes this criterion by precluding the consideration of possible information that one party knows to be false (counterfactual) but the other party believes is likely. For this reason, the standard version of the prescriptive/descriptive approach is hard-pressed to handle the signaling that accompanies and ultimately dispels informational disparities. An additional dose of the modeling methods and the qualitative insights from game theory could remedy this. However, I do not argue here for the full application of game-theoretic methods. As Raiffa implies, in normative contexts it is often difficult for a client to accept the strong assumptions about common knowledge and rationality invoked by game theory, let alone the predictions derived from equilibria calculated from simplified models. Nevertheless, I think that prescriptive/descriptive analysis can be improved by considering counterfactuals and invoking criteria of incentive compatibility.

In this paper, I first review some examples that illustrate the relevance of private information and the important role of signaling to communicate credibly. I then suggest how the prescriptive/descriptive style of negotiation analysis can be amended to evaluate signaling strategies, and, in particular, to establish the conditions required for credibility.

## Examples

This section describes the role of private information in three prominent contexts: open-ended wage negotiations, binding final-offer arbitration, and litigation.

### Wage Negotiations

After the strike by the major league baseball players' association led to the cancellation of a portion of the 1994 season, a sportswriter wrote about the president of the San Francisco Giants club:

> As a fan, Peter Magowan was devastated when the plug was pulled on the baseball season yesterday. As a businessman, he thought it was inevitable and necessary. "We owners didn't have much credibility," he said. "The players simply didn't believe us when we told them we were feeling economic stress. . . ."[2]

This is a familiar lament by employers: the strike is regrettable but necessary. Management's view is that a strike is necessary to convince the union that the firm cannot afford to pay the wages demanded. On the other hand, union leaders rally members for the strike with visions of their fair share of the profits they think the firm is hiding. For instance, the baseball players' consultant concluded his review of the owners' financial condition with the statement that, "Baseball is financially healthy. . . . The claim of widespread disaster is pure fiction."[3]

Of course, not all negotiations are afflicted with distrust, and in long-term relationships it can be valuable to build and maintain a reputation for forthright disclosure. Nor do all bargaining impasses and strikes fit the scenario of the baseball strike. But from those that do, I conclude that signaling is an important ingredient.

The dispute often stems from the union's belief that the firm has profits sufficient to pay higher wages, which the firm denies. An examination of accounting data cannot dispel the union's hopes. Such historical data do not reveal crucial information, such as the marginal contribution of union workers, nor reveal the future, especially the profitability of the firm's other options—such as hiring replacement workers, reorganizing or moving operations, or investing elsewhere. For example, the tragic 1985–1986 Hormel strike occurred at a time of increased overall profitability for the firm, but also substantial wage cuts at competing plants. The firm argued that reductions in the prevailing industry wage justified concessions at Hormel's Austin plant, as well as the use of replacement workers if necessary.[4] Accounting data cannot reveal Hormel's estimates of its costs of hiring and training a new non-union workforce operating under new work rules. More generally, opening the books to the union usually reveals little about the firm's opportunity costs, which ultimately determine wage settlements.

Alternatively, a dispute may stem from a union's unrealistic view of the firm's patience for a favorable settlement, or more generally its willingness to bear short-term costs to obtain longer-term gains. Here again, there is little prospect that the firm can provide any documentary evidence of its patience. A willingness to sustain the costs of a strike is the only sure evidence of patience.

Such impasses are resolved through credible communication. Unfortunately, strikes or work-to-rule slowdowns are apparently the only communications that are credible. By enduring the cost of disrupted operations long enough, the firm signals credibly that it cannot afford the wage demanded by the union, or that it values long-term gains more than current costs. The failure to win concessions early convinces the union that its initial rosy conjectures about the firm's profitability, or impatience to settle, were mistaken.

Casual evidence that strikes are a means of credible communication can be seen in the pervasive regret expressed by both sides. After a settlement is reached, the firm deplores lost production and union members lament foregone wages, but both (and the local press) express sorrow and regret at the realization that the same contract could have been concluded initially, without the costs of a strike. What happened in the interim? The firm conveyed credibly to the union its valuation of the union's services. Having resolved that informational disparity, the parties could settle on a base wage.[5]

I imagine that the sense of tragedy is more acute for the firm. After all, it knew initially that the union's conjectures were unfounded; moreover, it is locked into fulfilling the union's expectation of the strike long enough to disprove the existence of hidden profits.

As evidence for this view of the role of signaling, I mention three statistical studies from a growing collection. First, David Card and John Kennan observe that a contract reached after a short strike is more likely to be followed by another strike than is a contract concluded after a long strike.[6] This is consistent with the view that the shortness of the previous strike revealed the firm's profit or impatience to be high, so that, presuming profitability or impatience tends to persist, the union has good reason to hope that another strike will again extract wage gains.

Second, Peter Cramton and Joseph Tracy observe that more than half the average delay in reaching settlements is due to non-strike in-plant holdout tactics such as work-to-rule slowdowns.[7] Provided the expired contract's wage is high enough, this is a good strategy because state labor laws require the firm to pay the previous wage until an impasse is reached. Cramton and Tracy show that data on wage disputes in the United States are explained well by a bargaining model that recognizes the union's option to choose between a holdout and a strike. The key feature of this model is the firm's signaling by sustaining the productivity losses imposed by a holdout or a strike. The model also explains the decline in strike incidence and the concomitant increase in holdouts since the 1981 strike by air traffic controllers, which effectively legitimized the hiring of permanent replacement workers.

Third, a natural experiment began in 1977 in Quebec (and later British Columbia, Manitoba, and Ontario), when the provincial legislature passed a law banning the hiring of replacement workers. Proponents argued that banning replacements would shorten strikes by forcing firms to bargain.[8] Actually, strikes have been more frequent and longer, and wage settlements higher. Cramton, Morley Gunderson, and Tracy estimate that the replacement ban increased strike incidence by 50 percent, duration by 37 percent, and wages by 12 percent, or 4.3 percent after controlling for the previous wage.[9] The wage increase over the contract period is five times greater than the union's increased strike costs, which provides some measure of the profitability of striking when the firm cannot replace the union.[10] Strategic models predict these consequences; the removal of firms' options to replace striking workers encourages more price discrimination by unions.

These studies support the view that many holdouts and strikes reflect a rational strategy of price discrimination by the union, especially if its monopsony is ensured by a ban on hiring replacements. By forcing the firm to bear productivity losses to justify low wages, the union can obtain higher wages from a more profitable firm impatient to settle quickly. For the firm, the essential ingredient of its negotiation strategy is signaling: enduring a strike to make credible its insistence on wages lower than those first demanded by the union. The credibility of this signal stems from the fact that a more profitable or impatient firm would find it advantageous to settle earlier rather than bear the costs of a long strike. Thus, it is the demonstration of endurance, bearing the strike long enough to avoid advantageous imitation by a more profitable or impatient firm, that confers credibility.

A peculiar feature of most strikes is that serious negotiations are deferred until near the end. Initial offers are rarely improved until some event transforms the situation to make it ripe for settlement. The signaling interpretation provides a plausible explanation of this phenomenon: the situation alters after a strike sufficient to exclude inaccurate conjectures by the union. A settlement can be reached only after the parties' assessments of what the firm can afford to pay converge sufficiently to leave the union's prospects for better terms too low to justify the costs of continuing the impasse.

In other cases, it is employers who learn about the unions during strikes. During the 1994 strike by university professors in Israel, the government was uncertain about the salaries professors would accept and how long they could sustain the strike. After an initial demand for 100 percent raises, and a government offer of 20 percent, the strike continued for eight weeks without serious negotiations. The professors' union explicitly avoided making a counteroffer. Then a vote at the Hebrew University revealed that a 98 percent majority favored continuing the strike. This vote precipitated negotiations that quickly reached an agreement to split the difference between the initial offers.[11] The vote transformed the situation by demonstrating the union's cohesion, resolve, and patience.

### Arbitration

The impact of transforming events can be seen also in wage negotiations subject to final-offer arbitration. In major league baseball up to 1994, if an eligible player's remuneration is not settled by a certain date, each party files a supposedly final offer. An arbitrator then selects one of the two proposals after a hearing. Over the years, about 25 percent of the bargaining pairs filed for a hearing. During the three weeks before the hearing, 80 percent of the filed cases were settled; thus, the total settlement rate was 95 percent.[12] Some arbitrators had no cases to hear.

The filing of final offers is a transforming event. Because there is little pressure in the off-season for serious negotiations until the filing date in January, the final offers typically represent the first credible signals about what the parties will accept. In addition to signaling the range over which agreement could occur, the offers establish the basis for an immediate agreement, and the choices available to the arbitrator. The revelation of the offers establishes a common informational basis on which to conclude a salary agreement. These signals are credible because an uncompromising offer is unlikely to be chosen by the arbitrator. Thus, the quasijudicial character of final-offer arbitration is possibly less important than the fact that it creates an explicit mechanism for credible signaling, and imposes a date by which the negotiation must be ripe for settlement.

### Litigation

Pretrial negotiations to settle civil litigation provide further examples of the key role of informational effects. As in arbitration, serious offers signal the range of feasible settlements. The design of offers, moreover, is affected strongly by the "winner's curse," which is familiar from studies of auctions. Each party bases its offer on a private estimate of the trial judgment, so each must take account of the risk that its settlement offer is more likely to be accepted if it has underestimated its prospects at trial. For instance, the plaintiff realizes that her offer is more likely to be accepted by the defendant when her estimate of the judgment is on the low side. Indeed, regret may follow acceptance; acceptance reveals that her estimate was probably low compared to the defendant's, and therefore the judgment would probably have been higher than she estimated initially—though now she will never know.

The process of discovery in litigation is a prime example of the role of informational disparities. Discovery is usually initiated by the plaintiff, because at trial she bears the burden of proof (say, of negligence). In response, the defendant may seek discovery to counter the plaintiff's claim (say, to establish contributory negligence by the plaintiff). However, these motives alone cannot explain the proliferation of discovery in commercial litigation. For present purposes, the main explanation is that discovery promotes settlement. That is, its cost is justified by the prospect that the results will enable the litigants to agree to withdraw the suit, thus avoiding the costs of trial. The prospects for settling are enhanced by discovery that reduces the disparity between the parties' assessments of the consequences of trial, or resolves conjectures about undisclosed damaging information.[13]

Some game-theoretic models of litigation predict that the likelihood of settlement increases in proportion to the precision of each party's estimate of the judgment. In particular, each party's benefit from additional discovery increases with the precision of the *other* party's estimate, because the terms of settlement are less favorable for the party with the less precise estimate.[14] Thus, discovery that increases one party's precision provides an expected savings in trial costs by increasing the prospects of settling, but it also encourages the other to redress the balance with its own discovery.[15] This process continues until for each party the costs of further discovery are not justified by the additional savings in expected trial costs—whereupon the dispute is ripe for settlement negotiations.

Steven Shavell has shown that voluntary disclosure (or acquiescence to discovery) has an important signaling role that affects settlement negotiations.[16] Failure to disclose supports the other's inference that unfavorable information is being withheld, and thereby encourages less favorable settlement offers and increases the risk of a costly trial. Consequently, each party has an incentive to disclose information that is credible prima facie. Enforced discovery is therefore relevant mainly when credible disclosure is infeasible. For example, a claim that "these are copies of all the documents in my files relevant to this suit" may lack credibility because only an exhaustive search of the files can verify the truth of such a claim; in contrast, disclosure of a receipt for a purchase removes essentially all doubt about the nature and amount of the purchase.

## Signaling and the Role of Counterfactuals

These examples suggest two features that the prescriptive/descriptive style of negotiation analysis should include. The first is the pervasive role of signaling, in which one party tries to convince the other of what it knows to be true, via inferences from observable actions that derive their credibility from the observer's consideration of the actor's incentives. The second is that substantial progress in negotiation often depends on the dispute's ripeness for settlement. Ripeness can result from the conclusion of some information-acquisition phase, or a signaling phase that requires delay to sustain credibility, or serious offers that directly reveal the basis for settlement. Occasionally, ripeness can be precipitated by a deadline or an escalation in the cost of continued delay, but even so, the potential gain from continuing the impasse diminishes as communication and learning progress. In any case, negotiations tend to have an initial phase focused on exchanging private information in a credible fashion, followed by a phase that fixes the terms of trade. If delay is the only credible means of signaling then the initial phase can be long relative to the concluding phase; similarly, if the initial phase is devoted to discovery then it can be long and expensive, at least until the prospective gains outweigh the costs.

These conclusions contradict Ariel Rubinstein's seminal model of bargaining, in which the prevalent mode is alternation of serious offers, or a series of serious offers from one side to accomplish price discrimination, in the fashion of the proverbial Moroccan bazaar.[17] At least in the case of strikes, the empirical evidence refutes this scenario. The "Coase property" of bargaining games with alternating offers established by Faruk Gul and Hugo Sonnenschein explains why: the union's expected wage gains are small unless it can sustain long intervals between its offers.[18] If it is to garner a substantial wage premium, the union must impose a significant penalty on the firm for rejecting an offer, and this penalty is a costly delay before a better offer is proposed. My guess is that union leaders would find it difficult to sustain members' morale with the argument that "we must punish them for yesterday's rejection by waiting another month before improving our offer." The more plausible tactic is to sustain a strike until the firm proves that its profitability is as low as it claims, and then split the pie evenly.[19]

In the empirical studies of strikes by Cramton and Tracy, the best explanation for the data is that signaling is the dominant mode. To this I add the casual evidence that there is a notable absence of continually improving offers in journalistic accounts. For instance, each side hardly budged from its initial demands during the 1994 baseball strike during the five weeks before the cancellation of the remainder of the season.

The asymmetric, normative style of prescriptive/descriptive analysis can address these features by taking account of incentive compatibility considerations. To do so requires expanding the formulation to include analyses of contingencies that the client knows to be false. Prescriptive approaches have usually avoided this game-theoretic approach. Yet some amendment of this kind is necessary if prescriptive approaches are to capture the elements of signaling that are central to many negotiations. Because delay is one of the most costly and prevalent forms of signaling, it provides a useful illustration of how to amend the prescriptive/descriptive approach.

To illustrate, I use the example of the strike described previously, and suppose that the firm is the decision analyst's client. I suppose that the firm wants to achieve a fair settlement after dispelling the union's unrealistic conjectures about the feasibility of a high wage. I envision the penultimate stage of the strike as a dialogue in which the firm's negotiator presents not an offer, but a line of argument:

> I recognize that this strike has been hard on your members and their families, and they are disappointed—and some are embittered or angry. It has been costly for the firm too, and that is what I want to talk with you about. I ask you to recognize that if your claims were true, our shareholders would have been better off if we had quickly negotiated a settlement based on your initial demand. We did not do that; we've borne our share of the costs of the strike. We knew we had to, to dispel your hope that we might be sufficiently profitable to be impatient to settle. Otherwise, we'd only reinforce your initial beliefs and you'd have every reason to reiterate your initial demand. We think it's time for you to recognize that we have done what was necessary to demonstrate that we can't afford such high wages. I hope you will conclude now that those claims were unrealistic, that they have been disproved by our willingness to sustain the costs of the strike. If you do, then we can agree on a wage that fairly divides the pie that is really there, rather than the one that now we both know is not there.

This particular speech might not be effective, and probably no strike ends with the degree of mutual trust it implies, yet its ingredients are essential to a resolution of the strike. The argument is that the union's claim is disproved by actions of the firm that would injure its self-interest were the union's claim true. The substance of this argument is incentive compatibility: the firm's professed motivations are compatible with its actions. The union's reasonable inferences from the observed actions dispel those conjectures which, if true, imply actions different from those observed. A further essential requirement is that the firm could not otherwise profit from imitating the observed actions.

The full apparatus of game theory is not required to construct such an argument. Prescriptive/descriptive analysis can accommodate a similar argument if it examines the counterfactual situation that the union's claim is true, and undertakes a decision-theoretic analysis of the firm's strategy for that case too. To do this, the formulation must include false "types" of the client that the other party might consider likely. In addition, the strategy of each type must be incentive compatible, so that no type could gain by imitating another type.[20] This

**Table 22-1**
*Payoffs to the Firm*

| Type | Strategy | Payoff |
|------|----------|--------|
| High | High Wage, Early Settlement | 4 |
|      | Low Wage, Later Settlement | $6 - 2T$ |
| Low  | High Wage, Early Settlement | 0 |
|      | Low Wage, Later Settlement | $2 - T$ |

constraint assures the credibility of signals: in making inferences from observed actions, one can safely ignore the possibility of self-serving deception.

To illustrate, suppose there are two types of the firm corresponding to low and high profitability, and that each type has two feasible strategies, one that aims for a high wage early, and another that aims for a low wage later. If delay is costly in some proportion to profitability, and "later" is late enough, then the high-profit firm prefers the high wage early, whereas the low-profit firm prefers the low wage later. These differing strategies for the two types are feasible if the union can infer from the differing preferences of the two types that it is not being deceived into accepting a low wage from a high-profit firm. This conclusion fails if "later" is not late enough, for then the high-profit firm incurs insufficient costs during the strike to keep it from seeking the low wage later, in effect imitating the low-profit firm. In this case, the union need not be convinced to forego its demand for the high wage. Thus, incentive compatibility requires that the strike borne by the low-profit firm is long enough to convince the union that its type is not high-profit.

This construction strips away most of the usual game-theoretic equilibrium analysis, but preserves the role of counterfactual types. On the presumption that the settlement of the dispute depends ultimately on establishing a common informational basis for an agreement, it enforces the minimal requirement of incentive compatibility to ensure that the types are ultimately revealed by their actions.

A numerical example is shown in Table 22-1, which shows the payoffs to the firm depending on its type and strategy, where $T$ represents the duration of a strike. These payoffs are presumably derived from a strategy of the union that reflects a willingness to accept a low wage only after receiving convincing evidence that the firm's profits are really low. In particular, the union initially assigns a sufficiently high probability to the prospect that the firm's profits are high to justify a strike. For a strike to provide convincing evidence to the union, the duration must satisfy the incentive-compatibility constraint ensuring that the firm's High type prefers the High Wage, Early Settlement strategy; that is, $4 > 6 - 2T$, or $T > 1$. In turn, this requires the firm's Low type to endure a strike of duration greater than 1 to convince the union to accept the low wage. The union's preference for a higher wage whatever the duration rules out other strategies for the firm, such as Low Wage, Early Settlement (corresponding to $T < 1$); the union interprets an early low offer as uninformative because both types of the firm prefer this outcome, so it renews the strike in an attempt to gain the high wage. Thus, when the client's type is Low, consideration of the counterfactual case that its type is High introduces the constraint $T > 1$ on the strategies that are feasible. These are the only strategies the Low type can expect to implement with the concurrence of the union. An argument from the firm at $T = 1/2$ to the effect that "let's stop this nonsense and settle now; there's no sense waiting further" is not credible, because this argument could be imitated profitably by the High type.

This formulation does not invoke the strong assumptions required by the full game-theoretic analysis of negotiation, and it avoids the "iterative, back-and-forth, gamelike thinking" involved in equilibrium reasoning that Raiffa found impractical. Its advantage, from the pragmatic perspective that motivates asymmetric prescriptive/descriptive analysis, is its incorporation of some of the key qualitative insights about the role of signaling when there are informational disparities. Its basic premise is that differences in information must be reduced to enable a settlement, and this requires that actions credibly signal each party's private information that cannot be verified otherwise. Credibility is ensured by enforcing incentive compatibility for all types considered likely by the other party, including those contrary to the facts known by the client. Ultimately, incentive compatibility constrains the set of feasible strategies for the client's true type.

Thus amended, prescriptive/descriptive analysis could be useful also in final-offer arbitration and litigation. I do not develop them in detail here, but briefly sketch the arbitration case. A piece of each party's strategy is a specification of the final offer to be filed if prefiling negotiations fail. Recognizing that this will be a crucial signal affecting subsequent negotiations between the filing and the hearing, it is important to predict how it will be interpreted by the other party. In particular, each party must ask, "What is the estimate of my reservation price that the other party will infer from my filed offer?" This question can be addressed by examining a range of possible reservation prices (types) that includes the true one, and by imposing incentive-compatibility constraints on the strategies used by these various types. Based on a supposition that the other party will infer correctly and settle, say, for a split-the-difference deal whenever gains from the trade exist, this construction identifies for each type an optimal relationship between the reservation price and the corresponding offer filed. In particular, it specifies the offer that the true type should file, and predicts that this offer will enable the other party to infer the true type.

While this construction requires elaborate calculations and resembles the analogous game-theoretic construction—both of which are anathema to practitioners of the standard prescriptive/descriptive analysis—something of this kind seems essential to unraveling the implications of offers that signal information relevant to negotiations.

## NOTES

1. Howard Raiffa, *The Art and Science of Negotiation* (Cambridge, MA: Harvard University Press, 1982).
2. Glenn Dickey, *San Francisco Chronicle*, September 15, 1994, p. B1.
3. Roger Noll, quoted in the *Wall Street Journal*, September 15, 1994, p. A10.
4. The Hormel strike is portrayed in Barbara Kopple's Oscar-winning documentary film *The American Dream*, Miramax Films, 1991. The film describes the plight of hundreds of union workers who lost their jobs after a largely fruitless strike.
5. One might argue to the contrary—that any failed strategy or acquiescence to a compromise is likely to engender regret from both parties. However, I presume that some communication and learning took place; otherwise, the parties could have predicted the outcome of a protracted struggle, and would have elected to settle quickly.
6. David Card, "Strikes and Wages: A Test of an Asymmetric Information Model," *Quarterly Journal of Economics* 105 (1990): 625–659; David Card, "Strikes and Bargaining: A Survey of the Recent Empirical Literature," *American Economic Review* 80 (1990): 410–415; and John Kennan, "Repeated Contract Negotiations with Persistent Private Information," Department of Economics, University of Wisconsin, 1994.
7. Peter Cramton and Joseph Tracy, "Strikes and Holdouts in Wage Bargaining: Theory and Data," *American Economic Review* 82 (1992): 100–121; Peter Cramton and Joseph Tracy, "The Determinants of U.S. Labor Disputes," *Journal of Labor Economics* 12 (1994): 180–209; and Peter Cramton and Joseph Tracy, "Wage Bargaining with Time-Varying Threats," *Journal of Labor Economics* 12 (1994): 594–617.
8. Proponents also argued that a ban would reduce violence on picket lines.
9. Peter Cramton, Morley Gunderson, and Joseph Tracy, "The Effect of Col-

lective Bargaining Legislation on Strikes and Wages" (Economics Department, University of Maryland, 1994).

10. A ban on permanent replacements was defeated in the 1994 Congress only by a threatened filibuster in the Senate. Cramton and Tracy use U.S. data to estimate that a ban on replacements would increase strike incidence by a third. See Peter Cramton and Joseph Tracy, "The Use of Replacement Workers in Union Contract Negotiations: The U.S. Experience 1980–1989" (Economics Department, University of Maryland, 1993).

11. It took three more months to iron out the details of the final agreement, which allowed greater increases for younger faculty.

12. The implications of this statistic are surprising; it indicates that gains from trade were positive in nearly all cases. This runs counter to the view that final-offer arbitration is costly to the employer, who presumably is sometimes forced by the arbitrator's decision to pay wages above his reservation value. In the baseball strike, this consideration was presumably a factor in the owners' demand to abolish arbitration. On the other hand, after arbitration the owner still has options to trade the player to another team. Moreover, the occasional cost of excessive wages is offset by the savings in the costs of holdouts and strikes without arbitration.

13. Discovery can also aid the construction of trial arguments, but under the new rules of civil procedure adopted by most federal courts, each party is obligated to disclose voluntarily all information that is potentially useful to the other party's argument at trial.

14. For instance, in the extreme case that the defendant knows the judgment perfectly, the plaintiff cannot do better than make a single take-it-or-leave-it offer that leaves the residual surplus to the defendant if he accepts it.

15. An empirical study of discovery that emphasizes the recurrent leader-follower pattern of discovery by the plaintiff and defendant is by George Shepherd, "The Economics of Pretrial Discovery: An Empirical Study" (Department of Economics, Stanford University, 1994).

16. Steven Shavell, "The Sharing of Information Prior to Settlement or Litigation," *RAND Journal of Economics* 20 (1989): 183–195.

17. Ariel Rubinstein, "Perfect Equilibrium in a Bargaining Model," *Econometrica* 50 (1982): 97–110.

18. Faruk Gul and Hugo Sonnenschein, "On Delay in Bargaining with One-Sided Uncertainty," *Econometrica* 56 (1988): 601–612.

19. Such tactics are often accompanied by "cheap talk," such as claims that the other side is not bargaining in good faith; indeed, labor laws typically impose requirements for good-faith bargaining, but this does not obviate the prevalent absence of serious offers.

20. This is just the revelation principle used in many game-theoretic applications based on separating equilibria.

# PART 4

# The Art and Science of Howard Raiffa

# CHAPTER 23

# The Art and Science of Howard Raiffa

## Irving H. LaValle

Howard Raiffa possesses the very rare ability to assimilate large fields of study, extract the prescriptively useful concepts, augment them as necessary, and communicate his synthesis to a wide audience. The effectiveness of his individually and jointly authored publications is perhaps best judged by noting that few people called themselves "decision analysts" before 1968, while many do now, and that the asymmetrically prescriptive approach to strategically fraught decision situations now generally known as "negotiation analysis" was neither respectable nor cohesive before 1982. Raiffa's *Decision Analysis* (**R68** hereafter) and *The Art and Science of Negotiation* (**R82a**) have inspired many to make better decisions and deals and to improve their effectiveness in helping others to do the same.[1]

Raiffa's 1957 book *Games and Decisions*, written with R. Duncan Luce, made the central concepts of game and individual decision theories accessible to many social scientists for the first time, and also inspired advances in game theory through its penetrating critique of extant solution concepts. *Applied Statistical Decision Theory*, with Robert Schlaifer, and *Introduction to Statistical Decision Theory*, with John W. Pratt and Robert Schlaifer, were the first books to present complete Bayesian statistical decision theoretic treatments of many of the core problems of statistical inference—with, it is regrettable to note, a some-

Valuable advice from Ralph L. Keeney, Arthur Schleifer, Jr., and a referee is gratefully acknowledged.

what less dramatic effect upon statistical practice than the previously mentioned works had upon their intended audiences. The 1976 *Decisions with Multiple Objectives: Preferences and Value Tradeoffs,* with Ralph L. Keeney, made a convincing case for the practicality of formal analyses using multi-attribute utility functions of simplified structures that are implied by various frequently pertinent "utility-independence" assumptions.

The next section attempts to extract the kernel of the Raiffa philosophy and the Raiffa message, with reference to the evolution of the sorts of problems on which he has focused his attention. If this kernel and its evolution constitute the "Theorem," then the survey of publications in the third section is the "Proof." This section considers Raiffa's work in six areas: mostly game theory; statistical decision theory; foundations of choice under uncertainty; utility and MAU; general issues in decision analysis; and negotiation analysis. The reader is presumed to have some acquaintanceship with the basic concepts of game theory, statistical decision theory, decision analysis, and multi-attribute utility. The fourth section concludes with some observations on Raiffa's writing style and his approach to new problems. The references for this paper are divided into two parts. The first consists of publications by Raiffa and coauthors, arranged chronologically. The second consists of works in which Raiffa does not appear as an author; it is arranged alphabetically by first author.

This chapter focuses on Raiffa's publications, but we should not ignore his many other scholarly contributions. One is his parental role in the establishment of the International Institute for Applied Systems Analysis (IIASA), which has supported the work of scholars from many nations. A second consists of several unpublished working papers, NSF committee reports, and congressional testimony transcripts on issues in public-risk assessment. Among these are **R80**, **R82b**, and **GRV83**, which, together with **KR72** and **RSW77**, could be reworked as a fine text on policy analysis.

Another very major contribution has been his role as mentor to numerous doctoral students. Raiffa has been exceptionally generous with his ideas and his time. Seeing him on short notice was never a problem, and he gave his complete attention and participation to his students' intellectual struggles. In due course, he assisted with good placements and, unlike most mentors, refused coauthorship of publications based on the dissertation. This generous and modest refusal, together with his insistence on alphabetical listing of his coauthors, makes it impossible ever to take a complete inventory of Raiffa's original ideas. Only glimpses appear, typically in footnotes, of his role in the work of others.

Richard Feynman wrote in 1950 that he felt obligated to know the solvability of a problem before turning a Ph.D. student loose on it, and cited "the old saying that 'a Ph.D. thesis is research done by a professor under particularly trying circumstances.'"[2] Since this view is appropriate for theoretical topics in our field, and to an only somewhat lesser degree for empirical ones, it is reasonable to infer that Raiffa at least suspected the shape of the answers that his questions would elicit. Thus it is reasonable to impute a sliver of Raiffa in the dissertation-based early contributions of most of his students.

Raiffa has had a significant effect on others' students at Harvard and elsewhere and on more mature scholars through his public lectures and private communications. Not every lecture has become a book, as were those in 1964 that led to **R68** and in 1980 that led to **R82a**, but the engaging nature of a Raiffa lecture ensures that, in an audience of any reasonable size, at least one person leaves with the resolve to mend erroneous ways of thinking.

As his student in the early mid-1960s, it was my impression that Raiffa was much consulted by colleagues in other areas. I attribute this in part to his exceptional communication skills, and in part to his engagingly inquisitive open-mindedness. These same qualities cause him to be much in demand for discussions at professional meetings.

## The Raiffa Message and Its Evolution

Stripped of all slippery normative/prescriptive/descriptive terminology, the Raiffa message is: unless one is an exceptionally good holistic thinker, some systematic analysis can be of considerable help in making better decisions and in striking better bargains. Such analysis does not require superhuman rationality. It rests on certain principles of consistent behavior that most people find perfectly reasonable in the simple contexts in which they are asked to evaluate them. It calls upon them to constructively supply their own preferences and their own judgments, so that the resulting implications for action are ones that are good according to their own lights. And Raiffa warns of the common cognitive traps, such as overconfidence in quantifying judgments (**AR80**) and too-hasty overweighting of anticipated feelings such as regret (**R85a**). The analytical framework is broad enough to deliver on the claim that, if something matters to one, it *can* and it *should* be taken systematically into account. In the realm of negotiations, it implies that one should make a real effort to see things from the other parties' points of view and interests, one should seek ways to enlarge the pie at least as much as one strives to attain a goodly share of it, one should never neglect the linkages of the present situation with other current and future situations (the reputation you save may be your own), and one should explore mutually beneficial ways of utilizing outside parties as mediators or arbitrators, all the while keeping in mind the observed realities of how people actually behave in negotiation settings.

This is an oversimplification. **BRT88b** is indispensable reading on the nuances of descriptive, normative, and prescriptive approaches, and, as Tversky is recorded on page 2 of **BRT88a** as maintaining, suitable clarification of the normative category would obviate the prescriptive. In recent years, much controversy has arisen concerning these and related terms.[3] Some confusion may be due to a failure to distinguish between an *approach* and a *theory* or *model*. At the level of approach, it is true that game theorists and economists are interested in the implied behavior of superhumanly intelligent agents, usually in order to establish an ideal against which to measure the approximating behavior of mortals. This would qualify as a "normative" approach. Also at the level of approach, many scholars are concerned with actual choice behavior. This is "descriptive." And many in academe and elsewhere apply and develop methods intended to be used by real people, constructively, to help them make those rare choices that merit painstaking consideration. This is "prescriptive" in approach, but often labeled "normative" because the predominant strain is grounded in the subjective-expected-utility (SEU) model of choice under uncertainty, considered as having been first axiomatized by Ramsey (1931) and, independently, by Savage (1954).

Much of the confusion about the normative/prescriptive (as a single category) versus the descriptive may arise from a tendency to label any "mathematical model" of the choice problem—not to mention any *axiomatic* derivation of a representation model from preference as a primitive—as normative. Howard (1988) relates how his students have confused the descriptive virtues of prospect theory with normative superiority.[4] Aside from the motivations of its creator or creators, a theory stands on its own feet, and you can make of it what you will. The descriptive usefulness of a choice model is determined by empirical testing. Its prescriptive usefulness is judged partly by one's agreement in principle to conform to its axioms or constraints, and partly by the model's ability to accommodate all pertinent preferences and judgments in a framework that is intuitively meaningful and leads to clarity of ultimate choice.

The origins of Raiffa's prescriptive orientation are perhaps best sketched in the prologue of **R82a**, in which he describes how his interest in the *externally prescriptive* arbitration approach to non-zero-sum games was kindled by a lecture on labor arbitrations. The result was his dissertation (**R51**) and **R53**, which contributed one of the earliest solution concepts for cooperative games. The penetrating critiques in **LR57** of various axioms of cooperative behavior, the careful demonstration of nonequivalence and noninterchangeability of Nash equilibria except in two-person zero-sum games, and the painstaking development of axioms for individual decision making, all reflect a great respect for the applicability of theory, even though he disclaims interest in applications at that time. In **R88**, Raiffa describes himself as a "closet Bayesian" during his years at Columbia, intellectually accepting SEU but not emotionally compelled by it; this changed after he came to Harvard in 1957 and met Robert Schlaifer, who had independently developed, for Schlaifer (1959), the foundations of SEU without knowledge of the work of Savage. Collaboration with Schlaifer, and then also with John Pratt, followed and resulted in **RS61** and **PRS65**.

Compared to game theory, the statistical decision problems on which Raiffa concentrated his attention around 1961 are very clean. The prototypical sampling problem concerns obtaining information about a state of nature $\tilde{\theta}$ that takes a "disinterested" form such as market demand, fraction defective, or crude-oil content. Most (but not all) such problems are small enough that one need not worry excessively about risk aversion or linkages with other decisions under uncertainty. **RS61** takes von Neumann–Morgenstern (1944) utility as given and devotes most of its space to developing useful models for optimally treating several of the most common problems in statistics in common sampling contexts. Natural-conjugate distributions for $\tilde{\theta}$ made updating prior judgments easy when computation was laborious and expensive. And the notation, while complex, is remarkably denotive: clearly, $\tilde{\omega}''$ denotes the (prior) expectation of posterior variance.

It was during this period that the very constructive joint axiomatization of utility and subjective probability (**PRS64**, and Chapters 3 and 8 of **PRS65**) was developed. This work evinces a prescriptive orientation in not presuming completeness, and in making explicit the calibration lotteries appearing only implicitly in Savage's (1954) axiomatization.

It was also during this period that Raiffa's attention was increasingly called to decisions under uncertainty that lacked a primarily statistical focus. Grayson (1960) and Christenson (1965) were concerned with decisions in oil exploration and competitive bidding contexts. Problems of risk sharing addressed by Wilson (1968) and others in the context of group decisions were broached in a 1961 seminar in which Raiffa credits himself with having asked the right questions. Many of these topics are lucidly introduced in **R68**. The prefaces to all these books indicate a clear commitment to the prescriptive approach. It is fair to say that the theme has not changed, but it has been played increasingly artfully over time.

In 1964, Raiffa became more actively interested in developing the asymmetrically prescriptive approach broached in **LR57** to interactive (not to say competitive) decision situations. A principal feature of such situations is the mutual interestedness of the participants and the potential for infinite regress as each tries to second-guess the others' judgments about their judgments.[5]

According to **R88**, Raiffa's association with the Kennedy School sparked his interest in what has come to be known as multi-attribute utility (MAU). **R69**, work with Ralph Keeney, and **KR76** were the results. The effect of **KR76** in summarizing the substantial extant body of MAU material and illustrating the pertinence and practical useful-ness of MAU structurings under various independence assumptions is hard to overestimate. This work is also prescriptive: far fewer assess-ments are required when, say, utility may be assumed expressible in the additive form $u(x_1, ..., x_n) = \sum_{i=1}^{n}\lambda_i u_i(x_i)$ derived by Fishburn (1965), with only one more assessment required for the multiplicative form.

The substantial negotiations content of his work as first managing director of IIASA rekindled Raiffa's interest in negotiations and in the asymmetrically prescriptive approach to games that has come to be called negotiation analysis, the title of the preliminary draft of **R82a**. As Sebenius (1992) notes, one can view negotiation analysis as "deci-sion analysis plus" or as "game theory minus." The descriptive, be-havioral treatment of the other parties in a negotiation that is charac-teristic of negotiation analysis, and the experiments Raiffa performed along the way to **R82a**, led to a deepening of his interest in behavioral choice phenomena and the publications **BRT88a** and **R85a**, in which feelings of regret, elation, and disappointment are allowed to constitute attributes that affect preferences, provided that they are to be evaluated carefully.

With some cautions about the desirability of leaving good holistic choosers alone and about the difficulty of separating preference from judgment, Raiffa has not discernibly strayed from allegiance to SEU as the normative framework upon which to weave prescriptive advice. His as-yet unpublished work is unlikely to prove surprising in this regard.

## Survey of Raiffa's Publications

In this section, Raiffa's publications are discussed in six topic-area subsections that roughly correspond to the chronological evolution of his scholarly activities and interests.

## Mostly Game Theory

In this subsection we examine **CRT54** and **MRTT53** briefly, and **R53** and **LR57** somewhat less briefly, with a comment on **R51**. **CRT54** is an early exposition of the representational theory of measurement for relations such as preference that, in 1954, was still in its infancy.[6] Measurement theory includes the familiar taxonomy of nominal, ordinal, interval, and ratio scales identified by Stevens (1946) as well as the ordinal and cardinal utility familiar to economists and decision theorists. With an eye toward introducing Hausner (1954) in the same volume, **CRT54** leads up to linear lexicographic utility scaling, and then to von Neumann–Morgenstern utility. The authors admit that their individual efforts may be identifiable in places. It is of interest to speculate as to who illustrated the nontransitivity of "loves" by writing, "We cannot conclude from $a$ loves $b$ and $b$ loves $c$ that $a$ loves $c$, or that $b$ loves $a$, or that $b$ does not love $a$. For example, if John loves Mary and if Mary loves Peter, it may well be that, far from loving him, John would like to see Peter transported to the south pole" (p. 29).

    **MRTT53** introduces the "double description method" for solving two-person zero-sum games and linear programs. The basic idea is that each vertex $x$ of the (evolving) maximum envelope is described both by its coordinates in $\mathbb{R}^n$ and by the hyperplanes of which it is the common intersection. This leads to some efficiency in testing whether as-yet unaddressed hyperplanes can affect provisional (maximin) game value; see Appendix A1 in **LR57** for an exposition. As an algorithm, the double-description method does not seem to have found a niche vis-à-vis the simplex method, but its bookkeeping may be related to that which is associated with the apparently hard problem of characterizing the boundary facets of the convex hull of a finite set of points in $\mathbb{R}^n$.[7]

    **R53**, based on Raiffa's dissertation, **R51**, introduces the *externally prescriptive* arbitration approach as a distinct orientation for evaluating solution concepts in two-person game situations. It identifies an arbitration scheme with a rule $T$ for mapping status quo points $v = (v_1, v_2)$ to arbitrated, cooperative-game solutions $T(v)$ in the convex hull $H$ of the set of utility pairs corresponding to the two players' choices of pure strategies. There are two main parts to **R53**. The first, and apparently less well recognized, concerns taking $T$ as given and using it to determine the status quo point $v$ by solving the "threat" game of strictly opposing interests. This approach is more commonly associated with Nash (1953), but Raiffa shows that interchangeable and equivalent equilibria in the induced threat game obtain for a far broader class of transformations $T$ than Nash's, since it is only necessary that $T(v)$ be

Pareto-efficient, $T(v) \geqq v$, $T(\cdot)$ be continuous, and $\{v: T(v) = t\}$ be convex for all $t$. The last condition allows one to invoke the Kakutani Fixed-Point Theorem.[8]

The second main part of **R53** exhibits several definitions of arbitration schemes $T$ that satisfy individual rationality, Pareto efficiency (as noted), symmetry as regards player identities, irrelevance of pure-strategy labeling, and a stability condition (his third) that is motivated by prescriptive considerations that foreshadow the orientation of **R82a**. He writes, "If a slight perturbation of the payoff entries would result in a drastic change in the arbitrated solution, then the convention would not be stable enough to be practical. After all, payoff entries are at best only hazy appraisals of the possible terminal outcomes of the game" (p. 374).

One more condition (his fifth) concerns solution invariance with respect to transformations of players' utilities, and comes in two forms to apply to the cases in which interpersonal comparisons of utility are or are not meaningful. For the meaningless case, **R53** exhibits a $T$ that is in fact Nash's (1953) cooperative solution, although it is clear that other definitions of $T$ are possible and would satisfy the stipulated conditions, or "desiderata," a favorite Raiffa word that appears for the first time on page 381. For the case of meaningful interpersonal comparisons, **R53** exhibits arbitration schemes $T$ that are particularly simple to use directly, whether utility is transferable (via side payments) or not.

For details of these arbitration schemes, and others not discussed in **R53**, Sections 6.10 and 6.11 of **LR57** cannot be improved upon. A major concern in such arbitration schemes is how to establish an ad hoc but appropriate interpersonal comparison by using the game's definition. Raiffa's preferred method is to rescale utilities so that the worst and best possible outcomes for a player have transformed utilities 0 and 1 respectively. All arbitration schemes that use an interpersonal comparison of utility appear to violate the independence-of-irrelevant-alternatives condition.

**R53** concludes with the differential-equation, nonlinear arbitration scheme the linearization of which coincides with Nash's cooperative solution. The motivation for this is discussed on pages 343–344 of **R82a**, where the scheme is called the "balanced-increments solution." A technical problem is raised by the nonconvexity of $\{v: T(v) = t\}$ and resulting inapplicability of the Kakutani Fixed-Point Theorem to the induced threat game, as Raiffa recognizes. This problem and the identification of other appealing and amenable arbitration schemes $T$ deserve further attention.

**LR57** was the first book on game theory that was accessible to individuals with mathematical tolerance but not much training. Through its careful exposition and painstaking critique, it communicates the central approach, concepts, and findings of game theory to social scientists, while calling the attention of game theorists to various gaps that could be profitably filled. As the preface (p. viii) explains, "our aim is to warn and challenge the reader at just those points where the theory is conceptually weak."

Through this book, Luce and Raiffa furnished fuel to a generation of scholars. For example, Aumann and Maschler (1964) cite **LR57** repeatedly in developing their theory of bargaining sets (sets of utility allocations with the property that every "objection" has a "counterobjection"); and Harsanyi (1977, p. 243) argues that his modified Shapley value remedies the finding (**LR57**, pp. 140, 252) that the unmodified Shapley value is insensitive to threat potential.

**LR57** is generally credited with doing an exceptional job of identifying the big issues of game theory at the time. Besides those already mentioned, three others are particularly important. One concerns how to approach $n$-person cooperative theory when utility is not transferable: how does one go about defining the characteristic function? As a set of utility allocations.[9] A second concerns the nonequivalence and noninterchangeability of Nash equilibria in noncooperative games. Over the past two decades, a large number of "equilibrium refinements" have been defined with the objective of declaring that one equilibrium is better than others.[10] But is the refinement game worth the candle? The non-optimistic views of an active refiner are expressed in Chapters 12 and 13 of Kreps (1990). The third big issue is how to handle games of incomplete information, which led to Harsanyi's (1967–1968) formulation in terms of player types with a common prior distribution over the type profiles, this prior distribution being common knowledge.[11]

For its time, **LR57** devoted an unusual amount of space to two-person non-zero-sum games, and to many different approaches to solution concepts for $n$-person games that explicitly envision the formation of nontrivial coalitions. Luce's $\psi$-stability theory appears prominently; it imposes constraints on the coalitions that can form given a current partition of the player set into coalitions. The "coalitional naivete" of Nash equilibrium for $n$-person games is stressed early in the $n$-person treatment. As to von Neumann–Morgenstern "solutions," usually nowadays called "stable sets," the big open question of existence was settled in the negative by Lucas (1969). The germinal context of two-person zero-sum games accounts for only one of 14 chapters; this reflects their rarity in the real world and stands as a harbinger of books to be written. Recent books on game theory, especially those oriented toward economic applications, mention zero-sum games only tangentially if at all.[12] In one instance, however, a prediction in **LR57** went unfulfilled: contrary to the second paragraph on page 115, most applications to economic problems have taken the form of *non*cooperative games.

The initial and final chapters of **LR57** deserve mention as well. Chapter 2 contains a constructive axiomatization of von Neumann– Morgenstern utility, while Chapter 3 carefully exposits the extensive and normal forms; it should be studied by anyone under the delusion that decision trees are inherently more general than decision tables. Chapter 14 concerns group decision making from the social choice, Arrow-impossibility viewpoint, while Chapter 13 scrutinizes axioms for individual decision making under uncertainty, with utility assumed given for the most part (except as regards Savage's theory). Also introduced, in remarkably few pages, are the extant competitors of SEU, such as maximin, minimax regret, and Hurwicz $\alpha$; statistical decision theory, including complete classes and the accurate prediction that future books on this subject would deemphasize game theory; a comparison of the approaches of classical inference and "modern" statistical decision theory; and the discussion on pages 306–309 concerning treating games asymmetrically as decisions under uncertainty for a given player:

> The decision maker's very selection of an *a priori* distribution for his adversary sets up indirect forces to alter this initial choice. If such is the case, one can argue that the decision maker should keep on modifying the *a priori* distribution until this alleged indirect feedback no longer produces any change—until there exists an equilibrium in the decision maker's mind. We suspect that, roughly, this is the way games of strategy are actually played. (p. 306)

This is followed by a reconsideration of the subjective-probability axioms when the state is determined by an intelligent opponent rather than disinterested "nature."

Aumann (1989) terms **LR57** "enormously influential," while noting that the **LR57** definition of complete information should be strengthened to include common knowledge of complete information. Friedman (1990, p. xi) writes, "Luce and Raiffa have written the sort of classic book to which many of us must aspire. Although much out of date due to the developments of more than thirty years, it is a superb source for much of the central material of the field. The writing is lucid, the intuition supporting various models and the criticisms of them are insightful and illuminating, and the technical demands are never more than the minimum necessary for the subject."

Many have assumed that **R53** subsumed **R51**, especially since they have the same title. But **R51** also contains much then-original material on noncooperative two- (and $n$-) person games, including the first appearance and use of iterated dominance, which he called "complete reduction," the concept of psychological dominance of one equilibrium over another, and the first detailed examination of the Prisoner's Dilemma game.[13]

### Statistical Decision Theory

This subsection concerns **R61b**, **RS61**, and **PRS65**. **R61b** is actually of 1956 vintage, as the volume's preface indicates. **R61b** deals with the two-state (such as qualified and unqualified), two-action (such as accept and reject) problem, along with which there are available $k$ experiments $e_i$, such as items in a test bank, that are each binary, with $P(z_i = 1|e_i, \theta j) = p_{ij}$. To work through this paper, which develops the analysis (sequential choice of items but without replacement when $k$ is small, with heuristics for when $k$ is large) in normal form, is a kinder and gentler way to absorb the principal conceptual content of Wald (1950). In places, correlation of $(z_i, z_h)$ given $\theta$ is permitted.

It is worth mentioning that, in a footnote on page 209, Raiffa stresses the restrictiveness of the assumption that (in effect) terminal loss and the cost of experimentation are additive. Moreover, in the section on heuristics for large $k$, he allows for cost of analysis and computation as well: an early prescriptive recognition of cognitive limitations.

*Applied Statistical Decision Theory*, **RS61**, codified Bayesian statistical decision theory. In effect, it is three books in one. The first establishes the framework for the now familiar extensive-form, two-stage statistical decision problem, which is to find

$$u^\circ = \max_e E_{z|e} \max_a E_{\theta|z,e} u(e, \tilde{z}, a, \tilde{\theta}),$$

where $\tilde{\theta}$ is the uncertain state, $a$ the terminal action, and $\tilde{z}$ the outcome of experiment $e$. The second part of the book specializes $u$ to the additively separable form

$$u(e, z, a, \theta) = u_t(a, \theta) - c(e, z),$$

and obtains concrete results for several decision-theoretic versions of the point estimation, hypothesis testing, and choice-of-treatments problems of statistics, under several important data-generating-process assumptions such as the Bernoulli, Poisson, and Normal processes. The third main part is a carefully worked out handbook of the distribution theory to support the second part.

The theoretical innovations in **RS61** include natural-conjugate distributions, noninformative stopping and a Bayesian definition of sufficiency, and a codification and naming of "preposterior" distributions, which were explicitly called "prior distributions of the posterior mean" in Schlaifer (1959). In addition, some of the distribution theory in the third part is surely novel; the multivariate Student distribution was probably new, because it is obtained by generalizing the authors' derivation of the univariate Student as a Gamma mixture of Normals.[14]

One could argue that noninformative stopping is conceptually close to Birnbaum's (1962) Conditionality Principle. Raiffa argues in **R68** that the Conditionality Principle is equivalent to the Likelihood Principle.[15] Indeed, one cannot help being amused by the peculiarity of inferential procedures sensitive to the choice of a particular noninformative stopping rule. Such sensitivity is analogous to the sensitivity to decision-framing minutiae that crops up when one tries to prescriptively apply most non-SEU choice models.[16]

Natural-conjugate prior distributions, the parameters of which combine easily with the sufficient statistics to yield the (updated) parameters of the resulting natural-conjugate posterior distribution, were Raiffa's individual discovery (see **R88**). In an age of rare and expensive computing, they represented an essential contribution to making Bayesian methods practical. They are still of conceptual usefulness, since they permit one to interpret prior judgments as judgments posterior to a fictitious sample given a conventional prior distribution. Nowadays, the computational mandate has waned,[17] but the conceptual role remains. In fact, a mild generalization of the idea of natural-conjugacy idea is easy to define: take as the prior density function a weighted average $\Sigma_{i=1}^{I} w_i' f(\theta|p_i')$ of natural-conjugate priors $f(\theta|p_i')$ with different prior parameters $p_i'$. Then, as **R68** shows apropos of the panel of experts problem, the resulting posterior density function is of the same form, with $p_i'$ updated to $p_i''$ by the natural-conjugate operation, and $w_i'$ updated to $w_i''$ by, in effect, rewarding those constituents $i$ that did relatively good jobs predicting the sample outcome. These generalized conjugate distributions are hierarchical prior distributions,[18] in which the "hyperparameter" $p'$ is itself accorded the discrete distribution $w_1',...,w_I'$. Special cases for several of the standard data-generating processes appear in Exercise 14.20 of LaValle (1970).

The additive-utility specialization $u_t(a,\theta) - c(e,z)$ underlying the second and more applied part of **RS61** is fully justifiable when, to use terminology not then in existence, the only relevant attribute is money and the decision maker is risk neutral. It also obtains when there is a numeraire that fully captures preferences for terminal-outcome lotteries, a numeraire for experimentation cost, and additive independence for joint lotteries over pairs of these numeraires—and, for most subsequent results, linearity of the experimentation-cost numeraire in the number of observations. In fact, the authors' suggestion to price out variations in the nonmonetary attributes and deal with money henceforward is sound only when, letting $x$ be money and $y$ be everything else, utility is expressible in the form $u(x,y) = g(x + h(y))$.[19] For terminal-action problems of modest size, however, the additive-utility specialization is perfectly adequate; for others, general utility and the more complex information-evaluation theory in LaValle (1968) are appropriate, but then preposterior theory is inapplicable and few concrete results are obtainable.

Under the additive-utility specialization, and with distribution theory under natural conjugacy for important data-generating processes, **RS61** obtains closed-form solutions $(e°,\{a°(z): z \in Z(e°)\})$ for the decision-theoretic versions of point estimation (infinite-action problems with quadratic and with linear terminal loss) and hypothesis testing (finite and then two-action problems with linear terminal value and hence also linear loss), although in the latter context closed-form optima were obtained only for the Normal process with known variance; the unknown-variance case was soon dealt with by Bracken and Schleifer (1964). Selection of the best of several processes, with sampling possible on the individual processes, was set up, with concrete results on optimal sample sizes obtained only for the case of two processes whose linear terminal value-determining "yields," or "qualities," are independently Normally distributed. In all cases, however, the terminal analysis—what to do after the sample has been gotten—is easy; with preposterior distribution theory, obtaining the expected net gain of sampling (ENGS) of a given number of observations (or profile of observations on the several processes) is not exceptionally hard.

Even readers with some background in probability, statistics, and basic calculus are apt to be somewhat intimidated by **RS61**, which in places bristles with iterated integrals, linear algebra, and references to tables and graphs. These reflect the authors' determination to be as complete and explicit as they could in characterizing solutions to these problems of real importance. To some extent, **PRS65** represents an effort to exposit the main results of **RS61** in text rather than monograph form.

As a text, the core of **PRS65** concerns the same statistical decision-theoretic problems treated by **RS61**, with some variations: the Poisson process is not covered, and Normal sampling is restricted to the known-variance case. In three major respects, however, it goes much further than **RS61**. First, Chapters 21 and 22 carefully develop multivariate distribution theory and the multivariate-Normal distribution. Chapter 23 provides four applications of multivariate-Normal theory: selecting the best of several processes (as in **RS61**); allowance for uncertain bias (not in **RS61** but broached in Schlaifer, 1959); stratification (in neither previous work); and a remarkably lucid introduction to the portfolio problem, which in part uses the constantly risk-averse exponential utility form of which the virtues were unrecognized when the earlier works appeared but which, as Pratt (1964) had shown by then, was free of the contra-intuitive increasing risk aversion inherent in quadratic utility. The section on the portfolio problem also improves upon the treatment in many finance texts by expositing the efficient frontier for the case in which borrowing and lending can take place at different interest rates. The final chapter treats the Normal linear regression model with known common variance of the independent and identically distributed disturbances.

Second, Chapter 19 exposits normal-form statistical decision theory for infinite action (estimation) and for two-action problems with break-even values (also known as one-sided hypothesis-testing problems). In each case, the analysis goes as far as it can with neither losses nor priors, then introduces losses, and finally priors. Chapter 20, on classical methods from the Bayesian viewpoint, discusses hypothesis testing and confidence intervals explicitly, as well as topics such as unbiased estimation.

Third, **PRS65** extends to state spaces of arbitrary cardinality the unified axiomatization of SEU published as **PRS64** with restriction to finite state spaces (or equivalently, finite partitions of the state space). Further comment on this axiomatization is deferred to the next subsection, except for noting that this unified axiomatization makes the foundation of **PRS65** more seamless than that of **RS61**.

Other innovations concern careful coverage of how to assess utility functions (called "preference functions" in this book), probabilities, and cumulative-distribution functions. Surprisingly, for a text at this level, the pathologies of finitely but not countably additive probability measures are introduced.

To conclude this subsection, it is important to stress that "statistical decision theory" is as general as "decision theory" without an additional adjective. In terms of the two-stage $(e,z,a,\theta)$ tree of **RS61** and **PRS65** (with $\theta$ changed to $s$), the terminal-action stage $(a,\theta)$ can be regarded as the *normal* form of any decision problem under uncertainty, even the most important. The experimentation stage $(e,z)$ represents an add-on, with information acquisition considered to be one of several useful strategies for coping with uncertainty. Other strategies include trying to influence controllers of certain uncertainties, and acquiring insurance against bad outcomes.

Statistical decision theory focuses on the information acquisition problem and on the statistical sampling problems that constitute an important and analytically rich subset. But one should not lose sight of the forest for the trees. The forest is described well in Subsection 6.3.1 of **PRS65**, which introduces the oil-wildcatter problem; because of its prescriptive wisdom and potentially very great generality, pages 5–7 of this chapter are quoted at length:

> The psychological stimulus associated in the problem with an $(e,z,a,s)$ sequence is highly complicated. Different wells entail different drilling costs, and different strikes produce quantities and qualities of oil which can be recovered over different periods of time and sold at different prices. Furthermore, each potential consequence of the present drilling venture interacts with future potential drilling ventures. . . . At the tip of the branch $(e_1,z_1,a_1,s_2)$, for example, is the entry (+340) which is interpreted as follows: the wildcatter imagines at the beginning of the play of the game what his position would be like if, after taking the seismic sounding, he drilled and struck oil; he knows at that point in time he would have to pay the costs of the seismic sounding and drilling expenses which are in themselves uncertain, but he would then also be in the happy position of knowing that this particular site had oil deposits; the full monetary consequence associated with this $(e_1,z_1,a_1,s_2)$ sequence, however, would remain uncertain even *after* learning that oil has been struck; the +340 figure indicates that before the game starts the wildcatter's *selling price* for the *consequence* (or better yet, *lottery*) associated with this $(e_1,z_1,a_1,s_2)$ sequence is $340,000. . . . Actually the decision tree for this problem which extends only to the indication of "oil" or "no oil" is not complete; and in a general sense no decision tree is *ever* really complete. Life goes on after $(e_1,z_1,a_1,s_2)$ and in order to assign a selling price to the sequence one could always look ahead still further by adding additional uncertain elements and additional moves in the game of "life itself." In practice, however, it will not always be worth the effort of *formally* looking very far ahead.

The exposition then goes on to assume risk-averse preferences over the substantial range [$-110,000, $+340,000] of assessed certainty equivalents in the tree. As long as one adheres to SEU, so that one can substitute certainty equivalents for subtrees, it would be hard to improve upon this presentation.

### Foundations of Choice under Uncertainty

In this subsection we consider **BR88a**, **R61a**, **R85a**, and **PRS64** as extended in **PRS65**. According to the preface of **BRT88a**, in **BR88a** Bell and Raiffa "set themselves the goal of 'explaining' the axioms of von Neumann and Morgenstern in such a way as to leave all readers lifelong devotees of expected utility, at least for decisions under risk" (p. 3). It does a bit more and a bit less. Less, in that the domain is restricted to lotteries with monetary (or desirable-quantity) prizes and the formalism is restricted to "simple" lotteries, each with finitely many possible distinct prizes. More, in that stochastic dominance through the second degree is introduced and exploited along the way. An appealing feature of the authors' approach is that continuity enters the picture late rather than early, in the form of a "solvability principle."

Another interesting feature is that, in the formal proof of the expected-utility theorem, preferential independence and multi-attribute value theory are invoked (see **KR76**). Indeed, the authors argue that, in the context of their finite lotteries, preferential independence is equivalent to substitutability. Using preferential independence in deriving von Neumann–Morgenstern utility may seem strange and anachronistic, but it is perfectly natural if one views the ordered list of outcomes of a lottery as a multi-attributed consequence.

What is a bit puzzling is how to reconcile the characterization of **BR88a** in the preface of **BRT88a** as a normative paper with its stated intent to convert readers and with its urn-based exposition. These characteristics are clearly prescriptive, and reinforce Tversky's contention that the normative includes the prescriptive.

Turning back to **R61a**, with its famous randomized-act argument against normatively yielding to the perceptions induced by Ellsberg's trap, it is worth noting that Raiffa extols the normative virtues of SEU (pp. 690–691):

> The fact that most people can be shown to be inconsistent in their manifest choice behavior . . . clearly demonstrates how important it is to have a theory which can be used to aid in the making of decisions under uncertainty. If most people behaved in a manner roughly consistent with Savage's theory then the theory would gain stature as a descriptive theory but would lose a good deal of its normative importance. We do not have to teach people what comes naturally.

To scholars who seek to accommodate attitudes toward ambiguity by generalizing the SEU model, Raiffa's randomization argument is at least troubling. Hazen (1987, 1992) claims that it is without force if the randomizing is conducted and revealed before the subjective uncertainty is resolved rather than afterwards. However, Raiffa (**R61a**, p. 693) found that his subjects didn't much care whether the coin was flipped before or after the uncertainty was resolved, and, on page 112 of **R68**, he notes that a person who *did* care could easily arrange to defer revelation of the outcome of the randomization until after the subjective uncertainty was resolved.

The Choquet expected utility model of Schmeidler (1989) and Gilboa (1987) is perhaps the most prominent vehicle for accommodating non-neutral attitudes toward ambiguity. In the context of their model, the Choquet expected utility of an act is not linear in act-mixing probabilities, and Raiffa's randomized bets emerge as optimal choices because some genuinely randomized acts may be preferred to all pure acts.[20]

In **R85a**, Raiffa champions the SEU framework but argues that when psychological phenomena such as regret are anticipated and relevant to one's preferences, they must be accounted for in the utility assessment. But he cautions against overweighting them and advises a pricing-out procedure as well as "therapy," the latter particularly for people tending to succumb to probabilistic fallacies such as conjunction $(P(A \cap B) > P(A))$ and reversal of conditioning (quoting $P(A|B)$ when $P(B|A)$ is needed). All readers should enjoy this paper for themselves, and hence further comment is unwarranted, except for noting that it represents a considerable change in Raiffa's thinking since 1968. In **R68** (pp. 85–86), while discussing the Allais Paradox, Raiffa notes the argument about zero *with* regret not being the same as zero *without* regret, but he concludes that "this flexibility, however, has been bought at a price: No longer is zero the same as zero, the same as zero . . . [ellipses his]." One could interpret this worry as a slip into the numbers-oriented trap about which, later in **R68**, Raiffa registers Admiral Rickover's concerns. Raiffa cites Morrison (1967) as arguing that zero isn't zero, but he had heard this argument earlier; it had arisen in the summer of 1964 during the writing of Fellner (1965).

Finally, the axiomatization of SEU that constitutes **PRS64** and Chapters 3 and 10 of **PRS65** deserves particular note. Many axiomatizations of SEU have appeared in the years since Savage (1954). Fishburn (1981) surveys the then-extant theories critically and in depth, and awards very high marks to the **PRS** accomplishment, noting that **PRS65** may be the best of the theories that introduce scaling probabilities explicitly, since "their format allows general application with simple, interpretable axioms that tie in very closely with assessment" (p. 194).

A number of features are particularly noteworthy. First, the authors make explicit and put on the table the existence of conceptual randomization devices that are implicit (though clearly envisioned) in Savage's axiom P6, and they do this in a way that behaviorally embodies the notion of uniform distributions (on the unit square) independent of other variables constituting the state of nature. This is the work that gave us paired basic canonical lotteries, one component of which calibrates probabilities while the other calibrates utilities. Second, $\geqslant$ is not assumed to be complete on *all* lotteries, or even initially on all consequences, but the substitutability axiom, which says that every consequence can be "utility-calibrated," and every event "probability-calibrated," effectively gives completeness on the consequences. Together with transitivity of $\geqslant$ and substitutability, the SEU representation is obtained for finite state spaces $S$, or equivalently, for all acts measurable with respect to some finite partition of $S$. Uniqueness and finite additivity of subjective probability is proved. This is done in **PRS64** and in Chapter 3 of **PRS65**; Chapter 8 of the latter imposes dominance, general substitutability, and sequential-continuity axioms to obtain the Lebesgue Stieltjes integral representation $\int_S u(a(s))dP(s)$ for the SEU of an act $a$ that yields consequence $a(s)$ given state $s \in S$.

Third, this axiomatization presumes that the consequences are preference-bounded, in the sense that there exist $c_0$ and $c_1$ such that $c_0 < c < c_1$ for every consequence $c$, and hence that utility itself is bounded below and above by $u(c_0)$ and $u(c_1)$, which are taken to be 0 and 1 respectively to simplify the calibration. It should not be difficult to dispense with this assumption by extending the calibration of $u$ below $u(c_0)$ and above $u(c_1)$ in the familiar fashion and thus bring an increasingly wide class of lotteries into the domain of the model. Indeed, it is likely that this would enable the general-states **PRS** axiomatization to sidestep the boundedness of $u$ that Savage's (1954) axiomatization entails, since as Wakker (1993) shows, it is the presumed completeness of $\geqslant$ on the set of all *lotteries* that permits the construction (as in sections 14.1 and 14.5 of Fishburn, 1970) of the St. Petersburg sorts of examples that produce contradictions to presumed unboundedness of $u$ on the set of all *consequences*. Since **PRS** never presume completeness of $\geqslant$, the sidestepping should be graceful. Making this argument formally complete would legitimate linear, exponential, and other unbounded utility functions on the real line when coupled with probability measures of unbounded support such as the Normal distribution.

Fourth, the ultimate step in obtaining the usual SEU representation is to invoke the already proved finite additivity of subjective probability so as to reexpress the penultimate SEU representation; this is the Choquet expectation in Schmeidler's (1989) model. This means that there should be a weakening of the **PRS** axiomatization that yields the Schmeidler model. Suppose that $a(s) = c_i$ for all $s \in E_i$, $\{E_1,...,E_n\}$ is a partition of $S$, and $c_1 > c_2 ... > c_n$. Then **PRS**, and Schmeidler, obtain the expected utility $u(a)$ of $a$ as

$$u(a) = u(c_n) + \sum_{i=1}^{n-1} [u(c_i) - u(c_{i+1})]P(\bigcup_{j=1}^{i} E_j),$$

from which rearrangement yields the familiar formula

$$u(a) = \sum_{i=1}^{n} u(c_i)P(E_i),$$

provided that $P$ is additive so that $P(E_i) = P(\bigcup_{j=1}^{i} E_j) - P(\bigcup_{j=1}^{i-1} E_j)$ for $i > 1$.

To conclude this subsection, it should be noted that there is good reason for basing practice on the SEU model to which Raiffa has remained faithful, rather than using one of the numerous generalizations of SEU axiomatized since the mid-1970s.[21] Under these generalizations, normal-form and extensive-form analyses no longer produce the same optimal course of action, and similar peculiarities result from other arbitrary choices in problem representation.[22]

## General Issues in Decision Analysis

This subsection concerns **AR82**, **KR72**, **BRT88a** and **b**, and **R68**. This grouping is defined by excluding works that are primarily oriented towards statistical decision theory, game theory, utility, or negotiations.

**AR82**, "A Progress Report on the Training of Probability Assessors," written in 1969, reports what must have been among the earliest class-based experiments showing that probability assessors tend to be far too overconfident. Their assessed probability distributions are much too tight, so that they are surprised by the frequent occurrence of outcomes they had deemed very unlikely. The authors argue that for typical unimodal judgments, the intercentile-to-interquartile ratio $(x_{.99} - x_{.01})/(x_{.75} - x_{.25})$ should be in the interval from 2.25 to 4.50, noting that for Normal distributions this ratio is 3.50. The message to assessors is (p. 301): "For heaven's sake, Spread Those Extreme Fractiles! Be honest with yourselves! Admit what you don't know!" This quote illustrates the tone of the experiment's questionnaires and feedback memoranda recorded in this paper, and appears typical of Raiffa's pedagogical writing. The paper is a paragon of prescriptive communication.

In **KR72**, "A Critique of Formal Analysis in Public Decision Making," Keeney and Raiffa argue that public administrators cannot and should not try to avoid incorporating their subjective attitudes into the analysis, and that their active involvement in the process is essential if the possibly subconscious biases of the nonaccountable analysts are to be averted. After noting the strengths of formal decision analysis in furnishing a coherent framework for decomposing problems into manageable parts and in mandating hard thinking about formulation and assessment issues, the authors proceed to identify the difficulties as well as distinguishing features of the public administrator's role.

Public administrators have options for stalling and for changing the rules of the game that are not generally available to private administrators. They are typically free from the discipline of competition. Indeed, even the identity of "the decision maker" is often vague. Public scrutiny of subjective inputs can inflame rather than allay controversy, and excessive risk aversion can be induced by the public's judgments of the quality of the decision, which are often based on short-term results. Among the technical difficulties are the identification of objectives, measures of effectiveness, the consequences of alternative courses of action, the assessment of multivariate probability distributions on multi-attributed consequences, and the group-decision problem of synthesizing judgments and preferences of a decision-making group and of accounting responsibly for the interests of stakeholders outside the group. But the primary difficulty may be the main outstanding issue in decision analysis today: (p. 370) "There are no systematic procedures for isolating problems. This is especially true in the public sector, where there is an intricate web of overlapping and interacting agencies." However, the authors conclude that since the underlying theory is free from fundamental weaknesses and the technology for applying it is continually improving, the growing experience in public sector applications should lead to increasing demand for public sector decision analysis.

**BRT88b**, the introductory chapter to **BRT88a**, abounds with insights and wisdom from the prescriptive, here's-how-you-can-be-helped viewpoint that the authors seek to establish as a companion to the descriptive category and the category of superhumanly knowing, attentive, and calculating cogitation that they call normative. Since any brief summary would not do it justice, it should be read and pondered as a whole. It is worth noting that, in a section prefatory to discussing SEU, the authors discuss "willful choice models" in general (March's term). They note that:

Perhaps each of us, over the course of a lifetime, makes a dozen or so critical, deliberative, serious choices. That would add a vast pool of potential applications for the prescriptive uses of the willful-choice paradigm. But, granted, it would still be a terrible distortion to describe the denouement of most lifetime careers in terms of these deliberative choices. A lot else happens that can be better described in other ways (p. 19).

They then go on to note that only rarely is one sure of having all the alternatives on the table, but suggest that one can go ahead and analyze the known alternatives—thereby tacitly assuming that one's choice model satisfies the Independence of Irrelevant Alternatives property, or, in other words, that it cannot produce rank reversals of the remaining existing alternatives when others are deleted, new ones are introduced, or both. In the authors' view, however, the real difficulty lies in striking a good balance between creatively generating alternatives and in analyzing them.

The book as a whole, **BRT88a**, appeared some five years after the conference on which it was based, and a number of its 28 chapters had appeared elsewhere. Although it is a coherent set of papers on decision making, there are a few oddities, such as Seidenfeld's discussion of a paper by Good along with the chapter by Dempster. But this is a minor problem. The book can be sampled almost at random and contains material not readily available elsewhere; for example, the final chapter is a transcript of a discussion on medical decision making. Keeney's chapter on value-focused thinking; Edwards, von Winterfeldt, and Moody on simplicity in decision analysis; **BR88a**; **BR88b**; Schelling on the mind as a consuming organ; Fishburn on theories of decision making; and Argyris on problems of producing usable knowledge also appear only in **BRT88a**.

**R68**, *Decision Analysis: Introductory Lectures on Choices under Uncertainty*, was the book that codified the field in several respects. Most prominently, the almost universal convention of using boxes for decision nodes and circles for chance nodes in decision trees, and bigger versions of the same in influence diagrams, stems from **R68**. And while **RS61** and **PRS65** gave us EVSI and ENGS, **R68** gave us BRLTS (basic reference lottery tickets; it rhymes with "wilts").

Raiffa recalls in **R88** that he and Schlaifer developed decision trees jointly for **RS61**. Since decision trees appear in Schlaifer (1959), the chronology is doubtful, and Raiffa's initial contributions to this subject may be reflected in Schlaifer's general acknowledgment in his preface. Nevertheless, Raiffa was by then already an expert on trees and their normalization, given his work in game theory.[23]

For several years I used **R68** as the primary text in an MBA-level elective on decision analysis. There was only one troublesome aspect of the exposition: the "tollgates" that ascribe cash flows to branches along the way. For risk-neutral decision makers, they are an ideal means of concentrating on what is happening locally in the tree. But an enormous amount of unlearning and retraining seems to be required when novices must be convinced that one must cumulate cash flows to fashion the domain for utility assessment.

A substantial portion of **R68** is concerned with specifically *statistical* decision issues. The basic example, carried through most of the book, begins (in its tree form) with a choice of none, fixed, or sequential experimentation, and of course Bayes' Theorem is carefully developed and shown to pertain as much to subjective as to other sorts of probabilities, if there are any. What really differentiates **R68** from other works on Bayesian statistical decision theory are Raiffa's extensions and enrichments.

One such is Section 13 of Chapter 4, based on a Raiffa working paper. It concerns people whose pleasure from indulging in small gambles leads them to assess Friedman-Savage (1948) concave-convex-concave utility functions. Raiffa argues that, for decision-analytic purposes, such a curve should be "concavified," with the convex sag replaced by a linear segment. The reason is that if one received a payoff in the sag, one would be motivated to play a fair gamble with that payoff as the stake; the gamble has a higher expected utility; and hence that higher figure is what should be used to evaluate one's payoff in the immediate decision problem. Proceeding in this fashion is a practical alternative to continuing the tree out to the right to explicitly model such gambles.

The book abounds in prescriptive wisdom and tricks of the trade. For example, on pages 258–259, Raiffa shows how dependent random variables may be reexpressed as transforms of independent random variables: sales in two markets may be dependent, but their difference may be judged independent of their average. Later, this idea was applied in the context of utility independence; the **KR76** example of utility-dependent crime rates in two precincts is algebraically identical. Indeed, Raiffa notes in **R88** that he approached the multi-attribute utility problem by seeking to develop analogies to the practical simplifications of multivariate probability distributions obtained by exploiting probabilistic independence.

Among the long-lived quotes from **R68** are, "The spirit of decision analysis is divide and conquer" (p. 271, in the context of worrying about judgment-preference separability, creativity, etc.), and "When does a tree become a bushy mess?" (p. 240; von Winterfeldt and Edwards, 1986, answer: when it cannot be put on a single sheet of paper). To cope with a bushy mess, Raiffa recommends (pp. 242 ff.) artfully combining extensive and normal forms of analysis, as well as pruning act branches that are clearly unattractive. To some extent, influence diagrams and microcomputer software have mitigated the mess problem in recent years, but these tools do not provide a license to indulge in ponderous decision modeling.

To me, Chapter 8, on the group decision problem, is the high point of the book. Yet Raiffa had considered omitting it. In the preface (p. xiii), he states, "The results in Chapter 8 date back to a series of seminar talks I gave in 1961. While perhaps I posed a few fundamental questions for research, most of the relevant answers came from contributions by John Pratt, Robert Wilson, and Richard Zeckhauser." Chapter 8 presents Pratt's example of the nonexistence of a (financial) group utility function; Zeckhauser's demonstration that it can be optimal to do the opposite of what any number of experts unanimously recommend; the demonstration that experts' probability distributions should be averaged before obtaining sample evidence rather than afterwards; and a meaty and accessible explication of the financial group-decision problem treated by Wilson (1968).

Raiffa's treatment of the "syndicate" problem, in which $n$ individuals must jointly choose a monetary lottery, shows how coupling a lottery with all possible ways of sharing its proceeds conditional upon the event that will obtain, leads to an attainable region in the $n$-dimensional space of group members' expected utilities; how the availability of several lotteries can lead to crinkliness of the Pareto-efficient frontier of the union of the lotteries' separate attainable regions—and thus how a *randomized* choice of lottery-sharing rule pair may be in order; and how points on the resulting, convexified frontier are attainable by maximizing a weighted sum $\Sigma_{i=1}^{n} \lambda_i E_i u_i(\cdot)$ of members' expected utilities, where the weights $\lambda_i$ are all positive and can be normed to sum to 1.

Every arbitrated solution to the group members' bargaining problem thus corresponds to specifying the weights $\lambda_i$. Since these weights have meaning only relative to the members' individual utility scales, it is clear that suggestions such as "We're a democratic group, so let's just use equal weights" are useless. Instead of focusing on the weights, Raiffa suggested (p. 205) that attention be confined to the members' certainty equivalents of their shares, with one solution being that which produces equal certainty equivalents. The primal approach to determining the equal certainty equivalents solution by tracing out the conforming trajectory in the $n$-space of members' utilities is easily generalized to produce a large class of intuitively meaningful solutions.[24]

## Utility Assessment and Multi-Attribute Utility

There is a brief introduction to the multi-attribute problem in **R68**, in the context of medical decisions with generally constant rates of substitution, and it appears that it is Raiffa who introduced the now-universal "attribute" and "multi-attribute" terminology that expresses so well the subjective, constructed nature of the domain of preference assessment. This subsection concerns **BR88b**, **BKR77**, **RSW77**, **KR76**, and **R69**.

In **BR88b**, "Marginal Value and Intrinsic Risk Aversion," Bell and Raiffa revisit the old and somewhat quiescent notion of "utility" as measuring intrinsic preferences. They develop a structuring of von Neumann–Morgenstern utility $u$ as the composition of a risk attitude function $g$ and an intrinsic-preference-measuring value function $v$ on attributes $(x,y,z,...)$, so that $u(x,y,z,...) = g[v(x,y,z,...)]$. In essence, this paper melds Chapters 3 on value functions and 4 on von Neumann–Morgenstern utility of **KR76** in the same sense that Chapter 10 of **KR76** melds Chapter 4 and Chapter 6 on MAU. Bell and Raiffa consider alternative ways of assessing $v$ and, under appropriate additivity conditions on $v$, argue that $g$ should be linear or exponential; that is, that one should be constantly risk averse as regards value. It is surprising that more has not been made of this provocative idea, although there may be a tenuous connection in the recent work of Wakker (1994), who is primarily concerned with the rank-dependent non-SEU choice model and does not cite **BR88b**.

**BKR77**, *Conflicting Objectives in Decisions*, is a collection of papers presented at a workshop held in October 1975 under the auspices of IIASA. In addition to the generally rich methodological and applications papers, the discussions that followed many of them are included. Thus one finds bits of prescriptive wisdom from Raiffa, such as (p. 196): "By eliminating the alternatives that are obviously inferior, you can often limit the ranges [of the attributes] so that you can tolerate certain kinds of independence assumptions that were intolerable before. That is an aspect of the art of assessment." (See also p. 128 of **KR76**.) And: "I don't know of any procedure in these group problems that can prove that the optimal procedure is to tell the truth, but if you give a very, very complicated rule and then ask people for their beliefs, they cannot easily figure out how to subvert the analysis. In fact, most of the subjects that I have been involved with simply decide that the easiest thing to do is to tell the truth" (p. 387). This idea is elaborated at various points in **R82a**.

The book concludes with an edited general discussion of five topics, including checking independence conditions and tradeoffs over time. The methodological chapters include Luce's succinct survey of conjoint measurement, Fishburn's concise explication of the utility-structuring implications of the then-known independence conditions (few have appeared since), Meyer on state-dependent time preferences, Wallenius and Zionts on multiple criteria decision making, and MacCrimmon and Wehrung on the preferred-proportions approach to tradeoff analysis as contrasted with the indifference approach. Applications chapters include Dyer and Miles on the Mariner trajectory-selection problem, Bell on forest pests, Keeney and Nair on nuclear power plant siting, and Edwards on using his simple multi-attribute rating technique (SMART) for MAU in social-decision contexts.

RSW77 is a report on developing MAU structurings for societal decisions with health and mortality ramifications. According to Raiffa, Schwartz, and Weinstein, such decisions should be subjected to a "meticulous accounting" that includes all attributes germane to the decision, whether they concern mortality and morbidity, economic factors, or environmental considerations. The bulk of the paper concerns an analysis of tradeoffs within and between general categories such as "mortality/morbidity" and "economic," with particular emphasis upon dollar valuation of health status. Willingness to pay and willingness to accept are contrasted with the human capital approach, and the case for careful discounting of future lives saved or lost is made convincingly. The paper concludes with a profound analysis of *ex ante* and *ex post* attributability and identifiability, and on the decision maker's accountability. The authors treat the components and their relationships in the framework for structuring public decisions in a thorough and wise fashion. If the paper were slightly expanded to include worked-out examples and a primer on additive MAU and republished commercially, it would constitute a fine supplementary text for courses on decision analysis.

KR76, *Decisions with Multiple Objectives: Preferences and Value Trade-offs*, made a convincing case for the wide, practical applicability of structured multi-attribute utility in the real world. So convincing was this case that it won the Lanchester Prize for the most valuable publication in operations research that year. As is typical of Raiffa's work, the writing is lucid and well organized. His prescriptive commitment shows in the meticulous attention given to the development and illustration of methods for verifying the various independence conditions.

Many consider KR76 the bible of MAU, and appropriately so. No similarly comprehensive but updated book has appeared subsequently. Unlike the Judaeo-Christian Bible, however, KR76 is not completely self-contained. Some proofs are only sketched or heuristically argued, but in these cases references are provided.

One great strength of **KR76** is in showing just how universally applicable the EU-based approach of decision analysis is if the right prescriptive technology is available, and much of it is given here as regards preference assessment. (For judgments, consult **PRS65**, **R68**, and **RS61**.) A vast panorama of applications is set forth in Chapter 1. Chapter 2 distinguishes between objectives and attributes, and exposits the hierarchy that is generally called a value tree. Then comes the theoretical core of the book, Chapters 3 through 6. Chapter 3 concerns value (i.e., ordinal-utility) functions and tradeoffs under certainty, presents the "corresponding-tradeoffs condition" for two-attribute value functions and mutual preferential independence for value functions with more than two attributes, and explicates assessment techniques. Chapter 4 treats the cardinal, von Neumann–Morgenstern utility of a single real argument with the same care, devoting much more attention to functional forms and the implications of risk-aversion theory than any previous book. Since not all attributes are intrinsically desirable "goods," like money, this chapter also covers decreasing utility for intrinsically undesirable "bads," and nonmonotone utility for attributes that are good in moderation but bad in excess.

Chapters 5 and 6 contain the core theory of MAU, for two attributes in Chapter 5 and for arbitrary finite $n$ attributes in Chapter 6. The contents of these chapters, including the verification of independence conditions and the graphs of squares and cubes with heavy lines and dots denoting domains of minimally necessary utility assessment, are so well known that no further comment is necessary. Chapters 7 and 8 contain carefully explicated applications, with Chapter 8 devoted to the famous Mexico City Airport study that convinced the Office of Public Works to revise its position on the issue. Chapter 9, by Richard F. Meyer, develops MAU for cash flow streams and thus contributes importantly to financial theory; this chapter actually postdates his chapter in **BKR77**. Chapter 10, on the aggregation of preferences by a "supra-decision maker," exposits Arrow's impossibility theorem and the relationship of the aggregation "possibility" obtainable with cardinal MAU to Arrow's theorem.

The preface to **KR76** begins with a clear statement of the prescriptive orientation and notes the imbalance in contemporary analyses that devoted great effort to modeling probabilistic judgments but little if any to modeling utility preferences. It concludes by identifying its intended audience, as well as how the book may be read, and appears to focus on analysts and consultants. Surely, such individuals have been greatly helped by the wealth of approaches to assessment and other prescriptive aids contributed by **KR76**.

Written in July 1968, **R69** broaches the multi-attribute problem in its full generality. While its substantive content has been subsumed in **KR76**, this 107-page report is of historical interest, is a pleasure to read, and contains some developments and viewpoints not so easily accessible elsewhere.

After stating the problem, **R69** develops tradeoffs for two attributes, discusses value trees, and defines preferential and utility independence, which were then called weak and strong conditional utility independence, respectively. Next is a long section on the additive model $u(x_1,...,x_n) = \sum_{i=1}^{n} \lambda_i u_i(x_i)$, many useful observations on assessment, the additive value model and its relationship to utility, and a derivation of SEU when the $\lambda$s are interpretable as subjective probabilities. This section appears to introduce the "value function" terminology for ordinal utility (p. 55). In it, Raiffa clearly shows that $\lambda_i$ conveys nothing about the intrinsic importance of attribute $i$ to the decision maker. Beginning students seem to find this lack of relationship hard to appreciate, but Raiffa has a clear explanation: "Suppose, for example, in comparing jobs $S_i$ refers to monetary rewards and all jobs under consideration pay almost the same amount so that [the endpoints of the effective range of $S_i$] are close together; then $\lambda_i$ may be small but this does not mean that money is unimportant to the DM" (p. 43).

A shorter section introduces nonadditive utility-independent modeling, with credit to the very recent work of Keeney in this area. Then comes a section on the value of (primarily) one's life and vital functions, commencing with an example by Zeckhauser that shows that one should be willing to pay more for removing one cartridge from a Russian roulette gun if it contains more cartridges to start with. The willingness-to-pay argument here and in **RSW77** was later taken up by Howard (1980, 1984) with his white pill and black pill analyses. It is also worth noting that, in developing the model $u(x,p) = \lambda_1 u_1(x) + \lambda_2 u_2(p)$ for $(x,p) = $ (assets, probability of death), Raiffa observes that $u_2$ may be nonlinear in $p$ due to anxiety considerations; this is an early manifestation of sensitivity to psychological features of consequences.

The final section concerns intertemporal tradeoffs, with a clear statement of the temporal resolution issue, foreshadowing Spence and Zeckhauser (1972) and Kreps and Porteus (1978). Raiffa's treatment is to recursively assess certainty equivalents, taking intervening history and resolution timing into account. Given a suitably broad definition of certainty equivalents, this approach is as general as possible without explicit modeling of the reasons for preferring early (or late) resolution, but it raises the issue of changing tastes and predicting one's future preferences. On this issue, vexing to some, Raiffa's prescriptive orientation is clear:

One might still feel, however . . . that the utility number $u(x)$ [for a cash-flow stream $x$] is really uncertain. But still we have to act, and the problem ultimately boils down to: if we have to make up our minds *now*, all things considered, would we rather have [stream] $x$ or [stream] $y$? By answering such questions we essentially force ourselves to assess a certainty equivalent, $u(\hat{x})$, for this uncertain $u(\tilde{x})$ and this $u(\hat{x})$ is interpreted as our utility function as of this time that is relevant for making decisions *now*. (p. 106)

### Negotiations

This subsection concerns **R82a**, **R85b**, and **KR91**, in chronological order. It is desirable to put this body of work in the context of Raiffa's previous contributions.

As indicated above, Raiffa's interest in the *asymmetrically* prescriptive approach to games, viewed as decisions in which significant uncertainties are to be resolved by parties concerned with the decision maker's behavior, dates back at least to the writing of **LR57**. His interest in *external* prescription, involving intervenors such as arbitrators, dates even further back, to **R51** and **R53**.

**R68** also presents the asymmetrically prescriptive approach in Section 10.3, on "Game Theory, Gamesmanship, Gaming, and Decision Theory." In it, Raiffa expresses concerns about the difficulty of assessing probabilities to other players' actions, but he notes that "In one circumstance, however, we may be lucky, because the more realistic and complex a problem becomes, the more difficult it is to engage in this kind of iterative, destabilizing reflection" (p. 293). Then he goes on to note that direct assessment may be aided or even circumvented by gaming the problem, with experts playing the roles of the other participants.

Beginning in the late 1960s, there followed Raiffa's involvement in the negotiations which gave birth to IIASA, his experiences as an executive, his observations of the pitfalls along the way to happy outcomes of negotiations, and his experiences with the Competitive Decision Making course. These led to the publications considered here and to Raiffa's ongoing involvement with research and consulting in this field.

**R82a** differs from Raiffa's previous work in that it is oriented explicitly to practicing negotiators and intervenors:

This is *not* a book addressed primarily to analysts and academics; it neither introduces a new, nor enhances an old, theory of the negotiation process. Rather, it is addressed to practitioners of negotiation—and they are legion. It publicizes a need and an opportunity for them to think more systematically and consciously, in a more conceptually integrated fashion, about the dynamics of negotiation. The principal theme of the book is that analysis—mostly simple analysis—can help. . . . There are beautiful theories of the negotiation process that explain, to a first approximation, how negotiators do behave or should behave. But, as in the theory of the firm, these theories are not operational; and in spite of them, all too often no systematic analysis, or even partial analysis, is employed in practice. . . . A certain amount of analysis can be of help to negotiators and intervenors in many different ways. The need is not for the creation of new analytical techniques specially designed for the negotiation process, but rather for the creative use of analytical thinking that exploits simple existing techniques. (pp. 358–359)

His disclaimer notwithstanding, there does appear to be a methodological innovation in the book; namely, Raiffa's modification of Shapley Value for $n = 3$ players, presented in the context of an example and without examination of its general properties. But that his intended message to his intended audience came across was amply confirmed by **R82a**'s being awarded the 1985 Leo Melamed Prize of the *Journal of Business*.

**R82a** reads quite differently than Raiffa's other works; its style is much more that of the *Harvard Business Review* than *Management Science*. Its numerous cases are an inextricable part of the presentation, and one must recall their principal features to understand subsequent references to them. For the practitioner, this is fine; it is less helpful for theorists trying to follow the main steps of the argument.

The central message to practitioners comes through clearly: pertinent analysis is helpful and available—and one's ethical principles are *not* irrelevant. And **R82a** also served as a stimulus to scholars, as suggested by the appearance of the *Negotiation Journal* in 1985 and a burgeoning literature on issues touched upon in **R82a**. The field of negotiation analysis was recently surveyed by Sebenius (1992), while Young (1991) consists of eight chapters that focus on particular and important issues. Both of these works were inspired by **R82a** and constitute valuable supplements to it.

**R82a** consists of three principal parts. The first concerns two parties with a single issue, such as the price of a house or the settlement of a tort. Here we find BATNA (best alternative to negotiated agreement, or optimal threat strategy) and the "negotiation dance" of offers and counteroffers. Also in this part are the role of time and escalating commitments—for example, the infamous dollar auction in which the second-highest bidder also has to pay but gets nothing. The second part concerns settings in which two parties must negotiate many issues, typified by a bilateral treaty negotiation. Here we meet the SNT (single negotiation text); serious confrontation of situations in which outcomes are Pareto inefficient; and the dance of packages (p. 140) that results from successive improvements in the SNT. Finally, the third part concerns many-party negotiations and involves issues of fair division and willingness to pay for a public good.

Sebenius (1992) writes that negotiation analysis is "decision analysis plus." What are the plusses? First and most obviously, one must think hard about the interests (that is, the preferences) of the other parties. Second, opportunities for joint gains and enlarging the pie should be explored. Third, a host of issues involving communication, candor, and concealment require consideration, including in some cases stepping partially out of one's role as a participant and playing intervenor. Fourth, the linkage of a current negotiation to future situations, with its overtones of reputation, should be kept more constantly in mind than typical decision-analytic training would suggest.

Finally, the central position of other human beings in these problem settings raises unavoidable ethical issues that are well laid out in the book. To the discussion therein one might add three brief comments. First, nonspeciesists should replace "human beings" with "living creatures." Second, in enlarging the pie, one should keep in mind the source of the enlargement and assume some responsibility for stakeholders, possibly of future generations, who have no active say in the decision at hand. Third, deontologically conforming decision analysis is now possible, with the subjective expected lexicographic utility theory of LaValle and Fishburn (1992, 1994).

**R82a** does a superlative job in making the case for asymmetrically prescriptive and externally prescriptive approaches to negotiation contexts. For the practitioner, it redresses the imbalance in the literature, which hitherto had underemphasized the role of analysis. Some of the methodological issues raised in **R82a** are treated in depth, but at a generally accessible level, in Young (1991), which contains **KR91**.

**R85b**, "Post-Settlement Settlements," was the lead paper in the first issue of the *Negotiation Journal*. It elaborates on a suggestion on page 221 of **R82a**, that many settlements are improvable (for the active participants) if the parties share information in confidence with a "contract embellisher" who would try to devise a Pareto-superior settlement that would supplant the directly negotiated settlement if all parties agreed unanimously that they would be better off under it (net of the embellisher's fee). In **R85b**, Raiffa notes that the *post*-settlement feature obviates the objection to ab initio arbitration that a self-perceived strong negotiator would raise, and he expresses his belief that the pending, second-stage role of the contract embellisher would have little if any effect upon the outcome of the first, direct-negotiation stage.

This suggestion sparked prompt responses. First, Roth (1985), citing O'Neill (1981), shows that if there are $n$ parties and $m$ possible final settlements, and if the parties' rankings of the settlements are independently and uniformly distributed, then only for small $n$ is the proportion of inefficient settlements very substantial. Therefore, contract embellishment would be most useful in situations with two parties and a large number of possible settlements. Second, Bazerman, Russ, and Yakura (1987) argue, and present cases, to the effect that an outside party is not needed in many situations characterized by ongoing relationships; they argue that the very success of an ongoing relationship may depend in large part upon the parties' skills in devising post-settlement settlements and implementing them via contract modifications.

In **R82a**, a party's preferences for multi-attributed outcomes were taken to be representable by an additive value function; see footnote 2 on page 155, concerning Raiffa's increasing tolerance for using a value function as if it were a utility function. In **KR91**, this restriction is relaxed; the authors carefully outline the entire assessment process, including the estimation of other parties' preferences (possibly by specifying several value functions, and then looking at settlements that are efficient for at least one resulting profile of value functions). All aspects of the assessment process are considered, including those that determine the BATNA. In effect, **KR91** is a mini-course on preparing for, monitoring, and evaluating negotiations from the asymmetric perspective of one of the parties.

It contains too many insights and words of advice to summarize briefly, and so a small sample will have to do: nonadditivity of the value function can arise for several reasons, one of which is the need to satisfy intra-party constituencies. Some nonadditivities can be eliminated by intra-party compensation mechanisms or by redefining and perhaps adding issues—but highly sensitive issues may be irresolvable and should be kept off the table so as not to poison the proceedings. Computers can help with the more burdensome calculations in the presence of nonadditivity.

## Concluding Remarks

Helping decision makers clarify their thinking has long been a primary objective in Raiffa's publications. Stability of arbitration schemes in

**R53**, the penetrating critique and introduction of asymmetric prescription in **LR57**, natural conjugacy in **RS61**, the highly constructive axiomatization of **PRS64** and **PRS65**, the numerous probability- and utility-assessment techniques developed in **PRS65** and **R68**, the shepherding of MAU in **R69** and its codification in **KR76**, and the bringing of analytical thought to negotiations in **R82a**: all bespeak Raiffa's commitment to the prescriptive. This commitment should be no less evident in Raiffa's future work.

Of course, it helps to have as one's compass the impeccably beautiful and robust SEU model (**R85a**); according to it, a prescription must yield useful results that are either not too surprising, or surprising but serve to educate and deepen one's intuition—or they are wrong. No case of a correct but persistently contraintuitive fact about SEU comes to mind.

Ever since his emotional commitment to SEU developed in the late 1950s (**R88**), Raiffa appears never to have been tempted to turn his compass in for a new, generalized model. This asceticism probably stems from a firmly held distinction between the not-so-good descriptive status of SEU and its prescriptive ability to accommodate anything that affects one's preferences (**R61a**). And so, with prescriptive purposes dominant, the temptation to stray was never very great.

The widespread acceptance and effectiveness of Raiffa's publications are attributable to several factors. One is the inherent soundness and usefulness of his message. Second is Raiffa's effervescent writing style, which reveals his wise and kindly nature and actively engages the reader in the intellectual adventure at hand. His use of "we" is almost never imperial or editorial; it connotes an involved communication with the reader.

A third factor is Raiffa's open-minded approach to problems. He is not hasty in offering a recommended solution or even a recommended approach. Instead, he makes sure that he understands the problem as completely as possible from the vantage point of its proposer. And then he will cautiously probe the extent to which his current knowledge can be brought to bear. An example of this occurred in 1964, when he thought out in my presence the problems that arise if one wishes a group to behave just like a Bayesian individual, with a group utility function and a group probability function. Very carefully, he concluded that transitivity was no less appropriate in the group decision context, but that big difficulties arose concerning the validity of substitutability; see **R68**, Chapter 8.

Such a careful advisor will always be much in demand. One can only hope that the help that Raiffa agrees to continue giving will be of such a nature as to continue to contribute to his research and publication activities.

## Notes

1. References to works by Raiffa are given in boldface, with the first letters of authors' last names and the last two digits of the publication date, as well as letters a and b, if needed, to distinguish between publications in the same year.
2. In Gleick (1992).
3. See, for example, Brown (1992) and Howard (1992).
4. On prospect theory, see Kahneman and Tversky (1979).
5. LaValle (1966, 1967) considers this and related issues in treating all but one of the participants descriptively. On the infinite regress problem and associated considerations of iterated dominance, key references include Mertens and Zamir (1985), Bernheim (1984), and Pearce (1984).
6. See Roberts (1979) or the three-volume magnum opus Krantz, Luce, Suppes, and Tversky (1971), Suppes, Krantz, Luce, and Tversky (1989), and Luce, Krantz, Suppes, and Tversky (1990). Also, Narens (1985) is particularly relevant to those interested in relaxing Archimedean, or continuity, axioms and getting nonstandard representations.
7. On boundary facets, see, for example, Shachtman (1974) or Walker (1973).
8. But see footnote 7 on p. 373 of **R53**.
9. See Section 6.2.4 of Shubik (1982) for an introduction and further references.
10. See, for example, Van Damme (1991).
11. Again, see Kreps (1990), ch. 13, for discussion, including the dispensability of the common-prior assumption.
12. See, for example, Myerson (1991), Friedman (1990), and Fudenberg and Tirole (1991).
13. Raiffa attributes this game to Dresher (p. 29). It was later given its present name by Tucker.
14. Ando and Kaufman (1965) obtain the multivariate Student as a Wishart mixture of multivariate Normals.
15. There are some technical differences of opinion on this; see Berger and Wolpert (1988).
16. See, for example, LaValle (1989, 1992), Wakker (1988), and Sarin (1992).
17. See, for example, the papers in Flournoy and Tsutakawa (1991).
18. See, for example, Section 3.6 of Berger (1985).
19. See LaValle (1988).
20. See LaValle and Xu (1990), p. 266.
21. See, for example, Fishburn (1988a, 1988b).

22. That the SEU model is almost uniquely robust as regards flexibility in specifying the decision horizon, flexibility in choice of strategically equivalent problem representation, and the like, was shown in LaValle (1992), with other survivors of these prescriptively-motivated criteria limited to consequentialist (Hammond, 1988) generalizations that preserve cancellation/linearity/independence/substitutability and transitivity. However, continuity can be relaxed; see LaValle and Fishburn (1991, 1992, 1994).

23. See Chapter 3 of **LR57**. On techniques for partially or fully normalizing *decision* trees in various ways, see LaValle (1978, Chapter 7) and LaValle and Fishburn (1987).

24. See Chapter 11 in LaValle (1978); Thomson and Myerson (1980) develop trajectory-based solutions to the bargaining problem from a somewhat different viewpoint.

## REFERENCES

### Works by Raiffa and Coauthors

Raiffa, H. (1951). "Arbitration Schemes for Generalized Two-Person Games." Engineering Research Institute, University of Michigan. Report No. M720-1, R30. Ann Arbor, MI. **R51**

Raiffa, H. (1953). "Arbitration Schemes for Generalized Two-Person Games." In H. W. Kuhn and A. W. Tucker, eds., *Contributions to the Theory of Games II* [*Annals of Mathematics Studies* 28]. Princeton, NJ: Princeton University Press. 361–387. **R53**

Motzkin, T. S., Raiffa, H., Thompson, G. L., and Thrall, R. M. (1953). "The Double Description Method." In H. W. Kuhn and A. W. Tucker, eds., *Contributions to the Theory of Games II* [*Annals of Mathematics Studies* 28]. Princeton, NJ: Princeton University Press. 51–73. **MRTT53**

Coombs, C. H., Raiffa, H., and Thrall, R. M. (1954). "Some Views on Mathematical Models and Measurement Theory." In R. M. Thrall, C. H. Coombs, and R. L. Davis, eds., *Decision Processes*. New York: Wiley. 19–37. **CRT54**

Luce, R. D., and Raiffa, H. (1957). *Games and Decisions*. New York: Wiley. **LR57**

Raiffa, H. (1961a). "Risk, Ambiguity, and the Savage Axioms: Comment." *Quarterly Journal of Economics* 75. 690–694. **R61a**

Raiffa, H. (1961b). "Statistical Decision Theory Approach to Item Selection for Dichotomous Test and Criterion Variables." In H. Solomon, ed., *Studies in Item Analysis and Prediction*. Stanford: Stanford University Press. 187–220. **R61b**

Raiffa, H. and Schlaifer, R. (1961). *Applied Statistical Decision Theory*. Boston: Division of Research, Harvard Business School. **RS61**

Pratt, J. W., Raiffa, H., and Schlaifer, R. (1964). "The Foundations of Decision

Under Uncertainty: An Elementary Exposition." *Journal of the American Statistical Association* 59. 353–375. **PRS64**

Pratt, J. W., Raiffa, H., and Schlaifer, R. (1965). *Introduction to Statistical Decision Theory.* New York: McGraw-Hill (preliminary edition). Final edition scheduled to be issued by MIT Press, November 1994. **PRS65**

Raiffa, H. (1968). *Decision Analysis: Introductory Lectures on Choices Under Uncertainty.* Reading, MA: Addison-Wesley. **R68**

Raiffa, H. (1969). "Preferences for Multi-Attributed Alternatives." RAND Memorandum RM-5868-DOT/RC. Santa Monica, CA: RAND Corp. **R69**

Keeney, R. L., and Raiffa, H. (1972). "A Critique of Formal Analysis in Public Decision Making." In Drake, A. W., Keeney, R. L., and Morse, P. M., eds., *Analysis of Public Systems.* Cambridge, MA: MIT Press. 64–74. **KR72**

Keeney, R. L., and Raiffa, H. (1976). *Decisions with Multiple Objectives: Preferences and Value Tradeoffs.* New York: Wiley. **KR76**

Bell, D. E., Keeney, R. L., and Raiffa, H., eds. (1977). *Conflicting Objectives in Decisions.* New York: Wiley. **BKR77**

Raiffa, H., Schwartz, W. B., and Weinstein, M. C. (1977). "Evaluating the Health Effects of Societal Decisions and Programs." *Decision Making in the Environmental Protection Agency, Selected Working Papers, Volume* IIB. Washington, DC: National Academy of Sciences. **RSW77**

Raiffa, H. (1980). Testimony on H.R. 4939. (Unpublished.) **R80**

Raiffa, H. (1982a). *The Art and Science of Negotiation.* Cambridge, MA: Harvard University Press. **R82a**

Raiffa, H. (1982b). "Policy Analysis: A Checklist of Concerns." Working Paper, International Institute for Applied Systems Analysis. Laxenburg, Austria. **R82b**

Alpert, M., and Raiffa, H. (1982). "A Progress Report on the Training of Probability Assessors." In D. Kahneman, P. Slovik, and A. Tversky, eds., *Judgment Under Uncertainty: Heuristics and Biases.* New York: Cambridge University Press. 294–305. **AR82**

Graham, J. D., Raiffa, H., and Vaupel, J. W. (1983). "Science and Analysis: Roles in Risk and Decision Making." Draft. Washington, DC: National Science Foundation. **GRV83**

Raiffa, H. (1985a). "Back from Prospect Theory to Utility Theory." In M. Grauer, M. Thompson, and A. P. Wierzbicki, eds., *Plural Rationality and Interactive Decision Processes.* Heidelberg: Springer-Verlag. 100–113. **R85a**

Raiffa, H. (1985b). "Post-Settlement Settlements." *Negotiation Journal* 1. 9–12. **R85b**

Raiffa, H. (1988). "Reminiscences." Videotaped address as the first Frank P. Ramsey Medalist. [Tape includes addresses of Ronald A. Howard, Peter C. Fishburn, and Ward Edwards, the three subsequent (as of 1988) recipients of the Ramsey Medal.] Baltimore: The Operations Research Society of America. **R88**

Bell, D. E., Raiffa, H., and Tversky, A. (eds.) (1988a). *Decision Making: Descriptive, Normative, and Prescriptive Interactions.* New York: Cambridge University Press. **BRT88a**

Bell, D. E., Raiffa, H., and Tversky, A. (1988b). "Descriptive, Normative, and Prescriptive Interactions in Decision Making." In **BRT88a**. 9–30. **BRT88b**

Bell, D. E., and Raiffa, H. (1988a). "Risky Choice Revisited." In **BRT88a**. 99–112. **BR88a**

Bell, D. E., and Raiffa, H. (1988b). "Marginal Value and Intrinsic Risk Aversion." In **BRT88a**. 384–397. **BR88b**

Keeney, R. L., and Raiffa, H. (1991). "Assessing Tradeoffs: Structuring and Analyzing Values for Multiple-Issue Negotiations." In H. P. Young, ed., *Negotiation Analysis.* Ann Arbor: University of Michigan Press. 131–151. **KR91**

## Other Works Cited

Ando, A., and Kaufman, G. M. (1965). "Bayesian Analysis of the Independent Multinormal Process—Neither Mean nor Precision Known." *Journal of the American Statistical Association* 60. 347–358.

Aumann, R. J. (1989). "Game Theory." In Eatwell, J., Milgate, M., and Newman, P., eds., *The New Palgrave: Game Theory.* New York: Norton. 1–53. (Original edition, McMillan, 1987.)

Aumann, R. J., and Maschler, M. (1964). "The Bargaining Set for Cooperative Games." In Dresher, M., Shapley, L. S., and Tucker, A. W., eds., *Advances in Game Theory* [*Annals of Mathematics Studies* 52]. Princeton, NJ: Princeton University Press. 443–476.

Bazerman, M. H., Russ, L. E., and Yakura, E. (1987). "Post-Settlement Settlements in Two-Party Negotiations." *Negotiation Journal* 3. 283–292.

Berger, J. O. (1985). *Statistical Decision Theory and Bayesian Analysis* (2nd ed.). New York: Springer-Verlag.

Berger, J. O., and Wolpert, R. L. (1988). *The Likelihood Principle* (2nd ed.). Hayward, CA: Institute of Mathematical Statistics.

Bernheim, D. (1984). "Rationalizable Strategic Behavior." *Econometrica* 52. 1007–1028.

Birnbaum, A. (1962). "On the Foundations of Statistical Inference" (with discussion). *Journal of the American Statistical Association* 57. 269–326.

Bracken, J., and Schleifer, A., Jr. (1964). *Tables for Normal Sampling with Unknown Variance.* Boston: Division of Research, Harvard Business School.

Brown, R. V. (1992). "The State of the Art of Decision Analysis: A Personal Perspective." *Interfaces* 22, 5–14; and "Reply [to Howard (1992)]," *ibid.* 25–27.

Christenson, C. J. (1965). *Strategic Aspects of Competitive Bidding for Corporate Debt Securities.* Boston: Division of Research, Harvard Business School.

Fellner, W. (1965). *Probability and Profit.* Homewood, IL: Richard Irwin.

Fishburn, P. C. (1965). "Independence in Utility Theory with Whole Product Sets." *Operations Research* 13. 28–45.

Fishburn, P. C. (1970). *Utility Theory for Decision Making.* New York: Wiley.

Fishburn, P. C. (1981). "Subjective Expected Utility: A Review of Normative Theories," *Theory and Decision* 13. 139–199.

Fishburn, P. C. (1988a). Ramsey Medalist address. On the same videotape as **R88**.

Fishburn, P. C. (1988b). *Nonlinear Preference and Utility Theory.* Baltimore: Johns Hopkins University Press.

Flournoy, N., and Tsutakawa, R. K. (eds.) (1991). *Statistical Multiple Integration.* Providence, RI: American Mathematical Society.

Friedman, J. W. (1990). *Game Theory with Applications to Economics* (2nd ed.). Oxford: Oxford University Press.

Friedman, M., and Savage, L. J. (1948). "The Utility Analysis of Choices Involving Risk." *Journal of Political Economy* 56. 279–304.

Fudenberg, D., and Tirole, J. (1991). *Game Theory.* Cambridge, MA: Harvard University Press.

Genest, C., and Zidek, J. V. (1986). "Combining Probability Distributions: A Critique and an Annotated Bibliography" (with discussion). *Statistical Science* 1. 114–148.

Gilboa, I. (1987). "Expected Utility with Purely Subjective Nonadditive Probabilities." *Journal of Mathematical Economics* 16. 65–88.

Gleick, J. (1992). *Genius: The Life and Science of Richard Feynman.* New York: Pantheon Press.

Grayson, C. J. (1960). *Decisions under Uncertainty: Drilling Decisions by Oil and Gas Operators.* Boston: Division of Research, Harvard Business School.

Hammond, P. J. (1988). "Consequentialist Foundations for Expected Utility." *Theory and Decision* 25. 25–78.

Harsanyi, J. C. (1977). *Rational Behavior and Bargaining Equilibrium in Games and Social Situations.* Cambridge: Cambridge University Press.

Harsanyi, J. C. (1967–68). "Games with Incomplete Information Played by Bayesian Players, Parts I, II, and III." *Management Science* 14. 159–182, 320–334, 486–502.

Hausner, M. W. (1954). "Multidimensional Utilities." In R. M. Thrall, C. H. Coombs, and R. L. Davis, eds., *Decision Processes.* New York: Wiley. 167–180.

Hazen, G. B. (1987). "Subjectively Weighted Linear Utility." *Theory and Decision* 23. 261–282.

Hazen, G. B. (1992). "Decision Versus Policy: An Expected Utility Resolution of the Ellsberg Paradox." In J. Geweke, ed., *Decision Making under Risk and Uncertainty: New Models and Empirical Findings.* Dordrecht: Kluwer Academic Publishers. 25–35.

Howard, R. A. (1980). "On Making Life and Death Decisions." In R. C. Schwing and W. A. Albers, Jr., eds., *Societal Risk Assessment.* New York: Plenum. 89–113.

Howard, R. A. (1984). "On Fates Comparable to Death." *Management Science* 30. 407–422.

Howard, R. A. (1988). Ramsey Medalist address. On the same videotape as **R88**.

Howard, R. A. (1992). "Heathens, Heretics, and Cults: The Religious Spectrum of Decision Aiding." *Interfaces* 22. 15–24.

Kahneman, D., and Tversky, A. (1979). "Prospect Theory: An Analysis of Decision under Risk." *Econometrica* 47. 276–287.

Krantz, D. H., Luce, R. D., Suppes, P., and Tversky, A. (1971). *Foundations of Measurement, Volume I: Additive and Polynomial Representations.* New York: Academic Press.

Kreps, D. M. (1990). *A Course in Microeconomic Theory.* Princeton, NJ: Princeton University Press.

Kreps, D. M., and Porteus, E. (1978). "Temporal Resolution of Uncertainty and Dynamic Choice Theory." *Econometrica* 46. 185–200.

LaValle, I. H. (1966). *Strategic Situation Theory: A Bayesian Approach to an Individual Player's Choice of Strategies in Noncooperative Games.* Dissertation. Boston: Harvard Business School.

LaValle, I. H. (1967). "A Bayesian Approach to an Individual Player's Choice of Bid in Competitive Sealed Auctions." *Management Science* 13. 584–597.

LaValle, I. H. (1968). "On Cash Equivalents and Information Evaluation in Decisions under Uncertainty." *Journal of the American Statistical Association* 63. 252–290.

LaValle, I. H. (1970). *An Introduction to Probability, Decision, and Inference.* New York: Holt, Rinehart & Winston.

LaValle, I. H. (1978). *Fundamentals of Decision Analysis.* New York: Holt, Rinehart & Winston.

LaValle, I. H. (1988). "Caution! Pricing Out Variation in Nonmonetary Attributes Is Dangerous to Your Optimality." Unpublished ms. A. B. Freeman School of Business, Tulane University.

LaValle, I. H. (1989). "New Choice Models Raise New Difficulties: Commentary on Sarin." In I. Horowitz, ed., *Organization and Decision Theory.* Boston: Kluwer. 63–81.

LaValle, I. H. (1992). "Small Worlds and Sure Things: Consequentialism by the Back Door." In W. Edwards, ed., *Utility Theories: Measurements and Applications.* Boston: Kluwer. 109–136.

LaValle, I. H., and Fishburn, P. C. (1987). "Equivalent Decision Trees and Their Associated Strategy Sets." *Theory and Decision* 23. 37–63.

LaValle, I. H., and Fishburn, P. C. (1991). "Lexicographic State-Dependent Subjective Expected Utility." *Journal of Risk and Uncertainty* 4, 251–269.

LaValle, I. H., and Fishburn, P. C. (1992). "State-Independent Subjective Expected Lexicographic Utility." *Journal of Risk and Uncertainty* 5. 217–240.

LaValle, I. H., and Fishburn, P. C. (1994). "On the Varieties of Matrix Probabilities in Nonarchimedean Decision Theory." *Journal of Mathematical Economics* (forthcoming).

LaValle, I. H., and Xu, Y. (1990). "Information Evaluation under Nonadditive Expected Utility." *Journal of Risk and Uncertainty* 3. 261–275.

Lucas, W. F. (1969). "The Proof that a Game May Not Have a Solution." *Transactions of the American Mathematical Society* 137. 219–229.

Luce, R. D., Krantz, D. H., Suppes, P., and Tversky, A. (1990). *Foundations of Measurement, Volume III: Representation, Axiomatization, and Invariance.* San Diego: Academic Press.

Mertens, J.-F., and Zamir, S. (1985). "Formulation of Bayesian Analysis for Games with Incomplete Information." *International Journal of Game Theory* 14. 1–29.

Morrison, D. G. (1967). "On the Consistency of Preferences in Allais' Paradox." *Behavioral Science* 12. 373–383.

Myerson, R. F. (1991). *Game Theory: Analysis of Conflict.* Cambridge, MA: Harvard University Press.

Narens, L. (1985). *Abstract Measurement Theory.* Cambridge, MA: Harvard University Press.

Nash, J. F. (1953). "Two-Person Cooperative Games." *Econometrica* 21. 128–140.

O'Neill, B. (1981). "The Number of Outcomes in the Pareto-Optimal Set of Discrete Bargaining Games." *Mathematics of Operations Research* 6. 571–578.

Pearce, D. (1984). "Rationalizable Strategic Behavior and the Problem of Perfection." *Econometrica* 52. 1029–1050.

Pratt, J. W. (1964). "Risk Aversion in the Small and in the Large." *Econometrica* 32. 122–136.

Ramsey, F. P. (1931). "Truth and Probability." In Ramsey, F. P., *The Foundations of Mathematics and Other Logical Essays.* New York: Harcourt, Brace. Reprinted in Kyburg, H. E., and Smokler, H. E. (eds.), *Studies in Subjective Probability.* New York: Wiley (1964). 61–92.

Roberts, F. S. (1979). *Measurement Theory.* Reading, MA: Addison-Wesley.

Roth, A. E. (1985). "Some Additional Thoughts on Post-Settlement Settlements." *Negotiation Journal* 1. 245–247.

Sarin, R. K. (1992). "What Now for Generalized Utility Theory?" In W. Edwards, ed., *Utility Theories: Measurements and Applications.* Boston: Kluwer. 137–163.

Savage, L. J. (1954). *The Foundations of Statistics.* New York: Wiley.

Schlaifer, R. (1959). *Probability and Statistics for Business Decisions.* New York: McGraw-Hill.

Schmeidler, D. (1989). "Subjective Probability and Expected Utility Without Additivity." *Econometrica* 57. 571–587.

Sebenius, J. K. (1992). "Negotiation Analysis: A Characterization and Review." *Management Science* 38. 18–38.

Shachtman, R. H. (1974). "Generation of the Admissible Boundary of a Convex Polytope." *Operations Research* 22. 151–159.

Shubik, M. (1982). *Game Theory in the Social Sciences: Concepts and Solutions.* Cambridge, MA: MIT Press.

Spence, M., and Zeckhauser, R. (1972). "The Effect of the Timing of Consumption Decisions and the Resolution of Lotteries on the Choice of Lotteries." *Econometrica* 40. 401–403.

Stevens, S. S. (1946). "On the Theory of Scales of Measurement." *Science* 103. 677–680.

Suppes, P., Krantz, D. H., Luce, R. D., and Tversky, A. (1989). *Foundations of Measurement, Volume II: Geometrical, Threshold, and Probabilistic Representations.* San Diego: Academic Press.

Thomson, W., and Myerson, R. B. (1980). "Monotonicity and Independence Axioms." *International Journal of Game Theory* 9. 37–49.

Van Damme, E. (1991). *Stability and Perfection of Nash Equilibria* (2nd ed.). Berlin: Springer-Verlag.

von Neumann, J., and Morgenstern, O. (1944). *Theory of Games and Economic Behavior.* Princeton, NJ: Princeton University Press.

von Winterfeldt, D., and Edwards, W. (1986). *Decision Analysis and Behavioral Research.* Cambridge: Cambridge University Press.

Wakker, P. (1988). "Nonexpected Utility as Aversion of Information." *Journal of Behavioral Decision Making* 1. 169–175.

Wakker, P. (1993). "Unbounded Utility for Savage's 'Foundations of Statistics.'" *Mathematics of Operations Research* 18. 446–485.

Wakker, P. (1994). "Separating Marginal Utility and Probabilistic Risk Aversion." *Theory and Decision* 36. 1–44.

Wald, A. (1950). *Statistical Decision Functions.* New York: Wiley.

Walker, M. R. (1973). "Determination of the Convex Hull of a Finite Set of Points." Master of Science in Operations Research Thesis. Chapel Hill, NC, University of North Carolina.

Wilson, R. (1968). "The Theory of Syndicates." *Econometrica* 36. 119–132.

Young, H. P. (1991). *Negotiation Analysis.* Ann Arbor: University of Michigan Press.

# Index

ABB, 335–336, 337
acceptance principle, 8
actional thought, 83
advertising, 23, 37n.12, 39–40n.28
agreement(s)
  no-alternative, 335–337
  no-deal alternative, 333–335
agriculture, 339
aids
  decision, 42–43
  graphical estimation, 43–57,
    58nn.5, 6
AIDS, 174
airlines, 34, 41n.37
Alaska, 381
Allais, Maurice, 17
American Cancer Society, 171
amniocentesis, 171, 177
  birth defect detection and,
    185–186, 188
  costs of, 192–195
  optimal risk and, 190–192
analysis, xvi, 19

negotiation, xv, xvi, xvii, 400,
  401–402, 407–412, 444–447
  prescriptive, 42, 421–422
  prescriptive/descriptive, 400,
    401–402, 407–412
  systematic, 419–420
Antarctica, 377
*Applied Statistical Decision Theory*
  (Raiffa and Schlaifer), 417
Arab states, 327
arbitration, 386n.7, 405–406, 413n.12,
  446–447
  prescriptive, 420–421, 423
Argentina, 377
arms control, 336–337
Arrow-Debreu theory, 120–121
*Art and Science of Negotiation, The*
  (Raiffa), 290, 400, 401, 417
Asea, 335
assessment: integrated, 242–245
atmosphere, 372–373
attributes: and indivisibles, 374–375,
  376

457

# About the Contributors

**Arthur Isak Applbaum** was the first rapporteur of Howard Raiffa's Negotiation Roundtable. He is now an associate professor of public policy at the Kennedy School of Government at Harvard, where he directs the graduate ethics fellowship program. His work on political authority and on professional ethics has appeared in *Philosophy & Public Affairs* and *Harvard Law Review*. Applbaum is currently a Rockefeller Visiting Fellow at the Princeton University Center for Human Values, and was an ethics fellow at Harvard's Program in Ethics and the Professions. He is completing a book, entitled *Ethics for Adversaries,* on role morality in politics and the professions.

**David E. Bell** was an undergraduate at Oxford University and a graduate student at M.I.T. before being hired by Howard Raiffa as one of the first scientists at the International Institute for Applied Systems Analysis (IIASA) in Austria. He joined the Harvard Business School faculty in 1977 and since that time has taught courses on decision analysis and risk management. His research has been largely devoted to understanding how utility functions can become a panacea for all human decisions. With this current paper he feels close to a solution.

**Gary E Bolton** is an assistant professor of management science at Pennsylvania State University, University Park. He received a Ph.D. in economics from the Graduate School of Industrial Administration, Carnegie-Mellon University. He uses experimental methods to investigate issues pertaining to bargaining and conflict resolution and also teaches courses on negotiations and decision analysis to M.B.A. students.

**Adam M. Brandenburger** is a professor of business administration at the Harvard Business School. He researches, teaches, and consults in the areas of game theory and business strategy. He is the author of *Co-opetition* (1996) and of numerous articles on game theory and its application to business. Brandenburger teaches in the M.B.A., doctoral, and executive programs at the Harvard Business School; he has also brought game theory to a variety of business audiences. He received his B.A., M.Phil., and Ph.D. degrees from Cambridge University, England, and was the recipient of a 1983 Harkness Fellowship.

**Rex V. Brown** is a research professor of public policy at George Mason University, in Fairfax, Virginia. He was trained as a social scientist and statistician and was a student and colleague of Howard Raiffa at the Harvard Business School in the 1960s. Since then he has been a decision consultant to policy makers in government and business, a researcher in interdisciplinary decision-making methods, and a member of university departments of psychology, statistics, systems engineering, marketing, and management. He is the author of *Research and the Credibility of Estimates* and co-author of *Decision Analysis for the Manager* and *Teaching Decision Skills to Adolescents*.

**Rivka Carmi** is the head of the Clinical Genetics Unit at the Soroka Medical Center, Ben-Gurion University of the Negev in Beer-Sheva, which provides all the genetic services to the Negev region, population of about 250,000. She is also an associate professor of pediatrics and the vice dean for student affairs in the Faculty of Health Sciences, Ben-Gurion University, as well as the incumbent of the Kreitman Foundation Chair in Pediatric Genetics. She graduated from the Hebrew University Hadassah Medical School in 1975. She had her pediatrics residency and neonatology fellowship at the Soroka Medical Center and her medical genetics fellowship at the Children's Hospital Medical Center in Boston. She is board certified in pediatrics, neonatology, and medical genetics. Dr. Carmi's research interests are in syndrome delineation, the mapping of rare recessive genes, genotype/phenotype correlations, the human midline, and community genetic counseling.

**Kalyan Chatterjee** is the Distinguished Professor of Management Science at Pennsylvania State University, University Park, where he has been since 1979. In that year, he received his D.B.A. from Harvard, with Howard Raiffa as adviser. He worked then on bargaining and incentive compatibility under incomplete information, as well as on final-offer arbitration. He is currently interested in models of coalition formation and teaches a course in negotiation to second-year M.B.A. students, along with courses in game theory to other graduate students from different fields.

**Dana R. Clyman** is on the faculty of The Darden School, the graduate school of business at the University of Virginia, where he teaches and conducts research on decision theory, negotiations, and international finance. In 1994, his second year at Darden, he was named the Outstanding Faculty Member by the Darden student body. Dr. Clyman holds a bachelor's degree from New College; master's degrees in mathematics and engineering science from Dartmouth and Harvard, respectively; an M.B.A. from Stanford; and a Ph.D. issued jointly by Harvard University and the Harvard Business School. He has more than seventeen years of general management and consulting experience, and he serves on the board of directors of FINEX, the financial instruments subsidiary of the New York Cotton Exchange.

**James K. Hammitt** teaches decision theory and benefit-cost analysis at the Harvard School of Public Health. His research addresses the effects of risk and uncertainty on environmental-policy choice; current topics include policies toward global-scale threats like climate change and stratospheric-ozone depletion, economic valuation of health risks and environmental quality, and the effect of environmental liability on firms' cost of capital. Professor Hammitt was previously at RAND and a faculty member at the RAND Graduate School of Policy Studies. He received his A.B. and Sc.M. in applied mathematics and his M.P.P. and Ph.D. in public policy from Harvard University.

**Heather A. Hazard** is an associate professor at the Institute of International Economics and Management, Copenhagen Business School. Prior to moving to Copenhagen, she held faculty appointments at the Harvard Business School and at M.I.T.'s Sloan School of Management. She has also worked in consulting and manufacturing. Dr. Hazard has contributed articles and commentary on international trade theory and conflicts to numerous books, journals, newspapers, and news programs. Her work focuses on the international trade and industrial organization questions faced by firms and governments in industries dominated by a few multinationals actively engaged in foreign direct investment and trade. She has won numerous awards for both her research and her teaching.

**Ronald A. Howard** is a professor of engineering-economic systems at Stanford University, where he directs the Decision Analysis Program and the Decisions and Ethics Center. His experience includes decision analysis projects that range over virtually all fields of application. He has been a consultant to several companies and is a founding director and chairman of Strategic Decisions Group. Professor Howard has written three books and dozens of technical papers, has provided editorial service to seven technical journals, and was founding editor of the *Journal of the Society for Scientific Exploration*. In 1986 he received the Operations Research Society of America's Frank P. Ramsey Medal for Distinguished Contributions in Decision Analysis. His current research interests are improving the quality of decisions, life-and-death decision making, and the creation of a coercion-free society.

**Ralph L. Keeney** is a professor of systems management at the University of Southern California and a private consultant in San Francisco. He has been a professor in engineering and in management at M.I.T., a research scholar at the International Institute for Applied Systems Analysis in Austria, and the founder of the decision and risk analysis group at Woodward-Clyde Consultants. Dr. Keeney is co-author, with Howard Raiffa, of *Decisions with Multiple Objectives* and author of *Value-Focused Thinking: A Path to Creative Decisionmaking*. In 1995 Dr. Keeney was elected to the National Academy of Engineering.

**Irving H. LaValle** is the Francis Martin Professor of Decision Theory at Tulane's A. B. Freeman School of Business. His interests span most topics concerned with wise choices. At various times they have centered on information evaluation, dominance-optimality alternatives, nonlinear choice theories, and, most recently, the linear generalization of the familiar subjective-expected-utility model in which the subjective probabilities appear as matrices that premultiply utility vectors, ordered lexicographically. Besides teaching in decision theory and microeconomics, he has been active in university governance, was the founding chair of the Decision Analysis Section of INFORMS (formerly TIMS/ORSA), and has served as Decision Analysis Department editor for *Management Science*.

**Joanne Linnerooth-Bayer** studied industrial management at Carnegie-Mellon University and received her Ph.D. in economics from the University of Maryland in 1977. Her doctoral dissertation was on valuing human life, and Howard Raiffa served on her Ph.D. committee. She joined the International Institute for Applied Systems Analysis (IIASA) in 1974 and is presently leader of IIASA's Risk, Policy and Complexity Project. During 1989–1990 she was also affiliated with the Institute for Risk Management at Resources for the Future in Washington, D.C. Dr. Linnerooth-Bayer has published widely on environmental risk policy making, including articles on the valuation of public programs that affect population mortality, the siting of hazardous facilities, the role of scientific expertise in the policy process, and the control of transborder environmental risk. Her current interest is "fairness" concerning the distribution of environmental risk burdens.

**David V. P. Marks** is an economist and holds a J.D. and a Ph.D. from Harvard. He is co-author of *Competition in the Investment Banking Industry.*

**Richard F. Meyer** is a professor of business administration at the Harvard Business School. He received his Ph.D. from Harvard University and spent the first ten years of his career in the Management Services Division of Arthur D. Little, Inc., serving as a consultant to major corporations both in the United States and in Europe. On the faculty of the Harvard Business School since 1965, Professor Meyer has been chairman of the Admissions Policy Committee and chairman of the managerial economics area. He has also served as associate dean for research at INSEAD. In recent years, Professor Meyer has been teaching and doing research in financial risk management, managerial economics, and competitive strategy. His current research and course development focus on the use of derivatives to hedge financial risk in corporations.

**Edward A. Parson** is an assistant professor of public policy at Harvard University's John F. Kennedy School of Government and a research scholar in the International Environmental Commitments project of the International Institute for Applied Systems Analysis (IIASA) in Laxenburg, Austria. His research concerns negotiations and environmental policy, particularly in international settings. He has published recently on international cooperation to protect the ozone layer, methods and institutions for scientific assessment, and the use of simulation-gaming methods to study institutional design for global environmental change.

**Joseph S. Pliskin** is the Sidney Liswood Professor of Health Care Management at Ben-Gurion University of the Negev, Beer-Sheva, Israel. He is a member of the Department of Industrial Engineering and Management and is head of the Health Policy and Management Unit of the Faculty of Health Sciences. He is also an adjunct professor of health policy and management at the Harvard School of Public Health. Dr. Pliskin received his B.Sc. degree from the Hebrew University in Jerusalem and his S.M. and Ph.D. degrees from Harvard University. His Ph.D. thesis was supervised by Professor Howard Raiffa. Dr. Pliskin's research interests include decision analysis, cost-benefit and cost-effectiveness analyses in health care, operations research applications to health care, and utility theory.

**John W. Pratt,** the William Ziegler Professor of Business Administration at the Harvard Business School, specialized in mathematics and statistics during his education at Princeton and Stanford. Except for two years at the University of Chicago and a Guggenheim year in Kyoto, his entire career has been at Harvard. A fellow of five professional societies and a member of the American Academy of Arts and Sciences, he served as editor of the *Journal of the American Statistical Association* from 1965 to 1970; chaired National Academy of Sciences committees on environmental monitoring, census methodology, and the future of statistics; and co-authored or edited books on statistical decision theory, pollution, social experimentation, nonparametric statistics, and principals and agents. His current interests include risk, incentives, and statistical causality.

**Orit Refaely** is a senior engineer at Telrad, a company specializing in electronic communication. She received her B.Sc. and M.Sc. degrees in industrial engineering and management from Ben-Gurion University of the Negev, Beer-Sheva, Israel.

**Yitzhak Romem** is the director of the Genetics Institute at Soroka Medical Center, Ben-Gurion University of the Negev. He received his M.D. degree from the Hadassah Medical School, Hebrew University, Jerusalem, where he specialized in obstetrics and gynecology. From 1982 to 1985 he was a fellow in maternal fetal medicine at Women's County Hospital, Los Angeles, University of Southern California. Dr. Romem is interested mainly in prenatal diagnosis of congenital disorders and established the prenatal screening for Down's syndrome for the population of southern Israel. His interests also include the use of computers in medicine.

**William F. Samuelson** is a professor of economics and finance at Boston University's School of Management. He received his A.B. in applied mathematics and his Ph.D. in economics from Harvard University. His research and teaching interests include microeconomics, decision theory, and game theory. He is co-author of the textbook *Managerial Economics,* and his research in decision making, experimental economics, competitive bidding, and bargaining has been published in leading economics and management science journals.

**Thomas C. Schelling,** Ph.D. (Harvard, economics, 1951), joined the Marshall Plan in 1948 and served abroad and in Washington in the administration of foreign aid until 1953. He joined the Yale Department of Economics in 1953, the Harvard Department of Economics in 1958, Harvard's Kennedy School in 1969, and the University of Maryland in 1990. His work during the 1960s in nuclear weapons policy led, through an interest in nuclear proliferation, to the subject of nuclear energy, and in the 1970s and 1980s to energy policy. In 1981–1983 he participated in the National Academy of Sciences study of greenhouse gas and climate change, the subject of his contribution to this volume.

**James K. Sebenius** is the Gordon Donaldson Professor of Business Administration at the Harvard Business School, the director of the Negotiation Roundtable at the Harvard Business School, and a member of the Executive Committee of the Harvard-M.I.T.-Fletcher Program on Negotiation. A graduate of Vanderbilt University and Stanford University (where he earned his master's degree in engineering-economic systems), he holds a doctorate from Harvard in business economics. After working in a venture capital firm in 1984, Professor Sebenius helped to found the Blackstone Group, a private investment banking firm based in New York, where he worked until returning to Harvard four years later. Previously, he served as a member of the U.S. State Department delegation to the Law of the Sea negotiations, worked for Ambassador-at-Large Elliot L. Richardson, and was a personal assistant to Dr. Robert M. White, administrator of the National Oceanic and Atmospheric Administration. Elected as a team member of the Council on Foreign Relations, he is the author of *Negotiating the Law of the Sea* and *The Manager as Negotiator: Bargaining for Cooperation and Competitive Gain* (with David Lax) as well as numerous professional journal articles.

**Amos Tversky** is the Davis-Brack Professor of Behavioral Sciences at Stanford University. He is also a principal investigator of the Stanford Center for Conflict and Negotiation and a member of the Sackler Institute for Advanced Study at Tel Aviv University. His research focuses on individual decision making and judgment under uncertainty; it attempts to uncover the cognitive processes underlying the construction of preferences and the formation of beliefs. Professor Tversky is a member of the National Academy of Sciences. He received the McArthur Prize and the Distinguished Scientific Contribution Award of the American Psychological Association.

**Milton C. Weinstein** is the Henry J. Kaiser Professor of Health Policy and Management at the Harvard School of Public Health, where he teaches decision analysis to physicians and public health professionals and conducts research on resource allocation in health care. He earned A.B. and A.M. degrees in 1970 from Harvard University's Decision and Control Program, an M.P.P. in 1972 from the Kennedy School of Government, and a Ph.D. in public policy in 1973. He is the principal author of two books and more than one hundred articles in the medical, public health, economics, and operations research literatures. Professor Weinstein is an elected member of the Institute of Medicine of the National Academy of Sciences, and he recently co-chaired the Panel on Cost-Effectiveness in Health and Medicine for the U.S. Public Health Service.

**Robert Wilson** is the McBean Professor of Economics at Stanford Business School. He is a principal of the Stanford Center on Conflict and Negotiation and a member of the National Academy of Sciences. His research on negotiation strategies includes applications to wage bargaining and strikes, and in legal contexts to pretrial settlement negotiations. He received the D.B.A. degree from the Harvard Business School in 1963.

**H. Peyton Young** is a professor of economics at Johns Hopkins University and a research scholar at the Brookings Institution. He has written on game theory, bargaining and negotiation, public finance, political representation, and distributive justice. His most recent book, *Equity in Theory and Practice,* analyzes how institutions allocate scarce resources according to standards of fairness, and contrasts these revealed approaches to justice with theories in the philosophical and economics literature. His other books include *Fair Representation* (with M. L. Balinski), *Fair Allocation* (editor), *Cost Allocation: Methods, Principles, Applications* (editor), and *Negotiation Analysis* (editor). He is currently working on a book about the evolution of social norms. Professor Young is an associate editor of *Games and Economic Behavior, Social Choice and Welfare,* and *Mathematical Social Sciences.* He serves on the Council of the Society for Social Choice and Welfare and is a fellow of the Econometric Society.

**Richard J. Zeckhauser** is the Frank P. Ramsey Professor of Political Economy at the John F. Kennedy School of Government, Harvard University, where he teaches also in the Law School and Economics Department. His research addresses the challenges of creating appropriate commitments, making effective decisions under uncertainty, and governing the modern corporation. Health and finance issues provide a frequent focus. His recent edited books include *Principals and Agents: The Structure of Business, American Society: Public and Private Responsibilities, Privatization and State-Owned Enterprises,* and *Strategy and Choice.*